Listening Devices

Listening Devices

Music Media in the Pre-Digital Era

Jens Gerrit Papenburg

BLOOMSBURY ACADEMIC
NEW YORK • LONDON • OXFORD • NEW DELHI • SYDNEY

BLOOMSBURY ACADEMIC
Bloomsbury Publishing Inc
1385 Broadway, New York, NY 10018, USA
50 Bedford Square, London, WC1B 3DP, UK
29 Earlsfort Terrace, Dublin 2, Ireland

BLOOMSBURY, BLOOMSBURY ACADEMIC and the Diana logo are trademarks of Bloomsbury Publishing Plc.

First published in the United States of America 2023
This paperback edition published 2025

Copyright © Jens Gerrit Papenburg, 2023

For legal purposes the Acknowledgements on p. vii constitute an extension of this copyright page.

Cover design: Louise Dugdale
Cover image © Max Alt

All rights reserved. No part of this publication may be reproduced or transmitted in any form or by any means, electronic or mechanical, including photocopying, recording, or any information storage or retrieval system, without prior permission in writing from the publishers.

Bloomsbury Publishing Inc. does not have any control over, or responsibility for, any third-party websites referred to or in this book. All internet addresses given in this book were correct at the time of going to press. The author and publisher regret any inconvenience caused if addresses have changed or sites have ceased to exist, but can accept no responsibility for any such changes.

Whilst every effort has been made to locate copyright holders the publishers would be grateful to hear from any person(s) not here acknowledged.

A catalog record for this book is available from the Library of Congress.

ISBN: HB: 978-1-5013-4670-5
PB: 979-8-7651-0482-8
ePDF: 978-1-5013-4672-9
eBook: 978-1-5013-4671-2

Typeset by Newgen KnowledgeWorks Pvt. Ltd., Chennai, India

To find out more about our authors and books visit www.bloomsbury.com and sign up for our newsletters.

Contents

Acknowledgements — vii

Part I Theory of Listening Devices: A Sound and Music Historical Survey — 1

1 Introduction — 3
  What are listening devices? Five theses — 5
  What is a sound and music history of listening devices? A sixth thesis — 22
  (Popular) music's listening devices, music listening as record listening,
    outline of the book and signposts for the reader — 27

Part II Listening Devices in (and before) Rock 'n' Roll Culture, c. 1940–60 — 37

2 Single-listening: The single is not single — 39
  Music as record: Listening to Little Richard's *Long Tall Sally* — 39
  Defining single and LP by musical forms and listening practices in the 1940s — 50
  Mastering industry standards and non-listening: 'Hot' rock 'n' roll singles — 62

3 Limited choice: Listening through jukeboxes in the 1950s — 73
  The jukebox sound: Rock 'n' roll and beyond, belly resonance and tuned
    playlists — 74
  The jukebox's modelling and managing of record listening — 88
  Coda: Listening subjects and practices, discourses and nostalgia — 101

Part III Listening Devices in (and before) Disco and Club Culture, c. 1970–90 — 105

4 The 12-inch single as listening device: Music history, margins of
    listening and mastered sound — 107
  'A great idea after the fact': Finding the 12-inch single in 1970s New York
    disco culture — 107
  Listening at the margins: Reading and feeling 12-inch singles — 120
  Maxi-sound: Mastering disco, house and techno — 126

5 Sound system listening: Histories, enhanced disco sound, listening
    techniques — 137
  Sound system history as sound and music history (and vice versa) — 137

Disco's enhanced sound systems	146
Listening techniques in disco and club culture	159
Conclusion and outlook: Towards listening devices in the digital era	167
Notes	175
Sources	277
Index	317

Acknowledgements

Writing a book is difficult without allies, but also without opponents. Opponents mark differences that do not always have to be sublated. Sometimes such differences have to be simply endured; sometimes they become productive again and again as problems and can thus drive one's own work. Allies comment, accompany, support and build up. The first ideas for this book emerged as early as 2005. I was in the process of developing the topic of my PhD dissertation. The subject of my reflections increasingly shifted: from an investigation of music production to post-production and to listening. Two things became more and more clear to me: first, I did not want to pit history against theory or theory against history in my research. Instead, I wanted to integrate both. Second, I wanted my work to connect to the interest in sound that I had found at Berlin's Humboldt University in musicology, especially in popular music studies there, but also in media studies, which had just been institutionalized at that university. The academic environment in which I was moving at that time (and in which I wanted to move further) was open, but by no means undefined. My PhD project finally landed at Humboldt University in musicology. I owe a special debt of gratitude to my academic teacher Peter Wicke. Wicke supervised my PhD dissertation, which I defended in 2011 and from which — after more than ten years — the present book would finally emerge. I also thank Veit Erlmann very much, who wrote the second review of my doctoral dissertation, for his feedback, which was as committed as it was trenchant, and for the many fruitful conversations we had as temporary office neighbours. I thank Wolfgang Ernst for keeping the conversation going and for keeping his media archaeology an important point of reference. Finally, I would like to thank Holger Schulze, who brought sound studies to Berlin and to the University of the Arts already in 2006, who always remained an important discussion partner for me, and who encouraged me (next to Veit Erlmann) to turn my PhD dissertation, which I had written in German, into an English language book.

This book then gained further contours in terms of content in the context of my work in the international research network "Sound in Media Culture. Aspects of a Cultural History of Sound" (2010–16) and in the context of two visiting professorships I was offered at the universities of Lüneburg and Düsseldorf between 2017 and 2019. I would like to thank all members and guests of the international research network founded by Holger Schulze, Maria Hanáček (1981–2013), and myself and generously funded by the German Research Foundation (DFG), especially: Karin Bijsterveld, Susanne Binas-Preisendörfer, Jochen Bonz, Michael Bull, Thomas Burkhalter, Diedrich Diederichsen, Franco Fabbri, Golo Föllmer, Marta García Quiñones, Thomas Hecken, Anahid Kassabian, Carla J. Maier, Carlo Nardi, Thomas Schopp, Jonathan Sterne and Simon Zagorski-Thomas. At the network's workshops, I was able to present for discussion and sharpen key ideas that have been incorporated into this book. I also thank my colleagues at the Institute for Media and Cultural Studies at the Heinrich-Heine-Universität in Düsseldorf, who brought me to the institute as a visiting professor from April 2018 to March 2019. In the colloquium in Düsseldorf, my book project received further productive input. I thank Kathrin Dreckmann in particular, Maximilian Haberer and Tomy Brautschek, and last but not least my esteemed colleague Dirk Matejovski, who is never at a loss for a clear stance. Thanks are also due to Rolf Großmann, Malte Pelleter, Sarah-Indriyati Hardjowirogo, Sebastian Vehlken and Leslie Post for the exchanges and work on the topic and everything else during my visiting professorship at ICAM at Leuphana Universität Lüneburg during the summer semester of 2017.

The final phase of work on the present book then began with my professorship at the University of Bonn, which I took up in April 2019. I thank my colleagues there – especially Tobias Janz, Jens Schröter and Britta Hartmann – and the team of my professorship: Steffen Just and Valentin Ris for discussions and conversations on the margins of the book topic; José Gálvez and Max Nicolas Schmidt for their comments on and corrections of the manuscript, for investigations and the creation of the index; Max Alt for his drawings that can be seen on the book's cover and the exchange on digital perspectives of listening devices. I thank Luisa Glees for her organizational support. To the translator and editor Gloria Custance, thanks for the linguistic polish and fine-tuning and good collaboration. Leah Babb-Rosenfeld of Bloomsbury is thanked for her patient support of the book project. To the anonymous reviewers of the book proposal and manuscript, I thank you for your close readings and productive criticism. Moreover, I thank Bodo Mrozek, with his unerring sense for trenchant texts and highly readable books, especially for his comments on considerations of possible (and impossible) titles for the book. Finally, my thanks go to the students who, from the winter semester of 2005 to the winter semester of 2016–17, allowed themselves to be stimulated and excited by my seminars, primarily at the Humboldt University, but also, since 2019, at the University of Bonn, thus leading the work on the book via detours, the goal of which is now here as a result. I dedicate the book to my family – Anima, Ophelia and Nicolas, my mother and my sister.

Part I

Theory of Listening Devices: A Sound and Music Historical Survey

1

Introduction

The aim of this book may sound quite simple – writing a history of music listening based on a history of the devices used for listening. However, such a project develops an appealing form of complexity if we are willing to entertain the fact that certain listening devices are integral and even constitutive parts of certain music cultures. As such, listening devices model and manage listening (thus, they are not only instruments used for listening). They are actively involved in the formation of the listener as well as of the music heard (thus, they are not only mere reproduction or playback technologies). However, even though listening devices are a constitutive part of music and sound culture, how they developed is co-determined by the history of music and sound. Finally, listening devices, time and again, remove themselves from listening – for only in this way can music be heard. By developing and picking up, knotting and linking these threads in the book, I seek to develop a new and unconventional method for a historiography of listening in sound and (popular) music studies, a historiography which is strongly informed by media and cultural theory. This method should allow me to reconstruct historical conceptualizations of music listening that gain shape more and more in relation to technology and devices.

In the Introduction, I explore some fundamental theoretical and methodological considerations upon which the book's case studies can build that engage with selected crucial listening devices of two popular music cultures – rock 'n' roll culture and disco and club culture. Considerations that address the following questions: What are listening devices? What is a sound and music history of listening devices? Which methods can we use to study this history? Since when has music listening been organized in relation to listening devices in general and record listening in particular? When and in which sound and music culture did the corresponding forms of listening become normative? Based on these aspects and questions, the goal of my book is to write a history of listening by setting a few spotlights that are trained on historical case studies. Using these case studies, I aim to carve out the specificity of music listening that is organized as record listening. Ever since the invention of the flat disc record in the late nineteenth century, music listening was organized more and more as record listening. This lasted at least until the late 1980s, when record listening came to a temporary end, only to have a nostalgic revival about twenty years later, a revival that is still ongoing. However, the book is not about record listening in general, but more precisely about listening to two types of vinyl single records: the small singles or 45s (45 revolutions per minute

[rpm]) with huge holes in the centre that the US company RCA Victor launched on the market in 1949; and the huge single records with small holes in the centre, the 12-inch singles or maxi singles that arrived on the scene in the 1970s, which were not developed solely by one major company. I shall study these two types of single records mainly in connection with jukeboxes in the United States and in West Germany from the late 1940s to the early 1960s, and in connection with loudspeaker systems chiefly in the United States from roughly 1970 to 1990. The small 45s will be my starting point for the analysis of rock 'n' roll culture, and the large 12-inch singles for the study of disco and club culture.

For a few years now, more and more voices in the booming discourse of sound studies have been claiming that the research field has moved into a 'postsonic' phase.[1] In its prior, that is, in its sonic phase, sound studies critiqued the hegemony of visuality in Western modernity, or rather the concept of Western modernity as a visual era, by reconstructing the presence of sound, listening and hearing in multiple domains such as science and politics, work and art, the economy and everyday life. Sound studies eagerly indulged in bashing 'visualism',[2] the 'primacy of the visual' [*Visualprimat*],[3] an approach to cultural analysis based on overt and implicit visual concepts such as 'enlightenment' or 'panopticism'[4] as well as – more basically – the separation and hierarchization of the senses with vision in the first place and – even more fundamentally – a 'visually based epistemology'[5] and a 'world as text' paradigm.[6] In the transdisciplinary field of sound studies, such criticisms were fielded by identifying sound and hearing as important and integral parts of modernity; by excavating the 'cultural and political agendas' that correlate with hierarchization of the senses;[7] or by developing an emphatic 'sonic epistemology'.[8] To counter the paradigm of the world as text, sound studies as well as its neighbour sensory studies proposed a 'sensory standpoint'.[9] Sound studies showed that 'the auditory is deeply caught up in the modern project'.[10] Sensory studies exposed 'the senses for what they are: historically and culturally generated ways of knowing and understanding'.[11] However, as Michael Bull and Les Back state in the introduction to the second edition of their influential book *The Auditory Culture Reader*: 'The intervening years [of sound studies] has seen much "deep listening" in the arts, humanities, and social sciences. Today, there is no place for special pleading in order to understand the significance of sound in society. There has been a dramatic and impressive explosion of sound studies across the board in the form of monographs, journals, edited editions, readers, and indeed international research grants.'[12]

In its postsonic phase, sound studies 'must let go of its axiomatic assumptions regarding the givenness of a particular domain called "sound", a process called "hearing" or a listening subject'.[13] This describes also the theoretical starting point of this book in a nutshell. By letting go of axiomatic assumptions regarding the givenness of a process called 'hearing' or 'listening', my book explores how 'listening' is configured as an entity that is culturally, in terms of media, and historically specific. As a key to unlock these complex configurations, I have chosen to study selected listening devices – vinyl single records, jukeboxes and sound systems. On the one hand, such devices are concrete objects of study. On the other hand, such devices are conditioned by and intermixed with complex cultural, media and historical forces, and moreover, they have the potential to transform and shape such forces. That is, I propose in the following to study listening devices not as isolated technological objects, but rather to use them as keys to unlock an understanding of the music and sound cultures of which they are important parts. I propose to study these sound and music cultures not primarily by focusing on their 'works' or their 'practices', but by focusing on their listening devices. However, while we might have listening devices as objects quick and easily at hand or at ear, it is quite challenging, as already hinted above, to develop 'listening device' as a concept. The following parts of this introduction are devoted precisely to this endeavour. In these parts, I try to develop listening device as a concept or rather as a peculiar kind of keyword for sound studies, a key that enables sound studies to analyse how what listening is, is defined to a lesser extent by axiomatic assumptions or as a given object but rather as a process that includes media, culture and history, a process that gets analytically accessible through listening devices. I shall now outline significant contours of the concept 'listening devices' in the form of five theses that I later complement with a sixth thesis.

What are listening devices? Five theses

I. Listening devices are modelling peculiar forms of listening

As instruments, listening devices are used and employed by people to listen with or through them. For instance, people use records and soundfiles to listen to music. Ludwig van Beethoven used his hearing aids in order to be able to hear anything at all. Hermann von Helmholtz employed his resonators to listen to harmonics and overtones. And so on. However, such objects and instruments demand a certain form of usage; their materiality represents a certain kind of resistance that may make certain ways of handling them appear more obvious than others.[14] Thus, listening devices are not only used by people, but there is also some kind of feedback, a recursive relation, a collaboration between the device and the listener.

However, some of these listening devices are themselves listening. This is not just a metaphor like the ones we find in anthropocentric media theories that narcissistically identify media with human sense organs, that understand media as extensions.[15] Following this theory, for instance, satellite networks would be a new 'skin' in the age of tactile, electronic media.[16] In contrast to such metaphoric transhumanist narratives, listening devices are indeed listening themselves, if a certain model of listening becomes part of the device, if there is 'human–machine mimesis':[17] 'When Marshall McLuhan called media the extensions of the human nervous system, he thought he was simply offering a smart metaphor. He did not seem aware of a long tradition of physiological investigation that understands the human nervous system as precisely an extension of media.'[18]

This kind of mimesis is the core of the modelling function of listening devices. We can find lots of examples of this already in nineteenth-century physiological research: The phonautograph of the nineteenth century is a 'machine ... to hear for them',[19] a machine to which hearing was delegated, a machine that modelled the outer ear and the middle ear and even parts of memory.[20] Bruno Latour distinguishes between understanding of technology as an instrument and as a delegation.[21] As an instrument, technology is used, maybe even mastered, by intentional subjects. In this case, technological objects are, as Latour puts it polemically, 'pliable and diligent slaves'.[22] As a delegation, technology functions as an actant that is 'symmetrical' to human actors.[23] What is delegated to a machine in the case of the phonautograph is, certainly, not hearing in general or in itself – whatever that may be – but a specific form of hearing that can be built as a technological model. In the case of the phonautograph, it is a conceptualization of hearing as a 'tympanic function',[24] as a process that is organized by the outer and middle ear. And the mechanics of the ear were modelized in the form of the phonautograph. Other listening devices model listening in other ways. Take, for instance, the mp3 file:

The mp3 file is not a 'machine ... to hear for people',[25] but a machine 'to perceive for them'.[26] Whereas the phonautograph as well as the phonograph modelled hearing as a function of the middle ear, the mp3 models hearing as a function of psychoacoustic effects. Here we find two different models: physiological models and psychoacoustic models. Listening devices, such as the phonoautograph or the mp3 file, model and simulate specific forms of listening. They are the results of studying the physiology of the human (sometimes animal) sensory organs.[27] In the present-day 'algorithmic listening',[28] listening is modelled as a process that is also connected to memory and learning.[29] All these models and simulations of listening are a kind of technologized organs. In these cases, the organ of listening is not the ear or the brain; it is a technological device. However, these devices are not only anthropomorphic devices, but they also enable new forms of machinic listening. As Friedrich Kittler puts it for the phonograph: 'The phonograph does not hear as do ears that have been trained immediately to filter voices, words, and sounds out of noise; it registers acoustic events as such.'[30] We can add that the modelling function of listening devices includes both: the simulation of human organs and their functions in a very specific way – thereby they are technologized organs – and the exceedance of the organs' anthropological functions – thereby they become escalated organs.

The models and simulations of listening that listening devices offer include a specific knowledge about what listening is. As a result, they are 'epistemic things' that constitute listening as an object of knowledge.[31] Thus, listening devices can again and again be involved in the conceptualization of listening in a new way. This is especially the case in the experiential sciences when they burgeoned in the field of listening, particularly in the nineteenth century. An 'experimentalization' of listening and hearing was initiated in physiological, and later in psychophysiological and psychological, laboratories above all in the United States and in Germany.[32] Hearing became an 'experimental system',[33] something that could be tested or, more basically, that is constituted as an epistemic entity via testing operations.[34] Thus, 'listening' and 'hearing' did not precede these experimental systems. Rather, they were primarily produced by these systems.

This is not only the case with listening devices in the context of experimental science, but also with devices for listening to music.

If we study records as listening devices, for example, we conceptualize listening as an entity that includes processes of repetition, capturing and even of memory. If we study a phonautograph as a listening device, we conceptualize listening in a very specific way, as the above-mentioned 'tympanic function'. Current computer-based models of listening conceptualize listening as an entity that includes experience, learning and personal biographies.[35] Thus, the relationship between the organic listening apparatus and technology can be reversed if the knowledge about the first one is first created in reference to listening devices. Instead of assuming that in modernity there would be anthropological constitution independent of technology, due to listening devices as epistemic things, it is possible to conceive of a simultaneity of humans and technology, possibly even a 'pre-existence' [*Vorgängigkeit*][36] of technology.

Here the direction is reversed: listening devices are not 'added' to forms of listening and hearing that existed before them. Instead of being technologized organs, they turn into a technology that has turned into an organ.[37] That is, a theory of the perceiving organ – which is supposed to be fundamental – and a theory of the device – which is supposed to be secondary – merge.[38] The media anthropologist Stefan Rieger calls this 'technology becoming organ',[39] where technology does not function as an extension or addition but is invasive. This has the consequence that it is no longer the 'body as a fact that is ontologised', but that media participate in the 'program of invariant formations'.[40] Media or technology are then no longer 'historically invariably the Other of man',[41] but the distinction between human nature and technology is questioned in general. Media come first here.

We can find such a concept of invasive technologization that goes together with listening device's modelling function both in media epistemology and in media phenomenology. The philosopher Gernot Böhme uses the term 'invasive technification' in contradistinction to extension technology. According to Böhme, invasive technification is not causal and instrumental, but structural and transformative.[42] In terms of perception, Böhme outlines the structural and transformational by proposing that 'perception itself has come to be structured along technical lines'.[43] This connection between technology and perception is exemplified by Böhme as follows: 'The possibilities of perception itself are moulded by a vast range of technical media. Just as the categories of visual perception have long been moulded by photography (seeing something well has come to mean seeing it in sharp focus), what people are conditioned to hear has, in recent times, been increasingly moulded by acoustic technology as well.'[44] Here, listening devices are not only a means to an end or instruments that can be played and mastered – comparable to musical instruments. In addition, listening devices are generators of knowledge and models of listening.[45] Even if the models of hearing and listening that are implemented in the listening devices themselves bring us, as we have seen again and again, to the history of science, they also include political and economic agendas. For instance, statistical models of perceptual coding could include 'neoliberal market logics'.[46] I will return to this thread dealing with an economization of listening later, when discussing the management of listening (Thesis V).

II. Listening devices address the materialities of listening and organize listening as a cultural technique

Listening devices are affecting the materiality, the corporality, the hardware of listening and listening culture. By technifying the materialities of listening, they are modulating the listening capacity.[47] Thus, a study of listening through listening devices includes objects, artefacts, things and non-human actors. The term 'listening device' can thus be seen as the answer to the following problem, which became more and more relevant for music and sound cultures in the second half of the twentieth century: With what or with which devices and technologies were specific forms of music listened to? To study the materiality of listening, this book conceptualizes music listening as a cultural technique.[48]

Especially in musicology, there is a long tradition that understands listening in a rather idealistic, non-material way. From 'attentive' 'listening as a spiritual practice' in aristocratic circles in early modern Italy[49] to music critic Eduard Hanslick's 'deliberate, pure contemplation' of a musical work;[50] from Theodor W. Adorno's infamous 'structural listener'[51] who listens 'fully conscious'[52] and according to 'musical logic'[53] to Hugo Riemann's 'mental representations of tones' [*Tonvorstellungen*];[54] from a 'history of listening categories'[55] to listening as an 'operation of the intellect' [*Geistesoperation*][56] and Felix Salzer's 'structural hearing'.[57] Since the 1990s, such idealistic forms of listening became the objects of often harsh criticism through detecting their implicit normativity,[58] their cultural specificity as a part of a 'bourgeois experience'[59] and by showing that they are 'deeply interwoven with the Othering of the senses within the larger project of Western colonial domination', because 'proper listening ... was teleological listening, moving up from raw sensuousness to higher levels of transcendence'.[60] We can add here that despite all the pleas for 'spirit', 'logic', 'sense', 'interiority' and 'attention', there are even specific forms of materiality and corporality that condition these 'ideal' forms of listening. For instance, Riemann's mental representations of tones correlate with the score and the keyboard,[61] Adorno's structural listener has a body that is reduced to a thinking ear[62] and the contemplating, fully attentive listener relies on the real spaces of concert halls where 'absolute music' is presented.[63]

The core question raised by these idealistic approaches to music listening seems to be the question of how do, or rather how should, people listen to music.[64] By contrast, the study of music listening that takes the study of listening devices as its starting point begins with the question *through what* do people listen to music? This question addresses first and foremost the materialities of listening. Certainly, the study of these materialities has a long tradition as well. However, we do not find this so much in musicology, but primarily in the history of science, especially in anatomy, physiology and even psychology where the 'ear's rich physicality' is addressed.[65]

In the wake of research on cultural techniques, we can now stop perpetuating the dualism of hearing as a physical process on the one hand, and listening as an intellectual activity on the other. Instead, we can understand listening as a 'body-object-technique'.[66] The materialities of listening include the materialities of the listening organs of the hearing apparatus. Moreover, they include media, artefacts, things and devices for listening. The study of listening via listening devices analyses listening as a cultural technique. As a cultural technique, listening is not studied as a 'universal human capacity', but as a 'special case of acoustic perception',[67] a special case that is not defined by a normalized materiality of *Homo sapiens*' body nor as a mere 'intellectual technique' [*Geistestechnik*][68] as is the case in the above-mentioned rather idealized conceptions of listening. The objects that are part of listening as a cultural technique are contingent. Cultural techniques such as counting, calculating and writing presuppose objects for counting, calculating and writing. They are organized in very different and very specific ways depending on which objects are involved.[69] As with all cultural techniques, listening as a cultural technique 'cannot be derived from a body technique'.[70] Unlike an anthropological body technique, listening as a cultural technique is constituted in relation to an artefact. We can develop these considerations in reference to music and sound.

Likewise, the practice of making music, whether music is made with a piano or with a digital audio workstation, is different in each case.[71] Likewise, the practice of listening to music can have specificity depending on whether music is listened to, for instance, with a stereo system, a smartphone or a powerful sound system with sub-bass speakers. Depending on the music culture, such practices are based on specific normativities that are differentiated by media, materialities and instruments. Thus, listening as a cultural technique is not just a body technique,[72] a cultural practice,[73] a discourse or a text,[74] nor is it an art.[75] As a cultural technique, listening is organized in relation to devices, such as 'sonic skills'[76] or 'audile techniques'.[77] The materiality of listening is defined by devices.

Some approaches from sound studies have analysed the relationship of listening and technologies[78] and investigated 'how material objects prompt new ways of listening'.[79] The devices that are included in listening as a body-object-technique constitute listening in a *recursive* way. That is, the devices are not only used by listeners as mere instruments or are listening instead of the listener. In addition, listening is organized here primarily in the interaction between listeners and listening devices.[80] Thus, listening as a cultural technique is not projective – using prostheses, instruments and 'organ projections'[81] – but recursive. As shown earlier, listening devices (as instruments) are used to organize a specific form of listening. Moreover, they simulate a specific form of listening (as models), and ultimately, they can generate new knowledge about what listening is (as knowledge generators). Thus, the objects that listening as a cultural technique includes do not have to include an imitation, an extension, a mimesis of the human body or an anthropomorphic entity. In such a case, such objects and devices are involved in the constitution of peculiar forms of listening.

The study of listening as a cultural technique assumes a concept of culture that is constituted technically and materially. This is what distinguishes it from most praxeological and phenomenological approaches. The study of listening devices sets a different analytical focus than practice-based or praxeological approaches to listening. Rather than discussing listening as a cultural practice, a body technique, or in the form of rituals, behaviour or habits of listening, I deploy in this book – following the research on cultural techniques – a concept of listening informed by technology: 'Cultural techniques reveal that there never was a document of culture that was not also one of technology.'[82] The philosopher Sybille Krämer and the cultural studies scholar Thomas Macho have argued for an investigation of culture that starts with its 'factual and technical dimension'.[83] They distinguish such a conceptualization from approaches that ennoble culture as discursivized intellectual culture and the culture-as-text approaches: 'For a long time, perhaps too long, culture was considered a text!'[84] Listening devices are a part of the technical dimension of culture.

Even if a study of listening via listening devices starts with the question *through what* do people listen to music – and not with the question – *how* do people listen to music, the study of listening as a cultural technique does also include the how question. However, not at the most basic level, but more at a secondary level. As a cultural technique listening opens up and processes distinctions and thus includes practices with symbols. For instance, Jonathan Sterne discusses 'audile techniques' that are organized in relation to sonic technologies such as the stethoscope or the phonograph.[85] And beginning in the late eighteenth century, physicians developed listening techniques with the stethoscope that they used to code what they had heard as either sick or healthy.[86] We can also link such a processing of distinctions with Emily Thompson's discussion of the Tone Tests that Thomas Alva Edison's company initiated as a marketing campaign for the phonograph from 1915 to 1925. Through the Edison phonograph, the audience at the Tone Tests should develop a listening technique to distinguish 'creation from re-creation, authentic from imitation'.[87] Relying on such distinctions that cultural techniques establish and process, cultural orders can be built on.[88]

At a very basic level, listening as a cultural technique also opens up and processes the distinction between nature and culture. Traditional cultural techniques such as ploughing or draining turn 'nature into culture'.[89] In the wake of 'elementary cultural techniques' such as counting, calculating and writing, 'skills and aptitudes necessary to master the new media ecology' are a 'culturalization of technology'.[90] Moreover, the study of listening as a cultural technique reconstructs 'operative chains composed of actors and technological objects that produce cultural orders'.[91] Such operative chains 'give rise to notions and objects that are then endowed with essentialized identities',[92] notions and objects such as 'the listener' or 'listening'. The listener (as a subject of a specific culture) is constituted by listening as a cultural technique.[93] Thus, the study of listening as a cultural technique does not presuppose a listener or a concept of listening. Instead, it tends to reconstruct the 'basic operations and differentiations that give rise' to the listener and listening as 'conceptual and ontological entities which are said to constitute culture'.[94] Thus, following research on cultural techniques ontological entities and distinctions are produced by media processes: 'Underneath our ontological distinctions (if not even our own evolution) are constitutive, media-dependent ontic operations that need to be teased out by means of techno-material deconstruction.'[95] Thereby an analysis of listening as a cultural technique problematizes the distinction between the nature of listening/culture of listening as it is presented in the form of a physiology of listening and a technology of listening. Instead of a binarism of technology and physiology, this book analyses the intermixing of technology and organs, technology becoming organs as well as organs becoming technology. By addressing the materialities of listening, listening devices problematize the dichotomy of a 'natural' physiological hearing apparatus on the one hand and artificial listening technologies on the other. Thus, studying listening as a cultural technique means to analyse listening as a body-object-technique, that is as a technique which is constituted in the relation between the body and an object. As a cultural technique, listening opens up and processes specific distinctions. These processes and techniques precede concepts of the listener and listening.

III. Listening devices are combining a history of listening and its 'Other'; that is, a history of non-listening and a history of the unhearable

Increasingly sound studies defines its objects in relation to its 'Other', that is, in relation to deaf studies[96] or in relation to unsound studies.[97] By referencing phenomena such as infrasound, vibration and tactile or haptic sound experiences, and by studying events such as the deaf rave movement or bass cultures, such approaches critique an 'ear-centrism',[98] a 'cochlear-centrism'[99] or a 'sonocentrism' with its 'purely audiological conceptions of sound'.[100] Moreover, scholars such as Friedrich Kittler,[101] Wolfgang Scherer,[102] Wolfgang Hagen,[103] Jonathan Sterne[104] and Mara Mills[105] have shown that not only hearing and listening, but also their Other, that is, deafness, has been a driving force in the development of sonic media technologies. Referring to the fact that Thomas Alva Edison was hard of hearing, Kittler concluded: 'A physical impairment was at the beginning of mechanical sound recording – just as the first typewriters had been made by the blind for the blind, and Charles Cros had taught at a school for the deaf and mute.'[106] Sterne showed how the development of the ear phonautograph by Alexander Graham Bell and Clarence Blake in 1874 was motivated by Bell's interest in 'education of the deaf'[107] and his 'ultimate goal was training the deaf to speak'.[108] We can link our analysis of music's listening devices with these considerations, because such devices also have a close relationship to non-listening. For instance, this relationship addresses the modes of listening that do not rely on attention, such as the ubiquitous listening that Anahid Kassabian[109] has described in relation to the escalating presence of so-called background music, which also correlates with the success of mobile listening devices. However, the relation of listening devices to non-listening also includes other levels. As instruments, listening devices elude listening; as models, listening devices can hear and register sounds that exceed (or undercut) human listening and create knowledge about the peripheries of listening and the manipulability of the human senses.

As instruments for listening, listening devices give users sounds to hear, but themselves systematically elude being heard. Thus, the listening devices themselves remain unheard. Although it is common to speak of 'listening to a CD' or 'listening to a record', the CD or record itself is actually not being listened to, because only then is it possible to hear the music. On this level, the listening device itself only becomes hearable when disturbance, or interference, becomes audible as noise; for instance, the surface noise of a record, the glitches of a CD or the compression artefacts of a soundfile. However, technical and industry standards for listening devices function to render listening devices unhearable. 'Standards determine how media reach our senses.'[110] In terms of perception, such standards also have the function of making technologies imperceptible industry-wide.[111] Industrial standards in the 1950s sought to make technologies easier to be ignored or to cross over into the realm of the inaudible. However, in popular music cultures, there are now numerous examples of how technical standards that aimed to make certain media inaudible throughout the industry – such as the recording curve, that is, the curve that defines the degree in which certain frequencies are increased and decreased during cutting a record and during playback – were not accepted. Instead, recording curves were aestheticized in various practices, such as in practices like 'hot' mastering. In this volume, a history of non-listening is analysed by studying such an aestheticization of technical and industry standards of records. That is, by elaborating the development and implementation of industry standards, like for the vinyl record in the 1950s, I illustrate how that medium's functioning was rendered unhearable industry-wide and how such industry standards were ignored, time and again, in record production.

Further, I analyse the history of non-listening by exploring the visceral power of unheard sound.[112] In their modelling function listening devices include a specific form of listening. However, some listening devices also include sound at the periphery of listening. In his analysis of forms of 'sonic dominance'[113] in environments of Jamaican sound system culture, where the sound of the music dominates the other senses and a form of 'bass materialism' rules, Steve Goodman diagnosed something that he called a 'rearrangement of the senses'.[114] This includes not only a new hierarchy of the senses – Goodman is especially interested in club environments where sound seems more important than vision. It can also include a new arrangement of the connection of the senses and thus questions the organization of the sensorium in the form of discrete sensory channels. In what Goodman calls 'bass materialism', listening is closely connected by sound systems with touch, haptics and tactility. Thus, the non-listening that listening devices include is constituted via a link of listening to haptics.

Linking a history of listening and a history of non-listening listening devices establishes what media studies scholars have called an 'an-aesthetic' field.[115] Especially listening devices as epistemic things explore this field. We find many examples of this in the history of the physiology of hearing, the psychology of listening and in psychoacoustics.[116] These domains explore the peripheries of hearing and listening using technical measuring devices: What frequencies can/cannot be heard? How loud does a frequency need to be in order to be audible? How do different sounds mask each other? Thereby media-technical knowledge about the manipulability of human senses is constituted.[117] Listening is technologized when the listening technologies themselves go unheard, or rather systematically elude hearing. Nevertheless, they are constitutive for that which *is* heard.[118]

Against the backdrop of these considerations, in this volume I analyse the link of the history of listening to a history of non-listening that is explored by listening devices in relation to (a) industry standards that aim to make records imperceptible, (b) listening devices that sonically address sensory channels beyond the ears and (c) sensory knowledge of the 'an-aesthetic field' that the devices open up. Therefore, this book's exploration of listening devices implies a putative methodological paradox: Listening will also be analysed based on moments when it is actually systematically circumvented.

IV. Listening devices mediate actively between the (listening) subject and the object; thereby they co-constitute the music heard

Even if listening devices elude being listened to, they never simply go unheard, but instead continuously (co-)constitute both what is heard and the listeners themselves. Listening devices mediate actively between subject and object. Therefore, they are involved in the constitution of the listener and of the music heard. While the co-constitution of the listener is organized via listening as a cultural technique (see Thesis II above), the co-constitution of the heard music is organized at three other levels: in relation to the technical standards of the listening devices; in reference to music (post-)production processes (especially the final phase of music production is relevant here: mastering) and by the sonic activation of the devices themselves. In order for a sound to be heard as music in the first place, it must be adapted to particular listening technologies; only in this way can sound be made jukebox-, radio- or club-ready, for example. Nor is music strictly listened to with the ear. In fact, listening to music is a bodily practice that is transformed and (co-)constituted by technology. Just as today photos have to be 'instagrammable' and soundfiles have to be 'streamable' rock 'n' roll songs had once to be 'playlistable'. To this end, I shall pay particular attention to examining the mastering process and its theoretical substantiation.

In mastering, a sound is adapted to the specific physical properties of the recording format on which it is to be released. The mastering engineers surveyed in this book made vinyl record singles from magnetic audio tape. Mastering is the last stage in the music production process during which the sound is altered, and it mediates between the studio and the listener.

Yet listening devices are not only playback devices or devices for mere reproduction. They are an integral and even a constitutive part of the heard music. In contrast to playback technologies, listening devices do not only reproduce music, music that existed independently of and prior to the device, but the music is also attuned to a particular listening device. In contrast to the term listening device, 'playback technology' leads to a dead end: the term suggests that something which already exists – as a fixed entity, as something with a fully constituted identity – is simply being reproduced; that the identity of the music was already constructed prior to the playback. Thus, 'playback technology' does not admit enough consideration of the constitutive role of technology. By contrast, I argue for a concept of music that includes listening devices as constitutive parts. This can be explored analytically on the three levels already mentioned earlier. I will now elaborate on these levels:

At a very basic level, listening devices pre-hear that which is listened to through them. About eighty years ago, Adorno argued that in the case of popular music the 'composition hears for the listener', that popular music is 'pre-digested'.[119] Following on from this, we can analyse under the concept of the pre-heard, standardizations, normalizations, formalizations and formatting of popular music based on listening technologies. Such technical standards and norms, limitations and restrictions correlate with aesthetic norms: one striking example of this is the 45-rpm single's limited playing time and the standardization of song length to approximately three minutes. Moreover, music is produced and post-produced in relation to certain listening devices. Legendary music producer, rapper and business man Dr. Dre, for instance, said that he makes music 'for people to play in their cars' and added: 'You [are] in your car all the time, the first thing you do is turn on the radio, so that's how I figure. When I do a mix, the first thing I do is go down and see how it sounds in the car.'[120] Tuning music to a specific listening device is thus part of music's post-production. Especially mastering, a still understudied function in music's production process, is relevant here. Audio mastering is done on tunes that are produced in a studio or recorded 'live' in relation to listening devices. In the book's case studies, I shall analyse selected concrete tunings. In addition to the levels of presupposition of media materiality on the one hand, and the tuning of the (post-)production process on the other, listening devices can have a constitutive function for music and its sound on a third level: they can enhance the sound of music during listening. For example, in 1974, the movie *Earthquake* (United States, 1974), a disaster drama, was on general release. For that movie, a specific sound system was developed: the Sensurround system, a system that included powerful sub-bass speakers that enabled the audience to feel the tremors of the earthquake physically. However, the sub-bass vibrations were not on the film's soundtrack. Instead, the soundtrack included signals that controlled the generation of sub-bass signals by synthesizers included in the Sensurround system itself.[121] We also find such a sonic activation of listening devices in the 'enhanced' bass sound of disco's sound systems in the 1970s,[122] in bass booster apps and in current-day personalized equalization for smartphones.

If we are prepared to grasp such forms of tunings not as rather accidental in comparison to the 'real' music, we will require a quite complex and somewhat unconventional concept of music. We can develop this concept of music more precisely in reference to popular music studies,[123] especially popular music studies that are informed by actor-network theory[124] on the one hand, and by media theory[125] on the other. The musicologist Peter Wicke has sketched how the relevance of listening devices for the identity of music might look and how it can be conceptualized: 'The same song – listened to through headphones at home, or as part of a 90-minutes-long stage performance, or as material used for dancing in a club – is the same song in name only. A differently structured form emerges when the song is made accessible for dancing by the bassline, from, for example, in the case of the subject-centred aesthetic perception through headphones, which follows the relationship between text and sound.'[126] According to these considerations, listening devices do not have a reproductive but a constitutive function for that which is heard as music. Wicke outlines a concept of music that is different from an 'objectivist' concept of music shaped by categories such as work, form and authorship and is also different from a 'subjectivist' concept that understands music as a product of subjective perception.[127] Instead, music is understood as a relation: *Music is created in a relationship, mediated by listening devices situated between the sound event and the listener's body.*

Here the listening devices do not function as neutral tools that convey music which preceded them as free of all interference as possible. Rather, music is created in the relationship between the sound event, the listening device and the listener's body. Thus, music is conceptualized here as something that arises between the sound event and the listening subject. Listening body and listening device are both part of this concept of music: 'Musical experience results from the encounter with sound, which, at the moment of perception by the listening subject, is first of all nothing other than a sensory differentiated and self-structured sensual fact of experience.'[128] However, such a relationship between sound and the listening subject is not shaped exclusively by subjective idiosyncrasies. It is generalizable via conceptual schemes. Wicke adds: 'Basically, musical experience is conceptually organised. ... What reaches the ear is located in categorial ordering schemes.'[129] It remains to be investigated – and this is one of my book's central purposes – to what extent such schemata are supplemented by material mediations, that is listening devices, that have organized the relationship between sound events and the listener's body since the second half of the twentieth century. Such a listener-oriented concept of music does not point in the orthodox direction of composer- or artwork-oriented music historiography with its analysis of listeners that are implicated in the 'music itself'.[130] Listening devices are not to be studied as something that mediates pre-existing music: instead they are studied as something that is involved in the constitution of music.

The concept of music outlined here cannot be reduced to the listening subject, since the latter's experiences are mediated by schemata and technologies. These schemata and technologies, in turn, differentiate and structure the sound event, which is not determinable 'in itself'. This, of course, does not exclude an inherently indeterminable differentiation of the sound event; Wicke speaks of 'internal structural determinants' of the 'sound forms'.[131] Music is here conceptualized as a multiplicity or as a heterogeneous network, which is linked via sonic and also non-sonic nodes.[132] Thus – following Wicke – we can understand music as a network and not as a work of art. This notion of a network is contrary to the concept of the musical work, as well as its dialectically understood derivatives. Following these derivatives, 'music itself' exists only in relation to cultural contexts. The concept of music outlined here can be further elaborated by connecting it with the concept of music of various authors who have been working under the label 'theories of mediation'.[133] From the perspective of musical mediation theories, the identity of a work of art is dependent on technologies such as headphones, sound systems, mobile devices, records, jukeboxes and so forth.

In this regard, we can conceptualize listening devices as active 'material mediators'[134] that include a 'positive concept of mediation',[135] which discriminates it from conceptualization as an intermediary. As an intermediary, a listening device would be rather passive, and 'defining its inputs is enough to define its outputs'.[136] In approaches of popular music studies that are informed by an advanced concept of media,[137] we also find an understanding of technological media as a 'positive ... techno-cultural extension of musical design' and not a 'necessary malady of mass distribution'.[138] When Wicke points out that in the 1950s, the sound carrier became the 'normative paradigm of music',[139] this means that media are understood as a technology that is not external to music, but rather helps to constitute it. Thus, since the 1950s at the latest, music has not only been recorded in recording studios, but has also increasingly become 'produced music'; that is, a form of music not reducible to performed music and notated music.[140] Or, as the historian Susan Schmidt Horning puts it, placing the historical cut-off a decade later than Wicke: 'During the 1960s, the studio became an instrument in its own right, which musicians and producer–engineering teams exploited to create new sounds, rather than simply trying to capture them. This is often seen as the beginning of "engineered performances", that is, musical events that existed first as recordings, only later to be recreated by mimicking the record in concert.'[141]

To develop the thesis that listening devices co-constitute the heard music, that is, are not external to it, the conceptualization of listening devices as a mediator in the sense of actor-network theory is particularly useful. Sociologist and early popular music studies scholar Antoine Hennion, in particular, has developed the concept of the mediator with regard to music by showing that music does not exist in its own right, but only as mediated and not independent of mediators.[142] Hennion's project is 'a rewriting of music from the viewpoint of mediation'.[143] Mediators are more precisely defined by Hennion as 'active producers', which he distinguishes from 'passive intermediaries'.[144] According to Hennion's theory of mediation, there is no music that is prior to material mediation. Hennion states this in the following formula: 'Mediations in music ... are the art that they reveal.'[145] Hennion thus advances a concept of the mediator in which mediation is understood without an object, that is, intransitively. Mediation is not appropriated as a deficient disturbance of identity, but is written as a constitutive process.

We can find another example of a positive mediation concept that explicitly refers to technical mediators in a critical examination of Walter Benjamin's concept of technology, which Hennion developed with Bruno Latour. In contrast to Benjamin, Hennion and Latour do not want technology to be understood as a reproduction technology but as a production technology.[146] They exemplify this by taking the example of the sound engineer: 'Every sound engineer knows that his techniques produce music; they do not re-produce anything. Technique has always been the means of producing art.'[147] Moreover, by examining technique as a positive mediator, Hennion and Latour note that every technique of reproduction produces something: the original! There is no original work before technical mediation or reproduction. Thus, the original – and this is also true in Benjamin – is 'always constituted retrospectively, by the supplement of reproduction only as a supplemented'.[148] Hennion and Latour call the process that precedes the original 'an intense technical reproduction'.[149] Therefore, understanding music via the concept of the 'original work' is a product of reproduction techniques, used by both the recording industry and musicology.[150]

For the time being, we can summarize that with musical mediation theories an investigation of music via an investigation of material mediators can be embarked upon. These mediators are determined as active and non-human. The notion of a musical object or of 'music itself'[151] is rejected in favour of a relational concept of music: 'What remains is a view of music as a hardening mixture, a relationship which ties itself between humans while using material mediators.'[152] The musicologist Richard Middleton reformulates the concept of music that is hinted at here: 'The musical worlds that we inhabit, then, are not clear sets, filled with autonomous entities which are foreign to each other and connected only via neutral "links": rather, they are halfway worlds, without clear boundaries, filled with transient knots of variable meaning, practice, and status.'[153] Listening devices as mediators are involved in the constitution of such half-way worlds.

V. Listening devices are managing listening

Listening devices are managing listening.[154] In relation to listening devices, listening is organized as a process that is controllable, manageable. We encounter listening to music here not solely as a cultural practice.[155] In relation to listening devices, listening to music is increasingly becoming an economic issue. Yet the management of listening consists in more than economism. In addition to the capitalization and economization of perception, in addition to exploring listening as an exploitable resource, management also implies culturalization; that is, the transformation of a supposedly universal human capability into a culture-specific capability. In managing listening, economy and culture come together.

The process of managing listening began already with the increasing development of auditory technologies and media like the telephone and the phonograph in the late nineteenth century. Ever since then, listening has been co-organized by technologies and more and more listening is done via instruments. Present-day streaming services are also researching listening as an economic problem.[156] With this, they are carrying on an industrial tradition, which appeared in the US telephone industry in the early twentieth century and defined 'hearing as an economic problem'.[157] In the case of streaming services, the management of listening not only includes the physiology of hearing and psychoacoustics like the older audio technologies did, but to a greater extent the processes of segmentation, pattern recognition, cognition, learning, memory and expectation.[158] And, as has been ascertained in the context of a political economy of streaming, the transformation of listening into a strange form of unpaid labour.[159]

In this book, too, listening devices are analysed as being involved fundamentally in the transformation of listening into a resource that can be managed and controlled, explored and exploited. For a study of listening devices, this means that to study just the instrumental function of listening devices, which engages with the question of how and for which ends a specific listening device is used, would only scratch the surface.

To be able to conceptualize the transformation of listening into a manageable resource, a short excursus to Martin Heidegger's philosophy of technology is helpful. In his philosophy of technology, Heidegger famously problematizes an understanding of technology through an instrumental function. By contrast, Heidegger states far more fundamentally that (modern) technology challenges humans to place themselves in a very specific relation to the world. Technology, or rather the technicity of technology – Heidegger calls this the 'essence of technology' – sets up a certain framework for humans to be in the (modern) world. In modernity, according to Heidegger, this framework anticipates the individual who uses technology as an instrument. Heidegger defines this specific relation to be in the world as a relation that captures the world – he also speaks of 'reality' or 'nature' – as something that he calls a standing reserve [*Bestand*]. In this context, the world turns into something that is 'to be on call', 'orderable' [*bestellbar*] and 'nature' appears here as a 'calculable coherence of forces'.[160] Or, as the philosopher Oswald Spengler expressed it two decades before Heidegger, 'We think only in horsepower now; we cannot look at a waterfall without mentally turning it into electric power; we cannot survey a countryside full of pasturing cattle without thinking of its exploitation as a source of meat supply; we cannot look at the beautiful old handwork of a lively and primitive people without wishing to replace it by a modern technical process'.[161] Nature, as a 'calculable coherence of forces', is controllable, saveable and transmittable. Through modern technology the challenge of nature 'happens in that the energy concealed in nature is unlocked, what is unlocked is transformed, what is transformed is stored up, what is stored up is, in turn, distributed, and what is distributed is switched about ever anew. Unlocking, transforming, storing, distributing, and switching about are ways of revealing. ... Regulating and securing even become the chief characteristics of the challenging revealing'.[162]

However, according to Heidegger, technology not only challenges humans to place themselves in very specific relationship to the world. What is more, humans are challenged to place themselves in very specific relationship to themselves as humans. Thus, following Heidegger, we can conclude that technology in modernity challenges what is human, that it functions as a kind of framework – Heidegger employs the term 'enframing' [*Ge-stell*]. Unlike Jürgen Habermas's concept of technology, which understands technology through the concepts of instrumentality and rationalization, and as something that is used by humans, Heidegger's concept of technology assumes that modern technology does something with/to humans.

Heidegger's concept of technology as a frame or framework in which the real is concealed in a specific way – as a force, a standing reserve – and according to which technology is not dominated by humans, but instead challenges humankind, is quite close to the concept of media in media theory. The latter strives to uncover or archaeologically excavate the specific media conditions operative in literature,[163] music,[164] the soul,[165] the senses[166] or knowledge, for example.[167] Technology following Heidegger and media following media theory *do* something, they are – to say the least – active and, according to the thesis put forward in media theory, independent of human intentions and actions as well as independent of whether 'we have a concept of them'.[168] Kittler's triad of transmission or 'select, store, and process'[169] that should characterize his systems of recording can also arguably be understood as a variation on Heidegger's series of 'unlocking, transforming, storing, distributing, and switching about'.[170] However, in terms of media theory, Heidegger's concept of technology gets two updates. First, the relation of technology to nature, and thus Heidegger's adherence to the naturalness/artificiality schema, can be criticized.[171] Second, the essence of technology can be determined differently; in this determination, especially the relation between technology and time is accentuated.[172]

What do these considerations mean for our context; that is, for a study of listening devices? Against this backdrop, we can understand the technicity of listening devices more fundamentally as something that produces a specific relationship to the world and to oneself, that transforms listening into a standing reserve, into a resource.[173]

We can further carve out a managing of listening by listening devices by discriminating it from a pedagogy of listening. A pedagogy of listening is, for instance, part of musicological curricula as ear training, or of musical training and music theory. For pedagogy, frequently the musician or the composer is a kind of ideal type of listener. That is, the listener here shall listen like a musician or like a composer. Managing music listening again and again disengages listening from the listening of the musician or of the composer.

With the invention of listening devices for music listening, media industries developed a huge interest in music listening. This interest is part of an economization of listening. In the wake of this interest, concepts of listening emerged that are not oriented on forms of listening practised by musicians or composers. The managing of music listening that began in the nineteenth century became effective on a mass scale through the spread of radio and the gramophone. On the basis of these technologies, listening practices emerged in music culture that separated music listening from music making. This separation – driven primarily by the entertainment industry's approaches to listening that transform 'listeners into consumers'[174] – was long ignored by the discourses on listening in musicology as well as in cultural studies.[175] Particularly in musicology, the listener was not studied as a listener, but had to be ennobled as a composer or at least as a musician; as a listening composer or as a listening musician.[176]

This meant that the answer to the question 'Who listens?' quickly took on a slant in musicological and cultural studies discourses towards the musician or the composer. For Adorno, for example, the ideal music listener is not a listener at all in her or his own right, but actually a musician or even a 'professional musician'.[177] This strategy of elevation escalated in the discourse of musicology where the listener is even accorded the status of a composer.[178] We also find in Roland Barthes's and Peter Szendy's approaches to music listening, such strategies of elevation. However, in these cases, the strategies are guided by a productive modesty. Szendy, for instance, examines the listener not as composer but as an arranger: 'An arranger is a listener who signs and writes his listening'.[179] Barthes's listener is not a professional, but explicitly an amateur musician that Barthes placed in an amateur culture organized around the piano. Barthes locates its origins in an aristocratic milieu, and then sees it continued rather badly by the bourgeoisie of the nineteenth century. He takes up the cudgels for this culture's own music. He calls it 'muscular music'.[180] Muscular music, he argues, is a *musica practica*; a music that one makes and not music that one merely hears with one's ears: 'The sense of hearing is one only of ratification, as though the body were hearing – and not "the soul"'.[181] Barthes's listener, like Adorno's ideal listener, is ultimately a musician; but, in contrast to Adorno, not a professional. This leads to the fact that Adorno's ideal listener is not only a professional musician, but ideally hears like the composer of the piece of music heard. Whether Barthes denies the composer such a power of definition or authority and opens it up in favour of pluralized, equally coexisting modes of listening, remains open. Moreover, Barthes endows his listener with a specific corporeality. Whereas Adorno's ideal listener is condensed into the already above mentioned thinking ear,[182] listening for Barthes extends to the whole body, and finds a power centre, especially in the piano-playing and dexterity of the hands. Some organs or body parts are assigned a new function by Barthes. To summarize: in the discourses described here, the listener is not understood as a listener, but primarily as a musician, arranger or composer.

Adorno and Barthes carved out forms of listening that do not manage listening. In Barthes's case, listening is situated in a music culture of the eighteenth and nineteenth centuries. Its instrument is the piano and not media technologies. Barthes locates his listener/musician along with muscular music in a specific time period: 'This music has disappeared; initially the province of the idle (aristocratic) class, it lapsed into an insipid social rite with the coming of the democracy of the bourgeoisie (the piano, the young lady, the drawing room, the nocturne) and then faded out altogether (who plays the piano today?).'[183] In the course of the twentieth century, pianos had been replaced primarily by technical media such as records and radio (but also by the professionalized concert).[184] These new media changed listening not only in the musical culture of the aristocracy and the upper middle class, as Barthes mentions, but also in that of the American working class. At the beginning of the twentieth century, the US military bandmaster John Philip Sousa, who popularized the term 'canned music', also saw (his) musical culture endangered by the radio and the gramophone.[185] Historian William H. Kenney writes of Sousa: 'He [Sousa] proudly estimated that the American working class owned more pianos, violins, guitars, mandolins and banjos than in the rest of the world; but once they started listening to the phonograph, America's children would stop practicing and music teachers would be driven out of business.'[186]

Music sociologist Simon Frith points out that popular music culture became dominated by radio, film and the jukebox in the 1930s. Frith links the changes in the music business in that decade to changes in music making and music listening. In general, Frith surmises that the spatial and temporal distance between music making and music listening was increased by jukeboxes and radios. This distance also enabled new forms of subjects: a 'direct communication between artist and audience' had become a 'gap between star and consumer' in an industrial culture.[187] Like Barthes, Frith describes a change in the amateur culture of music making: 'The development of a large-scale record industry marked a profound transformation in musical experience, a decline in amateur music making, the rise of a new sort of musical consumption and use.'[188] Such a shift in musical culture as described by Barthes and Frith necessarily entails a fundamental change in listening culture. Musicians, composers and arrangers are no longer role models for the music listener. The music listener undergoes dissociation in relation to these role models.

The listening of this new listener was managed by media and entertainment industries. These industries developed an interest in listening. This became concrete not only in industry's research on hearing and listening,[189] in programmes that address listening practices and that train specific practices, but also in research on what this new listener wants and desires.[190] Already in the early twentieth century, the media industry began to cultivate listening. This not only competed with the pedagogical discourse, it was also organized differently. Whereas the pedagogical discourse of the time was normative as well as disciplinary and controlled by a 'Thou shalt!', the industry's discourses rather tried to anticipate what the listener wanted or desired. A shaping of listening moulded by state institutions, which could be assigned to Michel Foucault's disciplinary society,[191] got competition. The industry's strategies were not disciplinary strategies, but rather – to speak with William S. Burroughs or Gilles Deleuze – theirs have a controlling effect.[192]

We can find already at the beginning of the twentieth century, early examples of the management of listening in the form of advertising campaigns; for example, the Tone Tests conducted by Edison's company in the early twentieth century.[193] Thus, the media industry launched a training programme that competes in a certain way with music education. The listeners of rock 'n' roll in the 1950s were not musicians in disguise, but fans and teenagers; techno fans in the 1990s did not orient themselves on the model of a composer, but as ravers developed listening practices that were far removed from those of a composer or arranger.[194] In 1957, the programme *American Bandstand* popularized a television format that was broadcast throughout the United States, which focused less on musicians and performers and more on listeners. These were integrated into the broadcast as a dancing crowd of white teenagers. Thus, the reception of music was part of the medium. However, this was not due to calculation, but a coincidence: 'According to Clark [the show's host since 1956], dancing became part of 'Bandstand' quite accidentally. The station was located near a Philadelphia high school. After school, kids would drop in to watch Horn [the show's host until 1956] and then Clark as they announced records and read commercials. 'When records were played', Clark recalls, 'the kids got up and danced quite spontaneously'. In short, 'Bandstand' became a record hop, as it were, with entertainment almost incidental'.[195]

The management of listening described here did not, of course, only affect popular music culture, although it was there that it was most noticeable. Already at the beginning of the twentieth century, musicians and composers were often absent from the field of popular music. Wicke describes how, with the turn of the twentieth century, popular music forms – ragtime and tango, for example – were deterritorialized not only via the gramophone, but also through migration movements, and were thus 'withdrawn from established social and cultural instances of legitimation'.[196] In such decontextualizations, Wicke sees an 'increasingly self-aware audience'[197] or an adaptation of music to the 'needs of the audience'.[198] According to this view, forms of popular music were explicitly oriented towards the listener since about 1900. Through hit movies, according to Wicke, the relationship between music and listener changed to the relationship between star and fan.[199] Since the end of the nineteenth century, the composition has lost its importance in popular music in competition with the arrangement and, later, the production. Thus, the composition is adapted to a specific performance by an arranger – this practice was already around in the context of the Viennese waltz in the nineteenth century.[200]

Then, in the twentieth century, especially in the field of popular music, the listener moved farther and farther away from the musician, composer or arranger. The first traces of the orientation of sound on the listener can be found in the nineteenth century and resonate in the function of the arranger. Since the beginning of the twentieth century, the gramophone and radio not only increased the spatial and temporal distance between musician and listener, but also led to a listener who was detached from the musician. With the dominance of the radio and recording industries over the sheet music and piano industries – a process that began in the late 1920s and was completed in the late 1940s – the gap between musician and listener widened.

The music listener is managed by the media industry in the twentieth and twenty-first centuries. The topos of the listener as consumer, however, is an inadequate description of popular music's subjects. Managing listening now also includes forms of self-management that are crucial for today's streaming listening culture with all its fascination for neo-liberal self-improvement.[201] A history of listening or of the listener that does not want to be a history of the musician, composer or arranger began around 1900, gained in significance because of the dominance of listening devices in popular music cultures around 1930, and has been characteristic of the listening practices of popular music since 1950. Such a history is also a history of managing listening.

What is a sound and music history of listening devices? A sixth thesis

It is not another cultural history of music. The cultural turn is over.[202] In musicology, too: the 'belated' discipline.[203] However, this does not mean that musicology, in a kind of neo-conservative turn, has to transmute into the study of 'art itself' again; that musicology should get back to the era before new musicology and critical musicology, before sound studies and popular music studies.[204] Instead, recognizing the end of the cultural turn means that culture has become ubiquitous, including in musicology. Analogous to the diagnosis of media studies scholars that we are now living in a post-digital age because digital media are everywhere, 'every ware' or ubiquitous, we can argue for musicology that culture is now everywhere and ubiquitous, including in the humanities with an art tradition, such as art history or musicology. In view of this background, now is not the time for another cultural history of music. Instead, when it is now common knowledge that the cultural turn in musicology resulted in the study of music as culture[205] and even a 'new cultural history of music' has been written,[206] it is now time to write music history again. But certainly not in a neo-conservative way as a Western-centric history of 'great men' and 'great artworks', not as a history of 'music itself' whatever that might be. It is time to write music history as a history of things, entities and contexts that do not seem musical at first sight.[207] This approach will not lead to another cultural history of music but to a music history of culture; not to a media history of music but to a music history of media; not a device history of music but to a music history of devices, a music history of listening devices.

This approach or rather this research method does study *through* music, unlike a study *of* or a study *about* music; that is, a study which understands music as an object of research. A study *of* music, a study *about* music is turned into a study *through* music. In this approach, the analysis of music is developed as an analysis of cultural processes, for example, of subjectification and mediatization, globalization and industrialization. Research through popular music then asks to what extent cultural processes are integral components of music and, vice versa, whether and how music becomes a constitutive component of such processes.[208]

A technologization of listening takes place not only *within* popular music, but also *through* popular music, and in that sense can be observed through it. Around 1950, music production entered the era of post-production, thereby generating artificial sound worlds which did not seem to have 'real'-world counterparts anymore. In this book, I employ popular music as an investigative tool to explore aspects of the management of listening. Using music as an investigative tool was suggested by French economist Jacques Attali[209] and has been taken up by musicologists such as Robert Fink and Peter Wicke. Wicke explores the house and techno culture of the 1980s and 1990s in order to look at 'the shifting of perception relationships, new media and their ramifications'.[210] Fink explores minimal music and disco in order to analyse an 'excess of repetition', which he sees as a basic motive of a 'postindustrial, mass-mediated consumer society'.[211]

Using music as an investigative tool differs from other reflective approaches to music. These can be described (boldly over-schematizing): from the production perspective; from the fan's or music lover's perspective, who is concerned with a musician's increasing fame or with the proof of a work's greatness; from the historicist's perspective, who seeks to reconstruct bygone present days and to close gaps in knowledge; from the populist's perspective, who claims that for quantitative reasons, one must approach popular music academically (whereby, of course, there is basically nothing against taking an academic approach to subject matter that currently affects many people); and, finally, from the expert's perspective, who must presuppose a wide-eyed, knowledge-hungry public to whom the expert can explain the world. In research practice, of course, these perspectives do not appear in a pure form, but instead span the field of popular music studies as a complex structure in which specific research approaches can then be situated. It follows, then, that the subject of this book is not listening devices *in* popular music, but rather the peculiar organization of listening *through* popular music.

By contrast, the above-mentioned production perspective of popular music analysis tries to trace how popular music was made or produced. It is not always clear why this particular music production was chosen instead of another. In this case, the production perspective often implicitly plays together with the fan perspective. Scholarly discussions of popular music are often motivated by being a fan or music lover. Just as the old-school Wagner researcher usually worshipped Wagner, the popular music scholar who is also a fan, worships perhaps the Beatles or Pink Floyd or even an entire genre of music – heavy metal, techno, hip hop and so on. This perspective is followed in a couple of books published within the renowned Ashgate Popular and

Folk Music Series or Bloomsbury Publishing's 33 1/3 Series, which are dedicated to a single album, band or music style. The fan perspective is mainly concerned with increasing the fame of a musician or proving the aesthetic quality of a genre or the 'greatness' of a work. If the fan or enthusiast perspective argues that one should deal with selected popular music form academically because it is 'great' as music, then the populist perspective argues that one should deal with popular music academically for quantitative reasons. The urgency of this required engagement can then be fuelled by references to popular music forms being 'ubiquitous' or the 'representative music of our present'.[212] The historicist perspective is concerned with reconstructing past present-days and closing (historical) knowledge gaps. Thus, from this perspective, it can be ascertained that there are already countless works on, say, the life and work of the Beatles, but comparatively few on rock 'n' roll as a grassroots phenomenon in 1950s divided Germany. The claims for popular music studies articulated by these different perspectives remain as legitimate as they are unnecessarily modest. In contrast to the interests of these perspectives, research through popular music – the research perspective I am arguing for here – also aims to make its mark not only in music studies, but also in cultural and media theory. Music becomes a tool for cultural and media analysis.

We can outline the research interest of popular music studies, which reaches insights on culture and media through music or more precisely through the analysis of music, by the following examples: If, for example, an investigation and critique of the construction of masculinity and femininity or of a queer, non-binary determination of gender is to be developed, then a study of the voices of Antony Hegarty or Asaf Avidan, but also, let's say, of the blues singer Bessie Smith, offers a potential gain in knowledge. If research is conducted not only on the simulation of 'normality' and everydayness, but also on the emergence of cultural niches in totalitarian terror regimes, then it would pay to investigate the simulation of everyday life through the moderate sound of dance and light music under National Socialism.[213] If the search for an allegedly 'uninhibited' national self-relationship because it is mediated by popular music is to be analytically scrutinized, then an examination of terms such as 'Austro-Pop', 'Krautrock' or 'DeutschPoeten', and the soundscapes that interact with them would be productive. By studying listening devices through popular music, the latter turns into a tool for analysing forms of mediatized, technologized, managed perception.

However, writing a music history of listening devices does not only include a study of the dynamic relationship of listening and media. It also includes the question if and how listening devices are themselves musically conditioned. Is the development of listening devices also driven by a certain concept of music or a certain concept of sound? Do these devices already include a certain concept of music, a certain concept of sound?

We can situate a music history of listening devices both in contrast to a cultural history of music and, in addition, to a media history of music. Particularly in the historiography of popular music, we find a lot of examples for a media history of music, for a music history that is conditioned – although not determined – by media. Writing the history of music as a history of the media of music is an approach that has become established in music research in recent decades. For analysing popular forms of music from around 1900 to the present, it is obvious that technical media such as piano rolls, radio, microphones, amplifiers, records, audio tapes, CDs and computers should be examined, and not only as the means of mass dissemination of a music that exists largely independently of these means themselves. In this way, the constitutive function of media for music comes into view, and questions follow about concrete media as a prerequisite and condition of possibility for the development of certain forms of music, musical practices, sound worlds and music-related forms of knowledge. Then propositions like the following would have to be examined: without long-playing records (LPs) there would be no rock concept albums, without microphones and amplifiers no crooning, without audio tape no rock 'n' roll-typical slapback echo, without networked digital media no 'decentered sampling knowledge'.[214] Complementary to such a media history of music, however, would be a music history of media. To what extent is music history media history, and media history music history? And to what extent would a history of the sound of music be relevant to media development, design and engineering?[215]

Ironically, we can find such a music and sound history of media in the writings of Friedrich Kittler. This is ironic because Kittler is again and again classified as a 'techno-determinist', someone who argues that culture is driven by technology. Certainly, we can find techno-determinist arguments in Kittler's writings. For instance, in his essay 'Rock Music: A Misuse of Military Equipment', where Kittler argues that the origin of rock music is not, as most often assumed, the blues of the Mississippi Delta, but rather the audio and frequency technologies that emerged from two world wars or were decisively developed during them. For Kittler, rock music is at best superficially an expression of musicians' emotions or biographies.[216] Rather, rock music articulates and explores its condition of possibility defined by technical media. Or, in Kittler's words, 'what electrical information technology' accomplishes is the 'self-referential business of rock music'.[217]

In his rock music text, Kittler identifies the First and Second World Wars as the origin of news technology and technical media.[218] In the final version of the text, he then talks of a 'World War $N + 1$'.[219] According to this, the situation of music is determined by media, and these in turn are determined by war, whose innovative power Kittler emphasizes several times. In his book *Gramophone, Film, Typewriter* a 'medial a priori', which is transformed by wars, is probably most pointedly asserted: 'War appears as the father of all things technical; the medial a priori collapses into a martial a priori. *Gramophone, Film, Typewriter* is the most explicit text. The 1-3-1 narrative (writing differentiation into analogue media-digital sublation) is said to be caused by a succession of wars.'[220]

Thus, Kittler here conceptualizes rock music in relation to its 'medial a priori'. First come the media and then the music: 'To say it with slight exaggeration: music was always only as complex, dynamic, and rich in overtones as its technical media allowed.'[221] We can note, however, that a medial a priori need not be deterministic as long as it remains open as to how the transition from media conditions of possibility to sounding music takes place. Music does not necessarily have to resemble or exemplify its media conditions of possibility; it can also differentiate them.

However, and this brings us back to a music history of media, innovations in sonic media are not only put to use by Kittler as a result of warfare. There is another media genealogical thread. This one starts less from rock music and more from Wagner. More precisely, from Wagner's music dramas or, even more precisely, from the Bayreuth Festival Theatre on the Green Hill, where ten of these dramas have been performed in annual cycles since 1876, with interruptions. The musicologist Gundula Kreuzer has stated that for Kittler it is not so much Wagner's music dramas, but rather the Bayreuth's Festival Theatre that would transfer art into media. The 'proto-cinematic audiovisual synthesis' invoked by Kittler in relation to Wagner was primarily a synthesis accomplished by the Festival Theatre; the Festival Theatre was, in a sense, the hardware, and the music dramas were the software.[222]

Kittler marks this other media genealogy far less strongly than that of the media la priori. He uses rather inconspicuous temporal terms like 'anticipation' and the phrase 'avant la lettre'. With such temporal references, which articulate discontinuity instead of progressive development (anticipation is to be distinguished from invention!), media archaeological research will continue to contour its subject area into the present: 'In contrast to the teleologically conceived history of technology development or progression, it [media archaeology] is responsible not only for technical implementation, but also for mental anticipations, for the interweaving of science and fiction, and for the site of thought experiments and thought games that are not, as one might think, exhausted in the arbitrariness of the merely imagined, but that can conceivably inform precisely about the systematics of knowledge orders, because they themselves are informed by this systematics.'[223]

Kreuzer has shown that Kittler's Wagner analysis exhibits an astonishing tendency towards idealism and a concomitant tendency towards dematerialization.[224] Thus, Kittler would have focused primarily on Wagner's *ideas* about the Festival Theatre in Bayreuth, rather than on the real and concrete Festival Theatre and the performances that actually take place there: Kittler 'dealt with their idea [of technologies] rather than their actual working (or otherwise) – the creaks and smells, say, of Wagner's theater in operation'.[225] So it is Wagner's ideas about the Festival Theatre in which Kittler again finds a series of mental anticipations of sonic media and instruments. These anticipations, however, are not simply made up at random. Rather, they are connected to knowledge about listening and sound that resembles the order of knowledge about listening and sound that is laid out in the Festival Theatre.

Against this backdrop, Kittler does impute a whole series of anticipations to the *gesamtkunstwerk* and the Festival Theatre. Wagner's artwork of the future transforms into a 'monomaniacal anticipation of modern media technologies'.[226] Elsewhere, further anticipations are claimed for the music dramas and the Festival Theatre: the anticipation of the 'amplifier'.[227] The orchestral sound is no longer 'under the dominion of writing'.[228] It becomes part of a positive feedback with the voice, which thus becomes an 'orchestrally amplified voice'.[229] The orchestra thereby functions as a 'powerful amplifier'.[230] In addition, 'Wagner invented the radio play',[231] because Alberich, who has become invisible in the third scene of *Das Rheingold* by wearing his invisibility helmet, is identified by Kittler as a technician, an engineer, who sings with a disembodied voice that is, moreover, everywhere. Finally, there is the anticipation of the additive synthesizer:[232] the latter references the reproduction of the overtone series in the prelude to *Das Rheingold*.

Leaving aside the casualness of this empiricism, such anticipations of later technological development are irritating because they counteract a medial a priori: instead of citing a concrete material technology, they refer to a historically and culturally determined sonic assemblage that includes architecture (Festival Theatre) and practices (of sound production and sound perception), instruments and knowledge. It is this sonic assemblage to which the anticipation of media development is attributed. Or to put it another way: in Wagner's case, an 'amplifier' is said to have been in use that was not attached to the media materialities of the electron tube, microphone and loudspeaker, which were, after all, invented only later. In Wagner's case, there is said to be an amplifier 'avant la lettre', which is composed of a concrete sonic assemblage of architecture, practices, instruments and knowledge.

However, we should note that the anticipation thesis does not declare Wagner to be the inventor of amplifier, radio play, cinema and gramophone. It merely reconstructs that in Wagner's music dramas and in the synthesizer or the amplifier similar knowledge about sound was being used: knowledge, in the case of music drama and synthesizer, about the composability and design of overtone spectra; knowledge, in the case of music drama and amplifier, about feedbacks that build up pleasurably. In this respect, Kittler's media anticipations are only integrated at weaker points into a linear, progressive history of development, in which Wagner stands at the beginning and the massive loudspeaker systems of rock music festivals and techno clubs stand at the end. With its emphasis on the discontinuous, Kittler's media history differs fundamentally from approaches to popular music by historical musicologists, who think they have found the first disc jockey (DJ) in the silent film era just because two record players were once used in a picture palace, or who do not see the history of sampling as beginning in the post-colonial music cultures of dub and hip hop, but in avant-garde *musique concrète*. Against this background, we can add a sixth thesis about listening devices: *Listening devices are musically and sonically conditioned.* The reconstruction of these historical conditions is the task of a sound and music history of listening devices.

(Popular) music's listening devices, music listening as record listening, outline of the book and signposts for the reader

The devices and technologies through which popular music is listened to have been changing for a long time: shellac records (78s), piano rolls and player pianos, 7-inch singles (45s), jukeboxes, mono amplitude modulation (AM) radios, LPs, hi-fi stereo systems, maxi singles, public address (PA) systems in cinemas, music clubs and stadiums, boomboxes, compact discs (CDs), cell phones, iPods, smartphones, apps, (noise-cancelling) headphones and so on. Devices have been mediating listening to music at least since the late nineteenth century. They have increased in number and have become more and more important and ubiquitous. Thus, the question of *through what* music is listened to is moving into centre position in a history of listening. Before music's listening devices emerged, the materialities of listening stayed relatively constant. For this period, a history of music listening must frequently be limited to questions of *how* (by recourse to which practices, discourses and categories), *where* (in which architectures and situations), *what* (to expose implicit modes of listening) was listened to as well as to the question *who* listened (and how listening interacted with identity formation). However, we can distinguish between listening devices and listening circumstances such as architectures or listening situations.[233] Although the latter have existed for as long as there has been music, the devices have their origin in the sensory physiological research of the nineteenth century. They increased in significance when Thomas Alva Edison invented the phonograph in 1877, when Emile Berliner invented the gramophone in 1887 and with the advent of the phonographic and radio industries.[234]

There are a few listening devices in music cultures of the first half of the twentieth century – albeit in a period that most often lies outside the historical focus of this book. The rotating cylinders and revolving discs of phonographs and gramophones correlated – especially after the formation of a recording industry in the 1890s – with new practices of collecting music[235] – they interacted with marketing and education programmes that train people how to listen to the sound of a record and how to listen for 'fidelity',[236] they contributed to the identification of listening and consuming[237] and to the boom in allegedly more passive modes of background listening[238] and they occasioned the acousmatic replacement 'of an audiovisual event with a primarily audio one, sound without vision' or a disembodied 'voice without a face'.[239] Player pianos – enormously popular from around 1900 to 1925 – interacted with an 'economisation of perception'.[240] Radio – which began broadcasting regularly in the United States in 1920 and in Germany in 1923 – constituted a form of listening that was to include an 'unconscious' side of listening,[241] should foster 'atomistic' forms of listening,[242] supplemented by 'culinary' qualities[243] that listen for the 'softness and richness of sound'[244] instead of for musical structure. This kind of listening could potentially be involved in the constitution 'of national unity and, at the same time, a conspiratorial sense of subcultural difference'[245] or even of a fascist *Volksgemeinschaft* (racially based national community). Jukeboxes, which were booming in the United States after prohibition ended in 1933, interacted with a 'democratisation'[246] or a 'rationalisation'[247] of listening, a form of listening where the listener purportedly has the 'choice'; cinema connected sound and vision in a new way.[248] Lastly, in the first half of the twentieth century, a few minor listening devices emerged which were local phenomena such as the opera telephone.[249]

This book is about music listening that is organized as record listening in the time period from around 1940 to 1990. Especially in the second half of the twentieth century, specific forms of music emerged that were primarily listened to as records. When people talked about listening to music, they were above all talking about listening to records. Forms of popular music are particularly relevant in this context.

Art music was primarily listened to as a performance in the concert hall or with the 'inner ear' that silently 'listens' to a score. Record listening could also be organized as a kind of private performance; think of, for instance, the famous record listening scene in Thomas Mann's *The Magic Mountain*.[250] Popular music, however, from about 1950 was primarily organized as listening to records. Thus, record listening comes first, concert (hall) listening comes second and score reading – if anywhere – third.

This was evident, for instance, in 1950s rock 'n' roll culture. With the rapid rise of rock 'n' roll in that decade, the record became what can be called the 'normative paradigm of music'.[251] This paradigm resonates with a variety of levels. On the aesthetic level of music production and sound design, artificial sound worlds were produced in 1950s rock 'n' roll culture, most notably in the booming independent recording studios of the United States. Small studios such as Sam Phillips's legendary Memphis Recording Service where Elvis Presley recorded his first singles, or Bill Putnam's Universal Audio Studios in Chicago started to produce sounds which were no longer focused on their ability to be performed on a stage. In this context, the recording – or rather the production – became more important than the composition or song, and also more important than the performance. The emergence of post-production as a part of music production, which correlates with the introduction of magnetic audio tape in the recording studios of the late 1940s, must be emphasized here.[252] Post-production begins when the musicians have finished playing. Mastering is the aspect of post-production which involves a change of medium: the medium of audio tape, with which the music is produced, changes over to the record on which it will be released. At least until the CD was introduced, mastering engineers made vinyl records from audio tapes. Mastering makes it possible to analyse the difference between the production of music and the release of music.[253] On the performative level of music making, for instance, records were produced in the 1950s with musicians who had practically no experience of performing whatsoever – one of the most noted examples of this being Elvis Presley's first recordings for the Sun Records label. On the level of music listening, the record as normative paradigm raised the question of whether musicians could also play the music on their records 'live'; this issue surfaced in 1950s' music reception with increasing frequency. Primacy was therefore accorded to the record over the live performance, and music listening meant listening to records. Thus, rock 'n' roll fans started to listen to the sound of so-called live performances as compared with the sound of records. In 1950s rock 'n' roll culture, music listening was organized primarily as listening to records, and this fact changed listening in 'live' situations. Finally, the recording itself also turns up as a normative paradigm at the economic level. The recording industry became the dominant force in the music industry of the 1950s, and since then, 'music industry' has primarily meant recording industry, and not publishing industry, concert promotion or instrument manufacturing industry. The massive decline of the recording industry in the late 1990s, which lasted for about twenty years, has changed this dynamic.

In the first half of the twentieth century, we already find examples where record listening had become normative: In the 1920s, the Austrian tenor Richard Tauber was one of the most successful operetta stars in the Weimar Republic through his collaboration with composer Franz Lehár. Tauber often had to repeat the hit song of each operetta, its so-called *Tauber Lied* ('Tauber Song'), as an encore not only once, but up to five times.[254] Tauber, whose records produced and distributed by the label Odeon sold extremely well internationally in the 1920s and 1930s, turned into something like a living record for the audience, which could be played again, and again and again.[255] The songs in his late works, which Lehár wrote for Tauber, such as *Dein ist mein ganzes Herz* ['Yours Is My Heart Alone'] and *Gern hab' ich die Frau'n geküsst* ['Girls Were Made to Love and Kiss'] were extremely popular. In the multiple repetitions of the Tauber Song as an encore after a frenetically celebrated performance, a technified and mediatized listening practice was already being expressed, which pointed beyond the stage performance: the practice of listening to records, in which a hit is heard over and over again. In fact, the Tauber Song was highly compatible with technical media. The composer and conductor Paul Dessau was not the only one to observe that Tauber's voice was 'virtually predestined for technical fixation',[256] but Lehár provided Tauber with his 'radio-capable' operettas',[257] the material for broadcasting on the media channels of record, radio and sound film. Lehár's late operettas, according to musicologist Ingrid Grünberg, were no longer exclusively tied to the stage, even though they were hugely successful there. Despite their scenic character, they would also work with the 'technical-aesthetic conditions of radio'.[258] Thus, 'everything optical had to be transformed into the acoustic'.[259]

This means that in the first half of the twentieth century, we already find examples where record listening had become normative. In comparison to those years, the watershed year '1950' proved more significant in terms of music culture, because the record became normative at multiple levels: besides the economic, aesthetic and performative levels, also on the level of listening. And it is this normativity of the record for popular music listening that is one of the core subjects of this book.

As mentioned previously, I examine four different listening devices in the book: rock 'n' roll culture's jukebox of the 1950s, the PA or sound systems of the disco and club culture of the 1970s to the 1990s and the vinyl single records played in or on both of these devices. Jukeboxes, sound systems and their respective singles and maxi singles differ fundamentally from other listening technologies used in popular music, such as hi-fi stereo systems, in that neither jukeboxes nor sound systems were hi-fi technologies which focused on the sonic paradigms of fidelity, balance, transparency and documentation. The extreme emphasis on bass in the New York discos' sound systems of the 1970s, for example, runs again and again contrary to any sonic 'balance' paradigm. Moreover, there is no strong correlation between jukeboxes or sound systems and the individualization or privatization of listening. Listening to music via a jukebox or sound system was primarily a collective practice, not something practised by the isolated, privacy-seeking middle-class individual. Thus, an exploration of listening through jukeboxes and sound systems reveals the connection between technology and listening, independent of the increasing individualization and privatization ostensibly brought about by advances in technology. Furthermore, neither jukeboxes nor sound systems are technologies that are geared towards playing the closed, finished and self-contained works of 'great masters'. Instead, it is through these listening technologies that it is possible to hear what tend to be open structures of series of songs – as with 45s in a jukebox – as well as mixes of tracks – as with 12-inch singles on a sound system. These songs and tracks originate from diverse artists, producers, labels and studios. In order to become part of the rock 'n' roll, disco or club cultures, sound in these listening technologies must function as part of those kinds of series and mixes. This book will examine how this kind of functionality has been created.

The six theses on listening devices I developed in this first chapter can also be used as signposts by the reader. As signposts they show ways to connect the four case studies presented in the chapters, to compare different organizations of listening that correlate with different listening devices. As signposts they can offer the reader directions to a way to study and analyse a history of listening that is substantially informed by listening devices.

Chapter 2 is about the 7-inch single. In the first section of the chapter, I use the case of a classic rock 'n' roll production – *Long Tall Sally* by the singer and pianist Little Richard – to examine how small 45s became a constitutive component of rock 'n' roll productions. Thereby I develop one of the core theses of the book: that listening devices co-produce the music heard through them. I show how the short, concise and fragmentary nature of rock 'n' roll songs resonated with the architecture of the single. I reconstruct how listening in rock 'n' roll culture was primarily organized as listening to recordings and productions. Even when 'live' music was heard, the sound of performances often remained secondary or related to record productions. Produced sound became the norm for live sound. Moreover, I compare different releases of the production *Long Tall Sally* as LP, 78 shellac and vinyl 45 single. I demonstrate, that (i) *Long Tall Sally* was generated in a collective process in which human actors and non-human actors were involved as well as by an elaborate variation and adoption of techno-aesthetic norms and standards; (ii) that mastering practices are varying the sound of the 'original' production and tuning different releases to specific forms of listening and devices and, lastly, (iii) that the single release is characterized by a specific mid-accented, distorted and heavily compressed sound, which might be an advantage on radio and also in jukeboxes. In the second section of the chapter, I advance the thesis that the development of listening devices themselves is conditioned by music and sound history. For this, I deal with the development history of the 45s records by the US entertainment company RCA Victor. I am particularly interested in excavating the concepts of music and of listening on which the development of the single record was based: a concept of music that focuses on 'beautiful passages' and a concept of listening that is informed by automatic changes of the records. In this way, I also explore the premise that, in addition to an instrumental and epistemic function, listening devices have a modelling function. I argue that it is the materiality of the 7-inch single – its diameter, its large central hole, its easy portability – that already includes particular listening practices as well as particular musical forms. In order to contour more sharply the modelling function of the single and its music-and-sound-historical foundation, I also go into the history of the development of the LP. I show that the LP developed by RCA Victor's competitor CBS Columbia was based on another history of music and sound, and that listening was modelled quite differently by the LP. In the final section of the chapter, I take up the thesis that listening devices combine a history of listening with a history of non-listening. For this, I engage with the technical standards of vinyl records in the late 1940s and 1950s. I show how these standards were handled quite differently in the mastering practices of this period. Especially the sound of rock 'n' roll singles was repeatedly mastered during this time with a view to the greatest possible loudness, not with regard to the greatest possible sound fidelity. Thus, in mastering the standards of the record could be disregarded, and the singles became an integral part of the sound of music. With their loud and distorted sound, the 'hot' mastered singles were optimized for application in a series or playlist.

Chapter 2 is based on a close reading of the extensive literature on rock 'n' roll culture and literature dealing with a general cultural history of the 1950s. In addition, the key sources of the chapter include papers by RCA Victor and CBS Columbia concerning the development of the 7-inch single record and of the LP. Apart from these textual sources, the chapter accesses selected movies and relies on a close listening of rock 'n' roll records, specifically the different (re-)releases of the 'original' production of *Long Tall Sally* by Little Richard on different record and media formats.

Chapter 3 deals with the specificities of jukebox listening primarily in the 1950s in the United States and in Europe. In that decade, there were nearly half a million jukeboxes running in the United States. Moreover, in Europe the jukebox became a synonym for rock 'n' roll, and a symbol of Americanization. At the end of the 1950s, nearly fifty thousand jukeboxes were operating in West Germany. In this chapter, I analyse the jukebox of the 1950s as a listening device for the serialization, repetition and programming of single records. Although these records are called 'singles', in a jukebox they are not single in a numerical sense: they are a part of a series, a part of a playlist. Jukeboxes do not play closed programmes or coherent works. The playlist is an actualization of the selection the jukebox offers to the listener. The jukebox listener is a listener who, for a small amount of cash, selects from a pre-selected collection by choosing a title. As a part of a selection, records are not only things – like in large record collections – or objectified music. As part of a selection, records must be used, otherwise they will be sorted out.

The first section of the chapter offers an analysis of 1950s jukebox sound. Here I elaborate on the thesis that the jukebox as a listening device functions as a constitutive part of music. To this end, I ask how and why music and sound were attuned with and to the jukebox, how music and sound became jukebox-ready. Thereby I return to the premise developed in the book's introduction that listening devices mediate between heard object and listening subject and thus help to constitute the music listened to. The jukebox sound is defined by three factors: (i) a peculiar repertoire, which is played in the box; (ii) the adaptation of music productions and releases to the box and (iii) the sound of the technology of the box itself. Also, music was played on the jukebox that was not played on the radio. Around 1950, this made jukebox operators in the United States important customers for independent labels, which were active, for example, in the rhythm and blues market. Likewise in the UK and Germany, jukeboxes played a repertoire that was not played on public broadcasting. In the second section of the jukebox chapter, I focus on jukebox listening by reconstructing how the jukebox itself models and manages listening. In this section, I primarily develop three further theses of the book. First, the thesis that listening devices are not just instruments used by listeners, but more fundamentally that they model certain aspects of listening; that is, that they also listen for their human listeners. Second, that listening devices address the materiality of listening and organize listening as a cultural technique. As a cultural technique, jukebox listening opens up and processes the distinction between selection and scarcity, serialization and repetition, seeing and hearing, music making and music listening, the public and the private. Third, that listening devices are managing listening. As a recurrent theme, the hardware of the jukebox leads us through this section of the chapter. For instance, my investigation of the jukebox's ability to manage sound and music begins with an examination of the materiality of records, amplifiers and speakers of the jukebox, and my investigation of how the box models and manages listening begins with the record storage devices, the switching mechanisms, the play meters and the visual design of the box. I conclude the chapter then with a third section, a coda that opens up a larger vista on these materialities of jukebox listening. This wider view is opened up by discourses, practices and subjects of jukebox listening.

Chapter 3 is based on an analysis of the literature on the jukebox in light of an analysis of listening devices. This entails pertinent secondary literature on the jukebox by jukebox collectors and – the very few – publications on the jukebox written by academics. In addition, I draw on selected articles from the 1950s on the jukebox which were published by US magazines such as *Billboard* and *Audio* as well as by *Der Automatenmarkt*, a West German trade magazine for coin-operated businesses. I also include an analysis of the guidelines and handbooks for coin-operated businesses from the 1950s as well as descriptions of a close listening to the hardware of selected jukeboxes – the speakers, design, amplifiers, selection mechanisms and so on. Finally, the *Coda* is based on an analysis of jukebox listening in movies.

While Chapters 2 and 3 deal primarily with case studies from the 1940s and 1950s and focus consistently on rock 'n' roll sound and music and its culture, Chapters 4 and 5 move chronologically forward to the 1970s, 1980s and the early 1990s. These chapters focus on an analysis of disco and early house and techno culture. Chapter 4 is about the 12-inch single as a listening device. The first section is about the formation of the 12-inch single – which has the diameter of an LP but revolves at the higher speed of a 45 single. I argue here that the 12-inch single was not invented by an 'ingenious' engineer. Instead, I reconstruct how this record format was rather found in an incidental manner, albeit against a very specific music culture background: 1970s New York's booming disco culture. I show how in the early 1970s, that is, before the formation of the 12-inch single, new forms of releasing music became established, how discos transformed into spaces where songs can gain momentum to metamorphose into hits and how record companies became interested in producing sonic disco suitability. Further, specific bodily forms of listening arose that could be explored and developed by relying on new forms of managing the bass frequency. The diameter of the 12-inch single enabled a loud bass-accented cut as well as an encompassing expansion of breaks and rhythmic passages. By reconstructing the musical background against which the 12-inch single appeared, I offer a music history of the 12-inch single. Thereby I pick up the thread, once again, that listening devices themselves have a music and sound history. In the second section of the chapter the dynamics between a history of listening and a history of non-listening are analysed for the case of the 12-inch single. I argue that this single includes forms of perception beyond listening because the sound of the singles could be read, for instance, by DJs and, moreover, the singles combine listening with touching through exploring deep tactile bass frequencies. In the section of the chapter, I delve into the specific physics of the 12-inch single that coincides with a sound different from the sound of RCA Victor's 45 single or CBS Columbia's LP. The physics is explored aesthetically in mastering. The physics of the 12-inch single enables enhancement of the frequency range. Such enhancement is explored in disco culture, not within the context of an aesthetics of sound documentation, but as a part of sound production. A sophisticated resolution of bass frequencies contributes to the fact that the sound of the bass drum – after the rhythm was fixed as a four-to-the-floor beat – became the object of a sophisticated sound design. In contrast to such highly functional, differentiated disco productions, early house and techno productions were often the products of amateurs. I compare mastering practice in disco in New York in the 1970s with mastering practices in Chicago house and Detroit techno, especially in the 1980s. Thereby I again explore the thesis – here in the case of the 12-inch single – that listening devices actively mediate between the heard music and the listener and by doing so co-constitute the sound of the music.

Chapter 4 is based on primary and secondary sources on the genres of disco, house and techno as well as on the question of how these texts deal with the 12-inch single. Interviews with mastering engineers are an important resource for this chapter. Apart from these textual sources, I rely heavily on a close listening and analysis of disco records, especially the first officially released 12-inch single *Ten Per Cent* by Double Exposure and subsequent releases of this production in other formats. In addition, I draw on 12-inch singles of house and techno, focusing on releases in which the physicality of the record is used in a specific way – records with so-called endless grooves, records with signatures which are scratched on the vinyl and so on. I also examine specific cover sleeves for 12-inch records.

Chapter 5 is about loudspeaker systems as listening devices. I analyse selected sound systems of disco and club culture with a focus on the period around 1980. Like the jukebox, the sound system shaped a specific sound of popular music. Correlating with the sound system, specific forms of listening emerged and the materiality of perception was redefined. Like the other chapters with case studies, this chapter is also structured in three sections. The first section is a historical excursus on the history of loudspeaker systems: from early systems in political, musical and cinematic contexts in the 1920s and 1930s to sound systems of popular music in the 1960s, especially in rock music but also in reggae. This section elaborates on the question of how the development of sound systems and their media technologies is conditioned by the history of sound and music, and reconstructs which particular sound and which forms of music became decisive for such a development. In addition, I outline how sound systems became an integral and constitutive part of the sound of rock music and reggae. Using sound systems, I show how the history of listening devices and the history of sound and music are mutually dependent on each other. After this historical and theoretical foundation of sound systems, the chapter's second section is about the specific sound systems that were installed in discos and clubs, especially in the 1970s and 1980s. I analyse discos and clubs as 'empires of the senses',[260] where we find a tense and hierarchical order of the senses which is, again and again but not necessarily, characterized by a dominance of the sonic. I follow this with an analysis of the specific sound of disco's sound system. Here, I am especially interested in how sound systems around 1980 – I use the system of the Paradise Garage in New York as a case study – became sonically activated and produced enhanced sound relying on sophisticated hardware such as sub-bass speakers and bass enhancers. Sound systems (co-)produced the sound of disco. However, in the late 1970s, the designers of disco's sound systems began to address the question of whether their systems should merely reproduce sound or optimize sound according to a specific listening situation. These systems encompassed an excessive dimension – excesses of volume and escalation of high and low frequencies. Finally, the chapter reconstructs how there is feedback between disco's sound systems as listening devices and the sound of music as well as with specific aesthetic forms that combine music and technology – (re-)mixes, tracks and DJ sets. The third and last section of the chapter deals with the specificities of sound system listening by asking how this form of listening organizes listening's materialities and which distinctions contour this form of listening. Three distinctions in particular would appear to be relevant for such contouring: the opposition of individual and crowd, of hearing and feeling and of submission and liberalization. I elaborate on how disco's sound systems not only address dancing crowds, but also systematically body parts apart from the ear. They correlate with a new body of the listener: particular body parts are stimulated by particular frequencies in the sound system. A form of music listening which is not centred on the ear escalates through the sound system. In so doing, disco and club culture constitute a new body whose faculties of perception are defined beyond discrete sensory 'channels'. This body is marked by an ambivalent lust for volume. In addition, I show how these systems constitute collective sound spaces where dancing alone as part of the crowd has become common. Finally, I try to track down emancipatory potentials that lie in a sound system listening which strives to let oneself be overwhelmed by the sound of these systems, and partly even seeks to submit to it.

The key materials and sources I draw on in this chapter include a handful of scholarly publications on sound systems and their histories, discussions of sound systems and dancing and listening to sound systems in historiographies of disco, house and techno. I also consider articles by and interviews with the designers of disco's sound systems in periodicals such as the *Journal of the Audio Engineering Society*, articles on the work of these designers in *Billboard* magazine, as well as manuals for bass frequency-enhancing devices.

In the book's short last part, I not only offer a conclusion but, moreover, try to perspectivize the theses on listening devices that I developed and played through in the previous chapters in relation to current-day digital listening devices such as smartphones, apps and headphones. In this part, I try to show how multiple threads that are substantial for current soundfile or streaming listening were already present in the pre-digital era of single records, jukeboxes and sound systems.

Part II

Listening Devices in (and before) Rock 'n' Roll Culture, *c.* 1940–60

2

Single-listening: The single is not single

Music as record: Listening to Little Richard's *Long Tall Sally*

Recordings and listening devices as constitutive parts of rock 'n' roll

In a scene from the science fiction horror film *Predator* (directed by John McTiernan, United States, 1987), positioned between post-Vietnam trauma and pre-Glasnost, a military commando unit led by Arnold Schwarzenegger flies by helicopter through the Latin American jungle. Its mission seems clearly defined: members of the American government have crashed in a wilderness controlled by guerrillas, and now the unit has to bring them back to civilization. The mood on board is good. The jungle just flows by due to the military's superior flying technology and appears as a green and impenetrable sea over which the helicopter's technology triumphs effortlessly and confidently. This scene is not accompanied by *The Ride of the Valkyries* (like in *Apocalypse Now*), but by a rock 'n' roll song which could well be called a classic: Little Richard's *Long Tall Sally* (Specialty Records, United States, 1956). The soldiers fly deeper and deeper into the jungle at almost two hundred beats per minute.

Long Tall Sally is diegetically interwoven by a boombox, evidently brought along on board by the member of the unit who is responsible for radio engineering and media. The portable artefact is attached to the copter's wall with ropes. For the soldiers, Little Richard's 'crazy' voice quality, the hard backbeat, the shimmering high piano passages, and the rhythmized booming of the bass instruments seems to mediate between the jungle and home in the United States. Besides this exploitation of a reactionary cliché, here given a positive spin – rock 'n' roll as aestheticization of the jungle[1] – the crew thinks they hear a clear message in the song: 'We're gonna have some fun tonight, Everything's alright.' More enigmatic lines like 'I saw Uncle John with bald head Sally' are easily ignored by the hyper-masculine soldiers: they're heading for the hunt, and they're going to enjoy it.

Close to the end of the film, the song crops up again. This time, however, it is not transmitted by a boombox claiming a territory, but presented live. In the meantime, the film's action has been driven forward by the appearance of an extraterrestrial monster: the 'predator' referred to in the film title. The monster gives the elite troop a hard time in a manner that is both impressive and effective. Panic-stricken, a distracted soldier from the troop begins to sing in this scene: 'Long Tall Sally she's built sweet, she got everything that Uncle John needs, Oh Baby! Gonna have me some fun.' Stammering, he keeps repeating the last line, until he ultimately disappears into the jungle. The 'fun' of the helicopter scene has turned into a chalybeate bath, has turned deadly serious. From the safe bird's-eye view to immersion. From technical mediation using a boombox to a life-threatening presence. From professionally recorded music to live music by a panicking amateur. Surprisingly, the line 'Long Tall Sally, she's built sweet' does not appear in Little Richard's version.

Change of scene: from the jungle in the 1980s to a Hollywood film studio in the 1950s. One of the final scenes in the highly successful rock 'n' roll B movie – a genre which filled the movie theatres in the second half of the 1950s – *Don't Knock the Rock* (directed by Fred F. Sears, United States, 1956) consists of a 'live concert' at which DJ Alan Freed announces a performance by Little Richard to teenagers and to Bill Haley, who is also present. Little Richard and his band the Upsetters silently gesture and pose on the stage, while recordings of *Tutti Frutti* and specifically of *Long Tall Sally* are heard, though not through a boombox as in *Predator*, but, as it were, invisibly in the studio room from a record. The record is the one Little Richard recorded in February 1956 at Cosimo Matassa's J&M Studio in New Orleans for Art Rupe's Specialty Records.[2] Little Richard was not accompanied on this by the Upsetters who are in the film, but by the seasoned J&M studio band, who can also be heard, for example, on recordings by Fats Domino. The brass section of the studio band was not made up of the three tenor saxophones and one baritone saxophone that can be *seen* in the film, but of the one tenor and one baritone saxophone that can be *heard* in the film. Only the buzz of a party and clapping sounds on the so-called backbeats, that is, the second and fourth beats, are mixed into the 'live' version that is presented.

Thus what you see and what you hear in the scene diverge. To some extent, the audio and the video tracks run asynchronously as well. Both Little Richard and the Upsetters are moving for the most part synchronously to the audio track presented to them. In this respect, the playback seems to take the pressure off them, as it releases the musicians from the task of generating sound and thus motivates them to deploy an effusive repertoire of gestures: for instance, the saxophone soloist is presented standing on the grand piano.[3] Little Richard plays the keyboard instrument standing up; sometimes he even puts one leg on the piano. The clapping of the teenagers admiring the band definitely does not stress the backbeats typical of rock 'n' roll, but rather follows a number of tempi of their own: the rhythmic tightness is quite different. The sound's extreme emphasis on the backbeats is produced by the clapping and Earl Palmers's drums, which are mixed very much in the foreground. This is an example of an obvious paradox: overdubs, for example, the clapping and the buzz of a party, are intended to make 'live' music out of recorded music. Specifically, the clapping gestures disturb the distinction between diegetic and non-diegetic film music.

The scenes mentioned above from the films *Predator* and *Don't Knock the Rock* can be read as allegories on the relationship between performed and recorded music. Whereas in the film *Predator* live music appears atrophied compared to recorded music, there is no live music in the film *Don't Knock the Rock*. Instead, recorded music is sonically concealed and visually staged as live music. Sound recordings, or recorded music, have become the norm and are presented implicitly and explicitly as such in the films.

Long Tall Sally is heard in the two films over different devices: in *Predator* it is the boombox; in *Don't Knock the Rock* it is the (invisible) sound system that brings the actors and the acting musicians 'their' music into the studio club scene. In the helicopter scene in *Predator*, the jungle is technologically appropriated not only by the helicopter in a motor-driven way, but also aesthetically by *Long Tall Sally* from the boombox. In so doing, the boombox serves as a technology to appropriate space, comparable to how it is used in hip-hop culture.[4] The arrival of the special unit in the jungle does not take place silently under the guise of camouflage, but rather stridently with a chopper and rock 'n' roll. As if the Americans had to bring rock 'n' roll to the uncharted wilderness in order to symbolically appropriate it. Unlike the use of the boombox in hip-hop culture, the space appropriation strategy takes place from the distanced bird's-eye perspective of the helicopter and is acoustically restricted: the boombox is played in the safe space of the aircraft and thus only intervenes in the soldiers' symbolic realm and not in the real one of the jungle. *Don't Knock the Rock* is less about appropriating space using *Long Tall Sally* than an expression of the 'provocative nonconformity' that characterizes the rock 'n' roll experience.[5] This nonconformity is embodied in the 'crazy' poses and gestures of the actors and musicians. David Kirby writes on this: 'Teenagers use their bodies in new and morally dangerous ways.'[6] The music appears spontaneous, immediate and direct. However, its sound quality is co-defined by the norms of the studios and the sound recording medium. The use of *Long Tall Sally* in both films shows that the sound recording – as opposed to live music – has become the norm. Singles do not explicitly appear, however, in these scenes. Listening to *Long Tall Sally* via the boombox processes the distinction between civilization and wilderness, between 'my territory' and the outside world. Listening to it via the playback scene processes the distinction between conformity and nonconformity. Although the acting musicians conform to the rational playback standards of film production, they foreground their nonconformity by exhibiting a repertoire of wild gestures. For a study of listening devices, Little Richard's *Long Tall Sally* from 1956 offers a productive case study. Based on this music production, I try to show in the following how the single record as a listening device became an integral part of music and how it was involved in the organization of a peculiar form of listening in rock 'n' roll culture, a form of listening where records became normative (also for live music) and where music is presented in the form of series of single records.

Little Richard himself had a hard time with recordings.[7] Quite unlike other rock 'n' roll singers: Elvis Presley, for instance, hardly had any stage experience before recording his first records in Sam Phillips's studio. This is why Peter Doyle writes that Presley found his voice in the studio: 'He started out and learned his craft as a recording studio act; the famous stage presence came later.'[8] With Little Richard it was the reverse. Born in Macon, Georgia, in 1932 as one of twelve children, Little Richard (Richard Wayne Penniman) had his first experiences on stage in a neighbourhood setting with the

Penniman Singers, the family gospel choir. At the age of fourteen, he began to perform publicly in the American Southeast, sometimes in rather unorthodox settings, such as singing in a so-called medicine show advertising a 'miracle cure' and in a vaudeville-style minstrel show in which Little Richard performed in drag as 'Princess LaVonne'; and sometimes more above board when he sang in a variety show in Atlanta. For nearly ten years Little Richard barnstormed through the American Southeast as part of such shows and programmes. His first records – 1951 for RCA Victor and 1953 for Peacock Records – remained documentations of conventional rhythm and blues performances and did not go beyond the status of a regional achievement. His touring, eking out a living, would probably have continued for decades had Little Richard not landed a 'hit'. This success was linked to the record.

A demo tape that Little Richard had sent to the Californian independent label Specialty led in September 1955, after a few months' delay, to the label's owner Art Rupe getting his A&R (artists and repertoire) manager Robert 'Bumps' Blackwell in New Orleans to book the J&M Studio for two days for recordings with Little Richard. At the beginning, Little Richard was to be built up as a competitor to B. B. King, who was not signed to Specialty but to the label Modern Records, which was also located in Los Angeles. Blackwell recounts that the recordings with Little Richard were a disappointment at first, probably against the backdrop of expectations: 'I had heard that Richard's stage act was really wild, but in the studio that day he was very inhibited.'[9] Only after a break in the Dew Drop Inn did Little Richard thaw out: 'We walk into the place and, you know, the girls are there and the boys are there and he's got an audience. There's a piano, and that's his crutch. He's on stage reckoning to show Lee Allen [the tenor saxophonist of the J&M studio band] his piano style.'[10] Reportedly at this lunch break, Little Richard presented a raw version of 'Tutti Frutti' that was recorded later that day – although with a toned down text. This story of course cannot be proven![11] Nonetheless, one can find various statements from Little Richard referring to his difficulty with a studio without an audience and his preference for the stage.[12] *Tutti Frutti*, too (Specialty Records, United States, 1955), was actually a stage song for him: 'I'd been singing *Tutti Frutti* for years, but it never struck me as a song you'd *record*.'[13] For Little Richard, the site of his music was not the studio, but the stage. Also the fact that in the studio he couldn't play with his live band, the Upsetters, but instead with professional studio bands increasingly displeased him: 'But you know if Specialty had recorded me live with the Upsetters that would have been the most exciting rock 'n' roll of all.'[14] It was a different picture with Elvis Presley, who developed his vocal style – be it his hiccuppy singing style or his crooner voice – in dealing with studio technologies like the tape or the microphone, whereas Little Richard's frequently seemed to collide with the studio technologies: 'Richard screamed so hard. His dynamic range was so terrific. Richard would be singing like this [whispers] and then all of a sudden BOW!! The needles would just go off the dial.'[15] This voice, which could no longer be registered by measuring devices, can be heard on numerous Little Richard recordings as a distortion – for instance, in extreme form in the ballad *Shake a Hand* (Specialty Records, United States, 1959), but also in the master version of *Long Tall Sally* (Specialty Records, United States, 1989). Thus, for Little Richard recording signified more a domestication and an economic necessity. Little Richard's recordings are not, however – whether he intended this or not – the product of Little Richard, but rather the product of a larger network of many human actors and technologies. Music here is not so much a work of art that is supposed to endure 'in itself'. Rather, music is a network. And listening devices are also integrated into this network, which have a constitutive function for the music.

Despite Little Richard's antipathy towards the studio, his recordings can by no means be reduced to an economic function, but instead have an intrinsic aesthetic value. This involves on the one hand the overall sound of the recordings produced with Little Richard in the J&M studio, and on the other Little Richard's singing style. For example, the recordings in the J&M studio are characterized by a specific sound that makes them distinguishable on the sound level from productions made, for example, for Sun in Memphis or for Chess in Chicago.[16] Whether such distinctiveness was consciously intended or not is not relevant here. Peter Doyle describes the J&M sound primarily as a 'live' sound, distinguishing it from the artificial sonic spaces of the Sun and Chess productions.[17] Thus Sun and Chess productions created an intrinsic technological and aesthetic value of the recording in the 1950s, for instance, by exposing surreal worlds of sounds via tape echo or echo chamber and nesting several sonic spaces that were not consistent with each other. Unlike these sounds from Memphis and Chicago, the J&M sound tends to be characterized by relatively comprehensive instrumentation that also determines the sound of *Long Tall Sally*: drums, double bass, piano, guitar, baritone and tenor saxophone. If rock 'n' roll is a precursor of rock music, then this does not apply to the instruments of the New Orleans sound: the horns – Lee Allen's tenor saxophone and Alvin 'Red' Tyler's baritone saxophone – would play just as small a role in the rock music of the 1960s as the boogie piano, which was indispensable for this sound. For the rock bands of the 1960s, the distorted guitar sounds from Chicago and Memphis were more significant than the considerable instrumentation of the New Orleans productions.[18]

Nevertheless, New Orleans rock 'n' roll, substantially influenced by the J&M studio band, was characterized by a certain studio sound that cannot simply be described using an ideal of sound transparency. For instance, instruments are deployed that cannot always be heard distinctly on the recording produced. The characteristic ostinato bass figure – inspired by boogie-woogie – is frequently played by several instruments in unison. Langdon Winner quite aptly describes the sound this generates as a 'foggy rumble'. In the J&M studio, it was not a problem 'to load up the lower end of the scale with more instrumentation than seems reasonable. On top of that foggy rumble it becomes possible to contrast the higher range of a fine tenor sax or the voice of a good R & B shouter and generate a marvelous tension in the music'.[19]

The tenor saxophone is usually a so-called honking saxophone, which is exposed in the obligatory saxophone solo. From the foggy rumble mentioned – frequently produced by a combination of piano, double bass, guitar, bass drum and baritone saxophone – in addition to the voice and the tenor saxophone the extreme stress on the backbeat stands out. It is precisely the almost excessive backbeat by drummer Earl Palmer – which the recording technology helps to shape – that interacts with Little Richard's singing style. Blackwell points out that the extreme backbeat emphasis was deliberately shaped using a specific recording technique. Drummer Earl Palmer was placed in a separate room and recorded with a microphone of his own. In this way, it was possible to control separately the volume of the drums.[20]

This interaction of drums and voice becomes clear in *Long Tall Sally*. Already several months before he recorded the final version of the piece, Little Richard had recorded the song, then still called *The Thing* (Specialty Records, United States, 1989), in Hollywood at Radio Recorders with Guitar Slim's band.[21] Although nearly the same instruments were used, the sound produced is completely different. Instead of a foggy rumble, you hear here a consistently transparently aligned production in which individual instruments can be distinctly perceived. Rhythmically and in terms of tempo, 'The Thing' is fundamentally differently organized than the final version of *Long Tall Sally*.[22] *The Thing* flows and swings in a comfortable tempo, then the tempo in the J&M Studio is radically accelerated. While Little Richard in *The Thing* particularly stresses beats one and three, in the J&M version he changes over to backbeat emphasis. Here he's obviously adapting to Earl Palmer's drum playing, where studio technology contributed to the shape of the sound. In *Long Tall Sally*, the conventional 12-bar blues form – followed by all of Little Richard's hits from *Tutti Frutti* to *Slippin' and Slidin'* (Specialty Records, United States, 1956) to *Rip It Up* (Specialty Records, United States, 1956) and *Lucille* (Specialty Records, United States, 1957) – is divided into four-bar strophe sections and eight-bar refrain sections. In the refrain sections, Little Richard is accompanied by the entire band, whereas in the strophe sections, the continuous rhythm is interrupted by stop-time on the first beat. Precisely in these passages in which the drum also pauses, Little Richard emphasizes the backbeats excessively in the J&M version: functionally speaking, the voice becomes percussion. *Long Tall Sally*, too, is thus shaped by J&M's studio sound and is not the product of a stage. This studio sound, however, is not necessarily identical with the sound of the single. I will return to this difference soon. However, what can be concluded here is that aesthetically, the recording is already beginning to constitute a standard in the process of creating *Long Tall Sally*.

Strategies of serialization: Covering and versioning, (re-)mastering and (re-)releasing

Besides the relationship between recorded and live music, there is a second topic hinted at in the film *Predator* mentioned above, a topic that was central to popular music in the 1950s and the development of which also occurs related to the recording: the cover version. Connected to this topic are issues of how to deal with 'originality'. The soldier singing *Long Tall Sally* sings 'Long Tall Sally she's built sweet, she got everything that Uncle John needs …' and not 'Long Tall Sally she's built for speed she got everything that Uncle John needs ….' In this way what he performs is a softening of the song at the text level, and thus implicitly refers to the problem of cover versions, as were typical in the 1950s. The distinction 'built for comfort'/'built for speed' can be found in blues language – for instance, in Howlin' Wolf's *Built for Comfort*.[23] Applied to a person one desires, 'built for speed' was evidently too suggestive for the pop market in the 1950s.

Billboard announced Little Richard's *Long Tall Sally* on 17 March 1956. Just one week later, there were two announcements of cover versions in the same release: Marty Robbins's version on Columbia for the country market (Columbia, United States, 1956) and Pat Boone's version on Dot for the pop market (Dot, United States, 1956). Boone's version tones down what were apparently considered off-colour lines: 'Long Tall Sally she's built for speed' becomes 'Long Tall Sally has a lot on the ball', 'I saw uncle John with bald head Sally' turns into 'I saw Uncle John with long tall Sally'.

Depending on the listening situation, Little Richard's *Long Tall Sally* could be received both as 'good clean fun' and as an expression of primarily (homo-)sexual desire: in that case 'bald head Sally' was a man.[24] Little Richard embodies this ambivalence by performing the role of the 'freak' or 'trickster'. Little Richard pointed out that his image was constructed by Specialty in this direction: 'We decided that my image should be crazy and way-out so that the adults would think I was harmless. I'd appear in one show dressed as Queen of England and in the next as the pope.'[25] Little Richard was not marketed as a down-to-earth, racy musician, his image was formed by acting and a good dose of artificiality – miles away from the heroes of the 'authentic' blues.[26] In the worst case, Little Richard appears – with his little Menjou beard, the pompadour hairstyle, the heavily applied makeup and eye shadow – as a mere show object in a minstrel show: the message was probably supposed to be crazy but not gay! This 'craziness' takes place at the sound and dramaturgical levels as well.

At the vocal level, there's a lavish use of sounds not linked to meaning in language. For example, Little Richard uses a repertoire of completely affirmative and not at all desperate rock 'n' roll shouts, which he reverts to in various songs and which are also included in cover versions.[27] He develops a repertoire of vocal sounds that can be put into various songs. Little Richard frequently jumps from his chest to his head voice or switches from singing to shouting. At the text level as well *Long Tall Sally* emphasizes disruptions and discontinuities: a story is at best touched upon. In this, *Long Tall Sally* contrasts with texts by artists like Chuck Berry, who gave his texts a dramaturgical development which was closely related to the experience of high school teens.[28] In *Long Tall Sally*, Little Richard particularly emphasizes the fragmentary, slogans and shreds of action, and celebrates repetition: 'Little Richard was one of very few singers who became more expressive with meaningless sounds and disconnected phrases and images than he was with properly constructed songs.'[29] It may seem paradoxical considering the title, but everything about *Long Tall Sally* had to be concise and pithy. This pithiness resonates with the architecture of the single record.

The isolated soldier in *Predator* also falls back on practices of covering and varying. Ambiguities at the text level are rectified. The two cover versions are adapted to the sound conventions of their respective target markets.[30] The musicologist Albin Zak diagnoses that the problem, especially with Boone's cover versions of *Tutti Frutti* and *Long Tall Sally*, is neither the toning down of apparently objectionable text passages nor the singer's beaming nice-guy image, but rather 'the real problem is that it *sounds* all wrong'.[31] Bluntly, it can be said that Boone covered *Long Tall Sally* as a composition and not as a production. Nevertheless, Boone's version was more successful than Little Richard's. By contrast, Marty Robbins's adaptation in the rockabilly style, which was modern at the time, flopped completely. Whether this was due to Robbins's wilful emphasis on the first and third beats – in fact colliding with the stress on the second and fourth beats by his rhythm group – cannot, however, be proven.

Not only were sounds created in the studios that had not been heard previously, but also the technologies – the singles – on which these were released and with which they were heard were characterized by a sound of their own. The transfer from studio tape to the pressing matrix was part of mastering. If you compare different releases of Little Richard's *Long Tall Sally*, superficially no very significant differences catch your ear. Besides the releases of *Long Tall Sally* already mentioned in the framework of the films *Don't Knock the Rock* and *Predator*, the following will deal with eight different record releases by Little Richard of *Long Tall Sally* at different times and in different places.[32] These comprise two different productions and releases on 78 shellac, 7-inch single, LP and CD.[33]

In all record releases, the matrix number is inscribed in the area of the lead-out groove. On the Specialty releases, you search in vain for small icons, initials or symbols that give a hint about a specific mastering engineer. Such signs, which are also an indication that the mastering – initially a purely technical process – had become a technological *and* aesthetic one, can be found, for instance, on Capitol singles of the same period.[34] Overall, all releases are characterized by a sound that stresses the middle range and is strongly compressed.[35] The 78-shellac release, a European licensed release on London (London MSC.1443 (MSC 1443-1), UK, no date),[36] is articulated by strong surface sounds. The two 7-inch single releases (Specialty Records XSP-572-45 (45-XSP-572), United States, 1956; and Specialty Records XSP-572 (L-10723, 572-XSP), United States, 1968) stand out particularly because of a more brilliant high-frequency production, which highlights even more clearly, for example, the ride cymbal during the saxophone solo. This effect is even more strongly developed on *Long Tall Sally* on the LP re-release of Little Richard's first album *Here's Little Richard* by the audiophile label Mobile Fidelity Sound Lab (MoFi 1-287 (MFSL-1227-B1), United States, 2008).

The sound of *Long Tall Sally* released on the LP *Alan Freed's 'Golden Pics'* (End 313 (LP 313A), United States, 1961) is an exception. In the year this LP came out (unlike the single releases mentioned so far from the 1950s, the LP includes a reference to where it was mastered[37]), rock 'n' roll was old-fashioned and Alan Freed's career had basically ended at the latest with the payola scandal[38]: ideal prerequisites, therefore, for a rock 'n' roll revival under Freed's patronage! Freed presents this revival as a series of 'acoustic snapshots'. These snapshots are not new recordings of the old hits, but rather – as the record sleeve informs us – 'The 15 Original Hit Recordings'. This means that in this case a history of rock 'n' roll is being (co-)written not through re-enactment but through re-mastering. Freed's LP is thus a historiographical form, in sharp contrast to the revivals of rock 'n' roll as history. Thus, before the history of rock 'n' roll was written in book form following academic standards, there were already first efforts in 1959 to revive rock 'n' roll after it ceased to dominate the charts, in the form of compilation albums. Such a revival always carries as its complement a historicization.[39] The sound being released is adapted to the specifics of this form. Or in other words, reduced to economics, the LP can be categorized using the straightforward term 'secondary exploitation'.

Little Richard himself also took part in a revival of rock 'n' roll in the 1960s. – at the high point of his career and on tour in Australia, in 1957, he had a conversion experience and felt called to train as a preacher in the United States, to look for a woman, and get married – despite his obvious homosexuality – in order to correspond to his idea of 'normalcy' and 'naturalness'.[40] He got divorced shortly after his marriage and recorded gospel records, and then went back on tour with his rock 'n' roll songs – for instance, with the Beatles in 1963. Little Richard re-recorded his old hits for the Chicago label Vee-Jay Records in 1964.[41] His re-enactment was followed by a re-mastering. Specialty released the original recordings one more time on the LP *Little Richard's Grooviest 17 Original Hits* (Specialty Records, United States, 1968), from which once again the single *Long Tall Sally* was taken out; and Little Richard's re-enactment was itself re-mastered again in 1998. Such a re-mastering for CD would not be especially remarkable if the label responsible for it were not explicitly targeting audiophile forms of listening. The label Bell Records, located in southwest German Aichtal, re-mastered Little Richard's re-enactment from the 1960s as *Starpower* (Bell, Germany, 1998). Together with his fans' aging and social advancement, Little Richard's recordings had thus arrived in hi-fi listening culture. The re-release of Little Richard's first LP *Here's Little Richard* on 180 grams of vinyl in a limited and numbered edition of 2,500 copies by the label MoFi was also an attempt to serve audiophile listening practices. For this release that came out in 2008, the original tapes were cut on record using the half-speed mastering technique. The LP *Alan Freed's 'Golden Pics'* already bore the hi-fi promise on its cover.

Long Tall Sally is prominently positioned on *Alan Freed's 'Golden Pics'* in terms of dramaturgy and sound quality: the song is the opening track on Side 1 of the LP. Compared to the singles released in 1955 and 1968, it is striking that this LP version is cut significantly more quietly. While the single versions seem to stress the voice with a loud cut, to some extent already tending towards distortion,[42] the LP version seems intent on taking back the overly loud recording. The ambient sound of the single release from 1955 is unhearable on the LP release. The unheard of the single in the 1950s is thus characterized by a record cut positioned at the edge of distortion. Singles from other independent labels from the same period are also mastered according to this principle. Although Pat Boone's version of *Long Tall Sally* (Dot 45-15457 (MW9058), United States, 1956) is characterized by a tame production, the mastering, in which the produced sound was adapted to the physics of the single, generated an extremely aggressive result. Rock 'n' roll single releases from major labels look downright restrained by comparison. Such restraint in mastering can be heard, for instance, on the release of *Be-Bop-A-Lula* (Capitol F3450 (45-15230-D7), United States, 1956) by Gene Vincent. And this reserve can be heard in an even more enhanced form on the singles by West German rock 'n' roll stars released by Polydor, Deutsche Grammophon's pop music label.[43]

That the rock 'n' roll singles released by US independent labels in the 1950s did not follow a transparency or hi-fi ideal can also be explained by the devices with which these were primarily listened to. This can be shown in an exemplary way for the devices developed by RCA Victor together with the single. The playing devices that RCA Victor offered for the single in the late 1940s and 1950s were compact, low-priced and included a record changer. Their cases were frequently made of dark brown Bakelite. Fancier models were given a wooden case. The record players for the children's market – the entertainment group thought about this or rather set it up as well – were covered with cartoon characters. There were models that had no loudspeaker of their own and therefore had to be hooked up, for example, to a radio or a television. Portable models and combinations of radio and phonograph were soon on offer, as were console models that were frequently one component of pieces of furniture. At the beginning, high fidelity as a slogan did not play a major role. The models equipped with amplifier and loudspeakers were praised in advertising as a 'golden throat' – probably a paraphrase of the golden ears existing in hi-fi circles. RCA Victor's golden throat had a range of just 70 to 4,000 Hz.[44] This corresponds almost exactly to the frequency range that could be heard on the 7-inch rock 'n' roll singles. Only in 1956 did the group launch an explicit hi-fi product line on the market. RCA Victor ceased production of record players that played only forty-five 7-inch singles in 1957.

The target group that RCA Victor tried to address with its advertisements for the new system was primarily women and couples, but also children and sometimes young people of college age.[45] No pipe-smoking middle-class men in their wing chairs from hi-fi advertising were to be found in the marketing campaign created by J. Walter Thompson. RCA Victor also brought out a record player for singles that was dedicated to Elvis Presley.[46]

In Germany, at the end of the 1950s, there arose a market not only for portable radios – this is how the transistorized, battery-saving pocket radio came about[47] – but also for record players that specifically took into account young people and the ways they used them.[48] The portable Braun TP 1, designed by Dieter Rams and by now a design classic, even combines a radio and a single record player and directly targets the youth market.[49] The sound of the single had to work in connection with such devices and the listening practices connected with them.

In the course of this, various listening situations and listening devices have a constitutive function for the music. While *Long Tall Sally* remains the same piece notionally, it can reveal completely differently structured 'assemblages'.[50] These assemblages can be compared with each other, insofar as they are associated with one music production that, however, was processed and varied with differing mastering practices. In the film *Don't Knock the Rock* being a rebel and conforming come together in *Long Tall Sally*. The 'crazy', the flaunting of the physically expressive, comes to the fore. However, it ultimately remains without consequences, it's all 'good clean fun'. The sounds of the single being played get bodies to dance and awaken a new repertoire of gestures for the 1950s in the public realm. The playback performance in *Don't Knock the Rock*, however, willingly accepts that such a form of apparent spontaneous 'craziness' and 'being nuts' is always linked to and regulated by the repetitions of the recording. In the situation in the film *Predator*, *Long Tall Sally* can no longer mobilize any bodies and can at most trigger someone nodding their head or chewing gum. The crew member figuring as a 'media expert' even uses the flight time for contemplative reading of comics. Instead, the 200 beats per minute resonate with the beat of the helicopter. In this case, *Long Tall Sally* is not an instrument of a nonconformity that will provoke the older generation. Heard over a boombox, it becomes a means to appropriate space, announcing military 'bloody fun'. The high-end equipment by means of which the 180-gram vinyl of Little Richard's re-released first LP is heard by former teenagers who have come into money in the meantime, produced by MoFi using the 'half-speed mastering' technique, in turn, reveals another assemblage of *Long Tall Sally*. *Long Tall Sally* is no longer part of a series of singles, of a playlist of recordings from different artists, but is rather part of a 'high-quality' album that is received in private.

For this book's context, out of the number of various record releases of Little Richard's *Long Tall Sally*, three releases ultimately form fundamental parameters: the 7-inch release of 1956 (Specialty Records, United States, 1956) targets practices in which singles by different artists are heard in a series through listening devices like jukeboxes and record changers. The characteristic sound of the single, with a stress on the middle, highly compressed and cut on the edge of distortion, is taken back and tempered on the LP re-releases. This can be heard in particular on the LP release of the production on *Oldies but Goodies* (End, United States, 1961). This LP release is not made for listening devices on which recordings by different artists and producers are heard as a series. For this release, the sound of a range of productions was already homogenized: in this way, the sound of *Long Tall Sally* also had to be coordinated with the sound of the production that followed it on the LP – *Ship of Love* by The Nutmegs. The more or less complex recycled or re-mastered re-release of the original recording of *Long Tall Sally* as part of the re-release of Little Richard's first LP on the audiophile label 'MoFi' (MoFi, United States, 2008) targets in turn a different listening device – the sound system in a middle-class living room equipped with an expensive high-end record player.

The specific sound of the single is associated with the practices and devices of music listening, in which recordings of different artists and producers, no longer simulating performances, are played as a series. The versions of a production of *Long Tall Sally* are distinguished not only as regards listening practices but also – through mastering and the different listening devices – as regards the sound. The sound of the single in 1956 was never shaped by a fidelity paradigm – an orientation point, for instance, for mastering the MoFi release. The sound of the single was aligned to a listening practice of listening to single records by different artists in a series. The unheard of the single is associated with practices of music listening in which records were placed in a series and in which singles stopped being single. These series were brought about with the help of the radio DJ, the record changer for use at home or the jukebox. I will delve more deeply into the jukebox as a listening device in Chapter 3. For rock 'n' roll records in general and single records in particular became a constitutive part of music. However, even if 'music' in the case of rock 'n' roll also refers to individual hit singles, it increasingly refers to series of single records that are produced based on particular strategies of serialization.

Defining single and LP by musical forms and listening practices in the 1940s

The single's sound and music history

Today, with the impact of the internet and the success of downloads and later, streaming, time and again the 'death of the album' was diagnosed.[51] Along with its death, the disappearance of both the dramaturgies associated with that format and its corresponding listening practices are lamented in the field of popular music. However, when looking back at the 1950s, it is worth remembering that at that time popular music was in fact primarily concentrated on the single, not on the album. The link between popular music and the album format – which currently seems to be up for debate again – had not yet been established.[52] It was the small 45-rpm single, launched on the US market by the electronics and entertainment corporation RCA Victor in 1949 that would shape the sound of popular music in the 1950s. This record format ended up replacing the 78-rpm shellac disc, introduced together with the LP in 1948 by RCA Victor's competitor CBS Columbia.

In the 1950s, record companies which were also successful in the popular music market – such as Polydor or Telefunken in Germany, for example, or London Records in the UK (a subdivision of the US label Decca), or Atlantic Records in the United States – of course, also released LPs, or albums, in addition to singles. However, these albums did not yet captivate their audiences primarily through conceptual dramaturgies. Concept albums only became the focus of popular music business and journalism – as well as objects of desire for fans – starting in the late 1960s. The single's dominance is particularly evident in the catalogues of independent record labels, which were booming in the United States after the Second World War. As has often been remarked upon, this boom – experienced by labels such as Chess Records in Chicago, King Records in Cincinnati, Atlantic Records in New York, Sun Records in Memphis and Specialty Records in Los Angeles – was a main cause of the rise of rock 'n' roll.[53] Those labels' catalogues consisted predominantly of single records, and LPs were released only very rarely.[54] The pop albums of the 1950s were often compilations of singles that had already been released. The concept album format first established itself in the popular music business at the end of the 1960s with releases such as the Mothers of Invention's *Freak Out* (Verve, United States, 1966), the Beach Boys' *Pet Sounds* (Capitol, United States, 1966), and Beatles' *Sgt. Pepper's Lonely Hearts Club Band* (Parlophone, UK, 1967).[55] After that, it was regarded as a 'vehicle for artistic seriousness and experimentation within rock culture' in the youth market.[56] Yet the concept of these concept albums constituted more of a specific *sound* concept than one related to any particular content. Concept albums were popular music's first great 'masterworks',[57] which would soon resonate with musicology as defined by its hero- and genius-centric historiography[58] as well as with the newly emerging rock journalism – for example, the first issue of Jann Wenner's and Ralph J. Gleason's *Rolling Stone* was published in 1967. The aim of the concept album was 'to transcend the limitations of pop singles with a coherent extended work'.⁵⁹ In contrast to the album's coherence, singles represent a staging of the fragmentary.

The forms of popular music in the 1950s (focusing particularly on those which targeted the youth market) fall through the cracks of a historiographical framework that is based on great 'masterworks'. In such a framework, these musical forms can at best be regarded as less sophisticated antecedents of 1960s and 1970s rock music and its concept albums. Such an assessment gains support given the lack of artwork on – especially 1950s – singles: singles were not generally packaged in covers sporting elaborate artwork, their back covers emblazoned with liner notes – these are the hallmarks of the concept albums. Instead, a plain brown paper sleeve was initially the norm. Sleeves of this kind would later be replaced by modest printed covers, bearing either the label's logo or a photo of the artist.⁶⁰ Even when the stereo release became standard for the concept albums of the late 1960s,⁶¹ singles remained almost completely faithful to mono into the 1970s.

The popular music of the 1950s – rock 'n' roll being the most incisive example here – was primarily bound to the single and not to the LP: 'The single would become the main medium of popular music and dominated its development virtually uncontested until the end of the 1960s, whereas at first the long-playing record only took hold in the classical music sector.'⁶² The single not only superseded the LP in popular music in general and in rock 'n' roll in particular; it also dominated other manifestations of music, such as live performances or musical scores. Rock 'n' roll was not primarily transmitted from the stage as live music, or through musical scores meant for individual interpretation, but above all as single records. The US historian Carl Belz, who wrote the first history of rock music to be published by an academic press in 1969, stated that for rock music – which for him also included 1950s rock 'n' roll: 'Records were the music's initial medium.'⁶³ According to Belz, the performance is secondary in comparison with the recording in rock music – although he considers it primary in folk and jazz music. The aesthetic consequences of granting primacy to the recording were systematically expanded upon for the first time in the 1990s by the philosopher Theodore Gracyk, well informed with regard to the history of popular music and its sound.⁶⁴ More recently, the systematic analysis of recordings has been increasingly taken up by music studies.⁶⁵ In our context, Albin Zak's study about American popular music of the 1950s is especially worthy of attention.⁶⁶ Zak shows how the record acquired an intrinsic aesthetic value in the 1950s with the declining dominance of big band swing. The big band crooner Bing Crosby, who not only established the audio tape on US radio, but also saw to it that guitarist Les Paul received his first tape machine, understood this fact in a highly nuanced way: 'Those who are now in charge of production at the various recording companies tell me that to awaken popular interest in a record they've got to produce a new "sound": an unusual combination of instruments or voices which record buyers haven't heard before. If you can do this, they say, you've got a chance to turn out a hit record. It doesn't matter what the material is like or how good the song is or what it's all about, how it's done, or how it's performed. It's just whether it features an unusual sound which hasn't been heard before.'⁶⁷

Moreover, 1950s Hollywood cinema had already made the connection expatiated on here by Crosby. In Frank Tashlin's *The Girl Can't Help It* (United States, 1956), the 'slot machine king' mafioso, Marty 'Fats' Murdoch, sees Eddie Cochran on television. Murdoch, who wants to make the 'singer' Jerri Jordan (played by Jane Mansfield) into a star, remarks that Cochran cannot sing and has an untrained voice. And still he's a star. Murdoch immediately provides an explanation: Cochran has a 'new sound'. This insight ultimately leads to Jerri Jordan cutting a record on which her only contribution is a siren-like sound she emits at regular intervals.

Instead of live performance and musical scores, recording became the norm for 1950s rock 'n' roll in particular. This represented a first in music history: 'The triumph of the single was linked to the successful penetration of the United States by rock 'n' roll, which became the first music to be distributed in record form on a massive scale.'[68] At the same time, the single record established a new 'low-price segment' in rock 'n' roll,[69] which could be hailed under the watchword of 'democratization'.[70] Rather than once again focusing on a 'liaison between technology and the cultural industry',[71] and thus invoking discourse on heavily ideologically charged jargon such as 'reification', 'manipulation' and 'rationalization', in this part of the chapter, I follow the dynamics of 'technical and cultural media configurations' and 'aesthetic processes'.[72] In so doing, I show how the single exhibited an aesthetic specificity in the popular music of the 1950s that is relevant to listening history. Such an approach towards the single in rock 'n' roll culture integrates the link between media aesthetics and the history of listening that has thus far not been the subject of much research on popular music of the 1950s.[73]

The interdependencies among economy, technology and sound aesthetics constitute the focus of this analysis as they can be brought into focus in the single record. An analysis of popular music forms sheds more light on these connections. In this sense, popular music is more an epistemological instrument than an object of frustration or fascination for fans and music lovers.[74] As Simon Frith noted already at the end of the 1970s, 'only pop music is *essentially* a music which is communicated by a mass medium'.[75] According to Frith, that also has consequences for the ways in which this music is experienced: 'If in other musical experiences the musicians and their audiences are joined by the speed of sound, for recorded music the link is an elaborate industry'.[76]

But how does this 'essence' change exactly when the 'mass medium' is a specific form of vinyl record, and no longer – let's say – sheet music as it was in the case of a music industry dominated by music publishers such as Tin Pan Alley? By presenting the single as a listening device in its dynamics to the LP as well as the flourishing high-fidelity culture of the 1950s, I can describe the single more precisely as an aesthetic form by discussing how precisely the single becomes a constitutive part of the music, not only its formal structure, but also its sound.[77] By explicitly analysing the relationship between sound and the single as a listening device, I can understand music not 'merely as a kind of "black box" that is bound to social, technological, economic and cultural communicative relationships, without, however, divulging its own structure and character'.[78] Thus, it is also possible to address one of the gaps left open by Frith and mass communications research.

A sound and music history of the single record investigates what sounds, forms of music and listening practices were included and implemented in the materiality of the single. Such inclusion was part of the single's history of development that was made (and written) by the US entertainment company RCA Victor, its engineers, marketing and music business experts, and later by its archivists and its historians.[79] By studying this history, I aim to excavate to what extent RCA in the 1940s not only developed a mere technical device but also a fundamentally musical device, a device that already included and simulated a specific form of listening, a device that managed listening. In contrast to this sound and music history of media, a media history of music would analyse 'how technology has changed music',[80] how the single became a part of music, maybe even how the single turned into a condition of specific music forms. For instance, in popular music studies, we can find lots of examples that identify the single as a medium of rock 'n' roll.[81] The approach I take in the following is complementary to that. For this purpose, I focus on three areas: first, the formatting, normalization and standardization of the music's sound by the single, perhaps most evident in relation to the single's playing time. Second, the question of what conceptions of music listening and what listening practices are implemented in and modelled by the single. Third, the forms of music that are part of the history of development of the single. Which musical forms were inscribed in the single, and which of the single's material characteristics reflect those forms – such as diameter, large central hole and easy portability? These three levels constitute something that we might call the *pre-heard* of the single. By including these three levels, the single 'pre-listens' or 'pre-hears' the music that is listened to via the single. Thus, in the single's history of development, I argue, a very specific form of listening that is delegated to and modelled by the single, is already materialized in the single. Certainly, that does not mean that this form of technologized listening has to be reproduced in listening practices in popular music cultures of which this listening device became an important part. However, the listening materialized in the single record makes some practices more likely than others.

In order to be able to work out the peculiarities of this music history of the single record more precisely, I shall repeatedly place this history, as already mentioned, in relation to the music history of the LP.[82] Especially in popular music studies and in the history of music and media technology, the stories of the LP and the single record have been told many times.[83] If the LP correlates with a historiography centred on musical works, then the single interrupts that historiography – and not only by virtue of its length. This in turn leads to issues in historiographical representations, which put even a music culture such as rock 'n' roll (where the focus is more the catchy and intense song and less the album or the great 'masterwork') also on the aesthetic defensive in relation to more 'sophisticated' popular music forms such as rock music. In contrast to these historiographies, I shall reconstruct how specific forms of listening became the origins for the development of the single. Thus this chapter's focus is primarily on a history of listening, and not on the history of a variety of technological formats. The latter's story has been told multiple times. The former is still poorly studied.

With regard to music listening, I argue, the single was often more modern than the LP: unlike the LP, the single did not originate within a high-fidelity paradigm, even if it would later be marketed under one. Instead, the single stemmed from the concept of automatically playing songs – ideally hits – by various artists in a series. In this sense, the single refers primarily to jukebox listening, but also listening to radio DJs' playlists. If the LP's aim was again and again to simulate listening to music in a concert hall in a private space, then a technologization of listening is already inherent in the single.[84] Moreover, the two record formats correlated with different listening subjects: while the LP established itself with so-called music lovers – the subject of 1950s hi-fi culture was white, male, adult and relatively affluent[85] – the single established itself as the format of teenagers.

The listening practices and musical forms inherent in the single can be outlined as follows: the pieces of music are relatively short and – ideally – catchy. This has its material correlate in the diameter of the single. Music productions by various artists can be played automatically in series, which has its material correlate in the single's large central hole, which makes the single very suitable for smooth record changing.[86] High fidelity is not the priority when listening to singles; it is more important that music productions function as part of a series, and that it is possible to associate such musical series with activities other than contemplative music listening. The latter has its material correlate in portable playing devices, used not only in quiet listening environments – such as middle-class living rooms. When listening to singles, the records in the playlist refer to other records, not to performances, thus, single-listening is a form of listening where media refer to other media – not primarily to a non-mediated 'real' world.

CBS's development of the LP: Long-playing versus changing records

When examining listening devices, lumping together the single and the LP for the purpose of identifying the former's shortcomings – by referring to the record's length and diameter for instance – is not very productive. Hence, I start by exploring the single primarily from the inside out, not from the outside in; I shall use the same approach to compare it to the LP. The main characteristic of the single that distinguishes it from the LP, is not its diameter (7 inches vs. the LP's 10 or 12 inches), nor its playing speed (45 rpm vs. the LP's 33 1/3 rpm), nor its length,[87] but rather its large central hole. The large hole was necessary in order for the record to fit on a new device, namely, the 'world's fastest changer!' as it was dubbed in a blatant RCA Victor slogan on advertisements for its new record playing system. This 'fastest' changer required approximately nine seconds for the final sound of one single to be followed by the first sound of the next.[88] If the development of the LP was the response to problems such as 'transparency' and 'sound fidelity', then the development of the single was the response to the challenge of being able to automatically play short records containing hits in series; in other words, it was a response to the problem of rapid automatic record changing.

Although the changing of single records would later become a strictly manual task because the 'world's fastest changer!' failed to take off, the consequences of automatic record changing for the listening culture are not to be underestimated, a point to which Carl Belz alluded with respect to popular music: 'In comparison to 45s, LPs demanded a long-range decision – to hear twenty or twenty-five minutes of the same artist – and they resisted the spontaneous selection which was characteristic of the smaller records. Of course, listeners could nullify these demands by selecting one or two songs from an LP, but this contradicted the design of the record.'[89]

Cultural studies scholar Paul Willis, too, makes note of the specifics of listening to singles versus LPs in his study of the rocker subculture in late 1960s England, for which rock 'n' roll singles from the 1950s were an essential listening device: 'Singles were specifically responsive to the active, moving listener. They only lasted for 2 ½ minutes. If a particular record was disliked, at least it only lasted for a short time. It could also be rejected from the turntable more quickly without the difficulty of having to pick the needle up to miss tracks. Exact selection could also be made so that the order of records was totally determined by individual choice. To play an LP was to be committed – unless you were prepared to go to a great deal of trouble – to someone else's ordering in the music. By and large, LPs are more popular with an audience which is prepared to sit and listen for a considerable period, and with a certain extension of trust so that unknown material can be appreciated and evaluated …. [The concept album] implies an audience which is stationary, sitting, not engaged in other activities and prepared to devote a substantial length of time to the appreciation of the music alone.'[90]

In any event, characterizing the single as the 'response' to the LP can at best be limited to the point in time when the US media giants CBS Columbia and RCA Victor launched their respective technologies on the market. CBS Columbia introduced the LP to the public in June of 1948,[91] during the second strike by the American Federation of Musicians (AFM).[92] Challenged by this, RCA Victor followed suit in 1949 with the single, pushing it onto the market with a promotional campaign that was as well-financed as it was aggressive.[93]

The single was a response to the LP only in connection with its market launch. The development of the single had already been concluded several years prior to the introduction of the LP. RCA Victor's development of the single as technology took place at the same time but independently of CBS Columbia's development of the LP as technology. At the same time, both the single and the LP were never merely discrete technological artefacts, but always parts of technological *systems*: thus, both corporations developed new playing devices for their new record formats as well.[94] Each of these technological systems implied and integrated a specific form of music listening. The single and the LP were not simply new recording or reproduction mediums for music. Instead, they transformed the manner in which music was perceived and listened to. Those listening practices of the single's development differ from the listening practices that were propagated in the advertising for the single, as well as from the actual listening practices.

Accounts of the developmental history of the LP vary among the CBS Columbia employees who were involved in its development.[95] Hence there are various inconsistencies among the versions by former president of Columbia Records, Edward

'Ted' Wallerstein,[96] Peter Goldmark, then head of the research department at CBS,[97] and by other Columbia employees involved in the development and marketing of the LP.[98] The account by classical music fan Wallerstein that he already initiated the development of the technology for the LP in 1939 shortly after taking up his position at Columbia, nine years before it was launched,[99] is more probable than the version told by amateur cellist and classical music fan Goldmark. In his biography, Goldmark claims to have first had the idea for the LP in 1945 when record changing interrupted the recording of a piano concerto he was listening to.[100] At a press presentation of the LP on 19 June 1948, Wallerstein said that the development of the LP had begun nine years before, was interrupted by the war and resumed thereafter; the LP's development was not completed until 1948.[101] Goldmark is surely not the 'Father of Hi-Fi', as he proclaimed himself to be, and as the rock press declared him[102] – especially as he never held any patents for the LP.[103] A more likely scenario is that the LP was developed by an engineering team led by William S. Bachman, who was then head of research at Columbia Records.[104] As head of research at CBS, the parent company of Columbia Records, Goldmark was also responsible for this project: 'Peter Goldmark was more or less the supervisor, although he didn't actually do any of the work.'[105] Goldmark claims, however, that it was he who had the idea for the LP, and that he had to do a lot of persistent persuading to win Wallerstein over to the project, since it was Wallerstein who, as former head of RCA Victor, had had to discontinue that company's unsuccessful attempt to introduce an LP in the early 1930s.[106] The LP that RCA Victor introduced in the early 1930s ultimately failed due to two problems: first, there was no adequate playing device for this long-playing record made of vinyl, and the conventional playing devices of the time wore the new records out; second, the record market shrank at the beginning of the 1930s as a consequence of the Great Depression.

The story of the LP's development is not the stuff of heroic historiographies featuring a protagonist styled a genius. Most of the components that went into the LP were already in existence: records made of vinyl, records that play at 33 1/3 rpm, ultra-lightweight pickups and technical processes that made it possible to store the entire audible frequency spectrum on a record – the *full frequency range recording* (ffrr), developed by the British label Decca together with the British military.[107] Nevertheless, this story did create, at least nominally, a 'Father of Hi-Fi': Peter Goldmark. In this way, a history of technology is perpetuated that is particularly fixated on personal names: Edison invented the phonograph, Berliner the record and Goldmark is the father of the LP.

Regardless of who actually invented the LP, it is clear that the LP targeted a middle-class market in the United States with money to spend and the forms of listening established on this market. The catalogue of titles offered by Columbia consisted of 105 LPs at the time of market launch and comprised a classical and a popular repertoire – such as, for example, *The Voice of Frank Sinatra* (Columbia, United States, 1948). These productions were not, however, recorded as LPs, but as 16-inch transcription discs, sometimes years before.[108] They then had to be transferred to LP. The LP version of *The Voice of Frank Sinatra* was a re-release of a four 78-rpm shellac disc version, which had already been released back in 1946.[109]

In his biography, Goldmark mentions specific forms of listening on which the development of the LP was based: 'I simply had an instinctive feeling that the sound one hears directly in the concert hall should be and could be duplicated in quality and timbre by technology.'[110] Ultimately, then, the LP is about privatizing concert hall listening by transporting it into American homes. This type of listening is successful when the technology is not heard; that is, when the sound seems as transparent as possible and the technology does not intervene, for instance, with low fidelity or the necessity of changing the record. The technology through which one listens is intended to be turned on and then not heard. Goldmark describes the problem that the 78-gramophone record posed for the music lover and which the LP was to solve by as far as the necessity of changing the record goes: 'In the midst of listening to the first movement of this record [Brahms 2nd Piano Concerto, played by Vladimir Horowitz, conducted by Arturo Toscanini], a terrible thing happened. There was a click, silence, and strange noises, and then the movement continued. This happened again and again. I counted twelve sides for the four movements and eleven interruptions, of which eight were unplanned by Brahms .... There was no doubt in my mind that the phonograph ... was ... murdering Horowitz, Toscanini, and above all Brahms, and I felt somehow impelled to stop this killer in its shellac tracks.'[111]

But the hi-fi culture that was booming in the 1950s for which the LP was an important factor can by no means be reduced to 'concert hall realism', although this did become a catchword in the magazines of the 1950s.[112] The aspiration to high fidelity is not only confined to a concert hall experience, but may also refer to a recording studio[113] or to a lounge or bar experience[114] to be simulated in one's private environment. In this, however, certain spaces have definite limitations in terms of their auditive reproducibility in one's private environment: whereas the concert experience has been characterized by silent contemplation and individualization since the nineteenth century,[115] the distinctive feature of the lounge experience is its collectivity.

Not only the reference to the concert hall but also the reference to 'realism' or an ideal of documentation was to some extent a problem in hi-fi culture. Media studies scholar Tim J. Anderson points out a second significance of high fidelity: 'High fidelity offered a version of "the real" as a realizable fantasy. In this sense, high fidelity was always already positioned as a celebrated form of artifice and spectacle that, through the union of science and the arts, would provide listeners with sensational renditions of the real.'[116] According to this view, reality within the scope of high fidelity is a hyper-reality that is more real than reality. This invokes sonic signatures of over-presence, technically generated closeness and intimacy, and, since the introduction of stereophonic records in 1956, extreme Ping-Pong effects. Anderson also calls such sonic hyper-realities the 'campy, excessive aspects of the hi-fi movement'.[117] Such an acoustic hyper-reality is embodied, he continues, in the so-called lounge movement – by which he is referring to instrumentalists like the guitarist Tony Motolla or musical genres like 'exotica'.[118] Keir Keightley also observes that in the 1950s there were high-fidelity fans who were not searching for concert hall realism, but listening, for instance, to the 'sound effects LPs' that were extremely popular back then. The subject of the hi-fi culture of the 1950s – according to Keightley's argument – brings moments of the irrational and excessive to the American middle class: the listening practices of the '"adult" musical culture of the 1950s'[119] are also a search for imaginary journeys in sound; they are thus ultimately a precursor of the 'psychedelia in the 1960s' or rather the listening practices of the 'rock fan on LSD listening to a stereo LP on headphones'.[120] Such listening practices contrast with concert hall aesthetics inasmuch as they are searching for the hyper-real, the excessive or the surreal.

These forms of listening correlate with a specific musical repertoire. Already in the 1950s the repertoire of hi-fi culture included not only concert hall music, but also sound effects LPs and lounge music. The excessive components of a hi-fi culture can, however, easily be brought into the context of discourses about a retreat into the private sphere and a belief in technological progress that are unwaveringly upheld even today: 'Over the course of the 1950s, audiophiles, musicians, and critics became increasingly comfortable with recording artifices that dispensed with the documentary ideal. By 1960, the recording art was plainly directed not toward duplicating the sound of an original performance, but toward crafting a soundscape specifically for the home listener. Though some listeners continued to yearn for an effacement of technological mediation, many began to trumpet its benefits. A chorus of musicians and critics gloried in the advances of modern technology, declaring that the best seat was now at home, in front of the stereo.'[121]

The forms of listening on which the development of the LP was based were those of the middle class in the United States who had money to spend. The models of listening implemented in the LP were not just reproduced in the hi-fi culture of the 1950s, they were transformed.

RCA's development of the single record: Musical forms and listening practices

In contrast to the history of the development of the LP, we seldom find a clear-cut claim to origins in the history of the development of the single. The media format of the single tends to remain 'fatherless'. In an article in the in-house *RCA Review*, in which RCA's technological system, including the single, was presented in detail for the first time in June 1949, the authors also make this unequivocally clear: 'The system described in this paper is the result of the combined work of so many members of the RCA Victor Record and Home Instrument Departments that individual acknowledgments are impractical.'[122]

Thus, the single was not developed in RCA's legendary Acoustical Research Laboratory headed by Harry F. Olson in Princeton, New Jersey, which also went down in music history for developing the first modern synthesizer. To begin with, it was developed by the Advanced Development Group and, after company restructuring in 1945 from a functional to a product-based organization, by the development departments of the Record Department and the Home Instrument Department, which manufactured RCA Victor's radios, phonographs and televisions. Whereas Olson's research was isolated from the processes obtaining in one of the 'corporate profit centers' of RCA Victor,[123] the development team working on the single was always closely interlinked with other company departments.

Already in 1939 Benjamin R. Carson,[124] an engineer in the Advanced Development Group, was commissioned by Thomas F. Joyce, the head of marketing of RCA Victor's Home Instrument Department, to develop a new record system. The reason for assigning the task to Carson could have been a decline in RCA Victor's revenue from the gramophone record market before the Second World War,[125] the falling prices of radios and record players which the development of new functions for these devices was intended to counteract, or an increased demand for record changers.[126] For Alexander Magoun, former director of the David Sarnoff Library, increased demand arose because of playlists becoming popular in the form they were shaped by jukeboxes or radio: 'While prices dropped [for the record player combinations produced by RCA Victor at the end of the 1930s], rising sales of consoles with automatic record changers indicated that consumers liked programming their own selections. This demand arose in the response to the ways they heard records played outside the home. Jukeboxes flourished after the end of Prohibition in December 1933. ... At the same time [1939], radio programmers and disc jockeys responded to the jukebox's popularity and the sales listings in *Billboard* magazine by formatting playlists, as in "Make-Believe-Ballroom" and "Your Hit Parade". The syndication of these shows encouraged growing numbers of listeners to reproduce this programming at home.'[127]

Record changers were available for private use starting in the late 1920s – such as the Automatic Orthophonic Victrola, since 1927, or the high-end Capehart Deluxe Automatic Home Phonograph in the 1930s.[128] These machines were, however, very unreliable; in particular changing gramophone records from different manufacturers caused problems. Carson's objective – he is described by historian Alexander Magoun as the driving force behind the development of the single, thus in this respect the relatively anonymous development team does undergo personalization – was to develop an automatic record changer that worked reliably. The project was given the name 'Project X' and became the 'only secret consumer technology project in RCA's history';[129] in this way, it was possible to extend its 'patent life' for a long time.[130] The record system was only patented in 1949, when the market launch was decided.

Carson diagnosed that no record changer would work reliably with heavy 78-shellac records and concluded that for this project a new disc would have to be invented.[131] In their history of the phonograph Oliver Read and Walter Welch have commented that the lack of standardization of 78s caused problems for any changing mechanism: 'It must be remembered that the 78-rpm shellac discs were much bulkier than the present vinylite 45s, and often varied in thickness, diameter, and location of the starting groove.'[132] In particular the lack of a 'uniform stopping groove to actuate the cycling mechanism'[133] caused problems. Thus at the beginning of the single record's development was not the goal of simulating the music lover's concert hall experience, but primarily the listening to music through the jukebox experience.[134] As Richard Osborne points out, the jukebox in this respect is 'a device that also helped to inspire the 45 rpm single'.[135] We can distinguish jukebox listening both from concert hall listening and also from radio listening. When listening to music on a jukebox the listener chooses what they hear, but this is not the case when listening to the radio: 'Carson based his initial design on the intention of continuing to fulfill the slogan, "the music you want when you want it" that Victor Talking Machine Company's marketers had coined to combat broadcast radio in the 1920s.'[136] The listening practices that were adopted in developing of the single record were thus not cultivated in the institution of the concert hall as was the case with the LP, but in jukebox technologies. The model of music listening that the single includes is a technologized listening practice according to which records are played in a series.

RCA Victor's engineers determined the parameters of the single by the problem of changing records automatically: a lightweight and small vinyl disc that turned at 45 rpm – 78s were too fast for a changer to work reliably. The large middle hole of the single also had the function of ensuring a smooth change. In *The Story of Rock* Carl Belz observed that the large hole in the middle 'also produced a faster, easier listening'.[137] A prototype of RCA Victor's new record system was already presented to the marketing department of the Home Instrument Department in March 1944. However, the prototype and the project both ended up on the shelf because of internal restructuring at RCA Victor, competing technologies (particularly the television), and the fear of format wars – in the 1920s there had been a format war between the gramophone record and the cylinder. Instead, RCA Victor concentrated on improving the 78. It was only when CBS Columbia launched the LP and explicitly marketed it as hi-fi technology[138] that RCA Victor took the record system off the shelf and presented it to the public in 1949 as an answer to the LP. Thus the single was in competition with the LP for it was also placed within a hi-fi framework.[139] – Within the scope of a hi-fi culture of the 1950s, RCA Victor's system of course failed spectacularly!

In the mid-1940s, the later owner of the American independent label Specialty Records, Art Rupe, conducted an unconventional, extremely reduced form of music analysis for his first record label, Juke Box Records. The instrument used in this analysis was not a score but a stopwatch. The focus of the analysis was clear and pragmatic: 'He [Rupe] spent hours playing the records over and over and timing sequences – the length of intros, of choruses, of repeat choruses. He tried to discover correlations in the records that sold and in those that did not sell.'[140] Rupe's 'analyses' were not restricted to questions about the formal structure of songs, he also included questions about how to name titles and about distribution capacity: 'He [Rupe] noted that many popular records had the word "boogie" in the title and that the jukebox operators were the main customers. And so his first release was "Boogie #1" on the new Juke Box label by the Sepia Tones.'[141] We can read Rupe's data collections as a confirmation of Adorno's critical standardization hypothesis from the year 1941, turned economically positive.[142] According to Adorno, standardized music is pre-digested or pre-heard, and relieves the listener of listening or else reduces listening at most to a 'recognition experience'; in this, the recognition does not lead to anything new, but is rather the aim in and of itself.[143] For Rupe, however, the cultural or music industry was no longer the same sheet music and radio industry that it was for Adorno in 1941, but specifically the record industry. Rupe does not seek to criticize it from a cultural theory perspective, but to actively explore (and exploit) it. Rupe planned to become active in this industry himself as a player. In the record industry, the music listened to also correlates with the form of the record and is, as it were, pre-configured through this. This can also be shown for the single.

The playing time of the single was never an abstraction constrained by merely technical or economic necessities. Aesthetic components were already integrated into the development of the single. The definition of the playing time of the single also refers to a specific form of music. Through its playing time, the single standardizes the heard. Wicke writes on the correlation between technology and popular music: 'Technological conditions are thus directly set for the music, such as, for instance, the restriction of a song's length to the playing time of about three and a half minutes of the single record that dominated into the eighties. Overall, technological determinants of music-making play a much greater role than generally assumed, as only that which is technically feasible in the studio can or will be popular music.'[144]

Although the single became the primary record format of rock 'n' roll in the 1950s and was without significance for the classical music market, its playing time was not exclusively determined with regard to popular music.[145] From the outset, RCA Victor was targeting both the classical and the pop markets with the single. To decide on the single's playing time, RCA Victor's engineers examined two record catalogues: on the one hand Victor's complete catalogue, and on the other its catalogue titled 'The Music America Loves Best' (MALB). The latter was made up of RCA Victor records that included recordings of classical music pieces as well as popular standards. The engineers established that 70 per cent of the classical music pieces from the MALB catalogue – these had appeared as 'Red Seal' releases, presented in a high-quality way – and about 80 per cent of the popular standards lasted for less than five minutes. Further, 96 per cent of all records sold by Victor featured music pieces that lasted for far less than five minutes. The consequence drawn after analysing these statistics was to define the playing time of the single as five minutes and thirty seconds.[146] We can add here, that in terms of sound quality this is undoubtedly too long, because the extended bass frequencies can then find no place on the record.

This argument for fixing the single's playing time at five minutes is, of course, to a great degree circular reasoning. We can also argue that the music pieces that went into the MALB catalogue became popular because they were better adapted to the properties of a specific record – the 78 record – than longer music pieces were. The conclusion that many of the most popular music pieces heard as records do not last longer than five minutes is inappropriate if only five minutes of music fit on the record. Carson, Burt and Reiskind assume that here technology is external to music. For this reason, they define a piece of music as follows: 'By "music unit" is meant a selection or a part of a work, such as a movement of a symphony, that was *written* to be played without a break.'[147] However, the music pieces in the MALB catalogue are not just compositions whose technology is external; rather, they have already been formatted through the 78, inasmuch as their length is adapted to this record format. The MALB catalogue can be read as an example of how music was standardized by the record. This standardization not only affects popular music – even if it can be perceived most strongly there – but also classical music. What Adorno wrote about popular music now also applies to classical music: 'Popular music is "pre-digested" in a way strongly resembling the fad of "digests" of printed material.'[148]

At CBS Columbia, they had completely different notions about the properties of a classical music piece: 'Clearly, engineers at Victor had different ideas about what constituted a classical song, since their colleagues at CBS had determined that a record for classical music had to play at least 20 minutes.'[149] Goldmark, for instance, claims he had raised statistics that differed from those of his colleagues at RCA Victor and had used these as the basis for developing the LP. He measured the length of symphony movements: 'The average classical piece, I discovered, took thirty-six minutes from the first note to the last. Ninety percent of all works could be put into forty-five minutes of playing time on a record.'[150] The historian of technology David Morton writes: 'The new Columbia LP reflected not only technical concerns but also the interests of classical music listeners.'[151] Goldmark has described how the LP was developed against the background of simulating a concert hall experience.[152] Thus, the primary influence in developing the single was not a hi-fi paradigm, but the problem of changing records, and this leads back to the large middle hole of the single. It was intended to enable a listener to play a series of automatically changed, short, and catchy musical pieces. The development of the single was also driven by specific concepts of music and listening that its developers took as starting point. Thus, the single record is conditioned by music and sound history.

Mastering industry standards and non-listening: 'Hot' rock 'n' roll singles

Excursus: Mastering, a historical and theoretical positioning

From a historical point of view, mastering has long indicated a change of medium. When, for example, Enrico Caruso was recorded by Fred Gaisberg for and by Victor Records at the beginning of the twentieth century, the record format on which his tenor voice was stored was identical to the record format on which the recording was then released. In this respect, there was no mastering at that time, but there was only a master; namely, the record on which Caruso was recorded in April 1902 in a hotel in Milan.[153] Mastering in the narrower sense has only existed since the advent of audio tape in music production around 1950.[154] Since then, tape has been used in the recording studio, but records have been released.

Initially, the change from one medium to another seemed to be a purely technical transfer and was referred to as transferring or even re-recording.[155] In the 1950s, specific mastering rooms containing record cutting machines were set up in various recording studios.[156] This spatial separation soon corresponded to the distinction between sound engineer and mastering engineer.[157] In the second half of the 1960s, the first independent mastering studios were created, like the Frankford/Wayne Mastering Lab in Philadelphia in the vicinity of Joe Tarsia's Sigma Sound Studios, Doug Sax's Mastering Lab in Hollywood, and Sterling Sound in New York. The emergence of these studios marked the increasing professionalization and specialization in the field of mastering. These processes were followed by a stronger personalization of mastering. With the digitization of music production, mastering ceased to denote a change of medium and began to denote a change of format.

The function of the mastering engineer in the process of music production is comparable to that of the editor and proofreader in book production. Just as the editor and proofreader accompany the publishing process from the manuscript, typed script or text file to the finished book, the mastering engineer accompanies the process from the mixdown to the press matrix.[158] The mastering function is prominent in the music production process in the sense that it is the last stage in this process where the sound is modified. Unlike the sound engineer in the recording studio, the mastering engineer engages with audio technology primarily in its playback rather than its storage function. He or she articulates the relationship between sound, technology and listener. The mastering engineer fine-tunes sound in terms of the devices through which sound is listened to. In this respect, mastering creates potential or suitability. Mastering makes sound suitable for jukebox, radio, club or living room. Mastering is a part of post-production that does not rely on the presence of musicians.[159]

However, the fact that mastering emerged as a function in the music production process around 1950 is not only traceable back to the introduction of audio tape in music production and the accompanying necessary change of medium between music production and music release. Rather, mastering is also conditioned by the fact that music has entered – to quote Jacques Attali – an 'order of repetition': an order in which music basically plays together with a 'mould', that is, a specific form that is suitable for mass reproduction. It is as a factor in serial production that the mould acquires its central significance as a form for mass reproduction, and it undermines the distinction between original and copy by making a reproducible original possible: 'The repetitive economy is characterized first of all by a mutation in the mode of production of supply, due to the sudden appearance of a new factor in production, the mold, which allows the mass reproduction of an original.'[160] The mould is produced by the 'molder' whose work allows 'a great number of copies' to be made.[161] In the order of repetition, Attali sees the status of the musician devalued in relation to that of the moulder. The latter could certainly also achieve the status of an author.[162] Attali expresses this in the formula 'Music escapes from musicians.'[163] Musicians had become suppliers of material in a larger process in which sound engineers were gaining in importance.[164] However, the concepts of 'molder' and 'mold' ultimately remain hazy in Attali's work. Does the term 'molder' refer to the composer, the lyricist, the sound engineer, the producer, the musician, someone else entirely or even a collective? In this book, the mastering engineer will be examined as a moulder, since it is ultimately she or he who produces the form that is suitable for mass reproduction.

The fact that music escapes musicians becomes concrete on another level in the United States in the 1940s. There were two phases in the 1940s in which music was released on record even though the musicians had not recorded any music. Tim J. Anderson argues that the strikes of the AFM in 1942–44 and 1948 contributed to the fact that 'entertainment archives and catalogues'[165] became more important than performances, and that a 'recording-based media economy' emerged,[166] that is, recordings, became the focus of the music industry. With direct reference to Attali, Anderson offers a precise date when the order of repetition became dominant. He writes: 'I argue that the strikes are essentially a conflict between musicians, who are invested in an entertainment economy based on performances, and an advanced mass media economy, which is based on the production, reproduction, stockpiling, and repetitive playback of entertainment "molds".'[167]

The reason for the strikes initiated by union chief James C. Petrillo was the AFM's claim that the use of media in media like records in radio or jukebox, endangered the economic livelihood of musicians.[168] The AFM banned all of its members from making records. During the two strikes, significantly fewer records were released.[169] However, the record companies still found ways of putting records on the market in the pop sector: instrumentalists who were not represented by the AFM and singers who were organized in another union were recorded.[170]

Ultimately, according to Anderson, the strikes were counterproductive. They had the consequence, for example, that from then onward it was primarily records that were played on the radio – a condition for the emergence of the radio DJ of the 1950s. Anderson points to the changeover to a 'recording-based media economy'.[171] In such an economy, the status of the musician had changed: 'With each recorded performance, with each object that contains the potential of being repackaged in multiple fashions across time, control of the stockpile leaves the musician.'[172] Thus Attali's formula for the order of repetition – 'Music escapes from musicians' – became a concrete reality.

The 'mold makers' for Anderson are 'musicians, producers, and engineers'.[173] Anderson defines the mould more bluntly as a master recording: 'But unlike a publication of a specific composition, these objects' performance and reproduction are *intrinsically* removed from the musicians and composers who produce the initial master recording, or mold.'[174] This clear definition, however, differs from Attali's definition of mould as a mass reproducible form. Strictly speaking, it was not the master tape that is mass reproduced, but the master disc. In the 1950s, however, this matrix was not made by the composer, musician or producer, but by a specific engineer: the transferring or mastering engineer.

In this respect, even an oft-quoted comment by Jerry Leiber and Mike Stoller – 'We didn't write songs, we wrote records'[175] – acknowledges that music production fundamentally changed in the 1950s, but at the same time remained in the sphere of the metaphorical. Ultimately, Leiber and Stoller did not 'write' records. If records are written by anyone at all, it is by the mastering engineer. In the context of book production, this difference has been pointed out: 'Whatever they may do, authors do *not* write books. Books are not written at all. They are manufactured by scribes and other artisans, by mechanics and other engineers, and by printing presses and other machines.'[176]

Historians Roger Chartier and Guglielmo Cavallo emphasize in their edited history of reading that the text would never exists 'in itself', that is, 'separate from any material manifestation (an idea elaborated by literature itself that the more quantitatively inclined histories of the book have taken over), we should keep in mind that no text exists outside of the circumstance in which it is read (or heard)'.[177] This is also true for many forms of popular music, but their carriers are standardized. However, the form in which the carriers are mass-produced is not created by a composer, musician, or producer, but by the 'transfer of a recording onto a physical medium needed for industrial mass production (matrix for pressing records, magnetic tape or digital audio tape for producing music cassettes, glass master for producing CDs or DVDs)',[178] which has been provided by the mastering engineer since about 1950. The adaptation of sound events to the physics and standards of a technical medium is the responsibility of the mastering engineer.

Mastering thus emerged in the 1950s and indicates the establishment of post-production.[179] Since mastering is the final sound-altering stage in the music production process, the mastering engineer can potentially be said to have a gatekeeper function. On the other hand, the metaphor of mastering as the 'Supreme Court of audio' seems somewhat hypertrophic.[180]

On a systematic level, we can state that in mastering, a sound event does not exist in itself, but stands in a relation to technology. Such a relation can be specified in three ways for now: (i) The mastering engineer relates sound to a form that is suitable for mass reproduction. In this respect, a mastering engineer who masters records must know about cutting characteristics and their standardizations; a mastering engineer who masters CDs is familiar with the 'Red Book' standard. (ii) The mastering engineer relates sound to other sounds. This is done, for example, by homogenizing disparate sound material from different decades for a compilation or soundtrack. The mastering engineer can also make sound events suitable for use in a programme, such as for a jukebox, a DJ, or streaming playlist.[181] (iii) The mastering engineer relates sound to devices through and via which it is primarily heard or in which it is intended to function. These devices are examined in this book as listening devices.

Records becoming (Im)perceptible: Speeds and curves

In both the late 1940s and the 1950s, technical standards were newly defined and challenged on the US record and consumer electronics markets. As regards listening, such standards also had the function of making technologies imperceptible industry-wide. In the 1950s, industry standards were also intended to lead to sonic technologies being ignored more easily by the listener or else shifting over into the realm of the unhearable and non-listening. As already mentioned in Chapter 1 of this book, we can examine the domain of non-listening, characteristic of listening devices, by means of standardization processes and how they are dealt with. As part of introducing the LP and the single, two technical standards are predominantly up for discussion: the standardization of the playback speed and the standardization of the so-called recording curve.[182]

The challenge to the playback speed of records standardized across the industry by CBS Columbia and RCA Victor in the late 1940s also led to what the music press of the time subsumed under the dramatic slogan the 'battle of the speeds' or else 'war of the speeds':[183] CBS Columbia's LPs turned at 33 1/3 rpm, RCA Victor's singles at 45 rpm.

After record players no longer had to be cranked up by hand, 78 rpm established itself as the standard at the beginning of the twentieth century.[184] The prerequisite for this was the inclusion of at first self-controlling[185] and therefore constantly turning clockwork motors, and later reasonably precisely rotating electric motors in gramophones. The slogan 'battle of the speeds' implies the fatal economic consequences of this suspension of standardization by introducing the LP and the single, and thus also the destruction of the compatibility of records and playing devices of different manufacturers and labels. Reacting to the shrinkage of the market, finally RCA Victor began to release LPs and Columbia CBS singles. As far as the listening devices are concerned, two innovations ensured compatibility: 'Two minor innovations – the multi-speed turntable and the center hole adapter – rendered the 45-rpm and LP systems functionally compatible and effectively created a non-proprietary microgroove phonograph-disc system.'[186] Thus, record players soon played at all three speeds; in this way, the playing speed of records – after having been made perceptible – was again made unhearable. Only at the centre of the LP and the single did it continue to be hearable: because of their slower playing speed, LPs continued to tend towards greater distortions when the groove approached the middle hole than faster turning singles did. In this respect, placing hits at the end of an LP record side proved to be problematic.[187]

While the dispute about standardizing the playing speed was ended with the introduction of record players that could turn at three speeds and the spindle adapter, the standardization of the recording curve was more problematic. However, unlike the lack of standardization or compatibilization of the playing speed, the lack of standardization of the recording curve does not lead to records becoming almost unusable – apart from some experiments in sound art.

Every record, including every hi-fi record, comprises a distortion, amplifying the highs in order to suppress the static noise, lowering the level of the basses which require a lot of room on the record to cut; in this way, more sound can be put on a record. The intention is, when playing the record, that these distortions are rectified using corresponding filters. The standard that regulates such a distortion or equalization is called the recording curve. A lowering and raising or pre-emphasis and de-emphasis of frequencies is done by a mastering engineer when he or she cuts the record. There has been a characteristic curve that determines the exact ratio of the lowering and raising since the electrification of sound recording in the mid-1920s. However, throughout the 1950s a number of different curves were developed and used. The mastering engineers of the 1950s had to find a way to deal with such an abundance of curves.

Disregarding standards: Singles and rock 'n' roll mastering

What is striking about the attempts at standardizing the recording curve is that these were taken up and even driven by the hi-fi culture of the 1950s. Such attempts at standardization tended to be productively disregarded by those independent labels which covered rock 'n' roll. In this respect, the emergence of a standardized recording curve – one that is unhearable across the industry – in the United States in the 1950s cannot be explored without grappling with the numerous violations of such a standard. Referring to *Moanin' at Midnight* by Howlin' Wolf produced by Sam Phillips (Chess, United States, 1951), Albin Zak writes: 'the indies allowed more noise into a record's grooves than the majors would tolerate. Engineers at the big companies, for example, strove to prevent electronic distortion by carefully controlling input levels for microphone preamplifiers and tape machines.'[188] Such violations were not committed within the scope of the high-fidelity discourse that characterized the audio culture of the 1950s, which was committed to the telos of transparent, or rather unhearable technology.

The intentional violations can be examined in the releases from US independent labels that were booming in the 1950s. These labels also developed a sound aesthetic of their own again and again distinct from hi-fi sound, which they could not achieve given the limitations of their equipment. In the studios in which these releases were mastered, the top priority was not paradigms like 'high fidelity', 'transparency' and 'balance', but rather the competitive advantage when the record produced was used in a playlist. This competing power was not ensured through 'high fidelity', but rather through loudness. Notwithstanding, there were individual independent labels – such as Atlantic Records – that distinguished themselves by complying with the industry standards.[189]

In hi-fi culture, compliance with industry standards led to an increasing sonic transparency of the listening technologies.[190] The fact that listening forms emerged that, in turn, reduce this transparency – almost paradoxically given such escalating transparency – by provoking a listening to the technology, is noted by musicologist Alf Björnberg. In his examination of the hi-fi discourse in Sweden from 1950 to 1980, he diagnoses in a virtually dialectical way: 'the increased transparency of the medium tends to promote a mode of listening reducing transparency.'[191] In hi-fi jargon, this mode of listening is allocated an organ of its own: the 'golden ears'. These are not so much – to refer to the concepts I developed in Chapter 1 – technologized organs as rather technology that has become an organ:[192] the golden ears are able to hear the technology and materiality through which they are listening, without, however, hearing it exclusively: golden ears have as a *pars pro toto* the pretence of being music lovers. They are able to point out differences in sound in the technology although others claim that these differences not only cannot be heard, but they cannot be measured either. The golden ears can mock these others as 'meter readers'. Such readers of measuring instruments, it was said, were not able to hear, but only to measure or to see, and would try in this way – by, I can add hear, upholding every cliché of visually centred production of evidence – to attain 'epistemic authority'.[193] The golden ears, of course, also claim this authority for themselves. They also need to be differentiated from the 'tin ears'.[194] The distinction between golden ears and tin ears is also reproduced at the level of the music listened to. While golden ears primarily listen to classical music, tin ears would probably listen to Tin Pan Alley. Despite the compliance with standards usual in hi-fi culture, the technology is thus not of necessity unhearable. A discourse arose in hi-fi culture about how technically reproduced music should be listened to.

By contrast, in the production practices of the independent studios of the 1950s, we can find an almost systematic disregard for industry standards. The reasons for this seem to lie not only the specific hardware of these studios but also a peculiar concept of recorded sound that shaped the practices in the studio. Zak goes so far as to suggest that both the way that hardware rendered hi-fi impossible – this becomes concrete in the technology of the independent studios,[195] but also in listening technologies like the jukebox – and the way a virtue was made out of the negative relationship to hi-fi in the 1950s resulted in a new sound concept. This sound concept, he asserts, is indeed different from a hi-fi documentation ideal, but remains in a negative relationship to it. Recorded sound, in this new sound concept, is no longer related to a performance, but rather primarily to other recorded sound. Or in other words: because the technology of the independent studios as relates to a documentation aesthetics was not able to compete with the technology of the big studios, alternative aesthetics, or rather sound concepts, were established in the independent studios. The independent productions were thus not primarily compared with performances, but with other record productions: 'Surrendering to the medium's terms, pleasure could be taken in the sound of the record itself without the triangulating interference of comparative expectation. As records became the most common everyday mode of musical perception – spinning on radio, jukebox, and lo-fi record players – this kind of apprehension gradually changed the public's sense of recorded sound. Disembodied, electronically mediated pop sounds accumulated as members of a new sonic lexicon supporting a developing system of musical rhetoric. In the new world of pop record production, making a record meant making an aesthetic argument framed in terms not only of the natural sound world but of other records.'[196] Even if the listener is not the main focus of Zak's study, we can find there references to specific listening practices in rock 'n' roll culture. Zak proposes that listening in rock 'n' roll culture is not oriented towards transparency, but rather towards something he calls 'character'.[197] Such a sonic 'character' of records is also generated by disregarding industry standards.

The rejection of industry standards by many American independent labels of the 1950s that shaped the sound of rock 'n' roll resonates with the rebellious spirit, with the 'general Wild West atmosphere in which the indies operated',[198] as well as with the down-to-earth entrepreneurial spirit that was supposed to have been so characteristic for the operators of those very small companies.[199] We should note here, however, that this disregard for standards was not by any stretch about pursuing an artistic end in itself, but rather as constantly interlinked to their competitive advantage and thereby was aimed at a management of listening. The disregard for standards leads to the border formed by the unhearable and non-listening: as for standardizations like the recording curve that were also implemented in playing technologies, rock 'n' roll singles were mastered in a way that did not meet these standards, that ignored these standards in a targeted way. Here, sound was not primarily documented on the sound carrier, but primarily oriented towards its effect on the listener.

While RCA Victor's engineers developed the single as an answer to the problem of automatically playing records as a series, this problem can be found again with regard to mastering and in handling the recording curve in the 1950s.

In the mastering of popular music forms, records frequently did not operate as a hi-fi medium, but were instead intended to be competitive – mostly in terms of loudness – vis-à-vis the other records with which they were deployed on the radio or in the jukebox.

Thus, the correlation between unhearable and non-listening, mastering, standardization of the recording curve, listening devices and the concept of recorded sound can be found in the music culture of the 1950s. Susan Schmidt Horning, in her history of the culture and technology of the recording studio in the analogue age, describes how with the implementation of magnetic tape in the 1950s, the production of records was ever more strongly shaped by post-production.[200] Besides subsequent or post-mixing, such post-production also includes mastering. Whereas subsequent mixing of a recording is primarily caused by the multitrack tape, mastering is primarily caused by the fact that the medium on which the recording takes place in the studio is a different one than the medium on which the music is released and heard. The mastering engineer conveys this shift in media. There have been masters since there has been sound reproduction; mastering exists only since the introduction of the tape into music production.[201] The problem of the recording curve remained associated with mastering into the 1950s: 'Before magnetic tape became the standard recording medium, this master disc was made at the time of recording, just as mixing was done during the recording. When tape became the primary medium, the final mixed tape became the master and the lacquer master cut from it became the master sent for processing to vinyl LP or single disc .... Until 1954, when the Recording Industry Association of America (RIAA) established a standard recording curve, record companies had used a variety of different recording, or equalization curves, in cutting a master disc. Each company established its own curve to best suit playback on its own phonograph.'[202]

The fact that almost every record company in the United States into the 1950s used their own curve is probably justifiable, institutionally speaking, in that for a long time there was no formal organization of sound engineers, record companies and technology manufacturers. Schmidt Horning also writes the history of the recording studio in the analogue age as a history of its institutions. Work processes and procedures – for instance, the microphone array, mixing and mastering – were organized more through implicit than explicit knowledge until the formation of organizations like audio societies and professional institutions, until the first professional technical journals appeared.[203] In the United States, this institutionalization took place only at the end of the 1940s. In the first issue of the magazine *Audio Engineering* in May 1947, the editor, John H. Potts, defined the creation of standards as one of the aims of his magazine: 'This branch of the industry [audio engineering] is in sad need of standardization, different makes of records do not have the same cross-over frequencies, the degree of pre-emphasis at the higher frequencies varies, groove depth is not always the same, and there are still other factors which affect reproduction upon which no standards have been selected.'[204] Schmidt Horning describes how this desire for standardization ultimately led in January 1948 to the founding of the Audio Engineering Society (AES). Radio and jukebox operators in particular had to struggle with the lack of standardization.[205] The founding of the AES finally led to the creation of another standard among many. It was only the foundation of the RIAA in 1951 that succeeded in establishing a single industry standard. This was accepted in February 1954 by all the major and independent labels that were members of the RIAA; implementation was complete by the mid-1950s.[206] The RIAA standard had the objective that the capturing process of the record should be as unhearable as possible. It was especially dedicated to a high-fidelity paradigm. In this respect, after counting the various standards, American studies scholar William F. Shea remarked: 'With this much confusion and without an industry-wide standard there was little hope of achieving high fidelity.'[207]

Mastering rooms and studios: The Indies

Various independent labels, however, were not members of the RIAA; for instance, King Records.[208] Company founder Sidney Nathan wanted to economize on the annual membership fee. King had an 'in-house factory to record, master, press, design, print, and distribute records'.[209] Particularly fast production was guaranteed: 'A singer could walk into King in the morning and leave that night with a new record in his hands.'[210] Nathan had refused RCA Victor's single at the end of the 1940s as a format for the music he released. This was probably due to the fact that in the estimation of those operating the labels the market they served – following the *Billboard* jargon labelled 'race', or starting in 1948 'rhythm & blues' or 'hillbilly' – did not require the single: 'Sydney Nathan, who turned King Records into the sixth largest label by 1949, had no interest in new speeds of vinyl. Nathan estimated that fifteen percent of the country's phonographs were still springwound. Many of their owners lacked electricity, and some of them preferred their machines' "horrible tone". This was his market for King's lower-class "race" and "hillbilly" records, and he saw no reason for change from the 78 as the pop music format "for years and years to come … further than I can anticipate".'[211]

Usually, the independent studios did their mastering themselves. There were exceptions only in the 1940s and early 1950s. Thus, for instance, in the early days Sam Phillips sent the recordings he had made in his Memphis Recording Service to Bill Putnam's Universal Audio Studios in Chicago.[212] In his studios, Putnam set up two rooms with record-cutting machines for mastering in 1950. He also developed specific mastering procedures – for example, half-speed mastering. For this process, which enabled better resolution in the treble ranges, mastering was done at half the playing speed.[213]

For mastering, dedicated rooms were set up in the independent studios. Besides equalizers – usually from the film industry[214] – there were compressors for signal equalization and limiters for dynamics processing, usually a mixing console, and the record-cutting machine, which represented the heart of the mastering room. The main manufacturers of disc-cutting machines in the 1950s were the US companies Presto and Scully and the German Neumann company. The master records were cut with the hot cutting stylus of the cutting head.[215] These technologies were soon part of the standard equipment of independent studios like J&M[216] and Chess.[217] In the studios, there were soon specific engineers responsible for the mastering, such as Bill Stoddard at the Fine Sound Studio in New York, and Jack Wiener and Emory Cook at Universal in Chicago.[218]

Particularly when mastering productions of popular music, however, standards were not heeded, but rather sound was mastered mainly in terms of its effect; that means with a view to it being deployed in jukeboxes and on the radio. Schmidt Horning writes: 'Record companies, in fact, strove to produce the loudest records, at least in the popular field, so that they would be heard above the competition when played in jukeboxes, on the radio, or in the home.'[219]

Schmidt Horning's interviews with sound engineers also confirm this assumption. For example, the mastering engineer Bill Stoddard reports that even after introducing the RIAA curve his actions were not determined by technical norms and standards: 'In the mastering room we did what sounded best!'[220] The mastering engineers in the 1950s did not simply ensure that a single sounded 'good'. To a greater degree their actions were oriented towards a different objective: the effectiveness of a single on the jukebox or the radio. This led to strategies of 'hot' mastering, which sought to increase the competitive ability of sound: 'Making hot masters that could still track on most phonographs (play without skipping) was the goal of every mastering engineer and rarely would the artists or producer be involved at this stage.'[221]

The desire to make records suitable for jukeboxes soon resulted in one of the first jukeboxes appearing in a mastering room:[222] Randy Wood, the founder of Dot Records, had a jukebox delivered to one of the mastering rooms at Bill Putnam's Universal Audio Studios, where various rhythm and blues and rock 'n' roll classics released by Sun or Chess Records were mastered. After a mastering engineer compressed and cut a record with high levels, he immediately tested it in the jukebox as to whether it was still playable. If it was, the engineer increased the level until the maximum level that was still playable was found.[223]

Mastering engineers usually ignored not only standards but also again and again their clients' instructions.[224] As a result, the sound of a released record was no longer determined by the intention of the musician or the producer. However, some producers also preferred 'hot' mastering Thus, for instance, Sam Phillips speaks about how 'intended distortion' was achieved in the mastering.[225] On the box with the magnetic tape of Elvis Presley's recording of 'Mystery Train', Sam Phillips wrote for Bill Putnam and his team, who had started to master the recordings of Sun Records in Chicago since this record in 1955: 'Give me "hot" level on both 78 and 45s and as much presence peak and bass as possible!'[226] It was not fidelity that was to the fore here, but instead the competitive ability achieved via volume and loudness. 'Hot' mastering strategies were well established in the 1950s.

The hi-fi discourse of the 1950s is particularly linked to the existence of a private domestic space.[227] Such rooms offer a quiet listening environment in which a large dynamic range can develop. But the deliberate violation of standardizations and the orientation on competitive ability when mastering 7-inch singles is linked with specific forms of listening in which records by different performers are played in a series and in specific listening environments. These records were not intended to work only in a quiet living room but in louder and noisier listening environments as well. With regard to the forms of deployment in which the sounds of the rock 'n' roll productions have to function, complying with the standardized recording curve became less important, and disregarding it to preserve a competitive edge took over. Thus, the records in rock 'n' roll culture are not a transparent sonic medium, they are opaque. In mastering, the medium-specific sound of the single underwent crucial tuning.

3

Limited choice: Listening through jukeboxes in the 1950s

As coin-operated devices, for a long time jukeboxes were looked down upon, regarded as on the same level as other profanities or 'penny-diggers' of everyday life such as chewing gum, cigarette and slot machines, as well as their more extravagant relatives like the 'electric shocker', the pin-up machine or the 'voice-o-graph'.[1] Jukeboxes are very specific to their era and have corresponding nostalgic potential. When the later Nobel Prize winner Peter Handke wrote his 'Essay on the Jukebox' in the wintry north of Spain in 1989, a year so rich in events that ironically can also be considered the possible centenary of the jukebox,[2] he was constantly assailed by doubts because of his so 'unworldly topic', this 'mere plaything'.[3] The hasty modernity that the jukebox embodied in Europe after the Second World War as a sign of 'Americanization from below',[4] that is, Americanization driven primarily by the working class and by white-collar workers, became a feature of the unrestrainedly anachronistic impression this device makes today.[5]

West German cultural critics in the 1960s and 1970s regarded the jukebox as the emblem of unbridled commercialization of music: it stood for the 'incorporation of the Federal Republic of Germany [FRG] into the "international" – i.e., in this case English-language – hit market'[6] and the 'rigorous spread of the profit economy'.[7] Bearing this context in mind, statements by German jukebox operators – the people who set up and ran the jukeboxes and who stocked their selection of records – can be quoted with relish: 'Whether that's good or bad doesn't interest me. I only think commercially.'[8] Unsurprisingly, the culture-critical diagnoses are correspondingly drastic: The 'automaton monster' had 'spread like a plague over the whole world.'[9] Even the fact that some Germans might still be using a *Volksempfänger* from the Nazi era as their main listening device did not seem a pro for the jukebox to the narrow-minded cultural critics.[10] Compared to the current trend of miniaturization, to which developments in contemporary audio technology with its earpods and smartphones has often subscribed, the inflated jukeboxes look like a giant's toys, singing the praises of superficial glamour, untamed by any function and with forms blown up to the max. The non-sustainable material plastic is one of the main components of the jukebox, which it proudly displays and presents. In present-day Germany, the jukebox appears to be an icon of the 1950s, the era when most of today's jukebox collectors were young and could choose and listen to music for 'two pennies'.[11]

This chapter examines the jukebox as a listening device of the 1950s. In the first section, I elaborate on how the jukebox as a listening device is involved in the constitution of the music listened to. In the second section, I elaborate on how the jukebox models and manages listening, and thereby modulates the materialities of listening. While the first two sections of this chapter try to argue in close reference to the materiality of the jukebox itself, I close this chapter with a coda that opens up a wider vista on these materialities of jukebox listening. This unfolds through discourses, practices and subjects of jukebox listening.

The jukebox sound: Rock 'n' roll and beyond, belly resonance and tuned playlists

We can hardly overestimate the significance of the jukebox in the development of popular music from the 1930s to the 1950s not only in the United States, but also in West Germany and the UK. After the electrification of the phonograph in 1925 made its volume capability equal to that of automatic musical instruments, and after the US government finally repealed Prohibition in 1933, economic as well as sonic conditions were good for the jukebox – despite or perhaps because of the severe economic depression.[12] In the late 1920s and early 1930s, jukeboxes were already installed in the 'jook joints' of African American communities in the rural regions and cities of the US Southern states and in the 'honky tonks' of white communities in rural areas.[13] In the larger cities of the Northern United States, jukeboxes began to appear in Black communities in the late 1920s, where they were used primarily at 'rent parties', where dancing to records on a leased jukebox became common events.[14] However, especially in the 1940s and 1950s, jukebox manufacturers increasingly started to target the middle-class market.

By the 1950s, a significant proportion of records produced in the United States went into jukeboxes. For a history of listening, this fact raises the question of whether, and if so, to what extent, the music produced during this period was tuned to the jukebox; to its sound, economy and technology; to the forms of listening that emerged with it. Did music have to be of a certain texture in order to work in the jukebox, to be put into the boxes by the jukebox operators and to be selected at the boxes by the listeners? And if this was the case, how exactly did music acquire such 'jukeboxability', how did music become 'jukeboxable'? Ultimately, these questions refer to the thesis that listening devices have a constitutive function for what is heard through them as music; that jukeboxes as listening devices also (co-)produce the music heard via them. Especially for the records released by the numerous independent labels that were founded in the United States after the Second World War and that were crucial for the development of rock 'n' roll, the jukeboxes were key listening devices.[15] The releases of these labels also had to function in the boxes in order to become popular. In this context, the small, fast single records played an increasingly important role. Jukeboxability was central for the releases of these independent labels, because for a long time jukebox operators in the United States were one of the most important customers of record labels.

Indies, singles and jukeboxes

The development of rock 'n' roll was decisively boosted by a close link between independent labels, small single records and jukeboxes. From the 1930s to the 1950s, a large part of singles production went into the jukeboxes. In 1939, there were already between 225,000 and 300,000 jukeboxes in the United States, and thirteen to thirty million records passed through them, which is estimated to have been as much as half, or even more than 70 per cent of the total production of records.[16] On 8 January 1944, *Billboard* introduced music charts specifically for the jukebox – in addition to their charts for retail and radio – on a weekly basis. In 1950, there were around 400,000 boxes in the United States playing forty-six million records. This corresponded to 15 per cent of all releases or even 30 per cent of single output.[17] In 1956, Charlie Gillett stated that,[18] jukeboxes were responsible for 40 per cent of record purchases. In 1957, a total of 205 million singles are estimated to have been sold,[19] sixty million of which went into the jukeboxes.[20] In the 1950s, the jukebox market in the United States was saturated. There was only a modest increase in the number of machines during this decade. Manufacturers increasingly focused on exports. In the 1960s, jukeboxes lost their importance in the United States.[21] We can note that at least a quarter to a third of all single record production in the 1950s went into jukeboxes.[22]

For the independent labels that defined the sound of rock 'n' roll, the percentage of their total output that went into jukeboxes was even higher. For example, Joe Bihari, co-founders of the Modern Records label in Los Angeles, pointed out that in the early years of the label, half of the label's record output was for the jukeboxes.[23] Art Rupe, owner of Specialty Records, also notes that 'Jukebox operators were the main customers' of his label.[24] In the beginning, Rupe's label Specialty was even called Jukebox Records: 'I called it Jukebox Records ... because the jukebox was the medium then for plugging records. If you got a record into the boxes, it was tantamount to getting it on the top stations today. The jukebox operator was also important because he brought in volume. While a small operator might have twenty or thirty boxes, a big op would have a thousand or twelve hundred locations. It was a sizable sale if you made it.'[25] Even Rupe's removal of the jukebox from his label's name did not alter the fact that the boxes remained a central medium for the independent record labels.

Some of the independent label owners even had experience in the jukebox business before they switched to the record business. Both the Bihari brothers and Rupe operated jukeboxes before they started their own record labels. Cosimo Matassa, owner of J&M Studio in New Orleans, also had contacts in the jukebox business: 'Cosimo Matassa, son of a New Orleans jukebox operator and himself a field service engineer, witnessed the rocket-like ascendancy of the jukebox culture.'[26] Jukebox operators of the 1950s, who stocked their machines primarily with a repertoire for niche markets, also became active in other segments of the music business: 'As early as in 1953, a few [jukebox operators], especially those servicing locations that used a lot of black pop and country pop records, were actively creating publishing firms and developing new performers and new record labels. They were using the boxes to pre-test records pressed in their own factories and recorded by artists they controlled – a miniature, vertically integrated operation.'[27] Via the jukeboxes, for instance, record label owners were able to test a regional market: 'Local jukeboxes provided a vital testing ground for untried musicians and new styles' and even generated hits.[28]

Jukeboxes had been instrumental in fostering the mass start-up of independent labels in the United States: 'Jukeboxes played a vital role in the growth of independent record labels for R&B music, as jukebox operators could guarantee sales of 10,000 singles in the large cities.'[29] The jukebox thus relativized radio as a promotion channel for records to a certain extent, and this benefitted the new small record companies: 'Records were available in two places, in the jukebox and at the local record store. In the late 1940s and 1950s, before R&B disc jockeys, the jukebox was the main point of exposure.'[30] Thus in the 1950s jukeboxes and independent record labels were closely connected. In the 1950s, rock 'n' roll was not only promoted by radio DJs like Alan Freed with his *The Moondog Show* and later *The Rock 'n' Roll Party* in Cleveland, Ohio,[31] or Dewey Phillips's *Red, Hot and Blue* in Memphis, Tennessee,[32] it was also promoted by a network that consisted of jukebox, 7-inch single and independent labels.

The Seeburg Corporation in particular was quick to convert its boxes to RCA Victor's new record format. Seeburg, along with manufacturers such as Wurlitzer, Rock-Ola, Automatic Musical Instruments (AMI), Capehart and Evans, was a long-time leading jukebox manufacturer in the United States as well as worldwide. In the late 1940s, Seeburg introduced a new jukebox model, the M100A, that was years ahead of the other manufacturers' jukeboxes: 'In 1948, Seeburg unveiled a new jukebox which was at least three years ahead of anything that was being produced in the industry. It was called the M100A.'[33] In the 1940s, Wurlitzer had been the largest manufacturer of jukeboxes. Its legendary model 1015 sold extremely well, probably around 56,000 machines. This was likely also due to the fact that Wurlitzer launched a marketing campaign which not only targeted the jukebox operators but – and this was new – promoted the 1015 to a wider audience as being a crucial part of the American way of everyday life.[34] In the 1950s, however, Seeburg became the market leader and the M100A was an important factor in this. Designed by industrial designer Nils Miller, the angular shape of the M100A marked a clear visual break with Wurlitzer's 1940s arched forms. The angular appearance of the M100A, accentuated by narrow chrome trims and harsh fluorescent lighting, made older 'jukeboxes look like antiques'.[35] If the Wurlitzer 1015 represented the Golden Age of jukeboxes, then Seeburg's M100 series represented the Silver Age. In the Silver Age, the boxes almost exclusively ran the small singles with the big hole in the middle.

Most jukebox manufacturers had initially reacted to RCA Victor's 7-inch single with a wait-and-see attitude.[36] Unlike Seeburg, which saw the potential of this small and robust record for the jukebox immediately: 'As soon as RCA had presented their 7in [sic] disc, McKelvy [Seeburg's senior sales manager] knew at once that it was ideally suited for the jukebox operations. It was light, unbreakable and small.'[37] Seeburg immediately, in 1949, informed jukebox operators that the company considered the single a format suited to jukeboxes: 'The 45 r.p.m. record could, conceivably, in the years ahead become a factor in the coin-operated phonograph business because it has all the basic fundamentals which are required in our business.'[38] It was obvious that Columbia's LP was not very attractive for the jukebox manufacturers. Seeburg, for example, stated categorically that although the LP was appreciated, it was not suitable for the jukebox: 'With due respect to the many outstanding attributes of the long playing record, we do not feel that it will ever be a factor in the coin-operated phonograph business because the principle of the long playing record opposes the basic principles upon which the coin-operated phonograph business has been founded; namely, a single selection of music for five cents and each specific selection subject to selectivity by the public.'[39] Seeburg was the first jukebox company to see that the basic principles of successful jukebox business were explored by RCA Victor's new single record. Seeburg was already reliant on the small single when the future of this record format was still uncertain and the 'Battle of the Speeds' was still in full swing.

Although Seeburg had initially designed its M100A for old shellac records, the company assured the operators of its jukeboxes that a record changer mechanism for 45s had already been developed and that the changeover would be extremely inexpensive and easy to accomplish. The successor model of the M100A, the M100B,[40] which came on the market in 1950, was already designed to use only RCA Victor's 45s. The conversion of jukeboxes to 7-inch singles was as good as complete industry-wide by 1951: 'Before 1950 ended, conversion to the 45 rpm speed was proceeding so rapidly that operators anticipated that 45s would be used almost exclusively in boxes by the end of 1951.'[41] The advantages of the 45s for the jukebox business compared to the 78-shellac record would be: 'compactness and simplicity, nonbreakable, more durable, and easier to store, handle, and ship.'[42] In their history of the record, Oliver Read and Walter L. Welch even put forward the thesis that the jukebox was involved in the establishment of the 45 rpm record in general: 'Actually, the jukebox industry had a great deal to do with the survival of the 45 rpm record, for its engineers readily saw the advantages of multiple selection from the new, smaller-diameter discs offering equal playing time. The large hole in the center also offered opportunities for better changer design for automatic coin-operation. Moreover, had the ten- and twelve-inch LP records vanquished the 45 rpm discs, it might have been the death knell of the jukebox, for selectivity and frequent change of selections were proven to be requisites of successful coin-operation.'[43] As we saw in Chapter 2, RCA Victor had actually developed the small single as part of an automatic record changer. In the jukebox, too, the single's large centre hole facilitated efficient changing. For rock 'n' roll culture as it evolved in the 1950s, single records produced by independent record labels and jukeboxes became crucial listening devices.[44]

Repertoire and jukeboxability, sounding hardware and legal norming

As prominent listening devices of rock 'n' roll culture, small single records and jukeboxes coined the sound of rock 'n' roll decisively. Jukeboxes offered the listener a specific repertoire, resonated with short and concise hot mastered songs, stood out due to a peculiar sound, and helped to organize a form of listening where the sound of records no longer referred primarily to the sound of live performances. As a listening device, the jukebox was involved in the organization of a very different form of listening than, say, hi-fi systems. This is already indicated by different social reference frames: the term 'jukebox', which references an African American slang expression for dancing – 'jook' – had already appeared in the 1930s.[45] In the same period, terms such as 'automatic phonograph', 'commercial phonograph' or 'musicbox' were in circulation. These rather technical terms were due to the fact that the manufacturers of these listening devices – following racist and classist schemas – would not devalue their products through their designations: the manufacturers wanted to position their products on the solvent middle-class market. 'Jukebox' evoked associations with 'juke joints' or 'Southern road houses, poor whites, poorer blacks, race mixing, hillbilly music, and blues':[46] target groups that the jukebox manufacturers were probably happy to serve, but not primarily and not exclusively. When the term 'jukebox' finally became accepted, it did not cease to designate what was rejected by hegemonic music culture. This also affected the sound of the jukebox. Consequently, there are hardly any articles about the jukebox in the audio magazines of the 1950s – like *High Fidelity* or the *Journal of the Audio Engineering Society*. In one of the few exceptions in the magazine *Audio*, which is devoted to the oxymoron of a 'Hi-Fi Jukebox', it is made clear right at the beginning: 'Long used by audio engineers to describe bass, insufficient treble, and high distortion, the term has been understood by everyone.'[47] Music lovers with their 'golden ears' could reject the jukebox and its listeners with their 'tin ears' as well as their musical preferences – be they Tin Pan Alley or rock 'n' roll songs.

To date, there has not been a comprehensive study of the jukebox's sound aesthetics or its sound and music history. Most of the texts on the jukebox are chronologically ordered, stressing its visual design and compiling information on technical details and on the jukebox's manufacturers, for the most part echoing the perspective of the jukebox companies.[48] Some books and articles study the social history of the jukebox with a strong link to economics[49] or youth culture.[50] Only the musicologist Hanns-Werner Heister, who was one of the first and up to now one of the few musicologists ever to take on the jukebox, included an analysis of aspects of the box's aesthetics.[51] Which musical repertoire was primarily available in the jukebox? Which records were included in the jukebox selection by the jukebox operators, and which means and instruments were used to compile this selection? How did the specific sound of the jukebox differ from the sound of a hi-fi system or a transistor radio? Was the sound of music adapted to this sound of the jukebox in a certain way? Or, to put it another way: what made a single jukeboxable in the 1950s?

The programme or repertoire of the jukebox was compiled by the jukebox operator[52] and adapted – even if its programming also relied on specific record charts (more on these charts later in the text) – more individually to the preferences of the listeners than was possible in the mass medium of radio. Moreover, with the jukebox music could be played and find an audience that was not being played on the radio at the time – for example, certain forms of rhythm and blues or even country and western in the United States, or music in the UK that was ignored by the state-owned and controlled British Broadcasting Corporation (BBC).[53] Particularly in countries such as the UK and West Germany, whose broadcasting was organized under public law for a long time and did not want to relinquish their remit to educate and inform as well as entertain, jukeboxes offered access to a musical repertoire that was not available on the radio. In post-Second World War Britain, 'jukeboxes aided the dissemination of American music in raw form by bypassing the BBC's near-monopoly broadcasting position. BBC radio was broadly resistant to musical forms that did not conform to its ideals of public education.'[54] By the end of the 1950s, a national jukebox infrastructure had been established in England that made musical forms audible that were not played on the radio, such as rock 'n' roll: 'Jukeboxes bypassed cultural mediation to deliver American popular music, particularly rock 'n' roll, in an undiluted form.'[55] The jukebox was thus able to offer a repertoire that was peculiar to itself.

In West Germany, too, rock 'n' roll records were spinning in jukeboxes in the late 1950s that could not be heard on public radio.[56] Cultural critics of the jukebox, such as Heister, pass over such a potentially 'resistant' repertoire and claim that the records in the jukebox were 'narrowed down to a few genres of popular music',[57] regulated by 'the dialectic of standardization and pseudo-individualization, which Adorno for the first time worked out more precisely'.[58] Thus, here the jukebox is denied any emancipatory potential whatsoever. Yet, there is an empirical basis for claims such as Heister's: the charts for jukebox operators as published by the West German trade journal *Automaten-Markt* since 1954. These charts were especially dominated by German 'Schlager' music – a style of European pop music with a catchy instrumental and simple, carefree and sentimental lyrics.

In the 1950s, the charts published by *Automaten-Markt* were mainly dominated by hits from the likes of artists such as Freddy Quinn, Caterina Valente, Peter Alexander, Vico Torriani and Ralf Bendix. In February 1956, Bill Haley's 'Rock Around the Clock' briefly topped the charts.[59] On the basis of these charts, we can only speculate about the presence of US rock 'n' roll in jukeboxes in Germany in the 1950s: in the *Automaten-Markt*, which first and foremost addressed jukebox operators and not jukebox listeners, rock 'n' roll rarely appeared explicitly; if at all, there was talk of 'hot music'. However, it is very likely – the publication of the US jukebox charts in *Automaten-Markt* is also an indication of this – that releases from US independent labels, which were mostly licensed for Europe via the label London Records, also ended up in the jukeboxes. The *Automaten-Markt* wrote in June 1957 that the programming of the jukebox always had to be geared to the audience at the specific location where it was installed: 'There is *no universally valid* programme for the jukebox. At each installation site, the audience is different and wants different things. The collaboration of the operator with the host is a main prerequisite for putting together a successful programme, and it is gratifying that such collaboration actually operates practically everywhere.'[60] Jukebox charts, then, are at best a guide to the repertoire offered in the jukebox.

Despite their possibility to offer diverse repertoires, individual jukeboxes did repeatedly exclude certain forms of music – such as country blues: 'Even in the heart of the Mississippi Delta, the so-called country bluesman had limited appeal. A Fisk University sociologist who surveyed the black bars of Clarksdale late in the Depression

[1941 and 1942] found not a single Delta bluesman upon the jukeboxes. Instead, top sellers were the same as they were in black areas across the United States: Louis Jordan, Lil Green, Count Basie, Fats Waller, all patently urban and unabashedly sexual, their songs laden with double (and sometimes single) entendres, backed by a jazz-inflected sound that pulsed with the rhythms of city life.'[61] Rhythm and blues, on the other hand, became an increasingly important genre for the jukebox in the 1950s. In a 1955 *Billboard* survey, more than half of jukebox operators said they were putting more rhythm and blues records on their jukeboxes' programmes than they had the year before – so rhythm and blues had by far the largest growth rate over other genres that year.[62]

Special charts for the jukebox were not only found in industry journals such as *Variety*, *Billboard* and *Cash Box* in the United States or the *Automaten-Markt* in West Germany.[63] In addition, so-called one-stops provided jukebox operators in the United States with hints for shaping jukebox repertoires. In the 1950s, one-stops in the United States were regionally active record wholesalers who offered the records of various independent labels not only to local retailers, but also to jukebox operators.[64] In a 1955 *Billboard* survey, jukebox operators stated that they put together the programmes of their boxes primarily on the basis of information from relevant magazines; specific enquiries at the location of the jukebox as well as one-stops were also important sources of information.[65]

When we are dealing with the sound of the jukebox in general and its repertoire in particular, then one-stops quickly come into view. Beginning in the late 1940s, one-stops became increasingly important for jukebox operators as places to purchase records.[66] Prior to this, jukebox operators had increasingly purchased independent records directly from labels, from retailers and also from jukebox distributors, who were themselves part of a nationally operating distribution system that was partially used for record distribution. This network of jukebox distribution formed a structure from which a nationally networked distribution system for records from independent labels developed: 'The national distribution system [for records from independent labels] was an outgrowth of the jukebox distributors who frequently had a jukebox operating division.'[67] Against this backdrop, it is no wonder that it was a former player in the jukebox business, Jack Gutshall, who founded the first national independent distributor in the United States in Los Angeles in 1945.[68] In contrast to such national distribution structures, one-stops were regionally oriented. One-stops also had close ties to jukebox operators: 'one-stops were subdistributors that were set up initially for the purpose of serving jukebox operators from a single location.'[69] By 1957, 60 per cent of jukebox operators were buying from one-stops.[70] Initially, one-stops were primarily a response to the boom of independent labels in the 1950s in the United States: 'Distribution of rhythm and blues records by the new independents was difficult. It was accomplished piece by piece, using extensions of retail networks or the jukebox distribution routes to which many independents already belonged. The record distribution system itself responded to the rapid growth of small labels by elaborating a new kind of service. By 1952 the "one-stops", as the new firms were called, gave the small labels service to the jukeboxes *and* retailers.'[71]

However, national independent distribution only became truly attractive with the introduction of the vinyl record, which was held to be unbreakable.[72] The introduction of 'unbreakable' vinyl records in the late 1940s affected distribution: 'Technology changes, in the form of LPs and 45s, made the product deliverable to the consumer in new ways.'[73] This combination of vinyl singles, jukeboxes, one-stops, and independent labels formed a network that would have a lasting impact on popular music culture in the United States in the 1950s.

Record wholesalers existed even before the one-stops. However, they usually distributed only one label. Whereas one-stops offered records from several labels.[74] The importance of one-stops for the emergence of independent labels in the 1950s can hardly be overestimated.[75] The major record companies of the 1950s only distributed their own productions: 'But a jukebox operator needing multiple labels sold any label he could get, so the jukebox distributors were the original distributors for the independent record companies from the mid-1940s through the 1950s. They continued to expand and distribute more independent labels as the industry grew [leading to the one-stop].'[76]

The one-stops also had a great influence on the repertoire from which the jukebox operators could compose their selection. In Memphis, Tennessee, for example, Joe Cuoghi and John Novarese opened the one-stop Pop Tunes in 1946.[77] Pop Tunes – short for 'Poplar Tunes' derived from Poplar Avenue in Memphis where the store was located – not only provided important orientation for record entrepreneurs in the city such as Sam Phillips or rhythm and blues radio DJs like Dewey Phillips, they also informed jukebox operators about regional Top 40 charts. Historian Lewis Cantor, who specializes in the Memphis music scene of the late 1940s and 1950s, describes how Pop Tunes and jukebox sales in turn helped determine the repertoire policies of labels like Sun Records:[78] 'The one-stop was Sam's [Sam Phillips] favorite because there he could see what was being put into the jukeboxes and get a feel for what smaller stores were buying and selling. Jukeboxes were a reliable source of such information because they tallied the number of times each record was played. They were the musical barometer of the nation's taste during the early 1950s.'[79]

At Pop Tunes, records from various independent labels such as Atlantic, Modern or Chess could be purchased in one place. The advantage for jukebox operators that one-stops brought was obvious: 'Servicing the records for jukeboxes soon became a cottage industry in Memphis. Before Pop Tunes provided a "one-stop" service, dealers had to go to the various record distributors across town to acquire the latest material. Most one-stops today are wholesale, not retail', Pop Tunes co-founder John Novarese remembers: "Back then, a man who operated jukeboxes – say he had twenty or thirty of them around town – he would have to make five or six stops to get the latest records from the distributors." With a one-stop, a dealer like Southern Amusement Company, the major jukebox operator in the Memphis area, could stop by Joe and John's new place and pick up everything needed at one time.'[80] In addition to the charts and information from relevant trade magazines and regional one-stops, the tallies of the play metres[81] installed in the machines as well as the personal taste of the jukebox operator or perhaps even of the bar owner,[82] and, since the massive expansion of the selection in the 1950s to first 100, then later to 200 titles, specialized 'programming services'[83] were responsible for the repertoire.[84]

In addition to a specific repertoire selection, the sound of the jukebox is shaped by the jukebox suitability of singles. A jukebox-suitable single must be short and concise. Heister expressed this in the following jargon-like formulaic deliberation: 'The duration of the single piece of music is inversely proportional to the turnover rate of the capital. The shorter the piece, the more frequent the repetition of the act of numbers and the more rapid the turnover of capital.'[85] For an even greater acceleration of capital turnover, jukebox manufacturers are also said to 'often set the speed at slightly more than 45 rpm, allowing for more nickels per hour to go into the machines.'[86] Or, to put it as simply as possible: increasing the playback speed to just under 50 rpm can then potentially increase sales by up to 10 per cent. The playing time of these hit singles was shortened again with the implementation of the small single record in the jukebox. The short and, at best, concise single records, with a usual playing time of between two and three minutes, were ultimately ideal for the jukebox business of the 1950s, since jukebox operators did not earn money on the absolute playing time of their boxes, but rather on the number of records played.

Singles that were suitable for the jukebox were therefore those that contained concise and short pieces of music – that is, no music that is a great work, at least if great also means long, and no music that follows one of those 'large scale forms'.[87] Such short and concise singles also had to be suitable for use in a series – the playlist.[88] The music producer and studio owner Cosimo Matassa summed up the consequences of such jukebox suitability for his music production as follows: 'We made short records because jukebox operators wanted short records.'[89] Especially in the founding years of his J&M studio in New Orleans, 'the jukebox sales were a huge part of the market then'.[90] For Matassa's work, the listening device jukebox became a constitutive part of the music he produced.

In the case of the jukebox, we find feedback between economics and musical form: 'The mere duration itself, however, has in turn consequences for the nature of the music.'[91] Heister criticizes that against this background no elaborated musical syntax can develop. As true as this observation may be on the whole, the evaluation linked to it remains questionable. Implicitly, it absolutizes a classical-romantic concept of music, which measures the aesthetic value of music by structure and motivic-thematic development. Certainly, the brevity of jukebox singles is also strongly economically motivated. However, to deduce from this that musical narrowness is inevitable, is a short-circuited or a lumbering confrontation of art and commerce, which is also typical for a classical-romantic concept of art. In contrast, the brevity of the single and the often similar structure of the songs can put the focus on a sophisticated sound design, maybe anticipating an aesthetic of 'cult sounds';[92] that is, of concise and thoroughly designed individual sounds with a high recognition value. Such sounds are the results of music production and music post-production.

Thus, the brevity of the music pieces was not just a musical limitation. It also allowed for specific mastering of the single that has the potential to make an important sonic difference. Since the record – unlike the CD, for example – does not have a standardized volume, the volume at which it is cut is extremely variable. The louder the cut, the more the record develops a sonic life of its own. This life of its own not only is exploited, but also leads to new problems: 'It is fortunate that the length of the jukebox singles is only 2 to 3 minutes so that the recording engineer has plenty of space to spread out the recording. Even with this advantage, the demands for level have been known to outstrip the capability of the cutting stylus which, of course, leaves the playback stylus, with its spherical geometric limitations, in an impossible situation.'[93] Against this backdrop, it was obvious that the jukebox would soon find its way into a studio's mastering rooms to test whether a 'hot' mastered single was still playable in the box.[94] The jukebox changed the sound of popular music: 'As it [the jukebox] transformed the market for recorded music, the jukebox also altered its repertoire. Loud music was required for noisy meeting places. One of the early mainstays of the jukebox was country music, which in the "honkytonks" became louder, more percussive and was electrified. Race records were also favoured. ... The close relationship between black music and the jukebox is indicated by the fact that it is here that the machine earned its name.'[95]

Yet the sound of the jukebox does not only include certain repertoires, short and concise songs, and 'hot' mastered singles. The sound of the jukebox is also shaped by its technology, its speakers, its amplifier and filters, the clicking and whirring produced by its selection mechanism and the automatic putting on of a record. Matching the sound of record releases with this jukebox sound brings into play another aspect in relation to which jukebox suitability can be established. In his 'Essay on the Jukebox', Peter Handke distinguished the jukebox sound from the radio sound. According to Handke, a belly resonance [*Bauchklang*] is characteristic of the jukebox, which works from the depths or the 'underground', and not like the radio 'that stood at home in the corner with the shrine' [*Hergottswinkel*].[96] However, the belly resonance was not the only characteristic of the jukebox: 'It was not only the belly resonance: the "American hit" had also sounded entirely different to him back then on the jukeboxes of his native land than on the radio in his house.'[97] The jukebox's belly resonance resonated with the sound of US popular records: 'This was not for solitary listening at the record player in the small room; one also had to hear this body-emphasizing music prepared by the appropriate reproduction medium, that "belly resonance" of the amplified basses, whose power was concentrated in the depths of the musical furniture and could be experienced haptically, together with other people.'[98]

At the most basic level, the jukebox sound includes the inherent noise of the technology. Thus, specific grooves in and out of records not only ensured smooth record changes, but they also shaped the sound of the jukebox. This sound was not solely musical, it was also determined by the clicking and whirring of the technology. The pauses between the music also included sounds: 'Suddenly, after the pause between records, which, along with those noises – clicking, a whirring sound of searching back and forth through the belly of the device, snapping, swinging into place, a crackling before the first notes – constituted the essence of the jukebox, as it were, a kind of music came swelling out of the depths that made him experience, for the first time in his life, as later only in moments of love, what is technically referred to as "levitation", and which he himself, more than a quarter of a century later, would call – what? "epiphany"? "ecstasy"? "fusing with the world"?'[99] Sometimes even silence was part of the jukebox sound. The jukebox operators knew how to sell this as well. They then offered their customers a 'blank disk'.[100]

Until the 1950s, time and again the jukebox was associated with a strong bass-driven sound.[101] Even in that decade, most jukeboxes were still two-way systems equipped with a 12- or even a 15-inch speaker and a tweeter or horn; however, external smaller speakers could be added.[102] It was not only the speaker lineup that guaranteed a bass-driven sound – Handke's 'belly resonance' – it was also the activation of the bass boost on the amplifier. This combination made a proverbial 'jukebox bass' possible.[103] This bass boost was supplemented by the optional deactivation of the treble.[104] Thus, until the 1950s, the sound of jukeboxes was 'contrary to the concept of 'balance".[105] Jukeboxes were anything but hi-fi media, even though there were exceptions that were intended to establish themselves exactly in this gap.[106]

Further, the jukebox sound interacted with the environments in which the boxes were in use. The bass emphasis and simultaneous treble reduction or cutoff correlated with the places where the jukeboxes were located: bars, restaurants, ice cream parlours. In these places, music was not heard exclusively: the sound of the jukebox should not render speech incomprehensible,[107] yet at the same time it needed to be capable of asserting itself in such listening environments. Specific listening situations had to be taken into account in music production in order to make a single suitable for the jukebox: 'Jukeboxes reshaped not only which songs became popular, but how Americans listened to them. … Some songs simply sounded better on the jukebox or cut through the din of a crowded barroom better than others. Indeed, blues, jazz, and country musicians alike began to utilize more percussion and bass in order to make sure their songs got the attention of taverns patrons.'[108] However, a sound emphasizing bass and percussion was not only in demand in the jukebox, but also on the radio. Art Rupe commented: 'The sound technique I employed was identical for the two mediums [radio and jukebox]: lots of bass and accented rhythm.'[109] Nevertheless, bass-accented production did come into its own, especially on the jukebox.[110]

Up to this point I have analysed the sound of the jukebox in reference to the programming of a specific repertoire of singles, to the production of jukeboxability, and to the sound of the hardware of the jukebox. However, its sound does not only have an aesthetic dimension; it has a legal one, too: Does the sound of the jukebox correspond from a legal point of view to the sound of a performance or can it be distinguished from one? The answer to this question could potentially determine whether or not jukebox operators would have to pay royalties for performance rights. In the United States, this was not the case until the 1970s; in the UK and in West Germany jukebox operators had to pay most often for performance rights. Thus, the question of whether jukebox sounds were performances was answered in the negative by the US legal system. For jukeboxes in the United States, taxes only had to be paid at the local level – no additional royalties had to be paid to rights holders such as record companies, composers or musicians. It was not until the jukebox business had become almost insignificant that in 1978, the collecting societies of musical rights succeeded in claiming corresponding royalties; then a lump sum had to be paid for each jukebox that was set up.[111] Jacques Attali links this late introduction of royalties to the control of the jukebox business by 'underworld elements'.[112]

In 1937, the major record companies in the United States stipulated that their products had to state that they were for private and non-commercial use only. This initiative was also driven by protests from the US musicians' union AFM, which believed that recorded music played in public would put its members out of work.[113] Jukebox operators were exempt from this, with a few exceptions. Jukeboxes were not covered by copyright law in the United States.[114] Accordingly, no royalties had to be paid to the copyright holder of the music played in a jukebox in public, at least as long as no admission fee was charged for access to the location where the jukebox was located. The coins used to operate the jukeboxes were not considered by law as entrance fees. Thus, playing records in jukeboxes was not legally a performance in the United States.[115] From this perspective, the jukebox was not an electro-mechanical musical instrument that replaced musicians and thus made them redundant.

In the UK, as well as in West Germany, this was different. In England, jukebox operators paid royalties both to the collecting society that represented the record producers and to the society responsible for the performing musicians.[116] In Germany, jukebox operators paid both GEMA (Society for Musical Performing and Mechanical Reproduction Rights) fees and – in some federal states – entertainment taxes.[117] Legally, jukeboxes in West Germany provided 'musical performances'.[118] Thus, the connection between jukeboxes and live music was often short-circuited in West Germany – following a rationalization paradigm. The cultural criticism of the 1950s and 1960s and the statements of technocrats from industry and politics who believed in progress were two sides of the same coin. The music journalist Siegfried Schmidt-Joos, for instance, was outraged that the jukebox would put musicians out of work: 'In the average restaurant, the owner is happy that he has saved the costs of a band that would cost him 2000 marks per month – if it's a trio.'[119] In contrast, Elmar Michel – retired director of the Federal Ministry for Economic Affairs [Ministerialdirektor a. D. im Bundeswirtschaftsministerium] – praised the progressing rationalization in a technocratic way in the preface to the *Handbuch der deutschen Automatenwirtschaft 1956* [Handbook of the German Vending Industry]: 'I am convinced that these vending machines [jukeboxes, slot machines, etc.] have a great future in the course of the general rationalization and automation of processes in everyday life.'[120] I will show in a moment that this rationalization paradigm was negotiated in the United States primarily under the heading of increasing 'democratization'. For the time being, however, we can note that from a legal point of view, playing the jukebox was not defined as a performance in the United States – in contrast to West Germany and the UK. Behind this is a concept of technology that does not view technology exclusively as an instrument of rationalization.[121]

Thus, the different legal status of the sound of the jukebox – in the United States the sound of the jukebox was classified legally as the sound of a record, and in West Germany and the UK as the sound of a live performance – brings into play the dynamics between rationalization and democratization through technology. In historic as well as contemporary academic and journalistic texts that focus primarily on the jukebox in the United States, this technology is described as an instrument of rationalization. However, this rationalization is very often associated with tropes such as 'democratization' and sometimes even with ideas of the 'revolutionary'. Thus, coin-operated machines are 'basically a labor-saving device' but also 'a miniature box-office that harvests the millions of little coins of ordinary folk'[122] or even 'the people's orchestra'.[123] A grassroots organization of the jukebox business is praised in this context. The jukebox offered the possibility to react to demand much more individually than, for example, the mass medium of radio: 'Because jukeboxes could satisfy and measure popular taste, coin men boasted that these machines had fundamentally reshaped American popular music by shifting influence away from recording companies toward customers. For example, they insisted that automatic phonographs had identified and satisfied a demand for country music and blues that had been greatly underestimated by recording companies and radio stations.'[124] In this respect, the jukebox neither just mediated musical performance nor – thereby – substituted for the work of musicians. However, the jukebox is praised above all as a device for democratization. And democratization is understood here as a process that is characterized primarily by the fact that people have the choice. By referencing choice-having, voters and consumers can be short-circuited.

By contrast, especially in the German-speaking world, cultural criticism in the 1960s and 1970s classified the jukebox primarily as a technology that rationalized performances and made musicians redundant. In doing so, it starts from the rather non-complex concept of technology of critical theory,[125] and also remains in unreflected harmony with the legal status of the jukebox in Germany. One of the most concise examples of such a culture-critical view of the jukebox is Heister's already mentioned study published in 1974 – unmistakably inspired by Karl Marx and Theodor W. Adorno. For Heister, the jukebox is a 'technical objectification' of a 'music band' or even a substitute for 'living labour power'.[126] The listener is inevitably a manipulated one: thus the 'character of use' of the jukebox is defined as 'music request show put on by capitalism for the small man'.[127] Curiously, in Heister's analysis the materiality and the technology of the jukebox remain rather neutral. The jukebox is analysed solely as an instrument that is used – not as a listening device that models and manages listening, that mediates actively between the listener and the music heard. Against this backdrop, according to Heister – almost jargon-like and in all seriousness – a 'primarily musically oriented collective would take over the selection of the records'.[128] Here, then, practice obviously does not guide theory, but theory is to be 'implemented' in a top-down process, as it were. Dissident ways of using the jukebox, as they have been investigated, for example, by cultural studies in concrete reference to the UK,[129] are thus shifted into the realm of the purely hypothetical and theoretical. The extent to which the jukebox has served as a means of 'dissenting urban appropriation',[130] for example, in the environment of the rowdies or yobs in the 1950s, is ignored. In contrast to Adrian Horn's study, which is actually less about the jukebox and more about ways of using it, Heister's study does refer explicitly to the technology of the jukebox; however, it only understands this technology in an instrumental way.

Insight into the object status of the jukebox – and thus into the jukebox's relationship to performances and musical instruments – is not only gained from an examination of the legal and discursive definition of the jukebox but also from its sound. This differs fundamentally, especially in the 1950s, from the sound of instruments and performances. The sound of the jukebox is not (only) determined by the musical instruments used on the record played in the jukebox; in that case the jukebox would be a passive intermediary and simulate a performance. Rather, the sound of the jukebox appears as an abstract and disembodied sound which is designated – at least by the naming of the music's title and artist on the title strip. This sound, tailored to the needs of an audience, is not so much intended to simulate a performance as to evoke an effect in the listener.[131]

Tuning playlists

The jukebox as a listening device co-constituted, as I have tried to show, the music and its sound that is listened to through it. However, this includes not only single productions whose form and sound is tuned in reference to the jukebox. What is more, it includes the more extensive form of the music that is listened to with the jukebox. We can describe this form as a playlist. The production of jukebox capability of a single record is also established by making that record suitable for inclusion in a playlist. Actualizing the record selection set in the playing of a jukebox is accomplished by the selection mechanism and results in a playlist. In what way is the selection on the jukebox different from other collections of records such as those we find in archives of the entertainment industry or even in private record collections? What distinguishes a serialization of songs in a playlist from musical performances, musical programmes or even musical works?

In Chapter 2, I argued that the single is not single – even if its name suggests otherwise. The single does not stand for itself, is neither autonomous nor alone. Either it is part of a series or it is repeated. A device for serialization, but also for repetition of the single, is the jukebox. In the box, short pieces of music are sometimes endlessly repeated, but they are also capable of forming a series together with other short titles. Such a series is to be distinguished from a 'completed programme'[132] and from a coherent (art) work.[133] A playlist is an open structure while an artwork has an end. Repetitions create hits. Serializations playlists.[134] 'From their jukebox beginnings 45 rpm singles were made so that they would rub up against one another, both physically and aurally. They were always in competition, shouting against each other to be heard.'[135] In the course of the 1950s, playlists became programmable in the jukebox by the listener. The manufacturers integrated units in the boxes that could memorize and store choices. At first, these units worked with mechanical levers; later they used magnetic memory units without moving parts. Seeburg included these magnetic Tormat Memory Units for the first time in its Seeburg V200 from 1955.[136]

In the jukebox, 'hot' mastered records promised a competitive advantage: 'It is easy to imagine that these overcut records had no resemblance whatsoever to the original performance. It is my belief that a whole generation of Americans grew up believing that the raucous results of overcutting was the way music was supposed to sound.'[137] The 'loudness war' is thus by no means tied to digitization,[138] but is already found in the context of the small single record. By strong compression and loud record cut a single was to be made suitable for using in a series. This suitability was characterized above all by the assumption that loud pieces of music had a competitive advantage over quiet ones: 'It is easy to understand that because records are not all recorded at the same level further complications are added .... This condition is further burdened by the desire for performers whether they be vocal groups, solo instrumentalists, or any of the assorted combos to have their records sound loud on the jukebox so that they will be heard.'[139]

The fact that records were cut with different levels correlated with a flexibilization of the possibilities for volume control on the jukebox itself. In addition to automatic these also included manual control options: 'A remote volume control is useful for monitoring the music machine. It ... allows the volume to be controlled from a remote location, such as the bar. Since the volume must be adjusted to the changing occupancy of the premises and sometimes to the character of the piece being played, the remote volume control saves many a trip.'[140] Automatic regulation of jukebox volume began as early as the 1940s. In 1946, the smallish manufacturer Aireon attached an automatic volume control to its jukebox: a microphone hung in the 'noise centre' of the room and its output was used to automatically adjust the volume of the box.[141] Thus, this jukebox included a feedback system that adapted the volume of the box to the volume of its environment. It was not until the 1950s that compressors found their way into the jukebox – also as a reaction to the fluctuations in volume with which the various records had been mastered. Such AVCs – automatic volume controls – had been installed more and more in jukeboxes since 1953,[142] and extracted a control signal from the music signal: 'A level reduction of a 10 to 15 dB on a loud record was not uncommon.'[143] For example, the Rock-Ola 1455, launched in 1956, had a built-in equalizer and a compressor: 'The Rock-Ola 1455 has an automatic sound equalization system. This system (control dynamics) ensures a *constant volume level* when playing the various records.'[144] The use of such compressors made certain musical structures unsuitable for the jukebox. When songs had abrupt, extreme volume fluctuations, the AVC could leave quite lasting undesirable impressions on listeners: 'There were outstanding exceptions, however, where an extremely long and deliberate pause in the music allowed the level of the amplifier to build with ear-shattering results on the next loud passage. Fortunately, such records were uncommon and never attained great popularity.'[145]

The jukebox's modelling and managing of record listening

At the jukebox, listening to music is organized as listening to records. This is done in this device in a very peculiar way: for instance, the jukebox plays a certain repertoire, which is heard through it preferentially. In addition, the box is a device that is used for listening. However, a certain activity that characterizes record listening is also delegated to it – the changing of records. On the jukebox, this is no longer done by the listener's hand, but, for instance, by the Select-O-Matic mechanism of Seeburg, the Fireball 120 revolving changer by Rock-Ola or by Wurlitzer's old Simplex mechanism.

This delegation is the key point where the management of music listening by the jukebox begins. It becomes a constitutive component of what is listened to through the jukebox and how listening is organized. In so doing, it emphatically addresses the materialities of listening and opens up and processes distinctions that characterize jukebox listening. Thereby, listening at the jukebox is not a bodily technique, but differentiates itself only in relation to the box. As a cultural technique that relies on technology, devices, things and media, jukebox listening processes the distinction between selection and scarcity, serialization and repetition, seeing and hearing, music making and music listening, public and private. After it became established, jukebox listening could also be decoupled from the machine and coupled with listening in the context of live music: 'The jukebox style of listening to music also influenced the earliest rock 'n' roll concerts: these were package tours featuring a large number of artists who would perform their hits in rotation.'[146] In combination with the single record, the jukebox became a central listening device of rock 'n' roll culture in the United States as well as in Europe.

Hand and eye, ear and belly – materialities of listening

Jukeboxes are listening devices in which the process of changing records is delegated to a machine. After inserting a coin, the jukebox listener chooses from the jukebox selection and thus sets in motion a mechanism that puts on the selected record. This automation of putting records on by hand, becomes the basis for the management of listening. Bodily practices and techniques are delegated to, modelled and automated by the jukebox. Time and again, commentators on the jukebox have described this mainly in terms of a deficit. For instance, a contemporary in the 1950s speculating on the 'meaning' of the jukebox opined that this technology also derived its magic from the fact that with this 'prosthesis', it was capable of 'rising above stunted musical talent'.[147] The insertion of the coins would make the listener a 'programme creator' and 'produce the feeling of being productive oneself'.[148] Accordingly, the jukebox mechanizes the music-making body, but not the programming, which is left to the listener. This automation, however, is not so much a substitution – in that case the topos of the jukebox as a device that makes musicians redundant would merely be reproduced. Instead, it is a kind of supplement, a prosthesis of a body, a body that is not capable of making music itself. The jukebox strictly separates music making and music listening, and has even brought about this distinction historically in relation to music recording (more on this point later in the text). In this way, the jukebox fosters forms of listening to music – like record listening in general and also radio listening – that no longer need to come into contact with forms of making music, be it making music oneself or listening to and watching others make music. Against this backdrop, discourses on listening emerge in which listening to music is no longer oriented on the musician's listening: even when listening to jukeboxes, the musicians are generally absent. The jukebox listening of rock 'n' roll culture is not oriented towards the listening of the musician.[149] The jukebox enables group music listening that is not regulated by music experts such as professional musicians, not to mention music pedagogues. The distancing from musicians and listeners is already tangible in the 'coin actuated attachment for phonographs', which Louis T. Glass and William S. Arnold patented in the United States on 27 May 1890.[150]

In the historiography on the music industry, but also on music and technical media, a jukebox *avant la lettre* often gets a prominent mention, an appearance that is as clearly dated as it is localized.[151] The place is the Palais Royal Saloon in San Francisco, the date November of the year 1889, exactly 100 years before Peter Handke will try his hand at the jukebox.[152] This appearance of the jukebox *avant la lettre* gains its prominence mostly from the fact that it was through this event that the phonograph, invented a good ten years earlier, became a music machine. Louis Glass, the managing director of the offshoot of the North American Phonograph Company on the US West Coast – the Pacific Phonograph Company[153] – set up a battery-powered Edison phonograph in 1889 in the Palais Royal Saloon to which four stethoscope-like tubes were connected.[154] The individual tubes were disconnected by a weight until the blockage was removed by inserting a coin. A coin inserted unlocked a single blockage and allowed music stored on the cylinder to be heard through one of the four tubes. Glass filed a patent application for the mechanism on 27 May 1890.[155] He then presented 'the-nickel-in-the-slot machine' at the 'Convention of Local Phonograph Companies' on 28 and 29 May 1890, and drew attention to the lavish revenue generated by this machine.[156] This led Glass's colleagues, who ran other offshoots of the North American Phonograph Company, to dabble in the automatic phonograph market as well: 'In the early years, coin operation was so important to the infant record industry that in 1891, 16 of the 19 holders of franchises with North American Phonograph Co. were in the jukebox market with 1249 units in the field.'[157] However, these early automatic coin-operated phonographs did not offer a choice of what was heard.[158]

Closely linked to this success of the coin-operated phonograph was the increasing definition of the phonograph as a music machine. In 1889, this was at best in the air and, as is well known, Edison himself ranked it only fifth among the possible uses of his invention.[159] Edison and, following him, the entrepreneur Jesse H. Lippincott, whose North American Phonograph Company marketed both Edison's phonograph and Bell and Tainter's graphophone in the United States, had seen the future of the phonograph as a dictaphone. It was not until Glass's invention and its marketing through the Automatic Phonograph Exhibition Company that the phonograph became accepted as an entertainment technology, as a music technology. However, the success of the coin-operated phonograph changed the status of the phonograph not only in that it changed from a dictating machine to a music machine.[160] It also enlarged the distinction between music recording and music playback: 'The automatic phonograph reserved the recording function to the company and could only play back commercially manufactured records.'[161] The coin-operated phonograph thus processed the distinction between music making and music listening, or recording and playback, by assigning the recording function to record companies and allowing the playback function to be activated – for a fee – by music listeners.[162] The automatic phonograph is the unit of difference between music storage and music playback. This prefiguration of the jukebox thus limited and regulated a technical possibility of the Edison phonograph, which – in contrast to Berliner's gramophone – allowed both recording and playback. This regulation and differentiation would become a condition of the twentieth-century recording industry. The coin-operated phonograph and Berliner's gramophone stand at the beginning of this development.

However, the coin-operated phonograph was only able to hold its own on the market for a short time: 'By 1908, the public had virtually stopped dropping nickels into automatic phonographs …. During this period, the automatic band in its many wonderful manifestations was queen of the taverns. One such machine was a Seeburg "Solo Orchestrion" located in a roller-skating rink in Des Moines, Iowa.'[163] The early automatic, coin-operated phonographs were then, for the first time, replaced by automatic musical instruments such as orchestrions or player pianos. Only in the phonograph parlours, which came up in the United States from around 1890, was listening to phonographs for cash still successful for a while.[164] It was not until the electrification of the phonograph in the mid-1920s and the end of Prohibition in the United States in 1933 that the coin-operated phonograph returned in greater numbers. After the repeal of Prohibition in 1933, the jukebox market boomed in the United States. Manufacturers such as Seeburg, AMI and Wurlitzer switched from the production of automatic music instruments to the production of jukeboxes.[165] In the historiography on the jukebox, these developments mark the first three phases of coin-operated 'musical instruments'[166]: a first phase of the automatic phonograph (mostly without selection), a second phase of automatic pianos and other instruments (only a few would have allowed selection), a third phase of the electrically amplified jukebox. In addition to these three phases, Read and Welch also identify a fourth phase in which jukeboxes had very large selections, allegedly high-fidelity sound, remote controls and multiple speakers.[167]

As a listening device, the jukebox addresses and modulates the materialities of listening.[168] The jukebox integrates the hand, the eye and the ear, and also the stomach. The sound of the speakers, which are usually placed near the floor of the box, often do not seem primarily to address the ears at all, but first of all the legs and the abdomen. In jukebox listening, ear and eye, hand and belly, body and technology are constellated in a peculiar way. Just as the golden ears decisively gained contours in the interaction with hi-fi culture and its technologies in the 1950s, the jukebox also gives rise to a peculiar, engineered, we might even say galvanized, ear. However, this ear is not refined by any gold. The golden ears of the hi-fi culture of the 1950s explicitly rejected the jukebox because of its lack of sound transparency and its specific sound quality. There is hardly any mention of jukeboxes in the hi-fi magazines of the 1950s, and indeed only a few boxes claimed to be high fidelity.[169]

More appropriate than the refining them with gold seems to me, at least for the time being, the description of the ears involved in jukebox listening as *tin ears*. However, only if we are willing to reject its general pejorative meaning just as we reject – if we are dealing with popular music forms – terms such as Tin Pan Alley, punk, noise or, say, techno as pejoratives. Already in the 1940s tin ears is suggested by a *pars pro toto* also in the discourse on recorded sound to which listeners of non-hi-fi devices were tin ears.[170] In the following, I shall depart from the conventional meaning of tin ears, insofar as a *general* lack of discernment and ability to distinguish is not imputed to these tin ears, but merely a culturally *specific* lack of this ability. This latter, in turn, opens up the possibility of something new emerging in a different cultural space. In this case, the concept of tin ears can certainly develop a productive, even a resistant, potential. Just because the fine distinctions of hi-fi culture remained irrelevant to jukebox listeners does not mean that listening to the boxes cannot develop its very own distinctions.

Conventionally, tin ears mark the excluded and rejected. They are assumed to be incapable of attaining certain standards. In this way, they make norms visible *ex negativo*. The ethnomusicologist Dylan Robinson, for example, has referred to this. By 'tin ears' Robinson understands 'settler colonial forms of perception … that disallow us from understanding indigenous song as both an aesthetic thing and as more-than-song'.[171] This means that settler colonial forms of listening are determined by Robinson as tin ears, ears that are insensitive, even deaf, to idiosyncrasies of the indigenous musical forms that interest him. The colonial tin ears are thus only able to hear guided by a colonial aesthetic, an aesthetic that has received its outlines in relation to the tradition of Western art music. Listening takes its measure from the aesthetic normativity of this tradition. Robinson's polemical critique then proposes that the ear educated by Western art music, which also frequently sees itself as elaborate and differentiated, is itself a tin ear. This is the case when indigenous music forms are dismissed as 'inferior' because they appear aesthetically non-complex in relation to an understanding of music formed on the basis of Western art music.[172] By now attaching tin ears to what was formerly, at least for musicology, hegemonic musical culture, Robinson productively reverses the hegemony of Western and indigenous musical forms by marking the (unmarked) musical forms of settler colonialism via tin ears. However, this reversal perpetuates a tradition that devalues the reference to tin ears. The tin ears are passed on here like a buck. As already mentioned, especially in the history of popular music there is a certain tradition of positively reinterpreting and rearticulating the discarded – such as appreciating the tin of Tin Pan Alley, if you will.[173] Accordingly, I shall not refine the tin ears of jukebox listening as being actually golden ears in what follows. Instead, a differentiated, resistant description will take the place of their devaluation.

Both golden ears and tin ears include technology that has become an organ, or rather part of an organ: both types of ears hear through and with recourse to technology, they function in interaction with technology. In this respect, the two terms should by no means be understood only metaphorically. The golden ears of hi-fi culture correspond to an auditory practice that is dependent on technology. Golden ears claim to hear the finest differences in the technology over which something is heard. Golden ears simultaneously listen to technology – as hi-fi fans – and ignore the technology – as 'music lovers'[174] – in order to able to listen to the 'pure' music.[175] The technologies that became part of golden ears in the 1950s are hi-fi systems and LPs. The discourse that gave rise to the golden ears in the 1950s, embodied, for example, in the hi-fi journals that emerged during this period, not only included a training programme for how recorded sound should be heard. It also brought forth the tin ears as its 'other'. There is no scientific or journalistic discourse that defines tin ears positively. Tin ears, as a pejorative attribution rather than a positive self-description, are instead increasingly constituted by the listening practices that emerged in the 1950s to the technologies rejected by hi-fi culture: transistor radios, portable record players, singles and, of course, jukeboxes. However, to avoid misunderstandings and to relate to the materialities of jukeboxes of the Silver Ages, which were, obviously, not really made of silver (and also not of tin) but favoured chromium plate, we should take a more fitting concept and refer to *chrome ears* instead of tin ears.

The tin, or rather chrome, ears should not be considered merely under the auspices of something deficient; for example, as the forms of technology that have become organs, pleading for a limited bandwidth. Instead, I argue, the auditory practice of chrome ears is based on a different conception of recorded sound. Recorded sound is not heard by chrome ears primarily through a performance and transparency paradigm. Through the jukeboxes with large selections of the 1950s, a form of listening emerged that relates recordings to recordings in playlists or in series and repetitions of selected records. Such an aural practice resonates in the media aesthetic of rock 'n' roll. In the 1950s, chrome ears emerged through the organ-becoming of that audio technology which had been discarded by hi-fi culture. The jukebox as a listening device remains audible. But chrome ears also have to ignore it, close their ears to it, in order to hear the music. Furthermore, this is not 'pure' music but music that is co-constituted by listening devices. The sound of this music, in turn, is shaped by the jukebox itself. The jukebox constitutes an area that is ignored by listening. Nevertheless, this domain has consequences for what is heard. Especially in productions of rock 'n' roll culture, singles and jukeboxes did not become inaudible. Rather, they remained audible – for instance, by disregarding industry standards in mastering and by making the sound of music jukeboxable.

Besides the sound of the music, the jukebox as a listening device co-constitutes the physicality of the listener; changing records is no longer done manually, this is delegated to the jukebox. Listening is not only done through the ear, but also through the jukebox, which modifies the hearing ability of the ear. Listening with chrome ears here is also characterized by throwing open and processing the distinction between performance and production. In jukebox listening, such as in single-listening, the sound of records is compared to the sound of other records. Records constitute a norm in jukebox listening. This problematizes a conceptualization of recorded sound via the performance or fidelity paradigm. Such a paradigm is disturbed as well by all the noises and clicking sounds coming from the jukebox. As media historian, Lisa Gitelman already remarked in her analysis of the nickel-in-the-slot phonograph as follows: 'The first thing patrons heard was the medium itself, the whir of a motor and the scratch of the reproducer point against wax, then there was a quick announcement, and a recorded performance lasting about two minutes. Like the experience of listening to tinfoil records, the experience of listening to a nickel-in-the-slot phonograph is difficult to recover, largely because the issue of mimesis is so vexed in hindsight. ... Was the phonograph making music, or was it (just?) playing music?'[176] The jukebox listeners' chrome ears are especially sensitive to the music and the sound which is made by the machine.

The ear, technically modified by the jukebox, was increasingly linked to a peculiar way of seeing. Most books on the jukebox are devoted above all to its visual design.[177] The distinction between hearing and seeing is processed by the jukebox. The jukebox reproduces a separation of the senses on one level, but abolishes it on another: records and radio deliver sound in a quasi-disembodied way, thus separating the auditory from the visual.[178] The jukeboxes, lavish artefacts from the very beginning, interconnect sound with their blinking and burbling bodies, which are obviously designed to attract and command attention. 'Customers were supposed to enjoy *watching* the machine and its movements while *listening* to the recorded music.'[179] The virtually disembodied sound of records is embodied by the visually imposing appearance of the jukebox.

Visually, the jukebox effectively attempted to stage the selection mechanism and its functioning.[180] The selection of the record from the machine's record storage, which arranges the records in a revolving carousel-like ring (e.g. Rock-Ola and Wurlitzer), arranging them vertically (Seeburg) or piling them horizontally (Wurlitzer), is usually visible to the listener through a large window in the jukebox, as well as a 'robot record arm' that takes the selected record and puts it on a turntable.[181] Also in this respect, listening to records on the jukebox is not solely an auditory experience, but there is always something that distinctly connects the eye and the ear by relating them to each other via the device. This is also accomplished by its elaborate visual design, for which industrial designers were responsible: Nils Miller at Seeburg, Paul Fuller and his successor Joseph Clements at Wurlitzer[182] and even streamline design icon Raymond Loewy who restyled a jukebox at the end of the 1950s.[183]

The changing and selection mechanism was increasingly showcased visually in the 1950s. The playback technology was not removed from view, but given special prominence by means of panorama windows and mirrors – determining factors of jukebox design after the Second World War. With regard to the design of the jukebox cabinet, the *Handbuch der Automatenwirtschaft* 1956 points out: 'The playing of the records, however, takes place in the upper part, which is covered with a transparent hood made of Plexiglas, so that the interesting process of playing the records is visible.'[184] With the enlargement of the selections in the 1950s, categorization of records in the selection, for example, 'hit tunes' or 'popular hits' and 'old favorites', 'country and western', 'polkas' and 'religious music',[185] are then included on the title strips that assign a key combination for selecting a record. Thus, in 1950s jukebox listening, the technology being used for listening is by no means concealed, simulating a live performance; instead, the jukebox selection and playback processes become increasingly visible.

Although the shiny chrome and neon-glare visibility of the jukebox since the 1950s was able to stage the changing mechanism and the playing process ever more effectively and transparently,[186] from its first appearance until its disappearance in only nostalgic significance, the jukebox also constituted a constant invisibility. The flows of money and energy that fed it remained hidden from the eyes of the listener. Thus, in the case of jukebox listening, listening was placed in a very specific relationship to visibility/invisibility. In her analysis of Louis Glass's 1889 coin-operated phonograph, Gitelman has shown that this predecessor of the jukebox already created a certain relationship between visibility and invisibility, in which certain forms of the public and the private resonated.[187] For example, the battery and the coin mechanism were hidden from the view of customers, whereas the phonograph was always visible: 'The performance of these machines was public, while the (electrical and financial) power behind their performance was private and mystified in a bit of oak cabinetwork.'[188] Jukebox listening modulates the materialities of listening and articulates the ear with the eyes, the hand and even the stomach in special way.

Limited choice: The jukebox's selection, series and repetition

The jukebox is a device for controlling and programming music produced on records in semi-public spaces. Jukebox listening is characterized by the fact that the listener has a choice over what is heard. The choice is not free, however, but conditioned by the selection offered for listening as well as by the listener's ability to pay. The jukebox's selection conditions the possibilities of what can be listened to over it.[189] Playing records on the box is not an almost endlessly repeatable process, as was technically possible since the late 1940s at the latest with the introduction of low-wear vinyl records. Instead, playing is regulated, even rendered scarce, because it is linked to payment. Thus, jukebox listening acquires a distinctive contour in this dynamic of scarcity and choice. In addition, there is a second crucial dynamic for jukebox listening: the dynamic between series and repetition. The jukebox selection defines what can be heard on it; but what is actually heard is organized by the dynamics of series and repetition. If the selection is updated or actualized in the form of series of songs, then playlists are created. In such lists, the single does not stand alone. If the selection is organized in terms of repetitions, then hits can be created. The jukebox is a device that allows for the regulated serialization, but also the repetition, of single records.

Repetitions could be continued almost indefinitely on a technical level since the advent of the durable PVC 'vinyl' record. For a long time, the quality of a 78-shellac record deteriorated after fifty playbacks,[190] whereas the 7-inch single allowed very many times this number of playbacks without loss of quality. This was also undoubtedly due to the fact that the weight of the needle/stylus was getting progressively lighter.[191] In 1948, Wurlitzer had already included a new lighter weight tone arm in its jukeboxes – the Cobra tone arm of the Zenith Corporation which claimed that a record could be played about two thousand times without losing its sonic quality.[192] Thus, the jukebox, however, reclaims the 'technical possibility of the record or tape and cassette' to play a piece as often as desired.[193] It renders this possibility economically scarce. Therefore, the record changers used in jukeboxes differ from home record changers in one important aspect: a jukebox does not automatically play record after record, but only the selected and paid-for tracks. If a record has been played to the end, the playback process can be repeated automatically – provided it is paid for. Thus, the principle of regulated repetition was preserved in the jukeboxes, as it had been in the early coin-operated phonograph.

Gitelman has pointed out that the principle of repetition was already built into the 'nickel-in-the-slot phonograph' in the late nineteenth century: 'They [the nickel-in-the-slot machines] each had to contain a return device, so that when the reproducer (the mechanical part that "reproduced" the sound) reached the end of the record, it could return to the beginning and be reset for the next coin. Repetition was built into the machinery.'[194] Thus, what is heard through this device is a repeated thing. Jukebox listening is a form of listening that hears short and concise, serialized and repeated songs. What is heard via the jukebox is something technically serialized and repeated. Serialization and repetition depend on the listener's choice and the pre-selection by the jukebox operator. Repetition increasingly enters into what is heard and listened to.[195] The series of songs or the playlists heard through the jukebox play together with the principle of repetition.

In the 1930s, the record selection that conditioned customers' choices rarely included more than ten options. Even Wurlitzer's 1946 classic jukebox – the Wurlitzer 1015 – still offered only thirty choices – thirty records. It was not until around 1950 that the selection increased by leaps and bounds. Seeburg's M100A, launched in 1949, featured a change mechanism that archived fifty records vertically on an axis. Gripped by the selection mechanism, each of these records could be played from either side of the record magazine. Seeburg marketed this mechanism as Select-O-Matic; the 200-selection – that is, the selection of 200 titles on 100 records – then followed in the mid-1950s. Not only by its name, the Select-O-Matic combined a practice of listening to music – selecting records, with the 'O' symbolizing the record selected – via an automated process. Seeburg primarily developed this mechanism in order to offer a stream of background music and hoped to enlarge its market segment with the mechanism.[196] Unlike background music, however, the jukebox focuses on selectivity. This selectivity coincides with the selectivity of the single.

The enlargement of the selection also correlated with a change of repertoire in the jukebox's selection. This meant that not only the current as well as the old hits but also the future hits – and perhaps also the future flops – were selectable in the jukebox: 'This mechanism [100 selection mechanism] which selectively played both sides of 50 records, at last provided a showcase for new records on their way to popularity in addition to the top 10 or top 20 which previously enjoyed the full spectrum of the limited programming available for the 20- to 40-selection machines.'[197] The jukebox did not have to remain a mere '"hit tune" phonograph' any longer.[198] Thereby the jukebox could also blur the line between the current and the past: 'By storing what was fed into it, the music box blurred the line between current hit and timeless oldie. In this way, the jukebox contributed to the canonisation, even historicisation, of popular music.'[199] Even if the jukebox selection stays limited, it does not have to have restrictive features. That is the case if records are included in the jukebox selection that were not played on the radio. Thus, jukeboxes were able to contribute to the establishment of rock 'n' roll, especially in Germany and in the UK, but also in the United States – although the situation there was different, mainly because of the commercial radio landscape.

When they are a part of a jukebox selection, records have a very peculiar status. They are not only things. Their status differs fundamentally from records being part of archives or private record collections. In the jukebox, records are neither unregulated repeatable artefacts nor objects that are merely exchanged or collected and not used or listened to. In a certain way, the jukebox selection is a kind of record collection. However, it does not express individual taste. Moreover, in the jukebox selection unused records are consistently excluded from it – due to the device's limited scope. Thus, in a selection, records are never merely objects or a form of 'reified' music. Jacques Attali's abhorrence of records that are bought but not used[200] does not apply to records in the jukebox. The records in the jukeboxes must not only be 'exchanged', that is, bought, they must also be used, otherwise the jukebox operator earns no money! Unused records are sorted out. In this respect, the jukebox selection is fundamentally different from record collections, whose owners often oscillate between 'thing fetishism' and enthusiastic fandom.[201] The records that make up a record collection are often – as Attali laments – not used, but only possessed. In contrast, the records that are parts of the jukebox selection must always also have a non-objective dimension – the moment in which they are played – otherwise they are removed.

The jukebox selection has less similarities with private record collections expressing individual tastes and bears more resemblance to the archives and catalogues of radio stations and record labels. What media studies scholar Tim J. Anderson writes in relation to such archives and catalogues ultimately applies to jukebox selection as well: 'The modern mass media archive allows programming decisions to be made in an efficient and flexible manner.'[202] The records of the jukebox selection are programmable – in the playlist – and controllable – by inserting a coin. Here, music is a stock, or as Anderson puts it with Martin Heidegger's philosophy of technology more precisely, a *Bestand* [standing-reserve]. Music as a standing-reserve is controllable, transferable and storable. The jukebox does transform the status of music as record; it is 'self-acting'[203] or it plays.

The principle of compiling playlists from a short selection and relying heavily on repetition, which characterizes the jukebox, was also adapted by radio in the United States in the 1940s. The US radio producer Todd Storz, together with his assistant Bill Stewart, is said to have made a jukebox out of an entire radio station by observing the handling of a jukebox in a bar in Omaha, Nebraska – guests and staff always selected the same titles – and thus invented Top 40 radio.[204] This 'casual ethnography',[205] which is often repeated in pop historiography, can probably be called a 'legend'.[206] Radio historian Wolfgang Hagen writes: 'That professional radio producers infer people's listening behavior on the radio from what they do in a pub hardly seems plausible.'[207] It would also remain a mystery, we can add, why the selectivity of jukeboxes increased by leaps and bounds in the 1950s, if the observation attributed to Storz and Stewart were generalizable. Hagen asserts, contrary to casual ethnography, that a 1950 study of listening behaviour by sociologists working with an 'industrial office of psychological testing'[208] at the University of Omaha found that most US radio listeners wanted to hear hit singles again on the jukebox – even repeated several times on the same day – that they had already heard at home. On the basis of this study, and thus on the 'basis of statistical data interpretation ... and not by any pub observations', the Top 40 principle was developed.[209] Hagen also sees a connection between the singles boom of the 1950s and the aforementioned Omaha study: 'The Omaha study indirectly references this singles boom of the early 1950s insofar as it registered (once again) a marked increase in the popularity of hit parade broadcasts on the radio.'[210]

Despite the mere mythical connection of the Top 40 and the jukebox, the practices of Top 40 or hit parade listening – this arrived in US radio sporadically as early as 1935 with broadcasts such as 'Your Hit Parade' – and jukebox listening correlate. Hagen asks, 'How is one to understand that listeners primarily and initially want to hear again what they already know very well anyway?'[211] Hagen argues that a specific listening mode was a condition for the emergence of Top 40 radio. He describes this as a paradox[212] or as 'doubly negative': 'Listening to the radio is a non-listening that misses nothing.'[213] Compared to a 'passive, fleeting sidelistening',[214] this 'not-listening that misses nothing' allows for an engaged, loyal and active listener – as Hagen notes with reference to the high listener loyalty in Top 40 radio in the 1950s. It remains to be investigated as to what extent such a listening mode also occurs in the jukebox context.

Management and measurement of listening: Play meter as feedback, data traces and jukebox operators

The jukebox manages music listening and organizes it increasingly as an economic issue. The very first coin-operated phonographs only provided those who paid with something to listen to. At the jukebox, then, only those who can pay determine what they themselves and others hear. At the jukebox, however, listening is not only directly linked to payment, but since the 1930s also to its measurement. Jukebox manufacturers begin to install measuring devices, so-called play meters or 'popularity meters' in the machines. These instruments register how often a record has been selected on the jukebox. The jukebox operators evaluated these listening data and fed them back into what was available to the listener in the selection. In this way, a form of 'testing hearing' that had been increasingly employed since the nineteenth century entered the field of popular music, a form testing hearing that was as reductionist as it was effective.[215]

The management of music listening by the jukebox was initially quite abrasive: 'Those who don't pay hear nothing.'[216] Adorno noted this after visiting a phonograph parlour in 1920s Nice. The management of listening here initially goes hand in hand with its privatization. The listening tubes, which resembled a medical stethoscope, made possible a *private* form of listening in the *public* sphere and, moreover, contributed to a separation of the senses. On Glass's coin-operated phonographs and in the phonograph parlours of the early twentieth century, only those who paid listened. At the jukeboxes, as they boomed in the United States after the end of Prohibition, it was no longer only those who paid who listened. But those who paid could then determine what everyone else had to listen to. In contrast to the privatization of music listening that gained momentum with the Edison Home Model A – a phonograph introduced in the late nineteenth century especially for home use – and then increasingly again in the 1950s,[217] for example, in the hi-fi culture aimed at the living rooms of the middle classes, as well as in the increasing spread of portable radios and record players, the jukebox manages listening that takes place in public and semi-public spaces in the group.

As mentioned earlier, managing listening in the case of the jukebox also involves quantifying and measuring listening and incorporating the results of this quantification into a feedback system.[218] Therefore, the play meters in the jukeboxes are crucial. These devices count how often each record from the jukebox selection was played during a certain period of time. Based on the counting of the play meter, jukebox operators could then decide whether a record should remain part of the selection or whether it should be replaced by another one.

If a record is purchased, this says nothing about whether and how often it is listened to. In popular music studies, for example, it has been repeatedly pointed out that charts – manipulations aside – only record sales figures and identify sales potentials; such sales figures cannot be used to draw conclusions about the cultural significance, cultural use or even of the popularity of these records.[219] By contrast, in the jukebox records only become relevant if they are listened to, or at least selected and paid for. Play meters measure at least exactly that – how often each title was selected. Listening is reduced to selection and measured as such. The measurement results of the play meter not only differ from the listings of sales figures of records, but also from the radio charts; that is, the charts that indicate how often a title was played on the radio. If a title is played on the radio, it does not necessarily mean that people want to hear this title. However, when a title is selected on the jukebox, then it is obvious that it is exactly this title that someone wants to hear. In the case of the jukebox – in contrast to radio – it is the listener who leaves behind a data trace.

Wurlitzer began to incorporate play meters into its jukeboxes in the 1930s.[220] The results of the play meter could then form their own kind of charts for the specific location where the machine was in operation: 'When the record selection was restocked at regular intervals, the play frequency of each title registered by a counter served as orientation, so that in this way the music needs were transformed into quantifiable market structures according to a commercially oriented catalog of criteria, to which the record companies in turn adjusted. In this way, an economic control loop was finally created, which in its basic principle still dominates the music business today, except that the orientation variables are now provided by the charts with their listings of the best-selling recordings.'[221] However, it is not so much the music that is transformed into quantifiable market structures here, but more precisely the listening.

Since the 1920s and 1930s, music listening, organized in interaction with technical media such as records, radio and jukeboxes, has been increasingly quantified not only in the context of market research, but also on the borderline between social research, applied psychology and market research. Record companies and radio stations developed a pronounced interest in data on listening. To this end, they collaborated with research institutes in the fields of empirical social research and applied psychology. The Edison Phonograph Company launched The Edison-Carnegie Music Research Program as early as 1919 with Walter Van Dyke Bingham, founder of the Division of Applied Psychology at the Carnegie Institute of Technology in Pittsburgh, Pennsylvania, which sought, among other things, to quantify the mood-altering effects of selected music.[222] As part of radio listening research, specific measuring instruments were developed to register when a radio set was turned on and off and which station was listened to, like the Audimeter developed by two Massachusetts Institute of Technology (MIT) professors and deployed by the US market research analyst Arthur C. Nielsen and his company.[223] Devices were developed through which radio listeners could express whether they liked or disliked certain radio content.[224] Thus, the Stanton-Lazarsfeld Program Analyzer from the late 1930s, also known as 'Little Annie', was a 'rudimentary version of "like" or "thumb" buttons on contemporary music streaming services.'[225] Through devices such as the Program Analyzer or the Audimeter, listeners left data traces that they created either intentionally – in the case of the Program Analyzer – or more or less incidentally – in the case of the Audimeter. The play meters built into jukeboxes registered aspects of music listening behind listeners' backs. This listening data would have consequences for what will be heard in the future.

However, the feedback between the data generated during jukebox listening and registered by the play meter and the selection from which can be chosen during jukebox listening was still mediated by the jukebox operator. The *Automaten-Markt* defines the operator as follows: '*Operators* are members of a trade that has its legal basis in the trade regulations …. For their profession there is no prescribed job description with journeyman and master qualifications. They have to be technicians and merchants in one person. The eight-hour day or five-day week do not apply in this trade. Operators have to take care of all legal, fiscal, official, and operational matters themselves. The operator is truly "acting of itself", which is the literal translation of the Greek-derived "automaton" (emphasis in original).'[226] However, the operator's self-acting is modified because of its reliance on the activity of the play meter.

Moreover, the jukebox operator was part of an extensive network of record companies, record wholesalers and retailers, jukebox manufacturers and jukebox distributors, bar and hotel owners. The operator did not usually buy the equipment directly from the jukebox manufacturer, but from its distributor. Possibly, the jukebox operator gave the owner or the lessee of the installation site a share of the profits[227] or convinced them that such a device would be great advertising for their location. In 1955, the average jukebox operator in the United States operated around sixty jukeboxes.[228] Frequently, the operator had other coin-operated devices, such as slot machines and cigarette vending machines.[229] Weekly turnover was about ten dollars per jukebox. Operators bought around half of their records wholesale from the record distributors of the major record companies and half from the one-stops. In their mediation of feedback from play meters and stocking the selection, the jukebox operators especially included wholesalers such as the aforementioned one-stops, as well as charts from industry magazines. With the play meter, music listening became quantified and left behind data traces that were channelled by the jukebox operator into future listening.

Coda: Listening subjects and practices, discourses and nostalgia

The jukebox, then, mediates between music and listeners.[230] By doing this, the jukebox gives rise to what is heard through it, for example, by making and playing music that is supposedly exactly suited to being used in it. In addition, the jukebox modulates the materialities of listening, manages listening and integrates it into feedback mechanisms, beginning with the data trails that are created during listening itself. In this sense, the jukebox is not a playback technology but a listening device. Subsequently to the organization of listening as a cultural technique and the coordination of sound and music with the jukebox, we can identify certain subjects, practices and discourses that are differentiated in relation to the jukebox. Traces of these subjects, practices and discourses can be found, for example, in first-person accounts, in song titles and lyrics or in films.[231]

For our history of listening based on a history of listening devices, the study of jukebox listening in films cannot help us very much for the analysis of how the jukebox models and manages listening, how it modulates the listening's materialities, how listening is intertwined with non-listening and how it is itself conditioned by a sound and music history. However, a study of jukebox listening in films can help us to get a sense of the jukebox listener, of the listening subject that gains shape in reference to the jukebox. Moreover, films are a promising source for analytically examining practices of jukebox listening and cultural articulations in 1950s West Germany and the United States.[232] A history of listening that focuses on practices, subjects and the cultural 'meaning' of the jukebox repeatedly span our history of listening devices. However, the listening subject articulates both histories. Our history of listening devices analyses the formation of this subject primarily in reference to the materialities of listening and to listening as a cultural technique. In contrast, a history of listening can also study the formation of this subject by primarily relying on an analysis of practices and discourses of listening. It is especially this second approach to a history of listening that profits from films as resources for the history of listening. This is also the reason why I am presenting this last part of the chapter in the form of a coda.

The jukebox makes numerous prominent appearances in various 1950s rock 'n' roll and teenager films, the analysis of which is, in turn, informative for examining jukebox listening and its association with delinquency. In the music film *Loving You* (United States 1957), for example, Elvis Presley sings the song 'Mean Woman Blues' to the diegetically integrated sound of a Seeburg jukebox. In the film *G. I. Blues* (United States, 1960), the choice of a title on the jukebox in one scene leads to a conflict that results in a lively brawl: a G. I. has selected Elvis Presley's record *Blue Suede Shoes* (United States, 1960) on the jukebox with the words 'I wanna hear the Original!' and thus rudely interrupts Elvis Presley himself, who is appearing on stage in the same bar as G. I. Tulsa McLean, who does not want to put up with this. In the film *The Wild One* (United States, 1953), Marlon Brando as rocker boss Johnny selects a title on the box in a bar scene to create an adequate tonal background for making a rather intrusive approach to the waitress. In the film *Die Halbstarken* [Teenage Wolfpack] (FRG, 1956) with Horst Buchholz and Karin Baal, there is a jukebox in the café frequented by the teenager clique, which then provides the sound for one of the rock 'n' roll dance scenes.[233]

Part of the plot of Frank Tashlin's *The Girl Can't Help It* (United States, 1956) with Jane Mansfield is the prominent supporting role of a mafia 'slot machine king', Marty 'Fats' Murdoch, who is in the jukebox business. In a scene in Tashlin's film, the jukebox sound, freed from the bodies of the musicians, is embodied neither merely by the flashing of the box and by effective displays of record changing, nor, as in many other films, such as *Die Halbstarken*, by expressively dancing bodies, but by imagining a singer who is, after all, absent. The image of the jukebox, however, was by no means as clean as the pastel colours of the boxes made it out to be. There was another subject linked to the jukebox in the United States: the Mafia. This subject even occupied the US Congress: the so-called McLennan hearing revealed that the Mafia controlled the jukebox business in at least eight states. The Federal Bureau of Investigation (FBI) stated that in 1957 the Mafia was involved in the jukebox business in New York.[234] The association of jukebox listening with delinquency is also found in British cultural studies. Richard Hoggart cites the 'juke-box boys'[235] as an example of a strand of an Americanized, socially rather apathetic working-class culture that he rejects.[236]

The jukebox acquired even an uncanny dimension in a scene from the series *The Twilight Zone* (United States, 1959–64, Episode 1, Season 1, 'Where Is Everybody?'). In this scene, intense, physically affirming swing dance rhythms issue from a completely static jukebox sited in a deserted café. For the time being, this causes the protagonist to turn the jukebox down. We can also find the jukebox's association with loneliness and the absent, possibly even the uncanny and the dead, in the work of the recently deceased photographer Robert Frank. Frank's book *The Americans*[237] contains numerous photographs of jukeboxes. In the preface to the first edition of this book of photographs, Jack Kerouac wrote: 'After seeing these pictures you end up finally not knowing any more whether a jukebox is sadder than a coffin. That's because he's [Robert Frank], always taking pictures of jukeboxes and coffins.'[238]

More classic than the jukebox's association with the uncanny, or even with death, is surely its association with metropolitan loneliness. Especially a form of loneliness that can be experienced in bars. And it is surprising, as Peter Handke already noted in his *Essay on the Jukebox* that the night figures or revellers sitting at a bar counter in the cold neon light in Edward Hopper's famous bar painting Nighthawks (1942) do not listen to jukebox.[239] Perhaps they do, but in any case no jukebox can be seen. In films, too, the jukebox repeatedly provides the diegetic sound to a lonely, usually male city dweller looking deep into his glass at a bar. Such 'hanging out' to the jukebox sound can be found among the young people in Robert Frank's photos. Here, however, not alone, but in a group. Cultural and social historian Joe Moran describes the jukebox as a sign of juvenile delinquency in 1950s Britain: 'The jukebox became a powerful signifier of juvenile delinquency, not only because it was loud but also because it encouraged people to hang around, apparently doing nothing.'[240]

In films, however, the jukebox can also initiate new contacts and revive old acquaintances. Be it because a young woman has run out of 'nickels' and an old man is willing to help out with restrained wit (*The Asphalt Jungle*, United States, 1950), be it because the chosen title can be understood as an invitation to dance (such as in *Mad Men*, United States, 2007–15, Season 1, Episode 8, 'Long Weekend') or because the choice of a title on the box – or possibly on a jukebox remote control placed on one of the diner tables – specifically seeks contact with a person who is present, as in *Baby It's You* by John Sayles (United States, 1983). The jukebox thus plays together with metropolitan loneliness as well as with new possibilities of contact.

In addition, unusual and sometimes illegitimate uses of the jukebox are also presented in films. In the 1950s sitcom *Happy Days* (United States, 1974–84, Season 10, Episode 10, 'The Hobo Code'), for example, Fonzie, a leather-jacketed man who is as authoritarian as he is virile, not only knows how to rather ridiculously instruct women by snapping his fingers, but also how to get the jukebox in Arnold's Drive-In to work by delivering a precise blow, which then becomes known as 'The Fonz Touch' or 'Fonzie Bang', which bypasses putting a coin in the slot. A completely different form of rather unusual jukebox use can be found in the musical film *My Dream Is Yours* (United States, 1949). Here, Doris Day works in a kind of jukebox factory,[241] which is attached to a bar. This is vaguely reminiscent of the phonograph parlours that opened in the late nineteenth century, which featured several coin-operated phonographs with stethoscopes. Now, in *My Dream Is Yours*, it is not only those who pay who hear, but everyone present, and they hear what the payer has chosen. The jukebox in *My Dream Is Yours*, however, does not include an automatic changing mechanism, but a salaried player of records – Martha Gibson, played by Doris Day. In one film scene, a bar patron wants to hear a particular record. Doris Day then not only plays it, but uses it as an instrumental backing track for her own vocals presented by the jukebox. The jukebox thus gives rise to modes of use and listening practices that were not intended by either the producer or the installer.

In films, the jukebox, or rather the single records used in it, also often serves as a timer and measure of time. In the aforementioned *Asphalt Jungle*, after a policeman informs him that he has been watching him for three minutes in a bar with a jukebox, the protagonist states, 'see, as long as it takes to play a phonograph record', and then takes his leave for the length of a cigarette. What can happen while a record is playing in the jukebox? In his classic study *Profane Culture*,[242] cultural studies scholar Paul Willis examines the listening rituals of an English motorcycle club. These developed in confrontation with a jukebox stocked primarily with rock 'n' roll singles, which was installed in the café frequented by club members. Willis describes a ritual that is as simple as it is bizarre: club members select a song on the jukebox and attempt to cover a predetermined distance by motorcycle before the end of the track. The goal is to arrive back at the jukebox before the end of the song.[243] This can also take place while a single record is playing on the jukebox. Here, as in *Asphalt Jungle*, the jukebox acts as a bizarre timer.

But back to film: in movies and TV series, the jukebox is probably one of the obvious props when parts of the plot play out in a café or diner in 1950s United States – *A*

Bronx Tale (United States. 1993), *Back to the Future* (United States, 1985), *Pleasantville* (United States, 1998) – or to a milk bar or rock 'n' roll joint in West Germany in the same decade (*Ku'Damm 56*, FRG, 2016).

In various European films, contacts with US popular culture are sought through jukebox use up to the present day. For example, by Finnish director Aki Kaurismäki – *The Man Without a Past* (Finland, 2002), *The Match Factory Girl* (Finland, 1990) – and also by Wim Wenders. In his road movie *Alice in den Städten* [Alice in the Cities] (FRG, 1974), Wenders integrates a café jukebox scene in which a child leaning against it sings along to the psychedelic rock song *On the Road Again* by the West Coast hippie band Canned Heat. Jukeboxes also make their appearance in numerous Nouvelle Vague films (such as *Hiroshima Mon Amour*, France, 1959, or *Cléo de 5 a 7*, France, 1961). In Jean-Luc Godard's *Vivre sa vie* (France, 1962), there is a scene in which the protagonist, who has been forced into prostitution, in a billiard bar frequented exclusively by men, selects a pop tune on the jukebox, then begins to dance through the bar, but she is registered at most casually and furtively by the indolently self-sufficient male bar-goers. In the UK, historian Adrian Horn also points out that jukeboxes were primarily integrated into the everyday behaviour of adolescents or teenagers and into the subcultures formed by them, such as Teddy Boys, Teddy Girls or Spivs.[244]

Although the jukebox of the 1950s is increasingly coded in American terms in many European films, we can add that there were also numerous appearances of the jukebox in West German films in which the device was removed from its US context of origin.[245] The jukebox model Wiegandt Musikautomat 1954 (made in FRG), which can be seen in a pub in the film *Auf der Reeperbahn nachts um halb eins* (FRG, 1956) with Hans Albers set in Hamburg's entertainment and red-light district, is largely stripped of youth culture pop references. And even in the three-part German television film *Ku'Damm 56* (FRG, 2016), in which a family-owned dance school is the central setting of the action, the jukebox newly acquired for the dance school – it is a Wiegandt Tonmaster – does not play rock 'n' roll, but the music of the parents' generation. In the film, the purchase of the jukebox by the dance school means the end of the engagement of the dance music band, which consists of rock 'n' roll enthusiasts, who had had to supply the dance school with cultivated dance music, albeit with restraint. In *Ku'Damm 56*, the jukebox thus also becomes a symbol of rationalization: human labour is replaced by an automaton. In the rock 'n' roll dive Mutter Brause, which the TV film presents as a place of enthusiastic rock 'n' roll youth culture, there is also a jukebox: this is not a wooden Wiegandt, but a shiny chrome model with fluorescent light that is as colourful as it is hard, from the leading American manufacturer of jukeboxes in the decade – the Seeburg Company.[246]

Soon, in the 1960s, the jukebox became less important. In the 1970s, the manufacturer Wurlitzer ceased production of jukeboxes and its vice president, Ago Koerv, became a cultural critic: 'Nobody has time anymore, and in the modern feeding grounds nobody is encouraged to stay. Our whole lifestyle is changing.'[247] However, the past listening practices and cultural meanings of the jukebox have left their mark on the present – and certainly not only in films about the youth culture of the 1950s.

Part III

Listening Devices in (and before) Disco and Club Culture, *c.* 1970–90

4

The 12-inch single as listening device: Music history, margins of listening and mastered sound

'A great idea after the fact': Finding the 12-inch single in 1970s New York disco culture

Not all technologies are invented.[1] Some are found. In 1974, a new record format was discovered by accident rather than intended design in New York in connection with the disco culture that was booming – first there, and then soon everywhere in the Western world. In the city where popular music forms, from Tin Pan Alley hits to rhythm and blues, from rock 'n' roll to folk music, took on decisive contours, a music production was going to be transferred from magnetic tape to a record in a recording studio, as had been done many thousands of times before. Such a transfer was a necessary procedure: music had been produced in the studio with tape since the late 1940s, but was released on records. In the analogue era, this media transposition was the final step in music production in which the sound could be altered, and as mastering it mediates between the physics of the record and the sound aesthetics of the music. In music production with analogue technology, the mastering engineer turns tapes into records. The record to be cut in the aforementioned New York recording studio was to have just a single piece of music on one side of the disc. However, the mastering engineer had run out of the small vinyl blanks that usually came with a large hole in the centre. The only blanks still available were of a larger diameter. One of these was then used for the cut. Since there is room for more music on a larger record, the result looked curious: the record was nearly empty; only at the outermost edge had sound left its trace. Since in the analogue medium of the record it is true that the greater the excursion of the grooves or the more space individual grooves have available, the louder the record can be cut. The mastering engineer ramped up the volume and thus ensured that the space the record offered could be utilized by widely spaced grooves. The sonic intensity of the result was a real wow factor, and two years later – in 1976 – it became common practice for popular music to be released not only as 45 singles and LPs, but also as 12-inch singles. The 12-inch single is as large as an LP, but revolves most often at the higher speed of the smaller single, that is, at 45 rpm.[2] On 12-inch singles, longer pieces of music can be released as singles, and they also allow for a louder record cut with wider groove spacing. This mainly benefits the bass frequencies, which take up a lot of space on the vinyl. The louder a record is cut, the more it takes on a life of its own through sonic distortion that can be explored aesthetically. In addition, the relatively high playback speed of the 12-inch single enables a differentiated resolution of the high frequencies.

The case of the 12-inch single is a case of music history of media. The 'discovery' of the 12-inch single is tied to the specificities of disco culture. In disco culture, a connection emerged between specific sounds, technological development, auditory practice and music industry business models that conditioned the finding of the 12-inch single. Thus, here the history of popular music is not a history that can be exclusively understood through historical narratives oriented on categories such as 'work', 'style' or 'musician', nor can it be interpreted as the mere effect of a technological a priori. In contrast, here the history of popular music is shaped by ruptures, coincidences and discontinuities. The 12-inch single was not invented. It was found.

The reciprocal discontinuous structuring of popular music and media technological developments can be traced with reference to the example of the 12-inch single presented at the beginning of this chapter. All the technological components that make up the 12-inch single had been around since the late 1940s, when the US entertainment conglomerates CBS Columbia and RCA Victor put new record formats – LP and 7-inch single – on the market. However, no one saw any point in combining selected features of the LP and the single until the mid-1970s.

In this section of the chapter, I reconstruct the music cultural conditions and circumstances that led to finding the 12-inch single in New York's disco culture in the first half of the 1970s. At first, I show how new music industrial business models emerged in disco culture. These integrate discos as promotional channels, and record companies began to release specific, disco-ready versions of music for these channels. In a second step, I address the technologized auditory practices that became prominent in disco culture: dancers who dance alone as part of a crowd seeking immersive, tactile and corporeal sonic experiences. Such experiences correlate with a technical cultivation of the bass and sub-bass range, which was pursued in New York through specifically constructed loudspeaker systems from the early 1970s, which was then further developed with the 12-inch single. Finally, I elaborate on the 12-inch single as a case of a sound and music history of media.

Under music cultural conditions, a rather unsuspecting actor from the music and media industry, named Tom Moulton, accidentally stumbled upon a preform of the 12-inch single in 1974 in a recording studio, the New York Media Sound Studio, during a record test cut carried out by the mastering engineer José Rodriguez. This completes the proper names of the actors in the story told above. In historiographies on disco culture oriented on the actors, Moulton is transfigured ex post as the 'inventor' of the 12-inch single.[3] Moulton himself takes a more sober view of the situation: in retrospect, he regards the 12-inch single as 'a great idea AFTER the fact'[4] – at least if one believes one of the numerous grassroots disco historiographies circulating on the internet. Thereby, presumably without knowing it, he scotched the continuous chronology of narratives oriented on 'great ideas' and 'intentions'. In the case of the 12-inch single, music history is not conditioned by media history. Rather, the reverse is true: the listening device of the 12-inch single is conditioned by music history.

New forms of release and the production of disco suitability

In November 1974, the US music industry magazine *Billboard* reported in a cover story the transformation of discos into 'record "breakout" points', places where records can become 'hits'.[5] This even applied to records that were not played on the radio: earlier that year, Love Unlimited Orchestra's single *Love's Theme* (20th Century Records, United States, 1973), produced by Barry White, was highly successful in New York discos. Also, obscure imported records were finding their way into the US market in discos: for example, the founder of New York's legendary proto-disco Loft, David Mancuso, played an album released by RCA Victor in Spain – *Barrabas* (RCA Victor, Spain, 1972) by the band of the same name – at his influential parties, and also the single *Soul Makossa* (Fiesta, France, 1972) by Cameroonian saxophonist Manu Dibango, which was first released in France.[6] The Atlantic Records label responded to the success of the latter by licensing the single and releasing it extremely successfully in the United States in 1973.[7] Such success stories are an indication, says music journalist Peter Shapiro in retrospect, that discos had established themselves as promotional channels; Mancuso had proved that discos could sell records.[8] Media scholar Will Straw also points out that, from 1974, discos created an 'initial audience' for releases, which then conditioned radio use of the corresponding releases.[9] In *Billboard*, disco was finally given a permanent place: in October 1974, the magazine initiated the weekly column 'Disco Action'. In the column, proto-remixer, later producer, and finder of the 12-inch single Tom Moulton was tasked with informing the music industry about what music was being played in the booming discos.[10]

The establishment of the disco as a place where hits could be created led to US labels releasing records in 1973–74 that made explicit claims of sonic disco suitability. These releases went under labels such as 'Disco Mix' or 'Disco Version'. If a production is to function primarily in the large and complex loudspeaker systems of discos – and not, for example, in the small loudspeakers of radio sets – then the sound of the production must be specifically tuned or designed. In the claim of sonic disco suitability, the musical form was also varied: the short and compact three-minute pop song, characterized by the sectionality of verse, chorus and bridge, and its clear division of lead voice and accompaniment, was modulated in disco versions on a studio technical basis by so-called breaks and long-flowing instrumental passages that effectively staged the basic rhythm. In breaks, the entire instrumentation was broken down – usually abruptly – to one or a few instruments. From there, instruments could be gradually added again in a longer arc to produce 'a sense of excitement for the listener'[11] by returning to the full sonic texture. With disco, the focus shifted 'from the single, virtuoso produced sound event that leads into a melody or theme, to the sound fabric in its infinite differentiations, to the collective playing process.'[12]

A variation of the short and compact pop song can be found, for example, on the single *Dream World* (Scepter, United States, 1974) by soul singer Don Downing. The

A-side is a short version of the production for radio that conforms to all pop song conventions; the B-side is a longer version for the disco.[13] *Billboard* reported that 10,000 copies of this record were sold without it being plugged on the radio.[14] *Dream World* is an example of a release practice that began in relation to the booming New York disco culture, in which singles no longer contained two different songs, but two versions of a production which targeted different listening devices. Tom Moulton made a disco mix of *Dream World*.[15] Moulton's version is virtually identical to the initial release, but it is extended by an almost two-minute instrumental section in which the arrangement is not tailored to a solo voice but leaves that voice unoccupied. This section, inserted on the basis of the multitrack studio tape, consists of the instrumental backing tracks that provide a sonic stage for dancers and stretches the piece to over four minutes. In various disco histories, Moulton therefore figures – certainly somewhat hypertrophically – as the inventor of the disco break because of such mixing techniques.[16]

The 12-inch single by no means marks a break in terms of releasing music as records. Before Moulton found the 12-inch single and it established itself as a record format for popular music from 1976 onwards, record companies had released productions aimed at the disco context as small 7-inch singles or even as LPs. Atlantic Records, for example, released what it called a 'disco disc' for promotional purposes: a 7-inch single with a playing speed of only 33 1/3 revolutions per minute, which could thus accommodate longer mixes.[17] In the early 1970s, 7-inch singles were also increasingly released that no longer contained two different songs, but just one longer song split into two parts on the A- and B-sides.[18] The release of such singles had become necessary because the LP had been used in popular music since the second half of the 1960s not only for compilations of previously released singles, but also because it had to meet conceptual demands: only since then were songs lifted from albums and released as singles, and releases on an LP could claim a primacy vis-à-vis singles.[19] Mel Cheren, the later co-founder of West End Records, a label that was decisive for the development of disco, began to release instrumental versions of the A-side on the B-side of 7-inch singles in 1973 in view of DJ practices. The single *We're on the Right Track* by Ultra High Frequency (Wand, United States, 1973) appeared with an instrumental version of the song on the B-side. What is quite remarkable about this release is that the instrumental version claims almost no autonomy: A- and B-sides of the single are identical apart from the fact that the vocal tracks are heard on one and not on the other. This release form of Ultra High Frequency's single was not only extremely cost-effective, but it also worked as a tool for DJs.[20]

It was not only US 7-inch releases that targeted the disco context in the first half of the 1970s, but LP releases as well. Gloria Gaynor's first LP *Never Can Say Goodbye* (MGM Records, United States, 1975), released in January 1975, no longer contains various tracks on the A-side that are clearly distinguishable from each other, but a side-long mix.[21] This, in turn, consists of three tracks, but these flow seamlessly into each other. The driving force behind this mix was neither a DJ nor Gloria Gaynor herself, but again Tom Moulton. On the A-side of this LP you can read in large letters: 'A Tom Moulton Mix'. This designation established Moulton as a trademark. The LP *Love to Love You Baby* (Casablanca/Oasis, United States, 1975) by Donna Summer even contains just the title track on the A-side, which lasts for over sixteen minutes.[22]

These new release forms I mention here sought to stake their claim to disco suitability by referencing DJ practices that were established in parts of the gay and queer subculture in and around New York in the first half of the 1970s.[23] A remixing of records by the disco DJ was usually done with the goal of increasing the danceability of a release. In these remixes, the short and compact pop song form lost more and more of its contours. The resulting sound from these practices was then referred to as both a single and an LP, and later the disco versions were released as 12-inch singles. In June 1975, the first 12-inch single that was a promotional pressing for DJs was distributed in New York via so-called record pools – distribution networks or associations of DJs, which were specifically supplied by record companies for promotional purposes.[24]

DJ Walter Gibbons, who performed at the Galaxy 21 disco in Manhattan in 1972, developed a penchant for drum breaks and began – around the same time as proto-hip-hop DJ Kool Herc in the Bronx[25] – to isolate the percussion-accented passages and intros from songs and instrumentals using record players and to create loops on this technical basis. For this, he used two copies of a release.[26] New York DJs, like Francis Grasso and David Mancuso, already had a liking for rhythm-driven records. Grasso and Mancuso, however, mainly restricted their DJ skills to their elaborate choice of records and to minimizing the pause between two tracks.[27] Then DJs like Walter Gibbons or Nicky Siano perfected techniques for isolating and repeating rhythm passages or collaging and mixing different records in the Gallery, a disco that opened in early 1973.[28] Siano systematically intervened both in the structure and in the sound of the records, and thus remixed them.[29] For example, he was able to switch individual frequency ranges on and off that were coupled with his own amplifiers and loudspeakers: "I would turn everything off except the tweeter arrays and have them dancing to tss, tss, tss, tss, tss, tss for a while', says Siano. 'Then I would turn on the bass, and then I'd turn on the main speakers. When I did that the room would just *explode*."[30] Certain studios made unofficial test cuts – also called acetates or dubplates[31] – of the New York DJs' variations. With Sunshine Sound, a studio opened in New York at the end of 1974, where DJs had primarily self-made tapes cut in very small numbers as a record or acetate.[32] In addition, entire DJ mixes were recorded on tape: *Billboard* reported in October 1974 that DJs were recording their sets on tape and then selling these tapes without any involvement of rights holders. Buyers were not only discos but also stores and such venues that – one year before the release of Brian Eno's first ambient album *Discreet Music* (Obscure, UK, 1975) – were looking for 'hip background music' or a 'cool alternative to muzak'.[33]

Others, in addition to DJs, were producing sound streams of 'hip background music' at the beginning of the 1970s: since 1971, Tom Moulton had already produced several tapes for the Sandpiper venue on Fire Island, a barrier island off Long Island whose hamlets were a favourite haunt of the upper class of New York's gay community, where the tapes are said to have provoked both wild and enthusiastic reactions from the dancing crowd.[34] Moulton's tapes were modelled on DJ sets, which he certainly knew very well from New York discos and clubs, and were primarily concerned with minimizing the pauses between tracks.[35] These tapes are the automation of a DJ's work, and Moulton himself succumbed to the technocratic fascination of the perfectly running machine: 'Don't forget, humans make mistakes, whereas my tapes are perfect.'[36] Music journalist David Toop later portrayed Moulton first and foremost as a great marketer and rationalizer of disco culture.[37]

After the success of his mixtapes on Fire Island, Moulton contacted various recording studios and the label Scepter Records. He began to remix projected releases with a view to the disco context, whereby 'shift[ing] the simple principle of extension into the song itself' gave rise to the disco remix and the 'dominance of 'non-stop dancing'.[38] This spawned early practices of remixing.[39] With his extended mixes, Moulton encountered two constraints: first, musicians repeatedly rejected the mixes Moulton made of 'their' tracks;[40] – this, however, did not stop them from being released. Second, the length of Moulton's mixes – and this is crucial for the argument I seek to develop here – came up against the limits of the small 7-inch single. In 1973, for example, Moulton extended the playing time of the song *Do It ('Til You're Satisfied)* by B. T. Express from the originally about three to a lavish 5:52 minutes (Scepter, 1974).[41] So that the mix would still fit onto one side of a 7-inch single, the record had to be cut with a very low volume. In addition, the bass had to be radically filtered out. Especially towards the end of the track, the basses are missing and the treble is highly distorted. Regarding this single, *Billboard* reported in October 1974: 'Disco Play Starts a Hit.'[42] Moulton started writing his *Billboard* disco column, and the music industry began to exploit disco.

By releasing specific versions and remixes for the disco context, the record format of the 7-inch single reached its limits. In addition, ever since the prominence of disco versions, record releases had assumed the character of something unfinished: 'The advent of multitrack recording technology and the remixing of existing tracks that built upon it, resulted in the notion that a record was *never* finished …. From now on, will *all* records be remixed and reissued on a regular basis?'[43] The establishment of remixing practices created series of versions that did not have any 'originals': on the LP *Law and Order* by Love Committee (Gold Mind Records, United States, 1978), for example, there is a mix by Tom Moulton of the production *Just as Long as I Got You*. Another mix of the production – a disco mix by Walter Gibbons (Gold Mind Records, 1978) – was released as a 12-inch single. Moulton's and Gibbons's versions are no longer versions of a released 'original mix', they are versions of an unreleased multitrack tape. A music production comes to market in different versions on different recording formats.

By adopting a DJ practice – a specific form of mixing – in the recording studio, Moulton and other producers of specifically disco mixes contributed to the establishment of a musical practice in popular music that stretched instrumental passages of songs on a studio basis so that they would function more effectively as dance tracks. It is in relation to this practice and the musical form associated with it that the 12-inch single will be discovered.

That versions of song productions that vary and had abandoned the short and compact pop song form far more radically than Moulton's mixes were released only after the 12-inch single's 1976 launch was due to the fact that established DJs had themselves become remixers. Such DJ remixes entirely finished off the short and compact pop song and laid the groundwork for the 'tracks' of house and techno culture. The first regularly released 12-inch single, Double Exposure's *Ten Per Cent* (Salsoul, United States, 1976) with 'Disco Blending by Walter Gibbons', also integrated a three-minute song form in the remix, but literally let it drown in a mix lasting over nine minutes. This first remix released by Gibbons was a 'cut 'and' paste job'.[44] It was a stereo tape that was made by Gibbons in only three hours on behalf of Ken Cayre – the co-owner of the label Salsoul Records – in the Blank Tapes Studio in New York City, together with the sound engineer Bob Blank.[45] But for his further remixes, such as *Hit and Run* by Loleatta Holloway (Goldmine, United States, 1977), the DJ then had access to the multitrack master tape.[46] The 'inventor' of the disco break and 12-inch single, Tom Moulton, didn't understand Walter Gibbons's remixes. Moulton oriented his mixes sonically on live performances and rejected Gibbons's mixes as drug-influenced artificial soundscapes.[47] Gibbons's mixes focused on rhythm and sound. The 12-inch single farmed and cultivated the listening practices established in discos in an extended interplay of flowing repetitions, gradual modulations, abrupt breaks and sonic effects.

Disco bodies and managing the bass range

A second condition for the 12-inch single to be found was the organization of music listening as an explicitly bodily practice shaped by technology: in interaction with the disco sound, an immersive, tactile and bodily sound experience was created. We should remember here, of course, that discotheques existed before the 1970s. However, at the end of the 1960s, a new type of discotheque emerged in New York: 'The discotheque became a platform for marginalized groups excluded from rock culture, in particular for the various immigrant cultures and the African American gay scene. It was also in the African American gay discos that the practice arose of using non-stop music from records to make dancing, thus body experience, the actual content of the event.'[48] Art historian Douglas Crimp, who frequented New York nightlife venues in the 1970s, distinguishes between the old discos of the 1960s and the new discos of the 1970s. Regarding the former, he writes: 'They were private, or at least exclusive. They were expensive. They were straight.'[49] The new discos, on the other hand, bore 'traits of pariah culture'; 'they were located in out-of-the-way neighborhoods in quickly refurbished spaces with the palpable feeling of being susceptible to bust at any moment.'[50]

An immersive, tactile and physical sound experience was pivotal in New York disco culture even before the 12-inch single. The 12-inch single served and intensified this experience as well as the listening practices associated with it. The new sound format contributed to the further exploration and shaping of this experience through its loud, bass as well as treble-emphasized sound. In New York discos, sound had already been designed since the early 1970s in such a way that bodies could literally be physically immersed in it; moreover, dance forms in which people danced alone as part of a crowd, individual bodies immersed in a crowd of dancing bodies, were already becoming established in discos during this period.

Through the aforementioned practices, experiences and technologies, corporeality was produced as culturalized in the disco culture of the 1970s. Peter Wicke has argued that 'in a strange way, the turn to the body ... is arguably the most striking feature of popular 20th century music'.[51] According to Wicke, popular music forms segment, organize and constitute mutable, culturally specific forms of corporeality, which he calls 'body metamorphoses'.[52] These include listening practices and sound experiences.

We can add here that the complex formation of a specific corporeality through music is already indicated in the connection of body parts and organs to concrete musical forms before disco: thus the corporeality of Theodor W. Adorno's notorious 'expert' listener is constrained in the thinking ear, which listens preferentially to Anton Webern.[53] The philosopher Günther Anders wrote in the 1950s that jazz dancers 'lose their faces' or that in dance the face becomes a 'a mere *body part*, the naked and uncontrolled appearance of which no longer surpasses the likeness of a shoulder or a backside'.[54] The intention of the 'head music' of progressive and psychedelic rock of the late 1960s was primarily to produce a 'consciousness-expanding' effect in the head and, through such a reference, to be more than just a 'stimulating soundscape for dancing'.[55] Topoi of 'phallic' rock music and rock 'n' roll concentration on the hips – 'Elvis the Pelvis' – not only became established in pertinent discourses.[56] The structuring and segmentation of corporeality through music certainly harbours a fetishistic potential, which can be exaggerated in crude ways, for example, in so-called cock rock[57] or in Miami Bass, where it goes by the label 'booty music' – a type of hip-hop popularized in the 1980s and characterized by fast electronic rhythms and deep basses. Such body-related understandings of music often imply aesthetic evaluations that either ennoble by referring to the head or devalue aesthetically by referring to other parts of the body – especially those below the waistline – or seeking to act provocatively in a nonconformist way. A devaluation occurs, for example, through the reference to dancing feet, if dance music forms are classified as a principle as aesthetically inferior to music forms that are experienced sitting down and in a contemplative way. For an 'art of listening',[58] such body-related types of understanding music are of less significance.

In disco culture, the body makes scant claim to 'naturalness', as was demanded by the 'free-form abandonment of hippie dancing in the late 1960s'.[59] The disco body presents itself as something explicitly designable or designed. In disco culture, corporeality becomes – if we again follow Wicke here – a 'resource of pleasure and self-fulfillment' that is accessible to everyone, which is tapped into through 'playing with gender-specific identities'.[60] The historian Ulrich Raulff already points to games such as these in 1979 when he diagnoses that disco produced new '*techniques of the body*', a 'modeling of bodies', a 'new *technosex*' that 'certainly no longer has much to do with the heterosexuality of the couple'.[61] Sound is also involved in the shaping of this specific disco body, or rather this shaping is mediated by the 'systematic indexing of the somatic effects of sound and rhythm'.[62] Such systematic indexing implies sound technologies such as loudspeaker systems and – since the mid-1970s – precisely the 12-inch single.[63]

One of the first widely influential attempts to differentiate the physicality of disco also in relation to its sound was undertaken by British cultural studies scholar Richard

Dyer at the end of the 1970s.[64] In his classic text 'In Defence of Disco', Dyer correlates the organization of the disco body less with concrete sound technologies, such as the 12-inch single, and more with a musical form specific to disco. He describes this as characterized by an 'open-ended succession of repetitions'.[65] This distinguishes disco from other musical forms that aim at resolution, a single climax, or conclusion, and are centred. The disco-typical, open-ended sequences of repetitions, we can supplement Dyer here, are a central feature of the disco mixes and disco versions that record labels had been releasing since the first half of the 1970s. Dyer's unfinished repetition sequence thus corresponds with the variations of the short and compact pop song by DJs and remix pioneers described above, which became the template for the remixes released on 12-inch singles.

In 'Defence', Dyer focuses on the physical and sonic dimensions of the disco experience. He examines – as cultural studies scholar Jeremy Gilbert has pointed out – the 'organised but non-significatory nature of music's sonic effects'.[66] Thus Dyer does not ask how corporeality and desire are thematized and expressed in music – in song lyrics, for example – but how they are organized and produced in interaction with primarily non-textual musical forms and sounds.

Dyer terms the disco body '"whole body" eroticism'.[67] This term is suggestively contoured by a particular repertoire of gestures and movements – 'the expressive, sinuous movement of disco dancing'[68] – as well as by reference to a disco-specific culture of desire. Thus, such whole-body eroticism is to be distinguished from the phallic eroticism of rock music. Dyer finds these two contours reflected in the musical form of disco. However, we can sum up that Dyer, in his late 1970s, stimulating essay primarily provides a preliminary sketch of the disco body that jumps back and forth between polemical plain language and suggestive bon mots. Various disco releases function as an empirical basis in Dyer's text – for instance, Gloria Gaynor's *I've Got You Under My Skin* (Polydor, United States, 1976). Parts of this production focus on a simple phrase – 'I've got you' – from Cole Porter's song, and repeat it almost endlessly, without aiming for a harmonic conclusion.[69] Moreover, Dyer's essay was written specifically with reference to disco-like events he helped organize for the Gay Liberation Front in Birmingham, England, in the late 1970s.[70]

However, we can further differentiate Dyer's whole-body eroticism, or a decentralized and less hierarchized organization of the disco body, in empirical reference to the concrete visual and auditory design of discos. Thus, the disco body is not exclusively a listening one, it combines listening with other senses. The design of discos in 1970s New York is oriented on the 'mixed-media' environments of psychedelic rock as well as on the interiors of Las Vegas entertainment temples brushed with surface glamour.[71] Disco historian Tim Lawrence describes how the proto-disco Loft in New York in the early 1970s captivated with its multisensory orientation: 'Revelers refigured the dance floor as a site not of foreplay but of spiritual communion where, thanks to the unique combination of decor, space, music, drugs, lightning, and dance, as well as Mancuso's guiding party ethos, sensation wasn't confined to the genitals but was *everywhere* – in every new touch, sound, sight, and smell.'[72]

Dyer's disco body finds its limits not only in rock music that is headed for an explosive climax, but also in disco itself. Musicologist Robert Fink has noted that the musical forms of disco would by no means – as Dyer suggestively opines – be absorbed into a repetitive, anti-teleological and anti-narrative form that would correspond to a free-floating desire without telos or corporeal centre. Rather, Fink states – also with reference to the releases *Do It ('Til You're Satisfied)* by B. T. Express (Sceptor, United States, 1974) and *More, More, More* by Andrea True Connection (Buddah, United States, 1976), mixed by Tom Moulton: 'The build-up and breakdown of the basic groove *is* the narrative of electronic dance music.'[73] Disco does not bypass climaxes, it serializes them. According to Fink, the culture of desire that disco produces is characterized by an excessive and 'polymorphous-perverse teleology'.[74] This teleology goes beyond the time scale of 'quotidian bodily rhythms' and thus negates – we can add here – any claim to 'naturalness'.[75] Disco thus relates to central topoi of the 1970s and their techniques of the self-developed in the sub- and countercultures of the hippie and emerging New Age movement, to which a counterpart is constructed here through the negation of 'naturalness' – similar to punk. In this respect, disco is a phenomenon relevant to contemporary history that advances caesuras within cultural practices.

The disco body received its contours and dynamics largely through listening practices that incorporated technologies for cultivating the bass range. Such technologies were designed specifically for discos in New York: loudspeaker systems or sound systems that provoked the systematic exploration of the physical and immersive effects of sound.[76] Media scholar Keir Keightley has shown that engineered sound effects aimed at immersion were already central to the hi-fi culture that became prominent in the United States in the 1950s. In the living rooms of the white middle class, Keightley argues, technologized listening practices emerged that sought imaginary sound journeys: 'Immersion permits transportation into the world of music, away from domestic realities.'[77] He sees such listening practices continued in the recordings of psychedelic rock of the late 1960s. The followers of this form of music, he says, went on individual 'mind-expanding' sonic journeys equipped with headphones, an LP and a home stereo system. Such sound effects were collectivized in disco culture through sound systems and 12-inch singles in semi-public spaces: 'With the maxi-single, sound effects became audible outside the studio for the first time and, with gigantic four-digit wattages, unfolded a hitherto unknown effect that could previously only be imagined under stereo headphones.'[78]

Core players in the New York disco culture of the early 1970s, such as Loft founder David Mancuso, were self-confessed hi-fi fans. Nevertheless, hi-fi in the discos of this era were less oriented towards sonic paradigms such as 'fidelity' to a sound source or sonic 'balance'. Rather, hi-fi implied an excessive potential, which correlates with an immersive and physical sound effect, for instance, by amplifying bass and sub-bass frequencies. The targeted design of the (sub-)bass range began in disco culture with the construction of appropriate loudspeaker systems even before the 12-inch single. The 12-inch single was then found to be another means of cultivating the bass range.

It is true that releases of disco music often conformed to a typical hi-fi 'transparency' paradigm, which correlated with the multi-way systems of sound equipment in discos, in which three to four frequency ranges were each assigned to specific loudspeakers. At the same time, however, the music forms released as 12-inch singles were usually characterized by an extreme bass emphasis, which was opposed to a 'balance' paradigm, and which was also typical of hi-fi. Such a rejection of a balanced and harmonically balanced frequency arrangement was, however, in turn a condition for the tactile effect of sound. This was not always guaranteed by the small single record: on the aforementioned 7-inch single release of Moulton's nearly six-minute remix of B. T. Express's *Do It ('Til You're Satisfied)*, not much more than a click is audible from the bass drum. Low frequencies had to be filtered away in the mastering, otherwise Moulton's long mix would not have fitted on one side of the record.[79] The deliberate sonic management of the bass range and the production of an immersive and tactile sonic experience began in disco culture with the design of special loudspeaker systems by New York sound system designers, such as Alex Rosner and Richard Long, which emerged around 1970. Especially in the systems designed by Long, moments of excess and sonic escalation took precedence over an orientation towards harmonic balance of frequencies. These sound systems were involved in the design of the disco body.[80]

The 12-inch single is a technology whose emergence was provoked by concrete practices of listening to, producing and marketing music, which emerged in the New York disco culture of the first half of the 1970s. In terms of media and cultural history, the emergence of new sonic technologies and formats has been grounded in confrontations with disparate factors. If, for Friedrich Kittler, entertainment technologies such as radio and magnetic tape are a 'misuse of military equipment'[81] that owe their development to world wars, Jonathan Sterne sees the development of the MP3 format as decisively shaped by 'corporate capitalism'.[82] Wolfgang Hagen, on the other hand, emphasizes moments of non-incidental discovery in the technological history of radio.[83] The technological innovation represented by the 12-inch single is modest – not only in comparison with radio, magnetic tape and MP3. Nor was it developed in a military, scientific or industrial research laboratory. Attempts to explain the 12-inch single as a product of economic dynamics of supply and demand fall short. The position, argued emphatically, according to which the 12-inch single was the product of 'consumer demand',[84] finds its counterpart in the critical presentation of the 'promotional activism of small labels'.[85] Rather, the conditions and circumstances under which the 12-inch single was found encompass a historically as well as culturally specific structure of technological developments (LP, 7-inch single and disco sound system), auditory practices (a bodily perceptual practice correlating with a cultivation and management of the bass range), and music industry business models (the disco as a promotional channel supplied with specific releases). Then, from the late 1970s, the 12-inch single became a crucial format for the development of musical forms such as hip-hop, New Wave, house and techno. However, to present the specifics of this development is a different topic, which would be part of a popular music history told as a history of technology.[86] The 12-inch single, on the other hand, is itself already musically authored through its reference to a particular musical culture; in this respect, the inversion of these two histories applies to the finding of the 12-inch single: here technology history is music history.

Music history of the 12-inch single – disco inferno

The media historian Friedrich Kittler has been perceived by sound and music studies primarily in terms of his theses on the conditioning of music and sound by media. Kittler himself played this through mainly in relation to rock music.[87] However, in Kittler's work there is not only a media history of music, but also a music history of the media. We can also play such a history through in relation to disco and the 12-inch single. Kittler himself only had a few splinters of thoughts on disco. He treats disco in the main as an optical phenomenon and only incidentally as a sonic one. The lighting systems or – more precisely – the stroboscopic lights of the discos of the 1970s and early 1980s are the focus of interest: 'Whosoever is able to hear or see the circuits in the synthesized sound of CDs or in the laser storms of a disco finds happiness.'[88] Discos here apparently become places where both nineteenth-century perceptual-physiological experiments were repeated and the military 'retaliatory strike' was trained:[89] 'The stroboscopic effect at the beginning of film has left physiological labs and now chops up dancers twenty times per second into film images of themselves. The barrage of fire has left the major lines of combat and these days echoes from security systems – including their precise and simultaneous combination with optical effects. [Georges] Demeny's [chrono-]photography of speech continues as a videoclip, his "Vive la France!" as a salad of syllables: "Dance the Mussolini! Dance the Adolf Hitler!"'[90]

Ulrich Raulff, in his trenchant cultural studies essay on disco, already fancied he could hear 'the roar of war' in these places, 'when Kitty Hanson … describes the preparation for the stroboscopic blitzkrieg [in her 1978 bestseller *Disco Fever*]: pages and pages of 'Do's and Dont's [sic] for Surviving a Disco Night' and the résumé of Dr Berger, a discophilic psychiatrist ('The ultimate goal is to reach a total body experience that ruptures normal space and time') could just as well be from an army service manual for training solo combatants.'[91] However, we can add here, few people in the 1970s would have gone to the disco to play war games. Moreover, there is no reference to this in Tim Lawrence's superb history of popular dance music culture in the United States from 1970 to 1979.[92] Notwithstanding, this does not rule out the possibility that disco was a training programme for the senses, similar to the computer games that Kittler imagines (with Ronald Reagan) 'as a training ground for future bomber pilots'.[93] The purposive overloading of the senses, whether with strobe lights or loud and deep sounds, was characteristic of disco, and the thesis of the mobilization of the body is evident in the case of disco in diverse dance and bodybuilding practices, whether for '"good" gay disco' or '"bad" mainstream disco'.[94]

The mobilization of bodies and perception that interacts with disco has, unnoticed by Kittler, also become a condition of media transformation. However, it was a media transformation that was scarcely noticed outside of fan and specialist circles, a media transformation (which brings us back to the protagonist of this chapter) which combined technology that had existed for a longer time and led to a new media technology that was anything but disruptive: the 12-inch single. As we have seen, the 12-inch single is a media technology whose origin was conditioned by musical practices and new sounds. The 12-inch single is a case of a music and sound history of media.

Both popular music studies and media studies have engaged with the history of the 12-inch single. Media anthropologist Erhard Schüttpelz writes it as a *'history of media invention'*[95] which focuses on the 'priority of operational chains'.[96] By focusing on such chains of operations, this historiography – which is oriented on media anthropology – seeks to concentrate primarily on practices or the *'sporadically practiced alteration of previous practices'* or even the *'practical alterations of the operational chain'*.[97] This has in common with a music and sound history of the 12-inch single the fact that the emergence of the 12-inch single is not accounted for in the sense of a historical or media la priori by the mere existence of *'record blanks, long versions, and copyrights'*, but in the *'"a posteriori" combination'* and articulation of these components through new practices.[98] Here, Schüttpelz focuses on new practices of music making in the form of practices of (re)mixing recorded music. However, Schüttpelz somewhat ignores the new practices of releasing music. The fact that the 12-inch single was increasingly developed as a promotional and secondary exploitation tool by record companies, without, however, being reducible to such economic stakes,[99] is quickly lost sight of when this large and fast single is presented as an underground technology desired, concocted and then emancipated by fans and enthusiasts. Well, these remain problems of detail, which may be especially relevant for the case of the 12-inch single, but they do not fundamentally problematize an anthropological historiography of media. Decisively more problematic is Schüttpelz's talk of the 'history of media invention', for this suggests a subject-centred and subliminally intentionally guided history of the development of the 12-inch single. Be that as it may, Tom Moulton, who was close to industry, was rather the finder than the inventor of the 12-inch single. Nor did he find it alone, but together with mastering engineer José Rodriguez. Schüttpelz also remains conspicuously vague about the new practices of listening to music and perceiving the sound that characterized disco culture. It was precisely for these practices, however, that a specific sound was crucial, which could be developed not only in interaction with increasingly sophisticated loudspeaker systems, but also with the 12-inch single. It is precisely the 'sound of the widely deflected groove'[100] that can form the core of a music and sound history of the 12-inch single. For this sound not only depends on practices, but also on the 'technical-artefactual' or the 'specific mediality' of the 12-inch single.[101] The sound of the widely spaced grooves was probably also decisive for the fact that the 12-inch single 'was able to establish itself on the market, with DJs and in discos'.[102] Yet a sound history of the 12-inch single is not confined to exploring why this media technology became established. It attempts to argue why this new medium was found at a specific point in time. Apparently, disco culture was characterized by a demand, or to put it less economically, by a desire for loud, tactilely effective sound. For sound that exhibited an extensive bass spectrum and a differentiated treble presentation. This sound was concretized in pumping, jumping bass lines and powerful bass drums, in hissing hi-hats and rich overtone spectra. Bodies could literally immerse themselves in this sound. The desire for this sound was then developed by the 12-inch single.

Listening at the margins: Reading and feeling 12-inch singles

The 12-inch single is not only a sonic technology, but it also includes significant visual and even tactile aspects. The relationship between listening and seeing that is constituted via the 12-inch single concerned again and again the DJ; the relationship between listening and tactility addressed disco, house and techno dancers and listeners. Through these connections with visuality and tactility, the 12-inch single transcends the realm of the audible and links a history of listening with a history of non-listening. With reference to the visuality of the 12-inch single, popular music studies scholar Richard Osborne writes in his history of the vinyl record: 'The appeal of these records was visual as well as aural, and this visual appeal was both practical (enabling DJs to access passages of music within the grooves) and symbolic (to adopt the 12″ single meant identification with dance music genres).'[103] Thus, 12-inch singles increasingly allowed record grooves to be 'read' by DJs and were articulated to specific music forms; moreover, they came with a distinctive form of packaging. This packaging could, for instance, advertise the technical advantages of the format or, outside the United States, purport to be 'American disco imports'.[104] In addition to this visual dimension, 12-inch singles included a tactile dimension by the design of low-range sounds on the threshold of audibility; deep sounds that had a haptic, tactile effect. Before the advent of digitization in DJing, 12-inch singles were the central format for DJs. We find extensive archives of 12-inch singles in numerous legacies of DJs. For example, legendary house DJ Frankie Knuckles's collection of approximately five thousand records consists primarily of 12-inch singles.[105]

Reading records: Grooves and vinyl graffiti

The relationship between listening and seeing that the 12-inch single established is organized at several levels: The record cutting method in which the distance between the grooves is no longer constant but dependent 'on the level of the signal to be cut'[106] has been around since the 1950s. With such a record cut, the groove spacing of passages with bass drum is larger than that of passages without bass drum.[107] This difference is immediately recognizable visually. The extended cut of the 12-inch single compared to an LP or single intensified the optical effect of this procedure, and thus already facilitated a visual segmentation of music pieces for the DJ. Due to the more extensive cutting, DJs increasingly began to read records. If Adorno's analogy of phonography and 'writing' that could be 'read' not only by machines but possibly also by humans[108] remained just suggestive in the age of the shellac record, which was cut with constant groove spacing, then this analogy developed a pragmatic component in the age of the 12-inch single: for example, the DJ knows how to identify and decipher the places on the vinyl where the bass drum was faded out. The grooves can be made tighter in the cut at such points. This cut is clearly visible and gives the DJ targeted access to breaks or quiet spots, for example. Media theorist Mark Poster also refers to this readability of records: 'Because of this analogy [between record groove and writing], some people are even able to "read" the grooves on vinyl records and tell which piece of music is inscribed in them.'[109] Francis Grasso could even read LPs: 'If you look at an album carefully you can see which parts of the album are vocal and which parts are musical so you've already got a head start. Dark black grooves are instrumental sections and the lighter black is the vocal.'[110] However, the 12-inch single mediated the specific connection between hearing and seeing in a new, more explicit way.

The 'readability' of the 12-inch single includes both the analogue codes of the record grooves, its packaging and the usually colourful label stickers or labels in the centre of the record, as well as signatures consisting of alphanumeric characters and pictograms that were often hand-carved into the matrix. With the increasing personalization of post-production processes such as mixing and mastering, 'vinyl graffiti'[111] flourished in disco culture. This form of graffiti is placed in the so-called dead wax or inside margin; that is, in the area of the unmodulated run-out groove: mastering engineers inscribed their signatures there in the form of abbreviations and pictograms.[112] Especially in the form of dance music called 'techno' that mushroomed in Detroit in the late 1980s, mastering became an increasingly explicit process. This was personalized and indexed visually in the area of the run-out groove: in some cases, the signature even jumped over to the entire vinyl, turning it into a writing surface. Ron Murphy, who mastered a large part of Detroit's techno productions and cut them on vinyl at his mastering studio National Sound Corporation, which later functioned as Sound Enterprises, increased the space of the breaks between individual tracks on one side, for example, and carved inaudible but legible logos such as 'UR' or 'NSC' there,[113] and wrote 'the propaganda-style messages of Plus 8 and UR'[114] in the run-out groove and on the B-sides of the few releases of the label World Power Alliance, a sub-label of the legendary Detroit techno label Underground Resistance, and even a short manifesto.[115] The specific relationship between listening and seeing that the 12-inch single established thus enabled the DJ, on the one hand, to access individual sections of a piece of music, of a track, in a more targeted way and, on the other hand, encompassed strategies of authorization through which records were distinguished by mastering engineers. In these strategies, sound events do not speak for themselves, but are visually marked.

Tactile listening

With regard to the artificial sound worlds of 1990s techno culture, Peter Wicke has put forward the thesis that these were defined more by a connection to the tactile than to the visual. Such sound worlds would not be the outcome of body movements – think of disembodied sequencer-generated sound, samples and loops. Thus, a strong reference between 'the sonic event and its origin', between 'hearing and seeing, between the visible and the audible' is not given here.[116] Such disembodied sounds would be – this is the second part of Wicke's thesis on techno – primarily related to the bodies of the dancers, to the dancing crowd.[117] It is this reference that Wicke sees reinforced by the tactility of techno sound: 'Techno is literally *tactile* music. The enormous phonetic volumes, which literally take the breath away from outsiders and seem to make well-aimed blows to the pit of the stomach out of the bass, have nothing to do with volume as a dynamic quality of music making. That is why they always remain at the same high level. They are needed to generate a sound pressure that makes the rhythmic sound sequences palpable. It is a hearing through the skin that characterizes and carries this music, resulting in a symbiosis of sound and body .... The body has become the self-referential object of sonic perception.'[118] In the cultural context of 1990s techno clubs – such as Berlin's first Tresor club, opened in 1991, where the loud bass-heavy sounds were embedded in fog, darkness and strobe lights[119] – the sound of music provoked a hearing through the skin where the material impact of sound on the listening body became more important than the visualization of the physical source of the sound. In such an environment, listening was at least as strongly coupled with touch as with sight. Also the protagonist of this chapter, the 12-inch single was involved in the provocation of such a form of tactile listening and in the constitution of techno as a tactile music.

If we situate the tactility of sound described here in the case of techno within the history of listening devices, another specific feature of tactile sound emerges. The first technologies of sound transduction – such as the phonautograph or the telephone – were derived from the study of the human senses. They represented engineered organs abstracted from the body, to which corresponded to a differentiation of the sensorium into discrete 'sensory channels'.[120] Sound could thus be investigated independently of (its) physical 'source', but could be studied via its material effects. In the case of techno, but we can also add here disco and house, such a decoupling of the senses is problematized on a technical basis. This problematization does not appear against the background of an arbitrary reconnection of the senses – as in so-called multimedia products such as the music video. Rather, the 12-inch single is part of a strategy that escalates the sound of the record in its tactile and thus inaudible or at least not only audible dimension. Thereby, a form of 'presence' through touch can be generated in the context of disco, house and techno culture not only through content and certain vocal styles – think of Lil Louis's *French Kiss* (Diamond, United States, 1989) for instance – but precisely also through the escalation of the haptic dimension of sound.

Even if in the case of tactile listening, the contact between sound and the listening body seems, again and again, 'immediate', 'straightforward' and 'direct', it is most often heavily mediated. Such a form of sonic touch relies heavily on mediation. It is striking that tactile listening in relation to disco and electronic dance music is located in a musical culture characterized by a high degree of technological mediation. This holds paradoxical potential: 'presence' is generated through technological mediators. In popular music culture, this is by no means a phenomenon specific to electronic dance music. Popular vocal styles such as crooning[121] or more current vocal sounds impregnated by a desire for Autonomous Sensory Meridian Response (ASMR)[122] also represent strategies by which proximity and presence are precisely technologically produced and simulated, strategies by which the listener should be physically touched by sound. Such forms of presence correlate with a specific materiality of sound events.

Just as with the jukebox, the 12-inch single is also involved in the organization of a form of listening that includes body parts other than the ear. Such a form of tactile listening is defined by a physical contact of sound and the listening body, a listening body that is literally touched by sound. The 12-inch single also manages this touch, this contact. Thereby it is involved in a new configuration of the materialities of listening and the relations between the senses that can also coincide – as we will soon see – with a specific form of subjectivity in which the listening subject and the music listened to are sublated. Moreover, I shall argue that in disco and club culture tactile listening is not only provoked by tactile sounds but also by a certain form of temporality, a musical form that crosses the dualism of linear narrativity and one-way teleology on the one hand and repetition and circularity on the other. Such a musical form becomes prominent in disco, house and techno. In this musical form, tactile listening gets organized in time and becomes more than a repeating, intermittent touch.

Like other listening devices, the 12-inch single also combines listening with its Other; that is, with non-listening and the inaudible. However, the 12-inch single in disco, house and techno culture processes this relation prominently via a specific distinction, the distinction between listening and tactility. If the listening culture of the hi-fi LP was time and again motivated by a becoming inaudible of the technology itself[123] and the listening culture of the single in the 1950s in the context of rock 'n' roll culture was characterized by a retraction of the inaudible by disregarding industry standards in practices of 'hot mastering',[124] then the inaudible became tangible or tactile in relation to the 12-inch single. LP, single, and 12-inch single thus each form – certainly in relation to different musical cultures – a specific relationship to the non-audible, to non-listening, to sensory registers beyond the audible. A tactile effect of the sound of the 12-inch single was provoked by the emphasis on loud and deep (sub)bass.[125] In their cultural study of 1990s dance music, Jeremy Gilbert and Ewan Pearson describe how an exploration of the (sub)bass range in styles such as disco, house and techno resonated with the 12-inch single's technology: 'If one used the amount of vinyl traditionally employed for four or five tracks to reproduce just one, one could happily accommodate a ten-minute disco mix while also obtaining a large increase in amplitude. Wider grooves also allowed better reproduction of low frequencies: the bass that was traditionally emphasized by club speakers could be built into the record from the start without any danger of the needle jumping. The reproductive qualities of the new format were in concert with the requirements of the music it carried, and in turn gave that music vital space in which to develop sonically, to extend further into the lower reaches of the frequency spectrum, an opportunity which was eagerly taken up by the dance forms which followed disco, creating and utilizing ever heavier and deeper bass and sub-bass sounds.'[126] Such heavier and deeper bass and sub-bass sounds captivate through their tactile quality.

With regard to LP mastering, mastering engineer Bob Katz declared the high-pass filter to be the 'best friend' of his guild and he regarded 'excessive' groove excursion in the bass range as problematic: 'Historically, the high pass filter was our best friend when we made LPs, to prevent excess groove excursion and obtain more time per LP side.'[127] These limitations of LP mastering were put into perspective by the 12-inch single. For mastering of small single records, however, they still held. This is revealed, for example, by the above-mentioned releases of Tom Moulton's first mixes as 7-inch single records, where the sound of the bass drum had turned into a mere click. Everything else from it has been filtered away in the mastering, otherwise the mix would not have fitted on one side of the record.

However, it seemed it was not so much the extension of the frequency range as the volume that initially attracted Moulton to the 12-inch single. Fascinated by the volume, Moulton made the first informal test cut of what would later be called the 12-inch single. This cut was – as mentioned above – a product of serendipity: 'So, the thing is – one day I went in there to José – José Rodriguez – and I had "I'll Be Holding On" by Al Downing and I said: "José, I could really need some acetates." And he said: "Just Tom, I don't have any more 7″ blanks. All I have is like the 10″." And I said: "Well, if that's the only thing – we're gonna do it, what difference does it make?" So he cut one, I said: "It looks so ridiculous, this little tiny band on this huge thing. What happens if we just like … can we just like, you know, make it bigger?" He goes: "You mean, like spread the grooves?" And I said: "Yeah!" He goes: "Then I've got to rise the level." I said: "Well, go ahead – rise the level." And so he cut it like at +6. Oh, when I heard it I almost died. I said: "Oh my God, it's so much louder and listen to it. Oh! I like that – why don't we cut a few more?" So it was by accident, that's how it was created. But for the next song we cut, we went for the 12″ format instead of the 10″ and the song was "So Much for Love" by Moment of Truth. That was the birth of the 12″ single.'[128] Such a desire for volume was soon supplemented by a desire for bass.

I argue here that the 12-inch single as a listening device is involved in a peculiar organization of listening in which listening gains shape by pushing it to its boundaries, especially to its boundaries with haptics and tactility. The tactility of sound as a central aesthetic dimension of popular dance music forms such as disco, house and techno, but also of dub, dancehall and hip-hop, has been analysed many times in music and sound studies in recent years. Thus, for example, the 'vibrotactility' of reggae sound systems,[129] the 'bass materialism' of the popular music cultures of the Black Atlantic,[130] the '*tactilisation* of sound' in house and techno via 'percussion, texture, grain',[131] the 'intense musical and emotional experience occurring in the club context',[132] the 'low end theory'[133] and the 'booming basses of disco and club culture'[134] came into view. Against this background, there have been reflections on a 'musicology of bass culture' whose critical approach aims to counteract a 'mystification' of basses[135] as seen in the analysis of bass-heavy music cultures and their speech of 'myth-science' and 'bass cults'.[136]

To further explore the concept of tactile listening, musicologist Anahid Kassabian's considerations on 'hearing as a contact sense' are helpful. Kassabian brings the relationship between listening and tactility to the concept 'haptic hearing.'[137] She sees this form of listening as characterized by physical contact or proximity between the listener and what is heard. Here listening becomes associated with concepts such as touch, immediacy and intimacy. Relying most notably on affect theory, Kassabian understands music listening as a process that integrates primarily bodily reactions, 'somatic, haptic engagements',[138] which does not aim exclusively at 'consciousness' and 'attention'.[139] When hearing functions as a contact sense, Kassabian points out, boundaries are blurred, the difference between listening subject and heard object is suspended in a 'dynamic nonhuman subjectivity'.[140]

For Kassabian, haptic hearing becomes empirically manifest as well in forms of electronic dance music such as techno and dubstep, 'with their heavy emphases on bass and sub-bass frequencies'.[141] In these music forms, haptic listening is specifically addressed, and the provocation of this listening can even be declared a quality criterion of the music.[142] A good disco or house, techno or dubstep record must then have a physical effect, must be perceptible in the stomach, for example. We can add here that in the case of electronic dance music, haptic listening is co-constituted by certain listening devices that situate it culturally and historically. Thus, we can study haptic or tactile listening in reference to such devices. Devices in which sound is not only auditory but also tactile and which lies across discrete sensory channels are not only sound systems but also the 12-inch singles of disco and club culture. The specific relation between listening and non-listening that the 12-inch single constitutes then also constitutes hearing 'as a contact sense'.[143]

In addition to specific sounds, there seems to be – if we are willing to follow Kassabian once more – certain musical temporalities that are more suited to haptic or tactile listening than others. Against this backdrop, Kassabian discriminates this form of listening from forms of listening that exclusively concern the ear and which have learned to listen to the narrative and the semiotic: Adorno's structural listener, but also Susan McClary's narratological-feminist method serve here as negative foils.[144] Instead of a linear progressive narration of a musical object, as we find in musical forms such as the sonata form or also in a couple of rock productions peaking in the guitar solo or in a kind of scream of the singer, for tactile listening 'affective processes' and 'affective responses', which undermine subjectivity, significance and narration, ought to be crucial.[145]

However, in the case of disco we can add here – following Robert Fink's bold analysis of repetition in American minimal music mentioned above already – that disco is characterized by a peculiar kind of meta-dialectical temporality that includes both, narrative peaks *and* excessive repetitions. Fink argues that disco reshapes an essential aspect of Western listening experience: 'the sense that the music has a coherent *teleology*'.[146] However, he does not follow up this diagnosis with a duality of situative repetitive music on the one hand and dialectical music, which aims at memory, anticipation and development on the other.[147] Fink attempts to locate disco theoretically in French post-structuralism with reference to the free-floating desire of Gilles Deleuze and Félix Guattari's 'desiring machines' and with recourse to the distinction between *plaisir* and *jouissance*. He parallels this with the distinction between rock music based on narrativity and teleology and disco music based on repetition.[148] According to this, rock music's *plaisir* heads for a climax, whereas disco's *jouissance*, with its plateaus, streams, repetitions and loops, is presumed to be aimless and climaxless. However, such an opposition may sound problematic against the backdrop of Donna Summer's classic disco hit *Love to Love you Baby*. Fink notes that this is not a piece about climaxless 'floating erotic energy', but a piece about orgasms.[149] Teleology is not discarded in repetitive music, but serialized. Fink thus abolishes the dualism of teleological/non-teleological in the concept of 'recombinant teleology'.[150] There are narrative and teleological elements in disco – and we can find them in house and techno music as well. However, following Fink, repetitive music is about an 'expanse of teleology that the music does not articulate within time frames listeners can recognize as "normal" or "human". Perhaps this is why disco and minimalism are constantly imagined as the music of machines, androids, and cyborgs.'[151] The excessive time frames of repetitive music thus no longer have a human dimension.[152] Thereby, the 'dynamic nonhuman subjectivity' that corresponds to Kassabian's haptic listening can be more precisely defined in terms of its non-humanity in the context of electronic dance music. Corresponding to tactile listening, then, are musical forms that break with classical forms of musical narration.

Maxi-sound: Mastering disco, house and techno

The sound of the 12-inch single is also created in post-production. This means that what the 12-inch single gives us to hear does not just document a music performance or reproduce a music production. This brings mastering into play as well as remixing. For one thing, the 12-inch single makes the B-side of the single record more prominent: 'Artists created b-side material and they mixed 12″ versions of their songs.'[153] Osborne pointed out that the 12-inch single was initially used in the UK more as a 'gimmick',[154] but then gained acceptance in the early 1980s – Grandmaster Flash and The Furious Five's 'The Message' (Sugar Hill Records, United States, 1982) and New Order's 'Blue Monday' (Factory Records, UK, 1983) had been important here[155] – and finally, in relation to specific genres of music – New Wave, house and techno – a certain 'cult' had set in.[156] 'The 12″ single was the ultimate product of studio-based music.'[157] However, in the case of the 12-inch single in particular, sound is prominently reshaped in post-production both through remixing, and again and again in mastering. In this way, too, the 12-inch single became a constitutive part of music.

In disco, house and techno culture, as we have already seen in rock 'n' roll culture, mastering engineers turned tapes into records. Only the latter were released. The former found their way into the record companies' archives, to be re-released re-mastered soon if the demand was there. In disco and club culture, the 12-inch single was the central sound carrier format for a long time. Nevertheless, small singles and LPs were also pressed. A production came on the market in different versions and on different formats. The sales of 12-inch singles could 'cannibalise' the sales of albums.[158] In this respect, there was also a discussion in the recording industry about the release date of the 12-inch single in relation to the release date of the album. Whether a 12-inch single, which cost more than twice as much to manufacture as a single and almost as much as an album, should be released before the album, at the same time as the album, or only after sales of the album had slowed down was discussed within the industry.[159] In the 1980s, 12-inch singles gained greater economic and aesthetic autonomy in the context of house and hip-hop: 'By the 1980s, the 12″ (30 cm) single became the focus of a parallel music industry and a new creative underground. Its function was no longer limited to that of offering remixed versions of songs whose "real" or original versions were elsewhere (on albums or 7″ (18 cm) singles). Increasingly, dance tracks, released only as 12″ (30 cm) singles and bearing little textual resemblance to traditional song forms, were serving the new basis for new kinds of musical experimentation and live performance (as in scratching by hip-hop DJs). Just as the 12″ (30 cm) single became the focus of parallel structures of production, distribution, and review, so it nourished musical genres (such as house) whose viability in album form or mainstream broadcast media has remained doubtful.'[160]

With regard to house music, music journalist Kodwo Eshun has pointed out that a possible lack of usability of this music form for the album format is by no means seen as a deficit within this music culture. Rather, the 12-inch single occupies a prominent position there: 'The 12 [sic] is the hardback of music, the ltd-edn [limited edition] run of 2000 copies that sells out in 3 days, never to be seen again. The 12 [sic] is an elite product, frozen in a rigidly protected hierarchy of DJ, journalist and everyone else. Like paperbacks, compilations reverse this process, releasing tracks from their reverential and rarefied aura, dissolving journalistic reverence, bypassing hard-won connoisseurship by flooding the High Streets with anthologies anyone can buy.'[161] Interplaying with the 12-inch single is an understanding of music that no longer takes music to be a series of identifiable individual songs, as it is on the jukebox. Rather, music becomes a sound stream consisting of tracks that can be remixed again and again, as it also becomes concrete in the DJ set.[162]

In the sonic difference of different releases of a production the peculiar sound of the 12-inch single can be examined. However, it is not only in this dimension that this single reveals its own sound. The sonic difference between the master tape and the 12-inch single also reveals something that has been ignored by sound and music studies so far. In disco culture – as I have shown above in the wake of remixing – mastering evolved into an explicit function that became not only visible but also audible to listeners and fans. It became visible through corresponding authoritative information on the back of the record sleeve or on the label sticker on the vinyl and also through vinyl graffiti. It became audible through the almost simultaneous release of a production on up to three different sound carrier formats.

Physics of the 12-inch single

Technically, a 12-inch single has several advantages over the LP and 7-inch single. For example, it allows better resolution of both high and low frequencies. Low frequencies require the most space on a record – despite the bass reduction during cutting. Thus, the excursion of grooves analogous to bass frequencies is greater than the excursion of grooves representing mid-frequencies. Thus, fewer grooves representing low frequencies can be cut into a record than grooves representing mid-frequencies. Bass-heavy records cut at high levels must therefore be comparatively short.[163]

High frequencies can also be stored better on a record if there is more space available for their deflection, which has an analogous relationship to the volume, or if the needle scans the record at a greater speed – this stretches the slopes of the deflections. This situation is given as soon as the record revolves faster or is larger or the needle scans the record near the edge of the record.[164] Thus, the 12-inch single, that revolves at 45 rpm is faster than the LP and is larger than the 7-inch single, enables more comprehensive frequency range compared to other record formats.

Nevertheless, on the 12-inch single it is also difficult to reproduce strongly emphasized s-sounds and certain stereo sounds. Mastering engineer Andreas Lubich points out these difficulties and their consequences for physical sound effects: 'These s-sounds tend to tug on the record. Stereo effects on a bassline or bass drum can be problematic because of the resulting phase difference between the two stereo channels. It is advisable to keep the bass mono, especially for records that are to be played primarily in clubs. Otherwise, cancellations will occur on a club PA and the bass drum will no longer go to the legs.'[165] However, Lubich also emphasizes that vinyl ultimately integrates a spectrum that exceeds human hearing: 'Vinyl has a frequency range of 5 hertz to over 25 kilohertz … when handled correctly.'[166]

However, an expansion of the frequency range – compared to single and LP – by the 12-inch single is by no means simply explainable by the context of a hi-fi aesthetic and the common listening practices associated with it. For one thing, the low frequencies that can be stored on a 12-inch single – listened to with an appropriate system and at high volume – are not just perceived with the ears, but they become tactilely effective. In this respect, connections arise between auditory and tactile perceptions. On the other hand, the music in the environment where this medium arose is by no means a type of music in whose aesthetics the 'natural', or a highly faithful documentary ideal, constitute points of attraction. In the disco culture from which the 12-inch single emerged, the artificial, the constructed and the elaborately staged took precedence over any claims to naturalness, documentation and authenticity.[167] Even if components from hi-fi culture were repeatedly adopted in the sound aesthetics of disco – for example, the so-called Philly Sound which was characterized by its extreme transparency – both the listening practices and the techno-aesthetic forms that correlated with the 12-inch single were at a distance from hi-fi culture. In mastering, the specific physics of the 12-inch single have been made audible in various ways.

Music researcher Paul Jasen has pointed out that the 'bass cults' he analyses, by which Jasen means communities formed around low frequencies or bass-centred musical forms, often 'rely on just a small few engineers and mastering houses around the world that are known for their skill with the low end'.[168] The work of these mastering engineers – Jasen mentions Herb Powers Jr, Brian 'Big Bass' Gardner, Ron Murphy, and Dubplates & Mastering, for example – plus 'the system and room, via the sonic body, begin to exert a reciprocal influence on the sonic character of the music'.[169]

Disco, house and techno mastering

Mastering has a unique status in disco, house and techno culture. While the production of disco was highly professionalized and functionally differentiated, in which individual functions were taken over by respective specialists, the early house and techno producers were amateurs and generalists.[170] One of the first Chicago house 12-inch singles *On and On* (Jes Say JS9999, United States, 1984) was not only 'produced, arranged, and performed by Jesse Saunders' – as the label sticker informs us – but can also be understood in its sonic minimalism as an invitation to make music oneself.[171] The record 'was a cover of a rare, post-disco 12" promotional release from 1980 by an artist named MACH, supposedly stolen from Jesse Saunder's record collection'.[172] DJ and house producer Marshall Jefferson comments on this release: 'That was the single most important record to me of the twentieth century, because it let the non-musician know that he could make music.'[173] Who could have single-handedly released a disco record? Nobody! Strictly speaking, however, even Saunders could not have made his record alone. This does not mean that Saunders's label partner Vince Lawrence was involved, who also held copyrights to the production, but rather the fact that Saunders did not produce a record at all, he just produced a tape. The record was not made by Saunders, but by Chicago's only record pressing plant at the time, the Bridgeport Precision Pressing Plant, formerly Musical Products, which was owned by businessman Larry Sherman.[174] However, since Sherman later came to prominence because of his poor-quality vinyl pressings, it can probably be assumed that little value was placed on pressing this record, as well as on the mastering process, and that in this respect it remained – at best – a plain transfer. Early Chicago house records were thus not only produced by so-called non-musicians, often at home in the living room, but the amateur approach to music production was also preserved in the mastering.[175] The first producers of Detroit techno in the second half of the 1980s were also non-musicians.[176] However, from the late 1980s, the sound of their releases was adapted to professional standards by Ron Murphy's mastering. How the first productions of Derrick May, Juan Atkins and Kevin Saunderson sounded before they were modified in sound and cut on vinyl by Murphy is not known. In disco culture, then, mastering was gaining in importance and becoming personalized from the mid-1970s; in the early 1980s, mastering became a purely technical transfer process in Chicago house, whereas mastering was creating new sounds in Detroit techno since the late 1980s.

We can examine the peculiar and specific sound of the 12-inch single in disco culture on the first officially released 12-inch single: *Ten Per Cent* by Double Exposure (Salsoul 12D-2008 [12D-2008A-2], United States, 1976). Double Exposure's production Ten Per Cent was released on different formats and in different versions. I will examine five of these releases in more detail here: (i) the 12-inch single containing Walter Gibbons's 'Disco Blending'; (ii) the US single release (Salsoul SZ-2008 [SZ 2008 A], United States, 1976); (iii) a UK demo single release (Salsoul SZ 2013 [SZ 2013-A-1E], UK, 1976); (iv) the release of the production on the LP *Ten Percent* (Salsoul SZS-5503 [SZS 5503-A-1E], UK, 1976) and (v) another Walter Gibbons remix, not released officially in the

1970s, cut only as a dubplate. This has since been released on CD (Strut, UK, 2010). These five releases were not only on different recording formats – 7-inch single, 12-inch single, LP and CD – they also differ significantly in playing time.[177] These releases correspond to five versions of the production. Even the two single releases contain different versions: for example, the US single is slightly longer than the UK single, and the intro and outro of the production are arranged or mixed differently on these two releases.[178] Most radical on the level of musical form is the remix originally released as a dubplate. Here, almost all references to the song form have disappeared: there are no verses, and the chorus is only present in final fragments. The remix also sets accents on a spectral level: For example, the frequency response of the drum sound is heavily cut in the first twelve bars and is only opened up afterwards. The mastering of the different record releases is – albeit in nuances – specifically designed for each release. The two 7-inch singles were mastered by different engineers in different studios.[179] Al Brown mastered the US 7-inch single as well as the 12-inch single at the Frankford-Wayne Mastering Labs.[180] On the back of the LP *Ten Percent* Al Brown is also credited as mastering engineer. However, there are no signatures on the vinyl of the LP that point to Brown as mastering engineer. In this respect, we can assume that this LP release – the UK release not the US release – was not mastered by Brown. Al Brown's mastering of the 7-inch single, which is probably aimed more at radio use, and that of the 12-inch single, which is aimed at club use, exhibit some significant sonic differences. In reference to Gibbons's version released as a 12-inch single, popular music scholar Rietveld writes: '[This version] was pressed on a maxi-single, on which the grooves are further apart than on a conventional single or even an album. When nine minutes of music are placed on twelve inches, there is considerably more space to showcase the dynamics of the tracks. This brought a significant improvement in sound quality, allowing in particular a massive emphasis on bass, because for that you need a wide groove (as clearly visible under a magnifying glass). As a consequence Gibbons was able to foreground the bass, kick drum, and the rest of the rhythm section, making the track sound much better on a club's big sound system.'[181]

The volume of the 12-inch single and the 7-inch single differ only slightly. However, the spectrum of the 12-inch single is much broader. This is very noticeable in the treble: especially the hi-hat used in the production as well as the tambourine is more present or better audible on the 12-inch single. With regard to the hi-hat and tambourine, the mastering of the British 7-inch single and that of the US 7-inch single also differ: the mastering of the UK single attempted to give the hi-hat and tambourine greater presence by distorting them, which in turn affected the dynamics of the release. On the 12-inch single, the electric bass and bass drum, respectively, are more transparent and distinguishable. Also, the stereo image was exploited more there. The specific physics of the 12-inch single were used in the mastering in this case to produce a certain overall sound or for sharper rhythmic accentuation and differentiation of the percussion instruments. The specific sound of the 12-inch single here thus encompasses both an accentuated rhythm in the highs through hi-hat or tambourine sounds, and a more transparent resolution in the basses. This resolution in the basses contributes to the fact that the bass drum, after its rhythm had experienced fixation in the four-to-the-floor beat, increasingly becomes the focus of a differentiated sound design in the shape of its sound.[182]

Musicologist Charles Kronengold has noted that the sound of the bass drum in disco productions and releases has become the result of an extensive design process due to conventionalization of the bass drum pattern: 'Because conventions like four-on-the-floor are accepted without a fuss in disco, musicians can focus on how a convention is being used.'[183] For example, the bass drum in *Hit and Run* by Loleatta Holloway (Goldmine, United States, 1977) emphasizes the main two-measure riff: 'Because the song's main two-measure riff attacks the on-beats for the first six beats in succession, four-on-the-floor here seems to power this riff and thereby the whole arrangement.'[184] Thus, in Eurodisco productions, the bass drum is 'the clock or regulator to which the texture's human elements cohere'.[185] In *Keep on Dancing* by Gary's Gang (SAM, United States, 1978), 'the quality of percussion sounds becomes important, and we start to hear the bass-drum pattern partly as an assertion of the song's high production values'.[186] The sound of the bass drum, which Jimmy Simpson had designed in his remix for the Ashford & Simpson production *Found a Cure* (Warner, United States, 1979), in turn became a point of reference for other remixers such as John Luongo.[187] If bass drums are only audible as a lower click – as on the early 7-inch single releases of the disco mixes, for example – then such a design of the bass drum sound and thus such a treatment of a standardized bass drum pattern is not possible.

In contrast to disco 12-inch singles like *Ten Per Cent*, the early Chicago house 12-inch singles, especially those of the Trax Records label, which was founded in 1984, are not characterized by differentiated and professional mastering. This was mainly due to the fact that the only remaining record pressing plant in Chicago – the CD had been introduced in 1982 – was owned by Trax's co-founder Larry Sherman. Sherman did not attach great importance to the sound of the records released by Trax. A speedy and inexpensive release was the order of the day. This was not only true of Trax but also of Trax's competitor DJ International: 'Rocky Jones, head of the biggest house label, DJ International, says his 12-inch singles cost an average of $2,000 to make. One, Tyree's "I Fear the Night", which came out on his Underground affiliate, cost only $50 dollars.'[188]

Chicago house was characterized by recycling at several levels. First, most of the analogue synthesizers and programmable drum machines – such as the devices from the Japanese company Roland, especially the bass-synthesizer TB-303 and the rhythm machine TR-808 that soon achieved cult status – were used by early house producers and could be purchased extremely cheaply in second-hand stores after the introduction of the first digital synthesizer – the Yamaha DX-7.[189] Farley 'Jackmaster' Funk used a TR-808 in his radio show with the DJ team Hot Mix 5, for instance, and also integrated it into his DJ sets.[190] By contrast, synthesizers were rarely used in US disco productions. They rather shaped the sound of Eurodisco, such as Donna Summer's *I Feel Love* (Casablanca, United States, 1977), as well as European synthesizer music and New Wave, which in turn became important templates for Chicago house productions. Second, not only machines and instruments used to produce sound were recycled, but also melodies, bass lines and rhythms that entered early Chicago house productions. In some cases, bass lines from disco records were reprogrammed and replayed on an experimental basis or varied in these experiments.[191] There are numerous examples of re-recording as a practice in Chicago house: the house production with the perky title *You Can't Hide from Your Butt* by DJ Sneak recycles the disco hit *You Can't Hide from Yourself* by Teddy Pendergrass (PIR, United States, 1977). However, DJ Sneak's production is not a cover version. It contains various samples from Pendergrass's production. Moreover, it seems that DJ Sneak also re-recorded parts of *You Can't Hide from Yourself* with his rather low-tech set-up in a slightly different way. Third, recycling became a topic for Chicago house regarding the pressing of 12-inch singles. Record label boss and pressing plant owner Sherman allowed such recycling, which early house producers like Jesse Saunders did on a sonic level by simply replaying and recombining parts of disco productions for their productions, to take place on the level of record production: 'Sherman would go and buy records that had been pressed and manufactured that didn't sell – he'd go out and buy 'em for, like nothing, for a penny, two, two cents on the dollar or whatever. Then he'd grind 'em up and he'd reprocess them again in new record, which is why his records always had the opos, and they weren't very well pressed and they would warp and everything, because it wasn't virgin vinyl, you know.'[192] We can add here, that how the releases sounded was not Sherman's focus. Record stores such as Importes Etc. in Chicago received many complaints about the poor sonic quality of Sherman's records.[193] In one of the first journalistic portraits of Chicago's house scene published in the US magazine *Spin* in 1986, Barry Walters lists various tracks and concludes about their sound: 'These songs come on 12-inch singles (there are no house albums) in multiple versions called the House Mix, the Fierce Mix, the "Jack for Daze" mix, the a capella, The Houseapella, and the Dickapella mix.'[194] Walters then continues with a description of the 'original sound' of these records: 'Many house pressings are just like authentic Jamaican reggae rockers: they often snap, crackle, and pop louder than the percussion.'[195] Thus, recycling became audible also at this level.

Unlike disco productions, which were produced in professional recording studios with professional musicians – various labels even had their own orchestras, for example, the label Salsoul operated the Salsoul Orchestra – house was produced in home studios: Thus, the term 'house' can also be understood in this sense.[196] At the end of the 1970s, the Japanese company TASCAM launched a so-called Portastudio, a multitrack cassette recorder. These devices, as well as reel-to-reel tape machines, quickly gained importance in the emerging house culture. Producers made tapes at home, which then had to be mastered to record before being released. Lawrence points out that tape led a parallel existence alongside vinyl in early Chicago house: 'It was quite normal for a producer to lay down a track, distribute it on tape, and see it pressed up on vinyl several months later.'[197] Although Chicago house tracks were ultimately released as 12-inch singles, tapes produced in home studios could be tested in clubs before release. This distribution option required close contact between producers and DJs. In contrast to disco culture, this relationship in Chicago house was not necessarily mediated by record companies,[198] and accordingly depended on a different sound carrier format.

The track that was later released as *Acid Tracks* (Trax TX142A, United States, 1986), for instance, circulated in a pre-release version on cassette, and was tested by DJ Ron Hardy in the club Music Box.[199] Earl Smith, Herbert Jackson, and Nathaniel Pierre Jones, who went by the pseudonyms 'Spanky', 'Herb J.' and 'DJ Pierre', respectively, and who can be thought of as avid visitors to the Music Box and listeners to the Hot Mix 5 radio show – an important inspiration for many early house DJs and producers in Chicago – rather than music producers in a professional sense, had produced a cassette titled *In Your Mind*.[200] The Music Box was the place where the production should work. *In Your Mind* had emerged from the Music Box, and the perception of Smith, Jackson and Jones was shaped by the venue: 'We were already attuned – Ron Hardy has trained our minds – so the bass [the Roland TB-303] didn't sound like noise. It sounded like something you could dance to.'[201] Only after the piece had generated euphoric reactions in the Music Box, it was produced again – this time together with Marshall Jefferson, who had close contact with Trax Records. The new production was then finally released on 12-inch single by Larry Sherman.[202] Productions were thus first tested on cassette in the club before they were released as 12-inch singles. DJs not only played cassettes and tapes from other producers, they also made new mixes on tape themselves and incorporated these in their sets.[203] Tape was important for house music. Chicago DJ Ron Hardy integrated tapes from amateurs in his sets.[204] Tape was also important for the 'development of house music aesthetics' as well as for remembering it.[205] DJ sets were recorded on tape[206] and DJs not only mixed records, but also tapes. Frankie Knuckles used reel-to-reel tapes for the production as well as for the presentation of his own remixes.[207] 'Many local Chicago hits from the mid-1980s circulated first on cassette tapes before getting commercial releases on the city's burgeoning new indie labels.'[208] 'These revelatory opportunities to beta test may have inspired artists to tweak and adjust their compositions to better serve Chicago's dance floors prior to releasing them to the public on commercial 12″ singles.'[209]

In Detroit techno, too, tapes produced in the living room were the output of the first producers. However, in Detroit the mastering process soon moved more into focus in its productive function. As already mentioned, numerous Detroit releases were mastered by Ron Murphy. Murphy – a generation older than the 'Belleville Three'[210] and with 'side parting and moustache embodied the typical old-school businessman'[211] – had already gained considerable experience as a sound engineer in the music business.[212] In 1989, he and a business partner opened the record store National Sound Corporation. Part of the store included a disc-cutting lathe.[213] On this machine, Murphy mastered productions by Juan Atkins and Derrick May. Murphy adapted the productions to professional standards, also by listening again with a distanced ear to the home productions, to which the producers had often lost all distance.

Andreas Lubich points out differences between the hearing of the engineer and the hearing of the musician: 'A mastering engineer hears music differently than musicians, more analytically, and can make the final processing better and more effective.'[214] Mastering is especially important in relation to the 'classical one-man home recording approach' that is also so characteristic of house and techno producers.[215] In this respect, Murphy not only acted as a specialized engineer for the early techno producers, but as a consultant as well: 'When I started with NSC and was just slowly building up a business, I had quite a lot of time, which I then took to work with the guys on their tracks. In the early days, we would sometimes sit in my studio for a whole day until we had a result that was acceptable. They mostly just recorded their stuff on tape at home and the quality was really lousy.'[216]

Fairly soon Murphy closed the record store, focused only on mastering, and had to rename his micro-business Sound Enterprises after legal disputes. In 2004, he moved his studio from Detroit to Wayne, Michigan. In addition to Murphy's mastering studio, various micro-enterprises benefitted from the boom in electronic dance music from Detroit – for example, the Archer Record Pressing Plant.[217] Thus, a 'reindustrialization of at least one local business'[218] occurred at the local level.

Murphy made sure that the records he mastered would be associated with his studio: he carved 'NSC' in large letters in the area of the run-out groove. Murphy radically exploited the physics of the record in his mastering. He not only carved alphabetical codes on records, but also cut endless grooves or loops in the vinyl,[219] produced records that ran from the inside to the outside,[220] and records that had double grooves.[221] Murphy thus used the physics of the record to create a sound event that would not have been possible on CD, for example. Eshun identifies a productive dissonance in these practices: 'UR's and Jeff Mills's 12s play from the runout to the beginning of the vinyl, starting where the ordinary 12 ends, finishing where the needle usually launches itself. By switching direction to play forward from the end, the reverse-mastered 12 provokes acute cognitive dissonance.'[222] He specifies this dissonance as the inversion of the 'hifi consciousness inside out'[223] and with the appropriation of the disc cutting lathe.

In the meantime, there are various myths about the sound of Murphy's mastered records. One of the early historiographers of Detroit techno, Dan Sicko, for example, writes with regard to NSC mastering that it had a constitutive function for Detroit techno: 'This sound – the minute difference in the way its records are mastered – may be part of the Detroit techno mystique.'[224] Music journalist Julian Weber also takes the same line in his obituary for Murphy, who died in 2008, in which he enthuses about his 'warm' and 'dynamic' sound: 'With warmth and dynamics in his sound, Murphy also took the cliché of the cold, technological sound of electronic dance music ad absurdum. Detroit techno records are instead pulsating tools, raw, unfinished, but endowed with speaker-busting power.'[225]

The difference that Murphy's mastering made on a sonic level correlates to a specific technology. For record cutting, Murphy used very specialized equipment. Disc-cutting lathes from the Berlin-based company Neumann – such as the VMS 70 or the VMS 80 – had become the worldwide standard.[226] Nevertheless, Murphy increasingly relied on analogue, that is here, non-computer controlled, American equipment for cutting 12-inch singles: a record-cutting machine built around 1940 by the manufacturer Scully was the technological centre of his studio.[227] Murphy modified this machine several times, equipping it with a new cutting head and a new cutting amplifier, for example.

Murphy not only mastered records for Detroit's techno producers, but also productions that appeared on labels in Germany such as the Berlin-based dub techno label Basic Channel. The mastering studio Dubplates & Mastering, which opened in Berlin in 1995 and mainly masters electronic dance music on a Neumann VMS 70, was in close contact with Murphy.[228] An axis between Berlin and Detroit that was so significant for the second generation of Detroit techno producers – after the Belleville Three[229] – was not only mediated through clubs like Tresor, labels like Tresor Records, Basic Channel, Rhythm & Sound and Chain Reaction, and record stores like Hardwax, but also through Ron Murphy's mastering studio.

A loud record cut – made possible by the 12-inch single – was one motivation of NSC mastering: 'We wanted to have the absolute widest lpi (lines per inch). I had about 60 lpi in mind, which gave us a track length of about five minutes at a good volume and with passable bass.'[230] In this context, a loud record cut is not only motivated by the greater volume of the release, but it also allows for new sounds unheard during production. A record that is cut quietly makes little sonic impact. The louder a record is cut, the more it develops a life of its own. For example, a bass line that sounds rather restrained during music production can sound much more brutal when cut loudly, because it is enriched with harmonics during the cut. A louder record cut, therefore, does not simply result in sounds which already existed before mastering being made louder. Steve Beckett – one of the founders of the British label Warp Records – reports that it was only in mastering that loud record cutting of the label's releases created certain distorted bass sounds.[231] The disc cutting machine then not only transforms or transfers sound, but also becomes a active mediator and creates sounds that were not heard previously. This machine and the 12-inch single co-constituted techno as music.

5

Sound system listening: Histories, enhanced disco sound, listening techniques

Sound system history as sound and music history (and vice versa)

Loudspeaker systems have been crucial for the sound of popular music for a long time. For rock music ever since it was presented at festivals. These festivals began in the 1960s, first in the United States (the 1966 Trips Festival in San Francisco, in 1967 the Monterey International Pop Festival in California, and in 1969 the Woodstock Music and Art Fair in White Lake, Bethel, New York) and shortly thereafter in West Germany (Internationale Essener Songtage in 1968) and in the UK (Isle of Wight Festival in 1968, 1969 and 1970).[1] In Jamaica, sound systems for reggae and dub became must-haves,[2] and even today, electronic dance music in clubs and at festivals relies massively on extremely powerful loudspeaker systems.[3] Actually, the first loudspeaker systems were installed much earlier and were used primarily for amplifying speaking voices and sometimes for the transmission of music: in the United States since 1919; in Germany a couple of years later.[4] With the advent of the talkies in the late 1920s, increasingly complex loudspeaker systems found their way into cinemas; the forerunners of cinema sound systems such as Fantasound (1940), CinemaScope (1953), Sensurround (1974), Dolby Stereo (1975), Dolby Digital (1992), Digital Theater Systems (1993) and Sony Dynamic Digital Sound (1993).[5] Thus it took several decades before such complex loudspeaker systems would decisively condition the development of popular music forms.

Pre- and early history of sound systems

Yet not only music history is conditioned by media history – not only the history of music forms such as rock and reggae, dub, and electronic dance music (EDM) is conditioned by loudspeaker systems. The development of media technologies such as loudspeaker systems is also conditioned by the history of music and sound. This means that the powerful systems comprising microphones, massive loudspeakers and amplifiers as they have emerged since the 1910s to address sonically masses of people have a musical and a sonic prehistory. This prehistory has anticipated, possibly even challenged, the invention of such technologies. Acoustic experiments on 'amplification method[s]'[6] are already found in the early modern period, as well as phantasms and techno-utopias like those by the English statesman and philosopher Francis Bacon (1561–1626) and the German Jesuit Athanasius Kircher (1602–80). Bacon and Kircher imagined acoustic amplifier ensembles and developed sound volume not as an aesthetic, but primarily as a 'political category'.[7] The prehistory of electronic amplification gained massive momentum in the nineteenth century. In this century, for instance – if we follow Friedrich Kittler's bold thoughts on the subject – it integrates Richard Wagner and the Bayreuth Festival Hall on the Green Hill, where an amplification system *avant la lettre* was installed.[8] In a quest for musical 'monumentality'[9] and sonic 'megaphonics',[10] the prehistory of powerful loudspeaker systems relied on amplification by mechanical resonators, which were also in use at mass gatherings and in large concert halls. Then, the electrification of acoustics around 1900[11] conditioned the development of early electronic musical instruments and their connection to the loudspeaker systems of the 1920s and 1930s.

In addition, the development of loudspeaker systems is conditioned by the musical history of large venues and spaces as well as by the history of the concert. In contrast to the intimate tactility of radio, which was more involved with domestic space and the private sphere, sound reinforcement by loudspeaker systems targeted semi-public and public spaces. They thus echoed the '"large-scale concerts" or "mass concerts"' of the nineteenth century, for example, featuring military bands, such as the event in Munich in 1888 'with fireworks and other attractions for many thousands of listeners'.[12] Large orchestras also played 'people's concerts' at large venues; for example, in 1861 an orchestra of 101 musicians played at the Cirque Napoléon in Paris which had an auditorium capacity of 5,000 seats.[13] In New York, the first Madison Square Garden venue opened in 1879. In the early twentieth century, new gigantic halls were opened in Germany, such as the Frankfurt Festhalle, where symphony concerts for up to 15,000 people took place.[14] The concert – as a form or as a framework in which music is presented and performed – began to play a role in the development of popular music as early as the nineteenth century.[15] In the second half of the twentieth century, the popular music concert took place in even larger spaces, up to and including sports stadiums.

In popular music studies, the significance of loudspeaker systems for concerts and performances has at best received only scant attention so far.[16] As Philip Auslander has famously demonstrated, concepts such as 'performance' and also 'performance practice' need to be fundamentally rethought in relation to multi-media pop and rock concerts.[17] To describe popular music events, terms such as 'gig', 'tour' and 'festival' are more likely to be found, as well as terms that seem to only present tautologies but actually refer to the fundamental changes in 'performance in a mediatized culture':[18] 'live concert' or 'live performance'.[19] Further, the history of loudspeaker systems, which became a part of concerts and performances as early as the 1920s and 1930s, has been poorly studied so far.[20] Certainly, there were constant complaints from some contemporaries in those decades about increasing volume levels; for example, in connection with the then new jazz. Notwithstanding, a musical history of loudspeaker systems remains a desideratum of research.[21]

In terms of the history of media technologies, sound systems are conditioned by large loudspeakers, electronic tube sound amplifiers and microphones that integrate and interconnect these as their constituent parts. From the perspective of sound studies, this media history can be developed through the concept of 'transduction'.[22] The transduction of sound acquired a new specificity at the latest in the 1920s through electronic amplification: sound was electrified, that is, converted into electricity (via microphones), it could be amplified (via tube amplifiers) and then once again converted into sound (via loudspeakers). Although the conversion of sound into electricity had already been accomplished by the telephone, the amplification of electricity by tube amplifiers was a novelty. This also established a dichotomy between 'acoustic' and 'electric', 'which was in part always informed by crude notions of torsion and distortion.'[23] In the 1920s, the electrification of sound was implemented in various media; in sound films, radio, the record and particularly in sound reinforcement.[24] These media all used three technologies that were central to the electrification of sound in the 1920s: the condenser microphone, which converts sound into electricity; the electrodynamic loudspeaker, which converts electricity into sound; and the electron tube, which can amplify currents, that is, also sounds converted into electricity.

The first PA loudspeaker systems in the modern sense were presented to the public (which they aimed to address) in the late 1910s. By 1920, large corporations such as AT&T in the United States and Siemens & Halske in Germany had embarked on the development of PA systems. In the first half of the 1920s, both of these corporations launched loudspeaker systems on the market, which was established by the middle of that decade. However, the systems not only addressed an audience, but they also generated one. Such systems became technically possible due to the electronification of sound, and thus through electroacoustics that emerged in the nineteenth century, through technical forms of sound transmission as in the telegraph and the telephone, and above all by the technical sound amplification made possible by the triode patented by Lee de Forest in 1906 and Robert von Lieben's amplifier tube patented the same year.[25] These tubes enabled the electric current to be controlled, in the combination not only of electricity and acoustics, but of electronics and acoustics as well. Although the history of the connection between sound and electricity is ultimately transnational,[26] there were nevertheless centres where this connection was actively promoted. One of these was the US electrical giant AT&T. From 1913, after AT&T had acquired patent rights to the vacuum tube from the inventor de Forest, its companies Bell Laboratories and Western Electric had pushed ahead with research on electronic sound amplification through developing the triode further.[27] The combination of electricity and sound at AT&T was primarily in the context of telephony development and in the context of developing microphones and loudspeakers specifically for the telephone. The telephone industry played a pioneering role from which other industries benefitted, such as the film industry: 'The sciences and techniques, which have contributed to the constant progress of telephony, had by-products which culminated in 1926 in sound motion pictures.'[28] Another by-product was the electrification of sound recording and the reproduction of music.[29] In Germany, Siemens & Halske was instrumental in the electrification of sound. The company's founder, Werner von Siemens, had already presented research on the electromagnetic telegraph in the mid-nineteenth century; England set up a telegraph network in the second half of the nineteenth century which connected up its world empire.[30] Electrification of sound through electroacoustic technologies was a prerequisite that made three media possible in the 1920s: the talkies, the electrified gramophone and the radio.[31] Electrified sound is thus an entity that becomes tangible in a media-specific way, but it is not reducible to a specific medium.[32]

The large-scale loudspeakers, microphones and amplifiers that made up such systems made speakers' voices, in particular, audible for crowds of thousands of people. However, such systems, which I shall discuss in more detail in the course of this chapter, could also amplify music and were soon used at concerts. Whereas the amplifier tube around 1910 initially served 'exclusively to increase the transmission *distance*, not the sound *volume*',[33] from the second half of the 1910s it was also used to produce decidedly loud sounds. Systems for mass sound reinforcement, in contrast to the radio or the gramophone, aimed at increasing the volume of sound. Karl-Heinz Göttert, in his opulent history of the voice, has pointed out that a history of the loudspeaker has been increasingly studied in the context of the history of radio.[34] Göttert demonstrates, with regard to the use of loudspeakers at political events in the late 1910s and 1920s, that the history of the loudspeaker in this context was quite different from that in the context of radio. The key difference between these two histories of the loudspeaker is volume. Radio was initially listened to over headphones, and the volume of the early radio set equipped with a loudspeaker was a tempered one. In contrast, PA systems were aimed at 'speech amplification of mass addresses',[35] as well as at 'the communication of sports and other news to a large audience, for announcing trains, etc.'[36] and for church events (Cologne Cathedral got a PA system in 1927)[37] where listeners were present en masse. Göttert points out that although such systems received little attention in contemporary press reports, the 'installation of large loudspeakers'[38] continued apace.

Music was also transmitted and amplified by these installations. At the opening of the Deutsches Museum in Munich in 1925, a PA system was used to broadcast and amplify both speeches and musical performances – the sounds of an organ, a string and vocal quartet, a wind ensemble and a concert grand piano.[39] However, an aesthetic of volume or loudness did not play a role at the opening of the Deutsches Museum. Rather, the technicians of Siemens & Halske, who installed the system, were concerned with a 'sound reproduction true to tone by means of loudspeakers'.[40] Intrinsic sounds and aesthetic interventions of the technology – such as echoes, feedback, the divergence of acoustic and visual sources – were simply considered interference.

Without explicitly *loud* loudspeakers, the new volumes made possible by the amplifier tube remained theoretical musings at best. When Kittler points out that de Forest first 'fed the tube back to itself'[41] in 1910, that is, turned the tube into an oscillator, this means that so-called over one amplification became possible on 'a technically secure basis'.[42] However, it was not yet given that 'electric tube circuits [could] oscillate or swing up until damage occurs, until we end up at the auditory decibel pain threshold'.[43] Only through loud speakers was it possible to experience empirically that 'every echo comes back louder than its original'.[44]

We first find traces of the relevance of electronic amplification in the history of music and sound in the 1920s and 1930s. Amplification varied considerably, depending on whether it was part of the radio or of a sound system, and depending on the types of loudspeakers that were connected. Thus, electronic amplification did not necessarily have anything to do with loud sounds, but could be used – as in the case of early radio – to convey and transmit sound over long distances effectively. By contrast, electrical amplification in sound reinforcement systems also accentuated an increase in range and sound transmission, but this was done on the basis of changing the volume of sound – and this change correlated emphatically with an aesthetic dimension. Such an accentuation of volume played a role more in PA systems than in radio. Radio loudspeakers primarily played sounds in the private domestic context, but mass sound systems played sounds to subjects who were more concerned with decentring than with intimacy. At Siemens & Halske, the difference between quiet loudspeakers and loud loudspeakers was marked by the term 'large loudspeakers' [*Großlautsprecher*] in the 1920s.[45] The company had conducted research on such large loudspeakers since 1920,[46] and then in 1924 introduced the 'Blatthaller', an electrodynamic loud loudspeaker developed by Hans Riegger.[47] The company soon followed up with a larger model, the Large or Giant Blatthaller. For this last model, sound transmission was again relevant, but in a completely different sense than that for radio: 'With the largest model, distances of several kilometers were bridged in suitable weather conditions.'[48] In terms of media history, therefore, the 'leap into public address systems' had been taken in Germany by 1924 at the latest with the presentation of these large loudspeakers;[49] loudspeakers whose purpose was to provide sound to masses of people who were physically co-present.

The media aesthetics sounds of the loudspeaker include crooning voices, sounds of early avant-gardist electric and electronic instruments, and sounds resulting from experiments with recording and transmission technology. For example, conductor Leopold Stokowski's collaboration with Bell Laboratories from 1930 to 1940 resulted in 'enhanced music'.[50] The avant-garde's experiments with electricity and loudspeakers led to new musical instruments such as the Trautonium and the Theremin. Leon Theremin (1896–1983), for example, had to use loudspeakers at his concert on 27 August 1928 at New York's Lewisohn Stadium for the electric musical instrument he had invented and built.[51] In Germany, so-called electric music also had to rely on loudspeakers and amplification in the 1920s and 1930s, for otherwise nothing would have been heard of the performance given by an 'electric orchestra' at the Radio Exhibition in Berlin in 1933.[52] Amplifiers and PA systems thus became an 'integral part of musical performance'[53] not first in the 1950s, but as early as two decades earlier.[54]

It is only in recent years that sound systems have been studied in musicology and sound studies.[55] Musicologist Kyle Devine has emphasized that it is one of the 'mythologies of rock' that the loudspeaker first became culturally significant in the 1950s as part of rock 'n' roll.[56] In connection with his music and cultural history of loudness, Devine looked at the early history of the loudspeaker from 1915 to 1940. Already in this period, the loudspeaker had developed from being an 'incredible novelty' to a 'predictable ubiquity',[57] and in the 1930s the loudspeaker was already ubiquitous in music culture.[58] According to Devine, this ubiquity was evidenced by radio, jukeboxes, record players as well as in PA systems, and it correlated with the 'cultural configuration of the acoustic subject'[59] and with listening as a distinctive 'cultural practice'.[60]

Research on sound amplification before 1950 was focused on selected loudspeaker systems: for example, the loudspeaker system that the National Socialists, together with the Telefunken company, had installed on the *Reichssportfeld* [Imperial Sports Field], which was built for the 1936 Summer Olympics in Berlin to provide sound reinforcement for more than 400,000 people,[61] and the loudspeaker system of the Radio City Music Hall, which opened in New York City in 1932.[62] As Peter Doyle underlines, Emily Thompson has pointed out in her study of the amplified sound of the Radio City Music Hall that the installation of loudspeaker systems in concert halls, theatres and performance halls had proceeded 'relatively "behind-the-scenes"'.[63] Relatively, according to Doyle, compared to the much more explicit use of amplifiers in sound films, radio and record players that were accompanied by flashy advertising campaigns.[64] Thompson concludes that the Radio City Music Hall's loudspeaker system, which went into operation in New York in 1932, was ignored by the listener with a certain matter-of-factness and, to that extent, would have generated little controversy: 'Radio City Music Hall was wired for sound, and no one seemed to mind.'[65] Thompson attributes this to a certain cultural habituation effect. In the course of the 1920s, loudspeaker listening had become commonplace due to the radio, the electric record player and the sound film. In addition, a 'modern sound' that was characterized by directness and little reverberation was achieved by new acoustic damping materials and/or new architecture designed to be reverberation-free.[66] In the United States, such architecture was found in the Eastman Theatre in Rochester, New York, built in 1923, in which massive amounts of damping material was used, as well as in the Hollywood Bowl in California.[67] Thompson refers to such spaces as 'modern auditoriums'.[68] In her view, sound amplification by loudspeaker systems in the late 1920s and 1930s in the United States is not characterized by making loud sounds louder, but by making quiet or relatively quiet sounds audible. Otherwise, the installation of loudspeaker systems in entertainment venues in the United States would not have attracted such little notice.

That loudspeaker systems were only perceived when they were switched off was also reported by Hans Gerdien in 1926 for systems that had been installed in Germany. At the conference of the *Funktechnischer Verein* [Radio Technical Association] in Berlin's Konzerthaus in 1925, a Siemens & Halske system had been installed that initially appeared to be inaudible to the conductor: 'The conductor and his orchestra had the impression that nothing at all was added to their performances by the loudspeaker system. Of course, it was very easy to convince them otherwise by temporarily switching off the loudspeakers. Immediately the orchestral music, which had previously been quite full, became thin and unimpressive, as though it were being performed by a much weaker ensemble.'[69] Here, too, amplification systems, if they had to be used, were best not heard during performances, especially of concert hall music. Mediatized sound was a focal point for conflict. Thus, also when sound films were introduced in Germany, reservations were voiced about whether the ears of local audiences would be able to cope with mediatized sound: Ernst Hugo Correll, production director at UFA (Universum-Film AG), suggested that mediatized, so-called mechanical sound might not go down well in Germany: 'In particular, there was a widespread view that audiences in Germany, whose ears are not as accustomed to the reproduction of mechanical music as are American audiences, who for some time have entertained themselves to a more extended extent with radio screenings, would not enjoy mechanical music in the cinemas.'[70]

Even before 1950, loudspeakers, microphones and amplifiers played out in different discourses. Discourses that would continue to be perpetuated after 1950. Loudspeakers, for example, were articulated in subjects such as noise, rationalization, aesthetics and community. Within the discourse of rationalization, a concept of technology once again arose that understood technology as an instrument of rationalization, especially as an instrument for the rationalization of labour. From this perspective, utilizing loudspeakers primarily put musicians out of work because technically amplified smaller bands could play larger halls, for example, and expensive big bands could be replaced by smaller ensembles.[71] However, the '"all electric" small group'[72] that emerged in the late 1950s and that played a crucial role in the development of popular music forms certainly cannot be explained solely as part of a discourse of rationalization. Such examples, however, should not obscure the fact that this discourse has persistently accompanied the history of the loudspeaker. For example, the introduction of the loudspeaker in cinemas in the 1920s was already associated with rising unemployment: 'By the summer of 1929, the first major movie theaters had already disbanded their orchestras. By June 1930, 5000 cinema musicians had been laid off in Berlin alone.'[73] However, rationalization had already been initiated by the advent of organs and record players in cinemas. By contrast, a media-aesthetic discourse pointed to aesthetic changes in sound brought about by loudspeakers. Devine sums up both discourses: 'In the end, there was truth to both sides of the argument: sound systems did facilitate a shift from the semi-orchestral backing of big bands to smaller ensembles, and they also facilitated new musical tones and new roles for voices and musical instruments. The controversy of the loudspeaker thus continued.'[74]

In addition to the discourses of rationalization and aesthetics, the use of loudspeakers and amplifiers fuelled the conflict over 'noise' and 'noise control' that had been simmering in the early twentieth century.[75] Amplification technology also made it possible to simply drown out unwanted sounds. At the 1936 radio exhibition in Berlin, for example, a 'large tone organ' [*Großtonorgel*] powered by two 200-watt amplifiers was used. Amplification had also become necessary because of 'the noise in the exhibition hall.'[76] Finally, the loudspeaker was involved in the formation of new acoustic communities in the 1920s and 1930s. PA systems were used in places such as schools, factories and stadiums, as well as in politics. The loudspeaker had resulted in an 'expansion of the acoustic community', even contributing to 'nation building',[77] but it also led to the formation of a fascist 'Volksgemeinschaft'.[78] The PA community became an exceedingly ambivalent entity. The history of music and sound conditioned the development of loudspeaker systems as a listening device and the history of this listening device – vice versa – propelled the history of sound and music.

Popular music's sound systems: Rock and reggae

Loudspeaker systems began to be a part of popular music in the 1950s. In the late 1960s, a specific 'live sound industry' emerged in the United States, geared to the needs of popular music.[79] An important figure in the live sound industry was Bill Hanley, who founded Hanley Sound Inc. on the US East Coast in Meford, Massachusetts, in 1954, which specialized particularly in festival sound in the 1960s.[80] Hanley's company provided sound at the Newport Folk Festival, including in 1965 when Bob Dylan performed there with an electric guitar;[81] at the second Beatles performance at Shea Stadium in Queens, New York, in 1966;[82] at rock promoter Bill Graham's Fillmore East;[83] at the Woodstock Music and Art Fair in Bethel, New York in 1969[84] and also at anti-Vietnam War demonstrations.[85] Hanley did not develop new components, but reconfigured existing ones: 'He created systems of sound based on existing recording, cinema, and high-fidelity technologies.'[86] He established some practices and configurations that later became standards, such as: 'the introduction of large voice of the theater cinema speakers that were often raised into the air'; 'the use of construction-grade scaffolding for speaker tower deployment'; 'front of house (FOH) sound engineer and sound console positioning'; 'the construction, use, and placement of footlight stage monitor systems'; and 'the deployment of large sound systems with bi-amplification, and passive crossover.'[87]

We can find signs of the change of the aesthetic status of PA systems in music performances in relation to 1950s rock 'n' roll, where the PA system no longer merely served as 'amplification apparatus ... that provides small ensembles and instruments such as the double bass or the singing voice with the necessary volume in the problematic acoustic environment of the dance hall.'[88] Rather, PA systems went from being amplification devices to aids 'for the presentation of a studio production that is tuned to the conditions of loudspeaker reproduction.'[89] Loudspeaker reproduction, of course, not only includes certain artificial sound worlds produced in the studio, but also produces a desire for loudness or loud music, which had been consciously sought in the perception of some popular forms of music since 1950 – such as rock 'n' roll, rock music, or even electronic dance music. Paul Théberge writes with regard to the connection between music and amplification: 'It is only through the application of electrical amplification to loudspeakers (or headphones) that both public and private spaces can be invested with a musical intensity unprecedented in cultural history.'[90] Certain installations – such as the 'Wall of Sound' system Owsley Stanley developed with Dan Healy for the West Coast rock band Grateful Dead or the Azimuth coordinator used by Pink Floyd – attained legendary status.[91] Tom Wolfe has described the Grateful Dead's equipment in the late 1960s quite impressively: 'He [Owsley Stanley] started buying the Dead equipment such as no rock 'n' roll band ever had before .... The sound went down so many microphones and hooked through so many mixers and variable lags and blew up in so many amplifiers and rolled around in so many speakers and fed back down so many microphones, it came on like a chemical refinery.'[92] Grateful Dead still saw themselves primarily as a live band, who, after the popularization of the compact cassette, encouraged their fans to record their concerts and even set up 'taping areas' for this purpose.[93] Ultimately, however, loudspeaker systems also represent a response to the fact that, on the one hand, the vinyl record had become the norm[94] – musicians then tried to sound live 'like on the record', which in turn was optimized for loudspeaker reproduction – and, on the other hand, that an appetite for volume was technically constituted and tapped into.

Loudspeaker systems via which records were played in (semi-)public spaces then also appeared in the 1950s in the context of record hops. Such systems were not very successful in the 1950s and 1960s, even though they exceeded the performance of a jukebox many times over and could be used more flexibly: 'In the 1950s, record playback technology was not able to fill a large ballroom with high fidelity sound. Even in the early 1960s, few discotheques could provide all-around sound, highs or lows, or thumping bass.'[95] This changed, as we will see soon, in the 1970s with sound systems that were especially designed for discos.

The sound systems in Jamaica, as they emerged after the Second World War, were also places where records were played in public spaces over loudspeaker systems. In dancehall, dub and reggae culture, the term 'sound system' not only refers to a technological system, but also to a 'mobile entertainment collective'[96] in which music was played from records: 'From the 1950s onward, most Kingstonians enjoyed music via these sound systems: mobile outfits playing recorded music in dancehalls or outdoor clearings, which emerged as a more viable economic alternative to the large dance bands that they rapidly replaced.'[97] In the 1950s, the technologies of the sound systems were very modest: their output was in the lower two-digit watt range. Over the decades, however, systems emerged that were upgraded by local technicians to 'sonic powerhouses capable of delivering tens of thousands of watts of power'.[98] The musicologist Michael Veal sees the dub mixes of the 1970s as directly related to these sound systems. The mixes were not produced for home use, but for using on these systems. Producer, DJ and singer Michael Campbell aka Mikey Dread makes it clear how strongly the sound of dub depends on the technology through which it is heard: 'When you listen to a dub at your house, it sounds different than when you go to a Jamaican dance where they string up a series of maybe half a dozen double-sixteen or double-eighteen-inch woofers, and you have some horns playing midrange and some tweeters playing the top end. It sounds different outdoors than you can ever imagine it indoors, listening to a headphone or listening to a little boombox or in your car. So, the dub has a different dimension that you can't get through the speakers [at home].'[99] Sound systems here became a crucial, even a constitutive part of music.

The cultural studies scholar Julian Henriques coined his already mentioned concept of 'sonic dominance' based on the sound systems as they first emerged in Jamaica and later in England and the United States.[100] He understands the post-colonial sound systems in reggae as an 'experimental apparatus for producing the conditions for sonic dominance.'[101] Thus, the sonic in the sound system comes to the fore via other senses. Situations characterized by a dominance of the sonic would combine power and pleasure: 'The sheer physical force, volume, weight, and mass of it. Sonic dominance is hard, extreme, and excessive. At the same time the sound is also soft and embracing and it makes for an enveloping, immersive and intense experience. The sound pervades, or even invades the body, like smell.'[102] We shall now move from Jamaica to 1970s New York to explore the sonic dominance in the city's emerging disco culture.

Disco's enhanced sound systems

Sonic dominance: Discos and clubs as empires of the senses

Discos and clubs are environments that appeal to all the senses, not just to hearing:[103] 'Multi-pronged and complicated is the disco because it's more than a "sound". It's a total entertainment show, a bewildering whole of laser lights, strobe flashes, luminous floors, street glitter, phonetically strong music, and an atmospherically charged space – in short, an AMBIENCE whose appeal lies precisely in its systematicity, its simultaneous embrace of several senses.'[104] Nevertheless, sound and music in discos and clubs do not discreetly drift into ambience as ambient, in order to merge into an 'aesthetics of the background'.[105] In that case music becomes a subtle component of the interior design, a 'surrounding influence'.[106] Nor is the attention paid to music in discos and clubs focused in a form comparable to the concert and directed towards musical works presented in the foreground as aesthetic objects.[107] Although the ambience in discos and clubs is only created through the interaction of the senses, listening is usually accorded an exposed position. The relationship between seeing, hearing, tactility and other senses is shaped differently in specific places of disco and club culture. Clubs represent 'empires of the senses'.[108] In these, synaesthetic harmony does not prevail. Instead, the relationships between the senses are tense. Discos and clubs are places where 'the senses are typically ordered in hierarchies',[109] places where – as sensory studies call it – historically and culturally concrete forms of 'intersensoriality' have developed.[110]

The year 1977 was a transitional year for disco.[111] For one thing, disco became 'visible' in a new place – the cinema. In 1977, *Saturday Night Fever* (directed by John Badham, United States, 1977) premiered. Also, Studio 54 opened in New York and the Warehouse in Chicago. With its interior, probably inspired more by the casinos and entertainment temples of Las Vegas, Studio 54 exposed the visible (even though a complex sound system was included).[112] In turn, an excess of luminous floors, mirrors, balloons and mirror balls had consequences for the dynamics of the dancers: 'Whereas the dance floor was previously experienced as a space of sonic dominance, in which the sound system underpinned a dynamic of integration, experimentation and release, at Studio this became secondary to the theater of a hierarchical door policy that was organized around exclusion and humiliation, as well as a brightly-lit dance floor that prioritised looking above listening, and separation above submersion. ... Whereas the dance floor had previously functioned as an aural space of communal participation and abandonment, it was now reconceived as a visually-driven space of straight seduction and couples dancing, in which participants were focused on their own space and, potentially, the celebrity who might be dancing within their vicinity.'[113] In this description, disco historian Tim Lawrence only seemingly takes up essentializing clichés of a separating, parcelling sense of seeing and a community-creating sense of hearing, as we know them from the tradition of an 'audio-visual litany'.[114] Rather, the forms of seeing and hearing Lawrence describes, their relationship to each other and the understanding of self and world that correlate with them are massively technologically shaped and organized. Lighting and sound systems, possibly supplemented by air conditioning and fog machines, produce discos and clubs as artificial, mediatized environments.

If sound systems dominate these environments, then discos and clubs, as empires of the senses, are subject to 'sonic dominance'.[115] And exactly such a form of dominance, if we believe Lawrence, prevailed in some discos and clubs, but not in others. And it is the latter that Lawrence apparently sees as a problem. The concept of 'sonic dominance' opens a productive and critical space to a long asserted occidental visualism.[116] The fusion experiences of sound and body mediated by reggae sound systems, described by Julian Henriques as almost without alternative, thus certainly harbour a critical potential in this sense: 'There is no escape, not even thinking about it, just being there alive, in and as the excess of sound. Trouser legs flap to the bass line and internal organs resonate to the finely tuned frequencies, as the vibrations of the music excite every cell in your body.'[117]

We can also find spaces of sonic dominance in disco and club culture. In contrast to Studio 54, the Warehouse in Chicago constituted a different relationship between listening and seeing.[118] The DJ Frankie Knuckles describes the Warehouse: 'The room was dark …. People would say it was like climbing down into the pit of hell. People would be afraid when they heard the sound thumping through and saw the number of bodies in there, just completely locked in the music.'[119] Only a few strobe flashes twitched through the room: 'The main dance floor was pitch black, illuminated only by the intermittent pulses of strobe light.'[120] So there were clubs that focused on the sonic and sometimes even fetishized it. Jeremy Gilbert and Ewan Pearson refer here, for example, to the Paradise Garage in New York – its sound system will be discussed in more detail in a moment – or the Ministry of Sound in London.[121] The techno club Tresor, which opened in Berlin in 1991, was also characterized by a certain relationship between hearing and seeing. Dimitri Hegemann remembers the basement dance floor of the Tresor: 'There were hardly any light strobe flashes and a lot of fog. You had your own world to dive into and these incredible, heavy beats above it – that was already an acoustic narcotic. You could really fly away.'[122] Berlin's Berghain techno club has taken the fetishization of the sound system sound a step further since it opened in 2004. The sound system installed in the club, made by the British manufacturer Funktion One, is firmly integrated into the club's image and is a draw for numerous clubbers.

The sound of discos and clubs is co-constituted by the speaker systems installed in them. Such loudspeaker systems do not only play back music, but they also become a constitutive part of the music listened to. This takes place at different levels. First, they not only reproduce the sound of the records heard through them, but are themselves repeatedly sonically activated by producing 'enhanced sound'. Second, specific musical forms emerge in relation to loudspeaker systems: (re)mixes, tracks and DJ sets are particularly noteworthy here. In this context, the development of sonically dominated environments plays together with concrete loudspeaker systems. In the following, I will take a closer look at a disco loudspeaker system and its relationship to 'enhanced sound'.

Enhanced sound

In 1976, the US trade magazine *Billboard* started to organize annual 'disco forums'. In doing so, the magazine was exploring and exploiting the disco boom in the United States. Discussions about the sound of disco's sound systems also took place in these forums. In 1979, *Billboard* arranged a panel that was later summed up by the magazine under the heading 'Pure or "Enhanced" Sound Spurs Spark'.[123] Audio engineers who designed sound systems for discos – a profession which evolved in parallel to the genre's success – participated in that panel, including Alex Rosner and Ed King. The systems' designers discussed the normative question of whether disco's sound systems should reproduce sound, or if such systems should also actively modulate and enhance sound beyond the artistic practices of the disco DJ. Should a sound system (just?) be a form of transparent playback technology or should it also produce new sounds, should it be activated?[124]

On the *Billboard* panel, Rosner, who was already involved in building the sound system for the first proto-disco, David Mancuso's legendary Loft in Manhattan,[125] bemoaned the 'growing use of such sound enhancing aids as dynamic range expanders and boom boxes'.[126] He argued contra 'enhanced sound' and pro 'pure sound', citing the intention of the 'artist and recording engineer'.[127] However, an advocate for the intention of the artist was rather a surprising figure in the economy of 1970s disco culture. For what Rosner did not take into account in his reflections about the need to safeguard a particular musician's intentions was that no autonomous and intentional subject existed who expressed himself or herself in his or her music in the case of the production of disco music, but only an entire network of human and non-human actors who were collaboratively involved in the creation of a disco production. Therefore, this image of individuals who were 'stars' only existed in the context of disco's marketing – and it is also this marketing narrative that Rosner is echoing.

Mancuso also argued that the sound system should be ignored so that the artist's intention can be communicated: 'You don't want to hear the soundsystem. You want to hear the music.'[128] This makes a fundamental distinction between music and sound system, between music and listening device. The sound system should reproduce the music as smoothly as possible. The focus of the disco experience should be the music, not the sound system: 'I've been to clubs with soundsystems where you stand there and your clothes will be dry cleaned. It's like the sound system was more important than the music. It's totally unnecessary. It's not what the artist intended. Once you hear the soundsystem, it's a whole different story.'[129] As just mentioned, however, talk of artists' intentions in relation to disco productions raises more questions than it answers. In order that the sound system can be ignored when listening, a tremendous amount of technical effort is required. Furthermore, Rosner's and Mancuso's statements also indicate *ex negativo* that disco's sound systems are not reducible to the status of playback technologies anymore; that they have been transformed into active listening devices (which both of them bemoaned). As active listening devices, these systems did not pursue the sonic ideals of high fidelity, such as 'transparency' or 'harmonic balance'. Instead of a well-balanced sound, disco systems produce excessive moments of booming bass; and instead of high fidelity, they were more interested in moments of ultra high fidelity and sonic hyper-reality. Thus, the concepts of playback and sound reproduction are also problematized at a discursive level in relation to disco's sound systems.[130]

Rosner, who trained as an electrical engineer, founded the company Rosner Custom Sound Inc. in 1967, which soon began to build sound systems specifically for discos.[131] The sound of disco as a form of music was largely characterized by complex, loud, yet finely tuned loudspeaker systems, such as the ones that Rosner built. In the 1970s and early 1980s, certain sound systems in New York developed into reference systems for disco culture.[132] Two systems seem to have made a particularly strong impression. One was the system in Mancuso's proto-disco Loft, the private party series started in Mancuso's apartment in 1970, which was the 'incubator' for numerous clubs that became central to the development of DJ culture and music forms such as disco and house: the Gallery, SoHo Place, the Paradise Garage and the Warehouse in Chicago.[133] Another venue that became a reference system was the Paradise Garage, a members-only club that opened in SoHo, New York, in 1977.[134]

A lot of things come together in the history of these disco sound systems: hi-fi fans who were enthusiastic about certain types of speakers;[135] dancing crowds of the gay and queer New York subculture; esoteric aftermaths of a more 'psychedelic-adventurous' side of the 1960s counterculture coined by Timothy Leary[136] and their search for a 'psychedelic experience'[137] and for 'sexual energy' generated by the sexual revolution;[138] as well as entrepreneurial characters close to the scene like Rosner and Richard Long. Shortly after the establishment of an industry that built loudspeaker systems for live sound, for example, companies like Hanley Sound, disco sound design companies emerged, for example, Rosner Custom Sound Inc. and Richard Long & Associates. The difference to the live sound industry was that the disco sound systems usually did not amplify performances in the traditional sense, they amplified the sound of records that DJs were spinning. Rosner, Mancuso and Long were all hi-fi fans and were enthusiastic about the Klipschorn, a legendary loudspeaker that was first built in 1946 and is still being produced today. Its designer, Paul Klipsch, wanted 'to reproduce the sound of a live orchestra performance in his living room'.[139] Of course, disco sound systems did not aim at transforming discos into concert halls in the sense of hi-fi 'concert hall realism'. If anything, they should reproduce the sound that had been produced in the studio. With this orientation on the recording studio and the artificial sound worlds created in it, disco sound systems are more in the tradition of that part of the 1950s hi-fi movement that was enthusiastic about sonic hyper-realities.[140] A line of tradition leads from the US middle-class subjects of 1950s hi-fi culture, which indeed integrated moments of the excessive,[141] through sound-mediated psychedelia to the gay and queer disco culture of 1970s New York. In the discos of New York, headphones of hi-fi or rock fans listening to stereo LPs were then exchanged for sound systems. By then it was no longer necessary to go on a sound journey in isolation, but alone as part of a dancing crowd addressed by the sound system. The 'pure' sound faction relied on the disco sound systems to reproduce the sound of releases. The 'enhanced' sound faction counted on the system's own sound as well. Rosner belonged to the first faction; Long to the second: 'Alex's sound was very polished, like going to the theater. Richard's sound was funky and down-home, and bass was always a big component.'[142]

Whereas the systems of the first discos in New York were extended hi-fi home systems, like Mancuso's Loft, the success of disco then led increasingly to the construction of special sound systems that were optimized especially for this context. Sound system designers, such as Bob Casey, Rosner and particularly Long, were instrumental in shaping the sound of New York's discos and they left their mark on the design of club sound systems. Not only the DJ, the selection of records, the (optical) interior design or the audience made a club, but also its sound. This cannot be reduced to the personal styles or record selections of DJs. Rather, the sound is co-created by the sound system. Sound system and DJ then reciprocally constitute themselves. With reference to the system designed by Long in collaboration with an acoustic company for the Paradise Garage in New York,[143] where Larry Levan earned his legendary status as a DJ, Lawrence writes: 'Just as Long's electronics enabled Levan to become the most revered DJ of his time, so Levan's daring talent invariably drew attention to Long's unparalleled equipment.'[144] Thus, the systems Long designed were not necessarily about (high) fidelity to a sound source. Rather, it was a matter of creating a potential for sound to be able to evoke new effects – I shall discuss the texture of these effects in a moment. Especially in the systems designed by Long, moments of excess and escalation took precedence over balance and transparency. Moreover, the disco sound systems like the one Long built gave people something new to listen to: 'When you throw a record like Loleatta Holloway's "Love Sensation" on in that soundsystem you hear some frequencies, you hear some bass frequencies and some mids and highs that you never heard in your life. You hear things in the song that you could never hear again.'[145]

Both Rosner and Long came into contact with Mancuso early on, and both were involved in the original construction and ongoing construction of the system at the Loft.[146] In 1973, Long began hosting parties inspired by the Loft in his Broadway apartment. During these, his apartment became the SoHo Place. Levan played at the SoHo Place over a sound system that Long had assembled and installed himself. For Long, the SoHo Place served as a kind of first showroom for his systems.[147] Long built systems for various clubs that played a central role in the development of disco, house and techno: for example, Studio 54, the Paradise Garage and the Warehouse.[148] But he did not only design systems for discos in the United States; the system of the Dorian Gray in Frankfurt am Main, for example, originates from Long.[149] Outwardly anything but a scene type,[150] Long had worked for General Electric, electronics corporation, before founding his company Richard Long & Associates,[151] which specialized in building sound systems.[152] There was a brief collaboration between Rosner and Long in the early 1970s, the only consequence of which was that further collaborations were ruled out.[153]

The disco sound system is not merely installed in a room, it brings forth a peculiar spatiality, a specific sonic space. The loudspeakers of the sound system span the immersive listening or rather perception space of the disco dance floor. In this way, too, the sound effect described by Rosner with terms like 'engulf[ing]' and 'ensonify[ing]' becomes determinable.[154] Sound in this context is thus not a directional event – as is the case, for example, with a rock concert. The perceptual space produced by the disco sound system is organized horizontally by the boxes positioned separately on this plane, which are set up in the form of a quadrangle around the dance floor, but also vertically. For the organization of the vertical, the decomposition of the frequency spectrum is revisited, and 'high' tones actually come from above: in Rosner's typical disco sound system, the tweeters hung from the ceiling above the dance floor: 'Bursts of high-frequency energy are generated using omnidirectional arrays of high-frequency transducers mounted above the dancers' heads.'[155] The idea of placing the tweeters above the dancers' heads came from Mancuso. In the early 1970s, an initially unenthusiastic Rosner built 'an array of tweeters'[156] at his request that was suspended from the ceiling. Mancuso wanted the speakers to 'face north, south, east, and west.'[157] Thus, a new 'geography of listening'[158] was created: via the placement of the tweeters above the dance floor, sound acquired a peculiar spatial orientation, differentiated not in terms of mono or stereo, but increasingly in terms of frequency ranges: the mids came from the side, high frequencies came from above. The treble-emphasized sound of Mancuso's system in the Loft then challenged a redesign of the system's bass.[159] Mancuso involved Long in this, who will become a specialist in bass design during the 1970s. The 12-inch single can also be found in relation to this sonic management of the bass range and to the production of new listening geographies through sound systems, as well as the new forms of listening that correlate with them.[160]

We can get a deeper analytical insight into Long's bass design by turning to the system Long built for the Paradise Garage. The club primarily featured the DJ Larry Levan and an extensive sound system with considerable financial investment: 'By most estimates, the Garage was a half-million dollar soundsystem in the early 80s, and it was costly to maintain. If Levan was in a stormy mood, he might blow multiple speakers in a single night.'[161] With this system, Long ensured that the sound not only came from left and right, front and back, but also from above – here he took over Rosner's positioning of the tweeters – and even from below. In the Garage, the floor had to shake: 'The room was acoustically treated for sound, the walls were built on tracks to move throughout the night ... the floor was built on two-by-fours, so the floor would move too, so after several hours of dancing your feet didn't get tired. Everything was built around the dancing and the sound.'[162] Frankie Knuckles describes how Long incorporated the floor and ceiling into his sound systems as early as 1974 in his SoHo Place: 'This was right around the time that the movie *Earthquake* was coming out. And he [Long] designed the Earthquake bass speakers. For the [release of the] movie *Earthquake*, ... he had this big party and he had me play at that party and he was testing the speakers at that party. And I remember the first time he tried testing them out, the ceiling collapsed in his apartment from the vibration.'[163] The Sensurround sound system developed by film production company Universal Studios, which was used very selectively and ultimately relatively unsuccessfully in cinemas between 1974 and 1981, relied on a 'discrete low-frequency-only channel'.[164] This channel was intended to help movie audiences feel less like they were in the cinema and more like they were directly *in* the movie: 'Sensurround was used to create powerful ultra-low-frequency rumbles (some below the limits of human hearing) that shook audiences and theaters in concert with explosions and other appropriate onscreen stimuli (like *Earthquake's* titular event).'[165] The Sensurround system was sonically activated and relied on enhanced sound. It was designed to produce infrasound as well, down to 15 Hz. Initially, the bass and sub-bass frequencies of the Sensurround system were explicitly not part of the film soundtrack. The film merely contained control signals that drove low-frequency noise generators that were part of the sound system.[166] Long transferred parts of that system from the movie theatre to the disco and continued such exploration of the bass range with the Paradise Garage sound system. For this, he even developed his own sub-bass speaker, which proclaimed its cultural setting in its very name – the Levan Horn.

To design the sound of the Paradise Garage, Long collaborated with Alan Fierstein and his company Acoustilog Inc. Based on an acoustic survey, Fierstein's acoustical consulting firm was primarily concerned with improving the acoustics of the room in which Long's system was installed.[167] An immersive sound experience would not be created by a reverberant room sound – the Paradise Garage was housed in a former parking garage that originally had extremely high reverberation. It would be produced exclusively by the sound system and, accordingly, would also be controllable. To this end, the approximately 5,000 square feet hall in which the dance floor was located was fitted with large amounts of damping material.

Long installed in the Paradise Garage a four-way system in which the bass design was differentiated.[168] The system comprised separate bass boxes, and also separate sub-bass boxes – the aforesaid Levan horns. These, as well as the high frequencies, were playable by the DJ: 'The standard ranges are 20 to 100 Hz for sub-bass, 20 to 800 Hz for main bass, 800 to 20,000 Hz for mid range and 7,000 to 20,000 Hz for tweeters. Its most unique feature is that the two extreme ranges of 20 to 100 Hz and 7K to 20K Hz are controllable in volume by the Disc Jockey with up to 16 dB of gain built into the circuit.'[169] For decomposing the sound of the music into four frequency ranges, Fierstein designed a special electronic – that is, active – crossover according to Long's specifications. A breakdown of the frequency range like this also allows a new approach to volume. Long and Fierstein dismissed the accusation that it's too loud in discos as too sweeping. Even Rosner had become too loud in discos in the late 1970s. Whereas at his first visit to Mancuso's Loft in the early 1970s he 'just tore my shirt off and started to dance',[170] by the end of the decade he could only stand it for a few minutes in the Paradise Garage.[171] A sound pressure of no less than 135 dB had been measured there in the middle of the dance floor.[172] Why this excess?[173]

Fierstein and Long countered such a general condemnation of volume in discos with the frequency dependence of amplitude: 'For example, sub-bass in the range below 100 Hz when played at 110 dB SPL is not annoying at all whereas upper mid range from 2K to 4K Hz at 110 dB is extremely offensive.'[174] Therefore, the lowering of certain frequency ranges 'which can be offensive at the high sound pressure levels common in most discotheques'.[175] Volume is central to affecting body parts sonically apart from the ear: 'In order for a disco to be exciting, it is important for the *overall* level of the music to be loud. However, the highs that are present should be at a lower volume than the lows. If the highs were cut out altogether, the sound of the music would lose its crispness and become dull and lifeless. The reason the low frequencies should be boosted is that they cause pressure on the total body while the mid and high frequencies only create pressure on the ears.'[176] Thus, disco sound systems should not only address the ears of dancing crowds, but also the 'total body' of those dancing as part of this crowd.

Bass design, then, had anything but a secondary function in the Paradise Garage sound system. On this level, disco cannot be located in avant-garde or rock traditions, in which basses only have an accompanying function. Rather, a connection can be made to Jamaican sound systems. Steve Goodman names this as an alternative to music cultures that fetishize midrange frequencies: 'Unlike the futurist, avant-gardist legacy or rockist legacy of (white) noise music and its contemporary disciples, with its fetishization of midrange frequencies, the dancehall system simultaneously immerses/attracts and expels/repels, is hard and soft, deploying waves of bass, an immense magnet that radiates through the body of the crowd, constructing a vectorial force field – not just heard but felt across the collective affective sensorium.'[177]

The extensions of the frequency spectrum, as they correlate to the 12-inch single and the sound system, remain indifferent in terms of musical parameters such as melody and harmony. On the 12-inch single, it was precisely not that melodies become audible that were inaudible on the single or the LP. Rather, the 12-inch single correlates with a specific form of listening. Sound systems that divide the low frequencies into bass and sub-bass correspond to this form of listening.

The sound system of the Paradise Garage was a sonically activated one that relied on 'enhanced bass'.[178] That disco sound systems not only reproduced sound but also actively shaped it in relation to the listening practices of disco and club culture becomes clear through an examination of their loudspeakers and the spatial arrangement of them, as well as of the sound shaping devices that were integrated into the loudspeaker systems. Such devices also included the Boom Box Model 100 made by the US manufacturer DBX, which provided input to the Paradise Garage's Levan Horns. Such bass enhancers can be described, according to Kodwo Eshun, as a form of 'PhonoGlutamate' or 'low end glutamate', and they also contributed to the transformation of disco culture sound systems into active listening devices.[179] In this respect, such technologies not only reproduced sonic tactility, but also played a decisive role in generating it. The DBX Boom Box resonated with the perceptual practices and sound aesthetics of disco. This box, not to be confused with the boom box of hip hop culture, was marketed by DBX as a subharmonic synthesizer: a synthesizer designed not to tap the harmonic but the subharmonic spectrum; that is, the realm of the subharmonic. However, the DBX Boom Box was not playable like a conventional synthesizer; it was more like an effect device. When the box was activated, it added sub-basses to the basses of an incoming signal, such as a record. In this way, Long's Levan sub-bass boxes could be driven reliably. The bass enhancer, 'which provides a blend of 25–50 Hz bass synthesized from 50–100 Hz information present on the recording',[180] could be switched on and off by the DJ. This form of technical bass extension was necessary because most of the disco records released did not contain any sub-bass components themselves. The opening up of the subharmonic by the Boom Box played together with a type of listening that was organized on the border to the inaudible. Sound systems with bass enhancers were thus technologies in disco culture that managed the boundary between hearing and tactility. In this regard, the Boom Box aimed to create a 'totally pulsating atmosphere', according to a disco business manual from the early 1980s, and this atmosphere was to pulsate quite unmetaphorically at the frequency of the sub-basses.[181]

In disco sound systems, DJs had the possibility to adjust the sound of records via the mixing console to both the sound system and the track previously played in the mix.[182] The corresponding adjustments could be made either at the moment of playback through the sound system or anticipatively at the moment of headphone-mediated pre-listening to the record. The listening of the DJ was already different on the level of the technical equipment – through the headphones – to the listening of the dancer on the dance floor. Equalizers and other tools were available for sound adjustment, in addition to the already mentioned enhancers and exciters; these were devices for dynamics processing such as compressors and expanders.

In the course of the 1970s, this kind of sonic fine-tuning began to migrate from the studios where music was produced and mastered to the listening devices themselves. Enhancers and exciters added new frequency components to a music production, that is, frequency components that are not present in the original signal, whereas equalizers only boost or cut existing frequencies. As early as 1975, the US company Aphex launched the Aural Exciter on the market. Initially, the device had an almost mystical status, for its producers did not sell it, but rented it out in a sealed box for $30 per recorded minute.[183] It was only in the early 1980s that Aphex offered the device for sale, and then it made its way into numerous recording and mastering studios. Via distortion, the Aural Exciter adds additional overtones to the high-frequency spectrum of a production, which are 'essential for speech intelligibility (T and S sounds) and for the sense of direction when listening'.[184] Unlike the Aural Exciter, which started at the high frequencies, the Boom Box generated additional bass signals that could also be used to drive the sub-bass speakers. Also with an eye to the booming disco market, the US company DBX introduced its bass enhancer at the National Association of Music Merchants (NAMM) show in early 1978.[185] The exploration of listening on the border of the inaudible coincides with an economic exploitation of such a form of listening. The 12-inch singles, sub-bass boxes and bass enhancers are thus three technologies that are related to disco culture, where they manage the boundary between hearing and tactility.[186] The 'physical sensation' in discos was not only artistically managed by DJs, it was also increasingly capitalized on;[187] in this respect, it also became interesting for Doug Shannon's disco business manual, which in its second edition then acquired a plain text subtitle: 'The Handbook to Knowledge, Money and Success: Everything Related to Playing Recorded Dance Music in the Nightclub Industry'.[188] This nightclub industry integrates a sound system industry. These industries manage listening via sound systems as listening devices.

The enhanced sound of the disco speaker system is also relevant in terms of the importance of mastering in disco culture. Certain functions that in other contexts were done by the mastering engineer migrated to the listening devices themselves in disco culture. Compared to the equalizers and loudness controls found on home stereo systems, the sound processing options available to the DJ on the sound system were prolific. The DJ could tune the sound of different records that he brought into a mix by pre-listening to each. Such tuning was only possible to a very limited extent in the jukebox of the 1950s, for example, as a result of the automatic volume control that had been built into jukeboxes since the mid-1950s. This nevertheless led, at the mastering level, to practices in which records were cut as loudly as possible. In discos of the late 1970s, sound could be adjusted not only manually by the DJ, but also automatically – by the Boom Box, for example, to the sub-bass speakers through which it was being heard, at the moment of playback. Thus, the adaptation of sound to disco sound systems took place not only at the level of production and mastering. Rather, adjustments could also be made at the moment of spinning the record. The adaptation of sound to other sounds with which it is placed in relation and to the situation in which it is heard was thus also made in disco culture at the moment of pre-listening by the DJ. Although these adjustments were still made manually, it also suggests an automation of mastering functions – for example, through the Boom Box.

Finally, the sound of 12-inch singles was also adapted to the disco sound systems such as the ones built by Rosner and Long. For example, the tweeters suspended above the dancers reacted hardly at all to the mid-emphasized sound of the single. Likewise, the Levan horns remained muted. Of course, the DJ could counteract this with appropriate EQ settings and other forms of signal processing. On the 12-inch single, however, the sounds for the tweeter and sub-bass speakers were already included. The accentuated rhythm of the clear and present hi-hat and tambourine sounds, which can be heard on Double Exposure's *Ten Per Cent* 12-inch single,[189] for example, are in this respect not simply an expansion of the spectrum, they also opened up a new dimension of perception in Rosner's and Long's sound systems: the sound then came from above – from the tweeter speakers suspended from the ceiling. Such a new dimensioning of sound perception correlates both with the new musical forms of the time – the tracks and mixes – and with the specific sound of the 12-inch single. It is precisely in relation to the latter that club suitability was produced in the mastering process. In the end, of course, very few of the released 12-inch singles were heard in clubs via sound systems. The 12-inch singles not only went to DJs via record pools, but were also sold – sometimes extremely successfully – in the corresponding retail trade.[190] However, the form of the disco mix or the remix remained appealing, of course, also in relation to other listening devices.[191]

(Re)mixes, tracks, sets

So on a very basic level, the sound of sound systems was significantly shaped by the technologies of the systems, as well as by the configuration of these technologies in the room. Thereby the sound systems produced and processed the distinction between pure and enhanced sound. For the followers of pure sound as well as for the followers of enhanced sound, the systems had a decisive significance. For the former, the sound of the systems had to be anticipated already in the mixing and mastering of releases; for the latter, the sound of releases had to be modulated by the DJ and the enhanced sound system.[192]

On a further level, the sound of the disco and club sound systems was determined by the repertoire of records played on them.[193] This level does not have to be taken into consideration by analysing selected successful titles and productions. In the interaction with sound systems, peculiar musical forms gained contours – (re)mixes, tracks and sets. Even through these forms, which are both technically and musically informed, sound systems as listening devices brought forth what is listened to through them. What sound systems gave to hear were often DJ sets or mixes, which themselves always relied on songs and tracks mixed specially for this purpose. The fact that disco DJs did not mix was to remain rather the exception.[194]

In the sound systems of the disco and club culture, most often no series and repetitions of songs ran (as in jukeboxes), instead it was mixes of versions and tracks. In this case, it was not the listener who had limited choice over what is heard, as was the case with the jukebox. The choice was made by DJs. Through headphones, they auditioned what later became audible to the crowd through the sound system as part of a stream of sound. Whereas the choice of jukebox listeners was constrained by the selection of music on the jukebox, then the choice of the DJs was constrained by their respective record collections. DJs do not serialize and repeat songs – as jukebox listeners do – they mix versions and tracks. Various authors in cultural studies as well as in popular music studies have pointed out the differences between song and track with regard to electronic dance music[195] and have even tried to define a peculiar form of 'track music'.[196] If tracks are more likely to belong to musical forms such as house and techno, and in some cases have no reference to the form of the short and concise pop song, then such a reference often still remains in the versions of disco culture.

A house or techno track is not some kind of a pure musical form. A track is bound to technology. In the 1990s, for example, when a techno track was mentioned, it usually meant a 12-inch single. However, the term 'track' already referred to the connection between sound and technology before the 12-inch single. In cinematography, for example, the 'soundtrack' refers to the soundtrack positioned on the film stock next to the picture track since the introduction of the sound-on-film system in the 1920s. With the advent of magnetic tape in US sound studios after the Second World War, a 'track' is also an audio track on magnetic tape. This can then be divided into multiple tracks with the introduction of the multitrack process. Whereas the track runs vertically on the photographic film stock, it runs horizontally on magnetic tape. The titles on CDs and LPs – regardless of their content – are also referred to as 'tracks' in a broader sense. In connection with the sound film, the tape and the CD, however, the term 'track' is not to be equated with a piece of music. Rather, 'track' here denotes what Wicke calls a 'technical mode of existence of sound'.[197] This could potentially become music, but in principle it stands in difference to music.[198] In house and techno culture, a technical mode of existence of sound, which can also be found, for example, in relation to the LP in rock music, is no longer conceptually concealed as a 'song', but rather explicated as a 'track'. Techno tracks are a 'kind of semi-finished product ... from which music must first be made again in the DJ's mix'.[199] Such modularity will then become, albeit on a different level, an important aesthetic component of contemporary electronic dance music.[200] In contrast to being semi-finished products, songs represent self-contained structures. Discrete and self-contained units were not central to house and techno: 'The division of the musical sequence into self-contained sections was then replaced by a flow model with continuously building and breaking down tensions.'[201] The emergence of conclusions and pauses is consistently prevented and postponed by the DJ mix.

In contrast to the tracks of house and techno culture, the versions and (re)mixes of disco culture are still variations of the song form. They remain related to the song form, even if it is only a fraction of a remix. Parts and sections such as 'verse' and 'chorus' lose importance in disco versions compared to 'introduction' and 'breaks': 'Disco shifts the musical economy away from the chorus and verse towards sections like the introduction and the break.'[202] In the electronic dance music of the 2010s, 'build up' and 'drop' are then said to have a crucial aesthetic importance,[203] also in EDM pop: 'EDM pop songs score hits by soaring to climaxes or dropping to nadirs. Soars and drops are different tactical approaches to the same underlying strategy of building and exacerbating sonic and affective tension.'[204] In addition to such variations of song form through exposure of sections that only have a subordinate function in the short and concise song, in disco versions the moment of repetition is more central than a linear development aiming at a final conclusion or climax.

Disco productions repeatedly follow a modular layering principle, according to which several layers are arranged over a basic rhythm.[205] This gives rise to interactions, frictions and tensions between the individual layers, which tend to be organized in a cyclical manner and are in contrast to linear forms designed for a conclusion.[206] The form of disco productions then emerges 'by means of changing textures (bringing strata in and out), while its expansive forms facilitate the varied presentation of notably heterogeneous strata'.[207] The point of reference for all these layers, however, remains 'solidity of a groove'.[208] In contrast to musicologist Charles Kronengold, however, Carolyn Krasnow additionally describes disco as non-teleological and non-narrative; as a musical form that 'refuses the closure that is central to most European-derived music, including much seventies rock'.[209] Not least in relation to the praise and serialization of climaxes, including sonic ones, by numerous actors in disco culture, that we mentioned in Chapter 4 on the 12-inch single.[210]

Any connection to the song form dissipates increasingly in the tracks of house and techno culture. In reference to Chicago house, Will Straw writes: 'More and more, the idea of songs gave way to the notion of "tracks", records lasting from four to ten minutes in which the important things going on had to do with the relationship between a consistent rhythm and the wide variety of things which might be mixed over the top of it.'[211] Whereas the song still connotes the human body through the voice, the designation 'track' emphasizes the technical aspect of the music. Often tracks do without a singing voice and are therefore instrumental. In contrast to the song, the track is not determined by melody and harmony but primarily by rhythm and sound: 'In contrast [to the melodic emphasis of the song], rhythm and sound ... take the place of harmonic conventions in the track.'[212] Even when tracks integrate melodies and harmonies, these are there are to be modulated and modelled. They are, as Roland Barthes describes the material 'plastic' in his book *Mythologies*, 'more than a substance, plastic is the very idea of its infinite transformation ... it is less a thing than the trace of a movement'.[213] Music journalist Simon Reynolds coined the term 'jack track' for forms of music that are beyond the song.[214] The 'jack track' is to be distinguished from the 'song'. Glimmers of the latter would still shine through in disco as well as in some varieties of Chicago house – especially 'deep house' should be emphasized here.[215] The Jack Track – according to Reynolds – emphasizes the machine repetition. Voices are at most used as material, which the producer processes.[216] Verses or choruses would be condensed in the Jack Track to short commands and slogans. Sources of the music would be machines and synthesizers, not traditionally trained musicians.

The name of one of the most important Chicago house labels, Trax Records, in this respect is also the programme. House producer Jesse Saunders explains the name as follows: 'The reason we called it Trax Records was because we were doing a bunch of tracks .... So we just thought why not be true to what it's all about?'[217] Although Trax also released numerous productions that still reproduced the song form but also varied it – such as Marshall Jefferson's *Move Your Body* (Trax, United States, 1986) – the reference to the song completely vanished with the releases in the Trax catalogue, which was later subsumed under the term 'acid house'.[218]

Although a track is brought into the mix with other tracks and individual tracks seem to lose their contours in such a mix, within the house and techno culture individual tracks remained identifiable and could thus be used as DJ tools: 'Within the (re)mix culture of EDM, works cannot be associated with a single definitive recording in the manner of songs in rock. Although participants clearly viewed individual tracks as exhibiting particular formal behaviors, which DJs had to understand in order to create effective sets, this understanding was situated within consistent expectations regarding the larger context in which tracks would function. Participants frequently described records as "tools" to be employed in sets.'[219] In the DJ mix, therefore, the identity of the piece of music is not destroyed. Rather, a new identity of the mix is created.

The mixes and tracks became part of DJ sets. Various DJ sets are available digitally on relevant video and audio platforms. We find amateur archives of older DJ sets on specialized websites – for example, on the now deactivated deephouse page, on Soundcloud, or Mixcloud and, in addition, track lists of DJ sets on Gridface. On such websites, for example, we also find digitized recordings, probably made originally on cassette, of sets by DJ Ron Hardy in legendary Chicago clubs such as the Music Box.[220] DJ sets also became a subject for music analysis.[221] However, the length of selected DJ sets, which can last several hours, may present a problem here.[222]

To conclude, as listening devices disco and club sound systems mediated actively between the revelling subjects they addressed and the music listened to with them. At a very fundamental level, these systems were involved, time and again, in making the environments in which listening took place sonically dominant. Moreover, they co-constituted the music heard through them decisively via enhancing and tuning the sound of music. This turned them into systems of enhanced sound. Finally, there was feedback between the sound systems and the form of music heard through them. Here music was turned more and more into a mixed non-stop stream taken from tracks, remixes and versions.

Listening techniques in disco and club culture

When Colleen 'Cosmo' Murphy visited David Mancuso's Loft in New York in the early 1990s, she thought that she experienced a new kind of listening: 'The dance floor was dotted with ramshackle props including a Buddha and a Christmas tree, and was surrounded by seven columns made up of ten great big wooden loudspeakers, the bottom bass units of which sat on the floor wedged into "false corners", and the upper components lifted high above so they could beam the mid and high frequencies down over the dancers' heads. They were like mystical alien towers that emitted a beautiful and otherworldly language. Not only did I hear music new to my ears such as Dexter Wansel's "Life on Mars" and Code 718's "Equinox", but I also discovered a new way of listening.'[223] In the following, I try to trace this 'new way of listening' as it is called for here, but it will be at best outlined suggestively, starting from its materialities and the distinctions that characterize it. If this listening may seem new on a personal level, then its location – the Loft – refers back to its context of origin: the emerging disco culture in New York in the 1970s.

Sound systems significantly modulate the materiality of listening. We have already been able to establish in relation to the jukebox and the 12-inch single that its sound addresses the belly as well as the ears, and such a coupling of sound with organs beyond the ear applies to the sound systems to an intensified degree. This can culminate in the point where 'earcentrism' of hearing is decentred[224] or even escalated, when sound systems only produce sound in the ultra or infrasound range. We can think here, for instance, of Steve Goodman's Unsound System or Nik Nowak's Infra/Ultra.[225] Sound systems thus repeatedly address organs beyond the ear specifically on an individual level, but also transcend this individual level by addressing masses, collectives and publics. Unlike forms of popular music that fetishize individual body parts, this is not necessarily the case with disco and club sound systems. This already brings into play two distinctions that sound system listening opens up and processes: the distinction between crowd and individual and the distinction between hearing and feeling. Sound system listening is listening in which the listeners are part of a crowd. It thus differs from forms of listening that rely on isolation and contemplation. Moreover, in it the history of listening is connected with the history of non-listening. Finally, a third distinction of sound system listening can be added here: the distinction between submission and liberation. This refers primarily to the sound of systems designed to overwhelm, to the sonic dominance in some discos and clubs, which repeatedly, quasi-dialectically, assert an emancipatory potential, either in clubs and discos in the 1970s and 1980s where queer communities came together that otherwise possessed little space,[226] or that these places quite fundamentally offer an alternative to a dominance of visual culture. Concrete listening practices, also understood in a more comprehensive sense, for example, as dance practices as well as listening experiences, are then based on this level of listening as a cultural technique, which only differentiates itself in relation to materialities and processes peculiar distinctions.[227]

Articulating sound and body parts via sound systems

Sound system listening in disco and club culture is not centred on a single body part. Rather, sound systems as listening devices seek to address the listening body in a decentred way. Such a form of listening to music is then different from other forms of the management of listening, such as headphone listening in the middle-class living room as it developed, for example, in the hi-fi culture of the 1950s. If ears and headphones were central stations of individual sound journeys, then sound journeys in disco and club culture were collectivized by 12-inch singles and sound systems in semi-public spaces. DJ Francis Grasso had already played the 'head music' of psychedelic rock in the New York Sanctuary club around 1970, which, however, no longer addressed the head, but now tried to move the body through sound systems: 'With Grasso playing a kind of music that tempered the "head music" of the psychedelic era with "tribal" percussion that connected more with the feet and groin, and with the accompanying drugs moving away from mind-expanding psychedelics toward those that delivered a body high, the Sanctuary marked the transition between the expanded consciousness espoused by travelers going "further" in the sixties and the near loss of consciousness that many commentators said characterized the solipsistic seventies. Disco was a retreat back into the body – both the newly liberated body of its prime constituents and the body politic.'[228]

Certainly, every form of dance music starts by claiming to move the body. Through specific movement repertoires the body emerges here as something that is culturally constituted. However, it is a specificity of disco culture that it consistently implemented such body metamorphoses with technical means; that it brought technologies into play that engender an immersive listening experience and determine sound through its effect on the entire body via a technologization of the inaudible or a cultivation of the bass range through 12-inch singles, sub-bass boxes and bass enhancers. Such a determination of sound has been perpetuated in popular dance music such as house and techno since the 1980s, and is also prominent in more recent musical forms such as dubstep and EDM. These musical forms mobilize the body not only through groove and rhythm, but also by determining sound through a material and tactile dimension.[229]

As listening devices sound systems address a specific listening body, whose individual parts and zones are targeted by specific frequencies. Popular music studies scholar Hillegonda Rietveld has described how this occurs in the sets of house and techno DJs through mixers and equalizers, which leads to different strategies of filtering as well as specific sound effects: 'A great mixer allows the DJ to completely take out the frequency of a particular instrument, which can be used for dramatic effects. For example, if a bass line is suppressed with distracting partial tones, it means that people dance for a moment (usually eight or sixteen bars) without bass. When the bass comes back in, it triggers a high feeling in the dancers. Since the bass affects the lower parts of the body, the feet of the dancers seem to be able to carry them higher than before. Often the dancing then becomes more intense, and the hands wave in the air. In contrast, house DJ Carl Cox favours the complete withdrawal of the upper and middle frequency ranges, leaving a ponderous muffled drone as though the speakers were under water. This leaves a feeling of dejection that is alleviated when the upper frequency ranges return, eventually toning the body and infusing it with renewed energy.'[230]

What is stated here from the perspective of popular music studies on the coupling of sound and body parts mediated by sound systems has also come – with recourse to a different vocabulary – within the purview of sound system designers. At the end of the 1970s, Rosner, in an article in the prestigious *Journal of the Audio Engineering Society*, attempted to formulate the by no means merely technical performance requirements of a disco sound system. He describes the means by which these requirements can be implemented or how a typical sound system is constructed. Such a system should primarily achieve a specific effect: it must be able to flood the senses, must consist of technology capable of 'enabl[ing] the human body to be ensonified'.[231] In order to create such a physical capability, an extremely loud system is necessary, whose volume would also have to be guaranteed in the basses and in the trebles. Especially via the basses, a relatively direct coupling between the legs and pelvis of the dancers on the one hand and sound on the other hand should be possible: 'Strong, fundamental bass, originating low to the ground, is needed to vibrate the dancers' legs and pelvic area. The system should be able to reproduce 40 Hz information at 120 dB on the dance floor.'[232] Rosner goes on to say that this requires splitting the spectrum into at least three sections – bass, midrange and treble – using so-called crossovers. Divided in this way, the spectrum can then be reproduced via different types of loudspeakers, each of which is assigned specific amplifiers. The individual spectra would have to be controllable separately.

The theoretical location of dancing bodies in disco culture, and later also in house and techno culture, repeatedly emphasizes themes of the 'decentralised' and the 'comprehensive', for example, in '"whole body" eroticism' mentioned above.[233] Lawrence also emphasizes a decentralized and non-hierarchical organization of the disco dancer's body, drawing an arc to its theoretical constitution in the psychoanalytic sphere of the pre-oedipal. In this, he argues, the body is not yet organized by a binary symbolic order, for one thing, and sexuality is not yet centred on specific organs, for another.[234]

It is not only in discos and clubs that the perception of sound is coupled with other sensory modalities, but – strongly resonating here with the 12-inch single as a listening device – sonic perception itself becomes amodal: 'Bass figures as exemplary because of all frequency bands within the sonic encounter, it most explicitly exceeds mere audition and activates the sonic conjunction with amodal perception: bass is not just heard but is felt. Often sub-bass cannot be heard or physically felt at all, but still transforms the ambience of a space .... Bass demands more theoretical attention, as it is too often equated with buzzing confusion of sensation and therefore the enemy of clear auditory perception.'235 Music listening that is not centred on the ear is escalated by the multi-way sound system. This creates a body in disco and club culture whose perceptual capacity is determined beyond discrete sensory channels.236

Collective sound space

Sound systems open up a collective sound space in discos and clubs. There, they aim to create a dancing crowd rather than primarily individual listeners or dancing couples.237 The sound space here is usually determined less by the acoustics of the architectural space. Instead of being shaped by room acoustics, it is brought forth above all by sound reinforcement and its systems. The Paradise Garage, for example, was originally a parking garage and the task of the acoustician Alan Fierstein was to minimize the reverberant sound of this place, even to silence it as far as possible. The sound of the room in which the sound systems were installed was more of a problem for their designers: 'It's much easier to make an outdoor soundsystem [sic] than a sound system in a room. The soundsystem [sic] in a room is always affected by the room. The room is usually the enemy, not the friend.'238 Instead of room sound, sound system designers focused on sound reinforcement. This could lead to the almost paradoxical point that the result of the sound reinforcement should be perceived as room sound. Mancuso, for example, wanted to simulate a loudspeaker-free room sound through sound reinforcement: 'I would have to have a room where I could cover the speakers, but visually if you get my drift. You should not even know how many speakers are being used or where they are located. The room should just be filled with sound. When you go into a concert hall, like Carnegie Hall or any of those places, they don't even use a soundsystem, they use the room.'239 Such an intention corresponds first and foremost to the transparency phantasm of the audiophile world.

The sound spaces that sound systems open up through sound reinforcement patently address a crowd and focus less on the individual in terms of sound. This is also supported by the fact that the sound of the systems has no preferred direction. This, in turn, puts the sound spaces of sound systems at a remove from the sound spaces typical of concerts, where sound comes primarily from one direction, namely, from the stage. The disco sound system positions the listener in their physicality in a peculiar way to the sound event. This becomes especially clear in comparison to other sound systems, but also to other listening devices. The sound system of the Radio City Music Hall from the 1930s, for example, or the Woodstock sound system from 1969, created directional sound that – at least apparently – was supposed to come from the stage. Home stereo systems position the listener in the so-called sweet spot and only there make audible to the listener the 'phantom sound source' that is located opposite.240 The sweet spot is a position in the 'aural field centred on a lone auditor', an auditor that is stationary (to be able to take off for a sonic trip), gendered (masculine) and class-specific (middle-class).241 In contrast to this, the sound in the disco sound system comes from the front and from behind, from the sides, even from above and – as we have seen – from below. The perceptual space that this system spans experiences differentiations not only horizontally through the boxes positioned separately on this plane – which are set up in the form of a quadrangle around the dance floor – but also vertically. Here, the decomposition of the frequency spectrum is taken up again and 'high' tones come from the heights: 'The fizzing energy of the new tweeters resuscitated the sound system. Flat records could now be sharpened, enabling dancers to hear high-end frequencies that were being drowned out by the hullabaloo of the party, and the placement of the arrays above the dance floor produced a new geography of listening in which the treble emanated from the center of the room and moved outwards rather than downwards.'[242]

The collective sound space of the sound systems was not opened up exclusively through sound reinforcement. Although often a sound peculiar to the architectural space was supposed to be minimized as much as possible, sometimes the architectural space itself would become the loudspeaker. The starting point for this might be, for example, the Levan Horn loudspeaker. Long had designed this sub-bass loudspeaker based on the Klipschorn: 'This speaker virtually positions the listener in the speaker: The Klipschorn must stand in the corner and in this position uses the adjacent room walls as a horn mouth extension of the woofer, which is installed inside and coupled by multiple folding. In approximately freer interpretation, the listeners are thus not in front of, but quasi in the bass horn.'[243] This loudspeaker, extended by the architectural space, accommodated a dancing crowd. The disco sound system targets a dancing crowd submerged in the immersive listening space between the speakers and even in the speakers themselves.

The immersive experience of the disco body is not only sonically constituted, but also in relation to other dancing bodies. In disco culture, dance forms emerged in which people dance alone as part of a crowd. Lawrence describes how, at the beginning of that decade, 'a new practice of solo club dancing' appeared in New York discos like the Sanctuary or the Loft, which eventually became the 'enduring model for contemporary club culture'.[244] The dancer dances alone, but is not socially isolated. Douglas Crimp, referring to the New York disco scene in the mid-1970s, explains the function of the 'dance partner' in this context: '"Dance Partner" doesn't mean the same thing for disco as it does for, say, Fred and Ginger.'[245]

Disco dancing is individual and collective at the same time. Partners are found only temporarily, but they do not become couples.[246] Thus, these dance practices did not lead to isolation, but to the emergence of new forms of community beyond any reference to the couple. It was not until The Hustle dance forms came along, popularized in 1975 by the song of the same name by Van McCoy & The Soul City Symphony (Avco, United States, 1975) and made ubiquitous internationally in 1977 by the film *Saturday Night Fever* (directed by John Badham, United States, 1977) and a boom in dance instruction and dance classes, that improvised dance forms would again be supplemented by heavily choreographed couple and line dances.[247]

However, the problematization of the couple reference in the emerging disco culture also had very tangible, that is, legal, reasons. Men were not allowed to dance with men: a same-sex couple dancing was illegal. There had to be at least one woman present for every three men dancing.[248] Mel Cheren describes how such legal requirements regulated behaviour in the United States even in libertarian places like the bars on Fire Island in the 1960s: the owner of the Boatel, a hotel complex in Fire Island Pines, for example, made sure that men dancing in groups without a woman left the dance floor.[249] These practices, however, did not lead to singling out; instead, new forms of community emerged beyond the couple.

Liberation via submission

In addition to the distinction between individual and community, sound system listening also processes the distinction between overpowering and release, between submission and liberation. The sound of disco and club sound systems is always designed to overwhelm the listener – through extreme volume levels, through the exploitation of a comprehensive spectrum, through a technically generated, peculiarly immersive quality. Such forms of sonic overwhelming crystallize an emancipatory potential in disco, house and techno culture time and again.

Moments of overpowering through sound, even possibly forms of subjugation through music, can be found in various dance forms that have emerged in relation to disco or house. For example, in 'jacking' that emerged in house clubs in Chicago in the 1980s like the Warehouse or the Music Box: 'a frenetic dance in which the person taking part looks as though they've just plugged themselves into an electric mains socket',[250] 'the signature dance move of the city's teen party scene',[251] '"Jacking" also makes me think of jacking into an electrical circuit. Plugged into the sound system, the jacker looks a bit like a robot with epilepsy.'[252] The house dancer is thus said to be metaphorically 'jacked into' the sound system. Thus jacking was distinct from the increasingly less choreographed solo dancing in disco culture:[253] 'Jacking took this to the next stage, replacing pelvic-thrust and booty-shake with a whole-body frenzy of polymorphously perverse tics and convulsive pogo-ing.'[254] Thus, jacking does not highlight individual body parts – like other dance forms, such as twerking or the twist with its focus on the pelvis.[255] Jacking is characterized by a paradoxical combination of submission and liberation: 'freedom achieved by bonding subjectivity and self-will, the ecstasy of being *enthralled* by the beat'.[256] Consequently, jacking was not a dance form in which the dancer primarily masters the music through skilful movements. Rather, the dancers allow themself to be overwhelmed by the music by seeking as 'direct' a connection to the sound as possible. The overloud and immersive sound of the sound system corresponds to this form of dance.[257]

The motif of being captivated or enchanted by a beat that Reynolds cites for Chicago house was similarly presented in relation to disco by the literary scholar Walter Hughes, who died young of AIDS, in the early 1990s. Hughes explores a form of disco dancing in which the dancer – such as in Hustle – no longer masters and dominates the music. Instead, Hughes somewhat strikingly reverses the relationship between dancer and music: 'Dancing becomes a form of submission to th[e] overmastering beat.'[258] Autonomy and self-control would thus be surrendered to the beat. Hughes examines disco not as a form of immoderate or decadent enjoyment, but as a disciplining, regulating practice that paradoxically produces a peculiar form of freedom. The means of disciplining, according to Hughes, is the 'four-to-the-floor' beat. For Hughes, the form of freedom is a new form of explicitly gay male identity. Disco, he argues, was involved in turning the clinical identity of 'homosexuals' into a member of a '"gay" minority group'.[259] For Hughes, domination by the beat – we can add here – does not lead to masses marching in lockstep, but to an emancipated 'gay community'. A new form of community emerges, mediated by technologies such as records and sound systems: 'The transmission of the beat from disk to speaker, from speaker to dancer, from dancer to dancer, creates a kind of circuitry, an automatic community of technological communication that suggests an updating of Whitman's adhesive "body electric" as the gay body electronic'.[260] We can add here that the notion of the disciplining beat to which dancers surrender and thereby allay their subjectivity does not move exclusively within the framework of the demand for minority rights of gays. Rather, it is much more fundamentally about alternative determinations of subjectivity beyond a dominant subject form that experiences or must experience itself as self-determined, grounded in itself, and clearly separated from the outside world in order to endure.[261] Nevertheless, the dancer bodies Hughes refers to do not twitch to the beat like frog muscles in nineteenth-century electrophysiology experiments. Dance forms like jacking explore the game that the dancing crowd plays with the beat. Hughes's thesis, then, is that by being dominated by the beat, disco dancers free themselves from dominant notions of subjectivity.

Hughes follows up his remarks on the paradoxical relationship between disciplining and liberation in disco culture with fantasies according to which the dancers in their physicality – the beat is directed at them, not just at their ears – would become an extension of the beat-generating machine. Hughes sees in this a mechanization of the dancer: 'The fearful paradox of the technological age, that machines created as artificial slaves will somehow enslave and even mechanize human beings, is ritually enacted at the discotheque'.[262] Whether such automatisms actually occur remains to be seen. However, sound systems in clubs and discos certainly do create conditions that aim at such an excessive presence of the beat and provoke alternatives such as either dance or leave the club.

In jacking, too, moments of loss of control or, better, of renunciation of control seem to be sought. However, the beat does not control the movements of the dancing bodies. Rather, the beat is danced around. The early places where jacking arose were clubs in Chicago like the Warehouse, which opened in 1977, the Power Plant, which opened in 1983 – in both of which DJ Frankie Knuckles played – and the Music Box, which also opened in 1983 and where Ron Hardy mixed records. If disco and house culture still exhibited elements of a culture that worked off the norms of a dominant culture, not in a public space but in the semi-public spaces of discos and clubs, then such efforts were repeatedly suspended in 1990s techno. With regard to techno culture, however, this by no means signifies that it is free of control mechanisms. The dance studies scholar Gabriele Klein sees the combination of control and freedom at work in relation to the bodies of techno culture as well. Desire and control went hand in hand here as well, defining the status of the body in techno culture: 'It's no longer clothes that make people, but bodies, and that's why the body must also be constantly controlled'.[263]

In this context, bodies are something that can be manufactured: 'You don't have a body, you make it – this is the credo that distinguishes the techno scene from the bourgeois discourse about naturalness.'[264] Crimp had already made very similar observations in New York discos in the mid-1970s. He was astonished by a certain conformity and similarity that he could make out in the visitors, or rather in their bodies: 'The most striking aspect of the similarity was that these people have identical *bodies*, and these bodies are also strikingly different from other bodies. They seem as if honed for a particular activity, maybe a fairly athletic form of sex. In fact that activity is dancing, or what has become known as dancing. These bodies have been made into dancing machines.'[265] However, Crimp sees the bodies of such dancing machines – he also speaks of these bodies being synthetically produced – as not shaped exclusively by music, but above all by the new fitness equipment that was developed in the 1970s. These fitness machines made it possible to train individual and isolated muscle groups in an extremely targeted and efficient manner.[266] Crimp describes how this led to a fetishization of the pectoral muscles in New York's gay scene: corresponding competitions were also held in discos such as the Flamingo.

To conclude, in sound system listening the materialities of listening are configured by articulating the systems' enhanced sound with multiple body parts. The listening culture of disco, house and techno is heavily organized technically and materially. The listener as a subject of these cultures is constituted (and constitutes his, her or themself) in the dynamics propelled by the oppositions of submission and liberation, crowd and individual as well as of listening and touch.

Conclusion and outlook

Towards listening devices in the digital era

In this book, I have attempted to write a history of listening. Starting from the devices through which listening is done. To this end, I have focused on four listening devices that were relevant in selected popular music cultures. I have argued that popular music cultures offer themselves as a suitable object of investigation for such a history of listening because in these music cultures listening was increasingly done and continues to be done through devices, probably now more than ever. In addition, but also in connection with such a history of listening, a central concern of this book was to substantiate theoretically the concept of a listening device and to bring it to bear methodically. In Chapter 1, I set up five theses on the concept supplemented by a sixth. These theses run like red threads through the case studies of the book and link together to form a kind of network. This network can, at least to my purpose here, not only give consistency to the book as a whole, but also probe the radius of action and insight that the concept of a listening device opens up as a key to analysing and understanding music and sound cultures, and even crucial aspects of culture, media, and history in general. Listening devices model (Thesis I) and manage (Thesis II) listening; they co-produce both the music heard (Thesis III) and the listener (Thesis IV); they connect a history of listening to a history of non-listening (Thesis V); and they are grounded in music and sound history (Thesis VI). I explored some of these six theses in each case study, although others only run through two or three of the case studies. Nevertheless, by running through the four case studies, all of the theses ultimately developed.

The 7-inch singles and jukeboxes, 12-inch singles and sound systems are all devices of listening that can be used differently by listeners; in relation to all of these devices, specific knowledge emerges through each of them about what listening is. In the case studies, I was able to focus on the modelling function of listening devices and the specific knowledge about listening that is correlating with that function. In relation to listening devices as models of listening, I showed that such models included, time and again, economic knowledge that conceptualizes and manages music listening as a commercial resource. This epistemic function of listening devices transitions into the management of listening via listening devices. The 7-inch singles model music listening as a form of record listening, in which records by different performers, composers and producers are listened to automatically in series. Furthermore, jukeboxes model a form of record listening in that the process of changing records is not performed by the listener's hand but is delegated to a mechanism that is only activated if payment is made. The listening models, which are integrated into 12-inch singles and sound systems, seem to me to remain rather indeterminate, receiving at best a suggestive contour through their specific sonic addressing of body parts beyond the ear.

The four listening devices examined here each co-produce the music heard in their own way peculiar to them. In this respect, they are to be distinguished from playback technologies. I was able to show how such a co-constitution of the sound heard by listening devices included not only a sonic activation of these devices, which turned out very differently in each concrete case, but also an integration of listening devices into music production, and above all into music post-production; here mastering was the central factor. In the jukebox, the sonic activation of listening devices was still operationalized in a rather restrained way with recourse to adjusting dynamics, volume and frequency. With the sound systems of disco and club culture, however, this gained considerably in relevance and scope, so that the sound of the loudspeaker systems sought above all to be decidedly 'enhanced' sound. Both 7-inch and 12-inch singles, for one thing, became a constitutive part of the music heard over the sound systems through mastering. In Detroit techno, for example, the tracks produced on tape in the living room studio were always given a decisive sonic fine-tuning when they were mastered for 12-inch singles. In the mastering of rock 'n' roll productions, the record cut was pushed to the limit. I have also demonstrated that music was already being produced for jukebox, single and sound system suitability.

All four listening devices gained their contours specifically within commercial contexts. They are industrial products. They were developed by large US companies like RCA Victor or smaller ones like Seeburg and Wurlitzer. They emerged within the context of a music culture with an extremely high rate of turnover such as disco, and brought together different industries involved in the creation of sound, such as hi-fi, film and live sound. All four listening devices are expressions of an increasing commercial interest in listening. I have attempted to trace the forms this interest took concretely in relation to the four listening devices studied, and how it was organized. Thus, taking the example of the jukebox, listening was organized as something that left data traces, and these data co-determined what would be listened to in the future. The jukebox's management of listening begins with the delegation of the process of record changing from the hand to the machine. The management of listening through disco sound systems, which connected listening and tactility, also aimed at a specific 'disco experience' designed for saleability, a subject that featured prominently in disco business manuals published around 1980. However, the concrete analyses in this book have also demonstrated that a management of listening cannot merely be reduced to processes of capitalization, but that listening itself also generates something that is culturally specific.

In addition to the music heard, listening devices also bring forth the listener, or rather through them people generate themselves as listeners. I have investigated this dimension of listening devices in the four case studies primarily at the level of the materialities of listening as well as of listening as a cultural technique. Listening devices modulate the materialities of listening, for instance, by addressing certain parts of the body but also by modelling forms of listening peculiar to them. The sound systems of disco and club culture, for example, are designed to couple sound with body parts beyond the ear. The jukebox, too, already sought a connection with the belly through the positioning of its speakers. Moreover, listening devices bring forth listening as a cultural technique, opening up and processing differences. In doing this, I have outlined some distinctions that were processed by several listening devices. For example, the case study on the jukebox already touched on the distinction between listening and tactility, which was then also processed by the 12-inch single and the sound system. The distinction of individualization and collectivization, for instance, contours both jukebox and sound system listening. So does the distinction between series and repetition.

Listening devices connect a history of listening with a history of non-listening. In relation to the case studies, this connection has become concrete primarily in two forms. First, in technical standards, and second, in connections of listening to other senses. The small single record, for example, integrates technical standards in the form of so-called recording curves. These industrially standardized curves aim to make the records themselves sound as transparent as possible. I have shown how in the mastering practices of the highly independent record companies that were crucial to the development of rock 'n' roll in the 1950s these standards were deliberately ignored and instead the loudest possible record cut was made. Such a record cut no longer aimed for sonic transparency, but tried to evoke a sound peculiar to the single. The purpose of this loud record cut was to make records competitive for use in a playlist. In addition, this form of mastering resonated with an aesthetic of loudness and non-conformism that has always been found in rock 'n' roll culture. The thesis of combining a history of listening with a history of non-listening is thus linked to the theses of the management of listening and the co-production of what is heard.

Technical standards are also implemented in jukeboxes, 12-inch singles and sound systems; I have worked out the extent to which these three listening devices connect a history of hearing with a history of not-hearing, in that they relate hearing primarily to other senses. In the case of the 12-inch singles and the sound systems, this takes place mainly through the connection between sound and tactility. The listening devices, as well as the music forms of disco, house and techno, which increasingly interacted with them, address the borderline between the audible and the physically perceptible specifically through the production and design of tactile bass. The jukebox caught people's attention above all by its connection between hearing and seeing. Thus, jukebox listening is characterized by an effective visual staging of the process of selecting and changing records. In contrast to this staging, the monetary and electricity flows of the jukebox are largely hidden from view. The four listening devices examined thus combine, albeit each in a specific way, a history of listening with a history of non-listening.

I have been able to work out a music- and sound-historical conditionality of the listening devices especially for the small single record and for the maxi-single, and to outline one in a rather sketchy form for the sound systems. The development of the 7-inch single by the US company RCA Victor was based on certain musical forms and listening practices. In these, short pieces of music, mostly by different performers and composers, were to be listened to automatically in series. Based on these concrete forms and practices, RCA Victor then defined the material parameters of the single. Although these listening practices themselves had only emerged in conjunction with older listening devices, it was indeed concrete listening practices that conditioned the development of new listening devices. I was able to reconstruct the musical and sound conditionality of the 12-inch single even more extensively. I could show that the question of the development or even invention of the 12-inch single is misleading. It was not invented; it was found, related to the listening practices, forms of releasing music and loudspeaker systems peculiar to the disco culture emerging in New York in the 1970s. I have also uncovered a rudimentary music- and sound-historical conditionality for the development of loudspeaker systems, which began in the late 1910s, by sketchily reconstructing the conception of sound as a voluminous entity in the nineteenth century and the traces of this in the early modern period. Listening devices are thus conditioned by music and sound history, and/or by the listening practices that interact with them. This does not mean, however, that new sounds and musical forms cannot also emerge in close relation to listening devices. In my opinion, the six theses on listening devices are not confined to the four listening devices or to the music and sound cultures featured in this book. We can also play them through with regard to analysing contemporary listening cultures. In this respect, I would like to conclude my reflections in this book by putting the six theses into perspective with regard to selected listening devices of the present day.

Despite some limited vinyl revivals, records are at best of marginal relevance to contemporary music listening, and single records in particular. Jukeboxes have become expensive collector's items that rarely circulate outside of relatively closed and socially homogeneous collector circles. Every now and then, we do find them – in bars in 'trendy' districts in Berlin, for example, and also in favelas in Rio de Janeiro.[1] However, they do not usual play small single records, but CDs, or they access soundfiles stored in clouds. Three of the listening devices examined in this book are now yesterday's news. Only the loudspeaker systems can be found in various forms in contemporary listening cultures – at concerts, in clubs, at political events, in sports stadiums, at train stations. The fact that single records and jukeboxes have all but disappeared as objects has not, however, precluded their digital simulation and their metaphorization. When, for instance, in 1995 the Digital Performance Right in Sound Recordings Act in the United States attempted to create the first legal basis for the distribution of music recordings via the then still quite new internet, the platform for this distribution was presented as a 'celestial jukebox'.[2] This jukebox now no longer offered a mere 200 titles available as records to choose from, but like today's music streaming services, potentially included millions of titles (to say nothing of the additional offers that included other formats such as podcasts). The 12-inch single was also integrated into a digital environment, at least as a tool for DJs. However, the maxi-single no longer contained music, but a control signal with which DJs trained on the interface turntable could mix music in the form of soundfiles. A dynamic of singles and albums still frequently controls the release of recorded music today.

New listening devices eventually become old listening devices. Then they can have an existence comparable to 'dead media',[3] 'residual media'[4] or even 'zombie media'.[5] Although they are yesterday's news, obsolete and in a certain sense actually dead, they sometimes live on. Not only in the manageable framework of nostalgic revivals, in which singles are put on again and titles are selected on jukeboxes. Rather, the ways in which they managed and modelled listening, how they helped produce both the listener and the listened to, how they connected listening with non-listening, and even their respective specific musical and sonic conditionality may still stubbornly persist in the present and may possibly continue to do so in the future. The dominant listening devices of the present day – smartphones and streaming apps, noise-cancelling headphones and earbuds – also manage and model listening, and thus in a peculiar way bring it forth in the first place; they, too, implement technical standards that aim to ensure that the devices themselves are not heard, are ignored, and that instead music can be heard, thus linking a history of listening with a history of non-listening. They, too, co-produce what is heard through them as well as the listener. And they, too, are grounded in a specific history of sound and music. In this respect, smartphones, streaming apps, noise-cancelling headphones and earbuds by no means mark a clean break with the past. At a fundamental level, listening is organized through engaging with devices, even today. Probably today more than ever. Notwithstanding, at certain times, certain listening devices are dominant.

Present-day soundfile or streaming listening is characterized by the fact that listeners have a choice.[6] They can choose from a catalogue of several million titles. What can be heard in soundfile listening comes from this catalogue. The catalogue, or rather such a stock of music, becomes the condition of possibility of what can be heard in soundfile listening. This condition of possibility is actualized in the playlist. The network structure of the music database is linearized in the playlist.[7] Playlists show the listener concrete paths through the catalogue. Unlike record collections or archival collections, for example, the catalogue is neither personalized nor unique. There is a very high degree of similarity from streaming platform to streaming platform.[8] In contrast to this, however, the playlists always seek to impress with suggested personalization, reinforced by more or less 'smart' recommendation algorithms. In streaming listening, both what is being listened to and the environment in which it is being listened to are repeatedly fine-tuned in terms of sound. For example, the volume of the tracks linked together in a playlist, which are always based on different production standards and come from different genres and decades, is automatically adjusted. This can be done by the headphones producing a sound image that is personalized for the respective listener, which in turn brings headphones closer to the 'smart hearing' of medical hearing aids and their governing and standardizing practices,[9] or by the headphones cancelling out ambient noise. A further characteristic of soundfile listening is that, despite or perhaps because of all personalization, it organizes listening as a decidedly 'social' event. Whereby we can immediately add here – following Bruno Latour's caveat that the social does not explain anything, but has itself to be explained[10] – that the social is to be understood here in a very concrete sense; namely, in the sense of 'social' media. The social is then configured by operations of sharing, liking, following and commenting.[11] This configured relationship to others is supplemented by peculiar self-relationships of affect regulation and identity formation. The utilitarian character of these has been repeatedly pointed out,[12] yet algorithmic mediation also seems to be increasingly heard reflexively.[13] Lastly, soundfile listening is distinguished by a temporality peculiar to it. Everything that will be heard here in the future will come from the catalogue; that is, from the past. However, soundfile listening repeatedly gives rise to the question of which song will come next. Constantly, something is found, which the listener had not looked for at all. However, the recommendation system calculates that the soundfiles it has found will be desired by the listener. Soundfile listening is thus both strongly rooted in the past and oriented towards the future. In a certain sense, soundfile listening in this respect problematizes any history of listening. For it integrates a future in addition to a history.[14] This is perhaps the most striking peculiarity of soundfile listening, along with its statistical modelling of listening.

Nevertheless, listening via smartphones, apps and headphones takes up threads that we are now familiar with from the history of twentieth-century listening devices. The thread according to which what is heard gains contours through the dynamics of selection and abridgement as well as repetition and serialization in lists. The thread that the dynamics of repetition and serialization are in turn fed back into the sound of music in music production and post-production. The thread that listening devices not only reproduce music but are themselves sonically activated. The thread that listening devices address certain parts of the body, beyond the ear, even though control by hand has given way to control by the clicking and swiping thumb, even by programmes. Key features of today's listening culture such as listening to playlists and streams of sound, the integration of signal processing into listening devices themselves, or sonic practices such as the so-called loudness war all have a history. In this book, I have showed that this history did not start with digitization, MP3, or streaming, but goes far back into the history of popular music in the twentieth century.

Listening to music is increasingly managed by listening devices. Since the twentieth century, listening to music has become something that not only interests fans, music educators or music and sound scholars. Rather, the manufacturers of listening devices have developed a distinctive interest in music listening. Listening to music then becomes a resource that can be explored and exploited. In the past, it was companies from the music industry and consumer electronics that wanted to manage music listening. For some years now, it has increasingly been companies from the information technology sector. Here, music listening is modelled statistically to an increasing extent. This is based not only on the data of listening behaviour, but also on listening models that can classify sound data as listening machines via feature extraction, pattern recognition and learning algorithms. Such statistical models of listening – interacting with networked computers and big data, algorithms and artificial intelligence – certainly have a different quality than the mechanical modelling that was done for the jukebox or the small single record. Their history is currently being written, and their future and future history is being shaped and made.

Notes

1 Introduction

1. Jonathan Sterne and Mitchell Akiyama, 'The Recording That Never Wanted to Be Heard and Other Stories of Sonification', in *The Oxford Handbook of Sound Studies*, ed. Karin Bijsterveld and Trevor Pinch (Oxford: Oxford University Press, 2012), 546. Veit Erlmann, 'The Acoustic Abject: Sound and the Legal Imagination', in *Sound Objects*, ed. James A. Steintrager and Rey Chow (Durham, NC: Duke University Press, 2019), 157.
2. David Howes, 'General Introduction: Empires of the Senses', in *Empire of the Senses: The Sensual Culture Reader*, ed. David Howes (Oxford: Berg, 2005), 5.
3. Wolfgang Welsch, 'Auf dem Weg zu einer Kultur des Hörens?', *Paragrana – Internationale Zeitschrift für Historische Anthropologie* 2, no. 1 (1993). Welsch also points out that primacy of the visual means that seeing is inscribed in conceptualizations of cognition, in forms of behaviour, in technical-scientific civilization (Wolfgang Welsch, *Die Aktualität des Ästhetischen* [Munich: Fink, 1993]).
4. Michel Foucault, 'What Is Enlightenment?', in *The Foucault Reader*, ed. Paul Rabinow (New York: Pantheon Books, 1984). Michel Foucault, *Discipline and Punish: The Birth of the Prison*, trans. Alan Sheridan (New York: Vintage Books, 1977).
5. Michael Bull and Les Back, 'Introduction', in *The Auditory Culture Reader*, ed. Michael Bull and Les Back (Oxford: Berg, 2003), 3.
6. David Howes, ed., *Empire of the Senses: The Sensual Culture Reader* (Oxford: Berg, 2005), 1.
7. Veit Erlmann, 'But What about an Ethnographic Ear? Anthropology, Sound and the Senses', in *Hearing Cultures: Essays on Sound, Listening and Modernity*, ed. Veit Erlmann (Oxford: Berg, 2004), 4.
8. Holger Schulze, 'Sonic Epistemology', in *Sound as Popular Culture: A Research Companion*, ed. Jens Gerrit Papenburg and Holger Schulze (Cambridge, MA: MIT Press, 2016). Next to sound, listening is one of sound studies' main concepts. This differs from musicology, where sound and listening have just played rather minor roles for a long time.
9. Howes, 'General Introduction', 1. We can find an early critique of the world as text paradigm in Michel Serres: Serres warns against limiting the senses to their linguistic representation and construction and resorts to drastic comparisons: 'I live no differently from these drugged individuals. I am devoted to language, which anaesthetizes all five senses. Every group I am part of, needs it or lives by it'. In Michel Serres, *The Five Senses: A Philosophy of Mingled Bodies*, trans. Margaret Sankey and Peter Cowley (New York: Bloomsbury Academics, 2016), 89. The diagnosed tendency escalates in Serres: 'I fear those who go through life drugged, less than I fear those under the edict of language' (92).

10 Erlmann, 'Ethnographic Ear?', 5; Emily Thompson, *The Soundscape of Modernity: Architectural Acoustics and the Culture of Listening in America, 1900–1933* (Cambridge, MA: MIT Press, 2002); Jonathan Sterne, *The Audible Past: Cultural Origins of Sound Reproduction* (Durham, NC: Duke University Press, 2003). In musicology, where the study of listening had not been very prominent until the 1990s (see Rob Wegman, '"Das musikalische Hören" in the Middle Ages and Renaissance: Perspectives from Pre-War Germany', *The Musical Quarterly* 82, no. 3/4 [1998]), an inclusion of listening in modernity with its technical media, 'global' music forms and performance forms beyond the concert was discussed as a crisis of listening in the 1920s (Veit Erlmann, *Reason and Resonance: A History of Modern Aurality* [New York: Zone Books, 2010]; Hansjakob Ziemer, 'The Crisis of Listening in Interwar Germany', in *The Oxford Handbook of Music Listening in the 19th and 20th Centuries*, ed. Christian Thorau and Hansjakob Ziemer [Oxford: Oxford University Press, 2019]; Heinrich Besseler, 'Grundfragen des musikalischen Hörens', *Jahrbuch der Musikbibliothek Peters* 35 [1925]).

11 Mark M. Smith, *Sensing the Past: Seeing, Hearing, Smelling, Tasting, and Touching in History* (Berkeley: University of California Press, 2007), 3.

12 Michael Bull and Les Back, 'Introduction', in *The Auditory Culture Reader*. 2nd Edition, ed. Michael Bull and Les Back (New York: Bloomsbury, 2016), 1.

13 Sterne and Akiyama, 'Recording That Never Wanted to Be Heard', 556.

14 Especially approaches from science and technology studies are using the concept of 'affordance' here (for the use of affordance in music studies, see Tia DeNora, *Music in Everyday Life* [Cambridge: Cambridge University Press, 2000]; Georgina Born, 'On Musical Mediation: Ontology, Technology, and Creativity', *Twentieth Century Music* 2, no. 1 [2005]; Eric F. Clarke, 'The Impact of Recording on Listening', *Twentieth-Century Music* 4, no. 1 [2007]). In her cultural history and history of technology of portable radios, the Walkman and cell phones, Heike Weber operates with a 'user de-sign' approach that studies constructions of the user by the analysis of 'product catalogs, instruction manuals, or even the things themselves' (Heike Weber, *Das Versprechen mobiler Freiheit. Zur Kultur- und Technikgeschichte von Kofferradio, Walkman und Handy* [Bielefeld: transcript, 2008], 33). Via 'user constructions', the 'participation of the user in the development of technology' is to be taken into consideration (44). The following varieties of the user should be considered: real users, user images (e.g. in marketing and advertising), user images mainstreamed in the product, user images in public discourse (47), practiced versus prospective user constructs, user constructs that are implemented in things (63).

15 Marshall McLuhan, *Understanding Media: The Extensions of Man* (London: Routledge, 2008), 98.

16 Derrick de Kerckhove, 'Propriodezeption und Autonomation', in *Tasten*, ed. Uta Brandes and Claudia Neumann (Göttingen: Steidl, 1996), 333; Stefan Rieger, 'Organische Konstruktionen. Von der Künstlichkeit des Körpers zur Natürlichkeit der Medien', in *McLuhan neu Lesen. Kritische Analysen zu Medien und Kultur im 21. Jahrhundert*, ed. Derrick de Kerckhove, Martina Leeker and Kerstin Schmidt (Bielefeld: transcript, 2008).

17 John Durham Peters, 'Helmholtz, Edison, and Sound History', in *Memory Bytes: History, Technology, and Digital Culture*, ed. Lauren Rabinovitz and Abraham Geil (Durham, NC: Duke University Press, 2004), 189.

18 Ibid., 178.

19 Sterne, *The Audible Past*, 31–85.
20 Friedrich A. Kittler, *Gramophone, Film, Typewriter*, trans. Geoffrey Winthrop-Young and Michael Wutz (Stanford, CA: Stanford University Press, 1999); Viktoria Tkaczyk, 'Gedächtnis', in *Handbuch Sound: Geschichte – Begriffe – Ansätze*, ed. Daniel Morat and Hansjakob Ziemer (Stuttgart: J. B. Metzler, 2018).
21 Bruno Latour, 'On Technical Mediation. Philosophy, Sociology, Genealogy', *Common Knowledge* 3, no. 2 (1994).
22 Ibid., 31.
23 Ibid., 34.
24 Sterne, *The Audible Past*, 34.
25 Ibid., 40.
26 Jonathan Sterne, 'The MP3 as Cultural Artefact', *New Media and Society* 8, no. 5 (2006), 837.
27 Jonathan Crary, *Techniques of the Observer: On Vision and Modernity in the Nineteenth Century* (Cambridge, MA: MIT Press, 1990); Friedrich A. Kittler, *Optical Media: Berlin Lectures 1999*, trans. Anthony Enns (Cambridge: Polity, 2010); Peters, 'Helmholtz, Edison, and Sound History'.
28 Sebastian Klotz, 'Algorithmic and Nostalgic Listening: Post-Subjective Implications of Computational and Empirical Research', in *Musical Listening in the Age of Technological Reproduction*, ed. Gianmario Borio (Farnham: Ashgate, 2015).
29 Tristan Jehan, 'Creating Music by Listening', PhD dissertation, Massachusetts Institute of Technology, 2005, 36, https://web.media.mit.edu/~tristan/phd/pdf/Tristan_PhD_MIT.pdf.; Jens Gerrit Papenburg and Max Alt, 'Streamability: Überlegungen zu einer Ästhetik des Musikstreaming', in *Acoustic Intelligence: Hören und Gehorchen*, ed. Anna Schürmer, Max Haberer and Tomy Brautschek (Berlin: Düsseldorf University Press, 2022).
30 Kittler, *Gramophone, Film, Typewriter*, 23.
31 On the concept of the 'epistemic thing', see Hans-Jörg Rheinberger, *Experimentalsysteme und epistemische Dinge: eine Geschichte der Proteinsynthese im Reagenzglas* (Göttingen: Wallstein-Verlag, 2019). For an overview of epistemic things of acoustic and hearing physiological research in the nineteenth century, see David Pantalony, *Altered Sensations: Rudolph Koenig's Acoustical Workshop in Nineteenth-Century Paris* (New York: Springer, 2009).
32 Benjamin Steege, *Helmholtz and the Modern Listener* (Cambridge: Cambridge University Press, 2012); Alexandra Hui, *The Psychophysical Ear: Musical Experiments, Experimental Sounds, 1840–1910* (Cambridge, MA: MIT Press, 2013).
33 Julia Kursell, *Epistemologie des Hörens: Helmholtz' physiologische Grundlegung der Musiktheorie* (Munich: Fink, 2018).
34 Viktoria Tkaczyk, 'The Testing of a Hundred Listeners: Otto Abraham's Studies on "Absolute Tone Consciousness"', in *Testing Hearing: The Making of Modern Aurality*, ed. Viktoria Tkaczyk, Mara Mills and Alexandra Hui (Oxford: Oxford University Press, 2021). On experimental systems, see Rheinberger, *Experimentalsysteme und epistemische Dinge*.
35 Klotz, 'Algorithmic and Nostalgic Listening: Post-Subjective Implications of Computational and Empirical Research'; Jehan, 'Creating Music by Listening'.
36 Georg Christoph Tholen, *Die Zäsur der Medien. Kulturphilosophische Konturen* (Frankfurt am Main: Suhrkamp, 2002), 169.

37 With regard to the relationship between perception and media, Tholen concretized – in a somewhat apodictic tone – a pre-existence of technology in Heidegger, as follows: '[If we] define technology only as an instrument, we remain, as Heidegger's philosophy of technology and language has shown, bound to the blind will to only want to master and control it. Precisely because of this, however, we miss out on the predecessor of a perception and experience that is always caesuraed by the media. For there is no perception that would be sufficiently determined by its natural givenness. Perception is always mediated by media' (169). I shall return to Heidegger's philosophy of technology and to the pre-existence of technology in modernity later in the text.

38 In his analysis of mediated perception, the literature and media scholar Joseph Vogl has used the example of Galileo Galilei's telescope to distinguish between medium and instrument (see Joseph Vogl, 'Becoming-Media: Galileo's Telescope', *Grey Room* 29 [2007]). The telescope as an instrument is to be placed on the side of secondary experience. In this view, a theory of the eye is distinguished from a theory of the instrument – that is, the telescope (18). In the media view the telescope defines the sensory performance of the eye. Vogl introduces the term denaturation of the senses and follows it up with the thesis that media would enable a history of the senses (17–18).

39 Rieger, 'Organische Konstruktionen', 263.

40 Ibid., 264.

41 Ibid.

42 See Gernot Böhme, *Invasive Technification: Critical Essays in the Philosophy of Technology*, trans. Cameron Shingleton (New York: Bloomsbury Academic, 2012).

43 Ibid., 125.

44 Ibid., 7. Already in the sensory physiology of the nineteenth century, the relationship between organs and technology is reversed: 'Simple tools can perhaps still be derived from human organs, but in the case of complex machines and electrical media it is exactly the other way round, i.e. human organs become explainable at the latest since Müller, Du Bois-Reymond, and Helmholtz from their alleged projections' (Harun Maye, 'Was ist eine Kulturtechnik?', *Zeitschrift für Medien- und Kulturforschung: Schwerpunkt Kulturtechnik* 1 [2010]: 131).

45 At this point, a theory of listening devices touches base with a new or critical organology, that is, an organology that stresses next to the instrumental function of musical instruments its epistemic function; see John Tresch and Emily I. Dolan, 'Toward a New Organology: Instruments of Music and Science', *Osiris* 28, no. 1 (2013); Alexander Rehding, 'Three Music-Theory Lessons', *Journal of the Royal Musical Association* 141, 2 (2016).

46 Robin James, for instance, tries to show how the statistical models of perceptual coding include 'neoliberal market logics': Robin James, 'Sonic Cyberfeminisms, Perceptual Coding and Phonographic Compression', *Feminist Review* 127, no. 1 (2021). Not for listening devices but for the 'vocal apparatus' Iris Blake argues that this apparatus was a product of nineteenth-century physiological research and includes 'colonial fantasies and desires for scientific mastery of the body and the senses which relied on a delimited definition of both "the human" and "the human voice"'. Iris Sandjette Blake, 'The Vocal Apparatus's Colonial Contexts: France's Mission Civilisatrice and (Settler) Colonialism in Algeria and North America',

in *Sonic Histories of Occupation*, ed. Jeremy E. Taylor and Russell Skelchy (New York: Bloomsbury, 2022).

47 When we speak of materiality here, we are primarily following the tradition opened with the investigation of the 'materiality of communication' (Hans Ulrich Gumbrecht and Ludwig Pfeiffer, eds, *Materialität der Kommunikation* [Frankfurt am Main: Suhrkamp, 1988]), studies of 'aisthesis' (Karlheinz Barck and Peter Gente, *Aisthesis. Wahrnehmung heute oder Perspektiven einer anderen Ästhetik* [Leipzig: Reclam, 1990]) and a 'media materialism' (Kittler, *Gramophone, Film, Typewriter*), in the sense of a 'materialism of things'. The latter, however, is definitely brought together in the present book with a 'materialism of relations' (Jens Schröter and Till A. Heilmann, 'Zum Bonner Programm einer neo-kritischen Medienwissenschaft', *Navigationen. Zeitschrift für Medien- und Kulturwissenschaften* 16, no. 2 [2016]), thus bringing together 'not only epistemic or aesthetic, but also socio-economic inherent laws of the media' (17), as proposed, for instance, by the Bonn programme of a 'neo-critical media studies.' In sound studies, 'materiality' has become an often cited concept. Sterne writes: 'Reading around in the humanities and social sciences, we can find dozens of calls for materiality, but often little agreement over what the term entails' (Jonathan Sterne, '"What Do We Want?" "Materiality!" "When Do We Want It?" "Now!"', *Media Technologies: Essays on Communication, Materiality, and Society*, ed. Tarleton Gillespie, Pablo J. Boczkowski and Kirsten A. Foot [Cambridge, MA: MIT Press, 2014], 120). He proposes a concept of materiality that 'refers to both physical things and the irreducibly relational character of reality' (121), and sees the boom of materiality as a symptom of a 'fatigue with constructivism' (121). A call for materiality even brings together conflicting approaches by Christoph Cox and Marie Thompson (see Marie Thompson, 'Whiteness and the Ontological Turn in Sound Studies', *Parallax* 23, no. 3 [2017]; Christoph Cox, 'Sonic Realism and Auditory Culture: A Reply to Marie Thompson and Annie Goh', *Parallax* 24, no. 2 [2018]); even if so-called ontological approaches (such as Cox's) referring to 'new materialism' of sound studies and a 'materiality' of sound that should address a domain 'beyond representation and signification' (Christoph Cox, 'Beyond Representation and Signification: Toward a Sonic Materialism', *Journal of Visual Culture* 10, no. 2 [2011]) differ fundamentally from Thompson's approach. Steve Goodman's 'bass materialism' and its affective dimension can also be mentioned here (Steve Goodman, *Sonic Warfare: Sound, Affect, and the Ecology of Fear* [Cambridge, MA: MIT Press, 2010]). Also musicology studies the materialities of music: The research project 'Sound and Materialism in the 19th Century' studied the dynamics between 'scientific-materialist conception' and 'dominant culture of romantic idealism' (David Trippett, 'Sound and Materialism in the 19th Century', accessed 29 April 2022, https://sound-matter.com/dr-david-trippett/). Rebecca Wolf brings together material culture and organology: '"Matter", "material" and "materiality" are not among the central concepts in the humanities that deal with sound' (Rebecca Wolf, 'Materielle Kultur', *Handbuch Sound. Geschichte – Begriffe – Ansätze*, ed. Daniel Morat and Hansjakob Ziemer [Stuttgart: Metzler, 2018], 32). Here Wolf sees sounding objects and sound generators or the materials they are made of (such as glass, wood, plastic) as objects of material culture as much as sound itself or the 'scientific tools' with which it is studied as well as sheet music and music rolls for automatic pianos. Rolf Großmann studies the 'materiality of sound' (Rolf Großmann, 'Die Materialität des Klangs und die Medienpraxis der Musikkultur. Ein verspäteter Gegenstand der

Musikwissenschaft?', *Auditive Medienkulturen. Techniken des Hörens und Praktiken der Klanggestaltung*, ed. Jens Schröter and Axel Volmar [Bielefeld: transcript, 2013]). Kyle Devine, in his political economy of music, has examined music listening starting from materialities of music listening – shellac, plastic and data materialized, for example, through global communication infrastructures and server farms (see Kyle Devine, *Decomposed: The Political Ecology of Music* [Cambridge, MA: MIT Press, 2019]). The 'materiality of listening' is also the vanishing point of the contributions to the special issue of *Sound Studies* (Joeri Bruyninckx and Alexandra Supper, eds, 'Sonic Skills in Cultural Contexts: Theories, Practices and Materialities of Listening', *Sound Studies. An Interdisciplinary Journal* 2, no. 1 [2016]). In the research project 'Music Objects of Popular Culture' (Christina Dörfling, Christofer Jost and Martin Pfleiderer, eds, *Musikobjektgeschichten: Populäre Musik und materielle Kultur* [Münster: Waxmann, 2021]) materialities of 'musical experience' also play a major role – next to approaches to instruments in the context of material culture (Alan van Keeken, 'Sozio-technische Artefaktanalyse', in *Spurenlesen. Methodische Ansätze der Sammlungs- und Objektforschung*, ed. Ernst Seidl and Cornelia Weber [Humboldt-Universität zu Berlin, 2021], 61–71).

48 On cultural techniques, see Friedrich A. Kittler, *Discourse Networks 1800/1900*, trans. Michael Matteer (Stanford, CA: Stanford University Press, 1990); Wolfgang Scherer, 'Hörsturz 1900. Die Decodierung des Musikalischen Hörens', in *Welt auf tönernen Füßen. Die Töne und das Hören*, ed. Uta Brandes (Göttingen: Steidl, 1994); Sybille Krämer and Horst Bredekamp, 'Kultur, Technik, Kulturtechnik: Wider die Diskursivierung der Kultur', in *Bild – Schrift – Zahl*, ed. Sybille Krämer and Horst Bredekamp (Munich: Fink, 2003); Friedrich Balke, Bernhard Siegert and Joseph Vogl, eds, *Takt und Frequenz*, Archiv für Mediengeschichte 2011 (Munich: Fink, 2011); Bernard Siegert, 'Oszillationen zwischen Störung und Entstörung. Zur Kulturtechnik des Radiophonischen Hörens', in *Radiophonic Cultures*, ed. Ute Holl (Heidelberg: Kehrer, 2018).

49 Andrew Dell'Antonio, *Listening as Spiritual Practice in Early Modern Italy* (Berkeley: University of California Press, 2011).

50 Eduard Hanslick, *Eduard Hanslick's 'On the Musically Beautiful': A New Translation*, trans. Lee Allen Rothfarb and Christoph Landerer (Oxford: Oxford University Press, 2018).

51 Rose Subotnick, *Developing Variations: Style and Ideology in Western Music* (Minneapolis: University of Minnesota Press, 1991); Theodor W. Adorno, *Introduction to the Sociology of Music*, trans. E. B. Ashton (New York: The Seabury Press, 1976).

52 Ibid., 4.

53 Ibid., 5.

54 Hugo Riemann, 'Ideen zu einer Lehre von den Tonvorstellungen', *Jahrbuch der Musikbibliothek Peters* 21 (1914/1915).

55 Heinrich Besseler, *Das Musikalische Hören der Neuzeit* (Berlin: Akademie Verlag, 1959), 11.

56 Arnold Schering, *Musikalische Bildung und Erziehung zum Musikalischen Hören* (Leipzig: Quelle & Meyer, 1911).

57 Felix Salzer, *Structural Hearing: Tonal Coherence in Music* (New York: C. Boni, 1952).

58 Subotnick, *Developing Variations*; Andrew Dell'Antonio, *Beyond Structural Listening? Postmodern Modes of Hearing* (Berkeley: University of California Press, 2004).

59 Peter Gay, *The Naked Heart* (New York: Norton, 1995); Christian Thorau and Hansjakob Ziemer, eds, *The Oxford Handbook of Music Listening in the 19th and 20th Centuries* (Oxford: Oxford University Press, 2019).
60 Veit Erlmann, 'The Invention of the Listener: (An)Other History', in *Sound as Popular Culture: A Research Companion*, ed. Jens Gerrit Papenburg and Holger Schulze (Cambridge, MA: MIT Press, 2016), 167. Erlmann writes that the 'emergence of the (modern) listener is one of the key topics of sound studies' (164). Although Erlmann mentions different forms of the modern listener – a 'silent, inward-turned 'listener" (165), a listener who shaped the 'interplay of attentive listening and audio technology' (166), but also the 'discursive construction of modern subjectivity' through listening (166) – it is primarily the first one, the silent inward-turned 'listener', who Erlmann exposes as the modern listener. Erlmann dates the origin of this listener to the eighteenth century and points to preliminary forms in the seventeenth century. He shows that the modern listener 'rests on a hidden foundation' of 'difference and Otherness' (165); that for the modern listener 'race maintains an eerie presence, always lurking below the discursive surface' (166). Also Thorau and Ziemer are arguing in general – referencing Heinrich Besseler, Peter Gay and James H. Johnson – for 1750 'as the beginning of the modern listening tradition' (Christian Thorau and Hansjakob Ziemer, 'The Art of Listening and its Histories: An Introduction', in *The Oxford Handbook of Music Listening in the 19th and 20th Centuries*, ed. Christian Thorau and Hansjakob Ziemer [Oxford: Oxford University Press, 2019], 10).
61 Scherer, 'Hörsturz 1900'; Alexander Rehding, *Hugo Riemann and the Birth of Modern Musical Thought* (Cambridge: Cambridge University Press, 2003).
62 Adorno, *Introduction to the Sociology of Music.*
63 See Thorau and Ziemer, *The Oxford Handbook of Music Listening in the 19th and 20th Centuries.* Moreover, the listener can transform into a reader by listening through reading scores.
64 Over the how-question, phenomenological approaches can also be brought into play. Phenomenological approaches to music ask 'How is music?' (see Christian Grüny, *Kunst des Übergangs: Philosophische Konstellationen zur Musik* [Weilerswist: Velbrück, 2014], 7–9). According to this, the question 'How do people listen to music?' can also be also asked as a phenomenological one. However, the materiality, mediality and technicity of listening is not the core interest of phenomenological approaches. Moreover, agency beyond human agency is not always analysed in such approaches.
65 Erlmann, *Reason and Resonance,* 17. Listening becomes a prominent subject in physiology in the work of Hermann von Helmholtz ([1863], *On the Sensations of Tone as a Physiological Basis for the Theory of Music,* trans. Alexander J. Ellis [London: Longmans, Green, 1885]) and in the work of Carl Stumpf (*Tonpsychologie* [Leipzig: Hirzel, 1883–1890]) and Ernst Kurth (*Musikpsychologie* [Berlin: Hesse, 1931]).
66 Lorenz Engell and Bernhard Siegert, *Zeitschrift für Medien- und Kulturforschung: Schwerpunkt Kulturtechnik* (Hamburg: Meiner, 2010), 8.
67 Scherer, 'Hörsturz 1900', 388.
68 Engell and Siegert, *Zeitschrift für Medien- und Kulturforschung,* 8.
69 'However, operations such as counting or writing always presuppose technical objects on and with which these operations are performed, and which to no small extent determine the performance of these operations. An abacus allows a different counting than ten fingers, a computer again a different counting than an abacus' (Lorenz

Engell and Bernhard Siegert, 'Editorial', *Zeitschrift für Medien- und Kulturforschung* 1 [2010]: 7).

70 Siegert shows this using the example of cooking as a cultural technique: 'Simply put, you can't cook without some kind of vessel. The art of cooking – which, according to Claude Lévi-Strauss, is the most elementary of all cultural techniques – cannot be derived from a body technique. A pot is not a McLuhanesque extension of man, for example, of the hollow hand: You cannot boil anything in a hollow hand without losing your hand in the process' (Bernhard Siegert, 'Cacography or Communication? Cultural Techniques in German Media Studies', *Grey Room* 29 [2007]: 30). Following Siegert, listening turns into a cultural technique only when it is part of a media culture: 'Hearing itself is not a cultural technique. As is well known, the ear cannot close. Only in radiophonic cultures does hearing become a cultural technique' (Bernhard Siegert, 'Oszillationen zwischen Störung und Entstörung. Zur Kulturtechnik des radiophonischen Hörens', 233).

71 Alexander Rehding, 'Discrete/Continuous: Music and Media Theory after Kittler', *Journal of the American Musicological Society* 70, no. 1 (2017); Johannes Ismaiel-Wendt, *Post_PRESETS. Kultur, Wissen und Populäre MusikmachDinge* (Hildesheim: Universitätsverlag Hildesheim and Georg Olms Verlag, 2016); Alan van Keeken, 'Musik erzeugen', in *Audiowelten: Technologie und Medien in der populären Musik nach 1945: 22 Objektstudien*, ed. Benjamin Burkhart, Laura Niebling, Alan van Keeken, Christofer Jost and Martin Pfleiderer (Münster: Waxmann, 2021).

72 On the discrimination of body techniques and cultural techniques regarding sound, see also Britta Lange, 'Kulturwissenschaft', in *Handbuch Sound: Geschichte – Begriffe – Ansätze*, ed. Daniel Morat and Hanjakob Ziemer (Stuttgart: Metzler, 2018), 117–18. Lange emphasizes above all the production of symbolic meaning through cultural technology: 'In this sense, procedures of production, distribution, reception, and interpretation of sound can be studied as cultural techniques, such as colonial phonography for the generation of scientific knowledge or exoticizing show effects, the advertising of sound apparatuses with common cultural metaphors, and so on' (117).

73 See, for example, Dylan Robinson, *Hungry Listening: Resonant Theory for Indigenous Sound Studies* (Minneapolis: University of Minnesota Press, 2020).

74 In contrast to a couple of important sound and music studies scholars who studied listening in its cultural specificity (Veit Erlmann, ed., *Hearing Cultures. Essays on Sound, Listening and Modernity* [Oxford: Berg, 2004]; also Ola Stockfelt, 'Adequate Modes of Listening', in *Keeping Score: Music, Disciplinarity, Culture*, ed. David Schwarz, Anahid Kassabian and Lawrence Siegel [Charlottesville: University Press of Virginia, 1997], 129–46; Dell'Antonio, *Beyond Structural Listening?*; Rose Subotnik, *Developing Variations: Style and Ideology in Western Music* [Minneapolis: University of Minnesota Press, 1991]), studying listening as a cultural technique focuses on the objects that are involved in listening.

75 Thorau and Ziemer conceptualize such an art of listening by three threads: (1) 'art has been attributable to nearly every cultural practice that requires expertise and allows refinement' (Thorau and Ziemer, 'Art of Listening and Its Histories', 3); (2) 'an ability that belongs to the realm of the fine arts' (3); and (3) a normative meaning – 'the idea that music is the art that teaches us how to listen and refines our ability to do so' that correlates with the 'implicit listener' (5–8).

76 Karin Bijsterveld, *Sonic Skills: Listening for Knowledge in Science, Engineering and Medicine (1920s–Present)* (New York: Palgrave Macmillan, 2019). Bijsterveld defines sonic skills as follows: 'Sonic skills, as I use the term here, include not only listening skills, but also the techniques that doctors, engineers, and scientists need for what they consider an effective use of their listening and recording equipment. Examples of such skills would be the proper positioning of a stethoscope on a patient's body, the handling of magnetic tape recorders in bird sound recording, or simply archiving sound samples for easy retrieval. To understand listening for knowledge, therefore, we need to study not only the skills related to listening proper, but also those that ensure sounds can be amplified, captured, reproduced, edited, compiled, accessed, and analyzed' (ibid., 4).

77 Sterne, *The Audible Past*. Bijsterveld defines sonic skills as follows: 'Sonic skills, as I use the term here, include not only listening skills, but also the techniques that doctors, engineers, and scientists need for what they consider an effective use of their listening and recording equipment. Examples of such skills would be the proper positioning of a stethoscope on a patient's body, the handling of magnetic tape recorders in bird sound recording, or simply archiving sound samples for easy retrieval. To understand listening for knowledge, therefore, we need to study not only the skills related to listening proper, but also those that ensure sounds can be amplified, captured, reproduced, edited, compiled, accessed, and analyzed' (ibid., 4). Sterne coins the term 'audile or listening technique' in reference to Mauss's notion of body technique. He examines '"regimes" of listening practices' (Sterne, *The Audible Past*, 91) and thus the difference between specific listening ideals and their practical realizations in fields as diverse as otology, telegraphy and sound reproduction technologies in the nineteenth and early twentieth centuries. Thus, Sterne gives audile technique – 'it came to music rather late' (98) – a time index and classifies it as modern. The modernity Sterne specifies is as follows: 'Speaking generally, audile technique articulated listening and the ear to logic, analytic thought, industry, professionalism, capitalism, individualism, and mastery – even as it required a good deal of guesswork in practice' (95). In contrast to Siegert, who sees cultural technology as linked to an artefact, which is primarily not an extension of the body, Sterne tends to explain artefacts by social science: 'If media do, indeed, extend our senses, they do so as crystallized versions and elaborations of people's prior practices – or techniques – of using their senses' (92). Certain listening practices would thus precede the artefacts over which listening is performed: 'Over the course of the nineteenth century, hearing was constructed as a set of capacities and mechanisms, and that mechanical, objectified construct of hearing was crucial in the mechanical construction of sound-reproduction technologies' (96). In this respect, it is primarily such practices and not radio, film and sound recording that are 'agents of acoustic modernity' (95). Nevertheless, listening techniques are recursive for Sterne. To be sure, Sterne starts from social practices, which then sediment into techniques and technologies. The feedback of the technologies on listening as a bodily practice is also taken into account by Sterne. For a critique of Sterne's concept of 'audile technique', see Brian Kane, 'In Search of Audile Technique' (keynote lecture, EHESS, Paris, 26 January 2019) lecture audio available online: https://soundcloud.com/user-897145 586/brian-kane-yale-university (accessed on 18 February 2022). Kane shows that 'audile technique' is not a 'consistent object' because it oscillates between singular and plural, between a practice and a regime of knowledge. In his analysis of the mp3

format, Sterne gives up the link to Mauss's body techniques and thus also rejects the notion of auditory techniques: 'The encoded mathematical table inside the mp3 that represents psychoacoustic response suggests less a "technique of the body" as these authors [e.g. Bourdieu] would have it, than a concordance of signals among computers, electrical components and auditory nerves' (Sterne, 'MP3 as Cultural Artefact', 837). The mp3 file is not – at least not exclusively – about the organization and disciplining of a body as in the body techniques, but primarily about the modeling of a body: 'The mp3 uses a construct of the body to modify data, electrical signals and eventually sounds before they get to listeners' ears' (838).

78 Michael Bull, 'Personal Stereos and the Critical Theory of Urban Everyday Life', in *Sounding Out the City* (Oxford: Berg, 2000); Michael Bull, *Sound Moves: iPod Culture and Urban Experience* (London: Routledge, 2007) Thompson, *The Soundscape of Modernity*; Sterne, *The Audible Past*; Stefan Helmreich, 'An Anthropologist Underwater: Immersive Soundscapes, Submarine Cyborgs, and Transductive Ethnography', *American Ethnologist* 34, no. 4 (2007); Myles W. Jackson, 'From Scientific Instruments to Musical Instruments: The Tuning Fork, Metronome, and Siren', in *The Oxford Handbook of Sound Studies*, ed. Karin Bijsterveld and Trevor Pinch (New York: Oxford University Press, 2012); Anahid Kassabian, 'Listening and Digital Technologies', in *Sound as Popular Culture: A Research Companion*, ed. Jens Gerrit Papenburg and Holger Schulze (Cambridge, MA: MIT Press, 2016); Kursell, *Epistemologie des Hörens*; Bijsterveld, *Sonic Skills*; Alexandra Hui, 'First Re-creations: Psychology, Phonographs, and New Cultures of Listening at the Beginning of the Twentieth Century', in *The Oxford Handbook of Music Listening in the 19th and 20th Centuries*, ed. Christian Thorau and Hansjakob Ziemer (Oxford: Oxford University Press, 2019); Axel Volmar, 'Experiencing High Fidelity: Sound Reproduction and the Politics of Music Listening in the Twentieth Century', in *The Oxford Handbook of Music Listening in the 19th and 20th Centuries*, ed. Christian Thorau and Hansjakob Ziemer (Oxford: Oxford University Press, 2019). Moreover, there are a variety of approaches of music and sound studies which address the feedback between listening and technology. Terms such as 'listening technology' (Tim J. Anderson, *Making Easy Listening: Material Culture and Postwar American Recording* [Minneapolis: University of Minnesota Press, 2006], 114), '*instruments for listening*' (Peter Szendy, *Listen: A History of Our Ears* [New York: Fordham University Press, 2008], 72, original emphasis), 'technologies of reception' (Jeremy Gilbert and Ewan Pearson, *Discographies: Dance Music, Culture and the Politics of Sound* [London: Routledge, 1999], 128), 'technologically mediated forms of experience' (Michael Bull, *Sound Moves: iPod Culture and Urban Experience* 5) or 'hearing devices' (Don Ihde, *Listening and Voice: Phenomenologies of Sound* [Albany: State University of New York Press, 2007], 243–50) are introduced mostly in passing and are not systematically developed as concepts. Therefore, the present volume's treatment of a history of listening from the perspective of the 'listening device' concept represents a productive departure from those music and sound studies analyses of listening which have dealt only *en passant* for the most part with the assemblage of sound, corporeality and technology, and almost exclusively in the English- and French-speaking worlds.

79 Joeri Bruyninckx and Alexandra Supper, 'Sonic Skills in Cultural Contexts: Theories, Practices and Materialities of Listening', *Sound Studies* 2, no. 1 (2016): 1.

80 Schüttpelz, referring to the exteriorization concept of the anthropologist André Leroi-Gourhan (*Gesture and Speech*. Trans. Anna Bostock Berger [Cambridge, MA: MIT Press, 1993 [1980]]) calls this a 'recursive exteriorisation': 'For technical inventions, domestications, and media history, it is equally true that every exteriorisation strikes back at the exteriorisers and triggers a widely ramified series of contingent entanglements – between humans, animals, artefacts and media. Exteriorisation happens recursively or not at all; and its consequences – and indeed in the evidence of accumulating steps of invention – cannot be captured in any history of evolutionary stages' (Erhard Schüttpelz, 'Die medienanthropologische Kehre der Kulturtechniken', *Archiv für Mediengeschichte* 8 [2006]: 94).
81 Ernst Kapp, *Grundlinien einer Philosophie der Technik. Zur Entstehungsgeschichte der Cultur aus neuen Gesichtspunkten* (Braunschweig: Westermann, 1877); McLuhan, *Understanding Media*.
82 Geoffrey Winthrop-Young, 'Cultural Techniques: Preliminary Remarks', *Theory, Culture & Society* 30, no. 6 (2013): 6.
83 Krämer and Bredekamp, 'Kultur, Technik, Kulturtechnik', 12.
84 Ibid. Precursors of these positions can be found in the interwar period. The philosopher Oswald Spengler, in his essay 'Man and Technics' states: 'But even in Wilhelm von Humboldt we have the beginnings of that anti-realist, philological outlook upon history which in the limit reckons the values of a historical epoch in terms of the number of the pictures and books that it produced' (Oswald Spengler, *Man and Technics: A Contribution to a Philosophy of Life*, trans. Charles Francis Atkinson [New York: Alfred A. Knopf, 1932], 4). Technique and technology here seem to be excluded not only from the concept of history but also from the concept of culture.
85 At least at this point, the present work is at odds with Sterne's analysis of 'audile techniques' which continues to shape sound studies. Sterne sees the connection between listening and technology as determined by a progressive privatization, rationalization, and individualization (see Sterne, *The Audible Past*, 95). He examines privatized listening practices. In contrast, this book here rather follows Emily Thompson's investigation of technologized spaces of public listening (Thompson, *The Soundscape of Modernity*); see on this difference in Sterne and Thompson also Michele Hilmes, 'Is There a Field Called Sound Culture Studies? And Does It Matter?', *American Quarterly* 57, no. 1 (2005). Sarah Thornton also criticizes the short-circuit of increasing mechanization and increasing privatization in relation to music listening: 'Recorded music is as much a feature of public houses, stores, factories, lifts, restaurants and karaoke bars as it is an attribute of the private home' (Sarah Thornton, *Club Cultures: Music, Media and Subcultural Capital* [Cambridge: Polity, 1995], 34).
86 Sterne, *The Audible Past*, 94.
87 Emily Thompson, 'Machines, Music, and the Quest for Fidelity. Marketing the Edison Phonograph in America, 187–925', *The Musical Quarterly* 79 (1995): 133.
88 Cultural techniques are not assigned to one side of the distinction, but take the position of a third party, just as doors, for example, process the distinction between inside/outside (see Bernhard Siegert, 'Doors: On the Materiality of the Symbolic', trans. John Durham Peters, *Grey Room* 47 [2012]: 8–9; Bernhard Siegert, 'Door Logic, or, the Materiality of the Symbolic: From Cultural Techniques to Cybernetic Machines', in *Cultural Techniques: Grids, Filters,*

Doors, and Other Articulations of the Real, trans. Geoffrey Winthrop-Young [New York: Fordham University Press, 2015]).
89 Winthrop-Young, 'Cultural Techniques', 6.
90 Ibid., 5–6.
91 Geoffrey Winthrop-Young, 'Discourse, Media, Cultural Techniques: The Complexity of Kittler', *Modern Language Notes* 130, no. 3 (2015): 458.
92 Ibid., 459.
93 Of course, more examples can be found here: 'While phonetic writing is traditionally conceived as a simple and linear form of representation, writing is a cultural technique that makes visible a recursive network in which the one who writes and what is written down are not always already given, but are constituted for the very first time' (Maye, 'Was ist eine Kulturtechnik?', 125).
94 Winthrop-Young, 'Cultural Techniques', 3. Winthrop-Young mentions three different meanings, 'three different conceptual inflections' (Winthrop-Young, 'Cultural Techniques', 4) of the term cultural technique. The first refers to 'rural engineering' (5) such as agriculture or draining (transforming 'nature into culture') (6); the second 'skills and aptitudes necessary to master the new media ecology' (5) such as 'Kulturtechniken des Fernsehens' (6) supplemented by 'elementary cultural techniques' (9) ('culturalisation of technology' [6]), and the third 'to account for basic operations and differentiations that give rise to an array of conceptual and ontological entities which are said to constitute culture' (3).
95 Ibid., 11–12.
96 Michele Friedner and Stefan Helmreich, 'Sound Studies Meets Deaf Studies', *Senses & Society* 7, no. 1 (2012); Mara Mills, 'Deafness', in *Keywords in Sound*, ed. David Novak and Matt Sakakeeny (Durham, NC: Duke University Press, 2015); Rebecca Sanchez, 'Deafness and Sound', in *Sound and Literature*, ed. Anna Snaith (Cambridge: Cambridge University Press, 2020).
97 Steve Goodman, *Sonic Warfare: Sound, Affect, and the Ecology of Fear*; Steve Goodman, Toby Heys and Eleni Ikoniadou, eds, *AUDINT-Unsound:Undead* (Falmouth: Urbanomic, 2019); Julian Henriques, *Sonic Bodies: Reggae Sound Systems, Performance Techniques and Ways of Knowing* (New York: Continuum, 2011); Shelley Trower, '"Upwards of 20,000": Extrasensory Quantities of Railway Shock', *The Senses and Society* 3, no. 2 (2008); Shelley Trower, *Senses of Vibration. A History of the Pleasure and Pain of Sound* (New York: Continuum, 2012); Shelley Trower, 'Vibrations', in *Sound and Literature*, ed. Anna Snaith (Cambridge: Cambridge University Press, 2020); Paul C. Jasen, *Low End Theory: Bass, Bodies and the Materiality of Sonic Experience* (New York: Bloomsbury Academic, 2016).
98 Friedner and Helmreich, 'Sound Studies Meets Deaf Studies', 76.
99 Jasen, *Low End Theory*, 8 and 186; Will Schrimshaw, 'Non-Cochlear Sound: On Affect and Exteriority', in *Sound, Music, Affect: Theorizing Sonic Experience*, ed. Ian Biddle and Marie Thompson (New York: Bloomsbury Academic, 2013); Seth Kim-Cohen, *In the Blink of an Ear. Toward a Non-cochlear Sonic Art* (New York: Continuum, 2009).
100 Friedner and Helmreich, 'Sound Studies Meets Deaf Studies', 73 and 76.
101 Kittler, *Gramophone, Film, Typewriter*.
102 Scherer, 'Hörsturz 1900'.
103 Wolfgang Hagen, *Das Radio. Zur Geschichte und Theorie des Hörfunks – Deutschland/USA* (Munich: Fink, 2005), 150–1.

104 Sterne, *The Audible Past*; Jonathan Sterne, *Diminished Faculties: A Political Phenomenology of Impairment* (Durham, NC: Duke University Press, 2022).
105 Mills, 'Deafness'.
106 Kittler, *Gramophone, Film, Typewriter*, 22.
107 Sterne, *The Audible Past*, 36.
108 Ibid., 38. See also Mills, 'Deafness', 48–9.
109 Anahid Kassabian, *Ubiquitous Listening: Affect, Attention, and Distributed Subjectivity* (Berkeley: University of California Press, 2013).
110 Kittler, *Optical Media*, 36.
111 Ibid.
112 Next to the discourse of unsound I mentioned earlier, the discourse on listening as a vibrational practice (Nina Sun Eidsheim, *Sensing Sound: Singing and Listening as Vibrational Practice* [Durham, NC: Duke University Press, 2015]) is relevant here.
113 Henriques, *Sonic Bodies*; Julian Henriques, 'Sonic Dominance and the Reggae Sound System Session', in *The Auditory Culture Reader*, ed. Michael Bull and Les Back (Oxford: Berg, 2005); Julian Henriques, 'Auditory and Technological Culture: The Fine-Tuning of the Dancehall Sound System "Set"', *Journal of Sonic Studies* 1, no. 1 (2011).
114 Goodman, *Sonic Warfare*, 28.
115 Wolfgang Ernst, 'Der Anästhetische Blick? Wahrnehmung durch Medien', in *Ästhetik. Aufgabe(n) einer Wissenschaftsdisziplin*, ed. Karin Hirdina and Renate Reschke (Freiburg: Rombach, 2004), 74.
116 See, for instance, Jonathan Sterne, *MP3. The Meaning of a Format* (Durham, NC: Duke University Press, 2012).
117 Joseph Vogl, 'Becoming-Media: Galileo's Telescope; Kittler, *Optical Media*; Ernst, 'Der Anästhetische Blick?'. In the field of vision, Friedrich Kittler and Jonathan Crary explored such knowledge: An 'inhuman' technology in this sense can also be found in Kittler's work. Kittler examines the mode of operation of technology not only in the low-frequency range, but also and above all in the high-frequency range, that is, in 'ranges beyond the scope of human eyes and ears.' (Friedrich A. Kittler, 'Real Time Analysis, Time Axis Manipulation', *Cultural Politics* 13, no. 1 [2017]: 10). Such a technology, which seems to have lost the human measure, Kittler exemplifies in his discussion of optical media that are based on 'measurements of the abilities *and* inabilities of visual perception' (Kittler, *Optical Media*, 38, emphasis in original). Technology that has been 'developed strategically to override the senses' (36), is no longer directly related to the human body, but is 'escalated' (36). Crary has shown how 'optical devices that became forms of mass entertainment, such as the stereoscope and the phenakistiscope, originally derived from new empirical knowledge of the physiological status of the observer and of vision' (Crary, *Techniques of the Observer*, 14; see also 17). This empirical knowledge is also knowledge of the 'errors' of optical perception.
118 In this book, this point is developed by drawing particularly on media theory and media aesthetics. In media theory, it is taken into account that media constitute an 'anaesthetic' field (Vogl, 'Becoming-Media'; Kittler, *Optical Media*; Ernst, 'Der anästhetische Blick?'). Media aesthetics examines the effects of media on their perceptible 'contents' (with respect to auditory media see Rolf Großmann, 'Konstruktiv(istische)e Gedanken zur "Medienmusik"', in *Medien – Musik – Mensch. Neue Medien und Musikwissenschaft*, ed. Thomas Hemker and Daniel

Müllensiefen [Hamburg: Bockel, 1997]; Rolf Großmann, 'Die Geburt des Pop aus dem Geist der phonographischen Reproduktion', in *Popmusicology: Perspektiven der Popmusikwissenschaft*, ed. Christian Bielefeldt, Udo Dahmen and Rolf Großmann [Bielefeld: transcript, 2008]). With respect to media theory, the classification of perception technologies as 'empirical' proves to be problematic, as the perception technologies themselves are not 'given to the experience', at least during those moments when music is being heard through them. Technologies are nevertheless historically and culturally constituted materialities. Popular music forms have received selective attention in media theory (concerning this, see Jens Gerrit Papenburg, 'Rockmusik, Musikdrama, Disco. Klanggeschichte der Medien nach Friedrich Kittler', in *Friedrich Kittler. Neue Lektüren*, ed. Till A. Heilmann and Jens Schröter [Berlin: Springer, 2022]; Jens Gerrit Papenburg, 'Stop/Start Making Sense! Ein Ausblick auf Musikanalyse in Popular Music Studies und technischer Medienwissenschaft', in *Sound Studies: Traditionen – Methoden – Desiderate*, ed. Holger Schulze [Bielefeld: transcript, 2008]).

119 Theodor W. Adorno, *Current of Music: Elements of a Radio Theory* (Cambridge: Polity, 2009), 285.
120 Brian Cross, *It's Not about a Salary: Rap, Race and Resistance in Los Angeles* (London: Verso, 1993), 197.
121 Mark Kerins, *Beyond Dolby (Stereo): Cinema in the Digital Sound Age* (Bloomington: Indiana University Press, 2011), 29–30.
122 Jens Gerrit Papenburg, 'Enhanced Bass: On 1970s Disco Culture's Listening Devices', in *Sound as Popular Culture: A Research Companion*, ed. Jens Gerrit Papenburg and Holger Schulze (Cambridge, MA: MIT Press, 2016).
123 Peter Wicke, 'Popmusik in der Analyse', *Acta Musicologica* 75, no. 1 (2003).
124 Antoine Hennion, 'Baroque and Rock: Music, Mediators and Musical Taste', *Poetics* 24 (1997); Antoine Hennion, 'Music and Mediation: Toward a New Sociology of Music', in *The Cultural Study of Music: A Critical Introduction*, ed. Martin Clayton, Trevor Herbert and Richard Middleton (London: Routledge, 2003); Richard Middleton, *Reading Pop: Approaches to Textual Analysis in Popular Music* (Oxford: Oxford University Press, 2000); Born, 'On Musical Mediation'; Georgina Born, 'On Nonhuman Sound: Sound as Relation', in *Sound Objects*, ed. James A. Steintrager and Rey Chow (Durham, NC: Duke University Press, 2019); Antoine Hennion and Christophe Levaux, eds, *Rethinking Music through Science and Technology Studies* (London: Routledge, 2021).
125 Großmann, 'Die Geburt des Pop aus dem Geist der phonographischen Reproduktion'.
126 Wicke, 'Popmusik in der Analyse', 118. Keith Negus was in the same vein a few years before Wicke: 'The same musical genre or piece of music may be enjoyed and engaged with in completely different ways. Quite different audience experiences and activities are associated with listening to the same music in a performance event in stadiums, while driving or jogging with a Walkman, or while dancing to a jukebox in an open air bar. These studies suggest that the meaning of music is very hard to tie down, and indicate that we could learn much about music audiences by studying the same music in different contexts and among different people' (Keith Negus, *Popular Music in Theory* [Cambridge: Polity, 1996], 32). On the specificity of the musical experience shaped by sound systems in clubs, Gilbert and Pearson write: 'Obviously hearing a record at home, in a shop, or in the streets is vastly different to hearing it

in a club, not just because of this potentially various sonic kinaesthetic experience. The aural experience is just one dimension of a synaesthetic combination of space, sound, and sight which comprise the dancefloor's affective potential' (Gilbert and Pearson, *Discographies*, 138).

127 Hans Heinrich Eggebrecht characterizes 'the work' as a 'central category of musical thought and action' (Hans Heinrich Eggebrecht, *Musikalisches Denken. Aufsätze zur Theorie und Ästhetik der Musik* [Wilhelmshaven: Heinrichshofen 1977], 223) in the West, which is also valid for music after 1950. For Carl Dahlhaus, too, the concept of the work in 1985 is by no means 'fragile and outdated' (Carl Dahlhaus and Hans Heinrich Eggebrecht, *Was ist Musik?* [Wilhelmshaven: Noetzel, 1987], 49). In doing so, Eggebrecht and Dahlhaus fall back on a critical concept of the work, which they understand in a cultural – Occident! – and historically specific way: Eggebrecht discovers musical works already in the 'early modern 15th century' (Eggebrecht, *Musikalisches Denken*, 223), Dahlhaus sees the 'idea of an autonomous whole founded in an inner wealth of relationships', that is, of the 'classic' concept of the work 'formulated only in the 1780s by Karl Philipp Moritz' (Dahlhaus and Eggebrecht, *Was ist Musik?*). Philosophically, Eggebrecht and Dahlhaus draw on concepts from German Idealism – Hegel's 'ideal object' – and phenomenology – Ingarden's 'identity problem'. About the status of reception in Dahlhaus's and Eggebrecht's considerations, Klaus Kropfinger – systematically ignoring the mediations between the sound event and the listener – objects: 'The active role of the receiver shrinks towards zero' (MGG Online, 'Rezeptionsforschung', by Klaus Kropfinger, accessed 18 February 2022, https://www.mgg-online.com/article?id=mgg15962&v=1.0&rs=mgg15962). Thus, according to Kropfinger, only research on the effect of the work can be conducted, and no research on the active reception of the work by the listener. Complementary to Dahlhaus's and Eggebrecht's work concept is a critique of the work concept oriented towards Karl Marx, which ultimately led to complete rejection of the concept (see, e.g. Zofia Lissa, *Neue Aufsätze zur Musikästhetik* [Berlin: Henschel, 1975]). Dahlhaus dismisses Lissa's thesis as a 'postulate' (Dahlhaus and Eggebrecht, *Was ist Musik?*, 62) that modes of reception are socially grounded ('In every society divided into classes, the reception of music is also differentiated' [118]) and, moreover, are not external to music. Dahlhaus objects that to be 'empirically descriptive', it could be said that the claim to aesthetic autonomy is specific to modes of composition that aim at a 'self-contained and consistent form arising from the interaction of tonal harmony and thematic-motif development' – and modes of reception – Hanslick's and Schopenhauer's 'aesthetic contemplation' or even Wackenroder's 'aesthetic devotion.' The discussion about a musical concept of the work continued in the 1990s and 2000s. For a focus on classical music, see Lydia Goehr, *The Imaginary Museum of Musical Works: An Essay in the Philosophy of Music* [Oxford: Clarendon Press, 1992]) and also on 'aesthetic autonomy', Richard Taruskin, 'Is There a Baby in the Bathwater? (Part I)', *Archiv für Musikwissenschaft* 63, no. 3 (2006) and Richard Taruskin, 'Is There a Baby in the Bathwater? (Part II)', *Archiv für Musikwissenschaft* 63, no. 4 (2006); for a more comprehensive approach, see the essays in Michel Talbot, *The Musical Work. Reality or Invention?* (Liverpool: Liverpool University Press 2000). From the perspective of a musical theory of mediation, it can be objected that Goehr's approach does not take enough account of the destabilizing influence of technologies that are used increasingly in the production, performance and reception of the music concept

of the work (see Born, 'On Musical Mediation', 10). The concept of the work is also critically adjusted in an examination of the music of the Middle Ages (see Max Haas, *Musikalisches Denken im Mittelalter: Eine Einführung* [Bern: Lang, 2005]).

128 Peter Wicke, 'Sound Tracks. Popmusik und Popdiskurs', in *Was ist Pop? – Zehn Versuche* (Frankfurt am Main: Fischer, 2004), 116.

129 Ibid., 118.

130 Wicke elaborates the critique of such a musical object as follows: 'The assumption that "musical facts" are objective realities that are unquestionably accessible to "objective hearing" and thus only need to be brought to consciousness through analysis is untenable in view of the mediation of sound and its perception as music in complex, socially conditioned, technologically, economically, and discursively shaped cultural contexts' (Wicke, 'Popmusik in der Analyse', 112). Wicke emphasizes that such mediations, which ground and generalize the subject's idiosyncrasies supraindividually, yet not ahistorically and aculturally, have taken on a technological character, especially in popular music.

131 Wicke, 'Sound Tracks. Popmusik und Popdiskurs', 122.

132 Ibid.

133 Middleton, *Reading Pop*, 9; Benjamin Piekut, 'Actor-Networks in Music History: Clarifications and Critiques', *Twentieth-Century Music* 11, no. 2 (September 2014).

134 Hennion, 'Baroque and Rock', 432.

135 Hennion, 'Music and Mediation: Toward a New Sociology of Music', 83.

136 Bruno Latour, *Reassembling the Social: An Introduction to Actor-Network-Theory* (Oxford: Oxford University Press, 2005), 39. For a musical concept of mediation, see Hennion, 'Music and Mediation: Toward a New Sociology of Music', 90. A 'positive concept of mediation' (83) which is central to Hennion also features prominently in Bruno Latour's actor-network theory, which, in contrast to Hennion's writings, is not limited to music. Latour, a former colleague of Hennion at the Centre de Sociologie de l'Innovation distinguishes theorizing around mediators from theorizing around the subject–object schema. If intermediaries are locked into causal relations, then mediators tend to constitute conditions or milieus: 'For mediators, the situation is different: causes do not allow effects to be deduced as they are simply offering occasions, circumstances, and precedents' (Latour, *Reassembling the Social*, 58–9). Via the notion of mediator, which understands mediation as a process without an object that is mediated, distance is created from the subject–object schema on an epistemological level. By making mediators not 'mixtures of pure forms' but themselves the starting point of thought and theory, the subject–object schema is subverted: 'The explanations no longer proceed from pure forms toward phenomena, but from the centre toward the extremes. The latter are no longer reality's point of attachment, but so many provisional and partial results' (Bruno Latour, *We Have Never Been Modern*, trans. Catherine Porter [Cambridge, MA: Harvard University Press, 1993], 78). We find a comparable concept of the mediator, however, under another designation in diverse contemporary theories. For example, in the concept of media (see Stefan Münker and Alexander Roesler, *Was ist ein Medium?* [Frankfurt am Main: Suhrkamp, 2008]; in the concept of the 'quasi-object' (Michel Serres, *The Parasite* [Minneapolis, MN: University of Minnesota Press, 2007], 235–51); or in the concept of the 'virtual' or 'actualised virtualities' (see Gilles Deleuze,

Difference and Repetition [New York: Bloomsbury Academic, 2016], see also Latour, *Reassembling the Social*, 59–60). This notion of the mediator is close to studies that seek to understand technical media in popular music not just as recording media, but to examine them in their constitutive function for sound. For instance, Großmann calls such sounds – sounds that are shaped by mediators, 'media-reflexive sounds derived … directly from the storage, transmission, or electronic production of the media' – '*media sounds*' (Rolf Großmann, 'Spiegelbild, Spiegel, leerer Spiegel: Zur Mediensituation der Clicks & Cuts', in *Soundcultures. Über elektronische und digitale Musik*, ed. Marcus S. Kleiner and Achim Szepanski [Frankfurt am Main: Suhrkamp, 2003], 52, emphasis in original) or also 'the medium's own sound' (57). Stefan Heidenreich refers to them as the 'musical effects of technologies' (Stefan Heidenreich, 'Rauschen, filtern, codieren – Stilbildung in Mediensystemen', in *Das Rauschen*, ed. Sabine Sanio and Christian Scheib [Hofheim: Wolke, 1995], 24) and Mark Katz describes them via the term 'phonograph effect' (Mark Katz, *Capturing Sound: How Technology Has Changed Music* [Berkeley: University of California Press, 2010], 1–7).

137 Peter Wicke, 'Der Tonträger als Medium der Musik', in *Handbuch Musik und Medien. Interdisziplinärer Überblick über Die Mediengeschichte der Musik*, ed. Holger Schramm (Konstanz: Springer, 2019); Großmann, 'Die Geburt des Pop aus dem Geist der phonographischen Reproduktion'.

138 Ibid., 12. Such a specific form of media informed design has been studied in the 'musicology of record production' (e.g. Simon Zagorski-Thomas, *The Musicology of Record Production* [Cambridge: Cambridge University Press, 2014]; Simon Zagorski-Thomas and Andrew Bourbon, *The Bloomsbury Handbook of Music Production* [New York: Bloomsbury Academic, 2020]; in 'record musicology' (Amanda Bayley, *Recorded Music: Performance, Culture and Technology* [Cambridge: Cambridge University Press 2010], and in popular music studies (Immanuel Brockhaus, *Kultsounds: Die prägendsten Klänge der Popmusik 1960–2014* [Bielefeld: transcript, 2017]; Ismaiel-Wendt, *Post_PRESETS*).

139 Wicke, 'Der Tonträger als Medium der Musik', 4.

140 Jens Gerrit Papenburg, 'Popmusik als "produzierte" Musik', *Musik und Ästhetik* 23, no. 2 (2019).

141 Susan Schmidt Horning, 'Engineering the Performance: Recording Engineers, Tacit Knowledge and the Art of Controlling Sound', *Social Studies of Science* 34, no. 5 (2004): 704. Simon Frith has pointed out that popular music culture, before it was dominated by radio, film and the jukebox in the 1930s, had been shaped by printed music, piano manufacturers and concert hall owners (see Simon Frith, 'The Industrialization of Popular Music', in *Popular Music and Communication*, ed. James Lull [Newbury Park, CA: Sage, 1992], 55). Frith correlates such economic shifts with transformations in musical practice and sound. On the aesthetic consequences of this shift, Frith writes: 'The 1930s marked, in short, a shift in cultural and material musical power – from Tin Pan Alley to broadcasting networks and Hollywood studios, from the publisher/showman/song system to a record/radio/film star system – and the judgment of what constituted a good song or performance shifted accordingly – from suitability for a live audience to suitability for a radio show or a jukebox' (58).

142 Hennion, 'Baroque and Rock'.

143 Hennion, 'Music and Mediation', 90.

144 Ibid., 90.
145 Ibid., 84.
146 Antoine Hennion and Bruno Latour, 'How to Make Mistakes on So Many Things at Once – and Become Famous for It', in *Mapping Benjamin: The Work of Art in the Digital Age*, ed. Hans Ulrich Gumbrecht and Michael Marrinan (Stanford, CA: Stanford University Press, 2003).
147 Ibid., 94.
148 Bernhard Siegert, 'Es gibt keine Massenmedien', in *Medien und Öffentlichkeit. Positionierungen, Symptome, Simulationsbrüche*, ed. Rudolf Maresch (Munich: Boer, 1996), 108.
149 Hennion and Latour, 'How to Make Mistakes on So Many Things at Once – and Become Famous for It', 94.
150 In the middle of the twentieth century, fixed versions of Baroque operas were established because the first recordings of them were made. Before that, musicologists and publishers had already transformed composers' scores into '"exact" *Urtext* copies of an original piece written by a particular composer' (95, emphasis in original). However, the production of such 'original versions' or 'Urtexte' would contradict the approach of Baroque composers. Jean-Philippe Rameau, for example, rewrote his operas for every performance. A concept of the 'original' did not exist for Rameau. In summary, it can be said that only the production of reproducible editions of works as scores or recordings constituted a concept of the original.
151 See DeNora, *Music in Everyday Life*, 30.
152 Hennion, 'Baroque and Rock', 432.
153 Middleton, *Reading Pop*, 10.
154 The first two paragraphs of this "V. Listening devices are managing listening" adopt ideas and translations from Jens Gerrit Papenburg, 'Soundfile-Hören. Zukunft, Zeiterfahrung, Bewirtschaftung', in *Listening/Hearing*, ed. Raoul Mörchen and Carsten Seiffarth (Mainz: Schott, 2022).
155 Karin Bijsterveld and José van Dijck, eds, *Sound Souvenirs: Audio Technologies, Memory and Cultural Practices*, Transformations in Art and Culture (Amsterdam: Amsterdam University Press, 2009); David W. Samuels, Louise Meintjes, Ana Maria Ochoa and Thomas Porcello, 'Soundscapes: Toward a Sounded Anthropology', *Annual Review of Anthropology* 39, no. 1 (October 21, 2010).
156 Martin Scherzinger, 'The Political Economy of Streaming', in *The Cambridge Companion to Music in Digital Culture*, ed. David Trippett, Monique M. Ingalls and Nicholas Cook (Cambridge: Cambridge University Press, 2019).
157 Sterne, *MP3. The Meaning of a Format*, 45.
158 See the expanded model of listening in Tristan Jehan, 'Creating Music by Listening', PhD dissertation, Massachusetts Institute of Technology, 2005, 36, https://web.media.mit.edu/~tristan/phd/pdf/Tristan_PhD_MIT.pdf. Jehan is a co-founder of the company The Echo Nest, which was bought by Spotify in 2014. After this acquisition, the streaming service increasingly changed its business model from 'access' to 'recommendation'.
159 Scherzinger, 'Political Economy of Streaming', 274–97.
160 Martin Heidegger, 'The Question Concerning Technology', in *The Question Concerning Technology and Other Essays*, trans. William Lovitt (New York: Garland, 1977), 21.

161 Spengler, *Man and Technics*, 94.
162 Heidegger, 'Question Concerning Technology', 16.
163 Kittler, *Discourse Networks 1800/1900*.
164 Wolfgang Scherer, *Babbellogik. Sound und die Auslöschung der buchstäblichen Ordnung* (Basel: Roter Stern/Stroemfeld, 1983); Wolfgang Scherer, *Klavier-Spiele. Die Psychotechnik der Klaviere im 18. und 19. Jahrhundert* (Munich: Fink, 1989).
165 Friedrich A. Kittler and Georg Christoph Tholen, eds, *Arsenale der Seele. Literatur – und Medienanalysen seit 1870* (Munich: Fink, 1989).
166 Jochen Hörisch and Michael Wetzel, eds, *Armaturen der Sinne. Literarische und Technische Medien 1870 bis 1920* (Munich: Fink, 1990).
167 Axel Volmar, ed., *Zeitkritische Medien* (Berlin: Kulturverlag Kadmos, 2009).
168 Wolfgang Ernst, '"Merely the Medium"? Die Operative Verschränkung von Logik und Materie', in *Was ist ein Medium?*, ed. Stefan Münker and Alexander Roesler (Frankfurt am Main: Suhrkamp, 2008), 158.
169 Kittler, *Discourse Networks 1800/1900*, 369.
170 Heidegger, 'Question Concerning Technology', 16.
171 See on this Tholen, *Die Zäsur der Medien. Kulturphilosophische Konturen*, 173.
172 Wolfgang Ernst, *Chronopoetik. Zeitweisen Und Zeitgaben Technischer Medien* (Berlin: Kadmos, 2013).
173 That does not mean excluding symmetry of actor and actant. Bruno Latour criticized Heidegger's philosophy of technology, because Heidegger reversed the myth of technology as a neutral tool that is used by intentional human subjects into the myth of technology as an autonomous entity that cannot be controlled by humans (see Jim Johnson [Bruno Latour], 'Mixing Humans and Nonhumans Together: The Sociology of a Door-Closer', *Social Problems* 35, 3 [1988]).
174 Hui, 'First Re-creations', 376. Hui analyses Edison's tone tests as a programme for this transformation.
175 Certainly, there are important exceptions such as Holger Schulze, *The Sonic Persona: An Anthropology of Sound* (New York: Bloomsbury Academic, 2018).
176 For a critical account of an 'implicit listener', see Rainer Cadenbach, 'Der implizite Hörer? Zum Begriff einer "Rezeptionsästhetik" als musikwissenschaftlicher Disziplin', in *Rezeptionsästhetik und Rezeptionsgeschichte in der Musikwissenschaft*, ed. Hermann Danuser (Laaber: Laaber, 1991); see also Helga de la Motte-Haber, 'Der einkomponierte Hörer', in *Der Hörer als Interpret*, ed. Helga de la Motte-Haber and Reinhard Kopiez (Frankfurt am Main: Peter Lang, 1995); John Butt, 'Do Musical Works Contain an Implied Listener? Towards a Theory of Musical Listening', *Journal of the Royal Musical Association* 135, no. 1 (2010); Michele Calella, 'Musikhistorische Rezeptions-Forschung jenseits der Rezeptionstheorien', in *Zwischen Transfer und Transformation. Horizonte der Rezeption von Musik*, ed. Michele Calella and Benedikt Lessmann (Vienna: Hollitzer, 2020).
177 Adorno, *Introduction to the Sociology of Music*, 5.
178 Stockfelt, 'Adequate Modes of Listening', 129–46; Tobias Plebuch, 'Musikhören nach Adorno. Ein Genesungsbericht', *Merkur. Deutsche Zeitschrift für Europäisches Denken* 65 (2002): 675–87. Dahlhaus also ennobles when he states that 'reception as practised by composers' has always been the subject of music history (Carl Dahlhaus, 'Problems in Reception History', in *Foundations of Music History* (Cambridge: Cambridge University Press, 1983), 151.

179 Peter Szendy, *Listen. A History of Our Ears* (New York: Fordham University Press, 2008), 102.
180 Roland Barthes, 'Musica Practica', in *Image, Music, Text*, trans. Stephen Heath (London: Fontana, 1977), 149.
181 Barthes, 'Musica Practica', 149.
182 Adorno, *Introduction to the Sociology of Music*, 5.
183 Barthes, 'Musica Practica', 149.
184 A last resurgence of muscular music would have occurred in the interwar period. For Barthes, his singing teacher Charles Panzéra, whom he honored in his famous essay 'The Grain of the Voice' became the icon of this period. Barthes sees Panzéra as having been influenced by musical culture 'before the coming of the microgroove record' (Roland Barthes, 'The Grain of the Voice', in *Image, Music, Text*, trans. Stephen Heath [London: Fontana, 1977], 185).
185 Sousa's concern about the 'National Chest' shrinking as a result of the gramophone was later taken up again by Marshall McLuhan (see McLuhan, *Understanding Media*, 300).
186 William H. Kenney, *Recorded Music in American Life: The Phonograph and Popular Memory, 1890–1945* (New York: Oxford University Press, 1999), 31.
187 Simon Frith, *Sound Effects: Youth, Leisure, and the Politics of Rock 'n' Roll* (New York: Pantheon Books, 1981), 18.
188 Frith, 'Industrialization of Popular Music', 52.
189 Sterne, *MP3. The Meaning of a Format*.
190 However, a pedagogical discourse also attempts to access the listening practices that emerge with technical media. Apart from general remarks on music pedagogy (see Theodor W. Adorno, 'Zur Musikpädagogik', in *Gesammelte Schriften*, no. 14, ed. Rolf Tiedemann [Frankfurt am Main: Suhrkamp, 1990], 108–26), in response to a diagnosed convergence of music and technology Adorno proposed as early as 1928 to initiate a section on 'Mechanical Music' in the music journal *Anbruch* that would be dedicated to the consumer (see Theodor W. Adorno, 'Zum "Anbruch"', in *Gesammelte Schriften*, no. 19, ed. Rolf Tiedemann [Frankfurt am Main: Suhrkamp, 1984], 600–1). As Thomas Levin and Michael von der Linn write, Adorno wanted this column – to be understood as a 'critical and pedagogical forum directed toward the *consumers*, providing them with both technical advice and musicologically knowledgeable criticism of work produced for various new media' (Thomas Levin and Michael von der Linn, 'Elements of a Radio Theory: Adorno and the Princeton Radio Research Project', in *The Musical Quarterly* 78, 2 [1994]: 318, emphasis in original). Later, Adorno consolidated the impression that control over radio and record listening had already been lost to other contexts: In 1968, Adorno summarized in a *Der Spiegel* interview that his suggestions regarding a 'proper use of the so-called mass media' had not 'had many practical consequences' (Theodor W. Adorno, 'Musik im Fernsehen ist Brimborium', in *Gesammelte Schriften*, no. 19, ed. Rolf Tiedemann [Frankfurt am Main: Suhrkamp, 1984], 563).
191 Foucault, *Discipline and Punish*.
192 Gilles Deleuze, 'Postscript on the Societies of Control', *October* 59 (1992): 3–7.
193 Thompson, 'Machines, Music, and the Quest for Fidelity. Marketing the Edison Phonograph in America, 1877–1925'; Hui, 'First Re-creations'.
194 Other examples of entertainment industry management of listening can be found in television programmes that feature listeners rather than musicians. Musicologist

Andrew Dell'Antonio, in his analysis of a collective listening in the context of the programming of the music channel MTV, has pointed out that MTV itself would shape such listening through its programming. Shows like 'Yack Live' or 'Twelve Angry Viewers' would construct what Dell'Antonio calls ideal appraisers for music videos. Dell'Antonio cautions against hasty moral condemnation of such programmes. 'Ultimately, its [MTV's] ideology does not seem inherently more pernicious than modernist ideals of artistic autonomy' (Dell'Antonio, *Beyond Structural Listening?*, 226).

195 Arnold Shaw, *The Rockin' '50s: The Decade That Transformed the Pop Music Scene* (New York: Hawthorn Books, 1974), 177.
196 Peter Wicke, 'Soundtechnologien und Körpermetamorphosen. Das Populäre in der Musik des 20. Jahrhunderts', in *Handbuch der Musik im 20. Jahrhundert*, ed. Peter Wicke (Laaber: Laaber, 2001), 19.
197 Ibid., 20.
198 Ibid., 21.
199 Ibid., 28–31.
200 Ibid., 17.
201 Robin James, *Resilience & Melancholy: Pop Music, Feminism, Neoliberalism* (Winchester: Zero Books, 2015); Mack Hagood, *Hush: Media and Sonic Self-Control* (Durham, NC: Duke University Press, 2019).
202 On the cultural turn in social sciences and history, see Stephan Moebius, ed., *Kultur: Von den Cultural Studies bis zu den Visual Studies. Eine Einführung* (Bielefeld: transcript, 2012); Doris Bachmann-Medick, *Cultural Turns: New Orientations in the Study of Culture* (Berlin: de Gruyter, 2016). On 'Beyond the Cultural Turn' see Victoria E. Bonnell and Lynn Hunt, *Beyond the Cultural Turn: New Directions in the Study of Society and Culture* (Berkeley: University of California Press, 1999).
203 In an anthology he edited, Anselm Gerhard (2000) asked whether German language musicology was a 'belated' discipline (see Anselm Gerhard, *Musikwissenschaft – eine verspätete Disziplin? Die akademische Musikforschung zwischen Fortschrittsglauben und Modernitätsverweigerung*, ed. Anselm Gerhard [Stuttgart: J. B. Metzler, 2000]. Gerhard developed his thoughts on this primarily in relation to the long omitted confrontation of German language musicology with its position under National Socialism. Various contributions to this anthology, however, diagnosed musicological belatedness also on a theoretical and methodological level in relation to neighbouring disciplines.
204 For a critical view on critical musicology, see the special issue 'What Was, or Is Critical Musicology?' of the journal *Radical Musicology* (Richard Middleton and Ian Biddle, *Radical Musicology*, 5).
205 Martin Clayton, Trevor Herbert and Richard Middleton, eds, *The Cultural Study of Music: A Critical Introduction*, 2nd edition (London: Routledge, 2012).
206 Jane F. Fulcher, ed., *The Oxford Handbook of the New Cultural History of Music* (New York: Oxford University Press, 2011). The aim of this new cultural history is as follows: 'The new cultural history of music seeks to investigate precisely such arenas in which a close musical analysis must interact with a sophisticated understanding of the semiotic or linguistic dimension while maintaining a comprehensive grasp of the relevant social, cultural, and political dynamics' (Jane F. Fulcher, 'Introduction: Defining the New Cultural History of Music, Its Origins, Methodologies, and Lines of Inquiry', in *The Oxford Handbook of the New Cultural History of Music*, ed. Jane F. Fulcher [New York: Oxford

University Press, 2011], 12). If new musicology in the 1980s and 1990s produced cultural histories of music, this does not qualify for the claim of newness. However, the new cultural history of music does connect to new musicology's interest in interpretation, meaning, power and performances.

207 See also Kyle Devine, 'Musicology Without Music', in *On Popular Music and Its Unruly Entanglements*, ed. Nick Braae and Kai Arne Hansen (Cham: Palgrave Macmillan, 2020).

208 A combination of music analysis and cultural analysis has a longer tradition: thirty years ago, the musicologist John Shepherd summarized (and did not demand!) in his essay 'Why Popular Music Studies?' that for popular music studies that develops in dialogue with cultural studies and cultural theory, music is the object of cultural analysis and criticism. Popular music studies of this kind does not drift into a mere sociological description of contexts if it determines cultural differences by the sound events of music or examines practices of listening to and making music (John Shepherd, 'Warum Popmusikforschung?', in *PopScriptum. Texte zur populären Musik* 1 [1992]. Available online: https://edoc.hu-berlin.de/bitstream/handle/18452/20903/pst01_shepherd.pdf?sequence=1. Accessed 14 September 2022).

209 Jacques Attali, *Noise. The Political Economy of Music*, trans. Brian Massumi (Minneapolis: University of Minnesota Press, 1985), 4 and 18–20. Eric Drott remarks in his essay on this book that one of Attali's main theses that 'music is prophecy' (11) – 'turns the traditional Marxian understanding of the relation between base and superstructure on its head' (Eric Drott, 'Rereading Jacques Attali's *Bruits*', in *Critical Inquiry* 41, no. 4 [2015], 723) – is not very well developed: The 'book never fully spells out the mechanisms by which music performs this prophetic function' (725). This also holds true for Attali's methodological reasoning of research through music. Drott, however, attempts to show that Attali only superficially valorizes music as an approach to analysing culture and society. Ultimately, music for Attali has only an 'allegorical function' (733): 'Which means that Attali's statement that *Bruits* represents an attempt to theorise society "through music" is not entirely accurate because music already stands in for something other than itself in the text. And that something is the information/energy dialectic outlined in *La Parole et l'outil* [that is the book Attali wrote before *Bruits*]' (733).

210 Peter Wicke, '"Move Your Body": über Sinn, Klang und Körper', in *PopMusicology*. Available online: http://www.popmusicology.org/PDF/Move.pdf (accessed 30 April 2022).

211 Robert Fink, *Repeating Ourselves. American Minimal Music as Cultural Practice* (Berkeley: University of California Press, 2005), x. We find a comparable methodological approach in Alexander Weheliye's 'thinking through sound' (Alexander G. Weheliye, *Phonographies: Grooves in Sonic Afro-Modernities* [Durham, NC: Duke University Press, 2005], 8; Julian Henriques, 'Preamble: Thinking through Sound', in *Sonic Bodies. Reggae Sound Systems, Performance Techniques and Ways of Knowing*, xv–xxxii [New York: Continuum, 2011]); Steven Feld's 'acoustemology' (Steven Feld, 'Acoustemology', in *Keywords in Sound*, ed. Raphael Novak and Matt Sakakeeny [Durham, NC: Duke University Press, 2015], 12–21), and in the contributions in Jens Gerrit Papenburg and Holger Schulze, *Sound as Popular Culture: A Research Companion* (Cambridge, MA: MIT Press, 2016).

212 Ralf von Appen, Nils Grosch and Martin Pfleiderer, 'Einführung: Populäre Musik und Popmusikforschung: Zur Konzeption', in *Populäre Musik*.

Geschichte – Kontexte – Forschungsperspektiven, ed. Ralf von Appen, Nils Grosch, and Martin Pfleiderer (Laaber: Laaber, 2014), 7.

213 Jens Gerrit Papenburg, 'Nazis and Quiet Sounds: Popular Music, Simulated Normality, and Cultural Niches in the Terror Regime, 1933–1945', in *Made in Germany*, ed. Oliver Seibt, Martin Ringsmut and David-Emil Wickström (London: Routledge, 2020).

214 Ismaiel-Wendt, *Post_PRESETS*, 101–16. On the concept album, see Jens Gerrit Papenburg, 'Konzeptalben als "große Werke" populärer Musik?', in *Musik und Ästhetik* 21, no. 7 (2017); on crooning, see Allison McCracken, *Real Men Don't Sing: Crooning in American Culture* (Durham, NC: Duke University Press, 2015); on tape echo, see Peter Doyle, *Echo and Reverb: Fabricating Space in Popular Music Recording 1900–1960* (Middletown: Wesleyan University Press, 2005), 178–212.

215 The remainder of this section was adapted from Papenburg, 'Rockmusik, Musikdrama, Disco'.

216 Friedrich A. Kittler, 'Rock Music: A Misuse of Military Equipment', in *The Truth of the Technological World: Essays on the Genealogy of Presence* (Stanford, CA: Stanford University Press, 2014), 159.

217 Ibid.

218 Kittler, *Gramophone, Film, Typewriter*, 95–114.

219 Kittler, 'Rock Music', 164, emphasis in original.

220 Geoffrey Winthrop-Young, *Kittler and the Media* (Cambridge: Polity, 2011), 130–1.

221 Friedrich A. Kittler, 'Bei Tanzmusik kommt es einem in die Beine', in *Auditive Medienkulturen. Techniken des Hörens und Praktiken der Klanggestaltung*, ed. Axel Volmar and Jens Schröter (Bielefeld: transcript, 2013), 37–8.

222 Gundula Kreuzer, 'Kittler's Wagner and Beyond', *Journal of the American Musicological Society* 70, no. 1 (2017): 230.

223 Stefan Rieger, 'Medienarchäologie', in *Handbuch Medienwissenschaft*, ed. Jens Schröter (Stuttgart: J. B. Metzler, 2014), 140.

224 Kreuzer, 'Kittler's Wagner and Beyond'.

225 Ibid., 231.

226 Kittler, *Gramophone, Film, Typewriter*, 23.

227 Kittler, 'World-Breath: On Wagner's Media Technology', in *The Truth of the Technological World: Essays on the Genealogy of Presence*, ed. Hans Ulrich Gumbrecht (Stanford, CA: Stanford University Press, 2014), 128.

228 Ibid., 129.

229 Ibid., 133.

230 Friedrich Kittler, 'Wagners Untergänge', *Programmhefte der Bayreuther Festspiele*, no. 3 (1987): 9.

231 Kittler, *Gramophone, Film, Typewriter*, 104; Kittler, 'Wagners Untergänge', 16.

232 Kittler, *Gramophone, Film, Typewriter*, 24 and 48.

233 Stockfelt, 'Adequate Modes of Listening'.

234 Various studies in the fields of media theory and sound studies have suggested such an association of sonic media technology with sensory physiology, see Scherer, *Klavier-Spiele*; Bernhard Siegert, 'Das Amt des Gehorchens. Hysterie der Telephonistinnen oder Wiederkehr des Ohres 1874–1913', in *Armaturen der Sinne. Literarische und technische Medien 1870 bis 1920*, ed. Jochen Hörisch and Michael Wetzel (München: Fink, 1990); Peters, 'Helmholtz und Edison'; Sterne, *The Audible Past*; Matthias Rieger, *Helmholtz Musicus. Die Objektivierung der Musik im 19. Jahrhundert durch Helmholtz' Lehre von*

den Tonempfindungen (Darmstadt: Wissenschaftliche Buchgesellschaft, 2006); Erlmann, *Reason and Resonance*.
235 Sophie Maisonneuve, 'Between History and Commodity: The Production of a Musical Patrimony through the Record in the 1920–1930s', *Poetics* 29, no. 2 (2001).
236 Thompson, 'Machines, Music, and the Quest for Fidelity'; Sterne, *The Audible Past*, 215–86; Volmar, 'Experiencing High Fidelity'.
237 Hui, 'First Re-creations'.
238 Timothy Taylor, Mark Katz and Tony Grajeda, eds, *Music, Sound, and Technology in America. A Documented History of Early Phonograph, Cinema, and Radio* (Durham, NC: Duke University Press, 2012), 44–84.
239 Dave Laing, 'A Voice without a Face: Popular Music and the Phonograph in the 1890s', *Popular Music* 10, no. 1 (1991).
240 Marion Saxer and Leonie Storz, 'Die Ökonomisierung der Wahrnehmung. Wirtschaftsgeschichte der Medien', in *Spiel (mit) der Maschine: Musikalische Medienpraxis in der Frühzeit von Phonographie, Selbstspielklavier, Film und Radio*, ed. Marion Saxer (Bielefeld: transcript, 2016).
241 Adorno, *Current of Music*.
242 Ibid., 120–32.
243 Ibid., 123.
244 Ibid.
245 Susan Douglas, *Listening In: Radio and the American Imagination* (Minneapolis: University of Minnesota Press, 2004), 23.
246 Chris Rasmussen, '"The People's Orchestra": Jukeboxes as the Measure of Popular Musical Taste in the 1930s and 1940s', in *Sound in the Age of Mechanical Reproduction*, ed. David Suisman and Susan Strasser (Philadelphia: University of Pennsylvania Press, 2010).
247 Hanns-Werner Heister, 'Die Musikbox: Studie zur Ökonomie, Sozialpsychologie und Ästhetik eines musikalischen Massenmediums', in *Segmente der Unterhaltungsindustrie*, ed. Hanns-Werner Heister et al. (Frankfurt am Main: Suhrkamp, 1974); Hanns-Werner Heister, 'Musikbox', in *Handbuch Populäre Kultur*, ed. Hans-Otto Hügel (Stuttgart: J. B. Metzler, 2003).
248 Timothy Taylor, Mark Katz and Tony Grajeda, *Music, Sound, and Technology in America*.
249 Sonja Neumann, 'The Opera-Telephone in Munich: A Short History', in *The Oxford Handbook of Music Listening in the 19th and 20th Centuries*, ed. Christian Thorau and Hansjakob Ziemer (New York: Oxford University Press, 2019). See for further literature on listening devices of the first half of the twentieth century, Kenney, Recorded Music in American Life; Thomas Y. Levin, 'For the Record: Adorno on Music in the Age of Its Technological Reproducibility', in *October* 55 (1990); Laing, 'Voice without a Face'; Thompson, 'Machines, Music, and the Quest for Fidelity'; Theodor W Adorno, 'The Curves of the Needle', in *Essays on Music by Theodor W. Adorno*, ed. Richard Leppert, trans. Susan H. Gillespie (Berkeley: University of California Press, 2002); Theodor W. Adorno, 'On the Fetish-Character in Music and the Regression of Listening', in *Essays on Music by Theodor W. Adorno*, ed. Richard Leppert, trans. Susan H. Gillespie (Berkeley: University of California Press, 2002); Theodor W. Adorno, 'The Form of the Phonograph Record', in *Essays on Music by Theodor W. Adorno*, ed. Richard Leppert, trans. Susan H. Gillespie (Berkeley: University of California Press, 2002); Theodor W. Adorno, 'The Radio Symphony: An Experiment in Theory', in *Current*

of Music: Elements of a Radio Theory (Cambridge: Polity, 2009); Sterne, *The Audible Past*; Tony Grajeda, 'Early Mood Music: Edison's Phonography, American Modernity and the Instrumentalization of Listening', in *Ubiquitous Musics: The Everyday Sounds That We Don't Always Notice*, ed. Elena Boschi, Anahid Kassabian and Marta García Quiñones (London: Routledge, 2013); Clarke, 'Impact of Recording on Listening'; Hui, *First Re-creations* (on gramophones and phonographs); Taylor, Katz and Grajeda, *Music, Sound, and Technology in America*; on the phonograph, Eva Moreda Rodríguez, *Inventing the Recording: The Phonograph and National Culture in Spain, 187–914* (New York: Oxford University Press, 2021). For listening devices of the second half of the twentieth century, see Keir Keightley, '"Turn It Down!" She Shrieked: Gender, Domestic Space, and High Fidelity, 1948–59', in *Popular Music* 15, no. 2 (1996); Marc Perlman, 'Golden Ears and Meter Readers: The Contest for Epistemic Authority in Audiophilia', in *Social Studies of Science* 34, no. 5 (2004); Anderson, *Making Easy Listening*; Alf Björnberg, 'Learning to Listen to Perfect Sound: hi-fi Culture and Changes in Modes of Listening 1950–80', in *The Ashgate Research Companion to Popular Musicology*, ed. Derek B. Scott (Surrey: Ashgate, 2009); Eric D. Barry, 'High-Fidelity Sound as Spectacle and Sublime, 1950–1961', in *Sound in the Age of Mechanical Reproduction*, ed. David Suisman and Susan Strasser (Philadelphia, PA: University of Pennsylvania Press, 2010) (hi-fi-listening); Shuhei Hosokawa, 'The Walkman Effect', in *Popular Music* 4 (1984); Bull, *Sounding Out the City*; Bull, *Sound Moves*; Weber, *Das Versprechen mobiler Freiheit*; Anna Schultz and Mark Nye, 'Music Ethnography and Recording Technology in the Unbound Digital Era', in *The Oxford Handbook of Mobile Music Studies*, ed. Sumanth Gopinath and Jason Stanyek (New York: Oxford University Press, 2014); Rebecca Tuhus-Dubrow, *Personal Stereo* (New York: Bloomsbury Academic, 2017); on the iPod in the last US–Iraq War, see Suzanne G. Cusick, 'Musicology, Torture, Repair', *Radical Musicology* 3 (2008); and J. Martin Daughtry, *Listening to War: Sound, Music, Trauma and Survival in Wartime Iraq* (New York: Oxford University Press, 2015); on CD see Axel Volmar and Dominik Schrey, 'Compact Disc', in *Handbuch Sound: Geschichte – Begriffe – Ansätze*, ed. Daniel Morat and Hansjakob Ziemer (Stuttgart: J. B. Metzler, 2018) and Robert Barry, *Compact Disc* (New York: Bloomsbury Academic, 2020); on headphones see Hagood, *Hush: Media and Sonic Self-Control*; on listening apps see Anahid Kassabian, 'Listening and Digital Technologies'; Christian Thorau, 'Vom Programmzettel zur Listening-App. Eine kurze Geschichte des geführten Hörens', in *Das Konzert II*, ed. Martin Tröndle (Bielefeld: transcript, 2018); and Ben Ratliff, *Every Song Ever: Twenty Ways to Listen to Music Now* (London: Penguin, 2016). An overview can be found in Greg Milner, *Perfecting Sound Forever: The Story of Recorded Music* (New York: Faber & Faber, 2010); and Benjamin Burkhart, 'Musik wiedergeben', in *Audiowelten: Technologie und Medien in der populären Musik nach 1945: 22 Objektstudien*, ed. Benjamin Burkhart, Laura Niebling, Alan van Keeken, Christofer Jost and Martin Pfleiderer (Münster: Waxmann, 2021).

250 Volmar, 'Experiencing High Fidelity', 400–1.
251 Wicke, 'Der Tonträger als Medium der Musik', 59.
252 Susan Schmidt Horning, *Chasing Sound. Technology, Culture, and the Art of Studio Recording from Edison to LP* (Baltimore, MD: Johns Hopkins University Press, 2013), primarily 314–20.
253 Although in the meantime numerous studies concerning music production are available (e.g. Paul Théberge, *Any Sound You Can Imagine: Making Music/Consuming*

Technology [Hanover: Wesleyan University Press, 1997]; Mark Cunningham, *Good Vibrations. A History of Record Production* [London: Sanctuary, 1998]; Albin Zak, *The Poetics of Rock: Cutting Tracks, Making Records* [Berkeley, CA: University of California Press, 2001]; Virgil Moorefield, *The Producer as Composer. Shaping the Sounds of Popular Music* [Cambridge, MA: MIT Press, 2005]; Simon Frith and Simon Zagorski-Thomas, eds, *The Art of Record Production: An Introductory Reader for a New Academic Field* (Burlington: Ashgate, 2012); Zagorski-Thomas and Bourbon, eds, *The Bloomsbury Handbook of Music Production*), an analysis of mastering and the various forms of releasing popular music just started, see Russ Hepworth-Sawyer and Jay Hodgson, eds, *Audio Mastering. The Artists. Discussions from Pre-Production to Mastering* (London: Routledge, 2019); John Paul Braddock et al., eds, *Mastering in Music* (London: Routledge 2021).

254 Stefan Frey, 'Was sagt ihr zu diesem Erfolg'. *Franz Lehár und die Unterhaltungsmusik des 20. Jahrhunderts* (Frankfurt am Main: Insel, 1999), 233.
255 Also for performance the record becomes normative. As Hans Keller put it: 'Performance … is the improvisatory tail-end of composition, and improvisation can't be repeated. … The central truth about all creativity is indeed the meaningful contradiction of the recipient's expectations, which the creator arouses before he contradicts them. The gramophone record's repeatability has had a disastrous and well-definable effect not only on the sheer act of listening, but also on musical education and, thence, on performance itself' (Hans Keller, 'The Keller Column: The Gramophone Record', *Music & Musicians*, January [1985]: 13). Adorno writes for 1938 quite visionarily: 'The performance sounds like its own phonograph record' (Adorno, 'On the Fetish-Character in Music and the Regression of Listening', 301).
256 Frey, '*Was sagt ihr zu diesem Erfolg*', 242.
257 Ingrid Grünberg, 'Operette und Rundfunk. Die Entstehung eines spezifischen Typs', in *Angewandte Musik 20er Jahre. Exemplarische Versuche Gesellschaftsbezogener Arbeit für Theater, Radio, Massenveranstaltung*, ed. Dietrich Stern (Berlin: Argument Verlag, 1977), 70.
258 Ibid., 67.
259 Ibid., 68.
260 Jeremy Gilbert and Ewan Pearson, *Discographies. Dance Music, Culture and the Politics of Sound* (London: Routledge, 1999), 132; Howes, *Empire of the Senses*.

2 Single-listening: The single is not single

1 Little Richard, too, was first perceived by the record label that later signed him as 'Tarzan' because of his expressive exterior (Blackwell, cited in Charles White, *The Life and Times of Little Richard: The Quasar of Rock* [Boston, MA: Da Capo Press, 1994], 49). The articulation of African American music and an imaginary 'jungle' already began in the late 1920s with Duke Ellington's 'jungle style' (Kimberley Hannon Teal, 'Beyond the Cotton Club: The Persistence of Duke Ellington's Jungle Style', *Jazz Perspectives* 6, nos. 1/2 [2013]: 123–49).
2 When Wicke describes rock 'n' roll as a 'media phenomenon' (Peter Wicke, '"Heroes and Villains": Anmerkungen zum Verhältnis von Popmusik und

Musikgeschichtsschreibung', in *Zu Problemen der 'Heroen'- und der 'Genie'-Musikgeschichtsschreibung*, ed. Nico Schüler [Hamburg: von Bockel, 1998], 208) he means precisely such forms of marketing like using songs in teenager films. The exploitation of a song in a Hollywood film paid off for Specialty Records.

3   A couple of decades later, such a decoupling of music making and performance gestures becomes crucial for New Pop and the music video clip aesthetics of the 1980s: 'The New Pop openly acknowledged pop performance as a visual medium with a sound track. My point is that this has always been true, but it was made increasingly apparent by changes in music-making technology. Music video did not create the change; it was validated by it' (Andrew Goodwin, *Dancing in the Distraction Factory: Music Television and Popular Culture* [Minneapolis: University of Minnesota Press, 1992], 33; see also Jens Gerrit Papenburg, 'Körperlichkeit', in *Handbuch Sound. Geschichte – Begriffe – Ansätze*, ed. Daniel Morat and Hansjakob Ziemer [Stuttgart: Metzler, 2018], 26).

4   See, for instance, the films *Wild Style* (directed by Charlie Ahearn, United States, 1982) and *Do the Right Thing* (directed by Spike Lee, United States, 1989).

5   See Peter Wicke, 'Über die diskursive Formation musikalischer Praxis. Diskurs-Strategien auf dem Feld der Populären Musik', in *Festschrift Prof. Dr. Gerd Rienäcker zum 65. Geburtstag*, ed. Stephan Aderhold (Berlin, 2004).

6   David Kirby, *Little Richard: The Birth of Rock 'n' Roll* (New York: Continuum, 2009), 175. In this way some of the spectacular effects that were attributed to rock 'n' roll in the 1950s are demonstrated. Wicke goes so far as to understand this music primarily through its effects (see Peter Wicke, *Rockmusik. zur Ästhetik und Soziologie eines Massenmediums* [Leipzig: Reclam, 1989], 18).

7   Unlike artists such as Chuck Berry, Bo Didley, or Buddy Holly, Little Richard apparently never developed a keen interest in the recording process. He also never tried to adapt this process to his ideas. The coincidence of the artist's intention with the recording need not necessarily be concealed, but can also be integrated into the presentation of a record. Thus, for instance, the otherwise white cover of Howlin' Wolf's only psychedelic rock LP includes the following three sentences: 'This is Howlin' Wolf's new album. He doesn't like it. He didn't like his electric guitar at first either' (Cadet Concept, United States, 1969).

8   Doyle, *Echo and Reverb*, 184.

9   Blackwell, cited in White, *The Life and Times of Little Richard*, 49.

10 Ibid.

11 On the various stories about the origin of *Tutti Frutti*, see Kirby, *Little Richard*, 99–121. The story of origin mentioned shows certain narrative parallels to Elvis Presley's first recording session at Sun: this was also considered a thoroughly unsuccessful session, at which only the penultimate recording achieved the desired success (on this see also Albin Zak, *I Don't Sound Like Nobody: Remaking Music in 1950s America* [Ann Arbor: University of Michigan Press 2010], 184–5).

12 Instructions from label boss Art Rupe to his employees did nothing to enhance the studio situation without an audience. In guidelines he formulated in the mid-1950s, Rupe also sounds off about the principles of recording: 'Remember that a recording session costs money and requires extreme concentration of everybody involved. GET RID OF ALL SIGHTSEERS, HANGERS-ON, etc. TRY NOT TO HAVE VISITORS! That is also the way competitors learn your business. That is also the way such interference keeps you from getting good results' (Rupe cited in John

Broven, *Record Makers and Breakers: Voices of the Independent Rock 'n' Roll Pioneers* [Chicago: University of Illinois Press, 2009], 473, emphasis in the original).
13 Penniman cited in White, *The Life and Times of Little Richard*, 55, emphasis in the original.
14 Ibid., 78.
15 Blackwell, cited in White, *The Life and Times of Little Richard*, 75.
16 Art Rupe was not looking at this level at all for a uniform sound for his label. Under the point 'General Recording Principles', he gives his employees the following advice: 'Try to record in the following studios whenever possible: a. New Orleans (Cosimo's); b. Houston (ACA – Bill Holford's); c. Memphis (Sam Phillips) d. Chicago (Universal – Bill Putnam); e. Dallas (Sellers)' (Rupe cited in Broven, *Record Makers and Breakers*, 473).
17 Cogan and Clark also make this distinction between the J&M sound and the Sun sound: 'What sets Sam Phillips apart from people like Cosimo Matassa and Rudy Van Gelder, though, is that while they, of course, documented performances faithfully, Sam distorted, slapped, and tickled that shiny mono tape while seducing performances from artists they didn't even know they could give' (Jim Cogan and William Clark, *Temples of Sound: Inside the Great Recording Studios* [San Francisco, CA: Chronicle Books, 2003], 87).
18 *Long Tall Sally* by the Beatles (Parlophone, UK, 1964) attempts to bring together the sound of the two cities.
19 Langdon Winners, 'Little Richard', in *The Rolling Stone Illustrated History of Rock & Roll*, ed. Jim Miller (New York: Rolling Stone Press, 1976), 52–7. In Frankie Ford's *Sea Cruise* (Ace, United States, 1959) such a 'foggy rumble' actually transitions into the sound of a real foghorn.
20 See Blackwell cited in White, *The Life and Times of Little Richard*, 48; on the backbeat see also Martin Pfleiderer, *Rhythmus: Psychologische, theoretische und stilanalytische Aspekte populärer Musik* (Bielefeld: transcript, 2006), 219–26.
21 See Ray Topping, liner notes for Little Richard, *Little Richard: The Specialty Sessions*, SPCD 8508 (Specialty, United States, 1989).
22 *Long Tall Sally* was written by Little Richard, Robert 'Bumps' Blackwell, and E. Johnson (see on this White, *The Life and Times of Little Richard*, 60–3).
23 This title can be found, for instance, on *The Howlin' Wolf Album* (Cadet Concept, United States, 1969).
24 The texts of various Little Richard songs refer more or less directly to homosexual desire. Thus, for instance, *Lucille* is intended to be dedicated to a transvestite; the first versions of *Tutti Frutti* are also not within a heterosexual order. Although Little Richard describes himself as 'gay', a reader of his biography might be surprised about the excessive descriptions of various sexual practices that queer any hetero–homo dualisms.
25 Little Richard cited in White, *The Life and Times of Little Richard*, 65–6.
26 See Marybeth Hamilton, *In Search of the Blues* (New York: Basic Books, 2008).
27 Like, for instance, the shout with which Paul McCartney announces the first solo in the Beatles' version of *Long Tall Sally* or Little Richard's high 'whooo', which Paul McCartney also takes over in the outro.
28 See Wicke, *Rockmusik*, 57–8 and 73–5.
29 Charlie Gillett, *The Sound of the City: The Rise of Rock and Roll* (London: Souvenir Press, 1983), 86.

30 *Long Tall Sally* spawned not only various cover versions, but also numerous so-called answer songs. Thus along the axes of 'answer song' and 'cover version' a series of songs develops that appeal through variation. 'Answer songs' – such as Eddie Cochran's *Skinny Jim* (Crest, United States, 1957) or *Short Fat Fannie* from Larry Williams (Specialty Records, United States, 1957) – referred, however, only to the text of the titles. Songs by Little Richard also rarely seemed to originate in a stroke of 'genius', but more in varying and adapting existing material. This becomes particularly clear, for example, in *Heeby-Jeebies-Love* (Specialty Records, United States, 1989) and *Heeby-Jeebies* (Specialty Records, United States, 1956); it began as a version of *Tutti Frutti* and finally developed into a more or less stand-alone song.

31 Zak, *The Poetics of Rock*, 27, emphasis in the original. For a more statistically shaped depiction of Boone's cover versions, see Marc Pendzich, *Von der Coverversion zum Hit-Recycling. Historische, ökonomische und rechtliche Aspekte eines zentralen Phänomens der Pop- und Rockmusik* (Münster: LIT, 2004), 91–3, and for a study of selected cover versions in rock 'n' roll, that does not, however, go much into differences regarding the production of music see 101–9.

32 The production of *Long Tall Sally* [The Thing] mentioned already will not be taken further into account later in the text.

33 Five record releases and one CD release of the 'original production' of Little Richard's *Long Tall Sally* produced in 1956 will be examined: one CD, one 78 shellac, two 7-inch singles and two LPs. These releases will also be compared with a new production of the song with Little Richard, or rather its release on LP and CD produced in 1964. This means that in total eight releases of two productions of *Long Tall Sally*, released in four different formats, will be compared with each other. Besides the US original release as a 7-inch single (Specialty XSP-572-45 [45-XSP-572], United States, 1956) an English licensed release from the 1950s as a 78 shellac will be consulted (London MSC.1443 [MSC 1443-1], UK, no year). Furthermore, a release on the LP *Alan Freed's 'Golden Pics'* (End 313 [LP 313A], United States, 1961) will be examined. This can be situated in the context of a first attempted rock 'n' roll revival. Attention will also be paid to a re-release of the production as a 7-inch single from the late 1960s (Specialty XSP-572 [L-10723, 572-XSP], United States, 1968), as well as a more recent, lavishly re-mastered LP re-release of Little Richard's first album *Here's Little Richard* on an audiophile label (MoFi 1-287 [MFSL-1227-B1], United States, 2008). Finally, the release of the 'master version' of the production on CD will be consulted (Specialty, United States, 1989). After his epiphany and temporary retirement from the pop business, Little Richard again recorded his songs from the 1950s in the 1960s. These recordings were no longer released on the Specialty Records label from Los Angeles, but by Vee-Jay Records in Chicago. Two releases from this context will be consulted: a stereo release on the LP *His Greatest Hits* (Vee-Jay VJS 1124 [64933-1], United States, 1964) and a re-release of the version of 'Long Tall Sally' on his LP *His Greatest Hits* on a CD from a different audiophile label (Bell, Germany, 1998). Since not only different productions are being compared with each other but also differently mastered releases, the records are additionally specified here with their catalogue and matrix number.

34 Thus, for instance, on the single *Be-Bop-A-Lula* (Capitol F3450 [45-15230-D7], United States, 1956) by Gene Vincent.

35 This comprises about 100 to 3,500 Hz.

36 Here the matrix number is also indicated in addition to the catalogue number because reference is made to specific releases in the following section.
37 'Bell Sound' is stamped in the area of the lead-out groove.
38 On payola, that is, pay for airplay, see Reebee Garofalo, 'Payola', in *Continuum Encyclopedia of Popular Music of the World. Volume I: Media, Industry and Society*, ed. John Shepard, David Horn, Dave Laing, Paul Oliver and Peter Wicke (New York: Continuum, 2003). Alan Freed was indicted two times for payola and was financially ruined in the context of the 1959 and 1960 payola hearings after the American Society of Composers, Authors and Publishers (ASCAP), 'convinced Congress to investigate payola' (559). ASCAP represented primarily the old Tin Pan Alley Industry that 'fears to hold the line' with the success of rock 'n' roll (559).
39 Belz writes: 'At the end of the 1950s, rock became aware of its own history. "Oldies but Goodies" appeared' (Carl Belz, *The Story of Rock* [Oxford: Oxford University Press, 1969], 88). At the beginning of the 1960s, various labels released compilations of rock 'n' roll hits. For instance, Alan Freed compiled for End Records not only *Alan Freed's 'Golden Pics'* but also *Alan Freed's Memory Lane* (End, United States, 1962) and *Alan Freed's Top 15* (End, United States, 1962). The film industry as well was increasingly 'writing' a history of rock 'n' roll. The soundtracks of these films reconstruct the sound of the 1950s, unless they revert to so-called original versions – like, for instance, *Cadillac Records* (directed by Darnell Martin, United States, 2008) – or re-master it – such as, for instance, *American Graffiti* (directed by George Lucas, United States, 1973). Rock 'n' roll revivals have been cropping up since the 1970s with a certain tenacity: musicals like *Grease* (directed by Randal Kleiser, United States 1971), TV series like *Happy Days* (United States, 1974–84), or a resurrection of the Teddy Boys in Germany in the early 1980s with bands like the Spider Murphy Gang. Even rock 'n' roll is being revived again and again – for instance, by the British trio Kitty, Daisy and Lewis. They have certainly somewhat overshot the mark by offering their album *Smoking in Heaven* (Sunday Best Recordings, UK, 2011) in a version consisting of eight 10-inch discs operating at 78 rpm.
40 Little Richard perceived himself as profoundly 'unnatural': He described his homosexuality as 'unnatural affections' (Richard cited in White, *The Life and Times of Little Richard*, 101).
41 These new recordings were released on the LP *His Greatest Hits* (VeeJay VJS-1124 [64933-1], United States, 1964).
42 This voice, distorted already during the recording, can be heard blatantly, for instance, on the master of 'Long Tall Sally' released on CD in 1989 (Specialty, United States, 1989).
43 See, for example, the single *Sugar Baby* by Peter Kraus (Polydor 23 844 A [23844 A II], FRG, 1958).
44 Alexander Boyden Magoun, 'The Origins of the 45-RPM Record at RCA Victor, 1939–1948', in *Music and Technology in the Twentieth Century*, ed. Hans-Joachim Braun (Baltimore, MD: Johns Hopkins University Press, 2002), 33.
45 See Phil Vourtsis, The Fabulous Victrola '45' (Atglen, PA: Schiffer, 2007).
46 See Richard Osborne. *Vinyl: A History of the Analogue Record* (London: Routledge, 2016), 127.

47 The first transistor radio on the US market was the Regency TR1 in 1954 (David Attwood, *Sound Design: Classic Audio & Hi-Fi Design* (London: Mitchell Beazley, 2002), 12–13.
48 See on this Heike Weber, *Das Versprechen mobiler Freiheit*, 126–33.
49 Whereas the TP 1 was in the upper price segment. It cost DM 215. A survey of readers of the youth magazine *Bravo* revealed in 1961 that 12- to 16-year-olds had DM 20 a month that they could dispose of freely; and young adults up to the age of 24 had up to DM 100 per month to be used at their discretion (Ehrmann and Landgrebe cited in Weber, *Das Versprechen mobiler Freiheit*, 128). One 'Gerhard' is quoted in Fred Grimm's collection of quotations from young people between 1900 and 2010 as saying in 1960: 'I saved up several months' wages and bought myself a portable radio, the Grundig Boy. You could tune in for 5 hours, then the batteries were all empty. You had to buy batteries very frequently' (Gerhard, Norderstedt cited in Fred Grimm, *'Wir wollen eine andere Welt.' Jugend in Deutschland 1900–2010, Eine private Geschichte aus Tagebüchern, Briefen, Dokumenten* [Hamburg: Tolkemitt bei Zweitausendeins, 2010], 283).
50 On this concept of music as an assemblage or as a network, see Chapter 1, section, 'What Are Listening Devices?' or Peter Wicke, 'Popmusik in der Analyse', 118.
51 See, for example, Jemima Kiss, 'The Death of the Album', *The Guardian*, 29 August 2008, https://www.theguardian.com/media/pda/2008/aug/29/thedeathofthealbum.
52 The term 'album' has since established itself as a synonym for LP or CD – and I use it in that sense here. Into the 1950s, however, generic sleeves of clear plastic, bound together in book form and designed for the storage of records, were also referred to as albums, as were the compilations of multiple 78s or 45s available commercially as complete packages See Keir Keightley, 'Album', in *Continuum Encyclopedia of Popular Music of the World. Volume I: Media, Industry and Society*, ed. John Shepherd, David Horn, Dave Laing, Paul Oliver and Peter Wicke (London: Continuum, 2003); see also Rüdiger Bloemeke, *Roll over Beethoven. Wie der Rock 'n' Roll nach Deutschland kam* (Vienna: Hannibal, 1996), 36.
53 Independent labels were initially a US phenomenon. It was there that they experienced their first boom in the 1920s and 1930s, to be followed by a second in the 1950s. It was not until the 1960s that the first independent labels, such as Hansa Musik Produktion, emerged in West Germany.
54 For instance, from 1952 to 1968, Sam Phillips's label Sun Records released almost two hundred and fifty singles, but only seventeen EPs and twelve LPs (see Colin Escott and Martin Hawkins, *Good Rockin' Tonight: Sun Records and the Birth of Rock 'n' Roll* [New York: St Martin's Press, 1991], 249–63).
55 Of course, one can find forerunners of the concept album – Frank Sinatra's *In the Wee Small Hours* (Capitol, United States), 1955 or Joe Meek's *I Hear a New World* (Triumph, UK, 1960). These, however, primarily targeted the adult market.
56 Keightley, 'Album', 613.
57 Papenburg, 'Konzeptalben als "große Werke" Populärer Musik?'.
58 See, for example, Wilfrid Mellers, *Twilight of the Gods: The Beatles in Retrospect* (London: Faber & Faber, 1973). Mellers discusses the Beatles' musical scores, however, and not their recordings or performances.
59 Albin Zak, *I Don't Sound Like Nobody*, 238.

60 A selection of 500 single covers from 1950 on can be found in Spencer Drate and Judith Salavetz, *Five Hundred 45s: A Graphic History of the Seven-Inch Record* (New York: Collins Design, 2010). However, covers for singles from the 1950s are the absolute exception. Releases of singles and EPs on major labels such as RCA Victor or Capitol by stars – Frank Sinatra, Nat King Cole or Elvis Presley, for example – account for the majority of these exceptions. The 1960s are far more extensively documented by Drate and Salavetz.
61 After the second half of the 1950s, stereo records were primarily released for the classical music market.
62 Wicke, 'Der Tonträger als Medium der Musik', 23.
63 Belz, *The Story of Rock*, viii.
64 See Theodore Gracyk, *Rhythm and Noise: An Aesthetics of Rock* (Durham, NC: Duke University Press, 1996). Anderson correctly notes the problematic nature of Gracyk's thesis, which posits that rock music in particular is characterized by a complex relationship to recording technology, as compared to other forms of popular music. In this regard, Anderson is referring primarily to the 'easy listening' genre established in the 1950s (see Anderson, *Making Easy Listening*, 123–5).
65 For example, Nicholas Cook, Eric Clarke, Daniel Leech-Wilkinson and John Rink, eds, *The Cambridge Companion to Recorded Music* Enter spatium. (Cambridge: Cambridge University Press, 2009); Katz, *Capturing Sound*; Bayley, *Recorded Music*; Frith and Zagorski-Thomas, *The Art of Record Production*.
66 Zak, *I Don't Sound Like Nobody*.
67 Bing Crosby and Pete Martin, *Call Me Lucky* (Cambridge, MA: Da Capo Press, 2001), 142–3.
68 Peter Wicke, Kai-Erik Ziegenrücker and Wieland Ziegenrücker, *Handbuch der populären Musik: Geschichte, Stile, Praxis, Industrie* (Mainz: Schott, 2009), 667. In the United States, sales of singles grew in tandem with rock 'n' roll's success. Between 1954 and 1959, single sales in the United States nearly tripled: 213 million singles were sold in 1954; in 1959, sales were already at 603 million (data from Wicke, 'Der Tonträger als Medium der Musik' and Harvey Rachlin, *The Encyclopedia of Music Business* [New York: Harper & Row, 1981], respectively). As early as 1954, there were more 45-rpm singles sold than 78s in the US popular music market (see Belz, *The Story of Rock*, 53). From 1957, this was also the case in the R&B market (54). In Germany, the single did not come on the market until 1953 (see Bloemeke, *Roll over Beethoven*, 29, 32), although record players with three speeds had been available in the country since 1951 (31). At the Great German Radio, Phonograph and Television Exhibition held in Düsseldorf in 1953, Philips introduced the Philips Minigroove 45, a 7-inch vinyl record that played at 45 rpm (see 'Philips-Klein-Schallplatten für 45 Umdrehungen', *Der Automaten-Markt: Fachzeitschrift für die gesamte Automatenwirtschaft* 5, no. 12 [1953]: 352). Record players that only played 45s, such as Philips's Mignon or Grundig's Phono Boy, which were both specifically designed to be portable, came on the market in the second half of the 1950s (see Bloemeke, *Roll over Beethoven*, 35–6). In the UK, the 45s caught on more slowly than in the United States (see Adrian Horn, *Juke Box Britain: Americanisation and Youth Culture, 1945–60* [Manchester: Manchester University Press, 2009], 81 and Osborne, *Vinyl*, 126–41). Not until 1959 would the sale of 45s surpass that of 78s, and in certain subcultures, the 78 stubbornly held its ground. Paul Willis points out that in the English rocker subculture – which

seemingly possessed a nostalgic fondness for US rock 'n' roll – the 78 had a role to play in the search for 'originals', and was regarded in that scene as especially valuable well into the 1960s: 'Although their technical quality was demonstrably inferior to the more recent 45s, they had a bulk, a brittleness, a distinctive tactile presence that all spoke of genuine origins in the golden age' (Paul E. Willis, *Profane Culture* [Princeton, NJ: Princeton University Press, 2014], 85).
69 Wicke, 'Der Tonträger als Medium der Musik', 19.
70 Shaw, *The Rockin' '50s*, 229.
71 Großmann, 'Die Geburt des Pop aus dem Geist der Phonographischen Reproduktion', 122.
72 Ibid. With regard to the 1950s on this matter, see also Zak, *I Don't Sound Like Nobody*.
73 Osborne has argued that the single is a 'crassly commercial product', but that it also 'provides the perfect representation of recorded music' (Osborne, *Vinyl*, 117). But even in Osborne's analysis of different vinyl formats, the systematic analysis of the single as a listening technology remains a desideratum.
74 On popular music as an epistemological instrument, see Chapter 1, section, 'What Is a Sound and Music History of Listening Devices?'.
75 Simon Frith, *The Sociology of Rock* (London: Constable, 1978), 11, emphasis in original.
76 Ibid., 10.
77 There are now numerous publications which address the LP and high fidelity: Joseph O'Connell, 'The Fine-Tuning of a Golden Ear: High-End Audio and the Evolutionary Model of Technology', *Technology and Culture* 33, no. 1 (1992); Keightley, '"Turn It Down!" She Shrieked'; Perlman, 'Golden Ears and Meter Readers'; Anderson, *Making Easy Listening*; Shuhei Hosokawa and Hideaki Matsuoka, 'On the Fetish Character of Sound and the Progression of Technology: Theorizing Japanese Audiophiles', in *Sonic Synergies: Music, Technology, Community, Identity*, ed. Gerry Bloustien, Margaret Peters and Susan Luckman (Farnham: Ashgate, 2008); Björnberg, 'Learning to Listen to Perfect Sound'; Barry, 'High-Fidelity Sound as Spectacle and Sublime, 1950–1961'; Sara Jansson, '"Listen to These Speakers": Swedish Hi-Fi Enthusiasts, Gender, and Listening', *Journal of the International Association for the Study of Popular Music* 1, no. 2 (2010); Volmar, 'Experiencing High Fidelity'. High-fidelity culture can in no way be reduced to an aesthetic of documentation. This point will be examined more closely later in the text.
78 Wicke, 'Popmusik in der Theorie', 66.
79 Benjamin H. Carson, A. D. Burt and H. I. Reiskind, 'A Record Changer and Record of Complementary Design', RCA Review, June (1949), 173–90; Alexander Boyden Magoun, 'Shaping the Sound of Music: The Evolution of the Phonograph Record, 1877–1950', PhD dissertation, Department of History, University of Maryland, College Park, 2000; Magoun, 'The Origins of the 45-RPM Record at RCA Victor, 1939–1948'; Alexander Boyden Magoun, 'An In-Depth Look at the Origins of the LP, the "45", and High Fidelity, 1939–1950', in *The Fabulous Victrola '45'*, ed. Phil Vourtsis (Atglen: Schiffer, 2007). I refer here in particular to the developmental history of the single compiled by the historian Alexander Boyden Magoun (see Magoun, 'Shaping the Sound of Music'; Magoun, 'The Origins of the 45-RPM Record at RCA Victor'; Magoun, 'An In-Depth Look at the Origins of the LP, the "45", and High Fidelity'). However, despite his meticulous survey of this history, Magoun does not rigorously investigate its implications for a listening and music history.

80 This phrase is by Katz (*Capturing Sound*). Katz studies music production and not so much music listening and he tries to distinguish his approach from a technology deterministic approach.
81 For examples, see Wicke, 'Der Tonträger als Medium der Musik'.
82 The dynamics between the single record and the old shellac disc is also insightful here. Even if 78-rpm shellac records were listened to in series every now and then, this listening practice differed from the type of listening in series offered by the vinyl single. The 45-rpm single 'remediates' (Jay David Bolter and Richard Grusin, *Remediation: Understanding New Media* [Cambridge, MA: MIT Press, 1999]) the 78 record. Frith, for instance, emphasizes that those listening to the 45-rpm single were different from their 78-rpm single-listening counterparts: 'During the 1950s TV took over from the radio as the basic form of home entertainment leaving radio to specialize in its appeal. One of the most important "special" markets turned out to be the young and, with the simultaneous development of LPs, adults ceased to buy singles' (Frith, *The Sociology of Rock*, 98). Frith also refers elsewhere to the transformation of record listening in the 1950s: 'From the 1920s to the early 1950s the music industry aimed its products at the family audience; records reached the public on family radio and on the family phonograph – most homes only had one of each' (187). The difference between shellac and vinyl also made a difference in the making of music: 'Technical developments in manufacture [of records] have, as well, musical implications. When shellac was replaced by polyvinyl chloride as the new raw material of records, for example, the result was not simply that the easily breakable and weighty 78 was replaced by plastic discs: the new cutting process meant that much more sophisticated and complex sounds could now be reproduced' (86).
83 Time and again, the single is presented in the history of recording as the technologically conservative response to the LP. For example, the single only has commercial relevance for Gelatt (Roland Gelatt, *The Fabulous Phonograph: 1877–1977* [London: Cassell, 1977], 294–5): it was created for an uncritical mass market and not for the 'discriminating listener'. Gelatt claims that it was only due to an elaborate advertising campaign in the pop market that it was able to survive. Read and Welch describe the single as a conservative development (Walter L. Welch and Oliver Read, *From Tin Foil to Stereo: Evolution of the Phonograph* [Indianapolis, IN: Sams, 1976], 341). Even in more recent surveys of recording history – particularly in those from German-speaking countries – the single is for the most part neglected in comparison to the LP. This includes the unclear labels given to the single – for example, the nonsensical logo 'Single-LP/RCA' (Peter Overbeck, 'Die Entwicklung der Tonträgertechnologie', in *Handbuch der Musik im 20. Jahrhundert*, 10, ed. Arnold Jacobshagen and Frieder Reininghaus [Laaber: Laaber, 2006], 87). Further evidence of this neglect can be found in ignorance concerning the single, as evidenced by Adorno: as astute as his observations regarding the LP may have been ('Theodor W. Adorno, 'Opera and the Long-Playing Record', in *Essays on Music by Theodor W. Adorno*, ed. Richard Leppert, trans. Susan H. Gillespie [Berkeley: University of California Press, 2002]), the single escaped Adorno's attention. By the end of the 1940s, the response to the introduction of the LP and the single in consumer-oriented magazines had already proven to be disadvantageous for the latter (for an overview, see Jeffrey Donald Tang, 'Sound Decisions: System, Standards, and

Consumers in American Audio Technology, 1945–1975', PhD dissertation, University of Pennsylvania, 2004, 79–94). See also David Morton, *Off the Record: The Technology and Culture of Sound Recording in America* (New Brunswick, NJ: Rutgers University Press, 2000), 135–40; Andre Millard, *America on Record: A History of Recorded Sound* (Cambridge: Cambridge University Press, 2005), 199–208; Osborne, *Vinyl*, 117–41; Laura Niebling, 'Ernst Neger: Geb' dem Kind sein Nuddelche. Aus dem Mainzer Karneval in eine Jukebox in Flensburg', in *Audiowelten: Technologie und Medien in der populären Musik nach 1945: 22 Objektstudien*, ed. Benjamin Burkhart, Laura Niebling, Alan van Keeken, Christofer Jost and Martin Pfleiderer (Münster: Waxmann, 2021), 221–6. Hans Ernst Neger (1909–89) was a roofer who became famous as a singer in relevant circles with carnival songs, especially in the West German Rhineland.

84 Certainly there are other possible forms of listening to the single as well as to the LP. Of concern here, however, are those listening forms implemented in the phase of developing the technology.

85 See Keightley, '"Turn It Down!" She Shrieked'; see Anderson, *Making Easy Listening*.

86 When the single came on the market in Germany in 1953, several labels (among them Teldec, until 1960) delivered their singles with a built-in centre hole insert. This could be snapped out if the user had a record changer with a wide centre spindle; see Bloemeke, *Roll Over Beethoven*, 30).

87 For more on the length of records, see Susan Schmidt Horning, *Chasing Sound*, 107–11.

88 Tang, 'Sound Decisions', 89.

89 Belz, *The Story of Rock*, 55. Belz even sees a general 'speeding-up process' linked to the single: 'This was true for everyone connected with the records: manufacturers, distributors, shop owners, disk jockeys, and individual buyers' (54).

90 Willis, *Profane Culture*, 92.

91 'Columbia Diskery, CBS Show Microgroove Platters to Press; Tell How It Began', *Billboard* 60, no. 26 (1948): 3, 18, 21.

92 The timing of this market launch harbours a certain irony: while the musicians had stopped playing, that is, went on strike, CBS Columbia introduced a new record playing system while releasing material from its archives. Thus, CBS Columbia was temporarily independent of musicians' labour.

93 In the 30 July 1949 issue of *Billboard* music magazine, it was not only the title page of the NAMM Convention Section that heralded 'The Stars Who Make the Hits Are on RCA Victor 45 R.P.M.!' RCA Victor additionally used (and had purchased) the next twenty-three (!) pages of the magazine to promote its new record. RCA Victor's new system had been available on the market since 31 March 1949 (see Magoun, 'Shaping the Sound of Music', 262).

94 Unlike RCA Victor, CBS Columbia did not manufacture any electronic entertainment devices, so the record players for its new system were manufactured under licence by the Philco Radio and Television Company. RCA Victor had already attempted to introduce an LP in the early 1930s, although it was then not a part of a technological system. By contrast, Peter Goldmark describes the development strategy of CBS Columbia's LP as a 'system approach' (see Peter Goldmark, *Maverick Inventor: My Turbulent Years at CBS* [New York: Saturday Review Press, 1973], 132–3). With the LP, the company presented 'a plan to attack the entire system of record making' (132).

95 A comparative analysis of the different accounts can be found in Gary Marmorstein. *The Label: The Story of Columbia Records* (Boston, MA: Da Capo Press, 2007), 151–74. A survey of the LP's developmental history is found in Magoun, 'The Origins of the 45-RPM Record at RCA Victor, 1939–1948', 23–4. See also Peter Goldmark, R. Snepvangers and W. S. Bachman, 'The Columbia Long-Playing Microgroove Recording System', *Proceedings of the IRE* 37, no. 8 (1949), 923–7; Broven, *Record Makers and Breakers*, 73–90; and Osborne, *Vinyl*.

96 'Columbia Diskery, CBS Show Microgroove Platters to Press; Tell How It Began'; Wallerstein, Edward. 'Creating the LP Record (as Told to Ward Botsford)'. *High Fidelity Magazine* 26, no. 4 (1976): 56–8. Wallerstein was the first president of Columbia Records after it had been bought by CBS. He had previously worked for Victor and had been involved in the unsuccessful introduction of the LP there in 1931; see Marmorstein, *Label*, 71–2.

97 Goldmark, *Maverick Inventor*, 125–47.

98 William S. Bachman, 'The LP and the Single', *Journal of the Audio Engineering Society* 25, no. 10/11 (1977): 821–3; Howard Scott, 'The Beginnings of LP', *Gramophone*, July (1998), 112–13.

99 See 'Columbia Diskery, CBS Show Microgroove Platters to Press; Tell How It Began'; and Wallerstein, 'Creating the LP Record (as Told to Ward Botsford)'.

100 See Goldmark, *Maverick Inventor*, 125–47.

101 See 'Columbia Diskery, CBS Show Microgroove Platters to Press; Tell How It Began'.

102 Edward Zwick, 'An Interview with the Father of Hi-Fi: Dr. Peter Goldmark', *Rolling Stone* 27 (1973).

103 See Goldmark, *Maverick Inventor*, 147.

104 See 'Columbia Diskery, CBS Show Microgroove Platters to Press; Tell How It Began', 18. Pianist Howard Scott, who coordinated the first transfers to LP at Columbia (see Marmorstein, *Label*, 163), also confirms this version: 'No one invented the long playing record. It was developed by a team, ... Its leader was Bill Bachman', Scott, 'Beginnings of LP', 122; see also Wallerstein, 'Creating the LP Record (as Told to Ward Botsford)'.

105 Wallerstein, 'Creating the LP Record (as Told to Ward Botsford)'.

106 Goldmark, *Maverick Inventor*, 125–47.

107 RCA Victor had released records made of vinyl as early as 1945 (see Tang, 'Sound Decisions', 57). RCA Victor's engineers were already familiar with the material as they had made records from it for the Armed Forces Network (AFN) during the Second World War. These records were called 'V-Discs', although the 'V' stood for 'victory' rather than 'vinyl'. These were the only American records capable of surviving the long voyages over the world's oceans intact. V-Discs were the means to supply the US troops in Europe, Africa, Asia and on-board the warships with sounds from back home. Furthermore, a process would be developed parallel to and independent of the LP and single that would substantially lengthen the playing time of the record: variable groove spacing, invented by Eduard Rhein, physicist and editor-in-chief of the German magazine *Hörzu*. Rather than keeping the spacing between grooves consistent, Rhein's process varied it according to the actual groove excursion. Introduced in Germany in 1953, at the same time as the single, variable groove spacing made it possible to store eight minutes of music on one side of a single. Rhein entered into a licence agreement for his process with Teldec (Bloemeke, *Roll over Beethoven*, 23–7; 'Kleinere Schallplatten – Mehr Musik',

Der Automaten-Markt. Fachzeitschrift für die Gesamte Automatenwirtschaft 6, no. 9 [1954a]: 286) and Eduard Rhein, *100 Jahre Schallplatte. Vom Phonographen über die Laser-Disc – wohin?* (Berlin: Presse- und Informationsamt des Landes Berlin, 1987).
108 Bachman, 'LP and the Single', 822; see also Marmorstein, *Label*, 162–3.
109 See Osborne, *Vinyl*, 98. For an overview of the early repertoire of LPs, see 94–104; Knut Holtsträter, '"The Voice of Frank Sinatra" as the First Concept Album in the History of Popular Music. Musical (Large-Scale) Form on Records and Its Contexts of Use in the U.S. Popular Culture of the 1950s', in *Große Formen in der populären Musik: Large-Scale Forms in Popular Music*, ed. Christofer Jost and Gregor Herzfeld (Münster: Waxmann, 2019).
110 Goldmark, *Maverick Inventor*, 128.
111 Ibid., 127.
112 In the 1950s, for instance, various magazines dedicated to hi-fi came into existence. The first magazines of this time were published in the United States; for instance, the first edition of *High Fidelity* came out in 1951. Other Western countries followed several years later. On the development of hi-fi culture in Sweden, see Björnberg, 'Learning to Listen to Perfect Sound'.
113 Ibid., 113.
114 Anderson, *Making Easy Listening*.
115 See James H. Johnson, *Listening in Paris: A Cultural History* (Berkeley: University of California Press, 1995); Sven Oliver Müller, *Das Publikum macht die Musik: Musikleben in Berlin, London und Wien im 19. Jahrhundert* (Göttingen: Vandenhoeck & Ruprecht, 2014).
116 Anderson, *Making Easy Listening*, 114.
117 Ibid., 125.
118 Ibid., 151–78. The releases of the Grand Award Records label founded by Enoch Light in 1958 and Command Records (founded in 1959) are pertinent examples of generating such a hyper-reality. The extremely sophisticated sound design of these labels – the recordings were not recorded on magnetic tape but on 35-mm film – exceeded any concert hall realism.
119 Keightley, '"Turn It Down!" She Shrieked', 174.
120 Ibid.
121 Barry, 'High-Fidelity Sound as Spectacle and Sublime, 1950–1961', 120.
122 Carson, Burt and Reiskind, 'A Record Changer and Record of Complementary Design', 190.
123 Magoun, 'The Origins of the 45-RPM Record at RCA Victor, 1939–1948', 12.
124 See also James H. Kogen, 'Record Changers, Turntables, and Tone Arms: A Brief Technical History', *Journal of the Audio Engineering Society* 25, nos. 10/11 (1977): 749–58.
125 See David Morton, *Sound Recording: The Life Story of a Technology* (Baltimore, MD: Johns Hopkins University Press, 2004), 138.
126 Magoun, 'The Origins of the 45-RPM Record at RCA Victor, 1939–1948', 8. In an article in *Billboard* in 1944, jukeboxes for home use – under which the author understands a record player with an automatic record changer – were predicted to have a rosy future ('"Home Jukes" Will Boost Disk Sales', *Billboard* 26 [1944]). These devices, states the article, are particularly interesting for teenagers in a portable version: 'The biggest group of customers for recorded music in the home will be the teen-age group' (78).

127 Magoun, 'The Origins of the 45-RPM Record at RCA Victor, 1939–1948', 8. Magoun also refers here to the radio historian Susan Douglas: 'What began to emerge in the early 1950s and led to the invention of the Top 40 format was 'programming by the charts' – basing what was played on the air on record sales and jukebox plays. This was nothing new – as early as 1935, 'Your Hit Parade' offered performances of the top ten hits'; Douglas, *Listening In*, 246. However, it should be noted that the radio programme 'Your Hit Parade' was not designed around records, but around a live band that played hits.
128 Welch and Read, *From Tin Foil to Stereo*, 314.
129 Magoun, 'Shaping the Sound of Music', 9.
130 The name 'Project X' was changed to 'Madame X' by RCA Victor's advertising agency J. Walter Thompson after the market launch of the single record. She became the first promotional figure for the single (many thanks to Alexander Magoun for this observation).
131 See Magoun, 'The Origins of the 45-RPM Record at RCA Victor, 1939–1948', 9.
132 Welch and Read, *From Tin Foil to Stereo*, 307.
133 Ibid., 315.
134 'In June [1949] the magazine [*Consumer's Research Bulletin*] speculated that jukeboxes, with their power to promote new records, might tip the scales in favor of the 45, noting the irony that lovers of good music may have their choice of method of reproduction of music determined by the operations of a device that most of them have roundly cursed' (Tang, 'Sound Decisions', 88).
135 Osborne, *Vinyl*, 118.
136 Magoun, 'Shaping the Sound of Music', 208.
137 Belz, *The Story of Rock*, 54.
138 In the issue dated 26 June 1948, Columbia's LP is presented in detail for the first time, referring to a press presentation of the LP on 19 June in *Billboard*; see 'Columbia Diskery, CBS Show Microgroove Platters to Press; Tell How It Began'.
139 Carson, Burt and Reiskind, 'A Record Changer and Record of Complementary Design'.
140 Arnold Shaw, *Honkers and Shouters: The Golden Years of Rhythm & Blues* (New York: Macmillan, 1978), 183.
141 Broven, *Record Makers and Breakers*, 48.
142 See Chapter 1, section, 'What Is a Sound and Music History of Listening Devices?'.
143 Adorno, *Current of Music*, 299–307.
144 Peter Wicke, *Vom Umgang mit Popmusik* (Berlin: Volk und Wissen, 1993), 47.
145 The assumption that the playing time of the single was defined exclusively on the basis of the analysis of classical pieces of music released as records – as suggested in Magoun, 'Shaping the Sound of Music', and Morton, *Sound Recording*, for example – is, however, a supposition one must object to.
146 See Carson, Burt and Reiskind, 'A Record Changer and Record of Complementary Design'.
147 Ibid., emphasis added.
148 Adorno, *Current of Music*, 285.
149 Morton, *Sound Recording*, 138.
150 Goldmark, *Maverick Inventor*, 132.
151 Morton, *Sound Recording*, 135.
152 See Goldmark, *Maverick Inventor*, 127.

153 See Jerrold Northrop Moore, *Sound Revolutions: A Biography of Fred Gaisberg, Founding Father of Commercial Sound Recording* (London: Sanctuary, 1999), 94. The material of the record on which it was recorded – initially this was wax, later a metal plate covered with acetate lacquer, and since 1981 this can even be copper foil thanks to the Direct Metal Mastering (DMM) introduced by Telefunken (see Wicke, 'Der Tonträger als Medium der Musik', 9). On DMM, see also Christina Dörfling, 'Von der Liebe zum Hören. Direktschnitt, Direct Metal Mastering und die (Un-) Möglichkeit audiophiler Tonträger', *Musiktheorie. Zeitschrift für Musikwissenschaft* 36, no. 1 (2021): 32–45.

154 Reference should be made here to other preliminary forms of mastering. For example, as early as the beginning of the twentieth century, the French record company Pathé recorded on an enlarged wax cylinder running at double speed and transcribed it for release on vinyl or on another cylinder format (see Wicke, 'Der Tonträger als Medium der Musik', 9). The introduction of transcription records, originally from the radio industry, which had a diameter of sixteen inches and ran at 33 1/3 rpm, into recording studios around 1930 also made a change of media necessary before a record could be released (see Schmidt Horning, *Chasing Sound*, 50–4).

155 See Edward H. Uecke, 'The Control of Quality in Phonograph Records', *Journal of the Audio Engineering Society* 4, no. 4 (1956), 159–62.

156 For example, the studio complex opened in Hollywood in the late 1950s by Milton T. Putnam's United Recording Corporation included three studios for live recording, five echo chambers, and four studio rooms for transferring and mastering. Two of these rooms were equipped with 'automatic Scully, equalizing, and echo facilities' and were used for mono mastering. Another room was optimized for transferring – from three-track tape to two-track or mono tape – and mixing – with a nine-channel console with equalizers and echo facilities – a production. Finally, there was a room for stereo mastering. This contained a 'Neumann automatic lathe' with a 'Fairchild 641 stereo cutter system' and a 'dual limiter stereo mastering console' (Milton T. Putnam, 'Recording Studio and Control Room Facilities of Advance Design', *Journal of the Audio Engineering Society* 8, no. 2 [1960]). Sam Phillips's second studio in Memphis called Sam Phillips Recording Service Inc., which opened in 1960, also had specific rooms for mastering (see Peter Guralnick, *Sam Phillips: The Man Who Invented Rock 'n' Roll* [New York: Little, Brown, 2015], 430).

157 See Barbara Schultz, 'Sam Phillips', *Mix Online: Professional Audio and Music Production*, October (2000).

158 See on this Collins cited in Bobby Owsinski, *The Audio Mastering Handbook* (Boston, MA: Thomson, 2008), 179. The frequent designation of the mix-down as 'master' causes confusion. In the following, however, the master refers to the result of mastering.

159 On post-production, see also Nicolas Bourriaud, *Postproduction. Culture as Screenplay: How Art Reprograms the World* (New York: Lukas & Sternberg, 2007), who sees it as a general cultural paradigm since the 1990s.

160 Attali, *Noise*, 128, emphasis in original.

161 Ibid.

162 See ibid., 129.

163 Ibid., 115.

164 Ibid., 105.

165 Anderson, *Making Easy Listening*, 21.

166 Ibid., 22.
167 Ibid., xxxv, emphasis in original.
168 In 1940, the Federal Communications Commission made it easier to play sound recordings on the radio by overturning the restriction imposed by the Federal Radio Commission in 1927, which specified that records played on the radio had to be identified as records by an appropriate announcement before they were played (see Wicke, *Von Mozart zu Madonna*, 192).
169 See Anderson, *Making Easy Listening*, 18.
170 See ibid., and also Michael Chanan, *Repeated Takes: A Short History of Recording and Its Effects on Music* (London: Verso, 1995), 86.
171 Anderson, *Making Easy Listening*, 22.
172 Ibid., 21.
173 Ibid.
174 Ibid., xxxv, emphasis in original.
175 Jerry Leiber and Mike Stoller cited in Jon Pareles and Patricia Romanowski, ed., *The Rolling Stone Encyclopedia of Rock & Roll* (New York: Rolling Stone Press/Summit Books, 1983), 322.
176 Roger E. Stoddard cited in Guglielmo Cavallo and Roger Chartier, 'Introduction', in *A History of Reading in the West*, ed. Guglielmo Cavallo and Roger Chartier, trans. Lydia G. Cochrane (Cambridge: Polity Press, 2003), 5, emphasis in original.
177 Ibid.
178 Wicke, Ziegenrücker and Ziegenrücker, *Handbuch der Populären Musik*, 420.
179 On postproduction, see also Lars Nyre, *Sound Media: From Live Journalism to Music Recording* (London: Routledge, 2008), 25–6.
180 Anderton in Mitch Gallagher, *Mastering Music at Home* (Boston, MA: Thomson, 2008), 178.
181 Bobby Owsinski defines mastering accordingly: 'Mastering is the process of taking a collection of songs and turning them into a record by shaping them in sound, volume, and timing (spacing between songs) so that they belong together'. Owsinski, Bobby. *The Audio Mastering Handbook*, 2nd edn (Boston, MA: Thomson, 2008), 3.
182 The recording curve is a technical curve that defines the level of which frequencies are increased and decreased on a record. The recording curve has two technical functions: increasing the length of the music that can be stored on the record and enhancing the resolution of the higher frequencies. Because lower frequencies need more space on a record than mid or higher frequencies, the level of lower frequencies is decreased on the record. The degree of this reduction is defined by the recording curve. During playback, the lowering is compensated. For a better resolution of the high frequencies, these frequencies are increased on the record and decreased during playback.
183 Cf., e.g. Gelatt, *The Fabulous Phonograph*, 290–301; Welch and Read, *From Tin Foil to Stereo*, 333–42; Magoun, 'Shaping the Sound of Music', 251–68; and also Tang, 'Sound Decisions', 46–112.
184 The industry-wide standardization of 78 rpm or to be exact, 78.26 rpm, only took place in the mid-1920s when electrified recording systems were introduced (Warren R. Isom, 'Introduction: Before the Fine Groove and Stereo Record and Other Innovations', *Journal of the Audio Engineering Society* 25, nos. 10/11 [1977]: 815; see also Christian Büchele, *Geschichte der Tonträger: Von der Erfindung der Schallplatte zu den digitalen Medien* (Tutzing: Schneider, 1999). Before this the number of

revolutions was not standardized at all: for instance, Edison used 80 rpm for his records, and some other companies even used 82 rpm (Isom, 'Introduction', 815).
185 Millard, *America on Record*, 122.
186 Tang, 'Sound Decisions', 46–7. The microgroove technique had already been patented in 1924 by Frank Lewis Dyer. Improvements in the Art of Recording and Reproducing Sounds. UK Patent 215761A, filed 7 May 1924, and issued 7 September 1925.
187 Nonetheless, of course, exceptions can be found that rely on the dramaturgical effect intended by placing a hit as the last piece on a record side. Thus, for instance, on the LP *Visage* (Polydor, UK, 1980) by British synthi-pop band Visage, the hit *Fade to Grey* was cut as the last piece on the A-side.
188 Zak, *I Don't Sound Like Nobody*, 163.
189 Ray Charles's album *What'd I Say* (Atlantic, United States, 1959), for instance, offers the following tip for listeners: 'For best results observe the R.I.A.A. high frequency roll-off characteristic with 500 cycle crossover.'
190 Whether such transparency was desired on the market is another matter. Listening tests conducted by RCA Victor (Magoun, 'Shaping the Sound of Music', 163–4), but also by CBS Columbia (Howard A. Chinn and Philip Eisenberg, 'Tonal-Range and Sound-Intensity Preferences of Broadcast Listeners', *Proceedings of the IRE* 33, no. 9 [1945]) revealed that most listeners actually preferred a restricted bandwidth. Such findings were to be taken into account in technology development; in this respect, it was more a matter of 'limited' rather than 'high' fidelity. Harry Olson tried, however, to disprove such tests; increasingly after the Second World War (see Magoun, 'Shaping the Sound of Music', 239–42). For example, Carson, Burt and Reiskind noted when presenting the single in the *RCA Review* – referring to RCA's head acoustician Olson – that this new system would take into account the preference for an 'unrestricted frequency range' (Carson, Burt and Reiskind, 'A Record Changer and Record of Complementary Design'). Faced with the narrow frequency band which RCA Victor's playing devices produces, this provision can safely be regarded as an attempt to maintain harmony within the company. Market orientation – particularly towards the youth market – would probably have ensured a different alignment: for instance, psychologist Roger E. Kirk found in an empirical study with 210 college students in 1957 that they preferred a restricted to an unrestricted range of frequencies in reproduced music (Roger E. Kirk, 'Learning, a Major Factor Influencing Preferences for High-Fidelity Systems', *Journal of the Audio Engineering Society* 5, no. 4 [1957]).
191 Björnberg, 'Learning to Listen to Perfect Sound', 129.
192 See Chapter 1, section, 'What Are Listening Devices?'.
193 See Perlman, 'Golden Ears and Meter Readers'. Perlman made a point of emphasizing this difference between golden ears and readers of measuring instruments. Golden ears are hi-fi fans; readers of measuring instruments are more likely to be sound engineers.
194 This distinction can already be found in a *Newsweek* article from 1947 (see on this Magoun, 'Shaping the Sound of Music', 241; and also Welch and Read, *From Tin Foil to Stereo*, 336). I will come back to this distinction in the next chapter.
195 Zak points out that the standard of the technical equipment in independent studios made hi-fi virtually impossible in the 1940s and 1950s: 'As the large record companies rolled out their hi-fi campaigns, the surging sales of the independents

filled the music marketplace with sounds of another sort altogether. Fidelity was usually unattainable in the makeshift studios that sprang up across America in the late forties and early fifties' (Zak, *I Don't Sound Like Nobody*, 163).
196 Ibid., 153.
197 Ibid., 165.
198 Ibid., 83.
199 See Edward Kealy, 'From Craft to Art: The Case of Sound Mixers and Popular Music', *Work and Occupation* 6, no. 1 (1979).
200 Schmidt Horning, *Chasing Sound*, 185–91; Schmidt Horning, 'Engineering the Performance'.
201 Although there had been to some extent a media shift before the introduction of magnet tape – the shift from the transcription record revolving at 33 1/3 rpm to the 78 record – this was almost purely technical in nature and was referred to as transferring. Cosimo Matassa mentions this: 'The first thing we had was a Duo-Presto disc recorder, it was called a 28N, two Presto 8N recorders, and we used to do wild cuts on 33 1/3 and 16-inch discs. That means everything had to be transferred just once generally, that 16-inch to what was originally the 78 masters. We cut two simultaneously and we didn't play the one that hopefully was going to be transferred to the master disc. You made a master and a safety, and you played back the safety to see what you got' (Matassa cited in John Broven, *Rhythm and Blues in New Orleans* [Gretna, LA: Pelican Publishing, 1978], 14).
202 Schmidt Horning, *Chasing Sound*, 188, emphasis in the original.
203 Schmidt Horning points out that this institutionalization began earlier in Germany (ibid., 130). Starting in 1946, a study course Music Recording/*Tonmeister* (sound engineer) was available at the University of Music in Detmold.
204 Potts cited in Susan Schmidt Horning, 'Chasing Sound: The Culture and Technology of Recording Studios in America, 1877–1977', PhD dissertation, Case Western Reserve University, 2002, 131.
205 See Schmidt Horning, *Chasing Sound*, 71.
206 See on this William F. Shea, 'The Role and Function of Technology in American Popular Music: 1945–1964', PhD dissertation, Ann Arbor, University of Michigan, 1990, 108; see Tang, 'Sound Decisions', 147–52. With lower-priced devices it was possible to balance the varying curves in a provisional way using the machines' bass and treble controls. High-end devices featured switches with which various rectifications of the curves could be selected (see Shea, 'The Role and Function of Technology in American Popular Music', 108). An article in *Billboard* ('Diskeries Still Hold out against RIAA Standards', *Billboard* 28 [1954b]) reported in August that even large record companies like Columbia were still using different curves.
207 Shea, 'The Role and Function of Technology in American Popular Music', 107.
208 See Rick Kennedy and Randy McNutt, *Little Labels, Big Sound: Small Record Companies and the Rise of American Music* (Bloomington, IN: Indiana University Press, 1999), 59.
209 Ibid., 59–60, on King see also Broven, *Record Makers and Breakers*, 131–48.
210 Kennedy and McNutt, *Little Labels, Big Sound*, 60.
211 Magoun, 'The Origins of the 45-RPM Record at RCA Victor, 1939–1948', 26. Jim Wilson, manager at King Records in 1950, also points out the specific characteristics of the blues and country market in relation to 45s and the LP: 'The black and country record markets were some of the last to get the new equipment, so we didn't just

drop those [the 78s] overnight, but they began to get phased out' (Wilson cited in Broven, *Record Makers and Breakers*, 136).

212 Phillips also cites the difficulties that usually prevented him from doing the mastering himself in the early days of his studios: he simply lacked an equalizer, a limiter and a compressor (Phillips cited in Broven, *Record Makers and Breakers*, 151). Phillips, the owner of Sun Records, even sent his productions from Memphis to Chicago for mastering for a while: 'Initially I did some of the mastering myself, but the one deep-cut head on the Presto lathe I had just wasn't enough to do the level of mastering I needed, so I decided to have them done in Chicago. I sent them to Bill Putnam, who was a great operator, and he and his wife did most of the acetate mastering. He had some old Scully lathes, although I don't remember exactly what heads he used. Anyone who has anything to do with sound knows that you can lose a lot in mastering if you're not careful. For a while after the hot pickup became popular, I didn't allow a hot pickup to be used on my recordings because the presence of certain sounds could just be lost so easily' (Phillips in Schultz, 'Sam Phillips').

213 See Peter Sutheim, 'An Afternoon with Bill Putnam (Interview)', *Journal of the Audio Engineering Society* 37, no. 9 (1989). This mastering process was used, for example, for Mercury Records' 'Living Presence' series, which was dedicated exclusively to classical music (see Jim Cogan, 'Bill Putnam', *Mix Online. Professional Audio and Music Production*, 2003; on this series, see also Barry, 'High-Fidelity Sound as Spectacle and Sublime, 1950–1961', 127–32).

214 See Schmidt Horning, 'Engineering the Performance', 710.

215 See also Carlos Moura, 'Practical Aspects of Hot Stylus', *Journal of the Audio Engineering Society* 5, no. 2 (1957).

216 Broven, *Rhythm and Blues in New Orleans*, 14; Broven, *Record Makers and Breakers*, 182.

217 Ibid., 120.

218 On them, see Schmidt Horning, 'Chasing Sound', PhD dissertation, 316–20; on Cook see Cogan, 'Bill Putnam'.

219 Horning, 'Chasing Sound', PhD dissertation, 132.

220 Cited in Horning, *Chasing Sound*, 188.

221 Ibid., 189.

222 See on this, ibid., 188–9.

223 Wood was keeping very precisely in mind the channels through which his records would reach the listeners: for instance, his label Dot Records arose out of Randy's Record Shop in Gallatin, Tennessee, with which a mail order service was affiliated delivering to jukebox operators. Wood, who was extremely enterprising, sponsored a radio show in Nashville starting in 1947: Gene Noble's 'The Dance Hour', which consisted mainly of rhythm and blues records and was broadcast on the night program on WLAC in Nashville (see Broven, *Record Makers and Breakers*, 97–9). The records could be bought by mail order or directly in Randy's Record Shop 'in the heart of the segregated South' (101). WLAC, as well as WDIA from Memphis, were the favourite radio stations of Elvis Presley (see Nelson George, *The Death of Rhythm & Blues* [New York: Pantheon Books, 1988], 70). Little Richard also listened to the show sponsored by Randy's Record Shop (see White, *The Life and Times of Little Richard*, 28 and 55).

224 Horning, *Chasing Sound*, 189.

225 Phillips cited in Broven, *Record Makers and Breakers*, 152. 'Back then, I could make dubs that were adequate for anything except a master. With recording, you have to capture what's in that studio on tape. Then you've got to transfer it to where you can get the frequency responses that you need for the proper loudness. You do not overdo it and distort it, beyond intended distortion [laughs]' (152). Phillips also points out the volume problems of records deployed in jukeboxes and links these with the problem of standardization: 'With the first sessions [in the early days of his studio], it was a small Presto [mixing] board. It had an NAB curve on it before the RIAA had a standard curve, and that was something you had to pay attention to in those days. Otherwise, on jukeboxes, the level would be up and down, and somebody would put a nickel or a dime or a quarter in, and if it wasn't loud enough, they would be upset. Yet you didn't want to overdo the thing for loudness and kill some of the actual inflection by over-peak limiting and compression' (152). For Chess as well the jukebox sound – besides radio sound – became a reference: 'I remember we knew that [if it] sounded good in that mastering room, it would sound great on the radio. That was how you sold the records. … nobody was interested if it was stereo. It had to sound great on the radio; that's what made people buy it. And on the jukeboxes, it was the same idea' (120).

226 Cited in Guralnick, *Sam Phillips*, 258. It was probably the engineer Jack Wiener who mastered the Sun Records at Bill Putnam's Universal Audio Studio (258). For his new studio that Phillips opened in 1960, he bought two Neumann lathes for over $30,000 each and probably did the mastering in-house (399). The later producer of country music Billy Sherrill did the mastering for Sun Records: 'We had a little mastering room back there, and he'd [Sam Phillips] say, 'Now when you master a record and you think you got it right, get everything ready and then go to five thousand cycles and boost that up just a little bit, whether it needs it or not, and that'll give it that edge. Always boost everything up five thousand. That's someway or another in tune with the human ear' (cited after Guralnick, *Sam Phillips*, 445).

227 Keightley, '"Turn It Down!" She Shrieked'; Björnberg, 'Learning to Listen to Perfect Sound'; Volmar, 'Experiencing High Fidelity'.

3 Limited choice: Listening through jukeboxes in the 1950s

1 The voice-o-graph, a voice recording machine, is said to have been the 'highlight' at the 1956 Frankfurt am Main vending machine fair (cf. 'Die Messe-Neuheiten', *Der Automaten-Markt: Fachzeitschrift für die gesamte Automatenwirtschaft* 8, no. 4 [1956]: 208). A detailed overview of the diversity of different coin-operated machines in Germany in the 1950s can be found in the relevant volumes of the trade journal *Automaten-Markt*, which has been published since 1949. Starting in 1954, the journal was published with a special section on music vending machines.

2 Cf. Kerry Segrave, *Jukeboxes. An American Social History* (Jefferson, NC: McFarland, 2002), 277.

3 Peter Handke, *The Jukebox and Other Essays on Storytelling*, trans. Ralph Manheim (New York: Picador, 2020), 58.

4 Kaspar Maase, 'Amerikanisierung von Unten. Demonstrative Vulgarität und kulturelle Hegemonie in der Bundesrepublik der 1950er Jahre', in *Amerikanisierung: Traum und Alptraum im Deutschland des 20. Jahrhunderts*, ed. Alf Lüdtke, Inge Marssolek and Adelheid von Saldern (Stuttgart: Franz Steiner Verlag, 1996), 291–314.
5 In his cultural history of the jukebox in Great Britain, Adrian Horn traces the local characteristics of the use of this device for the period from 1945 to 1960 (cf. Horn, *Juke Box Britain*). According to estimates, the number of jukeboxes in Great Britain multiplied in the second half of the 1950s from 3,000 (1955), over 5,000 (1957) to 10,000–13,000 (1958) (cf. 50). Exports of US machines to West Germany also increased massively in the second half of the 1950s: for example, 348 units were exported from the United States to West Germany in 1953, 3,044 units in 1954, and 6,296 units in 1960 (cf. Segrave, *Jukeboxes*, 332–3; 'Richtige GEMA-Gebühren bezahlen', *Der Automaten-Markt: Fachzeitschrift für die gesamte Automatenwirtschaft* 7, no. 7 [1955]: 308; Bloemeke, Roll over Beethoven, 38). In 1952, US (Wurlitzer), German (Wiegandt Berlin) and Danish (Jensen) jukeboxes were presented for the first time in Germany at the Frankfurt Automata Fair. Cf. '"Musik wird störend oft empfunden ..." Automatenmesse – "musikalisch" wie noch nie – Schlacht der Juke-Boxes', *Der Automaten-Markt: Fachzeitschrift für die gesamte Automatenwirtschaft* 4, no. 10 (1952). The US jukeboxes were either imported via distributors holding exclusive rights – such as Helmut Rehbock GmbH from Hamburg (AMI), Gustav Husemann from Cologne (Wurlitzer), Nova Apparate Gesellschaft mbH Hamburg (Rock-Ola) or Löwen-Automaten Braunschweig (Seeburg) – or manufactured in Germany under licence. In 1960, Wurlitzer founded a branch in West Germany. The first jukebox imported from the United States to Germany was allegedly set up on Hamburg's Reeperbahn in 1951 (cf. Siegfried Schmidt-Joos, *Geschäfte mit Schlagern* [Bremen: Schünemann, 1960], 133). However, it can be assumed that the first jukeboxes came to Germany immediately after the end of the Second World War and were set up in the 'military canteens and clubs' of the US Army (cf. 'Historie von den Musikautomaten (II)', *Der Automaten-Markt. Fachzeitschrift für die gesamte Automatenwirtschaft* 11, no. 6 [1959]: 318). The *Automaten-Markt* mentions that Helmut Rehbock imported the first jukebox to West Germany already in 1950 and set it up in the Liliput bar on the Reeperbahn (318). In 1954, there were 3,000 jukeboxes in West Germany, and in 1960 already 50,000 (see Heister, 'Die Musikbox', 11). In the beginning, only the boxes imported from the United States were in use. Already by the mid-1950s, the jukeboxes installed in West Germany were – also because of the increasing licensed production – at the then current technical standard.
6 Heister, 'Die Musikbox', 12.
7 Ibid., 29.
8 Cited in Schmidt-Joos, *Geschäfte mit Schlagern*, 133.
9 Ibid., 134.
10 Peter Handke saw this point. See Alexander Honold, *Der Erd-Erzähler* (Stuttgart: J. B. Metzler, 2017) who points out that Handke argues for a comparability of the two artefacts by regarding them as *Platzhalter einer elektroakustischen Alltagsmystik* (placeholders of an electroacoustic everyday mysticism) (313).
11 See also exhibitions that integrate the jukebox, such as the exhibition 'Wenn der Groschen fällt ... Münzautomaten – gestern und heute' (cf. Cornelia Kemp and Ulrike Gierlinger, *Wenn Der Groschen Fällt ... Münzautomaten – gesten und heute* [Munich: Deutsches Museum IMS, 1989]) at the Deutsches Museum in Munich; the

exhibition 'Johann Strauß Meets Elvis: Musikautoautomaten aus zwei Jahrhunderten' (cf. Werner Reiß, *Johann Strauß Meets Elvis: Musikautomaten aus zwei Jahrhunderten* [Stuttgart: Arnoldsche, 2003]) at the Preußen Museum Nordrhein-Westfalen in Minden or the exhibition at Deutsches Automatenmuseum, Sammlung Gauselmann that opened in 1985 in Espelkamp. All three exhibitions were developed in contact with Paul Gauselmann. Gauselmann is a kind of doyen of the slot machine business in (West) Germany. His family is one of the richest families in Germany. Gauselmann started to work for the West German importer of Wurlitzer in the mid-1950s and operated jukeboxes. He then founded the Gauselmann Gruppe, an enterprise group that became extremely successful, especially in the 1970s with gaming arcades ('Merkur-Spielothek'). For nearly forty years, Gauselmann was also chairman of the Verband der Deutschen Automatenindustrie e. V. (VDAI), an important lobby association for slot machine business. Michael Adams, Thomas Lukas and Jürgen Maschke, *Musikboxen* (Augsburg: Weltbild, 1994), 113–23, provides insights on the milieu of jukebox collectors in Germany.

12 See Heister, 'Die Musikbox', 15.
13 See Katrina Hazzard-Gordon, *Jookin': The Rise of Social Formations in African-American Culture* (Philadelphia, PA: Temple University Press, 1990), 76–94; John Krivine, *Juke Box Saturday Night* (London: New English Library, 1977), 22, 98.
14 Hazzard-Gordon, *Jookin'*, 94–119. 'Rent parties' were events held in private rooms in African American working-class neighbourhoods until the 1950s. 'When jukeboxes appeared in black communities in the late 1920s and early 1930s, it provided an additional means of making money. Some rent parties had jukeboxes temporarily installed for the occasion. A jukebox could be leased for any period of time, no matter how short' (112). Jukeboxes 'were not fully accepted until the late 1940s or early 1950s. By that time rent parties had died out and the nature of music production and black entertainment had changed' (112).
15 On the history of rock 'n' roll and independent labels, see, for instance, the pertinent chapter in Wicke, *Von Mozart zu Madonna*, 186–213; Reebee Garofalo and Steve Waksman, *Rockin' Out: Popular Music in the USA* (Boston, MA: Pearson, 2014). See also John Broven, *Record Makers and Breakers: Voices of the Independent Rock 'n' Roll Pioneers* (Chicago: University of Illinois Press, 2009).
16 Peter Wicke, Kai-Erik Ziegenrücker and Wieland Ziegenrücker, *Handbuch der populären Musik*, 467. The low figures are taken from Gelatt, *The Fabulous Phonograph*, 272, and the high ones from 'Phonograph Records: Recovery in the Music Business' (after Magoun, 'Shaping the Sound of Music').
17 See Is Horowitz, 'Juke Box Influence on Record Business', *Billboard* 23 (1953): 91.
18 Charlie Gillett, *The Sound of the City: The Rise of Rock and Roll*, 41.
19 The figures for single sales vary widely depending on the authors. Rachlin, *The Encyclopedia of Music Business*, for example, states that 460 million singles were sold in 1957.
20 See Anonymous, according to Segrave, *Jukeboxes*, 208.
21 Ibid., 274–301.
22 In West Germany, this percentage was much lower than in the United States. Schmidt-Joos estimates that 6 per cent of West German record production went into jukeboxes in 1960 Schmidt-Joos, *Geschäfte mit Schlagern*, 133).

23 Cf. Broven, *Record Makers and Breakers*, 44.
24 Ibid., 48.
25 Rupe, according to Shaw, *Honkers and Shouters*, 180.
26 Broven, *Record Makers and Breakers* 16.
27 Philip H. Ennis, *The Seventh Stream: The Emergence of Rock 'n' Roll in American Popular Music* (Hanover: Wesleyan University Press, 1992), 164.
28 Horn, *Juke Box Britain*, 85. The question of whether jukeboxes also made hits – and not just exploited them – recurs in historical discussions of this listening technology.
29 Dave Laing, 'Jukebox', in *Continuum Encyclopedia of Popular Music of the World. Volume I: Media, Industry and Society*, ed. John Shepherd, David Horn, Dave Laing, Paul Oliver and Peter Wicke (London: Continuum, 2003), 514; see also Broven, *Record Makers and Breakers*, 16.
30 Ennis, *The Seventh Stream*, 177.
31 Thomas Schopp, 'Eine Klanggeschichte der Diskjockey-Show im US-Amerikanischen Radio von 1930 bis 1970', PhD dissertation, Universität Oldenburg, 2014.
32 Louis Cantor, *Dewey and Elvis: The Life and Time of a Rock 'n' Roll Deejay* (Champaign: University of Illinois Press, 2005).
33 Krivine, *Juke Box Saturday Night*, 88; on the M100-series, see also Christopher Pearce, *Vintage Jukeboxes: A Collector's Guide to the Much-Loved Musical Icons of the 1940s and 1950s* [1988] (Hamilton, MT: Eagle Editions, reprint edition, 2002), 68–75.
34 See ibid., 50–3.
35 Werner Mersch, 'Sprechmaschinen und Musikboxen', in *Wenn der Groschen fällt … Münzautomaten – Gestern und Heute* (Munich: Deutsches Museum IMS, 1989), 94.
36 *Billboard* reported already on 2 April 1949: 'New disks not to affect jukes' (see 'New Disks Not to Affect Jukes', *Billboard* 2 [1949]).
37 Krivine, *Juke Box Saturday Night*, 107.
38 'Seeburg States Its Policy to Music Operators', *Billboard* 17 (1949): 99.
39 Ibid.
40 With its new jukebox, Seeburg wanted to break with the tradition that had been common in the jukebox business until then, according to which a new model had to be put on the market every year. This led to the somewhat awkward sounding designations M100A, M100B and so on.
41 Segrave, *Jukeboxes*, 213. Krivine even claims that the other jukebox manufacturers did not consistently switch to the 7-inch single until 1953 (see Krivine, *Juke Box Saturday Night*, 112).
42 Segrave, *Jukeboxes*, 226.
43 Welch and Read, *From Tin Foil to Stereo*, 320.
44 The teenage market, which quite a few of the independent labels served and developed, was not only targeted by RCA Victor with its single record, but also by Seeburg with its M100 series, although not exclusively. The intended jukebox listener was outlined as follows: 'To listeners of every taste, every age from tots to teenagers to oldtimers – this amazing development [the Select-O-Matic] makes available to them the music of their choice' ('Seeburg States Its Policy to Music Operators', 98). Despite this integration of diverse age groups into the jukebox market, Seeburg differentiated the market with the introduction of the M100A in that Seeburg wanted their new product to be located in the upper price segment: 'We believe new equipment should be placed by operators in good income locations only. *We do not believe new equipment should be forced into low income locations*' (99, emphasis

in original). Seeburg marketed its KD to teenagers: 'It was only later, with its KD model, that Seeburg would dare to have teenagers shown in promotional material. By then, though, the 1950s jukebox had become synonymous with rock 'n' roll and the teenage rebel' (Pearce, *Vintage Jukeboxes*, 75).

45 See Hazzard-Gordon, *Jookin'*; Vincent Lynch, *American Jukebox: The Classic Years* (San Francisco, CA: Chronicle Books, 1990), 13.
46 Rasmussen, '"The People's Orchestra"', 183.
47 C. G. McProud, 'The Juke Box Goes Hi-Fi', *Audio* 38, no. 12 (1954): 33.
48 See Krivine, *Juke Box Saturday Night*; Mersch, 'Sprechmaschinen und Musikboxen'; Adams, Lukas, and Maschke, *Musikboxen*; Reiss, *Johann Strauss Meets Elvis*; Pearce, *Vintage Jukeboxes*.
49 See Segrave, *Jukeboxes*; Rasmussen, '"The People's Orchestra"'.
50 Horn, *Juke Box Britain*.
51 Heister, 'Die Musikbox'; Heister, 'Musikbox' 326–9. Recently, the object history of popular music has also discovered the jukebox. See Niebling, 'Ernst Neger: Geb' dem Kind sein Nuddelche'; Benjamin Burkhart, 'Rock-Ola Capri 100, Modell 404 (1963)', in *Audiowelten: Technologie und Medien in der populären Musik nach 1945: 22 Objektstudien*, ed. Benjamin Burkhart, Lara Niebling, Alan van Keeken, Christofer Jost and Martin Pfleiderer (Münster: Waxmann, 2021).
52 The jukebox business was organized by a system consisting of jukebox manufacturers, distributors, jukebox operators and innkeepers.
53 See Handke, *The Jukebox and Other Essays on Storytelling*, 50; Pearce, *Vintage Jukeboxes*, 89; Tim Wall, 'Rocking around the Clock: Teenage Dance Fads from 1955 to 1965', in *Ballroom, Boogie, Shimmy Sham, Shale: A Social and Popular Dance Reader*, ed. Julie Malnig (Champaign: University of Illinois Press, 2008), 186; Horn, *Juke Box Britain*, 66–89; Rasmussen, '"The People's Orchestra"', 193.
54 Horn, *Juke Box Britain*, 66. Horn points out that the BBC rejected jukeboxes after the Second World War: 'In an intellectual climate that was fierce of juke boxes … and believed in a link between amusement machines and delinquency, it is unsurprising that the BBC was antagonistic to the world of coin-operated amusements' (67). Only with the introduction of television formats such as 'Jukebox Jury' at the end of the 1950s – in this programme, 'celebrities' sitting in a television studio commented on songs played on a jukebox with regard to their hit potential – did this rejection disappear.
55 Ibid., 85.
56 See Bloemeke, *Roll over Beethoven*.
57 Heister, 'Die Musikbox', 38.
58 Ibid., 39. On the mentioned dialectic, see Adorno, *Current of Music*.
59 'Die Spitzenreiter des Monats', *Der Automaten-Markt. Fachzeitschrift für die gesamte Automatenwirtschaft* 8, no. 3 (1956): 137.
60 'Gäste, Wirte, Ober Antworten. Gedanken und Interviews zur Programmgestaltung in der Musikbox', *Der Automaten-Markt. Fachzeitschrift für die Gesamte Automatenwirtschaft* 9, no. 6 (1957): 300, emphasis in original.
61 Marybeth Hamilton, 'The Voice of the Blues', *History Workshop Journal* 7, no. 54 (2002): 125.
62 'The Billboard 8th Annual Juke Box Operator Poll', *Billboard* 26 (1955).
63 According to Osborne, *Vinyl*, 11, the first jukebox popularity charts were published by the US magazine *Variety*.

64 See Dave Laing, 'One-Stop', in *Continuum Encyclopedia of Popular Music of the World. Volume I: Media, Industry and Society*, ed. John Shepherd, David Horn, Dave Laing, Paul Oliver and Peter Wicke (London: Continuum, 2003), 558; See also Segrave, *Jukeboxes*, 227, and Robert A. Mittelstaedt and Robert E. Stassen, 'Structural Changes in the Phonograph Record Industry and Its Channels of Distribution, 1946–1966', *Journal of Macromarketing* 14, no. 31 (1994): 40.
65 'The Billboard 8th Annual Juke Box Operator Poll', 78.
66 In West Germany, the *Automaten-Markt* called on jukebox operators to buy their records only from the so-called *Automatenhandel* – and no longer from retailers. The operators were lured into the vending machine trade with discounts ('Schallplatten nur vom Automatenhandel beziehen', *Der Automaten-Markt: Fachzeitschrift für die gesamte Automatenwirtschaft* 8, no. 1 (1956): 13).
67 Rupe, according to Broven, *Record Makers and Breakers*, 479.
68 See Shaw, *Honkers and Shouters*, 185–6.
69 Broven, *Record Makers and Breakers*, 19.
70 See Krivine, *Juke Box Saturday Night*, 120.
71 Ennis, *The Seventh Stream*, 178, emphasis in original.
72 See Garofalo and Waksman, *Rockin' Out*, 85.
73 Mittelstaedt and Stassen, 'Structural Changes in the Phonograph Record Industry', 42.
74 Mittelstaedt and Stassen (ibid.) point out that in addition to the one-stop, a second new type of record wholesaler emerged in the United States in the 1950s – the rack jobber. Rack jobbers rented retail shelf space and stocked it with records. The supply of records to jukebox operators, however, ran primarily through the one-stops.
75 For an overview of the one-stops in 1955, see 'One-Stops', *Billboard* 26 March (1955): 84, 86, 142.
76 Rupe, according to Broven, *Record Makers and Breakers*, 479.
77 See Cantor, *Dewey and Elvis*, 96–105. See for another example *Stan's One-Stop* by Stan Lewis in Shreveport, Louisiana, where both retailers and jukebox operators bought (Broven, *Record Makers and Breakers*, 161–5).
78 In addition to jukebox sales, radio also influenced repertoire policy. Sam Phillips worked particularly closely with DJ Dewey Phillips. Cantor describes how potential Sun releases were tested in advance on Dewey Phillips's show 'Red, Hot and Blue': 'Bringing "straight-out-of-the-gate" studio dubs to WHBQ for Dewey to spin on "Red, Hot and Blue" before Sam cut the record that become, even before Elvis, standard operating procedure for the two Phillipses. That procedure was as simple as successful. Sam would first capture an artist on tape and immediately cut an acetate disc of the session, right in his tiny studio. Then – before pressing the master – he'd race down to the Gayoso Hotel, where Dewey was stirring the airwaves with "Red, Hot and Blue". The latest Sam Phillips offering would then blast out instantly to Dewey's captivated audience' (Cantor, *Dewey and Elvis*, 113).
79 Ibid., 103, see also Phillips in Escott and Hawkins, *Good Rockin' Tonight*, 57.
80 Cantor, *Dewey and Elvis*, 97.
81 More on these can be found later in the section 'The Jukebox's Modelling and Managing of Record Listening'.
82 See Segrave, *Jukeboxes*, 167–8.
83 Laing, 'Jukebox', 514.
84 Since the market launch of Seeburg's M100A in 1949, it had become common practice to play both sides of a single, so it was obvious that both A-side and B-side

of a single contained potential hits. Heister diagnoses a conflict of interest between vending machine operators and the record industry (see Heister, 'Die Musikbox', 31). A single with a hit on the A-side and a mere filler on the B-side would have been a waste of a slot for jukebox use.
85 Ibid., 28.
86 Evans, *Vinyl*, 2015, 93.
87 Christofer Jost and Gregor Herzfeld, eds, *Große Formen in der populären Musik: Large-Scale Forms in Popular Music* (Münster: Waxmann, 2019).
88 Wolfgang Kos, 'Intime Signale im anonymen Raum. Überlegungen zu Jukebox, Autoradio und Radiosignations', in *Abstracts, Tagung 'Ephemeres Erinnern'. Wiener Erinnerungsorte der Anderen Art, 15.–16.3.2002*, ed. Wolfgang Kos (2002).
89 Matassa, according to John Broven, *Record Makers and Breakers*, 17; see also Segrave, *Jukeboxes*, 246.
90 Matassa, according to Broven, *Record Makers and Breakers*, 16.
91 Heister, 'Die Musikbox', 30.
92 Brockhaus, *Kultsounds*.
93 A. G. Bodoh, 'The Jukebox, the Radio, and the Record', *Journal of the Audio Engineering Society* 25, nos. 10/11 (1977): 839.
94 See Chapter 2, section, 'Mastering Industry Standards and Non-Listening'.
95 Osborne, *Vinyl*, 119.
96 Handke, *The Jukebox and Other Essays on Storytelling*, 88 and 86.
97 Ibid., 88. Seeburg had launched a jukebox, the 'Hi Tone', in 1941. The speaker of this device was not installed at knee or belly level, but at the top of the device (see Krivine, *Juke Box Saturday Night*, 74). The 'Hi Tone' was a flop. Whether this failure – as Handke suspects (see Handke, *The Jukebox and Other Essays on Storytelling*, 87) – can be attributed to the lack of belly sound cannot, of course, ultimately be proven. Rock-Ola's 'Spectravox' also had its speaker at the top.
98 Alexander Honold, *Der Erd-Erzähler* (Stuttgart: J. B. Metzler, 2017), 313.
99 Handke, *The Jukebox and Other Essays on Storytelling*, 91.
100 See Segrave, *Jukeboxes*, 227; See also Schmidt-Joos, *Geschäfte mit Schlagern*, 137.
101 See, e.g., McProud, 'The Juke Box Goes Hi-Fi', 33–8, 42–3; Bodoh, 'The Jukebox, the Radio, and the Record'.
102 Stereo jukeboxes were available from the late 1950s, but they did not have any specific consequences.
103 Bodoh, 'The Jukebox, the Radio, and the Record'. Bodoh puts it as follows: 'The jukebox designers understood the public's need for adequate bass and provided up to 20 dB of electrical boost' (840). Bass boosting circuits have been built into jukeboxes since the 1950s: 'by 1950 this had significantly changed to bass boost circuits which raised the entire low-end response in the way generally recognized as optimum for the next 20 years in the audio industry' (840).
104 The AMI Model F hi-fi jukebox also had a so-called roll-off filter that allowed treble filtering starting from 10,000 Hz, 6,000 Hz or 3,500 Hz (see McProud, 'The Juke Box Goes Hi-Fi', 33–8, 42–3).
105 Bodoh, 'The Jukebox, the Radio, and the Record', 840.
106 See McProud, 'The Juke Box Goes Hi-Fi'.
107 See Bodoh, 'The Jukebox, the Radio, and the Record', 840.
108 Rasmussen, '"The People's Orchestra"', 194.
109 Rupe, according to Broven, *Record Makers and Breakers*, 480.

110 Of course, this did not preclude the use of high-fidelity jargon in relation to the jukebox. AMI's Model F was equipped with a 'fidelity equalizer' for adapting the jukebox sound to the room sound. A 'tone-quality control' was also integrated: 'The volume-control circuit provides compensation for the Fletcher-Munson effect …. As the volume level is reduced, the bass is automatically increased' (McProud, 'The Juke Box Goes Hi-Fi', 38). Virtually no test of a jukebox in the vending market of the second half of the 1950s is without a reference to high fidelity.
111 See Segrave, *Jukeboxes*, 293.
112 Attali, *Noise*, 84.
113 James Caesar Petrillo (1892–1984), former president of the American Federation of Musicians (AFM), also attacked the jukebox as an instrument that made musicians unemployed (Pearce, *Vintage Jukeboxes*, 40–1).
114 In the 1909 Copyright Act, 'coin operated machines' were explicitly mentioned, but only in order to be attributed a special status (Segrave, *Jukeboxes*, 121).
115 See ibid., 120.
116 Horn, *Juke Box Britain*, 162–9.
117 See Schmidt-Joos, *Geschäfte mit Schlagern*, 134; and Ganske, 'Aktuelle Fragen der Musikautomatenaufstellung', in *Handbuch der Deutschen Automatenwirtschaft 1956* (Cologne: Carl Heymanns Verlag, 1956), 271–3.
118 Licences for public performance rights had to be obtained in Germany for jukeboxes that were set up. The type of inn was an important factor in determining the amount of fees in 1956: There were three types: simple inns with no more than one operator, medium-sized establishments and luxury establishments (271). In 1955, *Automatenmarkt* found that 80–90 per cent of jukeboxes in Germany were located in the simplest inns ('Richtige GEMA-Gebühren bezahlen', 308). The fees for the performance rights were usually paid by the operator of the pub. At the end of 1956, a new contract was concluded between GEMA and the Arbeitsgemeinschaft des Deutschen Automatengewerbes e. V., which regulated the conditions of 'performance permission' by GEMA. The amount of fees to be paid to GEMA for an installed jukebox was determined in this contract depending on the size of the performance space and whether the 'musical performances' were without or with a 'public dance' or 'event character' ('Vertrag mit GEMA unterzeichnet', *Der Automaten-Markt: Fachzeitschrift für die Gesamte Automatenwirtschaft* 9, no. 1 [1957]: 12, 14) – this had also been taken into account in the first agreement with GEMA. The contract with GEMA was re-negotiated again and again, whereby the classification of playing a jukebox as a 'performance' was retained ('GEMA-Rahmenvertrag mit Wirkung 1. Januar 1959 in Kraft', *Der Automaten-Markt: Fachzeitschrift für die gesamte Automatenwirtschaft* 11, no. 3 [1959]: 120); a jukebox now meant 'amusement' and thus amusement taxes had to be paid, which was the occasion for endless quibbles (see Ganske, 'Aktuelle Fragen der Musikautomatenaufstellung'). Such legal discussions about the instrument status to clarify tax disputes were still being held in the present day, for example, in relation to the record player and the DJ (see Sarah Hardjowirogo, *'Instrumentalität': Der Begriff des Musikinstruments zwischen Klangerzeuger, Kultgerät und Körper-Technik* [Hildesheim: Olms, 2022], 69f).
119 Schmidt-Joos, *Geschäfte mit Schlagern*, 134. Whether this was actually the case can be doubted. In 1956, the magazine *Automaten-Markt* reported, with reference to the Deutscher Musikerverband (German Musicians' Association), that the jukebox

did not make professional musicians unemployed; jukeboxes were mainly to be found in small pubs where no concerts or performances took place anyway (see 'Die Musikbox befriedigt ein echtes Bedürfnis', *Der Automaten-Markt: Fachzeitschrift für die Gesamte Automatenwirtschaft* 8, no. 8 [1956]: 473–6; and '"Musikbox macht keine Musiker arbeitslos", Sagt der Deutsche Musikerverband', *Der Automaten-Markt: Fachzeitschrift für die gesamte Automatenwirtschaft* 8, no. 10 [1956]: 598). In 1959, however, such cost-cutting considerations did play a role for dance hall operators (see, 'Die Tanzbox ist groß im Kommen', *Der Automaten-Markt: Fachzeitschrift für die gesamte Automatenwirtschaft* 11, no. 12 [1959]: 717). The discussion whether the jukebox put musicians out of work also echoed the discussion from around 1930, after the introduction of the talkies, whether this kind of movie made musicians unemployed (see for this discussion Hardjowirogo, 'Instrumentalität', 65–7).

120 Elmar Michel, 'Zum Geleit', in *Handbuch der Deutschen Automatenwirtschaft 1956* (Cologne: Carl Heymanns Verlag, 1956), VIII.
121 The dependence of a 'jukebox music idea' ('Bacon Finds European Market Still Untapped', *Billboard* 5 [1952]: 78), whose absence in Europe was criticized by the vice president of Rock-Ola in 1952 after his trip to the Old World, on a concept of technology that did not shrink exclusively to a rationalization paradigm is obvious. US jukebox manufacturers discovered Europe as a jukebox market in the 1950s, probably because the US market was saturated in the 1950s. In 1954, for example, AMI and the Danish manufacturer Jensen signed a cooperation agreement (see 'IMA-AMI in Kopenhagen gegründet', *Der Automaten-Markt. Fachzeitschrift für die gesamte Automatenwirtschaft* 6, no. 1 [1954]: 13, 16).
122 Krivine, *Juke Box Saturday Night*, 7.
123 Rasmussen, '"The People's Orchestra"', 181.
124 Ibid., 186.
125 See Chapter 1, section 'What Are Listening Devices?'.
126 Heister, 'Die Musikbox', 25 and 49. Heister points out that the "Automaten-Aufstellungsvertrag" in Germany excludes other musical activities (55).
127 Ibid., 13.
128 Ibid., 64–5. Even though Heister's essay is penetratingly couched in the jargon of the West German left of the 1970s, we cannot deny that he has succeeded in creating an unprecedentedly versatile and well-researched picture of the jukebox that integrates economic, technological, socio-psychological and aesthetic components. In this respect, the essay is a pioneering achievement – not only in musicology. Heister's essay is virtually a prime example of an Adorno-influenced examination of everyday culture that is not informed by cultural studies.
129 See Horn, *Juke Box Britain*.
130 Kos, 'Intime Signale im anonymen Raum'.
131 The use of records on the radio also oscillates between simulating a performance and creating an independent sound reality. The proto-DJ Al Jarvis, who went on the air with his 'The World's Largest Make Believe Ballroom' in the summer of 1934, already simulated a performance with records and sound effects – such as recorded applause. Records were not presented by Jarvis as records on the radio, but were meant to simulate a performance – in this respect, the name of his programme spoke a pleasingly clear language (see Laurence W. Etling, 'Al Jarvis: Pioneer Disc Jockey', *Popular Music and Society* 23, no. 3 [1999]). That records were played and

presented as records – and not as a simulation of a performance – on US radio was dictated by a regulation of the FCC: the presenter had to identify the record as a record by announcement. Jarvis complied with this regulation by stating once at the beginning of his broadcast that all music played on the air would be from records. With the increasing emergence of radio DJs after the end of the Second World War, series of records were played on US radio with the sound referenced to other records rather than to performances. It was first during this period that recordings no longer had the whiff of something deficient attached to them. Records ceased to be mere copies of performances. This was audible, for example, in the strong variation of the spatiality of rhythm and blues or rock 'n' roll records: with these, no consistent spatial sound of a ballroom could be produced. Series of records – played on the radio or the jukebox – then no longer simulate the sound of a performance. Records, radios and jukeboxes transformed on the sonic level from intermediaries to active mediators. In a radio broadcast from the 1950s of his 'Red, Hot and Blue' show, DJ Dewey Phillips played the following titles in succession at the station WHBQ in Memphis: Ricky Nelson's *Teenager Romance* (Verve, United States 1957), Roy Brown's *Let the Four Winds Blow* (Imperial, United States 1957) and Lavern Baker's *Humpty Dumpty Heart* (Atlantic, United States 1959) (see the corresponding recordings on the CD 'Red Hot & Blue. Dewey Phillips Live Radio Broadcasts from 1952–1964' [Memphis Archives, United States 1995]). Each of these titles has its own characteristic spatiality.

132 See Heister, 'Die Musikbox', 62.
133 See Hagen, *Das Radio*, 284.
134 For a critical, historically informed overview of lists in popular music in the form of discographies, mixtapes, playlists, charts, setlists and their various economic, archival, canonizing, hierarchizing and emotional functions, see Kristoffer Cornils, 'On the History of the Playlist', in *Listen to Lists*, ed. Lina Brion and Detlef Diederichsen (Leipzig: Spector Books, 2021). On lists as a taxonomy of the popular, see Ralf Adelmann, *Listen und Rankings: Über Taxonomien des Populären* (Bielefeld: transcript, 2021).
135 Osborne, *Vinyl*, 125.
136 Pearce, *Vintage Jukeboxes*, 95.
137 Bodoh, 'The Jukebox, the Radio, and the Record', 839.
138 See Sterne, 'The MP3 as Cultural Artefact'; Bob Katz, *Mastering Audio: The Art and the Science*, 3rd edn (Burlington, MA: Focal Press, 2014); Milner, *Perfecting Sound Forever*.
139 Bodoh, 'The Jukebox, the Radio, and the Record', 839.
140 Kuno Callsen, 'Die Technische Gestaltung der Musikautomaten', in *Handbuch der Deutschen Automatenwirtschaft 1956* (Cologne: Carl Heymanns Verlag KG, 1956), 270.
141 'Juke's Boom Is Business Week Theme', *Billboard* 9 (1946): 98.
142 See Bodoh, 'The Jukebox, the Radio, and the Record', 840.
143 Ibid.
144 'Die Neue Rock-Ola Mit 200 Wahlmöglichkeiten', *Der Automaten-Markt. Fachzeitschrift für die gesamte Automatenwirtschaft* 8, no. 12 (1956): 702, emphasis in original. In the following years, Rock-Ola also pushed the installation of sound control devices in the jukebox. In 1960, for example, the company introduced a jukebox with a built-in 'reverb sound' – the system was also available as an option: as

a system for reverb generation that could be switched on and off ('Rock-Ola Bows 1961 Model', *Billboard* 3 October [1960]: 75).
145 Bodoh, 'The Jukebox, the Radio, and the Record', 840.
146 Osborne, *Vinyl*, 119.
147 'Eine Million [*sic*] Musikboxen Spielen für Millionen', *Der Automaten-Markt: Fachzeitschrift für die gesamte Automatenwirtschaft* 12 (1960): 811.
148 Ibid.
149 Moreover, the separation of music making and music listening enabled a decontextualization of music: the US rock 'n' roll records encountered a different environment in Europe than in the United States.
150 Louis T. Glass and William S. Arnold. *Coin Actuated Attachment for Phonographs*. US Patent 428570, filed 27 May 1890, and issued 27 May 1890.
151 Wicke, 'Der Tonträger als Medium der Musik', 4.
152 See Walter L. Welch and Leah Brodbeck Stenzel Burt, *From Tinfoil to Stereo: The Acoustic Years of the Recording Industry, 1877–1929* (Gainesville: University Press of Florida, 1994), 87, but especially Raymond R. Wile, *Proceedings of the 1890 Convention of Local Phonograph Companies* (Nashville, TN: Country Music Foundation Press, 1974).
153 The North American Phonograph Company commercially exploited the Edison phonograph patents. It consisted of several regional subcontractors.
154 See Welch and Read, *From Tin Foil to Stereo*, 105–18.
155 Glass and Arnold. *Coin Actuated Attachment for Phonographs*. Glass was by no means doing ingenious pioneering work here; he was merely picking up on an obvious possibility. Two years before Glass, the British engineer Charles Adams Randall had already applied for a patent for a coin-operated 'automatic parlophone'; see Paul Charbon, *Le Phonographe à La Belle Epoque* (Brussels: Libro-sciences SPRL, 1977). However, it was Glass's patent that first met with a response from the industry.
156 See Wile, *Proceedings of the 1890 Convention of Local Phonograph Companies*, 163–5.
157 Bodoh, 'The Jukebox, the Radio, and the Record', 836.
158 The Deutsches Museum in Munich exhibits a *Zungenspielwerk* ('reed organ') built in Leipzig, Germany, which could be seen and heard at the World's Fair in Paris in 1900, a Polyphon No. 5G built by Polyphon Musikwerke Leipzig (see also the Deutsches Automatenmuseum website, Gauselmann AG, accessed 9 May 2022, https://www.deutsches-automatenmuseum.de/). The Polyphon could be activated by inserting a coin. It did not play records, however, but punched metal discs of which the listener had ten to choose from. However, a few coin-operated phonographs were also built around 1900 that offered a selection (see Segrave, *Jukeboxes*, 3–19). Also the Gabel Automatic Entertainer was a coin-operated jukebox *avant la lettre* that offered a selection as early as 1906.
159 Thomas A. Edison, 'The Phonograph and Its Future [1878]', in *Music, Sound, and Technology in America: A Documentary History of Early Phonograph, Cinema, and Radio*, ed. Timothy D. Taylor, Mark Katz and Tony Grajeda (Durham, NC: Duke University Press, 2012), 33.
160 Lisa Gitelman points out that it was not only the automatic phonograph that prompted a new way of using sound reproduction technologies. Emile Berliner, for example, had already targeted the music market with his gramophone in 1888

(see Lisa Gitelman, *Always Already New: Media, History, and the Data of Culture* [Cambridge, MA: MIT Press, 2006], 44 and 46).
161 Kenney, *Recorded Music in American Life*, 24.
162 In the beginning, the automatic phonographs played mainly 'comic songs, monologs, whistling and band records' and also 'hymns' (Welch and Read, *From Tin Foil to Stereo*, 109). In 1889, the North American Phonograph Company's Washington, DC, offshoot – the Columbia Phonograph Company – launched the first catalogue of recorded music: 'Columbia issued the first-ever catalog of recordings in 1889. By 1891 the catalog contained 10 pages of cylinder recordings of marches, dance tunes, novelty and sentimental songs, and monologs, mainly for coin-in-the-slot jukeboxes at fairgrounds and exhibitions' (David Horn, Dave Laing and David Sanjek, 'Columbia', in *Continuum Encyclopedia of Popular Music of the World. Volume I: Media, Industry and Society*, ed. John Shepherd, David Horn, Dave Laing, Paul Oliver and Peter Wicke [New York: Continuum, 2003], 702). Such coin-in-the-slot jukeboxes by no means reflected the tastes of so-called music lovers. Cultural historian William Kenney writes that 'neither the machine nor its recordings yet echoed the music of the conservatory, concert hall, or *soirée musicale*' (Kenney, *Recorded Music in American Life*, 27, emphasis in original). On the repertoire of the automatic phonograph, see also Gitelman, *Always Already New*, 50–2). Kenney places automatic phonographs in a line of tradition with the minstrel show and the theatrical genre of vaudeville.
163 Krivine, *Juke Box Saturday Night*, 18. On the dominance of the player piano over the jukebox until 1933, see Segrave, *Jukeboxes*, 20–47. In the first decades of the twentieth century, this industry boomed: between 1904 and 1930, 2.5 million player pianos were sold (see Vanessa Bastian, 'Instrument Manufacture', in *Continuum Encyclopedia of Popular Music of the World. Volume I: Media, Industry and Society*, ed. John Shepherd, David Horn, Dave Laing, Paul Oliver and Peter Wicke [New York: Continuum, 2003], 527).
164 Kenney, *Recorded Music in American Life*, 26–8; Stefan Gauss, *Nadel, Rille, Trichter. Kulturgeschichte des Phonographen und des Grammophons in Deutschland (1900–1940)* (Cologne: Böhlau, 2009); Morton, *Sound Recording*, 28–9.
165 Seeburg started in 1907 as the J. P. Seeburg Piano Co. and built automatic instruments, especially orchestrions; it switched to the manufacture of jukeboxes in the late 1920s. Since 1909, AMI, as National Automatic Music Co., had produced automatic pianos with a selection mechanism for piano rolls, and from 1926 they produced jukeboxes (*The Facilities of AMI Incorporated*, accessed 9 May 2022, https://www.jukeboxhistory.info/ami/history/facilities_of_ami.pdf). Wurlitzer had produced musical instruments since 1856 and entered the market for automatic instruments in the late nineteenth century. The company also built coin-operated instruments and became famous for its large organs for cinemas in the days of silent films. It entered the jukebox business in 1933.
166 Welch and Read, *From Tin Foil to Stereo*, 304.
167 Ibid. An economic caesura in jukebox history is often made on the basis of the Golden Age/Silver Age distinction. Although this distinction is primarily design-oriented – the appearance of jukeboxes up to the end of the 1940s was dominated by the colour gold, while that of jukeboxes in the 1950s was dominated by silver – it actually designates a phase of rapid market growth – the Golden Age – and a phase of market stagnation – the Silver Age (see, e.g. Lynch, *American Jukebox*).

In this chapter, I focus primarily on the Silver Age. From a European perspective, the so-called Silver Age has also been called the 'Platinum Age' of the jukebox (see Adams, Lukas and Maschke, *Musikboxen*, 114).
168 Of course, the jukebox is not the only device that technologizes listening. Karin Bijsterveld and Trevor Pinch, 'Sound Studies. New Technologies and Music', *Social Studies of Science* 34, no. 5 (2004), with reference to Susan Schmid Horning's analysis of the recording studio since 1930, describe how sound engineers' listening has been increasingly mediated by new technology (see Horning, *Chasing Sound*). They frame this technology in terms of 'externalized ears'. With this term they refer to sociologist of science Michael Lynch's concept of the 'externalized retina', who understands this to mean a technologized organ that guides scientific inquiry.
169 On high-fidelity jukeboxes, see Pearce, *Vintage Jukeboxes*, 78–9, 83.
170 See Magoun, 'Shaping the Sound of Music', 237–8. The OED defines 'tin ear' as 'tone-deafness, aural insensitivity' and mentions a first use of the term from 1923, see *Oxford English Dictionary*, s. v. 'tin ear', accessed 7 September 2022, https://www.oed.com/view/Entry/202173?redirectedFrom=Tin+ears+#eid18466376.
171 Robinson, *Hungry Listening*, 45.
172 See also the criticism of popular music studies in the 1980s and 1990s of analytical approaches to pop music that superimpose popular music forms on musical concepts from the art music tradition (Richard Middleton, *Studying Popular Music* [Milton Keynes: Open University Press, 1990]).
173 Keir Keightley, 'Tin Pan Allegory', *Modernism/Modernity* 19, no. 4 (2013): 717–36; Dick Hebdige, *Subculture: The Meaning of Style* (London: Routledge, 1979).
174 See Chapter 2, section 'Mastering Industry Standards and Non-Listening'.
175 White and Louie include the distinction between 'golden' and 'tin ears' in their *Audio Dictionary* (Glenn D. White and Gary J. Louie, *The Audio Dictionary* [Seattle: University of Washington Press, 2005]). Golden ears are understood as people who have the ability 'to discern and appreciate subtleties and to identify defects in recordings and sound systems that ordinary people find elusive' (171). A 'tin ear', on the other hand, is a person who is unable 'to appreciate the fine points of quality sound reproduction' (395).
176 Gitelman, *Always Already New*, 50.
177 Krivine, *Juke Box Saturday Night*; Lynch, *American Jukebox*; Pearce, *Vintage Jukeboxes*; Werner Reiß, *Johann Strauß Meets Elvis*.
178 Laing, 'A Voice without a Face', 1–9; Jens Gerrit Papenburg, 'Körperlichkeit', in *Handbuch Sound: Geschichte – Begriffe – Ansätze*, ed. Daniel Morat and Hansjacob Ziemer (Stuttgart: Metzler, 2018), 26–7.
179 Kenney, *Recorded Music in American Life*, 25; emphasis added.
180 The Seeburg 148 is an exception; in Rock-Ola jukebox models, the record changing mechanism was often invisible up until the early 1940s.
181 Rock-Ola Manufacturing Corporation, 'Rock Ola 120 Fireball Model', advertisement, 1952, https://www.jukeboxhistory.info/rock-ola/jukeboxes/rock-ola_1436.pdf, accessed 7 September 2022.
182 On Fuller's groundbreaking art deco design for Wurlitzer until 1948, see Pearce, *Vintage Jukeboxes*, 24–39.
183 Loewy restyled the United Music Corporation's Model UPB-100.
184 Callsen, 'Die technische Gestaltung der Musikautomaten', 267.

185 Pearce, *Vintage Jukeboxes*, 92.
186 The jukebox designs of the 1950s visually emphasized the record changer and the selection mechanism, for example, with panoramic windows adopted from car design: 'It was the heyday of the "open" boxes that uncovered the selection mechanism so that the viewer had something to see: Not just that the music he wanted was playing. No, even before that, the open selection mechanism was a real feast for the eyes when it started to move, took the record out of the stack, and put it on the turntable. … It is a real spectacle what goes on there when the coin is inserted'; Adams, Lukas, and Maschke, *Musikboxen*, 47.
187 The listening tubes, which resembled those of a doctor's stethoscope, enabled private listening within public space – as Gitelman also argues in a critical reference to Sterne's 'audile technique' – and contributed to a separation of the senses: 'Customers listened privately to a record in much the same way that a doctor listens to a patient's lungs. … Users paid for private, even intimate, encounters with public machines. Much like the need to watch projected motion pictures in the dark a few years later, coin-operated phonograph parlors separated the senses and helped keep customers apart, even as they drew them into anonymous crowds. Visitors to the salons stood together, saw together, but heard alone' (Gitelman, *Always Already New*, 47). On these techniques, Sterne also writes with reference to the stethoscope and phonograph, 'The technicized, individuated auditory field could be experienced collectively' (Sterne, *The Audible Past*, 161).
188 Gitelman, *Always Already New*, 47.
189 Heister goes even further – certainly not without reason: 'The abstract freedom of choice, in turn, is doubly limited by the respective concretely existing record repertoire and the restrictions to which this repertoire is generally subject' (Heister, 'Die Musikbox', 60). Other authors – more or less directly influenced by Adorno's cultural criticism – also criticize the 'music request show' of the jukebox: the desire that guides the choice is 'prefabricated' (Schmidt-Joos, *Geschäfte mit Schlagern*, 134). All practices involving the jukebox or the 'culture industry' are considered in this theoretical setting subsumed under the vocabulary of 'manipulation'. That listening practices are formed around the jukebox which are not reducible to a manipulation paradigm was first noted by authors from cultural studies.
190 See Reiss, *Johann Strauss Meets Elvis*, 263.
191 See Bodoh, 'The Jukebox, the Radio, and the Record', 837. On the wear of vinyl records in the jukebox see also Niebling, 'Ernst Neger: Geb' dem Kind sein Nuddelche', 236.
192 Pearce, *Vintage Jukeboxes*, 61.
193 Heister, 'Die Musikbox', 26.
194 Gitelman, *Always Already New*, 46.
195 Gitelman also points out that phonograph listening correlates with a management of listening: 'I am suggesting that the design of nickel-in-the-slot and exhibition machines helped to create vastly intricate experiences of public and private – experiences animated by distinctions between performance and power, seeing and hearing, dead matter and living voices. These were repeated, repeatable experiences that suggestively tended to standardize and depersonalize exchange, to collect and yet atomize consumption, and thus effectively to essentialize the marketplace, making it more easily experienced as an abstraction: the market' (Gitelman, *Always Already New*, 48). On repetition in the age of mechanical or rather technical

reproducibility and music, see also Attali, *Noise*, 87–132; Suisman and Strasser, *Sound in the Age of Mechanical Reproduction*. Certainly, repetition is a feature of record listening in general; see Clarke, 'The Impact of Recording on Listening'.

196 Seeburg's Select-O-Matic mechanism, whose development as the Andrews mechanism is said to have begun as early as 1939, was tested in the 'industrial-commercial field' before being introduced into the jukebox business ('Seeburg States Its Policy to Music Operators', 97). One such field was the market for non-selectable background music such as that served by the Muzak Company. Seeburg also served this market, for example, with the Seeburg Industrial Music System (SICM) of 1948 (see Welch and Read, *From Tin Foil to Stereo*, 324), a system that provided background music. For the jukebox, the changer mechanism was marketed as the Select-O-Matic '100' Music System ('Seeburg States Its Policy to Music Operators').
197 Bodoh, 'The Jukebox, the Radio, and the Record', 837.
198 Welch and Read, *From Tin Foil to Stereo*, 326. Read and Welch point out the economic and cultural consequences of this enlargement of the selection: 'The multi-selection phonograph had a profound effect on the industry. Prior to this time, the jukebox had been looked upon primarily as a "hit tune" phonograph' (326).
199 Kos, 'Intime Signale im anonymen Raum'.
200 See Attali, *Noise*, 87–132. Sterne has pointed out that Attali's use-value/exchange-value distinction becomes problematic with regard to the .mp3 file: 'One could say that if recording shifted music from use-value to exchange-value, then digitization in the form of the mp3 liberates recorded music from the economics of value by enabling its free, easy, and large-scale exchange' (Sterne, 'The MP3 as Cultural Artefact', 831). Sterne then concedes, however, that the question of value remains, since playback and distribution hardware must be purchased. It would also be worth considering to what extent the concept of use value is still meaningful in the context of the jukebox or whether a concept such as 'experience value' (Gerhard Schulze, *Die Erlebnisgesellschaft: Kultursoziologie der Gegenwart* [Frankfurt am Main: Campus, 2005]) would be more precise. These developments are at odds with Attali's diagnosis that exchange value would have dominated over use value (see Attali, *Noise*, 84).
201 For a history of the record collector, see Roy Shuker, *Wax Trash and Vinyl Treasures: Record Collecting as a Social Practice* (Farnham: Ashgate Publishing, 2010).
202 Anderson, *Making Easy Listening*, 23.
203 Heister, 'Die Musikbox', 26.
204 See, e.g., Peter Fornatale and Joshua E. Mills, *Radio in the Television Age* (Woodstock, NY: Overlook Press, 1980), 27; Eric Rothenbuhler and Tom McCourt, 'Radio Redefines Itself, 1947–1962', in *Radio Reader: Essays in the Cultural History of Radio*, ed. Michele Hilmes and Jason Loviglio (London: Routledge, 2002), 381.
205 Douglas, *Listening In*, 247.
206 Hagen, *Das Radio*, 303.
207 Ibid.
208 Ibid.
209 Ibid., 305.
210 Ibid., 304.
211 Ibid., 305.
212 For Hagen, other forms of radio listening also have a paradoxical character: with reference to the 'serials' and early radio DJs, he speaks of 'dissimulative listening'.

Radio, he argues, is 'not a journalistic medium that provides any kind of observation of the world that the listener could accept or reject' (255). In 'serials', among radio DJs – here 'white people would play black people' – but also with the 'you' of 'Your Hit Parade', it would be about simulations (255). These simulations would be purposefully and benevolently ignored in dissimulative listening. However, Hagen wants to limit dissimulative listening to voices on the radio and does not apply it to music (see 257). This is questionable especially with regard to the use of sound carriers on the radio as a simulation of live music – as Hagen himself notes (see 258–9).

213 Ibid., 326.
214 Ibid.
215 Viktoria Tkaczyk, Mara Mills and Alexandra Hui, ed., *Testing Hearing: The Making of Modern Aurality* (New York: Oxford University Press, 2021).
216 Adorno, 'The Curves of the Needle', 273.
217 It is then only a small step from the phonograph parlour to the living room (see Gitelman, *Always Already New*, 49). As early as 1896, the first phonograph for home use came on the market with the Edison Home Model A (Peter Wicke, 'The Art of Phonography: Sound, Technology and Music', in *The Ashgate Research Companion to Popular Musicology*, ed. Derek B. Scott [Farnham: Ashgate Publishing, 2009], 147–70).
218 Wicke, Ziegenrücker and Ziegenrücker, *Handbuch der populären Musik*; Rasmussen, '"The People's Orchestra"'.
219 Attali, *Noise*, 106–9; Charles Hamm, *Putting Popular Music in Its Place* (Cambridge: Cambridge University Press, 1995), 116–30.
220 Rasmussen, '"The People's Orchestra"', 189.
221 Wicke, Ziegenrücker and Ziegenrücker, *Handbuch der populären Musik*, 467.
222 Hui, 'First Re-creations'.
223 Karen Buzzard, *Tracking the Audience: The Ratings Industry from Analog to Digital* (New York: Routledge, 2012), 24–6; Arthur C. Nielsen, 'Trends Toward Mechanization of Radio Advertising', *Journal of Marketing* 6, no. 3 (1942): 217–28; Max Alt, 'Die Datafizierung des Musikhörens durch die amerikanische Rundfunkforschung der 1930er und 1940er Jahre: Eine Musik- und Medienarchäologie des Musikstreaming', PhD dissertation (Universität Bonn, forthcoming).
224 Douglas, *Listening In*, 137–9; Mark R. Levy, 'The Lazarsfeld-Stanton Program Analyzer: An Historical Note', *Journal of Communication* 32, no. 4 (1982).
225 Robert Prey, 'Musica Analytica: The Datafication of Listening', in *Networked Music Cultures: Contemporary Approaches, Emerging Issues*, ed. Raphaël Nowak and Andrew Whelan, Pop Music, Culture, and Identity Series (London: Palgrave Macmillan, 2016), 31.
226 'Automaten-ABC', *Der Automaten-Markt. Fachzeitschrift für die gesamte Automatenwirtschaft* 12 (1960): 817.
227 See Laing, 'Jukebox', 514; see also Segrave, *Jukeboxes*, 172–4.
228 See 'The Billboard 8th Annual Juke Box Operator Poll', 71.
229 Seventy-six per cent of the operators had one to three employees. Only just under one-third of the operators were organized in a trade association such as the MOA (ibid., 72).

230 This Coda was adapted from Jens Gerrit Papenburg, 'Jukebox-Hören im Film. Strategien, Praktiken, Lokalitäten', in *Jugend, Musik und Film*, ed. Kathrin Dreckmann, Carsten Heinze, Dagmar Hoffmann and Dirk Matejovski (Berlin: de Gruyter, 2022), 455–75.

231 In song lyrics, jukebox listeners appeared in various forms – for example, as typologized female objects of desire, which were imaginarily fused with the jukebox – then there could be talk of the *Juke Box Baby* (Perry Como, RCA Victor, United States 1956) or the *Juke Box Mama* (on the LP *Link Wray* by Link Wray [Polydor, United States 1971]). Access to these objects of desire became possible through the jukebox. Then it could also be *Juke Box, Help Me Find my Baby* (Hardrock Gunter, Sun, United States 1956). But there were also male subjects of the jukebox – such as the *Jukebox Junkie* (on the LP *Killer Country* by Jerry Lee Lewis [Elektra, United States 1981]). Listening to jukeboxes as a practice in a pub in the northern German city of Flensburg is explored by Niebling, starting from the posts of the memories of contemporary witnesses in a Facebook group (Niebling, 'Ernst Neger: Geb' dem Kind sein Nuddelche', 234–6).

232 Relevant jukebox forums sometimes contain quite extensive overviews of jukeboxes in films. The websites Jukebox World, Hildegard Stamann, Stamann Musikboxen, accessed 9 May 2022, http://www.jukebox-world.de and 'Listal: Jukebox', Listal Limited, accessed 9 May 2022, https://www.listal.com/list/junkbox [*sic*] are particularly helpful here. In addition, dozens of colleagues were able to provide me with numerous references via the mailing list of the International Association for the Study of Popular Music (IASPM) on the use of jukeboxes in films and series for the investigation of central aspects of a listening culture of the 1950s or of jukebox listening. Thus, I was able to sift through a variety of film scenes of jukebox listening, some of which take place within the context of the youth cultures present during this decade.

233 In restaurants and ice cream parlours as well as milk and coffee bars, there were often jukeboxes or 'music boxes' as they were called in Germany: For example, the Italian ice cream parlour Giacomel from the 1950s, which is on display in the *House of the History of the Federal Republic of Germany* [Haus der Geschichte der Bundesrepublik Deutschland] museum in Bonn, includes a jukebox: an AMI 200 that came on the market in 1958, with an large selection of 200 tracks and a multi-channel speaker system, see Angela Stirken, *Eisdielen: 'Komm Mit Nach Italien …!'* (Bonn: Stiftung Haus der Geschichte Bonn, 2004). The localization of jukeboxes in West Germany in restaurants and ice cream parlours is also reflected in Heister: 'On the whole, the MB [jukebox] seems to be limited to restaurants just below the "good bourgeois" type …. In addition to student pubs and the smaller establishments, for example, pizzerias, prototypical (and also introduced with the gesture of a stereotype) is "the jukebox in the corner pub" and in the ice cream parlor, which replaced the "milk bar" in the FRG; to the latter corresponds the adult, to the latter the youth audience' (Heister, 'Die Musikbox', 45–6). Adrian Horn describes how the jukebox appeared in specific places in the UK and how meeting places for youth changed after the Second World War: 'In the fifteen years that followed World War II, casual youth meeting places went through a period of change and "crossed over", with jukeboxes, from amusement arcades into small-scale catering establishments' (Horn, *Juke Box Britain*, 161). Horn now sees the jukebox as being located primarily in such "unorganised" youth venues' (11). The US-influenced milk bars and primarily Italian-influenced

espresso bars that boomed in the UK after the Second World War, which were increasingly frequented by young people during this period more than the previously popular arcades, were such 'unorganised' venues (169–82), see also Joe Moran, 'Milk Bars, Starbucks, and the Uses of Literacy', *Cultural Studies* 20, no. 6 (2006), 552–73. Horn distinguishes such places, on the one hand from the 'adult male-dominated public house' (Horn, *Juke Box Britain*, 162), in which a jukebox was almost never found in the 1950s (see 180), from meeting places of young people organized by adults, such as youth clubs or rooms provided by the church. It can be added here that church and community youth work in Germany began to install jukeboxes in their youth centres or 'open houses' in the late 1950s. This does not seem to have been the case in England, according to Horn's comments. Dick Hebdige points out that the milk and coffee bars and the jukeboxes contributed to the spread of rock 'n' roll in England: 'It [rock 'n' roll] was heard in the vacant lots of the new British coffee bars where, although filtered through a distinctly British atmosphere of boiled milk and beverages, it remained demonstrably alien and futuristic – as baroque as the jukebox on which it was played' (Hebdige, *Subculture*, 50). It was only with the success of rock 'n' roll that jukeboxes also reached places in the United States where young people could handle music independently – for example, in 'ice cream parlors, bowling alleys and skating rinks' (Laing, 'Jukebox', 514).

234 See Laing, 'Jukebox', 514.
235 Richard Hoggart, *The Uses of Literacy: Aspects of Working-Class Life* [1957], (London: Penguin, 2009), 219.
236 Hoggart's descriptions allegedly go back to a personal experience in 1950 (see Moran, 'Milk Bars, Starbucks, and the Uses of Literacy'). In contrast to youth culture studies, which emerged in the context of later cultural studies, Hoggart's attitude towards the 'juke-box boys' is characterized by outright rejection.
237 Robert Frank, *The Americans* (Göttingen: Steidl, 2020).
238 Ibid.
239 Handke, *The Jukebox and Other Essays on Storytelling*, 61.
240 Moran, 'Milk Bars, Starbucks, and the Uses of Literacy', 561–2.
241 Thanks to François Ribac (Dijon) for this reference. The manufacturer AMI introduced an Automatic Hostess System in 1939 that looks a little bit like a jukebox (Pearce, *Vintage Jukeboxes*, 46). However, instead of a selection of records in the box, it included a microphone and a connection to the telephone network. After inserting a coin, the listener was connected via telephone line with a human 'hostess' in a central station, who put on the record. The selection available on this system was much more extensive than that of a standard jukebox. Probably *My Dream Is Yours* referred to the AMI system or a comparable system of AMI's competitor Rock-Ola.
242 Paul E. Willis, *Profane Culture*.
243 Ibid., 50.
244 See Horn, *Juke Box Britain*, 90–160.
245 Thanks to Hans-Jürgen Wulf (Westerkappeln) for relevant information.
246 In 1959, the industry-friendly *Automaten-Markt* magazine, which took the perspective of the jukebox setters and not that of the jukebox listeners, reported that 20 per cent of the jukeboxes set up in Berlin were so-called dance boxes [Tanzboxen] ('Die Tanzbox ist groß im Kommen'). Mainly young people were to be found at these. Meeting places of the 'dance-loving youth' were 'small and medium-sized pubs, sometimes bars', in which there was a jukebox. The sound of such dance boxes

consisted, for example, of Billy Vaughn, Ted Herold, Bill Haley, Peter Kraus and Elvis Presley. The vending machine market hailed the dance boxes as an unmitigated success. The youthful guests, for example, were taken with the large selection of music and the jukebox operators made lavish profits with their machines. In a pub in Braunschweig, dancing to the jukebox is said to have taken place every day of the week, with a dance competition on Wednesdays ('Die Tanzbox ist groß im Kommen', 717). The main attraction of the dance box was 'that the young people wanted to feel at home on the dance floor. But "at home" there is hardly any record collection that can compete with the assortment of a dance box stocked with skill.' Ibid., 718. Under the heading 'gesteuerte Ausgelassenheit der Jugend' (controlled exuberance of youth), an article in *Automaten-Markt* praises the installation of jukeboxes in a state-subsidised youth centre in Ahornstrasse in Berlin-Steglitz; this had replaced a dubious 'jazz cellar' ('Musikbox – Helfer der Jugend-Behörde', *Der Automaten-Markt. Fachzeitschrift für die gesamte Automatenwirtschaft* 12 [1960]). The purpose of installing a jukebox by Beromat GmbH with the programmatic name 'Harmonie' (harmony) was to exert control on the 'preferred means of entertainment' of young people: 'dance and hot music' were to be given a 'reasonable framework' (12). The hot music consisted predominantly of 'American numbers and popular jazz titles' (12). Youth shelters, ostensibly to shelters youth from delinquency and commercial forms of leisure, however, did not become the order of the day – despite their good facilities (see Detlef Siegfried, *Time Is on My Side: Konsum und Politik in der Westdeutschen Jugendkultur der 60er Jahre* [Göttingen: Wallstein Verlag, 2008], 133–45). At least in the case of the Steglitz example, this was probably also due to the fact that young people in 'robber's civilian clothes' or 'turtlenecks or jeans' were not wanted there at weekends ('Musikbox – Helfer der Jugend-Behörde', 576) and the 'youth care workers' made sure that the music selection in the jukebox 'as far as possible did not contain any records with shallow or not entirely faultless lyrics' (575). In other youth centres in Wedding and Berlin-Lichterfelde, the jukebox was blatantly used as a 'lure' (575): when the music machine was running, the crowd was huge. The Wiegandt Diplomat jukebox in Berlin-Lichterfelde was probably primarily a 'dance box' that encouraged young people to dance in pairs (see Adams, Lukas and Maschke, *Musikboxen*, 48).

247 'Unterhaltung: Die Jukebox verstummt', *Der Spiegel* 1, no. 14 (1974).

4 The 12-inch single as listening device: Music history, margins of listening and mastered sound

1 The introduction and the first two parts of this section of this chapter consist of translated, revised and supplemented passages from Jens Gerrit Papenburg, '"A Great Idea after the Fact": Das (Er-)Finden der Maxisingle in der New Yorker Discokultur der 1970er Jahre', in *Popgeschichte. Band 2: Zeithistorische Fallstudien 1958–1988*, ed. Bodo Mrozek, Alexa Geisthövel and Jürgen Danyel (Bielefeld: transcript, 2014), 179–98.
2 For this history of the 12-inch single, see Bill Brewster and Frank Broughton, *The Record Players: DJ Revolutionaries* (New York: Black Cat, 2010), 139–40; Claes Breitholtz Widlund, 'Tom Moulton', *Disco-Disco*. Available online:

http://www.disco-disco.com/tributes/tom.shtml (accessed 30 April 2022). The 12-inch singles have been distributed under a number of names since 1976; for example, as 'dance', 'giant' or 'super sound' singles. Few essays and book chapters exist in which the 12-inch single is situated in disco and club culture (see Straw, 'Value and Velocity'; Fikentscher, 'There's Not a Problem I Can't Fix'; Hillegonda C. Rietveld, 'Vinyl Junkies and the Soul Sonic Force of the 12-Inch Dance Single', in *Residual Media*, ed. Charles R. Acland (Minneapolis: University of Minnesota Press, 2007); Osborne, *Vinyl*, 143–59; Erhard Schüttpelz, 'Die Erfindung der Twelve-Inch, der *Homo sapiens* und Till Heilmanns Kommentar zur Priorität der Operationskette', Internationales *Jahrbuch für Medienphilosophie* 3, no. 1 (2017): 217–34; Till A. Heilmann, 'Der Klang der breiten Rille', *Internationales Jahrbuch für Medienphilosophie*. Available online: https://jbmedienphilosophie.de/2017/3-replik-heilmann/ [accessed 30 April 2022]). There are also various articles in relevant encyclopedias (e.g. Martin Elste, *Kleines Tonträger-Lexikon: Von der Walze zur Compact Disc* (Kassel: Bärenreiter, 1989), 75–6; Frank Wonneberg, *Vinyl Lexikon: Fachbegriffe, Sammlerlatein, Praxistipps* (Berlin: Schwarzkopf & Schwarzkopf, 2007), 104; Wicke, Ziegenrücker and Ziegenrücker, *Handbuch der populären Musik*, 667–8). With Elste, however, the brevity of the article offers no protection against wild speculation: 'Although the industry claims that maxi-singles are particularly suitable for high playback demands in discos, it is more likely that they were created primarily as a measure against shoplifting and to further uniformize distribution' (Elste, Kleines *Tonträger-Lexikon*, 75–6).

3 The body of research on disco has now reached prolific proportions and a wide scope. However, media history and sound studies have not yet informed disco's historiography strongly. For rock-centred music criticism and historiography with a preference for concept albums, live concerts, expressive aesthetics, brilliant individuals and virtuosos, disco has always been suspicious. A narrative quickly developed from this direction, according to which disco only emphasizes what is hedonistic, superficial, artificial, formulaic, serial, commercial and staged, and would sink into an apolitical dearth of content. This position also found support from some funk and soul musicians and journalists who once felt close to it: for Nelson George, for example, disco had turned into a 'sound of mindless repetition and textual idiocy', which in some varieties was appropriate to 'sex made of metal' (George, *The Death of Rhythm & Blues*, 153). Such statements construe funk and soul as quasi 'natural' musical forms that have been perverted by disco. With the misleading term 'disco sex rock', Reverend Jesse Jackson attempted to construct a defamatory and ultimately probably ill-informed conceptual synthesis of two musical styles that most rock fans would certainly object to in this form (see Fink, *Repeating Ourselves*, 8). The cultural studies scholar Richard Dyer was interested in defending disco at the height of the disco backlash (Richard Dyer, 'In Defence of Disco', *Gay Left* 8 [1979]: 20–3). This then served as a point of reference for further cultural studies examinations of this music form (Jeremy Gilbert, 'Dyer and Deleuze: Post-Structuralist Cultural Criticism', *New Formations* 58 [2006], 109–27; Tim Lawrence, 'In Defence of Disco (Again)', *New Formations* 58 [2006]). Of the historians of disco culture, Tim Lawrence has painted by far the most nuanced picture of the New York scene of the 1970s and early 1980s that shaped this culture (Tim Lawrence, *Love Saves the Day: A History of American Dance Music Culture, 1970–1979* [Durham, NC: Duke University Press, 2004] and Tim Lawrence, *Hold On to Your Dreams: Arthur Russell and the Downtown Music Scene, 1973–1992* [Durham, NC: Duke University

Press, 2009]). Lawrence's books literally overflow with material – interviews, references to records – and captivate with historical detail. The bibliographies, on the other hand, remain rather slim. Lawrence organizes the wealth of material primarily historically; that is, by attempting to reconstruct chronologically past presences, as well as by a mainstream–underground schematism that tends to be a rough outline. Nevertheless, Lawrence's work repeatedly reveals ambitious systematic and theoretical crystallization points: for example, he examines disco as an experimental field for new sexual identities that vary traditional, dualistically organized identity formations, and also transcend them. The fact that such identities are witnessed almost exclusively by men in Lawrence's work is surprising and a starting point for critique (Alice Echols, *Hot Stuff: Disco and the Remaking of American Music* [New York: W. W. Norton, 2010]; Diana L. Mankowski, 'Gendering the Disco Inferno: Sexual Revolution, Liberation, and Popular Culture in 1970s America' [PhD dissertation, University of Michigan, Ann Arbor, 2010]). Lawrence sees above all in the 'black gay downtown dance scene' (Tim Lawrence, 'Connecting with the Cosmic: Arthur Russell, Rhizomatic Musicianship, and the Downtown Music Scene, 1973–92', *Liminalities: A Journal of Performance Studies* 3, no. 3 [2007]: 62) – in contrast to the white gay disco scene but also to the hyperheterosexual disco world of *Saturday Night Fever* (RSO, United States, 1977) and Cerrone's *Love in "C" Minor* (Malligator, France 1976) – an environment in which sexuality and corporeality were determined beyond established opposites. Lawrence consequently posits that a disco aesthetic and experience was 'queer (rather than gay)' (see Lawrence, 'In Defence of Disco (Again)'): 'Plurality and openness were central tenants of New York's earliest black gay dance formations, where crowds were openly mixed and the dance floor was conceived as a space of open-ended community, non-normative expression, and body-sonic transformation' (Lawrence, 'Connecting with the Cosmic', 63). Lawrence examines different New York clubs in the 1970s as sites of the 'downtown party network' (Lawrence, 'In Defence of Disco (Again)', 129; see also Lawrence, *Love Saves the Day*, 55–81). His focus is on the 'dance floor dynamic' (xii); that is, the DJs and dancers in different clubs. Other approaches to disco culture include literary treatments (Nik Cohn, 'Tribal Rites of the New Saturday Night', *New York Magazine*, 7 June 1976; Andrew Holleran, *Dancer from the Dance* [New York: Perennial, 2001]) as well as accounts by contemporaries written during disco's boom period (Albert Goldman, *Disco* [New York: Hawthorn Books, 1978]; Hanson, *Disco Fieber*; Vince Aletti, *The Disco Files 1973–78: New York's Underground, Week by Week* [New York: Distributed Art Publishers, 2018]), and publications that seek to initiate into the disco business from an insider's perspective (Radcliffe A. Joe, *This Business of Disco* [New York: Billboard Books, 1980]; Doug Shannon, *Off the Record: The Disco Concept* [Cleveland, OH: Pacesetter Publishing, 1982]). These publications have been supplemented and critiqued since the late 1990s (Alan Jones and Jussi Kantonen, *Saturday Night Forever: The Story of Disco* [London: Random House, 2005]; John-Manuel Andriote, *Hot Stuff: A Brief History of Disco* [London: Harper Collins, 2001]; Peter Shapiro, *Turn the Beat Around: The Secret History of Disco* [London: Faber & Faber, 2020]). In the German-speaking world, in the late 1970s, none other than the former director of the German Literature Archive Marbach Ulrich Raulff wrote a trenchant cultural studies essay on disco (Ulrich Raulff, 'Disco: Studio 54 Revisited', *Tumult. Zeitschrift für Verkehrswissenschaft* 1, no. 1 [1979]: 55–66). Further, there are numerous studies on individual clubs such as Studio 54 (Anthony Haden-Guest, *The Last Party: Studio 54, Disco, and the Culture of the*

Night [New York: HarperCollins, 1997]) or Paradise Garage (Mel Cheren, *Keep on Dancin'*: *My Life and the Paradise Garage* [New York: 24 Hours for Life, 2000]), labels such as Philadelphia International Records (John A. Jackson, *A House on Fire: The Rise and Fall of Philadelphia Soul* [New York: Oxford University Press, 2004]) or West End (Cheren, *Keep on Dancin'*), and stars of the scene such as Chic (Daryl Easlea, *Everybody Dance: Chic and the Politics of Disco* [London: Omnibus Press, 2005]) and Donna Summer (Donna Summer and Marc Eliot, *Ordinary Girl: The Journey* [New York: Villard, 2003]). Cultural historical discussions of disco accentuate different aspects, such as gender, corporeality and subjectification (Walter Hughes, 'In the Empire of the Beat: Discipline and Disco', in *Microphone Fiends: Youth Music and Youth Culture*, ed. Andrew Ross and Tricia Ross [New York: Routledge, 1994]; Echols, *Hot Stuff*; Mankowski, 'Gendering the Disco Inferno'; Alexa Geisthövel, 'Anpassung: Disco und Jugendbeobachtung in Westdeutschland, 1975–1981', in *Zeitgeschichte des Selbst: Therapeutisierung – Politisierung – Emotionalisierung*, ed. Pascal Eitler and Jens Elberfeld [Bielefeld: transcript, 2015]). Histories of DJ culture also include chapters on disco (Ulf Poschardt, *DJ Culture*, trans. Shaun Whiteside [London: Quartet Books, 1998]; Bill Brewster and Frank Broughton, *Last Night a DJ Saved My Life: The History of the Disc Jockey* [London: White Rabbit, 2022]). Special issues of cultural studies journals on disco have appeared, such as the *New Formations* special issue 'Of Borders and Discos' (David Glover and Scott McCracken, eds, *New Formations* 58 [2006]) and the *Criticism* special issue 'Disco' (Jonathan Flatley and Charles Kronengold, eds, *Criticism: A Quarterly for Literature and the Arts* 50, no. 1 [2008]). In the aforementioned studies, the sound event of disco is repeatedly described in terms of regionally differentiated 'sounds': there is the 'Philly Sound', characterized above all by the Philadelphia International Records label, by lush, almost symphonic orchestral arrangements and hyper-transparent productions (see Jim Cogan and William Clark, *Temples of Sound*, 150–63), the Latin-influenced 'Miami Sound' of the T. K. Records label, or the 'Munich Sound' produced by Georgio Moroder from South Tyrol, northern Italy. With reference to the excessive use of synthesizers in the productions from Germany, France and Italy in the late 1970s that can be subsumed under the label Eurodisco and the use of samples in disco productions in the early 1980s, the sound of disco has been described along the synthetic–handmade axis (see Lawrence, 'In Defence of Disco (Again)', 144–6). However, this distinction remains questionable given the elaborate production of nearly all disco releases. Charles Kronengold also criticizes that a distinction between the synthetic and the handmade, or between the mechanical and the human, was often reduced in historiographies of disco culture to a juxtaposition of synthesizer and singing voice with regard to music types such as Eurodisco. However, there were synthesizers in various varieties of disco culture that created a 'human touch', as well as machine-repeated 'mechanic voices' (Charles Kronengold, 'Exchange Theories in Disco, New Wave, and Album-Oriented Rock'. *Criticism: A Quarterly for Literature and the Arts* 50, no. 1 [2008]: 52). Individual pieces of music are part of any disco history, but are usually not analysed in more detail. A distinctive reference to disco sound events – which, however, ultimately falls back on the adjectival cascades and metaphors of music journalism – motivates Shapiro (Shapiro, *Turn the Beat Around*). Musicological analyses of disco beyond the aforementioned cultural historical arguments are few and far between, and surprisingly unanimously call out Donna Summer as their icon (see Fink, *Repeating Ourselves*, 25–61; Martin Pfleiderer, *Rhythmus: Psychologische, theoretische und stilanalytische*

Aspekte populärer Musik [Bielefeld: transcript, 2006], 310–16; Sebastian Klotz, '"Love to Love You Music". Verschwendung, Begehren und kapitalistischer Realismus in Minimal Music und Disco', in *High–Low: Hoch- und Alltagskultur in Musik, Kunst, Literatur, Tanz und Kino*, ed. Corina Caduff and Tan Wälchli [Berlin: Kadmos, 2007]; Sebastian Klotz, 'Arcadia, Musicland: Variants of Eloquence in the Renaissance Madrigal and in Disco', in *Variantology 5. Neapolitan Affairs*, ed. Siegfried Zielinski and Eckhard Fürlus [Cologne: Walther König, 2011]). Nevertheless, there are, of course, breaks in this unanimity: in his investigation of the different ways in which sonic conventions are dealt with and exchanged in the music forms of disco, New Wave, and album-oriented rock (AOR), Kronengold presents some sonic disco conventions in a close examination of the Larry Levan remix of *Ain't No Mountain High Enough* by Inner Life (Salsoul, United States, 1982). Kronengold examines, for example, how disco conventions such as the four-to-the-floor beat were taken up and used in New Wave and in album-oriented rock. His thesis is that disco deals with conventions in a specific way: 'But disco requires that a song present the right convention in the right way at the right time; and among many ambitious producers a song must newly instantiate or revise a convention each time it's employed' (Kronengold, 'Exchange Theories in Disco', 56).
4 Breitholz Widlund, 'Tom Moulton', emphasis in original.
5 'Label Mix Records for Club Scene', *Billboard*, 2 November 1974, 1, 10. Even before that – in October 1973 and October 1974 – *Billboard* had been able to announce, but in less prominent places, that discos would make hits (see 'Discotheques Break Single', *Billboard*, 6 October 1973, 3, and 'Disco Play Starts a Hit', *Billboard*, 26 October 1974, 36).
6 Mancuso is certainly an impactful figure for the emergence of the New York disco scene. The critique of personalistic narratives presented here does not, of course, discount in principle that individual actors can be fundamentally important. However, it was certainly due to Lawrence's disco historiography that Mancuso was identified as a prominent actor; see Lawrence, *Love Saves the Day*.
7 See ibid., 114–16 and 124. See also Shapiro, *Turn the Beat Around*, 23–4, as well as Aletti, *The Disco Files*, 5–9.
8 See Shapiro, *Turn the Beat Around*, 28–34.
9 Straw, 'Value and Velocity', 166. See also Will Straw, 'Popular Music as Cultural Commodity: The American Recorded Music Industries 1976–1985' (PhD dissertation, Department of Art History and Communication Studies, McGill University, Montreal, 1990).
10 In 1974, various relevant US industry journals launched columns devoted to disco. In addition to Moulton's column Disco Action for *Billboard*, this includes Vince Aletti's column Disco File for Record World (see Aletti, *The Disco Files*; and Lawrence, *Love Saves the Day*, 205–11). In 1976, *Billboard* organized the First Annual International Disco Forum (see Lawrence, *Love Saves the Day*, 206). According to Lawrence, the term 'disco' became established around 1974 (Lawrence, 'In Defence of Disco (Again)', 129). Aletti reported on the New York disco scene in *Rolling Stone* as early as September 1973 (Aletti, *The Disco Files*, 5–9). By the end of 1978, there were about fifteen thousand to twenty thousand discos in the United States (see Lawrence, *Love Saves the Day*, 315). In 1980, the editor responsible for disco at *Billboard* – Radcliffe Joe – presented a book that

aimed to initiate into the disco business from an insider's perspective (Joe, *This Business of Disco*).

11 Chris Sedwell and Simon Bottom, 'Break', in *Continuum Encyclopedia of Popular Music of the World. Volume II. Performance and Production*, ed. John Shepherd, David Horn, Dave Laing, Paul Oliver and Peter Wicke (London: Continuum, 2003), 562. Prominent breaks can, of course, be found in popular music long before disco. However, the short breaks in jazz – for example, in Joe 'King' Oliver's Creole Jazz Band *Dipper Mouth Blues* (Gennett, United States, 1923) – or in funk and soul – for example, in *Amen Brother* by The Winstons (Metromedia, United States, 1969) – are not produced on a studio basis. A considerable temporal extension of percussion-emphasized passages as dance patterns is found in long funk and soul pieces of the early 1970s. However, these could only be released in a long version without interruption on LP: for example, the protodisco piece *Girl You Need a Change of Mind* (Tamla, United States, 1973) by Eddie Kendricks. In Frank Wilson's production of the track, two features are central that would later become constitutive of disco: the break and a four-on-the-floor beat. Wilson saw his breaks as inspired by gospel. 'Girl You Need a Change of Mind' contains two breaks, after which the song is built up again – starting from the basic rhythm. The starting point, however, is not a backbeat emphasis as in rock 'n' roll or a 'four-on-top' emphasis – so characteristic of 1960s Motown productions by Holland-Dozier-Holland – but a bass drum kicked on the quarters. Wilson commented in retrospect on this bass drum pulse as follows: 'At the time we did think, instead of four on top – which is what Holland-Dozier-Holland had been famous for – let's start with four on the floor and build it from there. Still, when I began hearing reports about what was happening with the record in the New York disco clubs, I was shocked. That was not what we were going for. We were after radio' (Wilson cited in Brewster and Broughton, *Last Night a DJ Saved My Life*, 225). Such four-to-the-floor patterns were then echoed on other Motown productions of the early 1970s. For example, in the Temptations's *Law of the Land*, produced by Norman Whitfield (Motown, United States, 1973).

12 Klotz, '"Love to Love You Music"', 85.

13 Don Downing's *Dream World* (Roadshow, United States, 1973) was also released in 1973 as a short and concise two-and-a-half-minute version conforming to pop song form conventions.

14 See 'Label Mix Records', 10.

15 Moulton's first disco mix made in the studio was *Do It ('Til You're Satisfied)* by B. T. Express (see Brewster and Broughton, *The Record Players*, 138). However, the mix of 'Dream World' by Don Downing was released first.

16 See Lawrence, *Love Saves the Day*, 146.

17 For instance, *Mad Love* by Barrabas (Atlantic, United States, 1974), *Disco Queen* by Hot Chocolate (Atlantic, United States, 1974) or *Ease on Down the Road* by Consumer Rapport (Atlantic, United States, 1975) were released in this series (see Aletti, *The Disco Files*, 86).

18 Motown released Eddie Kendrick's proto-disco track *Girl You Need a Change of Mind* (Motown, United States, 1973) as a single by pressing part one of the track on the A-side and part two on the B-side. The same form of release can be found on the single *The Love I Lost* by Harold Melvin and the Blue Notes (PIR, United States, 1973). The first isolated examples of splitting a production between the A- and B-sides of a single can be found as early as the 1950s – for example, Ray Charles's *What'd I*

Say (Atlantic, United States, 1959). Also in blues releases of the 1930s – such as Son House's *My Black Mama* (Paramount 13042, United States, 1930) – and prominently then in James Brown's funk singles from the mid-1960s, where a piece of music was split into two parts and released on the A- and B-sides of a record: 'It has been among the expansive rhythms of black music that the two-part single has been most common' (Osborne, *Vinyl*, 153).

19 The LP version of Eddie Kendrick's *Girl You Need a Change of Mind* for example, lasts 7:43 minutes. Part one of the single version runs 3:20 minutes, and part two 2:43 minutes.

20 See Cheren, *Keep on Dancin'*, 118–21. In West Germany, the practice of not adding a second independent track to B-sides of singles did not appear until 1976. In this context, the German trade journal *Musik-Informationen* mocked the 'cheating of the buyer' or 'B-side drudgery' through 'instrumental playback[s]' pressed onto the B-side and the practice of 'letting the A-side numbers run on endlessly like a tape worm, even on the second half of the record' (Peter Krebs, 'Kein Boom ohne B-Seiten', *Musik-Informationen* 12 [1976]: 1; thanks to Klaus Nathaus [Oslo] for this reference). On the 12-inch single in Great Britain, see Osborne, *Vinyl*, 156–8.

21 Soul LPs like *Hot Buttered Soul* by Isaac Hayes (Enterprise, United States, 1969), which contains only four tracks, or Barry White's *I've Got So Much Love to Give* (20th Century Records, United States, 1973), which contains only five tracks, should also be mentioned here; as well as the medley on Sly & the Family Stone's *Dance to the Music* (Epic, United States, 1968). We shall be silent about the symphonic excursions of rock music!

22 The first compilation album to appear as a mix is tellingly titled *Disco Par-r-r-ty. Non Stop Music* (Spring, United States, 1974).

23 On these practices as a template for the 12-inch single, see also Fikentscher, 'There's Not a Problem I Can't Fix' and Rietveld, 'Vinyl Junkies and the Soul Sonic Force'.

24 This is *(Call Me Your) Anything Man* by Bobby Moore (Scepter, United States, 1975) (see Aletti, *The Disco Files*, 97). *(Do you Wanna) Dance, Dance, Dance* by Calhoon (Warner Spector, United States, 1975) appeared in July 1975 (102). However, the play speed of the single released on Scepter was 33 1/3 rpm. The former contained a mix of the track by Tom Moulton lasting about six minutes. The latter contained a 'Special Disco Mix' of about the same length. Whether the Special Disco Mix was a studio mix or had already been recorded that way is not noted on the recording. Moulton claims that *Free Man* by Southshore Commission (Scepter/Ward, United States, 1975) was the first release of a 12-inch by a label for promotional purposes (see Moulton cited by Breitholtz Widlund, 'Tom Moulton').

25 Mark Katz, *Groove Music: The Art and Culture of the Hip-Hop DJ* (New York: Oxford University Press, 2012), 14–42. Katz's discussion also includes disco and Walter Gibbons, 32–3.

26 Gibbons mixed, for example, the drum and percussion grooves from *Happy Song* by the rock band Rare Earth (to be found on the LP *Back to Earth*) (Rare Earth [Motown], United States, 1975) and *2 Pigs and a Hog* from the soundtrack of the high school film *Cooley High* (Motown, United States, 1975) into an almost endless loop (see on this Lawrence, *Love Saves the Day*, 212–20]).

27 See ibid., 35–6.

28 On Siano, see ibid., 99–112, and also Shapiro, *Turn the Beat Around*, 37–9.

29 In 1974, Siano played with three turntables. The third record player was used to play sound effect records (see Lawrence, *Love Saves the Day*, 125).
30 Siano, according to ibid., 107–8, emphasis in original.
31 Acetates are aluminum discs coated with acetate lacquer. The soft lacquer wears off quickly, so the test cuts can only be played a few times.
32 On Sunshine Sound, see also Shapiro, *Turn the Beat Around*, 316.
33 Is Horowitz, '"Illegit" Disco Tapes Peddled by Jockeys', *Billboard*, 12 October 1974, 12.
34 See Brewster and Broughton, *Last Night a DJ Saved My Life*, 255–6.
35 The tapes were made with fairly modest means: Moulton claims to have made his first forty-five-minute mixtape in a time-consuming 80 hours stint with a reel-to-reel tape machine, a record player, and some 7-inch singles without tape editing using the sound-on-sound method (see Moulton, according to Brewster and Broughton, *The Record Players*, 137).
36 Moulton, according to Lawrence, *Love Saves the Day*, 72.
37 See David Toop, 'Lost in Music: Zwanzig Jahre Diskoproduktionen', in *Sound und Vision*, ed. Klaus Frederking (Reinbek bei Hamburg: Rowohlt, 1985).
38 Rolf Grossmann, 'Reproduktionsmusik und Remix-Culture', in *Mind the Gap: Medienkonstellationen zwischen zeitgenössischer Musik und Klangkunst*, ed. Marion Saxer (Saarbrücken: Pfau, 2011), 120–1.
39 On the remix, see ibid. In this article, Grossmann not only examines remix practices in disco, but also, for example, in Jamaican dub and in art music.
40 Gloria Gaynor, for example, was initially less than enthusiastic about Moulton's mixes (see Brewster and Broughton, *The Record Players*, 139).
41 B. T. Express also initially rejected Moulton's mix. But after the mix turned out to be extremely successful, the band stated in interviews that they had recorded the track in the long version (see ibid., 138). The boundary between recording and post-production thus became fluid or inaudible.
42 'Label Mix Records for Club Scene', 1. See also 'Discotheques Break Single', 3; 'Disco Play Starts a Hit', 36.
43 Toop, 'Lost in Music', 166, emphasis in original.
44 Shapiro, *Turn the Beat Around*, 34.
45 See Tim Lawrence, liner notes for Walter Gibbons, *Mixed with Love: The Walter Gibbons Salsoul Anthology* (Suss'd Records, UK, 2004) and Tim Lawrence, liner notes for Walter Gibbons, *Jungle Music (Mixed with Love: Essential & Unreleased Remixes 1976–1986)* (Strut, UK, 2010).
46 See Lawrence, *Love Saves the Day*, 263. Rolf Grossmann has noted that 'remix practice' aims above all at the 'texture' of sound events: 'The development of melody and harmony recedes into the background in favour of a rhythmically moving surface structure whose differentiation takes place according to the principle of layering parallel structures. Editing (cutting, copying, rearranging), layering (the superimposition of different tracks), and mixing (the remixing of these parallel structures) are already the basic elements of a new phonographic auditory design' (Grosmann, 'Reproduktionsmusik', 121–2).
47 See Moulton, according to Lawrence, *Love Saves the Day*, 268. For Mel Cheren, the extremely successful remix made by Walter Gibbons of Bettye Lavette's *Doin' the Best that I Can* (West End, United States, 1978) sounded 'like a musical acid trip' (Cheren, *Keep on Dancin'*, 213).

48 Wicke, Ziegenrücker and Ziegenrücker, *Handbuch der populären Musik*, 199.
49 Douglas Crimp, 'DISSS-CO (A Fragment): From *Before Pictures*, a Memoir of 1970s New York', *Criticism: A Quarterly for Literature and the Arts* 50, no. 1 (2008): 5.
50 Ibid.
51 Wicke, 'Soundtechnologien und Körpermetamorphosen', 41.
52 Ibid.
53 See Adorno, *Introduction to the Sociology of Music*, 4–5. See also Chapter 1, section 'What Are Listening Devices?'.
54 Günther Anders, 'On Promethean Shame', in *Prometheanism: Technology, Digital Culture, and Human Obsolescence*, ed. Christopher John Müller (New York: Rowman & Littlefield, 2016), 79, emphasis in original.
55 Peter Wicke, *Rock und Pop: Von Elvis Presley bis Lady Gaga* (Munich: Beck, 2011), 44.
56 See for instance, Simon Frith and Angela McRobbie, 'Rock and Sexuality', in *On Record: Rock, Pop, and the Written Word*, ed. Simon Frith and Andrew Goodwin (London: Routledge, 1990).
57 Ibid.
58 See Thorau and Ziemer, 'The Art of Listening and Its Histories'.
59 Will Straw, 'Dance Music', in *The Cambridge Companion to Pop and Rock*, ed. Simon Frith, Will Straw and John Street (Cambridge: Cambridge University Press, 2001), 160.
60 Wicke, 'Soundtechnologien und Körpermetamorphosen', 57.
61 Raulff, 'Disco', 65, emphasis in original.
62 Wicke, 'Soundtechnologien und Körpermetamorphosen', 57.
63 We should add here, however, that the disco body is not only cultivated through sound, but it is also trained by specific practices and body techniques such as body building or martial arts like kung fu. Body building was extremely popular in the New York disco scene of the 1970s, and definitely had a normative potential (see Crimp, 'DISSS-CO (A Fragment)'). In addition, the repertoire of martial arts moves, such as kung fu, is sonically and phonetically encoded and processed in Carl Douglas's hit 'Kung Fu Fighting' (20th Century Records, United States, 1974), for example.
64 On the contemporary historical setting in which Dyer's text was published, see Luis-Manuel Garcia, 'Richard Dyer, 'In Defence of Disco' (1979)', available online: http://history-is-made-at-night.blogspot.com/2008/05/in-defence-of-disco-richard-dyer.html.
65 Dyer, 'In Defence of Disco', 22.
66 See Gilbert, 'Dyer and Deleuze', 113.
67 Dyer, 'In Defence of Disco', 21.
68 Ibid., 22.
69 See also ibid.
70 See Tim Lawrence, 'Beyond the Hustle: 1970s Social Dancing, Discotheque Culture, and the Emergence of the Contemporary Club Dancer', in *Ballroom, Boogie, Shimmy Sham, Shake: A Social and Popular Dance Reader*, ed. Julie Malnig (Champaign: University of Illinois Press, 2008), 132.
71 See Gilbert and Pearson, *Discographies*, 136–7.
72 Lawrence, *Love Saves the Day*, 25, emphasis in original.
73 Fink, *Repeating Ourselves*, 40, emphasis in original.

74 See ibid., 43, and also Klotz, "'Love to Love You Music'".
75 See Lawrence, *Love Saves the Day*, 44.
76 Sound systems are also a central component of Jamaican dub and reggae culture (see Michael E. Veal, *Dub: Soundscapes and Shattered Songs in Jamaican Reggae* [Middletown: Wesleyan University Press, 2007] and Henriques, *Sonic Bodies*). However, the relationship of these to early New York disco culture cannot be discussed further here.
77 Keightley, "'Turn It Down!' She Shrieked'.
78 Wicke, *Von Mozart zu Madonna*, 272.
79 See Alex Rosner, 'Overview of Disco Sound Systems', *Journal of the Audio Engineering Society* 27, nos. 7–8 (1979): 584. However, it was not so much the extension of the frequency range, but primarily the volume that initially attracted Moulton to the 12-inch single (see Moulton, according to Breitholtz Widlund, 'Tom Moulton').
80 On these sound systems, see Chapter 5, section 'Disco's Enhanced Sound Systems'.
81 Kittler, 'Rock Music'. See also Chapter 1, section 'What Is a Sound and Music History of Listening Devices?'.
82 Sterne, *MP3. The Meaning of a Format*, 30.
83 See Wolfgang Hagen, *Das Radio*.
84 Brewster and Broughton, *Last Night a DJ Saved My Life*, 187.
85 Straw, 'Value and Velocity', 167.
86 In relation to house and techno, I develop this story in the third section of this Chapter ('Maxi-Sound: Mastering Disco, House and Techno).
87 This third part of this section is translated and adapted from Papenburg, 'Rockmusik, Musikdrama, Disco', 161–5.
88 Kittler, *Gramophone, Film, Typewriter*, xli.
89 Ibid., 140.
90 Ibid.
91 Raulff, 'Disco', 64.
92 Lawrence, 'Love Saves the Day'.
93 Kittler, *Gramophone*, 140.
94 Echols, *Hot Stuff*, 155. For a critique of this juxtaposition central to disco historiography, see ibid.
95 Schüttpelz, 'Die Erfindung der Twelve-Inch', 219, emphasis in original.
96 Ibid., 217.
97 Ibid., 233 and 229, emphasis in original.
98 Ibid., 233 and 232, emphasis in original.
99 Straw, 'Value and Velocity', 167.
100 Here I paraphrase and specify Heilmann, 'Der Klang'.
101 Ibid.
102 Ibid.
103 Osborne, *Vinyl*, 158.
104 Ibid. Record companies released 12-inch singles with a short accompanying text that explained the sonic advantages of the 12-inch single. The WEA record company, for example, marketed the 12-inch single as a 'super-sound single'. On a WEA release – *Groove Me* (WEA, Germany, 1979) by Fern Kinney – the 12-inch single was advertised as follows: 'Sound specialist and sound engineer Karl-Heinz

Kubitza on the subject of the Super-Sound Single: The visible distinguishing feature of this sound carrier is its larger diameter, which corresponds to that of an LP. The advantages of the Super-Sound Single with 45 revolutions per minute only become possible due to the larger surface available as a result. The most striking differences are: (1) higher modulation; (2) greater groove depth and width as well as (3) greater distance between the radii; and (4) greater dynamics. Thus, for the professional user or hi-fi fan, the Super-Sound Single is characterised by greater volume due to the high modulation, by smoother tonearm movement (no needle jumping) due to the greater groove depth and width even at extreme frequency mixes, and by a greater interference voltage spacing, which accounts for the greater dynamics; that is, by a greater ratio of useful noise to interference noise.' All forms of the vinyl record have a distinct relationship to the visual, but this is organized in a peculiar way in the 12-inch single. Osborne writes in his book on the vinyl record: 'This book devotes more space to the historical, visual, and tactile properties of the format than it does to its auditory qualities. When examining the latter I restrict myself to a discussion of the limitations that the format has set regarding duration, sound quality, volume and tonal range.' Osborne, *Vinyl*, 4.

105   See Maria Perevedentseva and Luis-Manuel Garcia, 'Chicago House Music, from Dance Floor to Museum: The Frankie Knuckles Vinyl Collection', *Sound Studies* 2, no. 1 (2016). See also the archival research perspective on the record collections of Afrika Bambaataa at Cornell University's Hip Hop Collection, Frankie Knuckles at the Stony Island Arts Bank in Chicago, and Larry Levan and Ron Hardy (Liam Maloney and John Schofield, 'Records as Records: Excavating the DJ's Sonic Archive', *Archives and Records*. Available online: https://doi.org/10.1080/23257962.2021.2001 319 [accessed 30 April 2022]).

106   Dirk Sommer, 'Die Georg Neumann GmbH', in *hifi tunes: Das Klassikerbuch*, ed. Roland Kraft (Gröbenzell: IMAGE Verlags GmbH, 2008), 16. See also Elste, *Tonträgerlexikon*, 130.

107   On this record cutting method see also Chapter 2, endnote 113.

108   See Adorno, 'The Form of the Phonograph Record [1934]'.

109   Mark Poster, '"Digitale" versus "analoge" Autorschaft', in *Heterotopien der Identität. Literatur in interamerikanischen Kontaktzonen*, ed. Hermann Herlinghaus and Utz Riese (Heidelberg: Winter, 1999), 269.

110   Grasso, according to Lawrence, *Love Saves the Day*, 36–7. Reading phonographic curves was already used in the nineteenth century in sensory physiology (Hermann von Helmholtz, *Die Lehre von den Tonempfindungen als physiologische Grundlage für die Theorie der Musik* [Braunschweig: Vieweg, 1913], 34) and in Alexander Graham Bell's early deaf pedagogy and in the experimental psychology of Edward Wheeler Scripture (Sterne, *The Audible Past*, 31–84). In addition, we find it in visual sound art by, for example, K. P. Brehmer – 'Composition for Tim Wilson II' (see Rolf Großmann, 'Phonographic Work: Reading and Writing Sound', in *Sound as Popular Culture. A Research Companion*, ed. Jens Gerrit Papenburg and Holger Schulze [Cambridge, MA: MIT Press, 2016], 359–62). The Englishman Tim Wilson demonstrated on talk shows his ability to identify music by merely reading record grooves. *The New York Times* reported in 1981 on a man – Arthur B. Lintgen – who could read records (Thomas Y. Levin, '"Tones from out of Nowhere": Rudolph Pfenninger and the Archaeology of Synthetic Sound', in *New Media, Old Media: A*

History and Theory Reader, ed. Wendy Hui Kyong Chun and Thomas W. Keenan [New York: Routledge, 2006], 52–3; and Bernard Holland, 'A Man Who Sees What Others Hear', *New York Times*, 19 November 1981, 28.

111 Chuck Miller, 'Herbie Was Here: Stories of the Mysterious Messages in the Runoff Grooves', *Goldmine*, 27 March 1998.

112 Besides the already mentioned abbreviation 'TM/JR' for Tom Moulton and José Rodriguez, the mastering engineer Herb Powers can be mentioned here. Powers began working at the Frankford-Wayne Mastering Labs in 1976 and marked the records he mastered with a unique pictogram (see Miller, 'Herbie Was Here'). Such visual indexing of the mastering engineer was historically preceded by references to the mastering studio or to the number of the pressing matrix in the area of the run-out groove. This type of information exhibits a high degree of media specificity, which is also relevant for the archiving of recordings: 'Vinyl records will typically include etched matrix numbers or pressing plant reference numbers that provide a modicum of information concerning the history of the musical material and the history of the physical disc's creation.' Maloney and Schofield, 'Records as Records'.

113 For example, on the LP *X-102 Discovers the Rings of Saturn* by X-102 (Underground Resistance, United States, 1992).

114 Dan Sicko, *Techno Rebels: The Renegades of Electronic Funk* (Detroit: Wayne State University Press, 2010), 111.

115 On this see also Kodwo Eshun, *More Brilliant Than the Sun: Adventures in Sonic Fiction* (London: Quartet Books, 1999), 122; and Mercedes Bunz, 'Das Mensch-Maschine-Verhältnis. Ein Plädoyer für eine Erweiterung der Medientheorie am Beispiel von Kraftwerk, Underground Resistance und Missy Elliot', in *Sound Signatures: Pop-Splitter*, ed. Jochen Bonz (Frankfurt am Main: Suhrkamp, 2001), 280–1. On Ron Murphy, see also Ashley Zlatopolsky, 'Behind the Groove: The Ron Murphy Story', *Red Bull Music Academy*. Available online: https://daily.redbullmusic academy.com/2015/05/ron-murphy-feature (accessed 30 April 2022).

116 Peter Wicke, '"Move Your Body"'. Even though this thesis may have critical limitations, it nevertheless is not reducible to these. For example, certain sound generators and instruments – such as the Roland TB-303 – possessed almost cult status in parts of the techno scene. By obtaining such a status, individual sounds are reconnected to a specific and well-defined source. Also, the disembodiment and de-subjectification on the part of music production, as applied for a while to the first and second generation of techno producers (see Beverly May, 'Techno', in *African American Music: An Introduction*, ed. Mellonee Victoria Burnim and Portia K. Maultsby [New York: Routledge, 2006]), was quickly replaced by a star system (see Tom Holert, 'Star-Schnittstelle: Glamour und elektronische Popkultur', in *Gendertronics: Der Körper in der elektronischen Musik*, ed. Club Transmediale and Meike Jansen [Frankfurt am Main: Suhrkamp, 2005]).

117 In the introduction to the anthology *Klang (ohne) Körper* [Sound (without) Body] they edited, Michael Harenberg and Daniel Weissberg point out that in popular electronic music forms, tension exists between the disembodied, synthetically generated sound sequences and the 'intended body and movement-related reception' (Michael Harenberg and Daniel Weissberg, 'Einleitung: Der Verlust der Körperlichkeit in der Musik und die Entgrenzung klanglichen Gestaltungspotenzials',

in *Klang (ohne) Körper: Spuren und Potenziale des Körpers in der elektronischen Musik*, ed. Michael Harenberg and Daniel Weisberg [Bielefeld: transcript, 2010], 8).

118 Wicke, '"Move Your Body"', emphasis in original.
119 I will get back to clubs as places of 'sonic dominance' in Chapter 5, section 'Disco's Enhanced Sound Systems'.
120 See Chapter 1, section 'What Are Listening Devices?'.
121 See Jacob Smith, *Vocal Tracks: Performance and Sound Media* (Berkeley: University of California Press, 2008); Knut Holtsträter, 'Der Crooner, das unbekannte Wesen', in *Musik und Popularität: Aspekte zu einer Kulturgeschichte zwischen 1500 und heute*, ed. Sabine Meine and Nina Noeske (Münster: Waxmann, 2011); McCracken, *Real Men Don't Sing*.
122 Paula Clare Harper, 'ASMR: Bodily Pleasure, Online Performance, Digital Modality', *Sound Studies* 6, no. 1: 95–8.
123 The fact that in the context of the listening culture of the hi-fi LP, minoritarian practices can also be found that claim an auditory sensitivity to technological differences is elaborated in Chapter 2 (section 'Listening to Little Richard's *Long Tall Sally*'). In the recent past, hi-fi critics and vinyl listeners have also drawn attention to the audibility of technology under positive auspices – for example, when sonic differences between LPs and CDs were highlighted (see Aden Evens, *Sound Ideas: Music, Machines, and Experience* [Minneapolis: University of Minnesota Press, 2005], 1–24 for a theoretical situating of this listener).
124 See Chapter 2, section 'Mastering Industry Standards and Non-Listening'.
125 Of course, there is also a haptic dimension to the artefact of the record. This dimension, on which the objects of desire of vinyl fans prone to fetishism and nostalgia are often arranged, includes, for example, the record cover or the haptic quality of the material vinyl. However, this form of haptics is not the focus of the present investigation.
126 Gilbert and Pearson, *Discographies*, 136. Wicke also points out the connection between the sonic characteristics of the 12-inch single and disco: 'The wider cut on the larger diameter record produced a significantly higher dynamic range, which benefitted the bass in particular when it was played in large rooms, creating a more transparent sound image, which in turn made possible the bass-heavy productions of the disco sound.' Wicke, 'Der Tonträger als Medium', 26.
127 Katz, *Mastering Audio*, 71.
128 Moulton, according to Breitholtz Widlund, 'Tom Moulton'.
129 See Henriques, *Sonic Bodies*.
130 See Goodman, *Sonic Warfare*.
131 Luis-Manuel Garcia, 'Beats, Flesh, and Grain: Sonic Tactility and Affect in Electronic Dance Music', *Sound Studies* 1, no. 1 (2015): 60, emphasis in original.
132 Ragnhild Torvanger Solberg, '"Waiting for the Bass to Drop": Correlations between Intense Emotional Experiences and Production Techniques in Build-up and Drop Sections of Electronic Dance Music', *Dancecult: Journal of Electronic Dance Music Culture* 6, no. 1 (2014): 64.
133 Jasen, *Low End Theory*.
134 Jens Gerrit Papenburg, 'Boomende Bässe der Disco- und Clubkultur: Musikanalytische Herausforderungen durch taktile Klänge', in *Techno Studies. Ästhetik und Geschichte elektronischer Tanzmusik*, ed. Kim Feser and Matthias Pasdzierny (Berlin: b-books, 2017).

135 Robert Fink, 'Below 100 Hz: Toward a Musicology of Bass Culture', in *The Relentless Pursuit of Tone: Timbre in Popular Music*, ed. Robert Fink, Melinda Latour and Zachary Wallmark (New York: Oxford University Press, 2018).
136 Jasen, *Low End Theory*, 14–20, 151–83.
137 Kassabian, *Ubiquitous Listening*, xvii. Kassabian developed the concept of the haptic from the Canadian film scholar Laura Marks (Laura U. Marks, *Touch: Sensuous Theory and Multisensory Media* [Minneapolis: University of Minnesota Press, 2002]), who was influenced by Deleuze and Guattari. I prefer the concept of tactile to that of haptic: if the latter primarily denotes a specific sensory and physiological quality, then the former has been used repeatedly in its proximity to the concept of the tactical. Such usage is prominent in Walter Benjamin's media aesthetics (cf. Tobias Wilke, *Medien der Unmittelbarkeit: Dingkonzepte und Wahrnehmungstechniken 1918–1939* [Munich: Fink, 2010], 189–219). Although the quality of tactility in Benjamin also aims at tactile perception, according to Wilke, Benjamin is concerned with the 'entry of tactile functions into the sphere of optics' (202); that is, not with the tactile per se, but primarily with its relationship to other sensory modes. Moreover, the tactile in Benjamin's work also implies a planned 'training of perception' (195), a 'tactile reconstruction of apperception' (196). On perception training through technology, see also Michael Bull, 'Technological Sensory Training', in *Sound as Popular Culture: A Research Companion*, ed. Jens Gerrit Papenburg and Holger Schulze (Cambridge, MA: MIT Press, 2016). According to this, the tactile in disco and in electronic dance music can be conceptually developed in the present book. We can add that the topic of the tactile also occupies a prominent position in the work of Canadian media theorist Marshall McLuhan. McLuhan sees the age that he describes as characterized by technical media beyond the book, as determined by a 'rumbles of audio-tactility' and no longer by visuality (Marshall McLuhan and Bruce R. Powers, *The Global Village: Transformations in World Life and Media in the 21st Century* [New York: Oxford University Press, 1992], 46). See also Frank Hartmann, 'Instant Awareness: Eine medientheoretische Exploration mit McLuhan', in *Soundcultures: Über elektronische und digitale Musik*, ed. Marcus S. Kleiner and Achim Szepanski (Frankfurt am Main: Suhrkamp, 2003); Thomas Schopp, 'Sonic FX: Klang, Körper, Kontrolle' (MA dissertation, Musikwissenschaftliches Seminar, Humboldt University of Berlin, Berlin, 2005); Wolfgang Ernst, 'Takt und Taktilität: Akustik als privilegierter Kanal zeitkritischer Medienprozesse', in *McLuhan neu lesen. Kritische Analysen zu Medien und Kultur im 21. Jahrhundert*, ed. Derrick de Kerckhove, Martina Leeker and Kerstin Schmidt (Bielefeld: transcript, 2008). Parts of this footnote are adapted from Jens Gerrit Papenburg, 'Boomende Bässe der Disco- und Clubkultur'.
138 Kassabian, *Ubiquitous Listening*, xvii.
139 Anahid Kassabian, 'Hearing as a Contact Sense' (Lecture, Music Forum at Keele University, Keele, UK, 3 June 2007).
140 Kassabian, *Ubiquitous Listening*, xvii. Kassabian refers here, once again, to Laura Marks.
141 Kassabian, 'Hearing as a Contact Sense'.
142 Music journalist Kodwo Eshun described such haptic sound sensations in electronic dance music between scholarship and literature: 'As beats ensnare you in the parallel complexity of the amplified jungle, your skin starts to feel what your ears can't. At these convergences, beats phase shift, cross a threshold, and become tactile

sensations that sussurate the body. Fleeting sensations of feeling skim across the skin, seizing the synapses. Senses swap so that your skin hears and your ears feel. Dermal ears. Your skin turns into one giant all-over ear. Ear tactility' (Eshun, *More Brilliant Than the Sun*, 76–7).

143 See Kassabian, *Ubiquitous Listening*, xvi.
144 Ibid., xxii.
145 Ibid., xviii and xviv.
146 Ibid., 31, emphasis in the original.
147 See ibid., 32–4.
148 See Fink, *Repeating Ourselves*, 34–8. Fink refers here to Dyer's 'whole body eroticism'. Such a phenomenon is highly ambivalent. Although it opens up a realm of the Other – here reference is made to subjectivity beyond a standard white, adult, heterosexual and male subject – it is also a gateway for the critique of reactionary factors: infantility, consumerism, or submission to technocratic authority (36). '*Plaisir*' stands for a symbolically regimented desire for an object or a climax that obeys the dynamics of tension and resolution. '*Jouissance*', on the other hand, stands for the maintenance of desire in symbolically unregulated repetition in the real. With his critique of the concept of '*jouissance*', Fink takes up a theoretically quite original position in the academic discussion of electronic dance music. After all, this mostly refers affirmatively or unregulatedly to the conceptual reservoir of French post-structuralism (see, e.g. the adoption of the term '*jouissance*' in Gilbert and Pearson, *Discographies*, 64–8 or in Jochen Bonz, *Subjekte des Tracks: Ethnografie einer postmodernen/anderen Subkultur* [Berlin: Kadmos, 2008]).
149 Fink, *Repeating Ourselves*, 42.
150 Ibid., 43.
151 Ibid., 44–5.
152 For Kronengold, the form of disco is constituted by the interaction of multiple temporal levels in the act of listening: 'narrative time, the time of conventional song forms, the time of memory, clock time, the time it takes for a generic signal or cultural reference to do its work, the temporalities of desire, and so on' (Kronengold, 'Exchange Theories in Disco', 55).
153 Osborne, *Vinyl*, 143. For a history of the B-side in various forms of music, such as rock music, dub, disco, see 143–59.
154 Ibid., 156.
155 Ibid., 157.
156 See ibid., 156–9.
157 Ibid., 159.
158 See Keir Keightley and Will Straw, 'Single', in *Continuum Encyclopedia of Popular Music of the World. Volume II. Performance and Production*, ed. John Shepherd, David Horn, Dave Laing, Paul Oliver and Peter Wicke (London: Continuum, 2003), 780. See also Straw, 'Value and Velocity', 168. Straw notes that such a cannibalizing function of the 12-inch single would not only have affected the sale of LPs. Rather, since the 12-inch single often exposed sound worlds that could no longer be reproduced in a live context, the 'promotional value of tours' was severely limited (169). In the end, by 1979, the record industry had to recognize the fact that disco fans understood music as an 'ongoing soundtrack to urban life rather than a series of separate songs to be identified as such' (169). This then led to disco fans having this soundtrack delivered via the radio or by buying compilation albums.

159 See Shannon, *Off the Record*, 208–10.
160 Keightley and Straw, 'Single', 780.
161 Eshun, *More Brilliant Than the Sun*, 97. Such a sonic claim for distinction through the 12-inch single can also be found in postpunk as well. Reynolds writes about the *Metal Box* release by Public Image Ltd (Virgin METAL 1, UK, 1979): 'In honour of reggae and disco's twelve-inch aesthetic and to ensure the highest possible sound quality, PiL insisted on releasing the album as three 45 r.p.m. records, rather than a single 33 r.p.m. disc. "We wanted to celebrate the twelve-inch singles, pre-releases, slates", says Levene [Keith Levene, PiL's guitarist]. "With that format, you got a better bass sound"' (Simon Reynolds, *Rip It Up and Start Again: Postpunk 1978–1984* [London: Faber & Faber, 2019], 268). If the British Northern Soul scene consistently relied on 7-inch singles, then postpunk was repeatedly released on 12-inch singles (288). The fact that postpunk or New Wave often ironically refracted elements of disco has been examined by Kronengold (see Kronengold, 'Exchange Theories in Disco', 66). However, Kronengold does not take into account that the reference also happens via the 12-inch single.
162 For DJ sets, see Mark J. Butler, *Unlocking the Groove: Rhythm, Meter, and Musical Design in Electronic Dance Music* (Bloomington: Indiana University Press, 2006), 13, 20–1, 33, 49–50 and 242; Hillegonda C. Rietveld, *This Is Our House: House Music, Cultural Spaces, and Technologies* (London: Routledge, 2018), 107 and 145; Lorenz Gilli, '"Navigate Your Set": Zur Virtuosität von DJs', in *Schneller, höher, lauter: Virtuosität in populären Musiken*, ed. Thomas Phleps (Bielefeld: transcript, 2017); José Gálvez, 'On Analyzing EDM DJ Sets: Problems and Perspectives for a Sociology of Sound', in *Contemporary Popular Music Studies*, ed. Marija Dumnić Vilotijević and Ivana Medić (Wiesbaden: Springer, 2019). Micah Salkind has done a close listening of a set by house DJ Ron Hardy (Micah Salkind, *Do You Remember House? Chicago's Queer of Color Undergrounds* [New York: Oxford University Press, 2019], 78–83).
163 The deflection of the grooves is greater for low frequencies because these have to be cut into the record material at a greater level than medium frequencies in order to be perceived as equally loud. This can be explained by the so-called 'hearing threshold'. This puts pitch and volume in relation to human hearing. The hearing threshold indicates how loud a sound must be for a person to hear it. For a person with normal hearing, for example, a 3,000 Hz tone must have a sound pressure of −3 dB in order to be perceived, while a 50 Hz tone must have a sound pressure of 40 dB.
164 The linear velocity decreases from revolution to revolution of the record. The speed of the needle relative to the record surface therefore decreases as the needle approaches the run-out groove.
165 Andreas Lubich, according to Thaddeus Hermann, 'Dubplates & Mastering. Von der Festplatte aufs Vinyl (Interview mit Andreas Lubich)', *DE:BUG Magazin für Elektronische Lebensaspekte*, 20 May 2006. Available online: http://www.de-bug.de/musiktechnik/archives/179.html (accessed 12 October 2011).
166 Ibid.
167 This weighting can also be found at other levels of disco culture. For example, terms such as 'realness' or 'authenticity' were meaningless for black gay men in the early 1970s as long as these vocabularies were appropriated by a white, heterosexual image of masculinity, such as that presented in rock music (Hugh Barker and Yuval Taylor,

Faking It: The Quest for Authenticity in Popular Music [New York: W. W. Norton, 2007], 229–61).
168 Jasen, *Low End Theory*, 167.
169 Ibid., 168.
170 Brewster and Broughton then define house accordingly: 'House was disco made by amateurs' (Brewster and Broughton, *Last Night a DJ Saved My Life*, 326). They add: 'Suddenly, everybody in Chicago became a producer, eagerly pushing tapes under DJs' noses' (327). Rietveld also specifies house via the status of its producers: 'the term "house music" was used to indicate a kind of urban DIY electronic disco music' (Rietveld, *This Is Our House*, 210).
171 By the mid-1980s, a scene had developed in Chicago around electronic dance music, with specific clubs (the Warehouse, which had already opened in 1977, the Music Box, and the Power Plant), radio programmes (the broadcasts of DJ Team Hot Mix 5), record stores (Paul Weisberg's Importes Etc.), record labels (Trax, DJ International), DJs (such as Frankie Knuckles and Ron Hardy), producers and dancers (for more on this, see Salkind, *Do You Remember House?*). House then soon became an international phenomenon. Also, the first journalists were soon reporting on the 'House Sound of Chicago'; see, for example Nelson George, 'House Music: Will It Join Rap and Go-Go?' *Billboard*, 21 June 1986, 27; Sheryl Garratt, 'Sample and Hold: The House Sound of Chicago', *The Face*, September 1986; Stuart Cosgrove, 'The DJs They Couldn't Hang', *New Musical Express*, 9 August 1986, 12–15; and Barry Walters, 'Burning Down the House', *Spin*, November 1986. The label DJ International signed a distribution contract with the British label London Records. First compilation albums such as *The House Sound of Chicago* (DJ International/London, UK, 1986) were released and productions from Chicago had international success – for example, *Love Can't Turn Around* by Farley 'Jackmaster' Funk feat. Darryl Pandy entered the British charts in September 1986. The first monographs – journalistic (Jonathan Fleming, *What Kind of House Party Is This? The History of a Music Revolution* [Slough: MIY, 1995]; Chris Kempster, *History of House* [London: Music Maker, 1996]; Sean Bidder, *Pump Up the Volume. The History of House Music* [London: Channel 4 Books, 2001]), and scholarly (Rietveld, *This Is Our House*) – began to appear in the mid-1990s. On the featuring of the term 'house' at the New Music Seminar (NMS) in New York in 1986, an industry gathering, by Farley 'Jackmaster' Funk, see Salkind, *Do You Remember House?* 112–13.
172 Salkind, *Do You Remember House?* 123.
173 Jefferson, according to Sean Bidder, *Pump Up the Volume*.
174 See ibid., 25–34, and Salkind, *Do You Remember House?* 123.
175 The Chicago house label DJ International obviously placed more emphasis on mastering than the Trax label as early as the mid-1980s. Various US releases by DJ International were mastered at the Trutone Mastering Labs in Haworth, New Jersey – for example, *If You Only Knew* by Chip E. (DJ International DJ 779, United States, 1986).
176 The international breakthrough of techno came with the release of the compilation album *Techno! The New Dance Sound of Detroit* (10 Records/Virgin Records, UK, 1988). Compiled by British Northern Soul DJ Neil Rushton, the album initially ran under the working title 'The House Sound of Detroit', but was later re-titled *Techno! The New Dance Sound of Detroit* to distinguish it from Chicago house (see

Brewster and Broughton, *Last Night a DJ Saved My Life*, 354–8). The liner notes for *Techno!* were provided by the same journalist – Stuart Cosgrove – who had written the liner notes for the compilation *House Sound of Chicago* two years earlier. It is quite remarkable how stubbornly the vocabulary has survived, which Cosgrove coined for techno in his liner notes (Stuart Cosgrove, liner notes for *Techno! The New Dance Sound of Detroit* [10 Records/Virgin Records, UK, 1988]) and for *The Face* magazine (Stuart Cosgrove, 'Seventh City Techno', in: *Night Fever: Club Writing in the Face 1980–1997*, ed. Richard Benson [London: Boxtree, 1997], 93–6) as well as his journalist colleague John McCready for the *NME* with their texts. McCready describes techno as the soundtrack to the supposedly de-industrialized former industrial city of Detroit (John McCready, 'Welcome to the Phuture: Techno', *New Musical Express*, 16 July 1988). He begins with a quote about the 'Techno Rebels' from Alvin Toffler's book, *The Third Wave*. McCready identifies the Techno Rebels as Atkins, May and Saunderson, respectively, as 'musical agents of the Third Wave who see the fusion of man and machine as the only future'. Toffler refers to the Third Wave as the Information Age, which followed agricultural and industrial modes of production. Detroit, with its industrial assembly line production à la Ford and Motown, is described in the McCready article as a second wave city and dramatized as 'a discarded set from *Robocop*'. European electropop by Kraftwerk and Gary Numan, among others, emerges as musical references of the techno sound, as well as synthesizer-heavy Italo disco. Detroit techno would have a pronounced future reference, would be 'future music', whereas house would refer to 1970s US disco. In Cosgrove's texts, May, Atkins and Saunderson are also referred to as the 'Belleville 3'. All three had grown up in the middle-class suburb of Belleville and gone to the same high school there. May's famous description of techno is also found here: 'The music is just like Detroit. A complete mistake. It's like George Clinton and Kraftwerk are stuck in an elevator with only a sequencer to keep them company.' Cosgrove describes techno as a 'hybrid of post-punk, funkadelia and electro-disco' and a 'post-soul sound' (Cosgrove, 'Seventh City Techno', 93, 95). The vocabulary coined in these three articles, as well as the definitions made there, have had a significant impact on techno reception to this day. On the history of techno, see Philipp Anz and Patrick Walder, eds, *Techno* (Zürich: Bilger, 1995), and Sicko, *Techno Rebels*.

177 The UK single release – 2:50 minutes – is the shortest, the 12-inch single release – 9:45 minutes – the longest. The naming of individual releases already indicates that in the version or series there is not simply repetition, but a potential for variation or difference: Thus the production on the 12-inch single trades under the spelling 'Ten Per Cent', and on the other release under 'Ten Percent'.

178 The intro of the UK release lasts almost 40 seconds, while that of the US release is only about half as long. The outro of the US release, however, is much longer.

179 In the area of the run-out groove of the US single, the abbreviations 'F/W' can be found next to the matrix number, supplemented by an apple symbol and the letter 'M'. This abbreviation stands for the fact that the record was mastered in the Frankford-Wayne Mastering Lab in New York by the engineer Al Brown – in addition the name is carved separately.

180 Mastering studios did not compete by claiming to have their own sound. Frankford-Wayne promoted their work via the axes of volume and playing time. A 1979 advertisement of the studio states that records could be cut there with up to 50 per cent more level and with up to 30 per cent more playing time (see 'Frankford/Wayne

Mastering Labs', *Billboard*, 27 October 1979, 65). The studio's equipment included the following: 'Gerry Block's CompudiskTM Multiple Microprocessor Computer Controlled Lathe; an optimized Ortofon/Ransteele Cutterhead and 1600 Watt Driver System; MCI JH-110M programmable tape playback system; Ransteele Control Console including three separate quasi parametric/-graphic equalizer systems, digitally controlled tracking limiter/compressors, filters, level control and specialized monitor controls with four selectable pairs of professional studio monitor speakers plus more' (65). The computer control was intended to ensure optimal use of space.

181 Hillegonda C. Rietveld, 'Im Strom des Techno. 'Slow-Mix'-DJ-Stile in der Dance Music der 90er Jahre', in *Handbuch der Musik im 20. Jahrhundert, Bd. 8: Rock- und Popmusik*, ed. Peter Wicke (Laaber: Laaber, 2001), 277–8.

182 Hans T. Zeiner-Henriksen compared different bass drums in disco, house and techno; Hans T. Zeiner-Henriksen, 'Chicago House and the "Democratization" of Music Production' (paper, conference on Music and Place, Manchester Metropolitan University, Manchester, UK, 8–10 June 2006).

183 Kronengold, 'Exchange Theories in Disco', 61. Kronengold uses the standardized bass drum pattern to explore the use of conventions specific to disco: 'Four-on-the-floor remains disco's most recognizable convention. As such it can provide a useful way to examine how this genre treats its conventions. It goes without saying that different genres possess different conventions, but we should add that the uses and understandings of conventions vary across genres as well' (56).

184 Ibid., 58.
185 Ibid., 59.
186 Ibid.
187 See ibid., 74.
188 Walters, 'Burning Down', 60.
189 See Wicke, *Von Mozart zu Madonna*, 281–3.
190 See Salkind, *Do You Remember House?*, 113–14.
191 In 1986 journalist Barry Walters identified the following sources of Chicago house tunes: 'Chip E.'s "Like This" takes its bass line and title from the South Bronx's ESG club hit "Moody". Farm Boys "Move" quotes Grace Jones's "Slave to the Rhythm", Farley "Jackmaster" Funk and Jesse Saunders's "Love Can't Turn Around" is a remake of Isaac Hayes's "I Can't Turn Around", J. M. Silk's "Music Is the Key" recalls Colonel Abrams's "Music is the Answer"; and Fresh's "Dum-Dum" (which ripped off Martin Circus's "Disco Circus") and snatches long excerpts from Shelia [sic] E.'s "The Glamorous Life" and Funkadelic's "One Nation under a Groove". House records generally get their bass lines and rhythms from lengthy early disco workouts like MFSB's "Love Is the Message" and First Choice's "Let No Man Put Asunder", while their barren synth textures and Eurodisco tempos come from Italian dance records. This is music born of digital sampling devices' (Walters, 'Burning Down', 60. See also Bidder, *Pump Up the Volume*, 49–52; Tim Lawrence, Liner Notes for *Acid: Can You Jack? Chicago Acid and Experimental House 1985–95* [Soul Jazz Records, UK 2005], 22; Brewster and Broughton, *Last Night a DJ Saved My Life*, 414–15). Samples are also central to Chicago house. In the mid-1980s, the first inexpensive samplers were produced. The cheap Casio SK-1 could sample just over a second of sound material

and play it modulated in pitch over four octaves. In short, chopped-up, often syncopated vocal samples, this device left its mark on Chicago house. For a recent portrait of the Chicago house scene and its sounds, see Salkind, *Do You Remember House?* Based on archival research, oral history and a critical review of the literature, Salkind focuses on a social history of house: 'House music must be contextualized within the queer, Black, maroon spaces of the Chicago underground to understand its cultural impact and social utility' (50). By reflecting on how house is remembered, Salkind gives his book an elaborate historiographical twist.

192 Saunders, according to Bidder, *Pump Up the Volume*, 32–3. See also Brewster and Broughton, *Last Night a DJ Saved My Life*, 418.
193 See Lawrence, Liner Notes for *Acid: Can You Jack?* 33.
194 Walters, 'Burning Down', 60.
195 Ibid.
196 Otherwise, 'house' is the music that was played in the Warehouse club by Frankie Knuckles (Bidder, *Pump Up the Volume*, 21). Another DJ, Farley Keith, claims that the term 'house' did not come from the Warehouse, but was derived from the import records he mixed on the radio. He called these records 'house' records because no one in Chicago played such records but him (Walters, 'Burning Down', 62). Farley Keith was a member of the 'Hot Mix 5' as Farley 'Jackmaster' Funk. Their radio show in Chicago in the early 1980s was not only an important source for house DJs, but also played the first house tracks on the radio a little later.
197 Lawrence, Liner Notes for *Acid: Can You Jack?* 17.
198 See ibid., 34.
199 See Salkind, *Do You Remember House?* 130.
200 On Hot Mix 5, see ibid., 106–17.
201 Jones after Lawrence, Liner Notes for *Acid: Can You Jack?*, 45.
202 See Brewster and Broughton, *Last Night a DJ Saved My Life*, 412–23; Bidder, *Pump Up the Volume*, 42–5; Lawrence, Liner Notes for *Acid: Can You Jack?* 44–6.
203 See Walters, 'Burning Down', 61.
204 Salkind, *Do You Remember House?* 48–9. On cassette tape use by Ron Hardy, see 71.
205 Ibid., 74.
206 The multiple DJ sets archived on platforms such as https://www.gridface.com/ or http://deephousepage.com were recorded on tape in the 1980s. See also Salkind, *Do You Remember House?* 74–83 on close readings of Ron Hardy's mix, and 67–8 on bootleg tapes.
207 Craig Cannon, according to Salkind, *Do You Remember House?* 65–6.
208 Ibid., 67.
209 Ibid., 77.
210 The 'Belleville Three', in the relevant literature, are the techno pioneers Juan Atkins, Derrick May and Kevin Saunderson. With their productions that were released under numerous pseudonyms and micro-labels – Metroplex, Transmat, KMS – they shaped the first wave of techno.
211 Julian Weber, 'Wärme und Dynamik. Kein Detroit-Techno oder House ohne ihn: Zum Tode von Ron Murphy, dem Meister des fetischisierten Klangs', *Die Tageszeitung*, 15 January 2008. Available online: https://taz.de/Zum-Tod-von-Ron-Murphys/!5188479/ (accessed 30 April 2022).

212 See Mizie Morales, 'Dubplate Special – Detroitstory', *DE:BUG Magazin für Elektronische Lebensaspekte*, 2000. Available online: http://www.de-bug.de/musiktechnik/archives/179.html (accessed 12 October 2011).
213 See Sicko, *Techno Rebels*, 109–11.
214 Lubich, according to Hermann, 'Dubplates & Mastering'.
215 See Robert Henke, 'Mastering', *Monolake*. Available online: http://www.disco-disco.com/tributes/tom.shtml (accessed 30 April 2022).
216 Murphy, according to Sven von Thülen, 'Detroit: Ron Murphy', *DE:BUG Magazin für Elektronische Lebensaspekte*, 2006. Available online: www.de-bug.de/mag/4224.html (accessed 12 October 2011).
217 See Sicko, *Techno Rebels*, 109.
218 George Lipsitz, *Footsteps in the Dark: The Hidden Histories of Popular Music* (Minneapolis: University of Minnesota Press, 2007), 248.
219 Endless grooves can be found, for example, on *The Rings of Saturn* by X-102 (Underground Resistance, United States, 1992). So *The Rings of Saturn* is not an arbitrary name for a record in this case. For various 'rings' can be found as loops on both records of the release. The A-side of Jeff Mills's *Cycle 30* (Axis AX-008, United States, 1994) even contains eight loops. A loop on a 12-inch single spinning at 33 1/3 rpm must have a tempo of 133 beats per minute to run smoothly.
220 *Funky Funk Funk/Bassline* (Network Records NWKT 23, UK, 1991) by Reese was mastered by Ron Murphy and runs inside out.
221 *Hidden in Plainsight EP* by Suburban Knight feat. Dark Energy and Chameleon (Underground Resistance UR-050, United States, 1999) has a double groove on the B-side. This side contains two tracks; they are not arranged one after the other on the vinyl, but run parallel to each other. On the record this procedure, which can already be found in the late 1970s – for example, on the 12-inch single *Pop Muzik* by M Factor (MCA Records 0900.138, DEU 1979) – is somewhat hypertrophically advertised as 'NSC-x2 Groove Technology'.
222 Eshun, *More Brilliant Than the Sun*, 132–3.
223 Ibid., 133.
224 Sicko, *Techno Rebels*, 110.
225 Weber, 'Wärme und Dynamik'.
226 The Neumann company, currently known almost exclusively as a manufacturer of microphones, developed record cutting machines from the 1920s until the early 1980s (see Sommer, 'Die Georg Neumann GmbH'). Neumann integrated various technological innovations into its machines: in the mid-1950s, for example, record cutting with variable feed was introduced, which significantly extended the playing time of the record. Also in the mid-1950s, Neumann developed stereo cutting heads. In the early 1980s, a system was introduced that could cut signals in copper foils. Here Neumann implemented the Direct Metal Mastering (DMM) technique introduced by Teldec. In 1993, Neumann discontinued the manufacture of record cutting machines due to lack of demand.
227 See Morales, 'Dubplate Special'; Tim Langham, 'National Sound Corporation: Ron Murphy', *Massive Mag*, 2008. Available online: http://massivemag.com/issue-20/national-sound-corporation-ronmurphy-issue-20.html (accessed 12 October 2011).
228 See von Thülen, 'Detroit'.
229 See May, 'Techno'.

230 Murphy, according to Morales, 'Dubplate Special'.
231 See Simon Reynolds, *Energy Flash: A Journey through Rave Music and Dance Culture* (London: Faber & Faber, 2013), 122–3.

5 Sound system listening: Histories, enhanced disco sound, listening techniques

1 On the Trips Festival and Buchla's PA system, see Trevor Pinch and Frank Trocco, *Analog Days: The Invention and Impact of the Moog Synthesizer* (Cambridge, MA: Harvard University Press, 2002), 94–9. On Woodstock's sound system, see Sergio Pisfil, 'Woodstock and the Live Sound Industry in the Late 1960s', *Popular Music and Society* 43, no. 2 (2020): 176–87. On the Internationale Essener Songtage, see Detlef Mahnert and Harry Stürmer, *Zappa, Zoff und Zwischentöne: Die internationalen Essener Songtage 1968* (Essen: Klartext, 2008); Siegfried, *Time Is on My Side*, 601–23. On the Isle of Wight Festival, see Simon Frith, Matt Brennan, Martin Cloonan and Emma Webster, *The History of Live Music in Britain, Volume II, 1968–1984. From Hyde Park to Hacienda* (Milton Park: Routledge, 2020).
2 See Veal, *Dub*; Henriques, *Sonic Bodies*.
3 Florian Gasser, 'Funktion-One: "Sound Doesn't Exist, Only the Truth"', *Groove*. Available online: https://groove.de/2017/05/29/funktion-one-tony-andrews-interview-english/2/ (accessed 30 April 2022).
4 See Ralf Gerhard Ehlert, 'Public-Address-Strategien von 1919 bis 1949', in *Politiken der Medien*, ed. Daniel Gethmann and Markus Stauff (Zurich: Diaphanes, 2005); John Kane, *The Last Seat in the House: The Story of Hanley Sound* (Jackson: University Press of Mississippi, 2020), 3–4.
5 Kerins, *Beyond Dolby (Stereo)*, 329–30. On loudspeaker systems for early sound films in the United States, see Frank H. Lovette and Stanley Watkins, 'Twenty Years of Talking Movies: An Anniversary', *Bell Telephone Magazine* 1946, and for Germany, see Günther Herkt, *Das Tonfilmtheater: Umbau, Neubau, Tongerät, Betrieb, Vorführung, Wirtschaftlichkeit* (Berlin: Deutsche Bauzeitung, 1931).
6 Jan-Friedrich Missfelder, 'Verstärker: Hören und Herrschen bei Francis Bacon und Athanasius Kircher 2016', in *Senseability: Mediale Praktiken des Sehens und Hörens*, ed. Beate Ochsner and Robert Stock (Bielefeld: transcript, 2016), 67.
7 Ibid.
8 See Kittler, 'World-Breath', 134. See also Chapter 1, section 'What Is a Sound and Music History of Listening Devices?'.
9 See Alexander Rehding, *Music and Monumentality: Commemoration and Wonderment in Nineteenth Century Germany* (New York: Oxford University Press, 2009).
10 See Timothy Hecker, 'The Era of Megaphonics: On the Productivity of Loud Sound, 1880–1930', PhD dissertation, Department of Art History and Communication Studies, McGill University, Montreal, 2014.
11 See Roland Wittje, 'The Electrical Imagination: Sound Analogies, Equivalent Circuits, and the Rise of Electroacoustics, 1863–1939', *Osiris* 28, no. 1 (2013): 40–63.
12 Walter Salmen, *Das Konzert: Eine Kulturgeschichte* (Munich: Beck, 1988), 183.
13 Ibid., 192.
14 Ziemer, 'The Crisis of Listening in Interwar Germany', 274.

15 See Salmen, *Das Konzert*; Wicke, *Von Mozart zu Madonna*; Derek B. Scott, *Sounds of the Metropolis: The Nineteenth-Century Popular Music Revolution in London, New York, Paris, and Vienna* (New York: Oxford University Press, 2001), 15–21 and 38–57. The steadily growing body of research on the theory and history of the concert has mostly taken little notice of sound amplification systems: Martin Tröndle, ed., *Das Konzert II: Beiträge zum Forschungsfeld der Concert Studies* (Bielefeld: transcript, 2018). Whether because they were not considered an integral part of the concept of music underlying this research, or because they were simply classified as a necessary instrumental means for mass distribution.

16 Challenged by another, the boom of the concert industry in the field of popular music that began in the late 1990s, Binas-Preisendörfer notes: 'Yet the history of (popular) music knows a never-ending fascination with the live concert as an important site of realisation of music: a promise of the unique and the singular, the fact of being live, the proximity to the artist, musician, whether in stuffy basement clubs, youth recreation centres, concert halls of all sizes, or at open air festivals' (Susanne Binas-Preisendörfer, '"Live Is Life". Faszination und Konjunktur des Popkonzerts, oder Überlegungen zur Performativität medienvermittelter musikkultureller Praktiken', in *Populäre Musik, mediale Musik? Transdisziplinäre Beiträge zu den Medien der populären Musik*, ed. Christopher Jost, Daniel Klug, Klaus Neumann-Braun and Axel Schmidt [Baden-Baden: Nomos, 2011], 131). A sound and media history of the concert, however, is found in Binas-Preisendörfer at best in rudimentary form in references to 'presence-enhancing media such as microphones, live mixing, PA, etc.' (137). Other discussions of the popular concert have a sociological-empirical orientation and examine, for example, audience typologies: Roland Hafen, 'Rockmusik-Rezeption in Live-Konzerten', in *Handbuch Jugend und Musik*, ed. Dieter Baacke (Opladen: Leske + Budrich, 1997) and Christoph Kalies, Andreas C. Lehmann and Reinhard Kopiez, 'Musikleben und Live-Musik', in *Musikpsychologie: Das neue Handbuch*, ed. Herbert Bruhn, Reinhard Kopiez and Andreas C. Lehmann (Reinbek bei Hamburg: Rowohlt, 2008); create concert typologies, give systematic overviews of functions that the concert fulfils for audiences: Martin Pfleiderer, 'Live-Veranstaltungen von populärer Musik und ihre Rezeption', in *Musikrezeption, Musikdistribution und Musikproduktion. Der Wandel des Wertschöpfungsnetzwerks in der Musikwirtschaft*, ed. Gerhard Gensch, Eva Maria Sröckler and Peter Tschmuck (Wiesbaden: Gabler, 2008); or examine the staging of star identity: Christian Jooß-Bernau, *Das Pop-Konzert als para-theatrale Form: Seine Varianten und seine Bedingungen im kulturell-öffentlichen Raum* (Berlin: de Gruyter, 2010). On performance in popular music, see fundamentally Philip Auslander, *Liveness: Performance in a Mediatized Culture* (London: Routledge, 2008), and also the anthology Dietrich Helms and Thomas Phleps, eds, *Ware Inszenierungen: Performance, Vermarktung und Authentizität in der populären Musik* (Bielefeld: transcript, 2013). On the history of live music in the UK, see Simon Frith, Matt Brennan, Martin Cloonan and Emma Webster, eds, *The History of Live Music in Britain, Volume I: 1950–1967: From Dance Hall to the 100 Club* (London: Routledge, 2013). In Hanns-Werner Heister's extensive study of the bourgeois concert, aspects of a media history of the concert certainly play a role: Hanns-Werner Heister, *Das Konzert: Theorie einer Kulturform* (Wilhelmshaven: Heinrichshofen, 1983). For example, Heister thinks of the 'invisible orchestra' in Bayreuth and the 'invisible orchestra' of the Edison phonograph together (510). Research on concerts in the field

of electronic music also addresses points of contact between the history of sound and the history of technology. Here, however, loud sounds play at best a subordinate role. For a critique of the concept 'loudspeaker concert', see Rolf Großmann, 'Verschlafener Medienwandel: Das Dispositiv als musikwissenschaftliches Theoriemodell', *Positionen: Beiträge zur Neuen Musik* 74 (2008). On the performance institutions of popular live music, see Fabian Holt, *Everyone Loves Live Music: A Theory of Performance Institutions* (Chicago, IL: University of Chicago Press, 2020).
17 See Auslander, *Liveness*, and also Großmann, 'Verschlafener Medienwandel'.
18 Auslander, *Liveness*.
19 Roy Shuker, *Popular Music Culture: The Key Concepts* (London: Routledge, 2012), 201, 247–8.
20 See Peter Doyle, 'Ghosts of Electricity: Amplification', in *The Sage Handbook of Popular Music*, ed. Andy Bennett and Steve Waksman (Los Angeles, CA: Sage, 2015).
21 Templates for a sound history of spaces are more likely to be found in the context of theatre history and the history of science: see, for example, Viktoria Tkaczyk, 'Listening in Circles: Spoken Drama and the Architects of Sound, 1750–1830', *Annals of Science* 71, no. 3 (2014): 299–334, and the research project 'The Acoustics of Historical Performance Spaces for Music and Theater' at the TU Berlin.
22 Stefan Helmreich, 'Transduction', in *Keywords in Sound*, ed. David Novak and Matt Sakakeeny (Durham, NC: Duke University Press, 2015).
23 Doyle, 'Ghosts of Electricity', 544. 'Torsion' is understood by Doyle here in the sense of 'cranking' (534), that is, in the sense of cranking or turning up the volume.
24 Steve Wurtzler, *Electric Sounds: Technological Change and the Rise of Corporate Mass Media* (New York: Columbia University Press, 2007).
25 We should note here that electron tubes already existed in the late nineteenth century. However, these could not be used to amplify electric current. Since 1948, the tube has been largely replaced by the transistor. On the history of electroacoustics, see Wittje, 'The Electrical Imagination'. From a media history perspective, we can point out that the history of electroacoustics or electrification of sound includes both concrete media technologies (electromagnetic telegraphs, telephones, radios), and electrical devices for measuring sound and even an 'electrical' conceptualization of sound. Physicists such as James Clark Maxwell (1831–79), Heinrich Hertz (1857–94) and Baron Rayleigh (1842–1919), Wittje argues, analogised sound and electricity so that electrical oscillations could be modelled by acoustic vibrations. Accordingly, Wittje has pointed out, electroacoustics began with a 'new electrical understanding of sound' (40). This new understanding operated with analogies of electrical and acoustic phenomena or with circuit diagrams that indicated functional relationships. The term 'electroacoustics' appeared in Germany around 1900, when a mechanical worldview had been replaced by an electromagnetic one (44). Wittje argues that electroacoustics was oriented on different sound events than nineteenth century acoustics: 'Precisely this work in electricity in the decade prior to the Great War made the rapid development and application of artillery ranging, submarine detection, wireless telephony, and other electroacoustic technologies for warfare possible. At the same time, the tradition of nineteenth-century acoustics, which was deeply rooted in the study of classical music and musical instruments, seems to have stagnated' (44).
26 Ibid., 41.
27 Wurtzler, *Electric Sounds*, 4.
28 Lovette and Watkins, 'Twenty Years of Talking Movies', 82.

29 Joseph P. Maxfield and Henry C. Harrison, 'Methods of High Quality Recording and Reproducing of Music and Speech Based on Telephone Research', *The Bell System Technical Journal* 5, no. 3 (1926): 493–523.
30 Wittje, 'The Electrical Imagination', 48.
31 On the development of the electrification of sound recording at Bell Labs under Joseph P. Maxfield and in other companies and research institutions since 1919, see Horning, *Chasing Sound*, 34–7. In addition to a condenser microphone, a tube amplifier and an electromagnetically driven cutting head, Maxfield and his colleague Henry C. Harrison integrated two other new components into their system: 'a volume indicator for measuring the power delivered to the recorder and an audible monitoring system, enabling the operator to listen during recording' (36). Western Electric presented its method for the electrical recording and playback of records to the record companies Columbia and RCA Victor in 1924; in 1925, both of them licensed the new process (see Lovette and Watkins, 'Twenty Years of Talking Movies', 94) and RCA Victor launched an electrified record player, the Orthophonic Victrola.
32 See Wurtzler, *Electric Sounds*.
33 Karl-Heinz Göttert, *Geschichte der Stimme* (Munich: Fink, 1998), 423, emphasis in original.
34 Ibid., 524–5.
35 C. W. Kollatz, 'Sprachverstärkung für Massenansprachen', *Funk-Anzeiger. Zeitschrift für die gesamte drahtlose Fermeldetechnik* 3, no. 29 (1925): 343–4.
36 'Lautsprecher der Western Electric Co.', *Elektrotechnische Zeitschrift* 38 (1920), 758–9. See also Göttert, *Geschichte der Stimme*, 423, and Ralf Gerhard Ehlert, '1920, Western Electric: Erste kommerzielle Public-Address-Anlage angekündigt', *Medienstimmen*; available online: https://www.medienstimmen.de/chronik/1911-1920/1920-western-electric-erste-kommerzielle-public-address-anlage-angekuendigt/ (accessed 30 April 2022).
37 Göttert, *Geschichte der Stimme*, 427.
38 Ibid., 428.
39 Ibid.
40 Hans Gerdien, 'Über klanggetreue Schallwiedergabe mittels Lautsprecher', *Telefunken Zeitung* 8, no. 43 (1926).
41 Friedrich A. Kittler, 'Echoes: Ein Prolog', in *Hörstürze: Akustik und Gewalt im 20. Jahrhundert*, ed. Nicola Gess, Florian Schreiner and Manuela K. Schulz (Würzburg: Königshausen & Neumann, 2005), 23.
42 Ibid.
43 Ibid.
44 Ibid., 13.
45 Gerdien, 'Über klanggetreue Schallwiedergabe'.
46 See Ehlert, 'Public-Address-Strategien', 325.
47 Ferdinand Trendelenburg claims that Riegger and Rice and Kellogg invented the electrodynamic loudspeaker in parallel; Chester W. Rice and Edward W. Kellogg, 'Notes on the Development of a New Type of Hornless Loud Speaker', *Transactions of the AIEE* 44 (1925): 461–80. The vibrating surface of Rice and Kellogg, who worked for General Electric, is a cone and Riegger's is a square surface; see Ferdinand Trendelenburg, 'Über Bau und Anwendung von Großlautsprechern', *Elektrotechnische Zeitschrift* 48, no. 46 (1927): 1688. Trendelenburg also mentions the Hewlett

loudspeaker, the Siemens ribbon loudspeaker, the Marconi loudspeaker and the Pathé loudspeaker.
48 Ferdinand Trendelenburg, *Einführung in die Akustik* (Berlin: Springer, 1939), 124.
49 Florian Schreiner, 'Laut – Ton – Stärke', PhD dissertation, Philosophische Fakultät III, Humboldt University of Berlin, Berlin, 2009, 218–23.
50 On this collaboration, see also Robert E. McGuinn, 'Stokowski and the Bell Telephone Laboratories: Collaboration in the Development of High-Fidelity Sound Reproduction', *Technology and Culture* 24, no. 1 (1983). Listening devices were already activated by filters as early as the mid-1920s in the wake of the electrification of sound recording. Bell Labs presented its system for the electrification of sound recording as part of several major semi-public events, amplifying recordings made with the system over a large speaker system. The acoustic department of Bell Labs worked with conductor Leopold Stokowski from 1930 to 1940 to test, develop and publicize the electrified recording system (McGuinn, 'Stokowski and the Bell Telephone Laboratories'; Milner, Perfecting Sound Forever, 50–73). For example, on 9 and 10 April 1940, Bell Labs presented not reproduced music, but rather 'enhanced music' in the form of a 'colossal record release party' at New York's Carnegie Hall (Milner, *Perfecting Sound Forever*, 50). At this presentation, Bell Labs recordings of the Philadelphia Orchestra conducted by Leopold Stokowski, among others, were played to a large audience over loudspeakers. Here, the loudspeaker system did not simply reproduce the sound of a performance, it was also intended to optimize it. Bell's and Stokowski's 'enhanced music' was intended to be 'actually louder – and in some cases softer – than life' (50). The technologies through which the recordings were heard in Carnegie Hall were sonically activated for this purpose and were operated by Stokowski himself: 'As the conductor listened, he made volume and tonal changes by using the electric controls, and simultaneously a new stereophonic record was made of the music as thus "enhanced"' (McGuinn, 'Stokowski and the Bell Telephone Laboratories', 64). Here, then, filters were in use through which a listening technology was activated and a form of 'enhanced music' was produced. This footnote is an adapted translation from Jens Gerrit Papenburg, 'Enhanced Sound. Filter der Musikproduktion und des Musikhörens', *Navigationen: Zeitschrift für Medien- und Kulturwissenschaften* 20, no. 2 (2020): 123–4. On Stokowski enhanced recordings, see also Gascia Ouzounian, *Stereophonica: Sound and Space in Science, Technology, and the Arts* (Cambridge, MA: MIT Press, 2021), 77–81. In view of the 'tone controls' and 'loudness' buttons that had been integrated into listening devices since the 1940s and 1950s, Glenn Gould was already thinking about the 'participational possibilities' of the listeners in the mid-1960s.
51 Albert Glinsky, *Theremin: Ether Music and Espionage* (Urbana: University of Illinois Press, 2005), 88.
52 On this form of music and the electric orchestra at the 1933 Radio Exhibition, see Peter Donhauser, *Elektrische Klangmaschinen: Die Pionierzeit in Deutschland und Österreich* (Vienna: Böhlau, 2007), 111–18.
53 Wicke, 'Soundtechnologien und Körpermetamorphosen, 35.
54 However, Wicke diagnoses this integration only for the 1950s.
55 Thompson, *The Soundscape of Modernity*; Ehlert, 'Public-Address-Strategien'; Cornelia Epping-Jäger, 'Stimmräume: Die phono-zentrische Organisation der Macht im NS', in *Politiken der Medien*, ed. Daniel Gethmann and Markus Stauff (Zurich: Diaphanes, 2005); Schreiner, 'Laut – Ton – Stärke'; Henriques, *Sonic*

Bodies, 39–62; Kyle Devine, 'A Mysterious Music in the Air: Cultural Origins of the Loudspeaker', *Popular Music History* 8, no. 1 (2013): 5–28; Jos Mulder, 'Making Things Louder: Amplified Music and Multimodality', PhD dissertation, University of Technology Sydney, 2013; Marta Herford, ed., *Booster: Kunst, Sound, Maschine* (Berlin: Kerber, 2014); Doyle, 'Ghosts of Electricity'; Pisfil, 'Woodstock'; Kane, *The Last Seat in the House*; Roland Wittje, 'Large Sound Amplification Systems in Interwar Germany: Siemens and Telefunken', *Sound & Science: Digital Histories*. Available online: https://soundandscience.de/contributor-essays/large-sound-amplification-systems-interwar-germany-siemens-and-telefunken (accessed 30 April 2022); Jens Gerrit Papenburg, 'Pleasure and Pain with Amplified Sound: A Sound and Music History of Loudspeaker Systems in Germany, ca. 1930' in *Techniques of Hearing: History, Theory and Practices*, ed. Michael Schillmeier, Beate Ochsner and Robert Stock (London: Routledge, 2022), 36–46.

56   Devine, 'A Mysterious Music in the Air', 7, 20.
57   Ibid., 5.
58   Ibid., 20.
59   Ibid.
60   Ibid.
61   Papenburg, 'Pleasure and Pain with Amplified Sound'.
62   Thompson, *The Soundscape of Modernity*, 229–35.
63   Doyle, 'Ghosts of Electricity', 536.
64   Ibid., 535–6.
65   Thompson, *The Soundscape of Modernity*, 231.
66   Ibid., 233–5.
67   On the Eastman Theatre see ibid., 249–52, on the Hollywood Bowl see ibid., 254–6. On the Hollywood Bowl, see also Kenneth H. Marcus: *Musical Metropolis: Los Angeles and the Creation of a Music Culture, 1880–1940* (New York: Palgrave Macmillan, 2004), 65–86; J. Christopher Jaffe, *Acoustics of Performance Halls: Spaces for Music from Carnegie Hall to the Hollywood Bowl* (New York: W. W. Norton, 2007), 118.
68   Thompson, *The Soundscape of Modernity*, 248.
69   Gerdien, 'Über klanggetreue Schallwiedergabe', 36.
70   Correll, according to Wolfgang Mühl-Benninghaus, *Das Ringen um den Tonfilm: Strategien der Elektro- und der Filmindustrie in den 20er und 30er Jahren* (Dusseldorf: Droste, 1999), 202.
71   See Devine, 'A Mysterious Music in the Air', 17.
72   Doyle, 'Ghosts of Electricity', 543.
73   Mühl-Benninghaus, *Das Ringen um den Tonfilm*, 201.
74   Devine, 'A Mysterious Music in the Air', 17.
75   On the aforementioned conflict, see Karin Bijsterveld, *Mechanical Sound: Technology, Culture, and Public Problems of Noise in the Twentieth Century* (Cambridge, MA: MIT Press, 2008).
76   Donhauser, *Elektrische Klangmaschinen*, 157.
77   Devine, 'A Mysterious Music in the Air', 14.
78   See Epping-Jäger, 'Stimmräume'; Carolyn Birdsall, *Nazi-Soundscapes: Sound, Technology, and Urban Space in Germany, 1933–1945* (Amsterdam: Amsterdam University Press, 2012); Papenburg, 'Pleasure and Pain with Amplified Sound'.
79   However, Pisfil also concludes that the 'history of live sound and its connections to popular music has yet to be written' (Pisfil, 'Woodstock', 186).

80 Both in the music arena and in the historiography of popular music sound system, designers have so far received at best only marginal attention: 'Sound engineers and production crews are often the forgotten people of the music arena, although they are usually the first and last to leave the venue, breaking their backs setting up and striking heavy equipment' (Kane, *The Last Seat in the House*, 9).
81 Ibid., 67–83.
82 Ibid., 133–5.
83 Ibid., 187–94.
84 Ibid., 280–92.
85 Ibid., 322–7.
86 Ibid., 447.
87 Ibid., 447–8.
88 Wicke, 'Soundtechnologien und Körpermetamorphosen', 35.
89 Ibid.
90 Paul Théberge, 'Amplifier', in *Continuum Encyclopedia of Popular Music of the World. Volume I. Media, Industry and Society*, ed. John Shepherd, David Horn, Dave Laing, Paul Oliver and Peter Wicke (London: Continuum, 2003), 506.
91 The Azimuth Coordinator System was 'a quadraphonic mixing and control system that Pink Floyd had developed for the live realization of their sophisticated sound dramaturgies' (Wicke, 'Soundtechnologien und Körpermetamorphosen', 37). Among other things, with this technology they had 'the technical conditions of the studio at their disposal on stage' (37). Kittler describes this dramatically: 'As the name indicates, the Azimuth Coordinator is a system that enables one to bring sonic events – tracks and layers within the mass of sound – directly to the listener's ear at will and in variable positions within all three dimensions of space. "Brain Damage" sings the device's praises' (Friedrich A. Kittler, 'The God of the Ears', in *The Truth of the Technological World: Essays on the Genealogy of Presence*, ed. Hans Ulrich Gumbrecht, trans. Erik Butler [Stanford, CA: Stanford University Press, 2014], 49). According to Kittler, the song 'Brain Damage' (on the Pink Floyd album *The Dark Side of the Moon* [Harvest, UK, 1973]) successively opens up three different spaces: a mono-space, a stereo space and finally even the head as a listening space – a sound event is placed in the head.
92 Tom Wolfe, *The Electric Kool-Aid Acid Test* (New York: Picador, 2008), 263.
93 See Robin James, ed., *Cassette Mythos* (New York: Autonomedia, 1992).
94 See Thornton, *Club Cultures*, 76–85.
95 Ibid., 58.
96 Veal, *Dub*, 5.
97 Ibid., 42.
98 Ibid.
99 Mikey Dread, according to ibid., 85–6.
100 Sound systems emerged in the 1970s in the United States and England not only in the context of reggae and dub. Both in the disco scene with its clubs in Manhattan and in the hip hop scene with its block parties in the Bronx, practices can be found in the 1970s, such as the mixing of records by DJs or the playing of records on powerful equipment, which are also found in the 'sound system' culture of Jamaica. Points of contact between these scenes have only been referred to selectively, and the areas of contact have hardly been explored at all.
101 Henriques, 'Sonic Dominance', 458.

102 Ibid., 451.
103 That in discos and clubs the senses were transformed not only technologically but also chemically has been emphasized and investigated by various authors; see, for example, Anz und Walder, Techno; Gilbert and Pearson, *Discographies*; Lawrence, *Love Saves the Day*.
104 Raulff, 'Disco', 59, emphasis in original.
105 Jens Schröter, Gregor Schwering, Dominik Maeder und Till A. Heilmann, eds, *Ambient: Ästhetik des Hintergrunds* (Wiesbaden: Springer, 2018).
106 Brian Eno liner notes for Brian Eno, *Ambient 1: Music for Airports* (EG, UK, 1979).
107 In disco and club culture, we can find a discussion about the positioning of the DJ and the difference between stage and DJ booth. In addition, the debate on the question of whether the DJ booth is more central than the dance floor in these places or vice versa.
108 Gilbert and Pearson, *Discographies*, 132.
109 Howes, 'General Introduction', 10.
110 Ibid., 7–12.
111 See Lawrence, 'In Defence of Disco (Again)'.
112 On the parallelization of Studio 54 and Las Vegas, see also Gilbert and Pearson, *Discographies*, 136–7.
113 Lawrence, 'In Defence of Disco (Again)', 130.
114 Sterne, *The Audible Past*, 15.
115 Henriques, 'Sonic Dominance'.
116 On occidental visualism, see Howes, 'General Introduction', 5. Paraphrasing Steve Goodman, we can note that the sound system as an apparatus for producing sonic dominance becomes an 'unsound system' that rearranges the senses via a bass materialism (see Goodman, *Sonic Warfare*, 27–9). The concept of sonic dominance was also taken up in further research on electronic dance music; see Jasen, *Low End Theory*, 98–9.
117 Henriques, *Sonic Bodies*, xv.
118 On the Warehouse, see Salkind, *Do You Remember House?*, 51–68.
119 DJ Frankie Knuckles, according to Brewster and Broughton, *Last Night a DJ Saved My Life*, 313.
120 Mike Winston, according to Salkind, *Do You Remember House?*, 47.
121 Gilbert and Pearson, *Discographies*, 136. However, Gilbert and Pearson also point out that there were clubs which were notorious for their bad sound, but nevertheless managed to achieve cultural relevance; for example, the Hacienda in Manchester (136). The sound system at the Ministry of Sound was built by employees of the sound system designer Richard Long: 'The main room at Ministry of Sound, you could almost land a plane in it, it's completely soundproofed, you can't hear it outside the room and it contains six twenty-two-foot high speaker stacks, each of which has probably got three or four hundred components in it. There's meteorological sensors in the ceiling which measure temperature, and adjust the sound all the way through the night, making sure it's at those perfect levels. It's sort of become a Disneyland attraction for clubbers' (Rodol, according to Bidder, *Pump Up the Volume*, 233–4.
122 Transcribed at 61:00 from *SubBerlin. The Story of Tresor* (directed by Tilmann Künzel, Germany, 2008).

123 'Pure or "Enhanced" Sound Spurs Sparks', *Billboard*, 11 August 1979, 40, 53. See also George Kopp, 'Sound Systems: Sound Experts Sound Off'. *Billboard*, 16 August 1980, 53.
124 This and the following paragraph are adapted from Papenburg, 'Enhanced Bass'.
125 See Lawrence, *Love Saves the Day*, 88–90.
126 'Pure or "Enhanced"', 40.
127 Ibid.
128 'Interview: The Loft Founder David Mancuso', *Red Bull Music Academy*. Available online: https://daily.redbullmusicacademy.com/2016/06/david-mancuso-interview (accessed 30 April 2022).
129 Ibid.
130 This paragraph is adopted and adapted from Papenburg, 'Enhanced Bass'. Rosner himself relied on transparency and liked to demonstrate this with the model of five glass panes placed one behind the other, which stand for sound carrier, player, preamp, amplifier, loudspeaker and room, and mediate between sound carrier and listener. If only one of the five components or glass panes is fogged, the quality of the entire system suffers (see 'Alex Rosner', *Red Bull Music Academy*. Available online: https://www.redbullmusicacademy.com/lectures/alex-rosner-systematic-sound [accessed 30 April 2022]).
131 Rosner, 'Overview of Disco Sound Systems', 584. Sound systems were not only built for discos, of course – otherwise Rosner would not have founded his company back in 1967. Sound systems for theatres, stadiums, cinemas, hotels, concert halls, churches, congress and exhibition halls, for example, preceded disco systems. Nevertheless, the disco sound systems – as I try to show in this second part of the chapter – have specificity. By the end of the 1970s, Rosner had built, developed and maintained more than 300 sound systems in discos (577); for all the sound systems that Rosner's company installed, see https://www.rosnercustomsound.com (accessed 30 April 2022).
132 These sound systems were reference systems not only for disco culture, but also for the hip hop culture that was developing in parallel in the Bronx: 'Part of the team that built the Zulu Nation sound system, [Africa] Islam made the Garage his primary reference point, acknowledging that "a lot of the stuff we copied came from Richard Long"' (Tim Lawrence, *Life and Death on the New York Dance Floor, 1980–1983* [Durham, NC: Duke University Press, 2016], 285).
133 Tim Lawrence, 'Loves Saves the Day. David Mancuso and the Loft'. Available online: https://static1.squarespace.com/static/519f4158e4b046d94a96e72e/t/52c8bc14e4b0df7dc79d5324/1388887060501/Loft-Placed-2007.pdf (accessed 30 April 2022). Mancuso's system was apparently a point of reference for other sound systems for a long time (91).
134 The Paradise Garage opened in 1977. Attempts had already been made to establish a disco in the building before. However, this had failed, probably also because of the extremely poor room acoustics. For the Paradise Garage, the space (20,000 square feet) was divided into several smaller ones, including a room with a dance floor (5,000 square feet) and a smaller lounge (2,000 square feet). Before the entire Paradise Garage was opened, smaller 'construction parties' were held in the lounge, which were also used to finance the remodelling of the entire club; see Alan Fierstein and Richard Long, 'State-of-the-Art Discotheque

Sound Systems: System Design and Acoustical Measurement' (paper, 67th AES Convention, New York, 31 October–3 November 1980), 1. On the Paradise Garage, see also Cheren, *Keep on Dancin'*.

135 For example, Mancuso, Long and Rosner were very enthusiastic about Paul Klipsch loudspeakers (see Colleen Murphy, 'David Mancuso hat uns gelehrt, dass Selbstlosigkeit der ultimative Akt der Rebellion ist', *Vice*. Available online: https://www.vice.com/de/article/bma5dw/david-mancuso-hat-uns-gelehrt-dass-selbstlosigkeit-der-ultimative-akt-der-rebellion-ist [accessed 30 April 2022]). From 1960, the loudspeaker manufacturer Paul Wilbur Klipsch published information sheets which addressed hi-fi fans and were dedicated to topics like 'Room Acoustics and Supplement', 'Distortion', 'False Corners' or 'Live Music'.

136 See Diedrich Diederichsen, 'Musikalische Stationen der Gegenkultur', in *The Whole Earth: Kalifornien und das Verschwinden des Außen*, ed. Diedrich Diederichsen and Anselm Franke (Berlin: Sternberg Press, 2013) 189. On Mancuso and Leary, see Lawrence, 'Loves Saves the Day'.

137 Timothy Leary, Richard Alpert and Ralph Metzner, *The Psychedelic Experience: A Manual Based on the Tibetan Book of the Dead* (New York: Citadel Press, 2017).

138 See Sven Reichardt, *Authentizität und Gemeinschaft. Linksalternatives Leben in den siebziger und frühen achtziger Jahren* (Berlin: Suhrkamp, 2014), 650, 693, and in general 629–720.

139 'Paul W. Klipsch'. Available online: https://www.klipsch.com/founder (accessed 30 April 2022).

140 Anderson, *Making Easy Listening*, 125 and 151–78. See also Chapter 2, section, 'Developing the Single and the LP Based on Musical Forms and Listening Practices in the 1940s'.

141 Keightley, '"Turn It Down!" She Shrieked', 149–77, and, once again, see also Chapter 2, section, 'Developing the Single and the LP Based on Musical Forms and Listening Practices in the 1940s'.

142 Siano, according to Andy Beta ('Magic Touch: Richard Long's Life-Changing Soundsystems', *Red Bull Music Academy*. Available online: https://daily.redbullmusicacademy.com/2016/05/richard-long-feature [accessed 30 April 2022]).

143 On the opening and the first year of the Paradise Garage, see Cheren, *Keep on Dancing*, 197–224. Michael Brody – for a time Mel Cheren's partner – opened the Paradise Garage. Cheren also used the club to test planned releases of his label West End Records.

144 Lawrence, *Love Saves the Day*, 357.

145 Carpenter according to Beta, 'Magic Touch'.

146 See Lawrence, *Love Saves the Day*, 7, 12, 88–91.

147 Ibid., 133–4. This showroom soon aroused the anger of the neighbours. Richard Long was unable to appease them, even with his generous methods: 'Richard told them [the neighbours] that he was showing the sound systems that he built and offered them money to go and stay in hotels' (Lord, according to Lawrence, *Love Saves the Day*, 134). Long's SoHo Place had to close again by the end of 1975 (196).

148 See Bidder, *Pump Up the Volume*, 10 and 16; Lawrence, *Love Saves the Day*, 345; Salkind, *Do You Remember House?*, 56–7.

149 See Brewster and Broughton, *Last Night a DJ Saved My Life*, 360.

150 See Lawrence, *Love Saves the Day*, 7.

151 Long's company was founded as 'Disco Sound Associates' and was renamed 'Richard Long and Associates' in 1977, see 'Reorganization for N.Y. Sound Firm', *Billboard*, 30 April 1977, 88.
152 The disco forums of *Billboard* also had their own panels then, where the forum was recruited exclusively from designers of sound systems; see 'Pure or "Enhanced"' and Kopp, 'Sound Systems'.
153 See Lawrence, *Love Saves the Day*, 89.
154 Rosner, 'Overview of Disco', 576.
155 Ibid., 578. The crossover that drives these loudspeakers can start at about 6 kHz.
156 See Lawrence, *Love Saves the Day*, 89.
157 Transcribed at 7:40 from 'Alex Rosner: Shaping the Sound of New York'. Available online: https://www.youtube.com/watch?v=Nv8mju2-gHI&t=0s (accessed 30 April 2022).
158 Lawrence, *Love Saves the Day*, 90.
159 Lawrence notes that Mancuso's system had long been a point of reference for other sound systems (see ibid., 91).
160 This paragraph is translated, adopted and adapted from Papenburg, '"A Great Idea after the Fact"', 179–98.
161 Beta, 'Magic Touch'.
162 DePino, according to Bidder, *Pump Up the Volume*, 10.
163 Knuckles, according to Kai Fikentscher, *'You Better Work!' Underground Dance Music in New York City* (Middletown: Wesleyan University Press, 2000), 85.
164 Kerins, *Beyond Dolby (Stereo)*, 30.
165 Ibid., 29, emphasis in original. Mark Kerins assumes that the Sensurround system was ultimately relatively unsuccessful precisely because it did not create an 'immersive' film experience, but rather ensured that the audience paid increased attention to the cinema space: 'Most audiences experiencing Sensurround would have been paying more attention (not less) to the space of the theater as they enjoyed the ride-like Sensurround rumblings' (157).
166 From the manual of Sensurround: 'Early in the project it was realized that none of the existing standard film recording techniques could effectively record and reproduce frequencies below 40HZ, the frequencies that could be physically felt in the body, so it was decided that each installation would be equipped with a low frequency noise generator. Low frequency control tones recorded on a special audio track were to regulate the timing and intensity of the low frequency rumble from the noise generator.' 'About Sensurround', *in70mm.com*. Available online: https://www.in70mm.com/newsletter/2004/69/sensurround/about/index.htm (accessed 30 April 2022). On Sensurround, see also Jasen, *Low End Theory*, 145–6; Stuart Swezey, 'Infrasound', in *Amok Journal: Sensurround Edition* (Los Angeles, CA: Amok, 1995), 373.
167 With Time Delay Spectrometry (TDS) from Richard C. Heyser.
168 See Fierstein and Long, 'State-of-the-Art Discotheque Sound'.
169 Ibid., 3.
170 Lawrence, *Love Saves the Day*, 88–9.
171 See ibid., 347.
172 See ibid., 348. In the design of discos, the question of whether visitors tended to dance to loud or soft music certainly played a role. However, this question was

decided in favour of loud music; see Shannon, *Off the Record: The Disco Concept*, 159–65.
173 'At the same time there is such a thing as too loud. But rarely have I ever heard a soundsystem that is too loud. What I have heard mostly is distorted sound, which sounds louder than it really is. So the idea is to create clean sound.' 'Alex Rosner', *Red Bull Music Academy*.
174 Fierstein and Long, 'State-of-the-Art Discotheque Sound', 4.
175 Ibid.
176 Fierstein, according to Shannon, *Off the Record: The Disco Concept*, 158, emphasis in the original.
177 Goodman, *Sonic Warfare*, 28.
178 Papenburg, 'Enhanced Bass'.
179 Eshun, *More Brilliant Than the Sun*, 88, 151.
180 Fierstein and Long, 'State-of-the-Art Discotheque Sound'.
181 Shannon, *Off the Record: The Disco Concept*, 159. This paragraph is translated, adopted and adapted from Papenburg, 'Boomende Bässe der Disco- und Clubkultur'.
182 Although this subsection primarily focuses on the sound systems that Rosner and Long developed, it should not go unmentioned that both were also involved in the development of other technologies that became prominent in disco culture, for example, in developing DJ mixing consoles. Together with Rudy Bozak, in 1971, Rosner had developed one of the first DJ mixers – the 'Bozak' (see Lawrence, *Love Saves the Day*, 108). Rosner also built a DJ mixer called 'Rosie'. Later, Long built – supported by JBL – his own DJ mixer, the 'Urei 1620', which had more stereo inputs than the Bozak (345).
183 See Wicke, Ziegenrücker and Ziegenrücker, *Handbuch der populären Musik*, 235.
184 Enhancers differ only marginally from exciters: 'Unlike exciters, enhancers use bandpass filters to select specific frequency ranges' (ibid., 227).
185 See Jim McCullaugh, '"Semi-pros" Eying Musical Instrument Outlets', *Billboard*, 4 February 1978, 73.
186 Fierstein and Long also included other effects in the Paradise Garage sound system, such as expanders and a 'Deltalab Acousticomputer and similar devices, used to alter or add to the sound of the recording'; they also mention other devices that they did not build into the Paradise Garage system, but which could be used in the system: an 'Audionics Space & Image Composer, a 4-channel synthesizer' and an 'Acoustilog Image Enhancer, which expands the stereo effect' (Fierstein and Long, 'State-of-the-Art Discotheque Sound', 5).
187 Shannon, *Off the Record: The Disco Concept*, 159.
188 Doug Shannon, *Off the Record: The Handbook to Knowledge, Money & Success: Everything Related to Playing Recorded Dance Music in the Nightclub Industry* (Cleveland, OH: Pacesetter Publishing, 1985).
189 See Chapter 4, section, 'Maxi-Sound'.
190 West End Records' first big hit – Karen Young's *Hot Shot* (West End, United States, 1978) – sold 800,000 copies as a maxi-single (see Cheren, *Keep on Dancin'*, 210–11). The 12-inch single of Walter Gibbons's remix of *Ten Per Cent* (Salsoul, United States, 1976) sold 110,000 copies in its first week (Ian Dewhirst, Liner Notes for *Salsoul 30th: 30 Years of Salsoul – 30 Classic Club Cuts – 30 World Class DJs* [Salsoul, United States, 2005]). Mel Cheren assumes that disco visitors were the main buyers of 12-inch singles: 'The people who are into the twelve-inch product are those who go

to discos and are much into disco music' (Cheren, according to Shannon, *Off the Record*, 1982, 209).

191 See the work of Bob Blank and Tee Scott (Bill Brewster, 'Better Than a Good Time. An Audience with Bob Blank', *Red Bull Music Academy*, 2019 [2006]. Available online: https://daily.redbullmusicacademy.com/2019/01/bob-blank-dj-history-interview [accessed 30 April 2022]).

192 Rosner points out, for example, that most disco releases had already been mixed by experienced disc jockeys (see Rosner, 'Overview of Disco', 582). The dynamic range of most disco releases is anyway lower than the dynamic range that a well-attended disco makes available to the music (582). Rosner states that in a disco without music there is a 'noise level' of 85 dB. This means that a system producing 120 dB leaves a dynamic range of 35 dB for the music (581–2). Rosner also largely rejects compressors in sound systems.

193 Detailed lists of the repertoire of records that went into DJ mixes in discos and clubs can be found in the relevant histories (see Lawrence, *Love Saves the Day*; Brewster and Broughton, *Last Night a DJ Saved My Life*). In the 1970s, industry journals such as *Billboard* – after the introduction of Moulton's disco column in October 1974 – and *Record World* began to publish charts for discos. Selected discographies of individual DJs were also printed there. If 'one-stops' had an important function in shaping jukebox repertoire in the 1950s in the United States (see Chapter 3, this volume), then the 'record pools' that began to emerge in the mid-1970s had a similar influence on the repertoire that DJs played in discos and clubs. Fikentscher's ethnography (Fikentscher, *'You Better Work!'*) of the New York disco and club scene of the 1980s and 1990s pointed to the continuing importance of record pools. On the transformation of the function of the record pool in the second half of the 1970s, see Straw, 'Popular Music as Cultural Commodity', 149–60. Straw points out that in the New York disco scene, record pools became less important from 1977 to 1979, as disco radio formats increasingly emerged during this period. Record pools were distribution networks or associations of DJs that were specifically supplied by record companies for promotional purposes (see Aletti, *The Disco Files*, 96). They mediated between record companies and DJs: 'Record pools were locally-based associations of disc jockeys who worked in discotheques, formed for the primary purpose of facilitating their contact with record companies' (Straw, 'Popular Music as Cultural Commodity', 150). In 1975, the first record pool – 'The Record Pool Inc.' – was opened in New York (see Aletti, *The Disco Files*; Lawrence, *Love Saves the Day*, 155–66). In 1977, there were already twenty-eight of these institutions in the United States; the largest record pool in New York had 300 members, who are said to have reached about 100,000 people a week via discos (see Mary E. Stibal, 'Disco: Birth of a New Marketing System', *Journal of Marketing* 41, no. 4 (1977): 84–5). The labels sent records to DJs via record pools and expected feedback from the DJs. However, this often failed to materialize. This, in turn, could lead to the labels limiting deliveries (see Jean Williams, 'Pools Decry Ebb in Record Flow', *Billboard*, 30 April 1977, 1, 88). In addition to record pools, contact between record companies and DJs was also established through mailing lists and independent promoters, such as Provocative Promotion (88). These forms of distribution largely determined what was played in discos and clubs.

194 For instance, the DJs Francis Grasso and David Mancuso did not mix the record, they spun.

195 See, for example, Poschardt, *DJ Culture*; Robin Mackay, 'Capitalism and Schizophrenia: Wildstyle in Full Effect', in *Deleuze and Philosophy: The Difference Engineer*, ed. Keith Ansell Pearson (London: Routledge, 1997); Wicke, 'Sound Tracks'; Simon Reynolds, 'Detroit Techno, Chicago House, and New York Garage', in *DJ, Dance, and Rave Culture: Examining Pop Culture*, ed. Jared F. Green (Detroit: Thomson Gale, 2005), 88; Bonz, *Subjekte des Tracks*; Johannes Ismaiel-Wendt, *Tracks 'n' treks: Populäre Musik und Postkoloniale Analyse* (Münster: Unrast, 2011), 54–6 and 208.

196 Ismaiel-Wendt, *Tracks 'n' treks*; Malte Pelleter, 'Funkologicalienatimepistomachinistics: Sensorisches Engineering und maschinische Heterochronizität bei Shuggie Otis', in *Musikformulare und Presets: Musikkulturalisierung und Technik/Technologie*, ed. Johannes Ismaiel-Wendt and Alan Fabian (Hildesheim: Olms, 2018), 149–66. 'The term track is used in music production for individual audio tracks as well as for the mix of audio tracks, that is, for the completed musical object' (Ismaiel-Wendt, *Tracks 'n' treks*, 208). Ismail-Wendt then follows this up with a cultural-theoretical examination of the track by combining tracks with treks, thereby arriving at a post-colonial concept of culture that would like to see culture 'understood as an accidental or strategic temporary connection of different tracks' (208). The 'TRX studies' (53–6), which Ismaiel-Wendt attempts to develop as a method, are ambitious in terms of both cultural and music theory, since they see the concept of a track, which originates in the analogue world, simply simulated in digital media, but not modified. Here, the differences between track and soundfile would have to be discussed in more detail. In relation to the music cultures discussed in this chapter, however, this difference is not (yet) relevant.

197 Wicke, 'Sound Tracks', 116.

198 Ibid., 116. See also Wicke, *Von Mozart zu Madonna*, 271–2. Wicke then follows up this diagnosis with a discourse analysis. He examines, for example, under the signum 'discourse of the virtual', how such soundtracks in technoculture 'arrive at all those dimensions, references and symbolic references' that then make music out of them (Wicke, 'Sound Tracks', 116).

199 Ibid., 134.

200 James, *Resilience & Melancholy*, 41–3. On modularity, see also Butler, *Unlocking the Groove*, 166–7.

201 Wicke, *Von Mozart zu Madonna*, 272.

202 Kronengold, 'Exchange Theories in Disco', 47. Kronengold shows this for example with the Larry Levan remix of Inner Life's *Ain't No Mountain High Enough* (Salsoul Records, United States, 1981). Only a good minute of this remix, which lasts just under eleven minutes, follows the form of verse and chorus. The song form appears here only as a residue.

203 Solberg, '"Waiting for the Bass to Drop"', 61–82.

204 James, *Resilience & Melancholy*, 29. On break-down and build up in electronic dance music, see also Butler, *Unlocking the Groove*, 224, 325; José Gálvez, 'Beschleunigte/euphorische Körper: Versuch einer Soundsoziologie von EDM-Livesets' (MA dissertation, Institute of Musicology and Media Studies, Humboldt University of Berlin, Berlin, 2017), 46–51.

205 Carolyn Krasnow, 'Fear and Loathing in the 70s: Race, Sexuality, and Disco', *Stanford Humanities Review* 3, no. 2 (1993): 37–45.

206 Ibid.

207 Kronengold, 'Exchange Theories in Disco', 50.
208 Ibid.
209 Krasnow, according to Fink, *Repeating Ourselves*, 40.
210 It is not only in disco culture that the players continue to look for climaxes, but in the emerging house and techno culture as well, climaxes are highly prized: for example, in the proto-techno track *Sharevari* by A Number of Names (Capriccio Records, United States, 1981), it says: 'Heading for the highest heights for the climax of the night'.
211 Straw, 'Dance Music', 172.
212 Bonz, *Subjekte des Tracks*, 127. Bonz then attaches an entire cultural theory to the concept of the track.
213 Roland Barthes, *Mythologies*, trans. Annette Lavers (London: Vintage Books, 2008), 79.
214 Reynolds, *Energy Flash*. *Jack Trax* is the title of an LP released by Mirage featuring Chip E. (House Records, United States, 1985). 'Jacking' refers to a dance form typical for Chicago house. On jacking, see later in the text.
215 The label Deep House was established in the late 1980s to distinguish house productions from Chicago from Acid House, which also originated in Chicago. In addition, Garage House music was associated with the Paradise Garage in New York.
216 For example, *You Used to Hold Me* (Hot Mix 5 Records, United States, 1987) by Ralphi Rosario featuring Xavier Gold starts after a long intro with a quite conventional verse/chorus scheme followed by a spoken bridge. About halfway through the track, however, Xavier Gold's voice is increasingly used as mere sampling material and the song form no longer provides order.
217 Saunders according to Bidder, *Pump Up the Volume*, 31.
218 Examples of this might be *I've Lost Control* by Sleezy D. (Trax, United States, 1986) or *Acid Tracks* by Phuture (Trax, United States, 1987).
219 Butler, *Unlocking the Groove*, 203–4.
220 On the significance of the cassette, the archiving of these mixes and their historiographical potential, see Salkind, *Do You Remember House?* 71–3. Salkind provides a detailed chronological description or 'close reading' (77) of a DJ set by Ron Hardy (77–83) from 1987 at the C.O.D. Club in Chicago, especially with regard to changes in the sound, such as transitions between the tracks, as well as musical references in the tracks played. 'I unpack Hardy's disbursal of cultural agency, "intense" playing style, and creative approach to programming by interrogating various semantic webs attached to each song that I understand him to have played, as well as the multiple potential meanings that he layered in his transitions between them' (77).
221 See Butler, *Unlocking the Groove*, 20–1; Mark J. Butler, *Playing with Something That Runs: Technology, Improvisation, and Composition in DJ and Laptop Performance* (New York: Oxford University Press, 2014), 8, 113–71; Gálvez, 'Beschleunigte/euphorische Körper', 32–71; Salkind, *Do You Remember House?* 69–83.
222 Luis-Manuel Garcia, 'As the World Turns: Time in Electronic Dance Music', *Little White Earbuds*. Available online: http://www.littlewhiteearbuds.com/feature/as-the-world-turns-time-in-electronic-dance-music/ (accessed 30 April 2022).
223 Colleen Murphy, 'Klipsch: No Bullshit', *Red Bull Music Academy*. Available online: https://daily.redbullmusicacademy.com/2016/11/klipsch-feature (accessed 30 April 2022).

224 Friedner and Helmreich, 'Sound Studies Meets Deaf Studies'. See also Mills, 'Deafness'.
225 See, for instance, the 'Unsound System' built by the 'art-research cell' AUDINT (Olaf Arndt, Moritz von Rappard, Janneke Schönenbach and Cecilia Wee, eds. 'Embedded Art. Kunst im Namen der Sicherheit. Eine Ausstellung der Akademie der Künste und der Künstlergruppe BBM', exhibition information [Berlin: Akademie der Künste, 2009], 24) or Nik Nowak's 'Infra/Ultra', which was installed in the Galerie alexander levy in Berlin from 24 June to 29 July 2017.
226 Tim Lawrence, 'Disco and the Queering of the Dance Floor', *Cultural Studies* 25, no. 2 (2011).
227 Such dance practices peculiar to disco, house and techno have been described many times and informed differentiatedly by cultural studies; see, for example, Fikentscher, 'You Better Work!'; Fiona Buckland, *Impossible Dance: Club Culture and Queer World-Making* (Durham, NC: Duke University Press, 2002); Gabriele Klein, *Electronic Vibration: Pop Kultur Theorie* (Wiesbaden: Springer, 2004); Lawrence, 'Beyond the Hustle'; Hans T. Zeiner-Henriksen, 'The "PoumTchak" Pattern: Correspondences between Rhythm, Sound, and Movement in Electronic Dance Music' (PhD dissertation, Department of Musicology, University of Oslo, Oslo, 2010); Sebastian Matthias, 'Groove feeling – somatischer Sound und partizipative Performance', in *Sound und Performance*, ed. Wolf-Dieter Ernst, Nora Niethammer, Berenika Szymanski-Düll and Anno Mungen (Würzburg: Königshausen & Neumann, 2015).
228 Shapiro, *Turn the Beat Around*, 18.
229 In dubstep, a particular listening experience is also (co-)constituted by the technology of the sound system. British journalist Derek Walmsley has described this as a low-end experience. For Walmsley, such an experience is dependent on the listening device of the sound system, and thus cannot be produced via other listening devices such as smartphones. The low-end experience affects the listener's body and mechanizes it by reorganizing the sensorium: 'No matter which pieces of vinyl you play them on, or how much you crank up the bass, the true low end experience can never be appreciated except in a proper club or sound system. It pulses through your body, prickles the skin, presses upon your face, confounds sensations of distance and depth. The feeling of bass is a crucial component of virtually all contemporary dance music. Dubstep is unique in the last 20 years, however, in taking the appreciation of bass to the level of obsession.' Derek Walmsley, 'The Primer: Dubstep', *The Wire*, May 2007, 44.
230 Rietveld, 'Im Strom des Techno', 285–6.
231 Rosner, 'Overview of Disco', 576.
232 Ibid., 577.
233 See Chapter 4, section "'A Great Idea after the Fact". Dyer, 'In Defence of Disco', 21. Gilbert and Pearson also see Dyer transgressing binary ordering schemes, and they distinguish such a transgression from possible pre-Oedipal essentialisms: 'Dyer presents the possibility of a music which would deconstruct the opposition between masculinity and feminity, and he suggests that disco is an example of such a form' (Gilbert and Pearson, *Discographies*, 101). In his essay, Dyer fundamentally questioned the dualism of categories such as 'masculinity' and 'femininity' and thus established connectivity to queer feminism.
234 Lawrence, 'Beyond the Hustle'.
235 Goodman, *Sonic Warfare*, 79.
236 See also Garcia, 'Beats, Flesh, and Grain', 59–76; Chapter 4, section 'Listening at the Margins'.

237 On crowds and electronic dance music, see also Ben Malbon, *Clubbing: Dancing, Ecstasy, Vitality* (London: Routledge, 1999); Fikentscher, *'You Better Work!'*; Butler, *Unlocking the Groove*.
238 'Alex Rosner', *Red Bull Music Academy*.
239 'Interview: The Loft Founder David Mancuso'.
240 The 'sweet spot' is the point in front of the two speakers of a stereo system where the signals from the speakers are not heard as two separate sound sources, but as a 'phantom sound source' localized between the two speakers.
241 Tony Grajeda, 'The "Sweet Spot": The Technology of Stereo and the Field of Auditorship', in *Living Stereo: Histories and Cultures of Multichannel Sound*, ed. Paul Théberge, Kyle Devine and Tom Everrett (New York: Bloomsbury Academic, 2015), 48.
242 Lawrence, *Love Saves the Day*, 90.
243 Cai Brockmann, 'Klipsch Klipschorn', in *Hifi tunes: Das Klassikerbuch*, ed. Roland Kraft (Gröbenzell: IMAGE Verlags GmbH, 2008), 117.
244 Lawrence, 'Beyond the Hustle', 200.
245 Crimp, 'DISSS-CO (A FRAGMENT)', 15.
246 This and the next paragraph are translated, adopted and adapted from Papenburg, '"A Great Idea After the Fact"'.
247 The images by photographers like Allan Tannenbaum and Waring Abbott, for example, impressively document the dance floors of the New York club and disco scene of the 1970s.
248 See Lawrence, *Love Saves the Day*, 31.
249 See Cheren, *Keep on Dancin'*, 60–1. The techniques with which 'illegal' behaviour was investigated were sometimes quite crass. In the Boatel in the second half of the 1960s, for example, there was an employee sitting on a ladder who had to monitor what was happening on the dance floor. He was ready to shine a lamp as offensively as possible in the face of anyone involved in 'illegal' behaviour (see Rodwell, according to Echols, *Hot Stuff*, 43). Echols assumes that because of such practices and because of the legal situation prevailing at the time, line dances in gay bars were so popular to begin with (256).
250 Bidder, *Pump Up the Volume*, 45–6.
251 Salkind, *Do You Remember House?* 191.
252 Reynolds, *Energy Flash*, 26. As with other vocabulary found in popular music, the word 'jacking' also has sexual connotations. Several authors have called attention to this. Reynolds (25), for example, writes that jacking 'may have some link to "jacking off"'. For Barry Walters, jacking is also a form of substitute for physical gratification: 'For Chicago's black gays threatened by AIDS, jacking the night away at an after-hours club has become the most physically gratifying alternative to sex' (Walters, 'Burning Down the House', 62). Moreover, the movement repertoire of jacking can also be found in other areas: '"Jacking" is a term specific to the type of sexualized dance movements made to the music' (Hillegonda C. Rietveld, 'The House Sound of Chicago', in *The Clubcultures Reader: Readings in Popular Cultural Studies*, ed. Steve Redhead, Derek Wynne and Justin O'Connor [Oxford: Blackwell, 1998], 109). Walters also sees such indistinguishability: '"Jacking your body" (moving up and down on a dance floor) can easily slide into sex' (Walters, 'Burning Down the House', 62).

253 The short boom of The Hustle, which was over by the end of the decade at the latest, has been described in recent historiographies of disco culture as 'the harbinger of a conservative revolution' (Shapiro, *Turn the Beat Around*, 181). The cultural orders reproduced in The Hustle are extremely traditional: for example, The Hustle as a couple dance in which a man 'leads' a woman and 'asks' her to dance can be understood as a 'practice of patriarchal heterosexuality' (Lawrence, 'Beyond the Hustle', 200). Lawrence sees practices of patriarchal heterosexuality undermined by dancers who 'faced the double marginalization of being black as well as gay' (202). With The Hustle – especially in its version as a couple dance – disco then became acceptable to an older generation and their values (Gilbert and Pearson, *Discographies*, 13). Parallel to The Hustle, however, less choreographed dance forms had always existed in discos (see Hanson, *Disco Fieber*, 190–6). Albert Goldman even reports that freestyle dancing ultimately remained the dominant dance form. The focus was on the 'one-man show' and self-dramatization (see also Goldman, *Disco*, 11). In relation to the club culture of the 1980s and 1990s, couple and line dances such as The Hustle remained insignificant. Prominent here was the 'solo dancer, moving to the collective rhythm of the room' (Lawrence, 'Beyond the Hustle', 200). Applause-inducing solo performances, in which individual dancers perform special and expansive combinations, are also discouraged by heavily frequented dance floors. Dancing in place that does not take up much space becomes predominant.
254 Reynolds, *Energy Flash*, 25.
255 See Ian Driver, *A Century of Dance: A Hundred Years of Musical Movement, From Waltz to Hip Hop* (London: Hamlyn, 2000), 193.
256 Reynolds, *Energy Flash*, 25, emphasis in original. Reynolds here takes up a thesis developed by Walter Hughes ('In the Empire of the Beat',) on disco.
257 This is to be set against forms of listening in which the listener thinks he or she has mastered what is heard. Such mastery takes place, for example, when a dancer sees the dance floor as a stage and heroically tries to elevate themself to the status of a star via a one-person show, or when the beat forms the mere background for the execution of firmly choreographed couple dance steps.
258 Hughes, 'In the Empire of the Beat', 149. See also on Hughes and the sonic subjectivation provoked by the four-to-the-floor beat. Malte Pelleter, *Futurhythmaschinen: Drum-Machines und die Zukünfte auditiver Kulturen* (Hildesheim: Olms, 2021), 338–41.
259 Hughes, 'In the Empire of the Beat', 148. In his critique of dominant forms of the subject, Hughes tends to act in defiance by simply reversing the relationship between sound events and the perceiving subject. It is not the listener who dominates the sound event – for example, by making categorical assignments – but the sound event of disco that dominates the listener: 'Allowing the beat to become a part of us disturbs the very foundations of conventional constructions of masculine selfhood; allowing ourselves to be penetrated and controlled by musical rhythm, by desire, or by another person is to relinquish the traditional conditions of full humanity and citizenship, and to embrace instead the traditional role of slave' (151).
260 Ibid., 152.
261 For Gilbert and Pearson, dance music is characterized in general by an oscillation of the dancer between subject and object status. The dancer is active and passive at the same time, they are danced and they dance: 'On the one hand, to dance to music is always (except in the highly circumscribed context of performance dance) to give

oneself up to the music, to allow the music *to dance us*. On the other hand, what more active response to music can there be than to actually move one's whole body in time to it?' (Gilbert and Pearson, *Discographies*, 106, emphasis in original). For Gilbert and Pearson, dancing is generally transverse to this subject form: 'Crucial to our discussion is the observation that dance in Western modernity tends to be an activity inextricably linked to the feminine. In postwar popular culture, dance cultures have been particularly associated with young women and gay men on the one hand, and with the cultures of the African diaspora and dispossessed young working-class men on the other. All of these groups, for one reason or another, were denied access to a fully masculine subjectivity as conceived by the dominant discourses of Western culture' (83–4).

262 Hughes, 'In the Empire of the Beat', 151–2. The motif of acting technology occupies a prominent position in arguments about the production of electronic dance music. For example, in Eshun's concept of 'AutoCatalysis', introduced in reference to acid house, in which the 'machine generates a new sound autonomously, without a human agent' (Eshun, *More Brilliant Than the Sun*, 19), in Kraftwerk, when technology is conceived there as an 'autonomous subject' (Bunz, 'Das Mensch-Maschine-Verhältnis'), or with reference to the Berlin techno scene of the early 1990s, when the techno fan is metaphorized there as a 'switching element' (Markus Konradin Leiner (Qrt), 'Tekknologic als Tekknowledge', in *Tekknologic Tekknowledge Tekgnosis. Ein Theoremix*, ed. Tom Lamberty and Frank Wulf [Berlin: Merve, 1999], 15) that optimizes communication between machines. Of course, it is still a step away from the recognition that technology is not merely used instrumentally, but also does something, to the postulation of the fact that technology 'dominates' people. Latour (see Chapter 1, section, 'What Are Listening Devices?') has pointed out that these two myths – the myth of technology as a neutral tool and the myth of the determination of man by technology – are two sides of the same coin and reproduce the subject/object schema. Latour, on the other hand, proposes to start from hybrid actors: A producer who uses a sequencer would thus no longer be the same producer, whereas the sequencer in the hands of the specific producer would no longer be the same sequencer.

263 Klein, *Electronic Vibration*, 175.
264 Ibid., 177.
265 Crimp, 'DISSS-CO (A FRAGMENT)', 6, emphasis in original.
266 Ibid., 6.

Conclusion and outlook

1 Pedro J. S. Vieira de Oliveira, 'Forbidden Music, Forbidden Jukeboxes: Listening Anxieties and the Hyper-amplification of Violence in Rio de Janeiro', in *Border Listening/Escucha Liminal*, vol. 1, ed. Alejandra Luciana Cárdenas (Berlin: Radical Sounds Latin America, 2020).
2 See Paul Goldstein, *Copyright's Highway: From Gutenberg to the Celestial Jukebox* (Stanford, CA: Stanford University Press, 2003), 21–5; 184–216.
3 Siegfried Zielinski, *Deep Time of the Media: Toward an Archaeology of Hearing and Seeing by Technical Means*, trans. Gloria Custance (Cambridge, MA: MIT Press,

2006), 1–2. Zielinski refers here to 'The Dead Media Project' by science fiction author Bruce Sterling.
4   Charles R. Acland, *Residual Media* (Minneapolis: University of Minnesota Press, 2006).
5   Garnet Hertz and Jussi Parikka, 'Zombie Media: Circuit Bending Media Archaeology into an Art Method', *Leonardo* 45, no. 5 (2012): 424–30.
6   I have tried to bring into view soundfile and streaming listening in their peculiarity (Jens Gerrit Papenburg, 'Soundfile: Kultur und Ästhetik einer Hörtechnologie', *Pop. Kultur und Kritik* 2, no. 1 [2013], 140–55; Jens Gerrit Papenburg, 'The File', in *The Bloomsbury Handbook of the Anthropology of Sound*, ed. Holger Schulze [New York: Bloomsbury Academic, 2021]; Jens Gerrit Papenburg 'Bewirtschaftung der Zukunft. Musikhören durch Apps, Kopfhörer und Smartphones', *Electronic Beats*, published by Deutsche Telekom [Berlin: Blumenbar, 2021], 92–9; Papenburg and Alt, 'Streamability', 227–42.
7   Eric Drott, 'Why the Next Song Matters: Streaming, Recommendation, Scarcity', *Twentieth-Century Music* 15, no. 3 (2018): 325–57.
8   Providers have been trying to differentiate their catalogues from those of their competitors for a few years now; not so much through music, but rather via podcasts.
9   Beate Ochsner, '"Die Zukunft smarten Hörens hat begonnen" (ReSound): Anmerkungen zu einer technosensorischen Regierungspraktik', in *Physiognomien des Lebens: Physiognomik im Spannungsverhältnis zwischen Biopolitik und Ästhetik*, ed. Vittoria Borsò, Sieglinde Borvitz and Luca Viglialoro (Berlin: de Gruyter, 2020), 161–82.
10 Latour, *Reassembling the Social*.
11 On these four characteristics of soundfile listening (catalogue/stock, playlist, fine-tuning, social event), see also Papenburg, 'Soundfile'.
12 Liz Pelly, 'Big Mood Machine', *The Baffler*, available online: https://thebaffler.com/latest/big-mood-machine-pelly (accessed 30 April 2022).
13 Maximilian Haberer, 'Versuch über Spotify, oder: Musikstreaming als Arbeit am Subjekt', in *Wissen im Klang: Neue Wege der Musikästhetik*, ed. José Gálvez, Jonas Reichert and Elizaveta Willert (Bielefeld: transcript, 2020).
14 I have attempted to delineate this future via three futures peculiar to soundfile listening – the present, the past and the open future: Papenburg, 'The File'; Papenburg 'Bewirtschaftung der Zukunft'.

Sources

'About Sensurround'. *in70mm.com*. Accessed 30 April 2022. https://www.in70mm.com/newsletter/2004/69/sensurround/about/index.htm.

Acland, Charles R. *Residual Media*. Minneapolis: University of Minnesota Press, 2006.

Adams, Michael, Thomas Lukas and Jürgen Maschke. *Musikboxen*. Augsburg: Weltbild, 1994.

Adelmann, Ralf. *Listen und Rankings: Über Taxonomien des Populären*. Bielefeld: transcript, 2021.

Adorno, Theodor W. *Current of Music: Elements of a Radio Theory*. Cambridge: Polity, 2009.

Adorno, Theodor W. 'The Curves of the Needle'. In *Essays on Music by Theodor W. Adorno*, translated by Susan H. Gillespie, edited by Richard Leppert, 271–6. Berkeley: University of California Press, 2002.

Adorno, Theodor W. 'The Form of the Phonograph Record'. In *Essays on Music by Theodor W. Adorno*, translated by Susan H. Gillespie, edited by Richard Leppert, 277–82. Berkeley: University of California Press, 2002.

Adorno, Theodor W. *Introduction to the Sociology of Music*. Translated by E. B. Ashton. New York: Seabury Press, 1976.

Adorno, Theodor W. 'Musik im Fernsehen ist Brimborium'. In *Gesammelte Schriften*, no. 19, edited by Rolf Tiedemann, 559–69. Frankfurt am Main: Suhrkamp, 1984.

Adorno, Theodor W. 'On the Fetish-Character in Music and the Regression of Listening'. In *Essays on Music by Theodor W. Adorno*, translated by Susan H. Gillespie, edited by Richard Leppert, 288–317. Berkeley: University of California Press, 2002.

Adorno, Theodor W. 'Opera and the Long-Playing Record'. In *Essays on Music by Theodor W. Adorno*, translated by Susan H. Gillespie, edited by Richard Leppert, 283–7, Berkeley: University of California Press, 2002.

Adorno, Theodor W. 'The Radio Symphony: An Experiment in Theory'. In *Current of Music: Elements of a Radio Theory*, 144–62. Cambridge: Polity, 2009.

Adorno, Theodor W. 'Zum "Anbruch"'. In *Gesammelte Schriften*, no. 19, edited by Rolf Tiedemann, 595–604. Frankfurt am Main: Suhrkamp, 1984.

Adorno, Theodor W. 'Zur Musikpädagogik'. In *Gesammelte Schriften*, no. 14, edited by Rolf Tiedemann, 108–26. Frankfurt am Main: Suhrkamp, 1990.

Adorno, Theodor W., and Thomas Y. Levin. 'The Form of the Phonograph Record'. *October* 55 (1990): 56–61.

Aletti, Vince. *The Disco Files 1973–78: New York's Underground, Week by Week*. New York: Distributed Art Publishers, 2018.

'Alex Rosner'. Red Bull Music Academy. Accessed 30 April 2022. https://www.redbullmusicacademy.com/lectures/alex-rosner-systematic-sound.

'Alex Rosner: Shaping the Sound of New York'. Accessed 30 April 2022. https://www.youtube.com/watch?v=Nv8mju2-gHI&t=0s.

Alt, Max. 'Die Datafizierung des Musikhörens durch die amerikanische Rundfunkforschung der 1930er und 1940er Jahre: Eine Musik- und Medienarchäologie des Musikstreaming". PhD dissertation, Faculty of the Arts, Rheinische Friedrich-Wilhlems-Universität Bonn, forthcoming.

Anders, Günther. 'On Promethean Shame'. In *Prometheanism: Technology, Digital Culture and Human Obsolescence*, edited by Christopher John Müller, 29–95. New York: Rowman & Littlefield, 2016.

Anderson, Tim J. *Making Easy Listening: Material Culture and Postwar American Recording*. Minneapolis: University of Minnesota Press, 2006.

Andriote, John-Manuel. *Hot Stuff: A Brief History of Disco*. London: HarperCollins, 2001.

Anz, Philipp, and Patrick Walder, eds. *Techno*. Zürich: Bilger, 1995.

Appen, Ralf von, Nils Grosch and Martin Pfleiderer, eds. 'Einführung: Populäre Musik und Popmusikforschung: Zur Konzeption'. In *Populäre Musik. Geschichte – Kontexte – Forschungsperspektiven*, edited by Ralf von Appen, Nils Grosch and Martin Pfleiderer, 7–14. Laaber: Laaber, 2014.

Arndt, Olaf, Moritz von Rappard, Janneke Schönenbach and Cecilia Wee, eds. *Embedded Art*. 'Kunst im Namen der Sicherheit. Eine Ausstellung der Akademie der Künste und der Künstlergruppe BBM'. Exhibition information, Berlin: Akademie der Künste, 2009.

Attali, Jacques. *Noise: The Political Economy of Music*. Translated by Brian Massumi, Minneapolis: University of Minnesota Press, 1985.

Attwood, David. *Sound Design: Classic Audio & Hi-Fi Design*. London: Mitchell Beazley, 2002.

Auslander, Philip. *Liveness: Performance in a Mediatized Culture*. London: Routledge, 2008.

'Automaten-ABC'. *Der Automaten-Markt: Fachzeitschrift für die gesamte Automatenwirtschaft* 12 (1960): 817.

Bachman, William S. 'The LP and the Single'. *Journal of the Audio Engineering Society* 25, no. 10/11 (1977): 821–3.

Bachmann-Medick, Doris. *Cultural Turns: New Orientations in the Study of Culture*. Berlin: de Gruyter, 2016.

Balke, Friedrich, Bernhard Siegert and Joseph Vogl, eds. *Takt und Frequenz*. Munich: Fink, 2011.

Barck, Karlheinz, and Peter Gente. *Aisthesis. Wahrnehmung heute oder Perspektiven einer anderen Ästhetik*. Leipzig: Reclam, 1990.

Barker, Hugh, and Yuval Taylor. *Faking It: The Quest for Authenticity in Popular Music*. New York: W. W. Norton, 2007.

Barry, Eric D. 'High-Fidelity Sound as Spectacle and Sublime, 1950–1961'. In *Sound in the Age of Mechanical Reproduction*, edited by David Suisman and Susan Strasser, 115–38. Philadelphia: University of Pennsylvania Press, 2010.

Barry, Robert. *Compact Disc*. New York: Bloomsbury Academic, 2020.

Barthes, Roland. 'The Grain of the Voice'. In *Image, Music, Text*, translated by Stephen Heath, edited by Stephen Heath, 179–89. London: Fontana, 1977.

Barthes, Roland. 'Musica Practica'. In *Image, Music, Text*, translated by Stephen Heath, edited by Stephen Heath, 149–54. London: Fontana, 1977.

Barthes, Roland. *Mythologies*. Translated by Annette Lavers. London: Vintage Books 2008.

Bastian, Vanessa. 'Instrument Manufacture'. In *Continuum Encyclopedia of Popular Music of the World. Volume I: Media, Industry and Society*, edited by John Shepherd, David Horn, Dave Laing, Paul Oliver and Peter Wicke, 526–9. New York: Continuum, 2003.

Bayley, Amanda. *Recorded Music: Performance, Culture and Technology*. Cambridge: Cambridge University Press 2010.

Belz, Carl. *The Story of Rock*. Oxford: Oxford University Press, 1969.
Besseler, Heinrich. *Das Musikalische Hören der Neuzeit*. Berlin: Akademie Verlag, 1959.
Besseler, Heinrich. 'Grundfragen des musikalischen Hörens'. *Jahrbuch der Musikbibliothek Peters* 35 (1925): 32–52.
Beta, Andy. 'Magic Touch: Richard Long's Life-Changing Sound Systems'. *Red Bull Music Academy*. Accessed 30 April 2022. https://daily.redbullmusicacademy.com/2016/05/richard-long-feature.
Bidder, Sean. *Pump Up the Volume: A History of House Music*. London: Channel 4 Books, 2001.
Bijsterveld, Karin. *Mechanical Sound: Technology, Culture, and Public Problems of Noise in the Twentieth Century*. Cambridge, MA: MIT Press, 2008.
Bijsterveld, Karin. *Sonic Skills: Listening for Knowledge in Science, Engineering and Medicine (1920s–Present)*. New York: Palgrave MacMillan, 2019.
Bijsterveld, Karin, and José van Dijck, eds. *Sound Souvenirs: Audio Technologies, Memory and Cultural Practices*. Amsterdam: Amsterdam University Press, 2009.
Bijsterveld, Karin and Trevor Pinch. 'Sound Studies. New Technologies and Music'. *Social Studies of Science* 34, no. 5 (2004): 635–48.
Billboard. 'Bacon Finds European Market Still Untapped'. 12 July 1952, 78.
Billboard. 'The Billboard 8th Annual Juke Box Operator Poll'. 26 March 1955, 71–82.
Billboard. 'Columbia Diskery, CBS Show Microgroove Platters to Press; Tell How It Began'. 26 June 1948, 3.
Billboard. 'Disco Play Starts a Hit'. 26 October 1974, 36.
Billboard. 'Discotheques Break Single'. 6 October 1973, 3.
Billboard. 'Diskeries Still Hold Out against RIAA Standards'. 28 August 1954, 62.
Billboard. 'Frankford/Wayne Mastering Labs'. 27 October 1979, 65.
Billboard. '"Home Jukes" Will Boost Disk Sales'. 26 February 1944, 78–80.
Billboard. 'Juke's Boom Is Business Week Theme'. 9 March 1946, 98.
Billboard. 'Label Mix Records for Club Scene'. 2 November 1974, 1, 10.
Billboard. 'New Disks Not to Affect Jukes'. 2 April 1949, 133.
Billboard. 'One-Stops'. 26 March 1955, 84, 86, 142.
Billboard. 'Pure or "Enhanced" Sound Spurs Sparks'. 11 August 1979, 40, 53.
Billboard. 'Reorganization for N.Y. Sound Firm'. 30 April 1977, 88.
Billboard. 'Rock-Ola Bows 1961 Model'. 3 October 1960, 75.
Binas-Preisendörfer, Susanne. '"Live Is Life": Faszination und Konjunktur des Popkonzerts, oder Überlegungen zur Performativität medienvermittelter musikkultureller Praktiken'. In *Populäre Musik, mediale Musik? Transdisziplinäre Beiträge zu den Medien der populären Musik*, edited by Christopher Jost, Daniel Klug, Klaus Neumann-Braun and Axel Schmidt, 131–46. Baden-Baden: Nomos, 2011.
Birdsall, Carolyn. *Nazi-Soundscapes: Sound, Technology and Urban Space in Germany, 1933–1945*. Amsterdam: Amsterdam University Press, 2012.
Björnberg, Alf. 'Learning to Listen to Perfect Sound: Hi-fi Culture and Changes in Modes of Listening 1950–80'. In *The Ashgate Research Companion to Popular Musicology*, edited by Derek B. Scott, 105–29. Surrey: Ashgate, 2009.
Blake, Iris Sandjette. 'The Vocal Apparatus's Colonial Contexts: France's Mission Civilisatrice and (Settler) Colonialism in Algeria and North America'. In *Sonic Histories of Occupation*, edited by Jeremy E. Taylor and Russell Skelchy, 25–49. New York: Bloomsbury, 2022.

Bloemeke, Rüdiger. *Roll Over Beethoven. Wie der Rock 'n' Roll nach Deutschland kam.* Wien: Hannibal, 1996.

Bodoh, A. G. 'The Jukebox, the Radio, and the Record'. *Journal of the Audio Engineering Society* 25, nos. 10/11 (1977): 836–42.

Böhme, Gernot. *Invasive Technification: Critical Essays in the Philosophy of Technology.* Translated by Cameron Shingleton. New York: Bloomsbury Academic, 2012.

Bolter, Jay David, and Richard Grusin. *Remediation: Understanding New Media.* Cambridge, MA: MIT Press, 1999.

Bonnell, Victoria E., and Lynn Hunt. *Beyond the Cultural Turn: New Directions in the Study of Society and Culture.* Berkeley: University of California Press 1999.

Bonz, Jochen. *Subjekte des Tracks: Ethnografie einer postmodernen/anderen Subkultur.* Berlin: Kadmos, 2008.

Born, Georgina. 'On Musical Mediation: Ontology, Technology, and Creativity'. *Twentieth Century Music* 2, no. 1 (2005): 7–36.

Born, Georgina. 'On Nonhuman Sound–Sound as Relation'. In *Sound Objects*, edited by James A. Steintrager and Rey Chow, 185–207. Durham, NC: Duke University Press, 2019.

Bourriaud, Nicolas. *Postproduction. Culture as Screenplay: How Art Reprograms the World.* New York: Lukas & Sternberg, 2007.

Braddock, John Paul, Russ Hepworth-Sawyer, Jay Hodgson, Matthew Shelvock and Rob Toulson, eds, *Mastering in Music*. London: Routledge, 2021.

Breitholtz Widlund, Claes 'Discoguy'. 'Tom Moulton'. *Disco-Disco.* Accessed 30 April 2022. http://www.disco-disco.com/tributes/tom.shtml.

Brewster, Bill. 'Better Than a Good Time. An Audience with Bob Blank'. *Red Bull Music Academy*, 2019 [2006]. Available online: https://daily.redbullmusicacademy.com/2019/01/bob-blank-dj-history-interview. Accessed 30 April 2022.

Brewster, Bill, and Frank Broughton. *Last Night a DJ Saved My Life: The History of the Disc Jockey.* London: White Rabbit, 2022.

Brewster, Bill, and Frank Broughton. *The Record Players: DJ Revolutionaries.* New York: Black Cat, 2010.

Brockhaus, Immanuel. *Kultsounds: Die prägendsten Klänge der Popmusik 1960–2014.* Bielefeld: transcript, 2017.

Brockmann, Cai. 'Klipsch Klipschorn'. In *Hifi tunes: Das Klassikerbuch*, edited by Roland Kraft, 117. Gröbenzell: IMAGE Verlags GmbH, 2008.

Broven, John. *Record Makers and Breakers. Voices of the Independent Rock 'n' Roll Pioneers.* Chicago: University of Illinois Press, 2009.

Broven, John. *Rhythm and Blues in New Orleans.* Gretna, LA: Pelican Publishing, 1978.

Bruyninckx, Joeri, and Alexandra Supper. 'Sonic Skills in Cultural Contexts: Theories, Practices and Materialities of Listening'. *Sound Studies: An Interdisciplinary Journal* 2, no. 1 (2016): 1–5.

Bruyninckx, Joeri, and Alexandra Supper, eds. 'Special Issue: Sonic Skills in Cultural Contexts: Theories, Practices and Materialities of Listening'. *Sound Studies: An Interdisciplinary Journal* 2, no. 1 (2016).

Büchele, Christian. *Geschichte der Tonträger: Von der Erfindung der Schallplatte zu den digitalen Medien.* Tutzing: Schneider, 1999.

Buckland, Fiona. *Impossible Dance: Club Culture and Queer World-Making.* Durham, NC: Duke University Press, 2002.

Bull, Michael. *Sound Moves: iPod Culture and Urban Experience*. London: Routledge, 2007.
Bull, Michael. *Sounding Out the City*. Oxford: Berg, 2000.
Bull, Michael. 'Technological Sensory Training'. In *Sound as Popular Culture. A Research Companion*, edited by Jens Gerrit Papenburg and Holger Schulze, 233–9. Cambridge, MA: MIT Press, 2016.
Bull, Michael, and Les Back, 'Introduction'. In *The Auditory Culture Reader*. 1st edn, edited by Michael Bull and Les Back, 1–18. Oxford: Berg, 2003.
Bull Michael, and Les Back, 'Introduction'. In *The Auditory Culture Reader*. 2nd edn, edited by Michael Bull and Les Back, 1–20. New York: Bloomsbury, 2016.
Bunz, Mercedes. 'Das Mensch-Maschine-Verhältnis. Ein Plädoyer für eine Erweiterung der Medientheorie am Beispiel von Kraftwerk, Underground Resistance und Missy Elliot'. In *Sound Signatures: Pop-Splitter*, ed. Jochen Bonz, 272–90. Frankfurt am Main: Suhrkamp, 2001.
Burkhart, Benjamin. 'Musik wiedergeben'. In *Audiowelten: Technologie und Medien in der populären Musik nach 1945: 22 Objektstudien*, edited by Benjamin Burkhart, Lara Niebling, Alan van Keeken, Christofer Jost and Martin Pfleiderer, 367–552. Münster: Waxmann, 2021.
Burkhart, Benjamin. 'Rock-Ola Capri 100, Modell 404 (1963)'. In *Audiowelten: Technologie und Medien in der populären Musik nach 1945: 22 Objektstudien*, edited by Benjamin Burkhart, Lara Niebling, Alan van Keeken, Christofer Jost and Martin Pfleiderer, 429–51. Münster: Waxmann, 2021.
Butler, Mark J. *Playing with Something That Runs: Technology, Improvisation, and Composition in DJ and Laptop Performance*. New York: Oxford University Press, 2014.
Butler, Mark J. *Unlocking the Groove. Rhythm, Meter, and Musical Design in Electronic Dance Music*. Bloomington: Indiana University Press, 2006.
Butt, John. 'Do Musical Works Contain an Implied Listener? Towards a Theory of Musical Listening'. *Journal of the Royal Musical Association* 135, no. 1 (2010): 5–18.
Buzzard, Karen. *Tracking the Audience: The Ratings Industry from Analog to Digital*. New York: Routledge, 2012.
Cadenbach, Rainer. 'Der implizite Hörer? Zum Begriff einer "Rezeptionsästhetik" als musikwissenschaftlicher Disziplin'. In *Rezeptionsästhetik und Rezeptionsgeschichte in der Musikwissenschaft*, edited by Hermann Danuser, 133–63. Laaber: Laaber, 1991.
Calella, Michele. 'Musikhistorische Rezeptions-Forschung jenseits der Rezeptionstheorien'. In *Zwischen Transfer und Transformation: Horizonte der Rezeption von Musik*, edited by Michele Calella and Benedikt Lessmann, 11–27. Wien: Hollitzer, 2020.
Callsen, Kuno. 'Die Technische Gestaltung der Musikautomaten'. In *Handbuch der Deutschen Automatenwirtschaft 1956*, edited by Harry von Rosen-von Hoewel and Gerhard Rauschenbach, 266–70. Cologne: Carl Heymanns Verlag KG, 1956.
Cantor, Louis. *Dewey and Elvis. The Life and Time of a Rock 'n' Roll Deejay*. Chicago: University of Illinois Press, 2005.
Carson, Benjamin H., A. D. Burt and H. I. Reiskind. 'A Record Changer and Record of Complementary Design'. *RCA Review* June (1949): 173–90.
Cavallo, Guglielmo, and Roger Chartier. 'Introduction'. In *A History of Reading in the West*, translated by Lydia G. Cochrane, edited by Guglielmo Cavallo and Roger Chartier, 1–36. Cambridge: Polity Press, 2003.
Chanan, Michael. *Repeated Takes: A Short History of Recording and Its Effects on Music*. London: Verso, 1995.
Charbon, Paul. *Le Phonographe à La Belle Epoque*. Brussels: Libro-sciences SPRL, 1977.

Cheren, Mel. *Keep on Dancin': My Life and the Paradise Garage*. New York: 24 Hours for Life, 2000.

Chinn, Howard A., and Philip Eisenberg. 'Tonal-Range and Sound-Intensity Preferences of Broadcast Listeners'. *Proceedings of the IRE* 33, no. 9 (1945): 571–81.

Clarke, Eric F. 'The Impact of Recording on Listening'. *Twentieth-Century Music* 4, no. 1 (2007): 47–70.

Clayton, Martin, Trevor Herbert and Richard Middleton, eds. *The Cultural Study of Music: A Critical Introduction*, 2nd edn. London: Routledge, 2012.

Cogan, Jim. 'Bill Putnam. The Art of Engineering. Part 1'. *Mix. Professional Audio and Music Production* 27, no. 11 (2003): 32–8.

Cogan, Jim. 'Bill Putnam. The Art of Engineering. Part 2'. *Mix. Professional Audio and Music Production* 27, no. 12 (2003): 46–52.

Cogan, Jim, and William Clark. *Temples of Sound: Inside the Great Recording Studios*. San Francisco, CA: Chronicle Books, 2003.

Cohn, Nik. 'Tribal Rites of the New Saturday Night'. *New York Magazine*, 7 June 1976.

Cook, Nicholas, Eric Clarke, Daniel Leech-Wilkinson and John Rink, eds. *The Cambridge Companion to Recorded Music*. Cambridge: Cambridge University Press, 2009.

Cornils, Kristoffer. 'On the History of the Playlist'. In *Listen to Lists*, edited by Lina Brion and Detlef Diederichsen, 17–32. Leipzig: Spector Books, 2021.

Cosgrove, Stuart. 'The DJs They Couldn't Hang'. *New Musical Express*, 9 August 1986, 12–15.

Cosgrove, Stuart. Liner Notes for Various, *Techno! The New Dance Sound of Detroit*. 10 Records/Virgin Records, UK 1988.

Cosgrove, Stuart. 'Seventh City Techno'. In *Night Fever: Club Writing in The Face 1980–1997*, edited by Richard Benson, 93–6. London: Boxtree, 1997.

Cox, Christoph. 'Beyond Representation and Signification: Toward a Sonic Materialism'. *Journal of Visual Culture* 10, no. 2 (2011): 145–61.

Cox, Christoph. 'Sonic Realism and Auditory Culture: A Reply to Marie Thompson and Annie Goh'. *Parallax* 24, no. 2 (2018): 234–42.

Crary, Jonathan. *Techniques of the Observer. On Vision and Modernity in the Nineteenth Century*. Cambridge, MA: MIT Press, 1992.

Crimp, Douglas. 'DISSS-CO (A FRAGMENT) from "Before Pictures", a Memoir of 1970s New York'. *Criticism: A Quarterly for Literature and the Arts* 50, no. 1 (2008): 1–18.

Crosby, Bing, and Pete Martin. *Call Me Lucky*. Cambridge, MA: Da Capo Press, 2001.

Cross, Brian. *It's Not about a Salary: Rap, Race and Resistance in Los Angeles*. London: Verso, 1993.

Cunningham, Mark. *Good Vibrations: A History of Record Production*. London: Sanctuary, 1998.

Cusick, Suzanne G. 'Musicology, Torture, Repair'. *Radical Musicology* 3 (2008). Available online: http://www.radical-musicology.org.uk/2008/Cusick.htm. Accessed 30 April 2022.

Dahlhaus, Carl. 'Problems in Reception History'. In *Foundations of Music History*, translated by J. B. Robinson, 150–65. Cambridge: Cambridge University Press, 1983.

Dahlhaus, Carl, and Hans Heinrich Eggebrecht, *Was ist Musik?* Wilhelmshaven: Noetzel, 1987.

Daughtry, J. Martin. *Listening to War: Sound, Music, Trauma and Survival in Wartime Iraq*. New York: Oxford University Press, 2015.

Deleuze, Gilles. *Difference and Repetition*. Translated by Paul Patton. New York: Bloomsbury Academic, 2016.
Deleuze, Gilles. 'Postscript on the Societies of Control', translated by Martin Joughin. *October* 59 (1992): 3–7.
Dell'Antonio, Andrew. *Beyond Structural Listening? Postmodern Modes of Hearing*. Berkeley: University of California Press, 2004.
Dell'Antonio, Andrew. *Listening as Spiritual Practice in Early Modern Italy*. Berkeley: University of California Press, 2011.
DeNora, Tia. *Music in Everyday Life*. Cambridge: Cambridge University Press, 2000.
Deutsches Automatenmuseum (website). Gauselmann AG. Accessed 9 May 2022. https://www.deutsches-automatenmuseum.de/.
Devine, Kyle. *Decomposed: The Political Ecology of Music*. Cambridge, MA: MIT Press, 2019.
Devine, Kyle. 'Musicology without Music'. In *On Popular Music and Its Unruly Entanglements*, edited by Nick Braae and Kai Arne Hansen, 15–37. Cham: Palgrave Macmillan, 2020.
Devine, Kyle. 'A Mysterious Music in the Air: Cultural Origins of the Loudspeaker'. *Popular Music History* 8, no. 1 (2013): 5–28.
Dewhirst, Ian. Liner Notes for Various, *Salsoul 30th: 30 Years of Salsoul – 30 Classic Club Cuts – 30 World Class DJ's*. Salsoul, United States, 2005.
Diederichsen, Diedrich. 'Musikalische Stationen der Gegenkultur'. In *The Whole Earth: Kalifornien und das Verschwinden des Außen*, edited by Diedrich Diederichsen and Anselm Franke, 189–91. Berlin: Sternberg Press, 2013.
'Die Messe-Neuheiten'. *Der Automaten-Markt: Fachzeitschrift für die gesamte Automatenwirtschaft* 8, no. 4 (1956): 208.
'Die Musikbox befriedigt ein echtes Bedürfnis'. *Der Automaten-Markt: Fachzeitschrift für die Gesamte Automatenwirtschaft* 8, no. 8 (1956): 473–6.
'Die Neue Rock-Ola mit 200 Wahlmöglichkeiten'. *Der Automaten-Markt: Fachzeitschrift für die gesamte Automatenwirtschaft* 8, no. 12 (1956): 702.
'Die Spitzenreiter des Monats'. Der Automaten-Markt. Fachzeitschrift für die gesamte Automatenwirtschaft 8, no. 3 (1956): 137.
'Die Tanzbox ist groß im Kommen'. *Der Automaten-Markt: Fachzeitschrift für die gesamte Automatenwirtschaft* 11, no. 12 (1959): 717.
Donhauser, Peter. *Elektrische Klangmaschinen: Die Pionierzeit in Deutschland und Österreich*. Wien: Böhlau, 2007.
Dörfling, Christina. 'Von der Liebe zum Hören: Direktschnitt, Direct Metal Mastering und die (Un-)Möglichkeit audiophiler Tonträger'. *Musiktheorie: Zeitschrift für Musikwissenschaft* 36, no. 1 (2021): 32–45.
Dörfling, Christina, Christofer Jost and Martin Pfleiderer, eds. *Musikobjektgeschichten: Populäre Musik und materielle Kultur*. Münster: Waxmann, 2021.
Douglas, Susan. *Listening In: Radio and the American Imagination*. Minneapolis: University of Minnesota Press, 2004.
Doyle, Peter. *Echo and Reverb: Fabricating Space in Popular Music Recording 1900–1960*. Middletown: Wesleyan University Press, 2005.
Doyle, Peter. 'Ghosts of Electricity: Amplification'. In *The Sage Handbook of Popular Music*, edited by Andy Bennett and Steve Waksman, 532–48. Los Angeles, CA: Sage, 2015.
Drate, Spencer and Judith Salavetz. *Five Hundred 45s: A Graphic History of the Seven-Inch Record*. New York: Collins Design, 2010.

Driver, Ian. *A Century of Dance: A Hundred Years of Musical Movement, From Waltz to Hip Hop*. London: Hamlyn, 2000.

Drott, Eric. 'Rereading Jacques Attali's *Bruits*'. *Critical Inquiry* 41, no. 4 (2015): 721–56.

Drott, Eric. 'Why the Next Song Matters: Streaming, Recommendation, Scarcity'. *Twentieth-Century Music* 15, no. 3 (2018): 325–57.

Dyer, Frank Lewis. Improvements in the Art of Recording and Reproducing Sounds. GB Patent 215761A, filed 7 May 1924, and issued 7 September 1925.

Dyer, Richard. 'In Defence of Disco'. *Gay Left* 8 (1979): 20–3.

Easlea, Daryl. *Everybody Dance: Chic and the Politics of Disco*. London: Omnibus Press, 2005.

Echols, Alice. *Hot Stuff: Disco and the Remaking of American Music*. New York: W. W. Norton, 2010.

Edison, Thomas A. 'The Phonograph and Its Future (1878)'. In *Music, Sound, and Technology in America: A Documentary History of Early Phonograph, Cinema, and Radio*, edited by Timothy D. Taylor, Mark Katz and Tony Grajeda, 29–36. Durham, NC: Duke University Press, 2012.

Eggebrecht, Hans Heinrich. *Musikalisches Denken: Aufsätze zur Theorie und Ästhetik der Musik*. Wilhelmshaven: Heinrichshofen 1977.

Ehlert, Ralf Gerhard. '1920, Western Electric. Erste kommerzielle Public-Address-Anlage angekündigt'. *Medienstimmen*. Accessed 30 April 2022. https://www.medienstimmen.de/chronik/1911-1920/1920-western-electric-erste-kommerzielle-public-address-anlage-angekuendigt/.

Ehlert, Ralf Gerhard. 'Public-Address-Strategien von 1919 bis 1949'. In *Politiken der Medien*, edited by Daniel Gethmann and Markus Stauff, 319–40. Zürich: diaphanes, 2005.

Eidsheim, Nina Sun. *Sensing Sound: Singing and Listening as Vibrational Practice*. Durham, NC: Duke University Press, 2015.

'Eine Million [sic] Musikboxen Spielen Für Millionen'. *Der Automaten-Markt: Fachzeitschrift für die gesamte Automatenwirtschaft* 12 (1960): 811.

Elste, Martin. *Kleines Tonträger-Lexikon: Von der Walze zur Compact Disc*. Kassel: Bärenreiter, 1989.

Engell, Lorenz, and Bernhard Siegert. 'Editorial'. *Zeitschrift für Medien- und Kulturforschung* 1 (2010): 5–9.

Engell, Lorenz, and Bernhard Siegert, eds. *Zeitschrift für Medien- und Kulturforschung: Schwerpunkt Kulturtechnik*. Hamburg: Meiner, 2010.

Ennis, Philip H. *The Seventh Stream: The Emergence of Rock 'n' Roll in America Popular Music*. Hanover, NH: Wesleyan University Press, 1992.

Epping-Jäger, Cornelia. 'Stimmräume. Die phono-zentrische Organisation der Macht im NS'. In *Politiken der Medien*, edited by Daniel Gethmann and Markus Stauff, 341–58. Zürich: diaphanes, 2005.

Erlmann, Veit. 'The Acoustic Abject: Sound and the Legal Imagination'. In *Sound Objects*, edited by James A. Steintrager and Rey Chow, 151–66. Durham, NC: Duke University Press, 2019.

Erlmann, Veit. 'But What about an Ethnographic Ear? Anthropology, Sound and the Senses'. In *Hearing Cultures: Essays on Sound, Listening and Modernity*, edited by Veit Erlmann, 1–19, Oxford: Berg, 2004.

Erlmann, Veit, ed. *Hearing Cultures: Essays on Sound, Listening and Modernity*. Oxford: Berg, 2004.

Erlmann, Veit. 'The Invention of the Listener: (An)Other History'. In *Sound as Popular Culture: A Research Companion*, edited by Jens Gerrit Papenburg and Holger Schulze, 163–72. Cambridge, MA: MIT Press, 2016.

Erlmann, Veit. *Reason and Resonance: A History of Modern Aurality*. New York: Zone Books, 2010.

Ernst, Wolfgang. *Chronopoetik: Zeitweisen und Zeitgaben technischer Medien*. Berlin: Kadmos, 2013.

Ernst, Wolfgang. 'Der Anästhetische Blick? Wahrnehmung durch Medien'. In *Ästhetik: Aufgabe(n) einer Wissenschaftsdisziplin*, edited by Karin Hirdina and Renate Reschke, 65–79. Freiburg: Rombach, 2004.

Ernst, Wolfgang. '"Merely the Medium"? Die Operative Verschränkung von Logik und Materie'. In *Was ist ein Medium?*, edited by Stefan Münker and Alexander Roesler, 158–84. Frankfurt am Main: Suhrkamp, 2008.

Ernst, Wolfgang. 'Takt und Taktilität – Akustik als privilegierter Kanal zeitkritischer Medienprozesse'. In *McLuhan neu lesen. Kritische Analysen zu Medien und Kultur im 21. Jahrhundert*, edited by Derrick de Kerckhove, Martina Leeker and Kerstin Schmidt, 170–80. Bielefeld: transcript, 2008.

Escott, Colin, and Martin Hawkins. *Good Rockin' Tonight: Sun Records and the Birth of Rock 'n' Roll*. New York: St Martin's Press, 1991.

Eshun, Kodwo. *More Brilliant Than the Sun: Adventures in Sonic Fiction*. London: Quartet Books, 1999.

Etling, Laurence W. 'Al Jarvis: Pioneer Disc Jockey'. *Popular Music and Society* 23, no. 3 (1999): 41–52.

Evans, Mike. *Vinyl: The Art of Making Records*. New York: Sterling, 2015.

Evens, Aden. *Sound Ideas: Music, Machines, and Experience*. Minneapolis: University of Minnesota Press, 2005.

The Facilities of AMI Incorporated. Accessed 9 May 2022, https://www.jukeboxhistory.info/ami/history/facilities_of_ami.pdf.

Feld, Steven. 'Acoustemology'. In *Keywords in Sound*, edited by Raphael Novak and Matt Sakakeeny, 12–21. Durham, NC: Duke University Press, 2015.

Fierstein, Alan, and Richard Long. 'State-of-the-Art Discotheque Sound Systems-System Design and Acoustical Measurement'. Paper, 67th AES Convention, New York, 31 October–3 November 1980.

Fikentscher, Kai. '"There's Not a Problem I Can't Fix, 'Cause I Can Do It in the Mix": On the Performative Technology of 12-inch Vinyl'. In *Music and Technoculture*, edited by René T. A. Lysloff and Leslie C. Gay Jr, 290–315. Middletown: Wesleyan University Press, 2003.

Fikentscher, Kai. *'You Better Work!' Underground Dance Music in New York City*. Middletown: Wesleyan University Press, 2000.

Fink, Robert. 'Below 100 Hz: Toward a Musicology of Bass Culture'. In *The Relentless Pursuit of Tone: Timbre in Popular Music*, edited by Robert Fink, Melinda Latour and Zachary Wallmark, 88–116. New York: Oxford University Press, 2018.

Fink, Robert. *Repeating Ourselves: American Minimal Music as Cultural Practice*. Berkeley: University of California Press, 2005.

Flatley, Jonathan, and Charles Kronengold, eds. *Criticism: A Quarterly for Literature and the Arts* 50, no. 1 (2008).

Fleming, Jonathan. *What Kind of House Party Is This? The History of a Music Revolution*. Slough: MIY, 1995.

Fornatale, Peter, and Joshua E. Mills. *Radio in the Television Age*. Woodstock, NY: Overlook Press, 1980.
Foucault, Michel. *Discipline and Punish: The Birth of the Prison*. Translated by Alan Sheridan. New York: Vintage Books, 1977.
Foucault, Michel. 'What Is Enlightment?'. In *The Foucault Reader*, translated by Catherine Porter, edited by Paul Rabinow, 32–50. New York: Pantheon Books, 1984.
Frank, Robert. *The Americans*. Göttingen: Steidl, 2020.
Frey, Stefan. '*Was sagt ihr zu diesem Erfolg*': Franz Lehár und die Unterhaltungsmusik des 20. Jahrhunderts. Frankfurt am Main: Insel, 1999.
Friedner, Michele, and Stefan Helmreich. 'Sound Studies Meets Deaf Studies'. *Senses & Society* 7, no. 1 (2012): 72–86.
Frith, Simon. 'The Industrialization of Popular Music'. In *Popular Music and Communication*, edited by James Lull, 49–74. Newbury Park, CA: Sage, 1992.
Frith, Simon. *The Sociology of Rock*. London: Constable, 1978.
Frith, Simon. *Sound Effects: Youth, Leisure, and the Politics of Rock 'n' Roll*. New York: Pantheon Books, 1981.
Frith, Simon, and Angela McRobbie. 'Rock and Sexuality'. In *On Record: Rock, Pop, and the Written Word*, edited by Simon Frith and Andrew Goodwin, 317–32. London: Routledge, 1990.
Frith, Simon, and Simon Zagorski-Thomas, eds. *The Art of Record Production: An Introductory Reader for a New Academic Field*. Burlington: Ashgate, 2012.
Frith, Simon, Matt Brennan, Martin Cloonan and Emma Webster, eds. *The History of Live Music in Britain, Volume I: 1950–1967: From Dance Hall to the 100 Club*. London: Routledge, 2013.
Frith, Simon, Matt Brennan, Martin Cloonan and Emma Webster, eds. *The History of Live Music in Britain, Volume II: 1968–1984: From Hyde Park to Hacienda*. London: Routledge, 2019.
Fulcher, Jane F. 'Introduction: Defining the New Cultural History of Music, Its Origins, Methodologies, and Lines of Inquiry'. In *The Oxford Handbook of the New Cultural History of Music*, edited by Jane F. Fulcher, 3–14. New York: Oxford University Press, 2011.
Fulcher, Jane F., ed. *The Oxford Handbook of the New Cultural History of Music*. New York: Oxford University Press, 2011.
Gallagher, Mitch. *Mastering Music at Home*. Boston, MA: Thomson, 2008.
Gálvez, José. 'Beschleunigte/euphorische Körper: Versuch einer Soundsoziologie von EDM-Livesets'. MA dissertation, Institute for Musicology and Media Studies, Humboldt University of Berlin, Berlin, 2017.
Gálvez, José. 'On Analyzing EDM DJ sets. Problems and Perspectives for a Sociology of Sound'. In *Contemporary Popular Music Studies*, edited by Marija Dumnić Vilotijević and Ivana Medić, 149–59. Wiesbaden: Springer, 2019.
Ganske, 'Aktuelle Fragen der Musikautomatenaufstellung'. In *Handbuch der Deutschen Automatenwirtschaft 1956*. Cologne: Carl Heymanns Verlag, 1956, 271–3.
Garcia, Luis-Manuel. 'As the World Turns: Time in Electronic Dance Music'. *Little White Earbuds*. Accessed 30 April 2022. http://www.littlewhiteearbuds.com/feature/as-the-world-turns-time-in-electronic-dance-music/.
Garcia, Luis-Manuel. 'Beats, Flesh, and Grain: Sonic Tactility and Affect in Electronic Dance Music'. *Sound Studies* 1, no. 1 (2015): 59–76.

Garcia, Luis-Manuel. 'Richard Dyer, "In Defence of Disco" (1979)'. *Geschichte der Gefühle – Einblicke in die Forschung*, November 2014. Accessed 30 April 2022. https://www.history-of-emotions.mpg.de/texte/in-defence-of-disco.

Garofalo, Reebee. 'Payola'. In *Continuum Encyclopedia of Popular Music of the World. Volume I: Media, Industry and Society*, edited by John Shepherd, David Horn, Dave Laing, Paul Oliver and Peter Wicke, 558–9. New York: Continuum, 2003.

Garofalo, Reebee, and Steve Waksman. *Rockin' Out: Popular Music in the USA*. Boston, MA: Pearson, 2014.

Garratt, Sheryl. 'Sample and Hold: The House Sound of Chicago'. *The Face*, September 1986, 18–23.

Gasser, Florian. 'Funktion-One: "Sound Doesn't Exist, Only the Truth"'. *Groove*. Accessed 30 April 2022. https://groove.de/2017/05/29/funktion-one-tony-andrews-interview-english/2/.

'Gäste, Wirte, Ober Antworten: Gedanken und Interviews zur Programmgestaltung in der Musikbox'. *Der Automaten-Markt: Fachzeitschrift für die Gesamte Automatenwirtschaft* 9, no. 6 (1957): 300.

Gauß, Stefan. *Nadel, Rille, Trichter. Kulturgeschichte des Phonographen und des Grammophons in Deutschland (1900–1940)*. Cologne: Böhlau, 2009.

Gay, Peter. *The Naked Heart*. New York: W. W. Norton, 1995.

Geisthövel, Alexa. 'Anpassung: Disco und Jugendbeobachtung in Westdeutschland, 1975–1981'. In *Zeitgeschichte des Selbst: Therapeutisierung – Politisierung – Emotionalisierung*, edited by Pascal Eitler and Jens Elberfeld, 239–60. Bielefeld: transcript, 2015.

Gelatt, Roland. *The Fabulous Phonograph: 1877–1977*. London: Cassell, 1977.

'GEMA-Rahmenvertrag mit Wirkung 1. Januar 1959 in Kraft'. *Der Automaten-Markt: Fachzeitschrift für die gesamte Automatenwirtschaft* 11, no. 3 (1959): 120.

George, Nelson. *The Death of Rhythm & Blues*. London: Penguin, 2004.

George, Nelson. 'House Music: Will It Join Rap and Go-Go?'. *Billboard*, 21 June 1986, 27.

Gerdien, Hans. 'Über klanggetreue Schallwiedergabe mittels Lautsprecher'. *Telefunken Zeitung* 8, no. 43 (1926): 28–38.

Gerhard, Anselm, ed. *Musikwissenschaft – eine verspätete Disziplin? Die akademische Musikforschung zwischen Fortschrittsglauben und Modernitätsverweigerung*. Stuttgart: J. B. Metzler, 2000.

Gilbert, Jeremy. 'Dyer and Deleuze: Post-Structuralist Cultural Criticism'. *New Formations* 58 (2006): 109–27.

Gilbert, Jeremy, and Ewan Pearson. *Discographies: Dance Music, Culture and the Politics of Sound*. London: Routledge, 1999.

Gillett, Charlie. *The Sound of the City: The Rise of Rock and Roll*. London: Souvenir Press, 1983.

Gilli, Lorenz. '"Navigate Your Set". Zur Virtuosität von DJs'. In *Schneller, höher, lauter: Virtuosität in populären Musiken*, edited by Thomas Phleps, 153–79. Bielefeld: transcript, 2017.

Gitelman, Lisa. *Always Already New: Media, History, and the Data of Culture*. Cambridge, MA: MIT Press, 2006.

Glass, Louis, and William S. Arnold. Coin Actuated Attachment for Phonographs. US Patent US428750A, filed 27 May 1890, and issued 27 May 1890.

Glinsky, Albert. *Theremin: Ether Music and Espionage*. Urbana: University of Illinois Press, 2005.

Glover, David, and Scott McCracken, eds. *New Formations* 58 (2006).

Goehr, Lydia. *The Imaginary Museum of Musical Works: An Essay in the Philosophy of Music*. Oxford: Clarendon Press, 1992.
Goldman, Albert. *Disco*. New York: Hawthorn Books, 1978.
Goldmark, Peter. *Maverick Inventor: My Turbulent Years at CBS*. New York: Saturday Review Press, 1973.
Goldmark, Peter, R. Snepvangers and W. S. Bachman. 'The Columbia Long-Playing Microgroove Recording System'. *Proceedings of the IRE* 37, no. 8 (1949): 923–7.
Goodman, Steve. *Sonic Warfare: Sound, Affect, and the Ecology of Fear*. Cambridge, MA: MIT Press, 2010.
Goodman, Steve, Toby Heys and Eleni Ikoniadou, eds. *AUDINT-Unsound: Undead*. Falmouth: Urbanomic, 2019.
Goodwin, Andrew. *Dancing in the Distraction Factory: Music Television and Popular Culture*. Minneapolis: University of Minnesota Press, 1992.
Goldstein, Paul. *Copyright's Highway: From Gutenberg to the Celestial Jukebox*. Stanford, CA: Stanford University Press, 2003.
Göttert, Karl-Heinz. *Geschichte der Stimme*. Munich: Fink, 1998.
Gracyk, Theodore. *Rhythm and Noise: An Aesthetics of Rock*. Durham, NC: Duke University Press, 1996.
Grajeda, Tony. 'Early Mood Music: Edison's Phonography, American Modernity and the Instrumentalization of Listening'. In *Ubiquitous Musics: The Everyday Sounds That We Don't Always Notice*, edited by Elena Boschi, Anahid Kassabian and Marta García Quiñones, 30–47. London: Routledge, 2013.
Grajeda, Tony. 'The "Sweet Spot": The Technology of Stereo and the Field of Auditorship'. In *Living Stereo: Histories and Cultures of Multichannel Sound*, edited by Paul Théberge, Kyle Devine and Tom Everrett, 37–63. New York: Bloomsbury Academic, 2015.
Grimm, Fred. '*Wir wollen eine andere Welt'. Jugend in Deutschland 1900–2010, Eine private Geschichte aus Tagebüchern, Briefen, Dokumenten*. Hamburg: Tolkemitt bei Zweitausendeins, 2010.
Großmann, Rolf. 'Die Geburt des Pop aus dem Geist der phonographischen Reproduktion'. In *Popmusicology: Perspektiven der Popmusikwissenschaft*, edited by Christian Bielefeldt, Udo Dahmen and Rolf Großmann, 119–34. Bielefeld: transcript, 2008.
Großmann, Rolf. 'Die Materialität des Klangs und die Medienpraxis der Musikkultur: Ein verspäteter Gegenstand der Musikwissenschaft?'. In *Auditive Medienkulturen: Techniken des Hörens und Praktiken der Klanggestaltung*, edited by Jens Schröter and Axel Volmar, 67–78. Bielefeld: transcript, 2013.
Großmann, Rolf. 'Konstruktiv(istische)e Gedanken zur "Medienmusik"'. In *Medien – Musik – Mensch: Neue Medien und Musikwissenschaft*, edited by Thomas Hemker and Daniel Müllensiefen, 61–78. Hamburg: Bockel, 1997.
Großmann, Rolf. 'Phonographic Work: Reading and Writing Sound'. In *Sound as Popular Culture. A Research Companion*, edited by Jens Gerrit Papenburg and Holger Schulze, 355–66. Cambridge, MA: MIT Press, 2016.
Großmann, Rolf. 'Reproduktionsmusik und Remix-Culture'. In *Mind the Gap: Medienkonstellationen zwischen zeitgenössischer Musik und Klangkunst*, edited by Marion Saxer, 116–27. Saarbrücken: Pfau, 2011.

Großmann, Rolf. 'Spiegelbild, Spiegel, leerer Spiegel: Zur Mediensituation der Clicks & Cuts'. In *Soundcultures: Über elektronische und digitale Musik*, edited by Marcus S. Kleiner and Achim Szepanksi, 52–68. Frankfurt am Main: Suhrkamp, 2003.

Großmann, Rolf. 'Verschlafener Medienwandel: Das Dispositiv als musikwissenschaftliches Theoriemodell'. *Positionen – Beiträge zur Neuen Musik* 74 (2008): 6–9.

Grünberg, Ingrid. 'Operette und Rundfunk: Die Entstehung eines spezifischen Typs massenwirksamer Unterhaltungsmusik'. In *Angewandte Musik 20er Jahre: Exemplarische Versuche Gesellschaftsbezogener Arbeit für Theater, Radio, Massenveranstaltung*, edited by Fritz Haug, 59–80. Berlin: Argument Verlag, 1977.

Grüny, Christian. *Kunst des Übergangs: Philosophische Konstellationen zur Musik*. Weilerswist: Velbrück, 2014.

Gumbrecht, Hans Ulrich, and Ludwig Pfeiffer, eds. *Materialität der Kommunikation*. Frankfurt am Main: Suhrkamp, 1988.

Guralnick, Peter. *Sam Phillips: The Man Who Invented Rock 'n' Roll*. New York: Little, Brown, 2015.

Haas, Max. *Musikalisches Denken im Mittelalter: Eine Einführung*. Bern: Lang 2005.

Haberer, Max. 'Versuch über Spotify, oder: Musikstreaming als Arbeit am Subjekt'. In *Wissen im Klang: Neue Wege der Musikästhetik*, edited by José Gálvez, Jonas Reichert and Elizaveta Willert, 145–61. Bielefeld: transcript, 2020.

Haden-Guest, Anthony. *The Last Party: Studio 54, Disco, and the Culture of the Night*. New York: HarperCollins, 1997.

Hafen, Roland. 'Rockmusik-Rezeption in Live-Konzerten'. In *Handbuch Jugend und Musik*, edited by Dieter Baacke, 369–80. Opladen: Leske + Budrich, 1997.

Hagen, Wolfgang. *Das Radio: Zur Geschichte und Theorie des Hörfunks – Deutschland/USA*. Munich: Fink, 2005.

Hagood, Mack. *Hush: Media and Sonic Self-Control*. Durham, NC: Duke University Press, 2019.

Hamilton, Marybeth. *In the Search of the Blues*. New York: Basic Books, 2008.

Hamilton, Marybeth. 'The Voice of the Blues'. *History Workshop Journal* 7, no. 54 (2002): 123–43.

Hamm, Charles. *Putting Popular Music in Its Place*. Cambridge: Cambridge University Press, 1995.

Handke, Peter. *The Jukebox and Other Essays on Storytelling*. Translated by Ralph Manheim. New York: Picador, 2020.

Hanslick, Eduard. *Eduard Hanslick's 'On the Musically Beautiful': A New Translation*. Translated by Lee Allen Rothfarb and Christoph Landerer. New York: Oxford University Press, 2018.

Hanson, Kitty. *Disco Fieber: Alles über die Disco-Welle*. Munich: Heyne, 1979.

Hardjowirogo, Sarah. *'Instrumentalität': Der Begriff des Musikinstruments zwischen Klangerzeuger, Kultgerät und Körper-Technik*. Hildesheim: Olms, 2022.

Harenberg, Michael, and Daniel Weissberg. 'Einleitung: Der Verlust der Körperlichkeit in der Musik und die Entgrenzung klanglichen Gestaltungspotenzials'. In *Klang (ohne) Körper: Spuren und Potenziale des Körpers in der elektronischen Musik*, edited by Michael Harenberg and Daniel Weissberg, 7–18. Bielefeld: transcript, 2010.

Harper, Paula Clare. 'ASMR: Bodily Pleasure, Online Performance, Digital Modality'. *Sound Studies* 6, no. 1: 95–8.

Hartmann, Frank. 'Instant Awareness: Eine medientheoretische Exploration mit McLuhan'. In *Soundcultures: Über elektronische und digitale Musik*, edited by Marcus S. Kleiner and Achim Szepanski, 34–51. Frankfurt am Main: Suhrkamp, 2003.

Hazzard-Gordon, Katrina. *Jookin': The Rise of Social Formations in African-American Culture*. Philadelphia, PA: Temple University Press, 1990.

Hebdige, Dick. *Subculture: The Meaning of Style*. London: Routledge, 1979.

Hecker, Timothy. 'The Era of Megaphonics: On the Productivity of Loud Sound, 1880–1930'. PhD dissertation, Department of Art History and Communication Studies, McGill University, Montreal, 2014.

Heidegger, Martin. 'The Question Concerning Technology'. In *The Question Concerning Technology and Other Essays*, translated by William Lovit. New York: Harper and Row, 1977.

Heidenreich, Stefan. 'Rauschen, filtern, codieren – Stilbildung in Mediensystemen'. In *das rauschen*, edited by Sabine Sanio and Christian Scheib, 17–26. Hofheim: Wolke, 1995.

Heilmann, Till A. 'Der Klang der breiten Rille'. *Internationales Jahrbuch für Medienphilosophie*. Available online: https://jbmedienphilosophie.de/2017/3-replik-heilmann/. Accessed 30 April 2022.

Heister, Hanns-Werner. *Das Konzert: Theorie einer Kulturform*. Wilhelmshaven: Heinrichshofen, 1983.

Heister, Hanns-Werner. 'Die Musikbox: Studie zur Ökonomie, Sozialpsychologie und Ästhetik eines musikalischen Massenmediums'. In *Segmente der Unterhaltungsindustrie*, edited by Hanns-Werner Heister et al., 11–65. Frankfurt am Main: Suhrkamp, 1974.

Heister, Hanns-Werner. 'Musikbox'. In *Handbuch Populäre Kultur*, edited by Hans-Otto Hügel, 326–9. Stuttgart: J. B. Metzler, 2003.

Helmholtz, Hermann von. *Die Lehre von den Tonempfindungen als physiologische Grundlage für die Theorie der Musik*. Braunschweig: Vieweg, 1913 [1863].

Helmholtz, Hermann von. *On the Sensations of Tone as a Physiological Basis for the Theory of Music*, translated by Alexander J. Ellis. London: Longmans, Green, 1885 [1863].

Helmreich, Stefan. 'An Anthropologist Underwater: Immersive Soundscapes, Submarine Cyborgs, and Transductive Ethnography'. *American Ethnologist* 34, no. 4 (2007): 621–41.

Helmreich, Stefan. 'Transduction'. In *Keywords in Sound*, edited by David Novak and Matt Sakakeeny, 222–31. Durham, NC: Duke University Press, 2015.

Helms, Dietrich, and Thomas Phleps, eds. *Ware Inszenierungen: Performance, Vermarktung und Authentizität in der populären Musik*. Bielefeld: transcript, 2013.

Henke, Robert. 'Mastering'. *Monolake*. Accessed 30 April 2022. http://www.disco-disco.com/tributes/tom.shtml.

Hennion, Antoine. 'Baroque and Rock: Music, Mediators and Musical Taste'. *Poetics* 24 (1997): 415–35.

Hennion, Antoine. 'Music and Mediation: Toward a New Sociology of Music'. In *The Cultural Study of Music: A Critical Introduction*, edited by Martin Clayton, Trevor Herbert and Richard Middleton, 80–91. London: Routledge, 2003.

Hennion, Antoine, and Bruno Latour. 'How to Make Mistakes on So Many Things at Once – and Become Famous for It'. In *Mapping Benjamin. The Work of Art in the Digital Age*, edited by Hans Ulrich Gumbrecht and Michael Marrinan, 91–7. Stanford, CA: Stanford University Press, 2003.

Hennion, Antoine, and Christophe Levaux, eds. *Rethinking Music through Science and Technology Studies*. London: Routledge, 2021.
Henriques, Julian. 'Auditory and Technological Culture: The Fine-Tuning of the Dancehall Sound System "Set"'. In *The Auditory Culture Reader*, 2nd edn, edited by Michael Bull and Les Back, 349–55. New York: Bloomsbury, 2016.
Henriques, Julian. 'Preamble: Thinking through Sound'. In *Sonic Bodies. Reggae Sound Systems, Performance Techniques and Ways of Knowing*, xv–xxxii. New York: Continuum, 2011.
Henriques, Julian. *Sonic Bodies: Reggae Sound Systems, Performance Techniques and Ways of Knowing*. New York: Continuum, 2011.
Henriques, Julian. 'Sonic Dominance and the Reggae Sound System Session'. In *The Auditory Culture Reader*, 1st edn, edited by Michael Bull and Les Back, 451–80. Oxford: Berg, 2005.
Herford, Marta, ed. *Booster: Kunst, Sound, Maschine*. Berlin: Kerber, 2014.
Herkt, Günther. *Das Tonfilmtheater: Umbau, Neubau, Tongerät, Betrieb, Vorführung, Wirtschaftlichkeit*. Berlin: Deutsche Bauzeitung, 1931.
Hermann, Thaddeus. 'Dubplates & Mastering: Von der Festplatte aufs Vinyl (Interview mit Andreas Lubich)'. *DE:BUG Magazin für Elektronische Lebensaspekte*, 20 May 2006. Accessed 12 October 2011. http://www.de-bug.de/musiktechnik/archives/179.html.
Hertz, Garnet, and Jussi Parikka. 'Zombie Media: Circuit Bending Media Archaeology into an Art Method'. *Leonardo* 45, no. 5 (2012): 424–30.
Hilmes, Michele. 'Is There a Field Called Sound Culture Studies? And Does It Matter?'. *American Quarterly* 57, no. 1 (2005): 249–59.
'Historie von den Musikautomaten (II)'. *Der Automaten-Markt. Fachzeitschrift für die gesamte Automatenwirtschaft* 11, no. 6 (1959): 318.
Hoggart, Richard. *The Uses of Literacy: Aspects of Working-Class Life*. London: Penguin, 2009.
Holert, Tom. 'Star-Schnittstelle: Glamour und elektronische Popkultur'. In *Gendertronics: Der Körper in der elektronischen Musik*, edited by club transmediale and Meike Jansen, 20–43. Frankfurt am Main: Suhrkamp, 2005.
Holland, Bernard. 'A Man Who Sees What Others Hear'. *New York Times*, 19 November 1981, 28.
Holleran, Andrew. *Dancer from the Dance*. New York: Perennial, 2001.
Holt, Fabian. *Everyone Loves Live Music: A Theory of Performance Institutions*. Chicago, IL: University of Chicago Press, 2020.
Holtsträter, Knut. 'Der Crooner, das unbekannte Wesen'. In *Musik und Popularität. Aspekte zu einer Kulturgeschichte zwischen 1500 und heute*, edited by Sabine Meine and Nina Noeske, 145–65. Münster: Waxmann, 2011.
Holtsträter, Knut. '"The Voice of Frank Sinatra" as the first Concept Album in the History of Popular Music. Musical (large-scale) Form on Records and its Contexts of Use in the U.S. Popular Culture of the 1950s'. In *Große Formen in der populären Musik: Large-Scale Forms in Popular Music*, edited by Jost Christofer and Gregor Herzfeld, 17–38. Münster: Waxmann, 2019.
Honold, Alexander. *Der Erd-Erzähler*. Stuttgart: J. B. Metzler, 2017.
Hörisch, Jochen, and Michael Wetzel, eds. *Armaturen der Sinne: Literarische und Technische Medien 1870 bis 1920*. Munich: Fink, 1990.
Horn, Adrian. *Juke Box Britain: Americanisation and Youth Culture, 1945–60*. Manchester: Manchester University Press, 2009.

Horn, David, Dave Laing and David Sanjek. 'Columbia'. In *Continuum Encyclopedia of Popular Music of the World. Volume I: Media, Industry and Society*, edited by John Shepherd, David Horn, Dave Laing, Paul Oliver and Peter Wicke, New York: Continuum, 2003, 702.

Horowitz, Is. '"Illegit" Disco Tapes Peddled by Jockeys'. *Billboard*, 12 October 1974, 1, 12.

Horowitz, Is. 'Juke Box Influence on Record Business'. *Billboard* 23 (1953): 91.

Hosokawa, Shuhei. 'The Walkman Effect'. *Popular Music* 4 (1984): 165–80.

Hosokawa, Shuhei, and Hideaki Matsuoka. 'On the Fetish Character of Sound and the Progression of Technology: Theorizing Japanese Audiophiles'. In *Sonic Synergies: Music, Technology, Community, Identity*, edited by Gerry Bloustien, Margaret Peters and Susan Luckman, 39–50. Aldershot: Ashgate, 2008.

Howes, David, ed. *Empire of the Senses: The Sensual Culture Reader*. Oxford: Berg, 2005.

Howes, David. 'General Introduction: Empires of the Senses'. In *Empire of the Senses: The Sensual Culture Reader*, edited by David Howes, 1–17. Oxford: Berg, 2005.

Hughes, Walter. 'In the Empire of the Beat: Discipline and Disco'. In *Microphone Fiends: Youth Music and Youth Culture*, edited by Andrew Ross and Tricia Ross, 147–57. New York: Routledge, 1994.

Hui, Alexandra. 'First Re-creations: Psychology, Phonographs, and New Cultures of Listening at the Beginning of the Twentieth Century'. In *The Oxford Handbook of Music Listening in the 19th and 20th Centuries*, edited by Christian Thorau and Hansjakob Ziemer, 373–94. New York: Oxford University Press, 2019.

Hui, Alexandra. *The Psychophysical Ear: Musical Experiments, Experimental Sounds, 1840–1910*. Cambridge, MA: MIT Press, 2013.

Hepworth-Sawyer, Russ, and Jay Hodgson, eds, *Audio Mastering. The Artists. Discussions from Pre-production to Mastering*. London: Routledge 2019.

Ihde, Don. *Listening and Voice: Phenomenologies of Sound*. Albany, NY: State University of New York Press, 2007.

'IMA-AMI in Kopenhagen Gegründet'. *Der Automaten-Markt: Fachzeitschrift für die gesamte Automatenwirtschaft* 6, no. 1 (1954): 13, 16.

'Interview: The Loft Founder David Mancuso'. Red Bull Music Academy. Accessed 30 April 2022. https://daily.redbullmusicacademy.com/2016/06/david-mancuso-interview.

Ismaiel-Wendt, Johannes. *Post_PRESETS. Kultur, Wissen und Populäre MusikmachDinge*. Hildesheim: Olms, 2016.

Ismaiel-Wendt, Johannes. *Tracks 'n' treks: Populäre Musik und Postkoloniale Analyse*. Münster: Unrast, 2011.

Isom, Warren R. 'Introduction: Before the Fine Groove and Stereo Record and Other Innovations'. *Journal of the Audio Engineering Society* 25, no. 10/11 (1977): 815–20.

Jackson, John A. *A House on Fire: The Rise and Fall of Philadelphia Soul*. New York: Oxford University Press, 2004.

Jackson, Myles W. 'From Scientific Instruments to Musical Instruments: The Tuning Fork, Metronome, and Siren'. In *The Oxford Handbook of Sound Studies*, edited by Karin Bijsterveld and Trevor Pinch, 201–23. New York: Oxford University Press, 2012.

Jaffe, J. Christopher. *Acoustics of Performance Halls: Spaces for Music from Carnegie Hall to the Hollywood Bowl*. New York: W. W. Norton, 2007.

James, Robin, ed. *Cassette Mythos*. New York: Autonomedia, 1992.

James, Robin. *Resilience & Melancholy: Pop Music, Feminism, Neoliberalism*. Winchester: Zero Books, 2015.

James, Robin. 'Sonic Cyberfeminisms, Perceptual Coding and Phonographic Compression'. *Feminist Review* 127, no. 1 (2021): 20–34.
Jansson, Sara. '"Listen to These Speakers": Swedish Hi-Fi Enthusiasts, Gender, and Listening'. *Journal of the International Association for the Study of Popular Music* 1, no. 2 (2010): 1–11.
Jasen, Paul C. *Low End Theory: Bass, Bodies and the Materiality of Sonic Experience*. New York: Bloomsbury Academic, 2016.
Jehan, Tristan. 'Creating Music by Listening'. PhD dissertation, School of Architecture and Planning, Massachusetts Institute of Technology, Cambridge, MA, 2005. https://web.media.mit.edu/~tristan/phd/pdf/Tristan_PhD_MIT.pdf.
Joe, Radcliffe A. *This Business of Disco*. New York: Billboard Books, 1980.
Johnson, James H. *Listening in Paris: A Cultural History*. Berkeley: University of California Press, 1995.
Johnson, Jim [Bruno Latour]. 'Mixing Humans and Nonhumans Together: The Sociology of a Door-Closer'. *Social Problems* 35, no. 3 (1988): 289–310.
Jones, Alan, and Jussi Kantonen. *Saturday Night Forever: The Story of Disco*. London: Random House, 2005.
Jooß-Bernau, Christian. *Das Pop-Konzert als para-theatrale Form: Seine Varianten und seine Bedingungen im kulturell-öffentlichen Raum*. Berlin: de Gruyter, 2010.
Jost, Christofer, and Gregor Herzfeld, eds. *Große Formen in der populären Musik: Large-Scale Forms in Popular Music*. Münster: Waxmann, 2019.
Jukebox World (website). Hildegard Stamann, Stamann Musikboxen. Accessed 9 May 2022. http://www.jukebox-world.de.
Kalies, Christoph, Andreas C. Lehmann and Reinhard Kopiez. 'Musikleben und Live-Musik'. In *Musikpsychologie: Das neue Handbuch*, edited by Herbert Bruhn, Reinhard Kopiez and Andreas C. Lehmann, 293–315. Reinbek bei Hamburg: Rowohlt, 2008.
Kane, Brian. 'In Search of Audile Technique'. Keynote lecture, EHESS, Paris, 26 January 2019. Lecture audio available online: https://soundcloud.com/user-897145586/brian-kane-yale-university. Accessed 18 February 2022.
Kane, John. *The Last Seat in the House: The Story of Hanley Sound*. Jackson, MS: University Press of Mississippi, 2020.
Kapp, Ernst. *Grundlinien einer Philosophie der Technik. Zur Entstehungsgeschichte der Cultur aus neuen Gesichtspunkten*. Braunschweig: Westermann, 1877.
Kassabian, Anahid. 'Hearing as a Contact Sense'. Lecture, Music Forum at Keele University, Keele, 3 June 2007.
Kassabian, Anahid. 'Listening and Digital Technologies'. In *Sound as Popular Culture: A Research Companion*, edited by Jens Gerrit Papenburg and Holger Schulze, 197–203. Cambridge, MA: MIT Press, 2016.
Kassabian, Anahid. *Ubiquitous Listening: Affect, Attention, and Distributed Subjectivity*. Berkeley: University of California Press, 2013.
Katz, Bob. *Mastering Audio: The Art and the Science*, 3rd edn. Burlington, MA: Focal Press, 2014.
Katz, Mark. *Capturing Sound: How Technology Has Changed Music*. Berkeley: University of California Press, 2010.
Katz, Mark. *Groove Music: The Art and Culture of the Hip-Hop DJ*. New York: Oxford University Press, 2012.
Kealy, Edward. 'From Craft to Art: The Case of Sound Mixers and Popular Music'. *Work and Occupation* 6, no. 1 (1979): 3–29.

Keeken, Alan van. 'Musik erzeugen'. In *Audiowelten: Technologie und Medien in der populären Musik nach 1945: 22 Objektstudien*, edited by Benjamin Burkhart, Lara Niebling, Alan van Keeken, Christofer Jost and Martin Pfleiderer, 19–190. Münster: Waxmann, 2021.

Keeken, Alan van. 'Sozio-technische Artefaktanalyse'. In *Spurenlesen: Methodische Ansätze der Sammlungs- und Objektforschung*, edited by Ernst Seidl and Cornelia Weber, 61–71. Berlin: Humboldt-Universität zu Berlin, 2021.

Keightley, Keir. 'Album'. In *Continuum Encyclopedia of Popular Music of the World. Volume I: Media, Industry and Society*, edited by John Shepherd, David Horn, Dave Laing, Paul Oliver and Peter Wicke, 612–3. London: Continuum, 2003.

Keightley, Keir. 'Tin Pan Allegory'. *Modernism/Modernity* 19, no. 4 (2013): 717–36.

Keightley, Keir. '"Turn It Down!" She Shrieked: Gender, Domestic Space, and High Fidelity, 1948–59'. *Popular Music* 15, no. 2 (1996): 149–77.

Keightley, Keir, and Will Straw. 'Single'. In *Continuum Encyclopedia of Popular Music of the World. Volume II. Performance and Production*, edited by John Shepherd, David Horn, Dave Laing, Paul Oliver and Peter Wicke, 779–80. London: Continuum, 2003.

Keller, Hans. 'The Keller Column: The Gramophone Record'. *Music & Musicans*, January (1985): 13.

Kemp, Cornelia, and Ulrike Gierlinger. *Wenn Der Groschen Fällt … Münzautomaten – gestern und heute*. Munich: Deutsches Museum IMS, 1989.

Kempster, Chris. *History of House*. London: Music Maker, 1996.

Kennedy, Rick, and Randy McNutt. *Little Labels – Big Sound: Small Record Companies and the Rise of American Music*. Bloomington, IN: Indiana University Press, 1999.

Kenney, William H. *Recorded Music in American Life: The Phonograph and Popular Memory, 1890–1945*. New York: Oxford University Press, 1999.

Kerckhove, Derrick de. 'Propriodezeption und Autonomation'. In *Tasten*, edited by Uta Brandes and Claudia Neumann, 330–45. Göttingen: Steidl, 1996.

Kerins, Mark. *Beyond Dolby (Stereo): Cinema in the Digital Sound Age*. Bloomington, IN: Indiana University Press, 2011.

Kim-Cohen, Seth. *In the Blink of an Ear: Toward a Non-Cochlear Sonic Art*. New York: Continuum, 2009.

Kirby, David. *Little Richard: The Birth of Rock 'n' Roll*. New York: Continuum, 2009.

Kirk, Roger E. 'Learning, a Major Factor Influencing Preferences for High-Fidelity Systems'. *Journal of the Audio Engineering Society* 5, no. 4 (1957): 238–41.

Kiss, Jemima. 'The Death of the Album'. *The Guardian*, 29 August 2008. https://www.theguardian.com/media/pda/2008/aug/29/thedeathofthealbum.

Kittler, Friedrich A. 'Bei Tanzmusik kommt es einem in die Beine'. In *Auditive Medienkulturen: Techniken des Hörens und Praktiken der Klanggestaltung*, edited by Axel Volmar and Jens Schröter, 35–42. Bielefeld: transcript, 2013.

Kittler, Friedrich A. *Discourse Networks 1800/1900*. Translated by Michael Matteer. Stanford, CA: Stanford University Press, 1990.

Kittler, Friedrich A. 'Echoes: Ein Prolog'. In *Hörstürze: Akustik und Gewalt im 20. Jahrhundert*, edited by Nicola Gess, Florian Schreiner und Manuela K. Schulz, 13–32. Würzburg: Königshausen & Neumann, 2005.

Kittler, Friedrich A. 'The God of the Ears'. In *The Truth of the Technological World: Essays on the Genealogy of Presence*, translated by Erik Butler, edited by Hans Ulrich Gumbrecht, 45–56. Stanford, CA: Stanford University Press, 2014.

Kittler, Friedrich A. *Gramophone, Film, Typewriter*. Translated by Geoffrey Winthrop-Young and Michael Wutz. Stanford, CA: Stanford University Press, 1999.
Kittler, Friedrich A. *Optical Media: Berlin Lectures 1999*. Translated by Anthony Enns. Cambridge: Polity, 2010.
Kittler, Friedrich A. 'Real Time Analysis, Time Axis Manipulation'. *Cultural Politics* 13, no. 1 (2017): 1–18.
Kittler, Friedrich A. 'Rock Music: A Misuse of Military Equipment'. In *The Truth of the Technological World: Essays on the Genealogy of Presence*, translated by Erik Butler, edited by Hans Ulrich Gumbrecht, 152–64. Stanford, CA: Stanford University Press, 2014.
Kittler, Friedrich A. 'Wagners Untergänge'. *Programmhefte der Bayreuther Festspiele*, no. 3 (1987): 1–19.
Kittler, Friedrich A. 'World-Breath: On Wagner's Media Technology'. In *The Truth of the Technological World: Essays on the Genealogy of Presence*, translated by Erik Butler, edited by Hans Ulrich Gumbrecht, 122–37. Stanford, CA: Stanford University Press, 2014.
Kittler, Friedrich A., and Georg Christoph Tholen, eds. *Arsenale der Seele. Literatur – und Medienanalysen seit 1870*. Munich: Fink, 1989.
Klein, Gabriele. *Electronic Vibration: Pop Kultur Theorie*. Wiesbaden: Springer, 2004.
'Kleinere Schallplatten – Mehr Musik'. *Der Automaten-Markt: Fachzeitschrift Für Die Gesamte Automatenwirtschaft* 6, no. 9 (1954): 286.
Klotz, Sebastian. 'Algorithmic and Nostalgic Listening: Post-Subjective Implications of Computational and Empirical Research'. In *Musical Listening in the Age of Technological Reproduction*, edited by Gianmario Borio, 69–90. Farnham: Ashgate, 2015.
Klotz, Sebastian. 'Arcadia, Musicland. Variants of Eloquence in the Renaissance Madrigal & in Disco'. In *VARIANTOLOGY 5: Neapolitan Affairs*, edited by Siegfried Zielinski and Eckhard Fürlus, 299–317. Cologne: Walther König, 2011.
Klotz, Sebastian. '"Love to Love You Music". Verschwendung, Begehren und kapitalistischer Realismus in Minimal Music und Disco'. In *High – low: Hoch- und Alltagskultur in Musik, Kunst, Literatur, Tanz und Kino*, edited by Corina Caduff und Tan Wälchli, 83–97. Berlin: kadmos, 2007.
Kogen, James H. 'Record Changers, Turntables, and Tone Arms: A Brief Technical History'. *Journal of the Audio Engineering Society* 25, nos. 10/11 (1977): 749–58.
Kollatz, C. W. 'Sprachverstärkung für Massenansprachen'. *Funk-Anzeiger. Zeitschrift für die gesamte drahtlose Fermeldetechnik* 3, no. 29 (1925): 343–4.
Kopp, George. 'Sound Systems: Sound Experts Sound Off'. *Billboard*, 16 August 1980, 53.
Kos, Wolfgang. 'Intime Signale im anonymen Raum. Überlegungen zu Jukebox, Autoradio und Radiosignations'. Conference programme. Conference: *"Ephemeres Erinnern": Wiener Erinnerungsorte der anderen Art* Internationales Forschungszentrum Kulturwissenschaften Wien, Vienna, 15–16 June 2002.
Krämer, Sybille, and Horst Bredekamp. 'Kultur, Technik, Kulturtechnik: Wider die Diskursivierung der Kultur'. In *Bild – Schrift – Zahl*, edited by Sybille Krämer and Horst Bredekamp, 11–22. Munich: Fink, 2003.
Krasnow, Carolyn. 'Fear and Loathing in the 70s: Race, Sexuality, and Disco'. *Stanford Humanities Review* 3, no. 2 (1993): 37–45.
Krebs, Peter. 'Kein Boom ohne B-Seiten'. *Musik-Informationen* 12 (1976): 1.
Kreuzer, Gundula. 'Kittler's Wagner and Beyond'. *Journal of the American Musicological Society* 70, no. 1 (2017): 228–33.

Krivine, John. *Juke Box Saturday Night*. London: New English Library, 1977.
Kronengold, Charles. 'Exchange Theories in Disco, New Wave, and Album-Oriented Rock'. *Criticism: A Quarterly for Literature and the Arts* 50, no. 1 (2008): 43–82.
Kursell, Julia. *Epistemologie des Hörens: Helmholtz' physiologische Grundlegung der Musiktheorie*. Munich: Fink, 2018.
Kurth, Ernst. *Musikpsychologie*. Berlin: Hesse, 1931.
Laing, Dave. 'Jukebox'. In *Continuum Encyclopedia of Popular Music of the World. Volume I: Media, Industry and Society*, edited by John Shepherd, David Horn, Dave Laing, Paul Oliver and Peter Wicke, 513–15. London: Continuum, 2003.
Laing, Dave. 'One-Stop'. In *Continuum Encyclopedia of Popular Music of the World. Volume I: Media, Industry and Society*, edited by John Shepherd, David Horn, Dave Laing, Paul Oliver and Peter Wicke, 558. London: Continuum, 2003.
Laing, Dave. 'A Voice without a Face: Popular Music and the Phonograph in the 1890s'. *Popular Music* 10, no. 1 (1991): 1–9.
Lange, Britta. 'Kulturwissenschaft'. In *Handbuch Sound: Geschichte – Begriffe – Ansätze*, edited by Daniel Morat and Hansjakob Ziemer, 113–19. Stuttgart: Metzler, 2018.
Langham, Tim. 'National Sound Corporation: Ron Murphy'. *Massive Mag*, 2008. Accessed 12 October 2011. http://massivemag.com/issue-20/national-sound-corporation-ronmurphy-issue-20.html.
Latour, Bruno. 'On Technical Mediation: Philosophy, Sociology, Genalogy'. *Common Knowledge* 3, no. 2 (1994): 29–64.
Latour, Bruno. *Reassembling the Social: An Introduction to Actor-Network-Theory*. New York: Oxford University Press, 2005.
Latour, Bruno. *We Have Never Been Modern*. Translated by Catherine Porter. Cambridge, MA: Harvard University Press, 1993.
'Lautsprecher der Western Electric Co.'. *Elektrotechnische Zeitschrift* 38 (1920): 758–9.
Lawrence, Tim. 'Beyond the Hustle: 1970s Social Dancing, Discotheque Culture, and the Emergence of Contemporary Club Dancer'. In *Ballroom, Boogie, Shimmy Sham, Shake: A Social and Popular Dance Reader*, edited by Julie Malnig, 199–214. Champaign, IL: University of Illinois Press, 2008.
Lawrence, Tim. 'Connecting with the Cosmic: Arthur Russell, Rhizomatic Musicianship, and the Downtown Music Scene, 1973–92'. *Liminalities: A Journal of Performance Studies* 3, no. 3 (2007): 1–84.
Lawrence, Tim. 'Disco and the Queering of the Dance Floor'. *Cultural Studies* 25, no. 2 (2011): 230–43.
Lawrence, Tim. *Hold On to Your Dreams: Arthur Russell and the Downtown Music Scene, 1973-1992*. Durham, NC: Duke University Press, 2009.
Lawrence, Tim. 'In Defence of Disco (Again)'. *New Formations* 58 (2006): 128–46.
Lawrence, Tim. *Life and Death on the New York Dance Floor, 1980–1983*. Durham, NC: Duke University Press, 2016.
Lawrence, Tim. Liner Notes for Various, *Acid: Can You Jack? Chicago Acid and Experimental House 1985–95*. Soul Jazz Records, UK, 2005.
Lawrence, Tim. Liner Notes for Walter Gibbons, *Jungle Music. Mixed with Love: Essential & Unreleased Remixes 1976-1986*. Strut, UK, 2010.
Lawrence, Tim. Liner notes for Walter Gibbons, *Mixed with Love: The Walter Gibbons Salsoul Anthology*. Suss'd Records, UK 2004.

Lawrence, Tim. 'Loves Saves the Day: David Mancuso and the Loft'. Accessed 30 April 2022. https://static1.squarespace.com/static/519f4158e4b046d94a96e72e/t/52c8bc14e4b0df7dc79d5324/1388887060501/Loft-Placed-2007.pdf.

Lawrence, Tim. *Love Saves the Day: A History of American Dance Music Culture, 1970–1979*. Durham, NC: Duke University Press, 2004.

Leary, Timothy, Richard Alpert and Ralph Metzner. *The Psychedelic Experience: A Manual Based on the Tibetan Book of the Dead*. New York: Citadel Press, 2017.

Leiner, Markus Konradin (Qrt). 'Tekknologic als Tekknowledge'. In *Tekknologic Tekknowledge Tekgnosis. Ein Theoremix*, edited by Tom Lamberty and Frank Wulf, 7–35. Berlin: Merve, 1999.

Leroi-Gourhan, André. *Gesture and Speech*. Translated by Anna Bostock Berger. Cambridge, MA: MIT Press, 1993, [1980].

Levin, Thomas Y. 'For the Record: Adorno on Music in the Age of Its Technological Reproducibility'. *October* 55 (1990): 23–47.

Levin, Thomas Y. '"Tones from out of Nowhere": Rudolph Pfenninger and the Archaeology of Synthetic Sound'. In *New Media, Old Media: A History and Theory Reader*, edited by Wendy Hui Kyong Chun and Thomas W. Keenan, 45–81. New York: Routledge, 2006.

Levin, Thomas Y., and Michael von der Linn. 'Elements of a Radio Theory: Adorno and the Princeton Radio Research Project'. *The Musical Quarterly* 78, no. 2 (1994): 316–24.

Levy, Mark R. 'The Lazarsfeld-Stanton Program Analyzer: An Historical Note'. *Journal of Communication* 32, no. 4 (1982): 30–8.

Lipsitz, George. *Footsteps in the Dark: The Hidden Histories of Popular Music*. Minneapolis, MN: University of Minnesota Press, 2007.

Lissa, Zofia. *Neue Aufsätze zur Musikästhetik*. Berlin: Henschel, 1975.

'Listal: Jukebox'. *Listal Limited*. Accessed 9 May 2022. https://www.listal.com/list/junkebox.

Lovette, Frank H., and Stanley Watkins. 'Twenty Years of Talking Movies: An Anniversary'. *Bell Telephone Magazine* 1946, 82–100.

Lynch, Vincent. *American Jukebox: The Classic Years*. San Francisco, CA: Chronicle Books, 1990.

Maase, Kaspar. 'Amerikanisierung von unten. Demonstrative Vulgarität und kulturelle Hegomonie in der Bundesrepublik der 1950er Jahre'. In *Amerikanisierung: Traum und Alptraum im Deutschland des 20. Jahrhunderts*, edited by Alf Lüdtke, Inge Marssolek and Adelheid von Saldern, 291–314. Stuttgart: Franz Steiner Verlag, 1996.

Mackay, Robin. 'Capitalism and Schizophrenia: Wildstyle in Full Effect'. In *Deleuze and Philosophy: The Difference Engineer*, edited by Keith Ansell Pearson, 247–69. London: Routledge, 1997.

Magoun, Alexander Boyden. 'An In-Depth Look at the Origins of the LP, the "45", and High Fidelity, 1939–1950'. In *The Fabulous Victrola "45"*, edited by Phil Vourtsis, 8–35. Atglen, PA: Schiffer, 2007.

Magoun, Alexander Boyden. 'The Origins of the 45-RPM Record at RCA Victor, 1939–1948'. In *Music and Technology in the Twentieth Century*, edited by Hans-Joachim Braun, 148–57. Baltimore, MD: Johns Hopkins University Press, 2002.

Magoun, Alexander Boyden. 'Shaping the Sound of Music: The Evolution of the Phonograph Record, 1877–1950'. PhD dissertation, Department of History, University of Maryland, College Park, 2000.

Mahnert, Detlef, and Harry Stürmer. *Zappa, Zoff und Zwischentöne: die internationalen Essener Songtage 1968*. Essen: Klartext, 2008.
Maisonneuve, Sophie. 'Between History and Commodity: The Production of a Musical Patrimony through the Record in the 1920–1930s'. *Poetics* 29, no. 2 (2001): 89–108.
Malbon, Ben. *Clubbing: Dancing, Ecstasy, Vitality*. London: Routledge, 1999.
Maloney, Liam, and John Schofield. 'Records as Records: Excavating the DJ's Sonic Archive'. *Archives and Records*. Available online: https://doi.org/10.1080/23257962.2021.2001319. Accessed 30 April 2022.
Mankowski, Diana L. 'Gendering the Disco Inferno: Sexual Revolution, Liberation, and Popular Culture in 1970s America'. PhD dissertation, University of Michigan, Ann Arbor, 2010.
Marcus, Kenneth H. *Musical Metropolis: Los Angeles and the Creation of a Music Culture, 1880–1940*. New York: Palgrave Macmillan 2004.
Marks, Laura U. *Touch: Sensuous Theory and Multisensory Media*. Minneapolis, MN: University of Minnesota Press, 2002.
Marmorstein, Gary. *The Label: The Story of Columbia Records*. Boston, MA: Da Capo Press, 2007.
Matthias, Sebastian. 'Groove Feeling – somatischer Sound und partizipative Performance'. In *Sound und Performance*, edited by Wolf-Dieter Ernst, Nora Niethammer, Berenika Szymanski-Düll and Anno Mungen, 591–607. Würzburg: Königshausen & Neumann, 2015.
'"Musik wird störend oft empfunden …" Automatenmesse – "musikalisch" wie noch nie – Schlacht der Juke-Boxes'. *Der Automaten-Markt: Fachzeitschrift für die gesamte Automatenwirtschaft* 4, no. 10 (1952): 179–81.
Maxfield, Joseph P., and Henry C. Harrison. 'Methods of High Quality Recording and Reproducing of Music and Speech based on Telephone Research'. *The Bell System Technical Journal* 5, no. 3 (1926): 493–523.
May, Beverly. 'Techno'. In *African American Music: An Introduction*, edited by Mellonee Victoria Burnim, 331–52. New York: Routledge, 2006.
Maye, Harun. 'Was ist eine Kulturtechnik?'. *Zeitschrift für Medien- und Kulturforschung* 1 (2010): 121–35.
McCracken, Allison. *Real Men Don't Sing: Crooning in American Culture*. Durham, NC: Duke University Press, 2015.
McCready, John. 'Welcome to the Phuture: Techno'. *New Musical Express*, 16 July 1988.
McCullaugh, Jim. '"Semi-pros" Eying Musical Instrument Outlets'. *Billboard*, 4 February 1978, 68, 73.
McGuinn, Robert E. 'Stokowski and the Bell Telephone Laboratories: Collaboration in the Development of High-Fidelity Sound Reproduction'. *Technology and Culture* 24, no. 1 (1983): 38–75.
McLuhan, Marshall. *Understanding Media: The Extensions of Man*. London: Routledge, 2008.
McLuhan, Marshall, and Bruce R. Powers. *The Global Village: Transformations in World Life and Media in the 21st Century*. New York: Oxford University Press, 1992.
McProud, C. G. 'The Juke Box Goes Hi-Fi'. *Audio* 38, no. 12 (1954): 33–8, 42–3.
Mellers, Wilfrid. *Twilight of the Gods: The Beatles in Retrospect*. London: Faber & Faber, 1973.

Mersch, Werner. 'Sprechmaschinen und Musikboxen'. In *Wenn der Groschen fällt ... Münzautomaten – Gestern und Heute*, edited by Cornelia Kemp and Ulrike Gierlinger, 88–95. Munich: Deutsches Museum IMS, 1989.

MGG Online, 'Rezeptionsforschung'. By Klaus Kropfinger. Accessed 18 February 2022, https://www.mgg-online.com/article?id=mgg15962&v=1.0&rs=mgg15962.

Middleton, Richard. *Reading Pop: Approaches to Textual Analysis in Popular Music.* New York: Oxford University Press, 2000.

Middleton, Richard: *Studying Popular Music*. Milton Keynes: Open University Press, 1990.

Middleton, Richard, and Ian Biddle, eds. *Radical Musicology* 5 (2010/11).

Millard, Andre. *America on Record. A History of Recorded Sound*. Cambridge: Cambridge University Press, 2005.

Miller, Chuck. 'Herbie Was Here: Stories of the Mysterious Messages in the Runoff Grooves'. *Goldmine*, 27 March 1998, 461.

Mills, Mara. 'Deafness'. In *Keywords in Sound*, edited by David Novak and Matt Sakakeeny, 45–54. Durham, NC: Duke University Press, 2015.

Milner, Greg. *Perfecting Sound Forever: The Story of Recorded Music*. New York: Faber & Faber, 2010.

Missfelder, Jan-Friedrich. 'Verstärker: Hören und Herrschen bei Francis Bacon und Athanasius Kircher 2016'. In *senseAbility – Mediale Praktiken des Sehens und Hörens*, edited by Beate Ochsner and Robert Stock, 59–80. Bielefeld: transcript, 2016.

Michel, Elmar. 'Zum Geleit'. In *Handbuch der Deutschen Automatenwirtschaft 1956*. Cologne: Carl Heymanns Verlag, 1956.

Mittelstaedt, Robert A., and Robert E. Stassen. 'Structural Changes in the Phonograph Record Industry and Its Channels of Distribution, 1946–1966'. *Journal of Macromarketing* 14, no. 31 (1994): 31–44.

Moebius, Stephan. *Kultur: Von den Cultural Studies bis zu den Visual Studies. Eine Einführung*. Bielefeld: transcript, 2012.

Moore, Jerrold Northrop. *Sound Revolutions: A Biography of Fred Gaisberg, Founding Father of Commercial Sound Recording*. London: Sanctuary, 1999.

Moorefield, Virgil. *The Producer as Composer: Shaping the Sounds of Popular Music*. Cambridge, MA: MIT Press, 2005.

Morales, Mizie. 'Dubplate Special – Detroitstory'. *DE:BUG Magazin für Elektronische Lebensaspekte*, 2000. Accessed 12 October 2011. http://www.de-bug.de/musiktechnik/archives/179.html.

Moran, Joe. 'Milk Bars, Starbucks, and the Uses of Literacy'. *Cultural Studies* 20, no. 6 (2006), 552–573.

Morton, David. *Off the Record: The Technology and Culture of Sound Recording in America*. New Brunswick, NJ: Rutgers University Press, 2000.

Morton, David. *Sound Recording: The Life Story of a Technology*. Baltimore, MD: Johns Hopkins University Press, 2004.

Motte-Haber, Helga de la. 'Der einkomponierte Hörer'. In *Der Hörer als Interpret*, edited by Helga de la Motte-Haber and Reinhard Kopiez, 35–41. Frankfurt am Main: Peter Lang, 1995.

Moura, Carlos. 'Practical Aspects of Hot Stylus'. *Journal of the Audio Engineering Society* 5, no. 2 (1957): 90–3.

Mühl-Benninghaus, Wolfgang. *Das Ringen um den Tonfilm: Strategien der Elektro- und der Filmindustrie in den 20er und 30er Jahren*. Düsseldorf: Droste, 1999.

Mulder, Jos. 'Making Things Louder: Amplified Music and Multimodality'. PhD dissertation, Faculty of Arts and Social Sciences, University of Technology Sydney, 2013.

Müller, Sven Oliver. *Das Publikum macht die Musik: Musikleben in Berlin, London und Wien im 19. Jahrhundert*. Göttingen: Vandenhoeck & Ruprecht, 2014.

Münker, Stefan, and Alexander Roesler. *Was ist ein Medium?*. Frankfurt am Main: Suhrkamp, 2008.

Murphy, Colleen. 'David Mancuso hat uns gelehrt, dass Selbstlosigkeit der ultimative Akt der Rebellion ist'. *Vice*. Accessed 30 April 2022. https://www.vice.com/de/article/bma5dw/david-mancuso-hat-uns-gelehrt-dass-selbstlosigkeit-der-ultimative-akt-der-rebellion-ist.

Murphy, Colleen. 'Klipsch: No Bullshit'. *Red Bull Music Academy*. Accessed 30 April 2022. https://daily.redbullmusicacademy.com/2016/11/klipsch-feature.

'Musikbox – Helfer der Jugend-Behörde'. *Der Automaten-Markt. Fachzeitschrift für die gesamte Automatenwirtschaft* 12 (1960): 575–6.

'"Musikbox macht keine Musiker arbeitslos", sagt der Deutsche Musikerverband'. *Der Automaten-Markt: Fachzeitschrift für die gesamte Automatenwirtschaft* 8, no. 10 (1956): 598.

Negus, Keith. *Popular Music in Theory*. Cambridge: Polity, 1996.

Neumann, Sonja. 'The Opera-Telephone in Munich: A Short History'. In *The Oxford Handbook of Music Listening in the 19th and 20th Centuries*, edited by Christian Thorau and Hansjakob Ziemer, 357–72. New York: Oxford University Press, 2019.

Niebling, Laura. 'Ernst Neger: Geb' dem Kind sein Nuddelche. Aus dem Mainzer Karneval in eine Jukebox in Flensburg'. In *Audiowelten: Technologie und Medien in der populären Musik nach 1945: 22 Objektstudien*, edited by Benjamin Burkhart, Laura Niebling, Alan van Keeken, Christofer Jost and Martin Pfleiderer, 215–43. Münster: Waxmann, 2021.

Nielsen, Arthur C. 'Trends toward Mechanization of Radio Advertising'. *Journal of Marketing* 6, no. 3 (1942): 217–28.

Nyre, Lars. *Sound Media: From Live Journalism to Music Recording*. London: Routledge, 2008.

Ochsner, Beate. "Die Zukunft smarten Hörens hat begonnen' (ReSound): Anmerkungen zu einer technosensorischen Regierungspraktik'. In *Physiognomien des Lebens: Physiognomik im Spannungsverhältnis zwischen Biopolitik und Ästhetik*, edited by Vittoria Borsò, Sieglinde Borvitz and Luca Viglialoro, 161–82. Berlin: de Gruyter, 2020.

O'Connell, Joseph. 'The Fine-Tuning of a Golden Ear: High-End Audio and the Evolutionary Model of Technology'. *Technology and Culture* 33, no. 1 (1992): 1–37.

Osborne, Richard. *Vinyl: A History of the Analogue Record*. London: Routledge, 2016.

Ouzounian, Gascia. *Stereophonica: Sound and Space in Science, Technology, and the Arts*. Cambridge, MA: MIT Press, 2021.

Overbeck, Peter, 'Die Entwicklung der Tonträgertechnologie'. In *Handbuch der Musik im 20. Jahrhundert*, 10, edited by Arnold Jacobshagen and Frieder Reininghaus, 77–112. Laaber: Laaber, 2006.

Owsinski, Bobby. *The Audio Mastering Handbook*, 2nd edn. Boston, MA: Thoson, 2008.

Oxford English Dictionary. s.v. 'tin ear'. Accessed 7 September 2022. https://www.oed.com/view/Entry/202173?redirectedFrom=Tin+ears+#eid18466376.

Pantalony, David. *Altered Sensations: Rudolph Koenig's Acoustical Workshop in Nineteenth-Century Paris*. New York: Springer, 2009.

Papenburg, Jens Gerrit. 'Bewirtschaftung der Zukunft. Musikhören durch Apps, Kopfhörer und Smartphones'. In *Electronic Beats*, edited by Deutsche Telekom, 92–9. Berlin: Blumenbar, 2021.

Papenburg, Jens Gerrit. 'Boomende Bässe der Disco- und Clubkultur. Musikanalytische Herausforderungen durch taktile Klänge'. In *Techno Studies. Ästhetik und Geschichte elektronischer Tanzmusik*, edited by Kim Feser and Matthias Pasdzierny, 195–210. Berlin: b-books, 2017.

Papenburg, Jens Gerrit. 'Enhanced Bass. On 1970s Disco Culture's Listening Devices'. In *Sound as Popular Culture. A Research Companion*, edited by Jens Gerrit Papenburg and Holger Schulze, 205–14. Cambridge, MA: MIT Press, 2016.

Papenburg, Jens Gerrit. 'Enhanced Sound: Filter der Musikproduktion und des Musikhörens'. *Navigationen – Zeitschrift für Medien- und Kulturwissenschaften* 20, no. 2 (2020): 115–32.

Papenburg, Jens Gerrit. 'The File'. In *The Bloomsbury Handbook of the Anthropology of Sound*, edited by Holger Schulze, 43–57. New York: Bloomsbury Academic, 2021.

Papenburg, Jens Gerrit. '"A Great Idea after the Fact". Das (Er-)Finden der Maxisingle in der New Yorker Discokultur der 1970er Jahre'. In *Popgeschichte. Band 2: Zeithistorische Fallstudien 1958–1988*, edited by Bodo Mrozek, Alexa Geisthövel and Jürgen Danyel, 179–98. Bielefeld: transcript, 2014.

Papenburg, Jens Gerrit. 'Jukebox-Hören im Film. Strategien, Praktiken, Lokalitäten'. In *Jugend, Musik und Film*, ed. Kathrin Dreckmann, Carsten Heinze, Dagmar Hoffmann and Dirk Matejovski, 455–75, Berlin: de Gruyter, 2022.

Papenburg, Jens Gerrit. 'Konzeptalben als "große" Werke populärer Musik?'. *Musik und Ästhetik* 21, no. 7 (2017): 30–45.

Papenburg, Jens Gerrit. 'Körperlichkeit'. In *Handbuch Sound: Geschichte – Begriffe – Ansätze*, edited by Daniel Morat and Hansjakob Ziemer, 25–31. Stuttgart: Metzler, 2018.

Papenburg, Jens Gerrit. 'Nazis and Quiet Sounds: Popular Music, Simulated Normality, and Cultural Niches in the Terror Regime, 1933–1945'. In *Made in Germany*, edited by Oliver Seibt, Martin Ringsmut and David-Emil Wickström, 39–47. London: Routledge, 2020.

Papenburg, Jens Gerrit. 'Pleasure and Pain with Amplified Sound: A Sound and Music History of Loudspeaker Systems in Germany, ca. 1930'. In *Techniques of Hearing: History, Theory and Practices*, edited by Michael Schillmeier, Beate Ochsner and Robert Stock, 36–46. London: Routledge, 2022.

Papenburg, Jens Gerrit. 'Popmusik als "produzierte" Musik'. *Musik und Ästhetik* 23, no. 2 (2019): 68–71.

Papenburg, Jens Gerrit. 'Rockmusik, Musikdrama, Disco: Klanggeschichte der Medien nach Friedrich Kittler'. In *Friedrich Kittler. Neue Lektüren*, edited by Jens Schröter and Till Heilmann, 145–69. Wiesbaden: Springer, 2022.

Papenburg, Jens Gerrit. 'Soundfile-Hören. Zukunft, Zeiterfahrung, Bewirtschaftung'. In *Listening/Hearing*, edited by Raoul Mörchen and Carsten Seiffarth, Mainz: Schott, 2022.

Papenburg, Jens Gerrit. 'Soundfile: Kultur und Ästhetik einer Hörtechnologie'. *Pop. Kultur und Kritik* 2, no. 1 (2013): 140–55.

Papenburg, Jens Gerrit. Stop/Start Making Sense! Ein Ausblick auf Musikanalyse in Popular Music Studies und technischer Medienwissenschaft'. In *Sound Studies: Traditionen – Methoden – Desiderate*, edited by Holger Schulze, 91–108. Bielefeld: transcript, 2008.

Papenburg, Jens Gerrit, and Max Alt. 'Streamability: Überlegungen zu einer Ästhetik des Musikstreaming'. In *Acoustic Intelligence: Hören und Gehorchen*, edited by Anna Schürmer, Maximilian Haberer and Tomy Brautschek, 227–46. Berlin: Düsseldorf University Press, 2022.

Papenburg, Jens Gerrit and Holger Schulze, eds. *Sound as Popular Culture: A Research Companion*. Cambridge, MA: MIT Press, 2016.

Pareles, Jon, and Patricia Romanowski, eds., *The Rolling Stone Encyclopedia of Rock & Roll*. New York: Rolling Stone Press/Summit Books, 1983.

'Paul W. Klipsch'. Accessed 30 April 2022. https://www.klipsch.com/founder.

Pearce, Christopher. *Vintage Jukebox: A Collector's Guide to the Much-Loved Musical Icons of the 1940s and 1950s*. Roysten: Eagle Editions, 2002.

Pelleter, Malte. 'Funkologicalienatimepistomachinistics: Sensorisches Engineering und maschinische Heterochronizität bei Shuggie Otis'. In *Musikformulare und Presets: Musikkulturalisierung und Technik/Technologie*, edited by Johannes Ismaiel-Wendt and Alan Fabian, 149–66. Hildesheim: Olms, 2018.

Pelleter, Malte. *Futurhythmaschinen: Drum-Machines und die Zukünfte auditiver Kulturen*. Hildesheim: Olms, 2021.

Pelly, Liz. 'Big Mood Machine'. *The Baffler*. Accessed 30 April 2022. https://thebaffler.com/latest/big-mood-machine-pelly.

Pendzich, Marc. *Von der Coverversion zum Hit-Recycling: Historische, ökonomische und rechtliche Aspekte eines zentralen Phänomens der Pop- und Rockmusik*. Münster: LIT, 2004.

Perevedentseva, Maria, and Luis-Manuel Garcia. 'Chicago House Music, from Dance Floor to Museum: the Frankie Knuckles Vinyl Collection'. *Sound Studies* 2, no. 1 (2016): 95–8.

Perlman, Marc. 'Golden Ears and Meter Readers: The Contest for Epistemic Authority in Audiophilia'. *Social Studies of Science* 34, no. 5 (2004): 783–807.

Peters, John Durham. 'Helmholtz, Edison, and Sound History'. In *Memory Bytes: History, Technology, and Digital Culture*, edited by Lauren Rabinovitz and Abraham Geil, 177–98. Durham, NC: Duke University Press, 2004.

Peters, John Durham. 'Helmholtz und Edison: Zur Endlichkeit der Stimme'. In *Zwischen Rauschen und Offenbarung: Zur Kultur- und Mediengeschichte der Stimme*, translated by Antje Pfannkuchen, edited by Friedrich A. Kittler, Thomas Macho and Sigrid Weigel, 291–312. Berlin: Akademie Verlag, 2002.

Pfleiderer, Martin. 'Live-Veranstaltungen von populärer Musik und ihre Rezeption'. In *Musikrezeption, Musikdistribution und Musikproduktion: Der Wandel des Wertschöpfungsnetzwerks in der Musikwirtschaft*, edited by Gerhard Gensch, Eva Maria Sröckler and Peter Tschmuck, 88–107. Wiesbaden: Gabler, 2008.

Pfleiderer, Martin. *Rhythmus: Psychologische, theoretische und stilanalytische Aspekte populärer Musik*. Bielefeld: transcript, 2006.

'Philips-Klein-Schallplatten für 45 Umdrehungen'. *Der Automaten-Markt: Fachzeitschrift für die gesamte Automatenwirtschaft* 5, no. 12 (1953): 352.

Piekut, Benjamin. 'Actor-Networks in Music History: Clarifications and Critiques'. *Twentieth-Century Music* 11, no. 2 (2014): 191–215.

Pinch, Trevor, and Frank Trocco. *Analog Days: The Invention and Impact of the Moog Synthesizer*. Cambridge, MA: Harvard University Press, 2002.
Pisfil, Sergio. 'Woodstock and the Live Sound Industry in the Late 1960s'. *Popular Music and Society* 43, no. 2 (2020): 176–87.
Plebuch, Tobias. 'Musikhören nach Adorno: Ein Genesungsbericht'. *Merkur. Deutsche Zeitschrift für Europäisches Denken* 65 (2002): 675–87.
Poschardt, Ulf. *DJ Culture*. Translated by Shaun Whiteside. London: Quartet Books, 1998.
Poster, Mark. '"Digitale" versus "analoge" Autorschaft'. In *Heterotopien der Identität. Literatur in interamerikanischen Kontaktzonen*, edited by Hermann Herlinghaus and Utz Riese, 261–74. Heidelberg: Winter, 1999.
Prey, Robert. 'Musica Analytica: The Datafication of Listening'. In *Networked Music Cultures: Contemporary Approaches, Emerging Issues*, edited by Raphaël Nowak and Andrew Whelan, 31–48. London: Palgrave Macmillan, 2016.
Putnam, Milton T. 'Recording Studio and Control Room Facilities of Advance Design'. *Journal of the Audio Engineering Society* 8, no. 2 (1960): 111–19.
Rachlin, Harvey. *The Encyclopedia of Music Business*. New York: Harper & Row, 1981.
Rasmussen, Chris. '"The People's Orchestra": Jukeboxes as the Measure of Popular Musical Taste in the 1930s and 1940s'. In *Sound in the Age of Mechanical Reproduction*, edited by David Suisman and Susan Strasser, 181–98. Philadelphia, PA: University of Pennsylvania Press, 2010.
Ratliff, Ben. *Every Song Ever: Twenty Ways to Listen to Music Now*. London: Penguin, 2016.
Raulff, Ulrich. 'Disco: Studio 54 Revisited'. *Tumult. Zeitschrift für Verkehrswissenschaft* 1, no. 1 (1979): 55–66.
Rehding, Alexander. *Hugo Riemann and the Birth of Modern Musical Thought*. Cambridge: Cambridge University Press, 2003.
Rehding, Alexander. *Music and Monumentality: Commemoration and Wonderment in Nineteenth Century Germany*. New York: Oxford University Press, 2009.
Rehding, Alexander. 'Three Music-Theory Lessons'. *Journal of the Royal Musical Association* 141, no. 2 (2016): 251–82.
Rehding, Alexander. 'Discrete/Continuous: Music and Media Theory after Kittler'. *Journal of the American Musicological Society* 70, no. 1 (2017): 221–56.
Reichardt, Sven. *Authentizität und Gemeinschaft. Linksalternatives Leben in den siebziger und frühen achtziger Jahren*. Berlin: Suhrkamp, 2014.
Reiß, Werner. *Johann Strauß Meets Elvis: Musikautomaten aus zwei Jahrhunderten*. Stuttgart: Arnoldsche, 2003.
Reynolds, Simon. 'Detroit Techno, Chicago House, and New York Garage'. In *DJ, Dance, and Rave Culture: Examining Pop Culture*, edited by Jared F. Green, 82–92. Detroit: Thomson Gale, 2005.
Reynolds, Simon. *Energy Flash: A Journey through Rave Music and Dance Culture*. London: Faber & Faber, 2013.
Reynolds, Simon. *Rip It Up and Start Again: Postpunk 1978–1984*. London: Faber & Faber, 2019.
Rhein, Eduard. *100 Jahre Schallplatte: Vom Phonographen über die Laser-Disc – wohin?*. Berlin: Presse- und Informationsamt des Landes Berlin, 1987.
Rheinberger, Hans-Jörg. *Experimentalsysteme und epistemische Dinge: Eine Geschichte der Proteinsynthese im Reagenzglas*. Göttingen: Wallstein-Verlag, 2019.
Rice, Chester W., and Edward W. Kellogg. 'Notes on the Development of a New Type of Hornless Loud Speaker'. *Transactions of the AIEE* 44 (1925): 461–80.

'Richtige GEMA-Gebühren bezahlen'. *Der Automaten-Markt: Fachzeitschrift für die gesamte Automatenwirtschaft* 7, no. 7 (1955): 308.

Rieger, Matthias. *Helmholtz Musicus. Die Objektivierung der Musik im 19. Jahrhundert durch Helmholtz' Lehre von den Tonempfindungen*. Darmstadt: Wissenschaftliche Buchgesellschaft, 2006.

Rieger, Stefan. 'Medienarchäologie'. In *Handbuch Medienwissenschaft*, edited by Jens Schröter, 137–44. Stuttgart: J. B. Metzler, 2014.

Rieger, Stefan. 'Organische Konstruktionen: Von der Künstlichkeit des Körpers zur Natürlichkeit der Medien'. In *McLuhan neu Lesen: Kritische Analysen zu Medien und Kultur im 21. Jahrhundert*, edited by Derrick de Kerckhove, Martina Leeker and Kerstin Schmidt, 252–69. Bielefeld: transcript, 2008.

Riemann, Hugo. 'Ideen zu einer Lehre von den Tonvorstellungen'. *Jahrbuch der Musikbibliothek Peters* 21 (1915/1914): 1–26.

Rietveld, Hillegonda C. 'The House Sound of Chicago'. In *The Clubcultures Reader: Readings in Popular Cultural Studies*, edited by Steve Redhead, Derek Wynne and Justin O'Connor, 106–18. Oxford: Blackwell, 1998.

Rietveld, Hillegonda C. 'Im Strom des Techno: "Slow-Mix"-DJ-Stile in der Dance Music der 90er Jahre'. In *Handbuch der Musik im 20. Jahrhundert, Bd. 8: Rock- und Popmusik*, edited by Peter Wicke, 267–99. Laaber: Laaber 2001.

Rietveld, Hillegonda C. *This Is Our House: House Music, Cultural Spaces and Technologies*. London: Routledge, 2018.

Rietveld, Hillegonda C. 'Vinyl Junkies and the Soul Sonic Force of the 12-inch Dance Single'. In *Residual Media*, edited by Charles R. Acland. 115–32. Minneapolis, MN: University of Minnesota Press, 2007.

Robinson, Dylan: *Hungry Listening: Resonant Theory for Indigenous Sound Studies*. Minneapolis, MN: University of Minnesota Press, 2020.

Rock-Ola Manufacturing Corporation. 'Rock Ola 120 Fireball Model 1436'. Advertisement, 1952. Accessed 7 September 2022. https://www.jukeboxhistory.info/rock-ola/jukeboxes/rock-ola_1436.pdf.

Rodríguez, Eva Moreda. *Inventing the Recording: The Phonograph and National Culture in Spain, 1877–1914*. New York: Oxford University Press, 2021.

Rosner, Alex. 'Overview of Disco Sound Systems'. *Journal of the Audio Engineering Society* 27, no. 7–8 (1979): 576–84.

Rothenbuhler, Eric, and Tom McCourt. 'Radio Redefines Itself, 1947–1962'. In *Radio Reader: Essays in the Cultural History of Radio*, edited by Michele Hilmes and Jason Loviglio, 367–88. London: Routledge, 2002.

Salkind, Micah. *Do You Remember House? Chicago's Queer of Color Undergrounds*. New York: Oxford University Press, 2019.

Salmen, Walter. *Das Konzert: Eine Kulturgeschichte*. Munich: Beck, 1988.

Salzer, Felix. *Structural Hearing: Tonal Coherence in Music*. New York: C. Boni, 1952.

Samuels, David W., Louise Meintjes, Ana Maria Ochoa and Thomas Porcello. 'Soundscapes: Toward a Sounded Anthropology'. *Annual Review of Anthropology* 39, no. 1 (2010): 329–45.

Sanchez, Rebecca. 'Deafness and Sound'. In *Sound and Literature*, edited by Anna Snaith, 272–86. Cambridge: Cambridge University Press, 2020.

Saxer, Marion, and Leonie Storz. 'Die Ökonomisierung der Wahrnehmung: Wirtschaftsgeschichte der Medien'. In *Spiel (mit) der Maschine: Musikalische*

Medienpraxis in der Frühzeit von Phonographie, Selbstspielklavier, Film und Radio, edited by Marion Saxer, 75–100. Bielefeld: transcript, 2016.
'Schallplatten nur vom Automatenhandel beziehen'. *Der Automaten-Markt: Fachzeitschrift für die gesamte Automatenwirtschaft* 8, no. 1 (1956): 13.
Scherer, Wolfgang. *Babbellogik: Sound und die Auslöschung der buchstäblichen Ordnung*. Basel: Roter Stern/Stroemfeld, 1983.
Scherer, Wolfgang. 'Hörsturz 1900: Die Decodierung des Musikalischen Hörens'. In *Welt auf tönernen Füßen: Die Töne und das Hören*, edited by Uta Brandes, 388–400. Göttingen: Steidl, 1994.
Scherer, Wolfgang. *Klavier-Spiele: Die Psychotechnik der Klaviere im 18. und 19. Jahrhundert*. Munich: Fink, 1989.
Schering, Arnold. *Musikalische Bildung und Erziehung zum Musikalischen Hören*. Leipzig: Quelle & Meyer, 1911.
Scherzinger, Martin. 'The Political Economy of Streaming'. In *The Cambridge Companion to Music in Digital Culture*, edited by David Trippett, Monique M. Ingalls and Nicholas Cook, 274–97. Cambridge: Cambridge University Press, 2019.
Schmidt Horning, Susan. 'Chasing Sound: The Culture and Technology of Recording Studios in America, 1877–1977'. PhD dissertation, Department of History, Case Western Reserve University, Cleveland, 2002.
Schmidt Horning, Susan. *Chasing Sound: Technology, Culture, and the Art of Studio Recording from Edison to LP*. Baltimore, MD: Johns Hopkins University Press, 2013.
Schmidt Horning, Susan. 'Engineering the Performance: Recording Engineers, Tacit Knowledge and the Art of Controlling Sound'. *Social Studies of Science* 34, no. 5 (2004): 703–31.
Schmidt-Joos, Siegfried. *Geschäfte mit Schlagern*. Bremen: Schünemann, 1960.
Schopp, Thomas. 'Eine Klanggeschichte der Diskjockey-Show im US-Amerikanischen Radio von 1930 bis 1970'. PhD dissertation, Fakultät III Sprach- und Kulturwissenschaften, Universität Oldenburg, Oldenburg, 2014.
Schopp, Thomas. 'Sonic FX. Klang, Körper, Kontrolle'. MA dissertation, Musikwissenschaftliches Seminar, Humboldt University of Berlin, Berlin, 2005.
Schreiner, Florian. 'Laut – Ton – Stärke'. PhD dissertation, Philosophische Fakultät III, Humboldt University of Berlin, Berlin, 2009.
Schrimshaw, Will. 'Non-cochlear Sound: On Affect and Exteriority'. In *Sound, Music, Affect: Theorizing Sonic Experience*, edited by Ian Biddle and Marie Thompson, 27–43. New York: Bloomsbury Academic, 2013.
Schröter, Jens, and Till A. Heilmann. 'Zum Bonner Programm einer neo-kritischen Medienwissenschaft'. *Navigationen: Zeitschrift für Medien- und Kulturwissenschaften* 16, no. 2 (2016): 7–36.
Schröter, Jens, Gregor Schwering, Dominik Maeder and Till A. Heilmann, eds. *Ambient: Ästhetik des Hintergrunds*. Wiesbaden: Springer, 2018.
Schultz, Anna, and Mark Nye. 'Music Ethnography and Recording Technology in the Unbound Digital Era'. In *The Oxford Handbook of Mobile Music Studies*, edited by Sumanth Gopinath and Jason Stanyek, 298–314. New York: Oxford University Press, 2014.
Schultz, Barbara. 'Sam Phillips'. *Mix Online. Professional Audio and Music Production*, October (2000).

Schulze, Gerhard. *Die Erlebnisgesellschaft: Kultursoziologie der Gegenwart*. Frankfurt am Main: Campus, 2005.

Schulze, Holger. 'Sonic Epistemology'. In *Sound as Popular Culture: A Research Companion*, edited by Jens Gerrit Papenburg and Holger Schulze, 111–20. Cambridge, MA: MIT Press, 2016.

Schulze, Holger. *The Sonic Persona: An Anthropology of Sound*. New York: Bloomsbury Academic, 2018.

Schüttpelz, Erhard. 'Die Erfindung der Twelve-Inch, der Homo Sapiens und Till Heilmanns Kommentar zur Priorität der Operationskette'. *Internationales Jahrbuch für Medienphilosophie* 3, no. 1 (2017): 217–34.

Schüttpelz, Erhard. 'Die medienanthropologische Kehre der Kulturtechniken'. *Archiv für Mediengeschichte* 6 (2006): 87–110.

Scott, Derek B. *Sounds of the Metropolis: The Nineteenth-Century Popular Music Revolution in London, New York, Paris, and Vienna*. New York: Oxford University Press, 2001.

Scott, Howard. 'The Beginnings of LP'. *Gramophone*, July (1998): 112–13.

Sedwell, Chris, and Simon Bottom. 'Break'. In *Continuum Encyclopedia of Popular Music of the World. Volume II. Performance and Production*, edited by John Shepherd, David Horn, Dave Laing, Paul Oliver and Peter Wicke, 561–2. London: Continuum, 2003.

'Seeburg States Its Policy to Music Operators'. *Billboard*, 17 September 1949, 97–100.

Segrave, Kerry. *Jukeboxes. An American Social History*. Jefferson, NC: McFarland, 2002.

Serres, Michel. *The Five Senses: A Philosophy of Mingled Bodies*. Translated by Margaret Sankey and Peter Cowley. New York: Bloomsbury Academics, 2016.

Serres, Michel. *The Parasite*. Translated by Lawrence R. Schehr. Minneapolis, MN: University of Minnesota Press, 2007.

Shannon, Doug. *Off the Record: The Disco Concept*. Cleveland, OH: Pacesetter Publishing, 1982.

Shannon, Doug. *Off the Record: The Handbook to Knowledge, Money & Success: Everything Related to Playing Recorded Dance Music in the Nightclub Industry*. Cleveland, OH: Pacesetter Publishing, 1985.

Shapiro, Peter. *Turn the Beat Around: The Secret History of Disco*. London: Faber & Faber, 2020.

Shaw, Arnold. *Honkers and Shouters: The Golden Years of Rhythm & Blues*. New York: Macmillan, 1978.

Shaw, Arnold. *The Rockin' '50s: The Decade That Transformed the Pop Music Scene*. New York: Hawthorn Books, 1974.

Shepherd, John. 'Warum Popmusikforschung?'. In *PopScriptum: Texte zur populären Musik* 1 (1992). Available online: https://edoc.hu-berlin.de/bitstream/handle/18452/20903/pst01_shepherd.pdf?sequence=1. Accessed 14 September 2022.

Shuker, Roy. *Popular Music Culture: The Key Concepts*. London: Routledge, 2012.

Shuker, Roy. *Wax Trash and Vinyl Treasures: Record Collecting as a Social Practice*. Farnham: Ashgate Publishing, 2010.

Sicko, Dan. *Techno Rebels: The Renegades of Electronic Funk*. Detroit: Wayne State University Press, 2010.

Siegert, Bernhard. 'Cacography or Communication? Cultural Techniques in German Media Studies'. *Grey Room* 29 (2007): 26–47.

Siegert, Bernhard. 'Das Amt des Gehorchens: Hysterie der Telephonistinnen oder Wiederkehr des Ohres 1874–1913'. In *Armaturen der Sinne. Literarische und technische*

Medien 1870 bis 1920, edited by Jochen Hörisch and Michael Wetzel, 83–106. Munich: Fink, 1990.

Siegert, Bernhard. 'Door Logic, or, the Materiality of the Symbolic: From Cultural Techniques to Cybernetic Machines'. In *Cultural Techniques: Grids, Filters, Doors, and Other Articulations of the Real*, translated by Geoffrey Winthrop-Young, 192–205. New York: Fordham University Press, 2015.

Siegert, Bernhard. 'Doors: On the Materiality of the Symbolic', translated by John Durham Peters, *Grey Room* 47 (2012): 6–23.

Siegert, Bernhard. 'Es gibt keine Massenmedien'. In *Medien und Öffentlichkeit. Positionierungen, Symptome, Simulationsbrüche*, edited by Rudolf Maresch, 108–15. Munich: Boer, 1996.

Siegert, Bernard. 'Oszillationen zwischen Störung und Entstörung: Zur Kulturtechnik des Radiophonischen Hörens'. In *Radiophonic Cultures*, edited by Ute Holl, 233–47. Heidelberg: Kehrer, 2018.

Siegfried, Detlef. *Time Is on My Side: Konsum und Politik in der Westdeutschen Jugendkultur der 60er Jahre*. Göttingen: Wallstein Verlag, 2008.

Smith, Jacob. *Vocal Tracks: Performance and Sound Media*. Berkeley, CA: University of California Press, 2008.

Smith, Mark M. *Sensing the Past: Seeing, Hearing, Smelling, Tasting, and Touching in History*. Berkeley, CA: University of California Press, 2007.

Solberg, Ragnhild Torvanger. '"Waiting for the Bass to Drop": Correlations between Intense Emotional Experiences and Production Techniques in Build-up and Drop Sections of Electronic Dance Music'. *Dancecult: Journal of Electronic Dance Music Culture* 6, no. 1 (2014): 61–82.

Sommer, Dirk. 'Die Georg Neumann GmbH'. In *Hifi Tunes: Das Klassikerbuch*, edited by Roland Kraft, 8–22. Gröbenzell: IMAGE Verlags GmbH, 2008.

Spengler, Oswald. *Man and Technics: A Contribution to a Philosophy of Life*. Translated by Charles Francis Atkinson. New York: Alfred A. Knopf, 1932.

Steege, Benjamin. *Helmholtz and the Modern Listener*. Cambridge: Cambridge University Press, 2012.

Sterne, Jonathan. *The Audible Past: Cultural Origins of Sound Reproduction*. Durham, NC: Duke University Press, 2003.

Sterne, Jonathan. *Diminished Faculties: A Political Phenomenology of Impairment*. Durham, NC: Duke University Press, 2022.

Sterne, Jonathan. 'The MP3 as Cultural Artefact'. *New Media and Society* 8, no. 5 (2006): 825–42.

Sterne, Jonathan. *MP3. The Meaning of a Format*. Durham, NC: Duke University Press, 2012.

Sterne, Jonathan. '"What Do We Want?" "Materiality!" "When Do We Want It?" "Now!"'. In *Media Technologies: Essays on Communication, Materiality, and Society*, edited by Tarleton Gillespie, Pablo J. Boczkowski and Kirsten A. Foot, 119–28. Cambridge, MA: MIT Press, 2014.

Sterne, Jonathan, and Mitchell Akiyama. 'The Recording That Never Wanted to Be Heard and Other Stories of Sonification'. In *The Oxford Handbook of Sound Studies*, edited by Karin Bijsterveld and Trevor Pinch, 544–60. New York: Oxford University Press, 2012.

Stibal, Mary E. 'Disco: Birth of a New Marketing System'. *Journal of Marketing* 41, no. 4 (1977): 82–8.

Stirken, Angela. *Eisdielen. 'Komm mit nach Italien ...!'*. Bonn: Stiftung Haus der Geschichte Bonn, 2004.

Stockfelt, Ola. 'Adequate Modes of Listening'. In *Keeping Score: Music, Disciplinarity, Culture*, edited by David Schwarz, Anahid Kassabian and Lawrence Siegel, 129–46. Charlottesville, VA: University Press of Virginia, 1997.

Straw, Will. 'Dance Music'. In *The Cambridge Companion to Pop and Rock*, edited by Simon Frith, Will Straw and John Street, 158–75. Cambridge: Cambridge University Press, 2001.

Straw, Will. 'Popular Music as Cultural Commodity: The American Recorded Music Industries 1976–1985'. PhD dissertation, Department of Art History and Communication Studies, McGill University, Montreal, 1990.

Straw, Will. 'Value and Velocity: The 12-Inch Single as Medium and Artifact'. In *Popular Music Studies*, edited by David Hesmondhalgh and Keith Negus, 164–77. New York: Oxford University Press, 2002.

Stumpf, Carl. *Tonpsychologie*. Leipzig: Hirzel, 1883–90.

Subotnik, Rose: *Developing Variations: Style and Ideology in Western Music*. Minneapolis, MN: University of Minnesota Press, 1991.

Suisman, David, and Susan Strasser, eds. *Sound in the Age of Mechanical Reproduction*. Philadelphia, PA: University of Pennsylvania Press, 2010.

Summer, Donna, and Marc Eliot. *Ordinary Girl: The Journey*. New York: Villard, 2003.

Sutheim, Peter. 'An Afternoon with Bill Putnam (Interview)'. *Journal of the Audio Engineering Society* 37, no. 9 (1989): 723–30.

Swezey, Stuart. 'Infrasound'. In *Amok Journal: Sensurround Edition*, edited by Stuart Swezey, 369–438. Los Angeles, CA: Amok, 1995.

Szendy, Peter. *Listen. A History of Our Ears*. New York: Fordham University Press, 2008.

Talbot, Michel. *The Musical Work: Reality or Invention?* Liverpool: Liverpool University Press, 2000.

Tang, Jeffrey Donald. 'Sound Decisions: System, Standards, and Consumers in American Audio Technology, 1945–1975'. PhD dissertation, University of Pennsylvania, Philadelphia, 2004.

Taruskin, Richard. 'Is There a Baby in the Bathwater? (Part I)'. *Archiv für Musikwissenschaft* 63, no. 3 (2006): 163–85.

Taruskin, Richard. 'Is There a Baby in the Bathwater? (Part II)'. *Archiv für Musikwissenschaft* 63, no. 4 (2006): 309–27.

Taylor, Timothy, Mark Katz and Tony Grajeda. *Music, Sound, and Technology in America: A Documented History of Early Phonograph, Cinema, and Radio*. Durham, NC: Duke University Press, 2012.

Teal, Kimberley Hannon. 'Beyond the Cotton Club: The Persistence of Duke Ellington's Jungle Style'. *Jazz Perspectives* 6, no. 1/2 (2013): 123–49.

Théberge, Paul. 'Amplifier'. In *Continuum Encyclopedia of Popular Music of the World: Volume I. Media, Industry and Society*, edited by John Shepherd, David Horn, Dave Laing, Paul Oliver and Peter Wicke, 505–6. London: Continuum, 2003.

Théberge, Paul. *Any Sound You Can Imagine: Making Music/Consuming Technology*. Hanover, NH: Wesleyan University Press, 1997.

Tholen, Georg Christoph. *Die Zäsur der Medien: Kulturphilosophische Konturen*. Frankfurt am Main: Suhrkamp, 2002.

Thompson, Emily. 'Machines, Music, and the Quest for Fidelity: Marketing the Edison Phonograph in America, 1877–1925'. *The Musical Quarterly* 79 (1995): 131–71.

Thompson, Emily. *The Soundscape of Modernity: Architectural Acoustics and the Culture of Listening in America, 1900–1933*. Cambridge, MA: MIT Press, 2002.
Thompson, Marie. 'Whiteness and the Ontological Turn in Sound Studies'. *Parallax* 23, no. 3 (2017): 266–82.
Thorau, Christian, and Hansjakob Ziemer. 'The Art of Listening and Its Histories: An Introduction'. In *The Oxford Handbook of Music Listening in the 19th and 20th Centuries*, edited by Christian Thorau and Hansjakob Ziemer, 1–34. New York: Oxford University Press, 2019.
Thorau, Christian, and Hansjakob Ziemer, eds. *The Oxford Handbook of Music Listening in the 19th and 20th Centuries*. New York: Oxford University Press, 2019.
Thorau, Christian. 'Vom Programmzettel zur Listening-App: Eine kurze Geschichte des geführten Hörens'. In *Das Konzert II*, edited by Martin Tröndle, 165–96. Bielefeld: transcript, 2018.
Thornton, Sarah. *Club Cultures: Music, Media and Subcultural Capital*. Cambridge: Polity, 1995.
Tkaczyk, Viktoria. 'Gedächtnis'. In *Handbuch Sound: Geschichte – Begriffe – Ansätze*, edited by Daniel Morat and Hansjakob Ziemer, 20–4. Stuttgart: J. B. Metzler, 2018.
Tkaczyk, Viktoria. 'Listening in Circles: Spoken Drama and the Architects of Sound, 1750–1830'. *Annals of Science* 71, no 3 (2014): 299–334.
Tkaczyk, Viktoria. 'The Testing of a Hundred Listeners: Otto Abraham's Studies on "Absolute Tone Consciousness"'. In *Testing Hearing: The Making of Modern Aurality*, edited by Viktoria Tkaczyk, Mara Mills and Alexandra Hui, 49–76. New York: Oxford University Press, 2021.
Tkaczyk, Viktoria, Mara Mills and Alexandra Hui, eds. *Testing Hearing: The Making of Modern Aurality*. New York: Oxford University Press, 2021.
Toop, David. 'Lost in Music: Zwanzig Jahre Diskoproduktionen'. In *Sound und Vision*, edited by Klaus Frederking, 144–67. Reinbek bei Hamburg: Rowohlt, 1985.
Topping, Ray. Liner Notes for Little Richard, *Little Richard. The Specialty Sessions*. Specialty, United States, 1989.
Trendelenburg, Ferdinand. *Einführung in die Akustik*. Berlin: Springer, 1939.
Trendelenburg, Ferdinand. 'Über Bau und Anwendung von Großlautsprechern'. *Elektrotechnische Zeitschrift* 48, no. 46 (1927): 1685–91.
Tresch, John, and Emily I. Dolan. 'Toward a New Organology: Instruments of Music and Science'. *Osiris* 28, no. 1 (2013): 278–98.
Trippett, David. 'Sound and Materialism in the 19th Century'. Accessed 29 April 2022, https://sound-matter.com/dr-david-trippett/.
Tröndle, Martin, ed. *Das Konzert II: Beiträge zum Forschungsfeld der Concert Studies*. Bielefeld: transcript, 2018.
Trower, Shelley. *Senses of Vibration: A History of the Pleasure and Pain of Sound*. New York: Bloomsbury, 2012.
Trower, Shelley. '"Upwards of 20,000": Extrasensory Quantities of Railway Shock'. *The Senses and Society* 3, no. 2 (2008): 153–67.
Trower, Shelley. 'Vibrations'. In *Sound and Literature*, edited by Anna Snaith, 287–314. Cambridge University Press, 2020.
Tuhus-Dubrow, Rebecca. *Personal Stereo*. New York: Bloomsbury Academic, 2017.
Uecke, Edward H. 'The Control of Quality in Phonograph Records'. *Journal of the Audio Engineering Society* 4, no. 4 (1956): 159–62.
'Unterhaltung: Die Jukebox verstummt'. *Der Spiegel*, no. 14 (1974).

Veal, Michael E. *Dub: Soundscapes and Shattered Songs in Jamaican Reggae*. Middletown: Wesleyan University Press, 2007.

'Vertrag mit GEMA unterzeichnet'. *Der Automaten-Markt: Fachzeitschrift für die Gesamte Automatenwirtschaft* 9, no. 1 (1957): 12, 14.

Vieira de Oliveira, Pedro J. S. 'Forbidden Music, Forbidden Jukeboxes: Listening Anxieties and the Hyper-amplification of Violence in Rio de Janeiro'. In *Border Listening/Escucha Liminal*, vol. 1, edited by Alejandra Luciana Cárdenas, 21–33. Berlin: Radical Sounds Latin America, 2020.

Vogl, Joseph. 'Becoming-Media: Galileo's Telescope'. *Grey Room* 29 (2007): 14–25.

Volmar, Axel. 'Experiencing High Fidelity: Sound Reproduction and the Politics of Music Listening in the Twentieth Century'. In *The Oxford Handbook of Music Listening in the 19th and 20th Centuries*, edited by Christian Thorau and Hansjakob Ziemer, 395–420. New York: Oxford University Press, 2019.

Volmar, Axel, ed. *Zeitkritische Medien*. Berlin: Kulturverlag Kadmos, 2009.

Volmar, Axel, and Dominik Schrey. 'Compact Disc'. In *Handbuch Sound: Geschichte – Begriffe – Ansätze*, edited by Daniel Morat and Hansjakob Ziemer, 324–8. Stuttgart: J. B. Metzler, 2018.

Vourtsis, Phil. *The Fabulous Victrola '45'*. Atglen, PA: Schiffer, 2007.

Wall, Tim. 'Rocking around the Clock: Teenage Dance Fads from 1955 to 1965'. In *Ballroom, Boogie, Shimmy Sham, Shale: A Social and Popular Dance Reader*, edited by Julie Malnig, 182–98. Chicago, IL: University of Illinois Press, 2008.

Wallerstein, Edward. 'Creating the LP Record (as Told to Ward Botsford)'. *High Fidelity Magazine* 26, no. 4 (1976): 56–8.

Walmsley, Derek. 'The Primer: Dubstep'. *The Wire*, May 2007, 42–9.

Walters, Barry. 'Burning Down the House'. *Spin*, November 1986, 60–3.

Weber, Heike. *Das Versprechen mobiler Freiheit: Zur Kultur- und Technikgeschichte von Kofferradio, Walkman und Handy*. Bielefeld: transcript, 2008.

Weber, Julian. 'Wärme und Dynamik. Kein Detroit-Techno oder House ohne ihn: Zum Tode von Ron Murphy, dem Meister des fetischisierten Klangs'. *taz*, 15 January 2008. Accessed 30 April 2022. https://taz.de/Zum-Tod-von-Ron-Murphys/!5188479/.

Wegman, Rob. '"Das musikalische Hören" in the Middle Ages and Renaissance: Perspectives from Pre-War Germany'. *The Musical Quarterly* 82, no. 3/4 (1998): 424–53.

Weheliye, Alexander G. *Phonographies: Grooves in Sonic Afro-Modernities*. Durham, NC: Duke University Press, 2005.

Welch, Walter L., and Leah Brodbeck Stenzel Burt. *From Tinfoil to Stereo: The Acoustic Years of the Recording Industry, 1877–1929*. Gainesville, FL: University Press of Florida, 1994.

Welch, Walter L., and Oliver Read. *From Tin Foil to Stereo: Evolution of the Phonograph*. Indianapolis, IN: Sams, 1976.

Welsch, Wolfgang. 'Auf dem Weg zu einer Kultur des Hörens?'. *Paragrana – Internationale Zeitschrift für Historische Anthropologie* 2, no. 1 (1993): 87–103.

Welsch, Wolfgang. *Die Aktualität des Ästhetischen*. Munich: Fink, 1993.

White, Charles. *The Life and Times of Little Richard. The Quasar of Rock*. Boston, MA: Da Capo Press, 1994.

White, Glenn D., and Gary J. Louie. *The Audio Dictionary*. Seattle, WA: University of Washington Press, 2005.

Wicke, Peter. 'The Art of Phonography: Sound, Technology and Music'. In *The Ashgate Research Companion to Popular Musicology*, edited by Derek B. Scott, 147–70. Surrey: Ashgate, 2009.

Wicke, Peter. 'Der Tonträger als Medium der Musik'. In *Handbuch Musik und Medien: Interdisziplinärer Überblick über die Mediengeschichte der Musik*, edited by Holger Schramm, 3–39. Wiesbaden: Springer, 2019.

Wicke, Peter. '"Heroes and Villains" Anmerkungen zum Verhältnis von Popmusik und Musikgeschichtsschreibung'. In *Zu Problemen der 'Heroen'- und der 'Genie'-Musikgeschichtsschreibung*, edited by Nico Schüler, 147–60. Hamburg: von Bockel, 1998.

Wicke, Peter. '"Move Your Body": Über Sinn, Klang und Körper'. *PopMusicology*. Accessed 30 April 2022. http://www.popmusicology.org/PDF/Move.pdf.

Wicke, Peter. 'Popmusik in der Analyse'. *Acta Musicologica* 75, no. 1 (2003): 107–26.

Wicke, Peter. 'Popmusik in der Theorie: Aspekte einer problematischen Beziehung'. In *Musikwissenschaft und Populäre Musik: Versuch einer Bestandsaufnahme*, edited by Helmut Rösing, Albrecht Schneider and Martin Pfleiderer, 61–73. Frankfurt am Main: Lang, 2002.

Wicke, Peter. *Rock und Pop. Von Elvis Presley bis Lady Gaga*. Munich: Beck, 2011.

Wicke, Peter. *Rockmusik: Zur Ästhetik und Soziologie eines Massenmediums*. Leipzig: Reclam, 1989.

Wicke, Peter. 'Sound Tracks. Popmusik und Popdiskurs'. In *Was ist Pop? – zehn Versuche*, edited by Walter Grasskamp, 115–40. Frankfurt am Main: Fischer, 2004.

Wicke, Peter. 'Soundtechnologien und Körpermetamorphosen: Das Populäre in der Musik des 20. Jahrhunderts'. In *Handbuch der Musik im 20. Jahrhundert*, edited by Peter Wicke, 11–60. Laaber: Laaber, 2001.

Wicke, Peter. 'Über die diskursive Formation musikalischer Praxis: Diskurs-Strategien auf dem Feld der Populären Musik'. In *Festschrift Prof. Dr. Gerd Rienäcker zum 65. Geburtstag*, edited by Stephan Aderhold, 163–74. Berlin, 2004.

Wicke, Peter. *Vom Umgang mit Popmusik*. Berlin: Volk und Wissen, 1993.

Wicke, Peter. *Von Mozart zu Madonna: Eine Kulturgeschichte der Popmusik*. Frankfurt am Main: Suhrkamp, 2001.

Wicke, Peter, Kai-Erik Ziegenrücker and Wieland Ziegenrücker. *Handbuch der populären Musik: Geschichte, Stile, Praxis, Industrie*. Mainz: Schott, 2009.

Wile, Raymond R. *Proceedings of the 1890 Convention of Local Phonograph Companies*. Nashville, TN: Country Music Foundation Press, 1974.

Wilke, Tobias. *Medien der Unmittelbarkeit: Dingkonzepte und Wahrnehmungstechniken 1918–1939*. Munich: Fink, 2010.

Williams, Jean. 'Pools Decry Ebb in Record Flow'. *Billboard*, 30 April 1977, 1, 88.

Willis, Paul E. *Profane Culture*. Princeton, NJ: Princeton University Press, 2014.

Winners, Langdon. 'Little Richard'. In *The Rolling Stone Illustrated History of Rock & Roll*, edited by Jim Miller, 52–7. New York: Rolling Stone Press, 1976.

Winthrop-Young, Geoffrey. 'Cultural Techniques: Preliminary Remarks'. *Theory, Culture & Society* 30, no. 6 (2013): 3–19.

Winthrop-Young, Geoffrey. 'Discourse, Media, Cultural Techniques: The Complexity of Kittler'. *MLN* 130, no. 3 (2015): 447–65.

Winthrop-Young, Geoffrey. *Kittler and the Media*. Cambridge: Polity, 2011.

Wittje, Roland. 'The Electrical Imagination: Sound Analogies, Equivalent Circuits, and the Rise of Electroacoustics, 1863–1939'. *Osiris* 28, no. 1 (2013): 40–63.

Wittje, Roland. 'Large Sound Amplification Systems in Interwar Germany: Siemens and Telefunken'. *Sound & Science: Digital Histories*. Accessed 30 April 2022. https://soundandscience.de/contributor-essays/large-sound-amplification-systems-interwar-germany-siemens-and-telefunken.
Wolf, Rebecca. 'Materielle Kultur'. In *Handbuch Sound: Geschichte – Begriffe – Ansätze*, edited by Daniel Morat and Hansjakob Ziemer, 32–8. Stuttgart, Weimar: Metzler, 2018.
Wolfe, Tom. *The Electric Kool-Aid Acid Test*. New York: Picador, 2008.
Wonneberg, Frank. *Vinyl Lexikon: Fachbegriffe, Sammlerlatein, Praxistipps*. Berlin: Schwarzkopf & Schwarzkopf, 2007.
Wurtzler, Steve. *Electric Sounds: Technological Change and the Rise of Corporate Mass Media*. New York: Columbia University Press, 2007.
Zagorski-Thomas, Simon. *The Musicology of Record Production*. Cambridge: Cambridge University Press, 2014.
Zagorski-Thomas, Simon, and Andrew Bourbon. *The Bloomsbury Handbook of Music Production*. New York: Bloomsbury Academic, 2020.
Zak, Albin. *I Don't Sound Like Nobody. Remaking Music in 1950s America*. Ann Arbor, MI: University of Michigan Press 2010.
Zak, Albin. *The Poetics of Rock: Cutting Tracks, Making Records*. Berkeley, CA: University of California Press, 2001.
Zeiner-Henriksen, Hans T. 'Chicago House and the "Democratization" of Music Production'. Paper, conference 'Music and Place' at Manchester Metropolitan University, Manchester, June 8–10, 2006.
Zeiner-Henriksen, Hans T. 'The "PoumTchak" Pattern: Correspondences between Rhythm, Sound, and Movement in Electronic Dance Music'. PhD dissertation, Department of Musicology, University of Oslo, Oslo, 2010.
Zielinski, Siegfried. *Deep Time of the Media. Toward an Archaeology of Hearing and Seeing by Technical Means*. Translated by Gloria Custance. Cambridge, MA: MIT Press, 2006.
Ziemer, Hansjakob. 'The Crisis of Listening in Interwar Germany'. In *The Oxford Handbook of Music Listening in the 19th and 20th Centuries*, edited by Christian Thorau and Hansjakob Ziemer, 97–121. New York: Oxford University Press, 2019.
Zlatopolsky, Ashley. 'Behind the Groove. The Ron Murphy Story'. *Red Bull Music Academy*. Accessed 30 April 2022. https://daily.redbullmusicacademy.com/2015/05/ron-murphy-feature.
Zwick, Edward. 'An Interview with the Father of Hi-Fi: Dr. Peter Goldmark'. *Rolling Stone*, 27 September 1973, 21–7.

Discography

Andrea True Connection. *More, More, More*. Buddah, United States, 1976, 12-inch single.
Ashford & Simpson. *Found a Cure*. Warner, United States, 1979, 12-inch single.
B. T. Express. *Do It ('Til You're Satisfied)*. Scepter SCE12395 (S-62102-2A), United States, 1974, 7-inch single.
Barrabas. *Barrabas*. RCA Victor, Spain, 1972, LP.
Barrabas. *Mad Love*. Atlantic DSKO 50, United States, 1974, 7-inch single.
Barry White. *I've Got so Much Love to Give*. 20th Century Records, United States, 1973, LP.
The Beach Boys. *Pet Sounds*. Capitol, United States, 1966, LP.
The Beatles. *Long Tall Sally*. Parlophone, UK, 1964, 7-inch single.

The Beatles. *Sgt. Pepper's Lonely Hearts Club Band*. Parlophone, UK, 1967, LP.
Bettye Lavette. *Doin' the Best That I Can*. West End, United States, 1978, 12-inch single.
Bobby Moore. *(Call Me Your) Anything Man*. Scepter SDT-12405, United States, 1975, 12-inch single.
Brian Eno. *Discreet Music*. Obscure, UK, 1975, LP.
Calhoon. *(Do You Wanna) Dance, Dance, Dance*. Warner Spector PRO 601, United States, 1975, 12-inch single.
Carl Douglas. *Kung Fu Fighting*. 20th Century Records, United States, 1974, 7-inch single.
Cerrone. *Love in 'C' Minor*. Malligator, France, 1976, LP.
Chip E. *If You Only Knew*. DJ International DJ 779, United States, 1986, 12-inch single.
Consumer Rapport. *Ease On Down the Road*. Atlantic DSKO 54, United States, 1975, 7-inch single.
Dewey Phillips. *Red Hot & Blue: Dewey Phillips Live Radio Broadcasts from 1952–1964*. Memphis Archives, United States, 1995, CD.
Don Downing. *Dream World*. Roadshow, United States, 1973, 7-inch single.
Donna Summer. *Can't We Just Sit Down (And Talk It Over)/I Feel Love*. Casablanca, United States, 1977, 7-inch single.
Donna Summer. *Love to Love You Baby*. Casablanca/Oasis, United States, 1975, LP.
Double Exposure. *Ten Per Cent*. Salsoul 12D-2008 (12D-2008A-2), United States, 1976, 12-inch single.
Double Exposure. *Ten Percent*. Salsoul SZ 2013 (SZ 2013-A-1E), UK, 1976, 7-inch single.
Double Exposure. *Ten Percent*. Salsoul SZ-2008 (SZ2008A-2), Single, United States, 1976, 7-inch single.
Double Exposure. *Ten Percent*. Salsoul SZS 5503 (SZS 5503-A-1E), UK, 1976, LP.
Eddie Cochran. *Skinny Jim*. Crest, United States, 1957, 7-inch single.
Eddie Kendricks. *Girl You Need a Change of Mind*. Tamla, United States, 1973, 7-inch single.
Elvis Presley. *G. I. Blues*. RCA Victor, United States, 1960, LP.
Fern Kinney. *Groove Me*. WEA, Germany, 1979, 12-inch single.
Frank Sinatra. *In the Wee Small Hours*. Capitol, United States, 1955, LP.
Frankie Ford. *Sea Cruise*. Ace, United States, 1959, 7-inch single.
Gary's Gang. *Keep on Dancing*. SAM, United States, 1978, 12-inch single.
Gene Vincent. *Be-Bob-A-Lula*. Capitol F3450 (45-15230-D7), United States, 1956, 7-inch single.
Gloria Gaynor. *I've Got You under My Skin*. Polydor, United States, 1976, LP.
Gloria Gaynor. *Never Can Say Goodbye*. MGM Records, United States, 1975, LP.
Grandmaster Flash & The Furious Five. *The Message*. Sugar Hill Records, United States, 1982, 12-inch single.
Hardrock Gunter. *Juke Box, Help Me Find My Baby*. Sun, United States, 1956, 7-inch single.
Harold Melvin & the Blue Notes. *The Love I Lost*. PIR ZS7 3533, United States, 1973, 7-inch single.
Hot Chocolate. *Disco Queen/Makin' Music*. Atlantic, United States, 1974, 7-inch single.
Howlin' Wolf. *Moanin at Midnight*. Chess, United States, 1951, 7-inch single.
Howlin' Wolf. *The Howlin' Wolf Album*. Cadet Concept, United States, 1969, LP.
Inner Life. *Ain't no Mountain High Enough*. Salsoul, United States, 1982, 12-inch single.
Isaac Hayes. *Hot Buttered Soul*. Enterprise, United States, 1969, LP.
Jeff Mills. *Cycle 30*. Axis AX-008, United States, 1994, 12-inch single.

Jerry Lee Lewis. *Killer Country*. Elektra, United States, 1981, LP.
Jesse Saunders. *On and On*. Jes Say JS9999, United States, 1984, 12-inch single.
Joe 'King' Oliver's Creole Jazz Band. *Dipper Mouth Blues*. Gennett, United States, 1923, 78-rpm shellac.
Joe Meeks. *I Hear a New World*. Triumph, UK, 1960, LP.
Karen Young. *Hot Shot*. West End, United States, 1978, 12-inch single.
Kitty, Daisy & Lewis. *Smoking in Heaven*. Sunday Best Recordings, UK, 2011. 8 10-inch 78 rpm.
Larry Williams. *Short Fat Fannie*. Specialty, United States, 1957, 7-inch single.
LaVern Baker. *Humpty Dumpty Heart*. Atlantic, United States, 1959, 7-inch single.
Lil Louis. *French Kiss*. Diamond, United States, 1989, 12-inch single.
Link Wray. *Link Wray*. Polydor, United States, 1971, LP.
Little Richard. *Heeby-Jeebies*. Specialty, United States, 1956, 7-inch single.
Little Richard. *Here's Little Richard*. MoFi 1-287 (MFSL-1227-B1), United States, 2008, LP.
Little Richard. *His Greatest Hits*. VeeJay 1124 (64933-1), United States, 1964, LP.
Little Richard. *Little Richard: The Specialty Sessions*. Specialty, United States, 1989, 3 CD.
Little Richard. *Little Richard's Grooviest 17 Original Hits!*. Specialty, United States, 1968, LP.
Little Richard. *Long Tall Sally*. London/Specialty (MSC 1443-1), GB 1956, 10-inch shellac, 78 rpm.
Little Richard. *Long Tall Sally*. Specialty XSP-572 (L-10723; 572-XSP), United States, 1968, 7-inch single.
Little Richard. *Long Tall Sally*. Specialty XSP-572-45 (45-XSP-572), United States, 1956, 7-inch single.
Little Richard. *Lucille*. Specialty, United States, 1957, 7-inch single.
Little Richard. *Shake a Hand*. Specialty, United States, 1959, 7-inch single.
Little Richard. *Starpower*. Bell, GER 1998, CD.
Little Richard. *Tutti Frutti*. Specialty, United States, 1955, 7-inch single.
Loleatta Holloway. *Hit and Run*. Goldmine, United States, 1977, 12-inch single.
Love Committee. *Law and Order*. Gold Mind Records, United States, 1978, LP.
Love Unlimited Orchestra. *Love's Theme*. 20th Century Records, United States, 1973, 7-inch single.
M. *Pop Muzik/M Factor*. MCA Records 0900.138, Germany, 1979, 12-inch single.
Manu Dibango. *Soul Makossa*. Fiesta, France, 1972, 7-inch single.
Marshall Jefferson. *Move Your Body*. Trax, United States, 1986, 12-inch single.
Marty Robbins. *Long Tall Sally*. Columbia, United States, 1956, 7-inch single.
Mirage featuring Chip E. *Jack Trax*. House Records, United States, 1985, LP.
Mothers of Invention. *Freak Out*. Verve, United States, 1966, LP.
New Order. *Blue Monday*. Factory, UK, 1983, 12-inch single.
A Number of Names. *Sharevari*. Capriccio Records, United States, 1981, 12-inch single.
Pat Boone. *Long Tall Sally*. Dot 45-15457 (45-M-9058), United States, 1956, 7-inch single.
Pat Boone. *Long Tall Sally*. Dot 45-15457 (MW9058), United States, 1956, 7-inch single.
Perry Como. *Juke Box Baby*. RCA Victor, United States, 1956, 7-inch single.
Peter Kraus. *Sugar-Baby*. Polydor 23844 A (23844 A II), FRG, 1958, 7-inch single.
Phuture. *Acid Tracks*. Trax TX142A, United States, 1987, 12-inch single.
Pink Floyd. *The Dark Side of the Moon*. Harvest, UK, 1973, LP.
Public Image Ltd. *Metal Box*. Virgin METAL 1, UK, 1979, three 12-inch singles.

Ralphi Rosario feat. Xavier Gold. *You Used to Hold Me*. Hot Mix 5 Records, United States, 1987, 12-inch single.
Rare Earth. *Back to Earth*. Rare Earth (Motown), United States, 1975, LP.
Ray Charles. *What'd I Say*. Atlantic, United States, 1959, LP.
Reese. *Funky Funk Funk/Bassline*. Network Records NWKT 23, UK, 1991, 12-inch single.
Ricky Nelson. *Teenager Romance*. Verve, United States, 1957, 7-inch single.
Roy Brown. *Let the Four Winds Blow*. Imperial, United States, 1957, 7-inch single.
Sleezy D. *I've Lost Control*. Trax TX113b (PRL 86113 B4), United States, 1986, 12-inch single.
Sly & The Family Stones. *Dance to the Music*. Epic, United States, 1968, LP.
Son House. *My Black Mama*. Paramount 13042, United States, 1930, 78-rpm shellac.
Southshore Commission. *Free Man*. Scepter/Ward, United States, 1975, 12-inch single.
Suburban Knight Feat. Dark Energy and Chameleon. *Hidden in Plainsight EP*. Underground Resistance UR-050, United States, 1999, EP.
Teddy Pendergrass. *You Can't Hide from Yourself*. PIR, United States, 1977, 7-inch single.
The Temptations. *Law of the Land*. Tamla Motown, United States, 1973, 7-inch single.
Ultra High Frequency. *We're on the Right Track*. Wand, United States, 1973, 7-inch single.
Van McCoy & The Soul City Symphony. *The Hustle*. H&L Records, United States, 1975, 7-inch single.
Various. *Alan Freed's 'Golden Pics'*. End LP 313 (LP 313A), United States, 1961, LP.
Various. *Alan Freed's Memory Lane*. End, United States, 1962, LP.
Various. *Alan Freed's Top 15*. End, United States, 1962, LP.
Various. *Cooley High*. Motown, United States, 1975, LP.
Various. *Disco Par-r-r-ty. Non Stop Music*. Spring, United States, 1974, LP.
Various. *Saturday Night Fever*. RSO, United States, 1977, two LPs.
Various. *Techno! The New Dance Sound of Detroit*. 10 Records/Virgin Records, UK, 1988, CD.
Various. *The House Sound of Chicago*. DJ International/London, UK, 1986, LP.
Visage. *Visage*. Polydor, UK, 1980, LP.
Walter Gibbons. *Jungle Music (Mixed With Love: Essential & Unreleased Remixes 1976–1986)*. Strut, UK, 2010, CD.
The Winstons. *Color Him Father/Amen, Brother*. Metromedia, United States, 1969, 7-inch single.
X-102. *Discovers the Rings of Saturn*. Tresor, Germany, 1992, two EPs.

Filmography

Alice in den Städten. Wim Wenders. Peter Genée, Germany, 1974.
American Graffiti. George Lucas. Lucasfilm Ltd., United States, 1973.
The Asphalt Jungle. John Huston. Metro-Goldwyn-Mayer, United States, 1950.
Auf der Reeperbahn nachts um halb eins. Wolfgang Liebeneiner. Kurt Ulrich, Germany, 1954.
Baby It's You. John Sayles. Paramount Pictures, United States, 1983.
Back to the Future. Robert Zemeckis. Universal Pictures, United States, 1985.
A Bronx Tale. Jane Rosenthal. Price Entertainment, United States, 1993.
Cadillac Records. Darnell Martin. TriStar Pictures, United States, 2008.

Cléo de 5 a 7. Agnès Varda. Georges de Beauregard, France, 1962.
Die Halbstarken. Georg Tressler. Inter West Film GmbH, Germany, 1956.
Do the Right Thing. Spike Lee. 40 Acres and a Mule Filmworks, United States, 1989.
Don't Knock the Rock. Fred F. Sears. Columbia Pictures, United States, 1956.
G. I. Blues. Norman Taurog. Paramount Pictures, United States, 1960.
The Girl Can't Help It. Frank Tashlin. 20th Century Fox, United States, 1956.
Grease. Randal Kleiser. Paramount Pictures, United States, 1971.
Happy Days. Garry Marshall. ABC Network, United States, 1974–84, TV Show.
Hiroshima Mon Amour. Anain Resnais. Anatole Dauman, France, 1959.
Ku'damm 56. Sven Bohse. UFA Fiction GmbH, Germany, 2016, TV Film.
Loving You. Hal Kanter. Paramount Pictures, United States, 1957.
Mad Men. Matthew Weiner. Lionsgate Television, United States, 2010–15, TV Show.
The Man without a Past. Aki Kaurismäki. Aki Kaurismäki, Finland, 2002.
The Match Factory Girl. Aki Kaurismäki. Aki Kaurismäki, Finland/Sweden, 1990.
My Dream Is Yours. Michael Curitz. Warner Bros. Pictures, United States, 1949.
Predator. John McTiernan. 20th Century Fox, United States, 1987.
Saturday Night Fever. John Badham. Paramount Pictures, United States, 1977.
SubBerlin. The Story of Tresor. Tilmann Künzel. Tresor Berlin GmbH, Germany, 2008.
The Twilight Zone. Rod Serling. CBS, United States, 1959–64, TV Show.
Vivre sa vie. Jean-Luc Godard. Pierre Braunberger. France, 1962.
The Wild One. László Benedek. Columbia Pictures, United States, 1953.
Wild Style. Charlie Ahearn. Submarine Entertainment, United States, 1982.

Index

12-inch single record 4, 30–4, 107–35, 153–7, 159–61, 167–71, 236 n.2, 242 n.20, 242 n.23, 242 n.24, 245 n.79, 245 n.104, 248 n.126, 250 n.158, 251 n.161, 256 n.219, 268 n.190
   visuality 120
45s, *see* 7-inch single record
45 rpm, *see* 7-inch single record
7-inch single record 3–4, 14, 27, 30–2, 46, 48–50, 54–5, 59–60, 65–6, 71, 76–7, 81–2, 87, 95, 107–8, 110, 112, 117, 124, 127–8, 130–1, 167–8, 170, 205 n.52, 206 n.68, 208 n.82, 216 n.211, 221 n.41, 243 n.35
78-rpm shellac, *see* shellac record
78s, *see* shellac record
(Call Me Your) Anything Man (record) 242 n.24
(Do you Wanna) Dance, Dance, Dance (record) 242 n.24
Acid: Can You Jack? Chicago Acid and Experimental House 1985–95 (record) 254 n.191
Acoustilog Inc. (company) 152, *see also* Alan Fierstein
actor-network theory 14, 16, 190 n.36
   and media theory 14
Adorno, Theodor W. 8, 14, 19–20, 60–1, 79, 86, 98, 114, 120, 125, 200 n.256, 208 n.83
Ain't No Mountain High Enough (record) 240 n.3, 270 n.202
Alan Freed's 'Golden Pics' (record) 46, 203 n.33
Alan Freed's Memory Lane (record) 203 n.33
Alan Freed's Top 15 (record) 203 n.33
Allen, Lee 42–3
Amen, Brother (record) 241 n.11

American Federation of Musicians (AFM) 55, 63–4, 85, 225 n.113
American Graffiti (film) 204 n.39
American Society of Composers, Authors and Publishers (ASCAP) 204 n.38
amplification 25–27, 33, 48, 83–4, 88, 111, 137–44, 258 n.15, 260 n.31
Anders, Günther 114
Anderson, Tim J. 57, 63–4, 97, 206 n.64
Aphex (company) 154
   Aural Exciter 154
Apocalypse Now (film) 39
Armed Forces Network (AFN) 210 n.107
Atkins, Juan 129, 133, 253 n.176, 255 n.210
Attali, Jacques 23, 63–4, 85, 97, 196 n.210
AT&T 139
audience, *see* listener
Audio Engineering (magazine) 69
Audio Engineering Society (AES) 69–70
audiophile, *see* hi-fi
Auslander, Philip 138
authenticity 128, 251 n.167
Automaten-Markt (magazine) 79–80, 100, 223 n.66, 235–6 n.246

Bachman, William S. 56
backbeat 39–40, 43–4, 202 n.20, 241 n.11, *see also* rock 'n' roll culture
Back to Earth (record) 242 n.26
Bacon, Francis 138
Barrabas (record) 109, 241 n.17
Barthes, Roland 19–20, 158, 194 n.185
Basie, Count 80
bass
   -accented cut (record) 33
   cultivation of 108, 160
   deep tactile 34
   design 151–3
   enhancement 14, 35, 153–4, 160, 268 n.184, *see also* disco; disco and club culture

enhancer DBX Boom Box Model 100 153
frequency 33, 35
of jukebox 83–4, *see also* belly resonance
materialism 12, 124, 179 n.47, 264 n.116
sonic management of the 117, 151
speaker 9, 14, 35, 151–5, 160
sub- 14, 35, 108, 116, 123, 125, 152–5, 160–3
sub-bass speaker 14, 35, 152, 154–5, *see also* Levan Horn
BBC 79, 222 n.54
B. B. King 42
Be-Bop-A-Lula (record) 47, 203 n.34
Beckett, Steve 135
Bell Laboratories 139, 141, 261 n.50
belly resonance, *see* jukebox
Belz, Carl 51, 55, 60, 204 n.39
Benjamin, Walter 16, 59, 249 n.137
Berlin (city) 122, 134–5, 141–3, 147, 170, 235 n.246, 275 n.262
Berliner, Emile 28, 91, 228 n.160
Berry, Chuck 45, 201 n.7
Bihari, Joe 75
Bijsterveld, Karin 7, 183 n.76
Billboard (magazine) 33, 35, 45, 59, 70, 75, 80, 109–10, 112, 148, 209 n.93, 211 n.126, 216 n.206, 221 n.36, 240 n.5, 267 n.152, 263 n.193
Bingham, Walter Van Dyke 100
Blackwell, Robert 'Bumps' 42, 202 n.22
Blank, Bob 113, 269 n.191
Blue Monday (record) 126
body
see under technique
dancing 102, 113–14, 161, 163, 165–6
designable 114
disco 114–17, 163, 244 n.63
Böhme, Gernot 7
Boone, Pat 45, 47
break (in music) 33, 42, 109–11, 113, 120–1, 157, 241 n.11
Brewster, Bill 239 n.3, 252 n.170
Broughton, Frank 236–7 n.1, 252 n.170
Brown, Al 130, 253 n.179
Buddy Holly 201 n.7
Built for Comfort (record) 44
Burroughs, William S. 21

Cadillac Records (film) 204 n.39
Campbell, Michael 'Mikey Dread' 145
Cantor, Lewis 81
Carnegie Hall 162, 261 n.50
Carson, Benjamin R. 59, 61
Caruso, Enrico 62
Casey, Bob 150
Cash Box (magazine) 80
Cavallo, Guglielmo 64–5
Cayre, Ken 113
CBS Columbia (media corporation), *see under* Columbia Records
Chartier, Roger 64
Cheren, Mel 110, 163–4, 243 n.47, 266 n.143, 268–9 n.190
Chess Records 43, 50, 70–1, 81, 218 n.225,
Chicago, Illinois 29, 34, 43, 47, 50, 70, 129, 131–3, 146–7, 149, 157–8, 164, 217 n.212, 252 n.170, 252 n.171, 252 n.175, 254 n.191, 245 n.196, 271 n.215, 273 n.252
chrome ears 93–4, *see also* golden ears; tin ears; jukebox
Cirque Napoléon 138
class identity 20, 30, 48–9, 54, 56, 58, 70, 73–4, 78, 99, 102, 111, 116, 149, 160, 162, 220 n.14, 252 n.176, 274 n.261
Clements, Joseph 94
clubs (famous)
Berghain 147
Dorian Gray 150
Flamingo 166
Galaxy 21 111
Gallery 111, 149
Loft 109, 115–16, 148–52, 159, 163
Ministry of Sound 147, 264 n.121
Music Box 133, 158, 164–5
Paradise Garage 35, 147–53, 162, 237 n.3, 265 n.134, 266 n.143, 268 n.186, 271 n.215
Power Plant 165, 252 n.171
Sanctuary 160, 163
SoHo Place 149–51, 266 n.147
Studio 54 146–7, 150, 237 n.3, 264 n.112,
Tresor 122, 135, 147
Warehouse 146–50, 164–5, 252 n.171, 255 n.196

Cochran, Eddie 52, 203 n.30
collectivization 30, 35, 57, 116, 159–60, 162–3, 169
Columbia Phonograph Company 56, 77, 229 n.162
Columbia Records 55–6, 210 n.96, 260 n.31
  CBS (media corporation) 31–4, 50, 55–6, 60, 62, 65–6, 77, 108, 209 n.92, 209 n.94, 212 n.138, 215 n.190, 229 n.162
compressor (audio) 70, 88, 154, 217 n.212, 253 n.180, 269 n.192
Cook, Emory 71
Cooley High (OST) (record) 242 n.26
copyright 85, 119, 129, 225 n.114
Correll, Ernst Hugo 143
Cox, Christoph 179 n.47
Crimp, Douglas 113, 163, 166
crooning 25, 122, 141, 197 n.215
Crosby, Bing 51–2
cultural studies 19, 86, 102, 156, 196 n.209, 226 n.128, 131 n.189, 235 n.236, 272 n.227
Cuoghi, Joe 81
Cycle 30 (record) 256 n.219

Dahlhaus, Carl 189 n.127, 193 n.179
danceability, *see* remix; disco and sound culture; DJ; 12-inch single record
Dance to the Music (record) 242 n.21
dancing crowd 21, 35, 111, 121, 149–50, 153, 162–3, 165, *see also* disco and club culture; DJ
deafness, *see* unhearable
deaf studies 11, *see also* unhearable
de Forest, Lee 139, 140
Deleuze, Gilles 21, 125
Dell'Antonio, Andrew 195 n.195
Detroit, Michigan 34, 121, 129, 133–5, 168, 252 n.176
Devine, Kyle 141–3, 179 n.47
Didley, Bo 201 n.7
disco and club culture 3–4, 34–5, 123–6, 146–7, 153, 156, 159–62, 168–9, 236 n.2, 264 n.107, *see also* sound system; 12-inch single record; disco; house; techno
disco (discotheque) 33, 35, 109–13, 116–19, 145–50, 152–4, 161, 163, 165–6, 240 n.5, 263 n.100, 264 n.103, 264 n.134, 269 n.192, 269 n.193, 274 n.253
  see also clubs (famous)
  loudspeaker systems of 14, 30, 35, 109, 116–18, 147–51, 153–6, 159, 161–4, 168, 265 n.131, 265 n.132
  visual design 115, 122, 162
disco (genre) 23, 34, 112, 114–16, 118, 122–6, 129, 131–2, 146–50, 153, 157–8, 164–5, 169, 237 n.3, 240 n.10, 241 n.11, 243 n.39, 249 n.137, 250 n.152, 254 n.183, 272 n.227, 274 n.253, 274 n.259
  see also body; sound systems; tactility; 12-inch single record; DJ; remix; New York
  mix 109–12, 115, 123, 131, 155, 241 n.15, 242 n.24
  suitability 33, 109, 111, 155
  teleology 116, 123, 125–6, 157, *see also* repetition
  version 109, 111–12, 115, 157
Disco Par-r-r-ty. Non Stop Music (record) 242 n.20
Disco Queen (record) 241 n.17
Discreet Music (record) 111
distortion (sound) 42, 47, 49, 66–7, 71, 78, 108, 139, 154, 218 n.225
DJ 27, 34–5, 40, 49, 64–5, 76, 81, 110–15, 119–21, 127, 132–3, 148–58, 160, 171, 225 n.118, 226 n.131, 232 n.212, 237 n.3, 255 n.206, 263 n.100, 264 n.107, 268 n.182, 269 n.193,
  set 35, 111, 127, 131, 133, 147, 156, 158, 251 n.162, 255 n.206, 271 n.220, *see also* remix; danceability
Doin' the Best that I Can (record) 243 n.47
Do It ('Til You're Satisfied) (record) 112, 116–7, 241 n.15
domestic space 71, 138
Domino, Fats 40
Don't Knock the Rock (film) 40–1, 46, 48
Do the Right Thing (film) 201 n.4
Douglas, Susan 212 n.127
Doyle, Peter 41, 43, 142, 259 n.23
Dream World (record) 109–10, 241 n.13
Drott, Eric 196 n.210

Dyer, Richard 115–16, 237 n.3
Dylan, Bob 144

Ease on Down the Road (record) 241 n.17
Eastman Theatre 142
Edison, Thomas Alva 10–11, 21, 28, 56, 90–1
Eggebrecht, Hans Heinrich 189–90 n.127
electronic dance music (EDM) 116, 122, 125–6, 134–5, 137, 144, 156–7, 249 n.137, 250 n.148, 270 n.204, 273 n.237, 275 n.262, *see also* house; techno
electron tube, *see* amplification
England 55, 79, 85, 115, 140, 145, 234 n.233, 263 n.100
equalizer 70, 88, 154–5, 160, 213 n.156, 217 n.212, 225 n.110
Erlmann, Veit 175 n.1, 176 n.10, 181 n.60, 181 n.65
Ernst, Wolfgang 187 n.115, 193 n.169, 193 n.173
Eshun, Kodwo 127, 134, 153, 249 n.142, 275 n.262
exciter (audio) 154, 268 n.184
exotica (genre), *see* hi-fi culture
expander (audio) 148, 154, 268 n.186

Fade to Grey (record) 215 n.187
Farley 'Jackmaster' Funk 131, 252 n.171, 254 n.191, 255 n.196
FCC (Federal Communications Commission) 226–7 n.131
Fierstein, Alan 152, 162, 265 n.134
Fillmore East 144, *see also* Bill Graham
Fink, Robert 23, 116, 125–6
Found a Cure (record) 131
Frankfurt am Main (city) 150, 219 n.5
Frankfurt Festhalle 138
FRC (Federal Radio Commission) 214 n.168
Freed, Alan 40, 46–7, 76, 204 n.38
Free Man (record) 242 n.24
French Kiss (record) 122
Frith, Simon 20, 52, 191 n.141, 208 n.82
Fuller, Paul 94
Funky Funk Funk/Bassline (record) 256 n.220

Gaisberg, Fred 62
Gardner, Brian 'Big Bass' 128
Gauselmann, Paul 220 n.11
GEMA 85
gender 24, 54, 114, 162, 237 n.3
General Electric 150, 260 n.47
Gerdien, Hans 142
Gerhard, Anselm 195 n.204
Germany 4, 6, 24, 28, 32, 48, 50, 73, 74, 79, 80, 84, 85, 86, 97, 101, 104, 135, 137–9, 141–3, 204 n.39, 205 n.53, 206 n.68, 209 n.86, 216 n.203, 218 n.1, 219 n.5, 219 n.11, 223 n.66, 225 n.118, 226 n.126, 234 n.233, 237 n.3, 242 n.20, 259 n.25, 261 n.55
Gibbons, Walter 111–13, 129, 242 n.25, 242 n.26, 268 n.190
Gilbert, Jeremy 115, 123, 147, 188 n.188–9
Gillett, Charlie 75
Girl You Need a Change of Mind (record) 241 n.11
Gitelman, Lisa 93, 95–6, 228 n.160, 231 n.187
Glass, Louis T. 90, 95, 98
Gleason, Ralph J. 50
Goehr, Lydia 189 n.127
golden ears 48, 67, 78, 91–3, 215 n.193, 230 n.175, *see also* chrome ears; tin ears; hi-fi
Goldmark, Peter 56, 209 n.94
Goodman, Steve 12, 153, 159, 179 n.47, 264 n.116
Göttert, Karl-Heinz 140
Gracyk, Theodore 51, 206 n.64
Graham, Bill 144
Grasso, Francis 111, 121, 160, 269 n.194
Grease (film) 204 n.39
Groove Me (record) 245–6 n.104
Großmann, Rolf 179–80 n.47, 190–1 n.136, 243 n.46
Grünberg, Ingrid 30
Gutshall, Jack 80

Habermas, Jürgen 18
Hagen, Wolfgang 11, 97, 117
Haley, Bill 40, 79, 235 n.246
Hamburg (city) 104, 219 n.5
Handke, Peter 73, 83, 90, 102, 219 n.10

Hanley, Bill 144
Happy Days (film) 103, 204 n.39
Hardy, Ron 133, 158, 165, 246 n.105, 251 n.162, 271 n.220
Hardwax (record store) 135, *see also* techno
Healy, Dan 144
Heeby-Jeebies-Love (record) 203 n.30
Hegemann, Dimitri 147
Heidegger, Martin 17–19, 97, 178 n.37
Heidenreich, Stefan 190–1 n.136
Heister, Hanns-Werner 78–9, 82, 86, 226 n.128, 231 n.189
Helmholtz, Hermann von 5, 181 n.65, 246 n.110
Helmreich, Stefan 186 n.96, 186 n.98, 186 n.100
Hennion, Antoine 16, 188 n.124, 190 n.134, 190 n.136, 192 n.152
Henriques, Julian 145, 147
Here's Little Richard (record) 46, 203 n.33
Hertz, Heinrich 259 n.25
Hidden in Plainsight EP (record) 256 n.221
hi-fi 47–8, 54, 57–8, 62, 66–9, 116–17, 211 n.112, 215 n.195,
   culture 54, 57–8, 60, 66–7, 91–3, 99, 116, 123, 128, 149, 160, 248 n.123,
   listener 47, 92, 116, 149, 198 n.250, 215 n.193, 245 n.104, 266 n.135
   stereo system 27, 30, 78, 93, 150
hip-hop 41, 111, 114, 117, 124, 127, *see also* 12-inch single record
His Greatest Hits (Little Richard) (record) 203 n.33, 204 n.41
Hit and Run (record) 113, 131
Hollywood, California 40, 44, 52, 62, 142, 191 n.141, 201 n.2, 213 n.156
Hollywood Bowl 142
Hot Buttered Soul (record) 242 n.21
Hot Shot (record) 268 n.190
Horn, Adrian 86, 104, 219 n.5, 234 n.233
Hot Mix 5 131, 133, 252 n.171, 255 n.196
house (genre) 23, 33–5, 113, 117, 120–33, 144–50, 152, 156–61, 164–6, 169, 252 n.170, 252 n.171, 252 n.176, 254 n.191, 255 n.196, 271 n.210, 271 n.215, 272 n.227
   see also sound system; Chicago
   jacking 164–5, 271 n.214, 273 n.252

Howlin' Wolf 44, 67, 201 n.7
Hughes, Walter 164
Humpty Dumpty Heart (record) 227 n.131

I Feel Love (record) 131
If You Only Knew (record) 252 n.175
Importes Etc. (record store) 132, *see also* house
inaudible, *see* unhearable
individualization 30, 57, 79, 169, 185 n.85
In the Wee Small Hours (record) 205 n.55
Ismaiel-Wendt, Johannes 270 n.196
I've Got So Much Love to Give (record) 242 n.21
I've Got You Under My Skin (record) 115
I've Lost Control (record) 271 n.218

Jackson 'Herb J.', Herbert 133
Jack Trax (record) 271 n.214
Jamaica 137, 145, 153, 263 n.100
James, Robin 178 n.46
Jarvis, Al 226–7 n.131
Jasen, Paul C. 128
Jefferson, Marshall 129, 133, 158
jook joints 74
Jones, Nathaniel Pierre 'DJ Pierre' 133
Jordan, Louis 80
Joyce, Thomas F. 59
jukebox 4, 13, 15, 20, 27–36, 49, 59, 63–5, 68–71, 73–104, 123, 127, 142, 145, 155–6, 159, 167–73, 211 n.126, 212 n.127, 212 n.134, 218 n.225, 219 n.5, 219 n.11, 220 n.14, 221 n.44, 222 n.51, 222 n.52, 222 n.63, 223 n.78, 224 n.102, 224 n.103, 225 n.113, 225 n.118, 225 n.119, 226 n.121, 226 n.131, 229 n.162, 229 n.163, 229 n.167, 231 n.186, 231 n.189, 234 n.231, 234 n.232, 234 n.233, 235 n.246
   see also repetition; serialization; sound of jukebox
   automatic regulation of jukebox sound 88
   business 75, 77, 80, 82, 84–6, 102, 221 n.40, 222 n.52
   changing mechanisms 89 (Fireball 120 revolving changer), 89, 96, 221

n.44, 232 n.196, (Select-O-Matic), 89
(Simplex)
distribution 60, 80–1
golden age of 76, 229 n.167,
listener 32, 79, 89, 92, 94, 101, 156, 234
n.231, 235 n.246
listening 32–3, 54, 59, 74, 88–98, 100–2,
168–9, 234 n.232
materiality of the 74
measurement 86, 98–9, 103, *see also*
play meter
operator 32, 60, 68–9, 73–85, 96–100,
217 n.223, 222 n.52, 223 n.66,
223 n.74, 223 n.77, 223 n.84,
233 n.229, 235 n.246
playlist 32, 54, 59, 82, 87, 93, 95–7
play meter 33, 98–100
regulated repetition 96
selection 78, 89, 94–9
of the Silver Age 76, 93, 229 n.167
suitability 82–3
volume control on 88, 155, 225 n.110,
jukeboxes (manufacturers)
Automatic Musical Instruments (AMI)
76, 91, 224 n.104, 226 n.121, 229
n.165, 235 n.241
Capehart 76
Evans 76
Rock-Ola 76, 88–9, 94, 226 n.121, 227
n.144, 230 n.180
Seeburg 76–7, 87, 89, 91, 94, 96, 101,
104, 168, 221 n.40, 221 n.44, 223
n.84, 224 n.97, 229 n.165, 230 n.180,
232 n.196
United Music Corporation 230 n.183
Wurlitzer 76, 89, 91, 94–6, 99, 104, 168,
229 n.165, 230 n.182
jukebox (models of)
AMI 200 233 n.234
AMI F 224 n.104, 225 n.110,
Rock-Ola 1455 88
Rock-Ola Spectravox 224 n.97
Seeburg 148 230 n.180
Seeburg Hi Tone 224 n.97
Seeburg KD 221 n.44
Seeburg M100A 76–7, 96, 221 n.40, 221
n.44, 223 n.84
Seeburg M100B 77, 221 n.40

Seeburg V200 87
United Music Corporation UPB-100
230 n.183
Wiegandt Musikautomat 1954 104
Wurlitzer 1015 76, 96
Juke Box Baby (record) 234 n.231
Juke Box Mama (record) 234 n.231
Juke Box, Help Me Find my Baby (record)
234 n.231
Jukebox Junkie (record) 234 n.231
*Jungle Music (Mixed with Love: Essential
& Unreleased Remixes 1976–1986)*
(record) 243 n.45
Just as Long as I Got You (record) 112

Kassabian, Anahid 7, 11, 124–6, 249 n.137
Katz, Bob 123
Katz, Mark 190–1 no. 136, 208 n.80, 242 n.25
Keep on Dancing (record) 131, 266 n.143
Keightley, Keir 57, 116
Keith, Farley 255 n.196
Keller, Hans 200 n.256
Kenney, William H. 20, 229 n.162
King, Ed 148
Kingston 145
Kircher, Athanasius 138
Kirk, Roger E. 215 n.190
Kittler, Friedrich 6, 11, 18, 25–7, 117–18,
138, 140, 263 n.91
Klipsch, Paul, *see* Klipschorn
Kool DJ Herc 111
Krämer, Sybille 10
Krasnow, Carolyn 157
Kreuzer, Gundula 26
Kronengold, Charles 131, 157, 239–40 n.3,
251 n.161
Kung Fu Fighting (record) 244 n.63

Latour, Bruno 6, 16, 172, 190 n.136,
193 n.174
Law and Order (record) 112
Law of the Land (record) 241 n.11
Lawrence, Tim 115, 118, 132, 146–7, 150,
161, 163, 237–39 n.3, 240 n.6, 240
n.10, 274 n.253
Lawrence, Vince 129
Leary, Timothy 149
Lehár, Franz 30

Let the Four Winds Blow (record) 227 n.131
Levan, Larry 150–1, 240 n.3, 246 n.105, 270 n.202
Lewisohn Stadium 141
Lieben, Robert von 139
Lil Green 80
limiter 70, 217 n.212, 253 n.180
Lippincott, Jesse H. 90
listener 3, 5, 8–15, 19–22, 28, 32–5, 55, 57–60, 62, 63, 65, 68, 74, 77–9, 86–109, 114, 120, 122, 124–7, 133, 138, 140, 142, 156, 159, 162–8, 171–2, 181 n.60, 181 n.63, 189 n.127, 195 n.195, 215 n.190, 221 n.44, 265 n.130, 272 n.229, 274 n.256, 274 n.259
  as composer 19–22
  expert 114
  ideal 19–20
  implicit 28, 41, 182 n.75, 193 n.177
  modern 181 n.60
  as musician 19–22
listening
  algorithmic 6
  as art 114, 182 n.75
  background 28
  body 15, 122–3, 160
  collective 195 n.195
  concept of 10, 19, 31
  culture 8, 20, 22, 47, 55, 123, 166, 170, 172, 234 n.232, 248 n.123
  as an economic problem 17
  in films 101
  form of 3, 5–9, 12, 28, 31, 33–5, 41, 47, 53–8, 71, 74, 78, 89, 93, 96, 98, 124–5, 153–4, 159–60, 209 n.84, 274 n.257
  as generator of knowledge 7, 9
  haptic 125–6, *see also* tactility
  history of music 3, 28
  immersive 151, 160, 163
  machinic 6
  management of 8, 17, 21, 23, 68, 89, 98, 100, 160, 167–9, 195 n.195, 231 n.195,
  models of 7, 58, 167, 173
  in modernity 176 n.10
  modes of 11, 20, 28
  music 3, 8, 19–20, 27–30, 33, 35, 49, 53–5, 60, 89–92, 98–100, 113, 125, 162, 167, 170, 172, 179 n.47, 228 n.149

pedagogy of 19
private 231 n.187
public 185 n.85
to records 3, 28–31, 88–9, 94, 168, 194 n.191, 208 n.82, 231 n.195
subject 4, 13, 15, 32, 54, 101, 123, 125, *see also* listener
tactile 121–6, *see also* tactility
technique 10, 183 n.77
technology 11–14, 30–1, 67–8, 184 n.78, 207 n.73, 261 n.50
ubiquitous 11
as a vibrational practice 187 n.112
listening devices (others than single records, jukeboxes, sound systems)
  apps 14, 27, 36, 171–2, 198 n.250
  boombox 27, 39–41, 49, 145
  CD 11, 12, 25, 27, 29, 46–7, 65, 82, 118, 130–1, 134, 156, 170, 198 n.250
  cell phone 27, 176 n.14,
  iPod 27, 198 n.250
  LP, *see* LP
  magnetic tape 65, 69, 71, 107, 117, 156, 183 n.76, 183 n.77, 211 n.118
  mp3, *see* mp3
  noise cancelling headphones 28, 171
  orchestrion 91, 229 n.165
  phonograph, *see* phonograph
  piano roll 25, 27, 229 n.165
  player piano 27–8, 91, 229 n.163
  smartphone 9, 14, 27, 36, 73, 171–2, 272 n.229
  tape machine 51, 67, 132, 243 n.35
  Walkman 176 n.14, 188 n.126
Little Richard 31, 32, 39–49, 200 n.1, 201 n.7, 202 n.24, 203 n.30, 203 n.33, 217 n.223
Little Richard: The Specialty Sessions (record) 202 n.21
Little Richard's Grooviest 17 Original Hits (record) 47
Loewy, Raymond 94
Long, Richard 149–52, 155, 265 n.132
Long Tall Sally (record) 31–2, 39–49, 202 n.18, 203 n.30, 203 n.32, 203 n.33, 204 n.42, 248 n.123
Los Angeles, California 42, 50, 75, 80, 203 n.33

loudness 32, 67, 69, 71, 88, 140–1, 144, 155, 169, 172, 218 n.225, *see also* mastering; sound system; bass enhancement
loudspeaker system, *see* sound system
Long Playing record, *see* LP
Love in "C" Minor (record) 238 n.3
Love to Love You Baby (record) 126
Love's Theme (record) 109
LP 25, 27, 31–4, 46–7, 49–58, 60, 62, 65–6, 69, 77, 93, 107–8, 110–12, 116–17, 120–30, 149, 153, 156, 207 n.77, 208 n.83, 209 n.84, 209 n.94, 210 n.95, 210 n.96, 210 n.104, 210 n.107, 212 n.138, 241 n.11, 248 n.123
Lubich, Andreas 128, 133
Lucille (record) 44, 202 n.24

Macho, Thomas 10
Madison Square Garden 138
Mad Love (record) 241 n.17
Magoun, Alexander Boyden 59, 210 n.95, 212 n.127, 212 n.130, 212 n.145
Mancuso, David 109, 111, 116, 148, 159, 266 n.135, 269 n.194
Mann, Thomas 29
Marx, Karl 86
mastering 12–14, 29, 31–2, 34, 44, 46–9, 62–72, 82–3, 93, 107–8, 117, 119, 121, 123, 126–35, 154–6, 164, 168–9, 200 n.254, 213 n.154, 213 n.156, 214 n.181, 217 n.212, 217 n.213, 218 n.226, 247 n.112, 252 n.175, 253 n.180
  Direct Metal Mastering (DMM) 213 n.153, 256 n.226
  engineers 13, 29, 34, 46, 62–6, 69, 71, 107–8, 119, 121, 123, 126, 128, 130, 133, 155, 247 n.112
  function 63, 155
  hot 12, 71, 123,
  with hot cutting stylus 70
  re- 46–7
  rooms 62, 70–1, 83, 218 n.225, 218 n.226
  studio 62, 121, 134–5, 154, 247 n.112, 253 n.180, *see* studio
  vinyl graffiti 121, 127
Matassa, Cosimo 40, 75, 82, 216 n.201
Maxfield, Joseph P. 260 n.29, 260 n.31

maxi-single, *see* 12-inch single record
Maxwell, James Clark 250 n.25
May, Derrick 129, 133, 255 n.210
McClary, Susan 125
McLuhan, Marshall 5, 194 n.186, 249 n.137
media
  anthropology 119
  archaeology 18, 26
  conditions 18, 25
  digital 22, 25, 270 n.196
  electronic 5
  epistemology 7
  as extensions 5
  formats 32, 58
  history of 119, 139
  industries 19, 21–2, 108
  materiality 9, 14, 27, 179 n.47
  music history of 22, 25–6, 53, 108, 119, 139
  phenomenology 7
  studies 12, 22, 119
  technologies 11, 20, 26, 34, 137, 139, 259 n.25
  theory 14, 18, 24, 187 n.118, 197 n.235
mediation, *see* actor-network theory
mediator, *see* actor-network theory
Meford, Massachusetts 144
Memphis, Tennessee 29, 43, 50, 76, 81, 202 n.16, 213 n.156, 217 n.212, 227 n.131
Metal Box (record) 251 n.161
Michel, Elmar 85
microphone 25, 27, 42, 44, 67, 69, 88, 137, 139–40, 143–4, 235 n.241, 260 n.31
Middleton, Richard 17, 190 n.133, 230 n.172
Miller, Nils 76, 94
Mills, Mara 11, 186 n.96, 187 n.105, 187 n.108
Mixed with Love: The Walter Gibbons Salsoul Anthology (record) 243 n.45
mixing console 70, 154, 268 n.182
Moanin' at Midnight (record) 67
modernity 4, 7, 18, 73, 176 n.10, 178 n.37, 183 n.77, 274 n.261
More, More, More (record) 116
Morton, David 62
Motolla, Tony 57

Moulton, Tom 108–13, 116–17, 119, 124, 241 n.15, 242 n.24, 243 n.35, 245 n.79
Move Your Body (record) 158
mp3
  file 6, 183 n.77, 200 n.232,
  format 117, 172, 183 n.77
MTV 195 n.195
Munich (city) 138, 140, 239 n.3
Murphy, Colleen 'Cosmo' 159
Murphy, Ron 121, 129, 133–5
music
  aesthetic value of 82
  as art 22
  as culture 22
  form of 16, 61, 116, 149, 159, 261 n.52
  history of 3, 22, 24–5, 28, 31, 53, 118, 137, 141, 143, 195 n.207
  as network 15, 25, 43, 148, 205 n.50
  publishing 29, 63
musicology 8, 16, 19, 22, 50, 92, 124, 141, 175 n.8, 176 n.10, 179 n.47, 191 n.138, 195 n.204, 195 n.205, 195 n.207
Muzak Company 232 n.196
My Black Mama (record) 242 n.18

Nashville, Tennessee 217 n.223
Nat King Cole 206 n.60
Nathan, Sidney 70
National Association of Music Merchants (NAMM) 154, 209 n.93
National Automatic Music Co. 229 n.165
National Sound Corporation 121, 133, *see also* techno
Neger, Hans Ernst 209 n.83
Negus, Keith 188 n.126
Neumann 70, 256 n.226
  lathe 134, 213 n.156, 218 n.226
  VMS 70 134–5
  VMS 80 134
Never Can Say Goodbye (record) 110
New Orleans, Louisiana 40, 42–3, 75, 82, 202 n.16
Newport Folk Festival 144
New Wave (genre) 117, 126, 131, 237 n.3, 251 n.161, *see also* 12-inch single
New York 30, 33–5, 50, 62, 71, 102, 107–17, 137–8, 141–50, 159, 160, 163, 166, 170, 237–40 n.3, 240 n.6, 241 n.11, 244 n.63, 245 n.76, 261 n.50, 269 n.193, 270 n.195, 271 n.215, 273 n.247
Nielsen, Arthur C. 100
noise 6, 12, 57, 66, 83, 93, 133, 143, 152, 145 n.104, 269 n.192
  see also loudness; cultural technique; hi-fi
  control 143
  -cancelling 28, 171
  of a record 12, 67, 83
normativity, *see* standard
North American Phonograph Company 90, 228 n.153, 229 n.162
Novarese, John 81
Nowak, Nik 159

Ochsner, Beate 276 n.9
Olson, Harry F. 58
Omaha, Nebraska 97, 98
On and On (record) 129
one-stop (shop), 80–1, 100, 223 n.74, 223 n.75, 269 n.193, *see also* jukebox
Osborne, Richard 59, 120, 126
overdub 40
Owsinski, Bobby 214 n.181

Pacific Phonograph Company 90
Palmer, Earl 40, 43–4
Panzéra, Charles 194 n.185
Paris (city) 138, 228 n.158
PA system, *see* sound system
Pathé 213 n.154, 261 n.47
Paul, Les 51
Penniman, Richard Wayne, *see* Little Richard
performance 14, 16, 21, 26, 29–31, 40, 42, 48–9, 51–2, 54, 58, 64, 68, 84–7, 93, 95, 126, 138, 140–5, 149, 176 n.10, 178 n.36, 181 n.69, 188 n.126, 189 n.127, 191 n.141, 192 n.150, 195 n.207, 200 n.256, 201 n.3, 202 n.17, 205 n.58, 225 n.118, 225 n.119, 226 n.131, 231 n.195, 258 n.16, 261 n.50
  live 29, 51–2, 78, 85, 94, 113, 127, 138
Petrillo, James C. 64, 225 n.113
Philadelphia, Pennsylvania 21, 62, 237–40 n.3, 261 n.50
Phillips, Dewey 76, 81, 223 n.78, 227 n.131

Phillips, Sam 29, 41, 67, 70–1, 81, 202 n.17, 205 n.54, 213 n.156, 217 n.212, 218 n.225, 218 n.226, 223 n.78
phonautograph 6–7, 11, 122
phonograph 6, 10, 17, 20, 28, 48, 56–9, 66, 69–71, 74, 77–8, 86, 90–100, 103, 120, 198 n.250, 228 n.153, 228 n.160, 229 n.162, 231 n.187, 231 n.195, 232 n.198, 233 n.217
   coin-operated 77, 90–1, 95, 98, 103, 228 n.158, 231 n.187
   parlor 231 n.187
Pinch, Trevor 230 n.168
Pink Floyd 23, 144, 263 n.91
playlist 13, 32, 49, 54, 59, 65, 67, 82, 87, 93, 95–7, 169, 171–2, 227 n.134, *see also* jukebox playlist; streaming; 7-inch single record; radio; top 40
Pop Muzik (record) 256 n.221
Pop Tunes (one-stop shop) 81
popular music studies 3, 14–16, 22–4, 53, 99, 119–20, 138, 156, 160–1, 196 n.209, 230 n.172
Poster, Mark 120–1
post-production, *see* mastering
Potts, John H. 69
Powers Jr, Herb 128, 247 n.112
Predator (film) 39–41, 44–6, 48
Presley, Elvis 29, 41–2, 48, 71, 101, 201 n.11, 206 n.60, 217 n.223, 236 n.246
Putnam, Bill 29, 70–1, 217 n.212

queerness 24, 111, 149, 159, 202 n.24, 237 n.3, 254 n.191, 272 n.233

race (construction of) 70, 74–5, 78–80, 83, 124, 181 n.60, 220 n.14, 232 n.212, 237 n.3, 251 n.167, 254 n.191, 273 n.252, 274 n.253
radio 13–14, 19, 20, 22, 25–32, 39, 48–9, 51, 58–60, 63–4, 68–9, 71, 75–9, 81, 83, 84, 86, 89, 93–100, 109–10, 117, 130–3, 138–43, 176 n.14, 191 n.141, 205 n.47, 208 n.82, 212 n.127, 214 n.168, 217 n.223, 218 n.225, 223 n.78, 226 n.131, 232 n.212, 252 n.171, 255 n.196, 269 n.193
   see also top 40

loudspeakers 141
   station 86, 97, 99, 217 n.223
Raulff, Ulrich 114, 118, 238 n.3
Rayleigh, Baron 259 n.25
RCA (media corporation) 42, 109, 206 n.60, 209 n.93, 210 n.107, 215 n.190, 221 n.44, 260 n.31
RCA Victor (record label) 4, 31–2, 34, 48, 50, 53–6, 58–70, 76–7, 108, 168, 170, 209 n.93, 209 n.94, 210 n.107, 212 n.130, 260 n.31,
Read, Oliver 59, 77, 208 n.83
record
   see also 7-inch single record; 12-inch single record; jukebox; sound system
   -cutting machine 62, 70, 134, 256 n.226
   changer 48–9, 54–6, 59, 77, 83, 95, 102, 168, 209 n.86, 211 n.126, 230 n.180, 231 n.186
   companies 33, 50, 64, 66, 69, 71, 76, 81, 84–5, 91, 99–100, 108, 110–11, 119, 126, 132, 169, 213 n.154, 215 n.195, 245 n.104, 260 n.31, 269 n.193
   cut, *see* mastering
   playback speed 65, 82, 108
   playback stylus 83, 95
   player 27, 48–9, 59, 66, 68, 83, 93, 99, 111, 142–3, 206 n.68, 209 n.94, 211 n.126, 225 n.118, 243 n.29, 243 n.35, 260 n.31
   pools 111, 155, 269 n.193
record label 50, 60, 75–7, 97, 115, 132
   see also Chess Records; Columbia Records; RCA Victor; Specialty Records; Sun Records
   Atlantic Records 50, 67, 109–10
   Basic Channel 135
   Bell Records 47
   Capitol Records 46, 206 n.60
   Chain Reaction 135
   Decca 50, 56
   DJ International 131, 252 n.171, 252 n.175
   Dot Records 71, 217 n.223
   Juke Box Records 60
   King Records 50, 64, 70, 216 n.211,
   KMS 255 n.210
   London Records 50, 79, 252 n.171

Metroplex 255 n.210
Mobile Fidelity Sound Lab 46
Modern Records 42, 75
Peacock Records 42
Polydor 47, 50
Rhythm & Sound 135
Scepter Records 112
Telefunken 50, 213 n.153
Transmat 255 n.210
Trax Records 131, 133, 158
Tresor Records 135
Underground Resistance 121
Vee-Jay Records 47
Victor Records 62
Warp Records 135
West End Records 110, 266 n.143, 268 n.190
World Power Alliance 121
Record Industry Association of America (RIAA) 69–71, 216 n.206, 218 n.225
recording curve 12, 65–6, 68–9, 71–2, 169, 214 n.182
remix 109, 111–13, 115, 117, 126–7, 129–33, 155, 157, 159, 243 n.39, 243 n.46, *see also* danceability
Reynolds, Simon 158, 164, 251 n.161, 273 n.252, 274 n.256
Rhein, Eduard 210 n.107
Rieger, Stefan 7, 197 n.224
Riegger, Hans 141, 260–1 n.47
Rietveld, Hillegonda C. 130, 160, 252 n.170
Rip it Up (record) 44
Robbins, Marty 45–6
Robinson, Dylan 92
Rock Around the Clock (record) 79
rock 'n' roll culture 3–4, 29–32, 41, 52, 68, 72, 77, 89–90, 93, 123, 126, 169, *see also* 7-inch single record; jukebox
Rodriguez, José 108, 119, 124
Rolling Stone (magazine) 50, 240 n.10
Rosner, Alex 117, 148–52, 155, 160, 265 n.130
Rupe, Art 40, 42, 60, 75, 84, 201–2 n.12, 202 n.16

Salkind, Micah 251 n.162, 254–5 n.191, 271 n.220

Salsoul 30th: 30 Years of Salsoul – 30 Classic Club Cuts – 30 World Class DJs (record) 268–9 n.190
sampling 25, 27, 254 n.191
  Casio SK-1 254 n.191
San Francisco, California 90, 137
Saturday Night Fever (film) 146, 163, 238 n.3
Saturday Night Fever (record) 238 n.3
Saunderson, Kevin 129, 253 n.176
Scherer, Wolfgang 11, 181 n.61, 181 n.67, 186 n.102, 193 n.165, 197 n.235,
Schmid Horning, Susan 16, 69, 71, 216 n.203
Schmidt-Joos, Siegfried 85
Schulze, Holger 175 n.8, 193 n.176
Schüttpelz, Erhard 119, 185 n.80
science and technology studies 176 n.14
sensory physiology 178 n.44, 197 n.235, 246 n.110, *see also* media archaeology
sensory studies 4, 146
serialization (of records) 32–3, 49, 87, 89, 95–6, 157, 172
Serres, Michel 175 n.9
Shake a Hand (record) 42
Shannon, Doug 154
Shapiro, Peter 109
Sharevari (record) 271 n.210
Shea Stadium 144
Shea, William F. 70
shellac record 27, 31, 46, 50, 56–7, 59–60, 66, 77, 95, 120, 179 n.47, 206 n.68, 208 n.82, 214 n.184
Sherman, Larry 129, 131–3
Short Fat Fannie (record) 203 n.30
Siano, Nicky 111, 243 n.29
Sicko, Dan 134
Siegert, Bernhard 180 n.48, 182 n.70, 183 n.77, 185 n.88, 197 n.235
Siemens, Werner von 139–40
Sinatra, Frank 205 n.55, 206 n.60
single, *see* 7-inch single record
Skinny Jim (record) 203 n.30
Slippin' and Slidin' (record) 44
Smith, Earl 'Spanky' 133
Smoking in Heaven (record) 204 n.39
So Much for Love (record) 124

sonic dominance 12, 145, 146–8, 159, 264 n.116
Soul Makossa (record) 109
sound
  see also 12-inch single record; disco; house; techno
  amplification 139, 142, 258 n.15
  concepts 50, 68
  electrification of 66, 139–40, 259 n.25, 260 n.31, 261 n.50
  engineer 16, 62–3, 69, 71, 113, 133, 144, 215 n.193, 216 n.203, 230 n.168, 263 n.80, *see also* mastering engineer
  history of 34–5, 143, 171, 258 n.16
  of jukebox 84
  Philly 128, 237 n.3
  reinforcement 138–42, 162–3
  space 35, 43, 151, 162–3
  of sound systems 155
  tactility of 122, 124, *see also* tactility
sound and music culture 3, 5
sound studies 4–5, 9, 11, 22, 124, 139, 141, 175 n.8, 179 n.47, 181 n.60, 184 n.78, 185 n.85, 197 n.235, 237 n.3
  postsonic phase of 4
sound system 4, 9, 12, 14–5, 30–1, 34–6, 41, 49, 116–17, 124–5, 130, 137, 139, 141, 143–70, 188 n. 126, 230 n.175, 245 n.76, 257 n.1, 263 n.80, 263 n.100, 264 n.116, 264 n.121, 265 n.131, 265 n.132, 265 n.133, 266 n.147, 267 n.152, 267 n.159, 268 n.182, 269 n.192, 272 n.229
  see also disco; hi-fi; sound of sound system
  industry 154
  listening 35, 159–66, 169
  multi-way 116
  of Radio City Music Hall 142, 162
  of Reichssportfeld 142
  sensurround sound system 14, 137, 151–2, 267 n.165, 267 n.166
  of Woodstock Music and Art Fair 137, 162, 257 n.1
sound system (manufacturers and famous designs)
  Azimuth coordinator 144, 263 n.91
  Funktion One 147

Hanley Sound Inc. 144, *see also* Bill Hanley
Klipschorn 149, 163, *see also* Paul Klipsch
Levan Horn 152–3, 155, 163, *see also* Larry Levan
Richard Long & Associates 149–50
Rosner Custom Sound Inc. 149, *see also* Alex Rosner
Siemens & Halske 139–42
Wall of Sound system 144, *see also* Owsley Stanley; Dan Healy
Sousa, John Philip 20
Specialty Records 39–50, 60, 75, 201 n.2, 203 n.33, *see also* Art Rupe
Spengler, Oswald 18, 185 n.85
Spin (magazine) 132
standard 12–14, 31, 44, 53, 59, 60–1, 65–70, 72, 79, 82, 92, 129, 131, 133–4, 144, 152, 218 n.225, 254 n.183
  industry 12–14, 65, 67–8, 70, 93, 123, 169, 214 n.184,
  technical 12, 32, 41, 51, 65, 69, 70–1, 169, 171, 215 n.195, 219 n.5, 267 n.166
Stanley, Owsley 144
Sterne, Jonathan 10, 11, 117, 179 n.47, 183–4 n.77, 185 n.85, 231 n.187, 232 n.200
Starpower (record) 47
Stewart, Bill 97
Stoddard, Bill, *see* Fine Sound Studio
Stokowski, Leopold 141, 261 n.50
Storz, Todd 97
Straw, Will 109, 157, 250 n.158, 269 n.193
studio (recording) 16, 29, 41, 57, 62–3, 69, 107–8, 112, 132, 149, 213 n.154, 230 n.168, *see also* mastering, *see also* record; listening devices (others)
studio (famous)
  Blank Tapes Studio 113
  Dubplates & Mastering 128, 135
  Fine Sound Studio 71
  J&M Studio 40–4, 75, 82, *see also* Cosimo Matassa
  Mastering Lab 62, 130, 247 n.112, *see also* Al Brown
  National Sound Corporation, 121, 133, *see also* Ron Murphy

Sigma Sound Studios 62
Sound Enterprises 121, 134, *see also* Ron Murphy
Sterling Sound 62
Sunshine Sound 111, 243 n.32
Universal Audio Studios 29, 70–1, *see also* Bill Putnam; Jack Wiener; Emory Cook
SubBerlin. The Story of Tresor (film) 264 n.122
Sugar Baby (record) 204 n.43
Sun Records 29, 50, 71, 81, 205 n.54, 217 n.212, 218 n.226, *see also* Sam Phillips
synthesizer 14, 27, 58, 131, 153, 158, 237 n.3, 268 n.186
    avant la lettre 141 (Theremin), 141 (Trautonium)
    Roland TB-303 131, 133, 247 n.116
    Roland TR-808 131
    subharmonic 153
    Yamaha DX-7 131

tactility 11–12, 34, 108, 113, 117, 119–26, 128–9, 138, 146, 153–4, 160, 168–9, 207 n.68, 246 n.104, 249 n.137, 249 n.137, 249 n.142, *see also* 12-inch single record; bass; disco; disco and club culture; mastering; sound system
Tarsia, Joe, *see* studio (Sigma Sound Studios)
TASCAM 132
Tauber, Richard 29–30
technique
    see also listening technique
    audile 9–10, 183 n.77, 185 n.85, 231 n.187
    body 9–10, 89, 114, 182 n.70, 182 n.72, 183 n.77, 244 n.63
    body-object 9–11
    cultural 8–11, 13, 33, 89, 101, 160, 169, 182 n.70, 180 n.48, 182 n.72, 182 n.74, 186 n.93, 186 n.94
    intellectual 9
    reproduction 16
technology
    culturalization of 10
    delegation 6, 89

democratization of 52, 85–6
as instrument 6, 17–18, 85–6, 143, 178 n.38, 275 n.262
rationalization of 52, 85–6, 143, 185 n.85
reproduction 16, 55, 63, 183 n.77, 228 n.160
techno (genre) 21, 23, 27, 33–5, 113, 117, 120–9, 133–5, 147, 150, 156–61, 164–6, 168–9, 247 n.116, 252 n.176, 254 n.182, 255 n.210, 271 n.210, 272 n.227, 275 n.262, *see also* sound system; Detroit
Techno! The New Dance Sound of Detroit (record) 252–3 n.176
Teenager Romance (record) 227
telephone 17, 28, 122, 139, 235 n.241, 259 n.25
television 21, 48, 52, 58, 60, 104, 195 n.195, 206 n.68, 222 n.54
Ten Per Cent/Ten Percent (record) 34, 113, 129–31, 155, 253 n.177, 268 n.190
Théberge, Paul 144
The Dark Side of the Moon (record) 263 n.91
The Girl Can't Help It (film) 52, 102
The House Sound of Chicago (record) 252 n.171
The Howlin' Wolf Album (record) 202 n.23
The Hustle (record) 163
The Love I Lost (record) 241 n.18
The Message (record) 126
The Thing (record) 44
The Voice of Frank Sinatra (record) 56, 211 n.109
Theremin, Leon 141
Thompson, Emily 10, 142, 185 n.85
Thompson, Marie 179 n.47
Thornton, Sarah 185 n.85
tin ears 67, 78, 91–3, 230 n.175, *see also* golden ears; chrome ears
Tin Pan Alley 52, 67, 78, 92, 107, 191 n.141, 204 n.38
tone tests (Edison) 10, 21, 193 n.175
Toop, David 112
top 40 radio 81, 97–8, 212 n.127
track (music) 31, 35, 40, 103, 110–13, 121, 123, 127, 130, 132–5, 147, 154–9, 168, 171, 241 n.11, 255 n.196, 256 n.221,

270 n.196, 271 n.210, 271 n.212, 210 n.220, *see also* DJ; disco and sound culture; 12-inch single record; remix
transduction (sound) 122, 139
Trendelenburg, Ferdinand 260 n.47
Tutti Frutti (record) 40, 42, 44–5, 201 n.11, 202 n.24, 203 n.30
Tyler, Alvin 'Red' 43

UK / Great Britain / United Kingdom 32, 50, 74, 79, 84–5, 97, 104, 126, 129, 130, 137, 206 n.68, 219 n.5, 234 n.233, 242 n.20, 253 n.177, 253 n.178, 258 n.16
unhearable 11–13, 47, 49, 65–70, 135, 159, 264 n.116, 272 n.225
  non-listening 11–13, 32, 34, 65, 68–9, 98, 101, 120, 123, 125, 159, 167, 169, 171
unsound, *see* unhearable
unsound studies 11, 187 n.112
USA / US / United States 4, 17, 20, 31, 33, 47, 50–1, 53, 55, 65, 67, 70, 74, 79, 83, 84, 85, 90, 97–8, 100, 102, 104, 108–10, 129–32, 139, 144, 148–9, 153–4, 156, 168, 170, 198 n.250, 203 n.33, 205 n.47, 206 n.68, 210 n.107, 219 n.5, 222 n.63, 226 n.121, 226 n.131, 228 n.149, 234 n.233, 240 n.10, 252 n.175, 252 n.176

Valente, Caterina 79
Variety (magazine) 80, 222 n.63
Veal, Michael 145
Verband der Deutschen Automatenindustrie e. V. (VDAI) 219 n.11
Visage (record) 215 n.187
Vogl, Joseph 178 n.38
voice 26–7, 28, 30, 39, 41–5, 47, 52, 62, 73, 109–10, 140, 144, 157, 178 n.46, 204 n.42, 218 n.1, 239 n.3, 271 n.216
  shouting 45, 87

Wagner, Richard 26–7, 138
Waller, Fats 80
Wallerstein, Edward 'Ted' 55–6
Walters, Barry 132, 252 n.171, 254 n.191, 273 n.252
Weber, Heike 176 n.14
Weber, Julian 134
Webern, Anton 114
Weissberg, Daniel 247 n.117
Welch, Walter L. 59, 77
Wenner, Jann 50
We're on the Right Track (record) 110
Western Electric 139, 260 n.31
What'd I Say (record) 215 n.189
Wicke, Peter 14, 15, 16, 21, 23, 61, 114, 156, 121, 190 n.130, 199 n.252, 201 n.2, 201 n.6, 202 n.28, 206 n.62, 206 n.68, 207 n.69, 207 n.78, 212 n.144, 214 n.178, 220 n.16, 228 n.151, 233 n.218, 233 n.221, 244 n.48, 244 n.51, 244 n.55, 244 n.60, 244 n.62, 245 n.78, 247 n.116, 248 n.118, 248 n.126, 254 n.189, 261 n.53, 263 n.88, 263 n.91, 268 n.183, 270 n.197, 270 n.198, 270 n.199, 270 n.201
Wiener, Jack 71, 218 n.226
Wild Style (film) 201 n.4
Williams, Larry 203 n.30
Willis, Paul 55, 103, 206 n.68
Wilson, Jim 216 n.211
Winner, Langdon 43
Wolfe, Tom 144
Wood, Randy 71, 217 n.223

X-102 Discovers the Rings of Saturn (record) 247 n.113

You Can't Hide from Your Butt (record) 132
You Can't Hide from Yourself (record) 132
You Used to Hold Me (record) 271 n.216

Zak, Albin 45, 51, 67
Zeiner-Henriksen, Hans T. 254 n.182

www.ingramcontent.com/pod-product-compliance
Lightning Source LLC
Chambersburg PA
CBHW070013010526
44117CB00011B/1554